Red Hat Certified Engineer Study Guide

Red Hat Certified Engineer Study Guide

Osborne/McGraw-Hill is an independent entity from Red Hat, and not affiliated with Red Hat, Inc. in any manner. This publication and CD may be used in assisting students to prepare for a Red Hat Certified Engineer exam. Neither Red Hat, nor Osborne/McGraw-Hill, warrants that use of this publication and CD will ensure passing the relevant exam.

Syngress Media, Inc.

Osborne/McGraw-Hill

Berkeley New York St. Louis San Francisco Auckland Bogotá Hamburg London Madrid Mexico City Milan Montreal New Delhi Panama City Paris São Paulo Singapore Sydney Tokyo Toronto

Osborne/**McGraw-Hill**
2600 Tenth Street
Berkeley, California 94710
U.S.A.

For information on translations or book distributors outside the U.S.A., or to arrange bulk purchase discounts for sales promotions, premiums, or fund-raisers, please contact Osborne/**McGraw-Hill** at the above address.

Red Hat Certified Engineer Study Guide

234567890 DOC DOC 019876543210

Book P/N 0-07-212153-X and CD P/N 0-07-212154-8
parts of
ISBN 0-07-212155-6

Publisher
Brandon A. Nordin

Associate Publisher and Editor-in-Chief
Scott Rogers

Acquisitions Editor
Gareth Hancock

Editorial Management
Syngress Media, Inc.

Acquisitions Coordinator
Tara Davis

Series Editor
David Egan, RHCE

Technical Editor
Paul Tibbitts

Copy Editor
Beth Roberts

Proofreaders
Brian Galloway
Rhonda Holmes

Indexer
Jack Lewis

Computer Designers
Roberta Steele
Gary Corrigan

Illustrator
Beth Young

Series Design
Roberta Steele

Cover Design
Regan Honda

This book was composed with Corel VENTURA™ Publisher.

FOREWORD

From Global Knowledge

At Global Knowledge we strive to support the multiplicity of learning styles required by our students to achieve success as technical professionals. In this series of books, it is our intention to offer the reader a valuable tool for successful completion of the RHCE Certification Exam.

As the world's largest IT training company, Global Knowledge is uniquely positioned to offer these books. The expertise gained each year from providing instructor-led training to hundreds of thousands of students worldwide has been captured in book form to enhance your learning experience. We hope that the quality of these books demonstrates our commitment to your lifelong learning success. Whether you choose to learn through the written word, computer-based training, Web delivery, or instructor-led training, Global Knowledge is committed to providing you the very best in each of those categories. For those of you who know Global Knowledge, or those of you who have just found us for the first time, our goal is to be your lifelong competency partner.

Thank you for the opportunity to serve you. We look forward to serving your needs again in the future.

Warmest regards,

Duncan Anderson

Duncan Anderson
President and Chief Operating Officer, Global Knowledge

ABOUT THE CONTRIBUTORS

About Syngress Media

Syngress Media creates books and software for Information Technology professionals seeking skill enhancement and career advancement. Its products are designed to comply with vendor and industry standard course curricula, and are optimized for certification exam preparation. Visit the Syngress Web site at www.syngress.com.

Contributors

Henry Maine is a principal consultant for Maine Consulting, Inc. In addition to providing consulting services for a number of corporate clients in the Charlotte, North Carolina region he also travels the United States offering Linux training as well as training in other subjects. He has a B.S. in Computer Science from Tennessee Technological University. Mr. Maine is a Red Hat Certified Engineer and Red Hat Certified Examiner as well as a Microsoft Certified Systems Engineer. He has more than ten years of systems administration and network management experience with various flavors of UNIX as well as OpenVMS and Windows NT. He has been an advocate of Linux for the past several years.

Kirk Rafferty is the Director of Operations at Fairplay Communications, a small ISP he started in 1999. He has been a Unix Systems Administrator for 11 years, and a rabid Linux fan since 1993. Kirk lives and works in Denver, Colorado, and enjoys spending time with his wife and three children, gaming, paintball, and "recreational hacking." He was a (minor) contributor to O'Reilly and Associates *Stopping Spam* book.

Chris Rogers has been configuring Linux servers since 1994. To give an idea of how long that is in terms of the computing industry, the web browser was Mosaic, Netscape 0.9 had just hit the FTP sites, and the Slackware distribution without X-windows could still fit on only three 3.5" diskettes. Chris now owns an ISP that runs exculsively on Red Hat Linux and caters to the web needs of small businesses. He also is the webmaster for a Fortune 500 financial company. Chris may be emailed at crogers@wyvernweb.com. Many thanks must go out to the Washington, D.C. and Northern Virginia Linux Users' Groups (www.tux.org). Without the help of several members such as Sam Chessman, Przemek Klosowski, David Niemi, and Paul Thomas, Chris's chapter would not be nearly as complete as it is.

Craig Smith currently works for Cincinnati State College as Network Analyst. He is also an outside consultant specializing in Linux server installations and custom programming. Craig started using Linux in 1994 and has since used many different distributions of Linux. He installs and configures around 75 Red Hat systems a year. He has written and released several OpenSource applications for the Linux community. Currently, Craig possesses the SAIR GNU Linux certifications for installation, configurations and administration of Linux systems.

Christopher Wedman works full time as a LAN Administrator for the University of Alberta and also does some freelance computer and network consulting. He is an experienced web administrator and is well versed in developing customized scripts for web sites. He has been using Linux since 1995 and advocates the use of Linux for custom business solutions. Christopher completed high school in 1997. He graduated with the highest grades in his class and plans to complete a university degree in computer sciences at the University of Alberta.

Series Editor

David Egan, P. Eng., BASc Engineering U of T 78, MCT 96, RHCE 99, has lived and worked in several countries and has worked with computers since the early days of the Apple and IBM type PC's. David's first "hobby-turned-job" was as a Z80 Assembler and C Language programmer for five years. David transitioned into a VMS / UNIX / NT / PC Systems Integration Consultant and Technology Instructor—"An Edutainer"—during the past 15 years. David is still consulting and writing the occasional book, but mostly contracting as a Course Director and Course Writer of UNIX-, NT- and Linux-based courses for Global Knowledge Inc. of Cary, North Carolina: http://www.globalknowledge.com.

When not on the road—preaching the virtues of Linux and NT from his stage or showing the plan—he resides near Vancouver, B.C. with his lovely wife Deborah, daughter Vanessa and son Callen.

They can be reached at either egand@istar.ca or egand@wwdb.org or through http://home.istar.ca/~egand.

ACKNOWLEDGMENTS

We would like to thank the following people:

- Richard Kristof of Global Knowledge for championing the series and providing access to some great people and information.
- All the incredibly hard-working folks at Osborne/McGraw-Hill: Brandon Nordin, Scott Rogers, and Gareth Hancock for their help in launching a great series and being solid team players. In addition, Tara Davis and Cynthia Douglas for their help in fine-tuning the book.

CONTENTS AT A GLANCE

CONTENTS

PREFACE

This book's primary objective is to help you prepare for and pass the required Red Hat Linux Certification exam so you can begin to reap the career benefits of certification. We believe that the only way to do this is to help you increase your knowledge and build your skills. After completing this book, you should feel confident that you have thoroughly reviewed all of the objectives that Red Hat has established for the exam.

In This Book

This book is organized around the actual structure of the Red Hat exam. Red Hat has let us know all the topics we need to cover for the exam. We've followed their list carefully, so you can be assured you're not missing anything.

In Every Chapter

We've created a set of chapter components that call your attention to important items, reinforce important points, and provide helpful exam-taking hints. Take a look at what you'll find in every chapter:

- Every chapter begins with the **Certification Objectives**—what you need to know in order to pass the section on the exam dealing with the chapter topic. The Certification Objectives headings identify the objectives within the chapter, so you'll always know an objective when you see it!

exam Watch

- Exam Watch notes call attention to information about, and potential pitfalls in, the exam. These helpful hints are written by individuals who have taken the exams and received their certification—who better to tell you what to worry about? They know what you're about to experience!

- **On the Job** notes point out procedures and techniques important for coding actual applications for employers or contract jobs.
- **Certification Exercises** are interspersed throughout the chapters. These are step-by-step exercises that mirror vendor-recommended labs. They help you master skills that are likely to be an area of focus on the exam. Don't just read through the exercises; they are hands-on practice that you should be comfortable completing. Learning by doing is an effective way to increase your competency with a product.
- **From the Classroom** sidebars describe the issues that come up most often in the training classroom setting. These sidebars give you a valuable perspective into certification- and product-related topics. They point out common mistakes and address questions from actual classroom discussions.
- **Q & A** sections lay out problems and solutions in a quick-read format. For example:

QUESTIONS AND ANSWERS	
A user wishes to save a file to a pre-existing filename.	Inform the user that the file exists and prompt them as to whether they wish to overwrite the file.
A CFile object throws an exception during construction.	Ensure that the program cannot go on to attempt to use that object.

- The **Certification Summary** is a succinct review of the chapter and a restatement of salient points regarding the exam.
- The **Two-Minute Drill** at the end of every chapter is a checklist of the main points of the chapter. It can be used for last-minute review.
- The **Self Test** offers questions similar to those found on the certification exams, including multiple choice and fill-in-the-blank. The answers to these questions, as well as explanations of the answers, can be found in Appendix A. By taking the Self Test after completing each chapter, you'll reinforce what you've learned from that chapter, while becoming familiar with the structure of the exam questions.

Some Pointers

Once you've finished reading this book, set aside some time to do a thorough review. You might want to return to the book several times and make use of all the methods it offers for reviewing the material:

1. *Re-read all the Two-Minute Drills*, or have someone quiz you. You also can use the drills as a way to do a quick cram before the exam.
2. *Re-read all the Exam Watch notes.* Remember that these are written by individuals who have taken the exam and passed. They know what you should expect—and what you should be careful about.
3. *Review all the Q & A scenarios* for quick problem solving.
4. *Re-take the Self Tests.* Taking the tests right after you've read the chapter is a good idea, because it helps reinforce what you've just learned. However, it's an even better idea to go back later and do all the questions in the book in one sitting. Pretend you're taking the exam. (For this reason, you should mark your answers on a separate piece of paper when you answer the questions the first time.)
5. *Complete the exercises.* Did you do the exercises when you read through each chapter? If not, do them! These exercises are designed to cover exam topics, and there's no better way to get to know this material than by practicing.
6. *Check out the Web site.* Global Knowledge Network invites you to become an active member of the Access Global Web site. This site is an online mall and information repository that you'll find invaluable. You can access many types of products to assist you in your preparation for the exams, and you'll be able to participate in forums, online discussions, and threaded discussions. No other book brings you unlimited access to such a resource. You'll find more information about this site in Appendix C.

INTRODUCTION

How to Take a Red Hat Linux Certification Examination

by David W. Egan, P. Eng, MCT, RHCE, RHCX
4Egans and Associates, A Division of Elegant Leasing

This article covers the reasons for pursuing industry-recognized certification, the importance of your RHCE certification, and prepares you for taking the actual examination. It gives you a few pointers on how to prepare, what to expect, and what to do on exam day.

Leaping Ahead of the Competition!

Congratulations on your pursuit of Red Hat Linux certification! Industrial certification has become a de facto standard in almost all networking and operating systems. The list of highly coveted certifications includes Cisco, Microsoft, Novell, SCO, and many more that are industry standard, industry and peer accepted, in demand, and an established mark of knowledge.

With the explosion in the Internet and intranet requirements of the last few years, and now the emergence of the "other" PC-based operating system called Linux, there is a huge need for skilled professionals with a proven "test" of knowledge and skill. This is what the Red Hat Certified Engineer examination provides.

This exam is not just a series of written exams. There are three parts to the exam:

- **Part 1**: A 2.5-hour troubleshooting section; worth one third of the score.
- **Part 2**: A 1-hour written part; worth one third of the final score.
- **Part 3**: A 2.5-hour hands-on covering installation and configuration.

Each section requires a minimum score of 75 percent, with an overall average of 80 percent or more for all three parts to pass the examination.

Why a Grueling Day Examination?

The main reasons for the certification exam is to provide a proven measurement of knowledge and competence. With the highly competitive nature of the computer industry today and the rapid evolution of the technologies, there is still a need for skilled professionals who are thoroughly grounded in the basics.

The basics for any operating system are installation, setup, management, and troubleshooting of the running or failed system. Although operating systems all provide the same generic services, each has peculiarities of how to troubleshoot and set up. There will always be a need for skilled networking and administrative people. The demand has been growing continuously as the computer revolution of the 1990s has exceeded all predictions. The boom has just begun in many experts' eyes. This means there are not enough people with "certified" skills available. This is where the Red Hat Certification is needed and accepted; the requirements provide proof of skill and knowledge.

Many networking and operating system companies started certification early in their product development life, such as Cisco, Novell, Microsoft, Sun, and SCO, to name a few. The reason was simple; in general, they provided a measured level of knowledge and skill. The exact levels varied between certifications, but the industry understood and accepted them as validation. The rest was left to the individual. The certifications progressed with the current developments and forced the students to prove they could keep up with technology.

The emergence of Linux as another "major" force in the operating systems wars of the late 1990s has provided a new skill shortage. The demand for Linux has skyrocketed as of late because it provides a rock-solid foundation with a plethora of industry-standard tools. Although Linux historically was an "erector set" design with no corporate support, Red Hat has changed that by providing support and customer service, making Red Hat Linux a viable alternative operating system to host networking services.

The certification test is a measurement of achievement and skilled knowledge. But like any test, there must be a high level of knowledge tested. The failure rate has been documented at about 40 percent, and this may be low; first-time test takers may see 50–60 percent failure rates. There are few third-party exam preparation books or courses currently available for RHCE because it is relatively new. It has been modeled after the Cisco exams, requiring the student to personally solve problems, install, administer, and set up the operating system and many of the standard component packages.

RHCE @dvice

This exam is very Red Hat Linux specific. Knowledge of BSD-based UNIX is most helpful ,as well as network services like Samba, NFS, DNS, and DHCP under Red Hat version 6.0 specifically. Experience with previous versions of Red Hat is always helpful. Real-life practice in setting up any of these versions is more important than memorizing the numbers and details. This information can be very helpful when you need to determine which areas of the exam will be most challenging for you as you study for the subsequent test.

Why One Linux Vendor Certification?

Over the years, vendors of other operating systems and network hardware operating systems have created their own certification programs because of industry demand for a proven knowledge base. When the marketplace needs skilled professionals for any product that is the leading or cutting edge, certification is an easy way to identify them. Vendor certification benefits both the skilled professionals and the purchasers; it shows the products are in demand and the people skilled in their products are in demand. Employers benefit because it helps them identify specifically qualified individuals.

Universities and colleges are changing their focus to provide more specifically skilled graduates for the growing computer-related industries. The corporation itself provides a more direct route for those who are not in the university and college stream, and is targeted for those who are already in the position of needing the skill now, this week, not in a few years.

With the steadily changing technology industries forging ahead, only the vendors can provide not only immediate, definable standards of certification, but maintain the evolutionary pace of their products and services within these certification standards. While most certifications are very specific to one vendor, they provide a solid measurement of essential skills and knowledge that is very much tuned to their products.

Corporate Recognition

Corporate America and the rest of the world have come to appreciate and stand by these vendor certification programs for the value, measured achievement, and recognition they provide. Employers also recognize that certifications do not guarantee an absolute level of knowledge, experience, or performance; rather, they establish a meaningful baseline for the comparison of development and professional achievement levels. By seeking to hire vendor-certified employees, a company can assure itself that, not only has it found a person skilled in the specific operating system or networking system, but it has also hired a person who has demonstrated a measured level of skill with the specific products the employer uses.

Professional Recognition

Just as university degrees and diplomas indicate a measured level of achievement in a given field of study, certification provides a recognized measurement of skill and knowledge in a specific product such as Red Hat Linux. The pursuit of these recognition levels has always been seen by peers and employers as incrementally more valuable, now and in future endeavors.

In today's "skills needed now" marketplace, certification becomes a foot in the door and an indication that this professional understands that development of leading-edge skills will lead to career and personal advancement and satisfaction.

RHCE @dvice

Red Hat and partner Global Knowledge provide convenient Web-based registration systems for the courses and test. To sign up for any of the Red Hat courses leading to certification and the RHCE exam, access http://www.redhat.com or http://am.globalknowledge.com, and register for the Red Hat Certification path. After the registration online, you will be e-mailed or telephoned to confirm that your request has been accepted.

After registering, a pretest of questions requiring written answers and multiple choice is sent to each student to prequalify him or her for the course. If you have problems with any areas of this pretest, you should spend time studying them before going to the class to solidify the concept in your mind.

Red Hat Linux Certification Program

At this writing, there are two certifications, with only one certification exam. There are three courses that lead up to the exam, each four to five days in length. The exam itself is a one-day, closed-book, individualized set of problems, questions, and an installation to perform in a time-limited environment.

The certification is dependent upon a candidate passing all three sections of the exam with at least 75 percent in each and an overall average of 80 percent or greater. With the right amount of all-around experience and study materials, each of these exams can be passed without taking the associated class.

There are three courses that cover the gambit of what is required to pass the Red Hat exam for those who may not have enough personal experience. There is also an accelerated four-day course that screams through all the material contained in the last two courses, the first course is assumed to be fully understood. This accelerated course, RH310, starts on Monday, and is immediately followed by the exam on Friday. For those individuals who are basically familiar with most but not all aspects of Red Hat Linux, then this is probably the best option currently until more extensive sets of pre-exam tests and books start to appear on the market. Nothing prepares you better for this exam than having covered the material immediately before taking the exam itself ,without the distractions of life and work to slow you down.

Table 1 shows the available hands-on, instructor-led courses that are optional but desirable prerequisites to the Red Hat Certified Engineer examination.

TABLE 1

Red Hat Courses and Certification

Course	Description
RH033	Introduction to Red Hat Linux (the fundamentals of the OS)
RH133	Red Hat Linux Systems Administration (basic network and user management)
RH253	Red Hat Linux Network and Security Administration
RH300	Rapid Track Certification (four days combining RH133 and RH253)
RHCE	The one-day, three-part certification examination (Fridays and Mondays)
Optionally to be a Red Hat Certified Examiner:	
RHCX	Red Hat Certified Examiner three-day course; must be RHCE to participate

Look for Updated Red Hat Coverage and Information Online

Chapter 1 of the text discusses the many advantages of Linux and its Open Source software development model, such as the benefits of peer review in improving the reliability and security of software. Linux has clearly benefited from this process; however, one practical challenge brought about by Open Source has been the difficulty of keeping up with the rapid - and accelerating - pace of change. With thousands of software developers around the world contributing to the software that forms the basis of the Red Hat distributions, updates are happening constantly. Dramatic reductions in software distribution costs (those of us who purchased early Linux distributions, consisting of dozens of floppies, can attest to this!) have enabled much more frequent revisions. Whether using this book to prepare for an exam or simply as a guide to installing, configuring, or maintaining Red Hat Linux, the importance of always seeking the latest available software updates and information cannot be over-emphasized. Recognizing the need to keep readers updated on these rapid and ongoing changes, Osborne (www.osborne.com) and Syngress Media (www.syngress.com) will continually monitor new releases of Red Hat Linux and will provide technology updates from their Web sites. Significant Red Hat updates may be coming in the future, so readers will want to check these web site frequently for details. We also encourage readers to utilize the links provided to Red Hat's errata and security patches, and to evaluate the significance of this information to their particular situation before installing or upgrading a Linux system.

Computer Simulated Testing

In a past experience, a three-day written, oral, and physical candidate evaluation set were used to determine the one candidate out of 10 who would be accepted for a position at a prestigious international company. Many tests were one on one, some were one on many, a few were psychological, and all were timed. Very few of the tests were of the easy "day-to-day" stuff; most were related to the ability to handle situations and problems that might arise in various areas related to the job. The candidate needed to be "well -suited" for the position, and all it entailed, within the company, as seen now and foreseen in the future by the company. Now that was an evaluation!

Measurement of anything always provides for variance. By measuring multiple levels of both skill and experience under pressure, like any good job would, the Red Hat Certification Exam is designed to cull out those with weaknesses in specific skill areas.

Prepare until it becomes second nature, and then relax. Good Luck!

1

Planning

CERTIFICATION OBJECTIVES

1.01 Open Source and Free Software

1.02 GPL and Open Source Licenses

1.03 About Linux

1.04 Starting Out

1.05 Hardware

Red Hat Linux is a modern, flexible, and mature operating system. Although it started life on the Intel platform, it has since been ported to many other platforms such as Amiga, DEC Alpha, Apple Power PC, Sun workstations, and others. Linux boasts many other features:

- **Multitasking** Linux is a true preemptive multitasking operating system. All processes run independently of each other and leave processor management to the kernel.
- **Symmetrical multiprocessing** Linux currently scales up to 16 processors.
- **Networking** Linux supports a multitude of networking protocols.
- **Multi-user** Linux handles multiple users at one time logged on to a machine.
- **Advanced memory management** Traditional UNIX systems use swapping to manage memory, where the entire memory structure of a program is written to disk when the system is running low on memory. Linux uses paging, a method that intelligently allocates memory when system memory is running low by prioritizing memory tasks.
- **POSIX support** POSIX defines a minimum interface for UNIX-type operating systems. Linux currently supports POSIX 1003.1. This ensures that POSIX-compliant UNIX programs will port easily to Linux.
- **Multiple file systems** Linux supports several different file system formats, including DOS/Windows, OS/2, and Novell formats. This makes interoperability a reality between operating systems.

CERTIFICATION OBJECTIVE 1.01

Open Source and Free Software

All Linux distributions are based on the same idea: Take the Linux kernel and surround it with freely available software, to create a usable operating system. Red Hat Linux is Red Hat Software's latest distribution and is no exception.

History

Although Linux traces its history back to 1991, it traces its heritage much further back. In 1969, a Bell Labs programmer named Ken Thompson invented the UNIX operating system. Around the same time, another programmer, Dennis Ritchie, was working on a new computer language called C. By 1974, the two had rewritten UNIX in the C language and ported it to several different machines. It is this combination of UNIX and C that Linux owes its heritage to.

UNIX and C are at the heart of Linux and the Open Source movement. While languages such as Perl, Python, Java, and others are making the headlines today, far more lines of Open Source code have been written in the C language than any single other language.

And, while many of these programs have been ported to other operating systems such as Windows NT, UNIX and UNIX-like operating systems have benefited from Open Source software the most.

Linux

In 1991, a student at Helsinki University in Finland posted this message to the Usenet group comp.os.minix:

```
From: torvalds@klaava.Helsinki.FI (Linus Benedict Torvalds)
Newsgroups: comp.os.minix
Subject: Gcc-1.40 and a posix-question
Message-ID: <1991Jul3.100050.9886@klaava.Helsinki.FI>
Date: 3 Jul 91 10:00:50 GMT
Hello netlanders,
Due to a project I'm working on (in minix), I'm interested in the posix
standard definition. Could somebody please point me to a (preferably)
machine-readable format of the latest posix rules? Ftp-sites would be
nice.
```

It was followed up a few months later with this post:

```
From: torvalds@klaava.Helsinki.FI (Linus Benedict Torvalds)
Newsgroups: comp.os.minix
Subject: What would you like to see most in minix?
Summary: small poll for my new operating system
Message-ID: <1991Aug25.205708.9541@klaava.Helsinki.FI>
Date: 25 Aug 91 20:57:08 GMT
Organization: University of Helsinki
```

```
Hello everybody out there using minix -
I'm doing a (free) operating system (just a hobby, won't be big and
professional like gnu) for 386(486) AT clones. This has been brewing
since april, and is starting to get ready. I'd like any feedback on
things people like/dislike in minix, as my OS resembles it somewhat
(same physical layout of the file-system (due to practical reasons)
among other things).
I've currently ported bash(1.08) and gcc(1.40), and things seem to work.
This implies that I'll get something practical within a few months, and
I'd like to know what features most people would want. Any suggestions
are welcome, but I won't promise I'll implement them :-)
Linus (torvalds@kruuna.helsinki.fi)
PS. Yes - it's free of any minix code, and it has a multi-threaded fs.
It is NOT portable (uses 386 task switching etc), and it probably never
will support anything other than AT-harddisks, as that's all I have
:-(.
```

The student of course was Linus Torvalds. Linus had just purchased a (then) state-of-the-art 386 PC, and wanted, among other things, to learn how it worked. The MS-DOS operating system was too limiting, and immediately discounted. At the time, he had been using another UNIX-like operating system called Minix, a microkernel-based teaching operating system. Minix had many limitations, however, so Linus set about writing a new operating system that did not suffer the limitations of MS-DOS and Minix.

Linus was by no means the first person to come up with the idea of a free UNIX-like operating system. Several years earlier The Free Software Foundation, headed by Richard M. Stallman, announced a kernel called The HURD. Unfortunately, efforts on this new kernel faltered, and it wasn't until 1996 that a stable version of The HURD was available. William and Lynne Jolitz in 1991 were also busy porting Berkeley UNIX, BSD, to the Intel platform.

But Linux was quickly propelled to the front of the pack by the large army of programmers from all across the world, who all pitched in their expertise for the Linux kernel. Instead of the project becoming chaotic and unmanageable, Linux actually benefited from the large number of coders and testers, and nearly instant feedback every time a new kernel was released, which was often. At times, several versions of Linux were released in a single day. A few years after development had begun on Linux, it was a full-featured, stable operating system.

Today, the Linux kernel is still developed as it was in the beginning. Programmers across the globe collaborate on discussion groups and e-mail lists to work on the Linux kernel. Most are not paid for their efforts, but do it out of a sense of the community that binds Linux developers.

CERTIFICATION OBJECTIVE 1.02

GPL and Open Source Licenses

The terms "Free" and "Open Source" software are commonly used to mean the same thing. While the differences are subtle, they are very important.

Free Software

"Free software" is the term typically used to refer to software that has been released under the GNU Public License, or GPL. The GPL (also called "Copyleft") was designed with the philosophy that all software should be free. Not free as in zero price, but free as in open. As the Free Software Foundation's Richard Stallman puts it in his essay "The GNU Operating System and the Free Software Movement,"

on the job

The term "free software" is sometimes misunderstood—it has nothing to do with price. It is about freedom. Here, therefore, is the definition of free software. A program is free software, for you, a particular user, if:

- ***You have the freedom to run the program, for any purpose.***
- ***You have the freedom to modify the program to suit your needs. (To make this freedom effective in practice, you must have access to the source code, since making changes in a program without having the source code is exceedingly difficult.)***
- ***You have the freedom to redistribute copies, either gratis or for a fee.***
- ***You have the freedom to distribute modified versions of the program, so that the community can benefit from your improvements.***

Since "free" refers to freedom, not to price, there is no contradiction between selling copies and free software. In fact, the freedom to sell copies is crucial: collections of free software sold on CD-ROMs are important for the community, and selling them is an important way to raise funds for free software development. Therefore, a program that people are not free to include on these collections is not free software.

The idea of free software is not new. In fact, back when mainframes ruled the data centers and universities, most software was free, and end users were free to modify it to suit their needs. In the same essay, Richard Stallman describes the situation at MIT in 1971:

"We did not call our software 'free software,' because that term did not yet exist, but that is what it was. Whenever people from another university or a company wanted to port and use a program, we gladly let them. If you saw someone using an unfamiliar and interesting program, you could always ask to see the source code, so that you could read it, change it, or cannibalize parts of it to make a new program."

In the 1980s, the trend reversed, and most new software was becoming proprietary. The idea that software should be shared soon turned into a criminal idea. Groups such as the "Software Publishers Association" sprang up, encouraging people to turn in colleagues and corporations whom they suspected of violating software copyrights.

In 1984, Richard Stallman began work on the GNU project. GNU stands for "GNUs Not UNIX, a self-recursive definition meant to imply that GNU software, unlike UNIX software, is open and free. Today, most of the software and utilities used in most Linux distributions, including Red Hat, are GNU utilities.

Here is the most recent version of the GNU Public License, which most Red Hat Linux software falls under. It can be found at http://www.gnu.org:

GNU GENERAL PUBLIC LICENSE

Version 2, June 1991

Copyright © 1989, 1991 Free Software Foundation, Inc.

59 Temple Place - Suite 330, Boston, MA 02111-1307, USA

Everyone is permitted to copy and distribute verbatim copies of this license document, but changing it is not allowed.

Preamble

The licenses for most software are designed to take away your freedom to share and change it. By contrast, the GNU General Public License is intended to guarantee your freedom to share and change free software—to make sure the software is free for all its users. This General Public License applies to most of the Free Software Foundation's software and to any other program whose authors commit to using it. (Some other Free Software Foundation software is covered by the GNU Library General Public License instead.) You can apply it to your programs, too.

When we speak of free software, we are referring to freedom, not price. Our General Public Licenses are designed to make sure that you have the freedom to distribute copies of free software (and charge for this service if you wish), that you receive source code or can get it if you want it, that you can change the software or use pieces of it in new free programs; and that you know you can do these things.

To protect your rights, we need to make restrictions that forbid anyone to deny you these rights or to ask you to surrender the rights. These restrictions translate to certain responsibilities for you if you distribute copies of the software, or if you modify it.

For example, if you distribute copies of such a program, whether gratis or for a fee, you must give the recipients all the rights that you have. You must make sure that they, too, receive or can get the source code. And you must show them these terms so they know their rights.

We protect your rights with two steps: (1) copyright the software, and (2) offer you this license which gives you legal permission to copy, distribute and/or modify the software.

Also, for each author's protection and ours, we want to make certain that everyone understands that there is no warranty for this free software. If the software is modified by someone else and passed on, we want its recipients to know that what they have is not the original, so that any problems introduced by others will not reflect on the original authors' reputations.

Finally, any free program is threatened constantly by software patents. We wish to avoid the danger that redistributors of a free program will individually obtain patent licenses, in effect making the program proprietary. To prevent this, we have made it clear that any patent must be licensed for everyone's free use or not licensed at all.

The precise terms and conditions for copying, distribution and modification follow.

TERMS AND CONDITIONS FOR COPYING, DISTRIBUTION AND MODIFICATION

0. This License applies to any program or other work which contains a notice placed by the copyright holder saying it may be distributed under the terms of this General Public License. The "Program," below, refers to any such program or work, and a "work based on the Program" means either the Program or any derivative work under copyright law: that is to say, a work containing the Program or a portion of it, either verbatim or with modifications and/or translated into another language. (Hereinafter, translation is included without limitation in the term "modification".) Each licensee is addressed as "you".

Activities other than copying, distribution and modification are not covered by this License; they are outside its scope. The act of running the Program is not restricted, and the output from the Program is covered only if its contents constitute a work based on the Program (independent of having been made by running the Program). Whether that is true depends on what the Program does.

1. You may copy and distribute verbatim copies of the Program's source code as you receive it, in any medium, provided that you conspicuously and appropriately publish on each copy an appropriate copyright notice and disclaimer of warranty; keep intact all the notices that refer to this License and to the absence of any warranty; and give any other recipients of the Program a copy of this License along with the Program.

You may charge a fee for the physical act of transferring a copy, and you may at your option offer warranty protection in exchange for a fee.

2. You may modify your copy or copies of the Program or any portion of it, thus forming a work based on the Program, and copy and distribute such modifications or work under the terms of Section 1 above, provided that you also meet all of these conditions:

   a) You must cause the modified files to carry prominent notices stating that you changed the files and the date of any change.

   b) You must cause any work that you distribute or publish, that in whole or in part contains or is derived from the Program or any part thereof, to be licensed as a whole at no charge to all third parties under the terms of this License.

   c) If the modified program normally reads commands interactively when run, you must cause it, when started running for such interactive use in the most ordinary way, to print or display an announcement including an appropriate copyright notice and a notice that there is no warranty (or else, saying that you provide a warranty) and that users may redistribute the program under these conditions, and telling the user how to view a copy of this License. (Exception: if the Program itself is interactive but does not normally print such an announcement, your work based on the Program is not required to print an announcement.)

These requirements apply to the modified work as a whole. If identifiable sections of that work are not derived from the Program, and can be reasonably considered independent and separate works in themselves, then this License, and its terms, do not apply to those sections when you distribute them as separate works. But when you distribute the same sections as part of a whole which is a work based on the Program, the distribution of the whole must be on the terms of this License, whose permissions for other licensees extend to the entire whole, and thus to each and every part regardless of who wrote it.

Thus, it is not the intent of this section to claim rights or contest your rights to work written entirely by you; rather, the intent is to exercise the right to control the distribution of derivative or collective works based on the Program.

In addition, mere aggregation of another work not based on the Program with the Program (or with a work based on the Program) on a volume of a storage or distribution medium does not bring the other work under the scope of this License.

3. You may copy and distribute the Program (or a work based on it, under Section 2) in object code or executable form under the terms of Sections 1 and 2 above provided that you also do one of the following:

   a) Accompany it with the complete corresponding machine-readable source code, which must be distributed under the terms of Sections 1 and 2 above on a medium customarily used for software interchange; or,

   b) Accompany it with a written offer, valid for at least three years, to give any third party, for a charge no more than your cost of physically performing source distribution, a complete machine-readable copy of the corresponding source code, to be distributed under the terms of Sections 1 and 2 above on a medium customarily used for software interchange; or,

   c) Accompany it with the information you received as to the offer to distribute corresponding source code. (This alternative is allowed only for noncommercial distribution and only if you received the program in object code or executable form with such an offer, in accord with Subsection b above.)

The source code for a work means the preferred form of the work for making modifications to it. For an executable work, complete source code means all the source code for all modules it contains, plus any associated interface definition files, plus the scripts used to control compilation and installation of the executable. However, as a special exception, the source code distributed need not include anything that is normally distributed (in either source or binary form) with the major components (compiler, kernel, and so on) of the operating system on which the executable runs, unless that component itself accompanies the executable.

If distribution of executable or object code is made by offering access to copy from a designated place, then offering equivalent access to copy the source code from the same place counts as distribution of the source code, even though third parties are not compelled to copy the source along with the object code.

4. You may not copy, modify, sublicense, or distribute the Program except as expressly provided under this License. Any attempt otherwise to copy, modify, sublicense or distribute the Program is void, and will automatically terminate your rights under this License. However, parties who have received copies, or rights, from you under this License will not have their licenses terminated so long as such parties remain in full compliance.
5. You are not required to accept this License, since you have not signed it. However, nothing else grants you permission to modify or distribute the Program or its derivative works. These actions are prohibited by law if you do not accept this License. Therefore, by modifying or distributing the Program (or any work based on the Program), you indicate your acceptance of this License to do so, and all its terms and conditions for copying, distributing or modifying the Program or works based on it.
6. Each time you redistribute the Program (or any work based on the Program), the recipient automatically receives a license from the original licensor to copy, distribute or modify the Program subject to these terms and conditions. You may not impose any further restrictions on the recipients' exercise of the rights granted herein. You are not responsible for enforcing compliance by third parties to this License.
7. If, as a consequence of a court judgment or allegation of patent infringement or for any other reason (not limited to patent issues), conditions are imposed on you (whether by court order, agreement or otherwise) that contradict the conditions of this License, they do not excuse you from the conditions of this License. If you cannot distribute so as to satisfy simultaneously your obligations under this License and any other pertinent obligations, then as a consequence

you may not distribute the Program at all. For example, if a patent license would not permit royalty-free redistribution of the Program by all those who receive copies directly or indirectly through you, then the only way you could satisfy both it and this License would be to refrain entirely from distribution of the Program.

If any portion of this section is held invalid or unenforceable under any particular circumstance, the balance of the section is intended to apply and the section as a whole is intended to apply in other circumstances.

It is not the purpose of this section to induce you to infringe any patents or other property right claims or to contest validity of any such claims; this section has the sole purpose of protecting the integrity of the free software distribution system, which is implemented by public license practices. Many people have made generous contributions to the wide range of software distributed through that system in reliance on consistent application of that system; it is up to the author/donor to decide if he or she is willing to distribute software through any other system and a licensee cannot impose that choice.

This section is intended to make thoroughly clear what is believed to be a consequence of the rest of this License.

8. If the distribution and/or use of the Program is restricted in certain countries either by patents or by copyrighted interfaces, the original copyright holder who places the Program under this License may add an explicit geographical distribution limitation excluding those countries, so that distribution is permitted only in or among countries not thus excluded. In such case, this License incorporates the limitation as if written in the body of this License.
9. The Free Software Foundation may publish revised and/or new versions of the General Public License from time to time. Such new versions will be similar in spirit to the present version, but may differ in detail to address new problems or concerns.

Each version is given a distinguishing version number. If the Program specifies a version number of this License which applies to it and "any later version," you have the option of following the terms and conditions either of that version or of any later version published by the Free Software Foundation. If the Program does not specify a version number of this License, you may choose any version ever published by the Free Software Foundation.

10. If you wish to incorporate parts of the Program into other free programs whose distribution conditions are different, write to the author to ask for permission. For software which is copyrighted by the Free Software Foundation, write to the Free Software Foundation; we sometimes make exceptions for this. Our decision will be guided by the two goals of preserving the free status of all derivatives of our free software and of promoting the sharing and reuse of software generally.

NO WARRANTY

11. BECAUSE THE PROGRAM IS LICENSED FREE OF CHARGE, THERE IS NO WARRANTY FOR THE PROGRAM, TO THE EXTENT PERMITTED BY APPLICABLE LAW. EXCEPT WHEN OTHERWISE STATED IN WRITING THE COPYRIGHT HOLDERS AND/OR OTHER PARTIES PROVIDE THE PROGRAM "AS IS" WITHOUT WARRANTY OF ANY KIND, EITHER EXPRESSED OR IMPLIED, INCLUDING, BUT NOT LIMITED TO, THE IMPLIED WARRANTIES OF MERCHANTABILITY AND FITNESS FOR A PARTICULAR PURPOSE. THE ENTIRE RISK AS TO THE QUALITY AND PERFORMANCE OF THE PROGRAM IS WITH YOU. SHOULD THE PROGRAM PROVE DEFECTIVE, YOU ASSUME THE COST OF ALL NECESSARY SERVICING, REPAIR OR CORRECTION.

12. IN NO EVENT UNLESS REQUIRED BY APPLICABLE LAW OR AGREED TO IN WRITING WILL ANY COPYRIGHT HOLDER, OR ANY OTHER PARTY WHO MAY MODIFY AND/OR REDISTRIBUTE THE PROGRAM AS PERMITTED ABOVE, BE LIABLE TO YOU FOR DAMAGES, INCLUDING ANY GENERAL, SPECIAL, INCIDENTAL OR CONSEQUENTIAL DAMAGES ARISING

OUT OF THE USE OR INABILITY TO USE THE PROGRAM (INCLUDING BUT NOT LIMITED TO LOSS OF DATA OR DATA BEING RENDERED INACCURATE OR LOSSES SUSTAINED BY YOU OR THIRD PARTIES OR A FAILURE OF THE PROGRAM TO OPERATE WITH ANY OTHER PROGRAMS), EVEN IF SUCH HOLDER OR OTHER PARTY HAS BEEN ADVISED OF THE POSSIBILITY OF SUCH DAMAGES.

END OF TERMS AND CONDITIONS

It is important to note that the Linux kernel, which is distributed under the GPL, contains the following preamble:

NOTE! This copyright does *not* cover user programs that use kernel services by normal system calls—this is merely considered normal use of the kernel, and does *not* fall under the heading of "derived work." Also note that the GPL below is copyrighted by the Free Software Foundation, but the instance of code that it refers to (the Linux kernel) is copyrighted by me and others who actually wrote it.
Linus Torvalds

Open Source Software

Open Source software, like Free software, requires that software source code be provided and readable. What Open Source does not promote, however, are the philosophical reasons behind Free software. Where the GPL makes freedom a central point, Open Source sidesteps the philosophy and sets only the guidelines for software to fit the Open Source definition. Richard M. Stallman in his essay, "Why Free Software is better than Open Source" states that:

"The obvious meaning for 'open source software' is 'You can look at the source code.' This is a much weaker criterion than 'free software'; it includes free software, but also includes semi-free programs such as Xv, and even some proprietary programs, including Qt, under its former license.

"That obvious meaning for 'open source' is not the meaning that its advocates intend. (Their 'official' definition is much closer to 'free software.') The result is that people often misunderstand them. Of course, this can be addressed by publishing a precise definition for the term. The people using 'open source software' have done this, just as we have done for 'free software.' However, this approach is only partially effective in either case. For free software, we have to teach people that we intend one meaning rather than another that fits the words equally well. For open source, we would have to teach them to use a meaning which does not really fit at all."

Here is the most recent version of the Open Source Definition, which can be found at http://www.opensource.org.

Open source doesn't just mean access to the source code. The distribution terms of an open-source program must comply with the following criteria:

1. **Free Redistribution** The license may not restrict any party from selling or giving away the software as a component of an aggregate software distribution containing programs from several different sources. The license may not require a royalty or other fee for such sale.
2. **Source Code** The program must include source code, and must allow distribution in source code as well as compiled form. Where some form of a product is not distributed with source code, there must be a well-publicized means of downloading the source code, without charge, via the Internet. The source code must be the preferred form in which a programmer would modify the program. Deliberately obfuscated source code is not allowed. Intermediate forms such as the output of a preprocessor or translator are not allowed.
3. **Derived Works** The license must allow modifications and derived works, and must allow them to be distributed under the same terms as the license of the original software. (rationale)
4. **Integrity of the Author's Source Code** The license must not discriminate against any person or group of persons. (rationale)
5. **No Discrimination Against Fields of Endeavor** The license must not restrict anyone from making use of the program in a specific field of endeavor. For example, it may not restrict the program from being used in a business, or from being used for genetic research. (rationale)

6. **Distribution of License** The rights attached to the program must apply to all to whom the program is redistributed without the need for execution of an additional license by those parties. (rationale)
7. **License Must Not Be Specific to a Product** The rights attached to the program must not depend on the program's being part of a particular software distribution. If the program is extracted from that distribution and used or distributed within the terms of the program's license, all parties to whom the program is redistributed should have the same rights as those that are granted in conjunction with the original software distribution. (rationale)
8. **License Must Not Contaminate Other Software** The license must not place restrictions on other software that is distributed along with the licensed software. For example, the license must not insist that all other programs distributed on the same medium must be open-source software. (rationale)
9. **Example Licenses** The GNU GPL, BSD, X Consortium, and Artistic licenses are examples of licenses that we consider conformant to the Open Source Definition. So is the MPL.

Bruce Perens wrote the first draft of this document as "The Debian Free Software Guidelines," and refined it using the comments of the Debian developers in a month-long e-mail conference in June, 1997. He removed the Debian-specific references from the document to create the "Open Source Definition."

Services and Applications

If you think that Free and Open Source software is a new or niche idea, it may surprise you to learn that most of the Internet runs on Free or Open Source software. Most of your e-mail is passed across the Internet using Sendmail, a free program written by Eric Allman in 1979. A survey done by Netcraft in May 1999 showed that over 60% of Web sites on the Internet are using the Apache Web Server, or Apache derivatives. (The survey can be found at http://www.netcraft.com/survey/.) And every time you type a Web address into your browser, there's a good chance it resolves the location of that Web address against a server running BIND, a free implementation of the Domain Name System that runs the Internet. The free news server Dnews handles much of the Usenet traffic, and many people read that news using free news readers such as rn, tin, and mutt. One of the most popular (and powerful) editors, GNU/Emacs, is used to compose documents and source code, read e-mail, news, and even program in LISP.

In the development space, languages such as C, C++, Perl, Python, Tcl/Tk, Pascal, Cobol, Fortran, and many others are freely available. And, if you're curious as to how these compilers are built, the source code is available for every one of them.

CERTIFICATION OBJECTIVE 1.03

About Linux

You hear people talking about Linux all the time. But you also probably hear about the "Red Hat" Linux distribution, and names like SuSE, Caldera, Debian, Slackware, and others. Are they all Linux?

Recall that Linux is the operating system kernel. That is, Linux is the very heart of the operating system. However, like all operating systems, to be useful Linux has to have utilities and programs to do the actual work. This is where distributions come in. All of the Linux distributions run the Linux kernel. But after that, the distributions vary from each other to some degree. For example, the Slackware distribution looks and feels much like Berkeley UNIX, whereas the SuSE distribution is much more System V'ish. Red Hat Linux tends to fall somewhere in between.

Current Support for Networking Services

Linux was built from the start to be a network operating system. This may seem obvious now, but consider that in 1991 nobody knew how important networking and the Internet would be to modern-day computing. This gives Linux a big edge, in terms of network stability and integration.

Today, Linux supports the following networking protocols (Table 1-1).

TABLE 1-1

Networking protocols supported by Linux

TCP/IP	This is the protocol used by the Internet, and on most local networks.
AppleTalk	The protocol used for Apple computers to communicate with each other.
CCITT X.25 Packet Layer	The X.25 networking protocol.
IP Version 6	This is the protocol that will eventually replace IP version 4 on the Internet.
Acorn Econet/AUN	An older protocol, used by Acorn computers to access file and print servers
IPX	The Novell networking protocol, used to access Novell file and print servers

Flexibility of Open Source Software

Much ado has been made about Free and Open Source software, but what do you really get that you can't get from closed operating systems such as Microsoft Windows?

- **Stability** When a version of an Open Source program is released on the Internet, there is a large peer review of the source code. With so many people looking at the code, there's a much better chance that somebody will see a bug, and even offer a correction. This type of peer review just isn't possible in the closed source world.
- **Modifications** In a closed source environment, you're at the mercy of the vendor. If you want or need a feature, you can submit a request for features, but you can only hope the vendor will agree with you. If not, you're stuck. With Open Source, you have the source code, and you can add the features yourself if need be. Or, you can hire a programmer to make the changes for you. Many times, you can post a message to the appropriate Usenet newsgroup saying "Gee, it sure would be nice if program Foo could do this." Sometimes somebody will have a patch written within a couple of days that does just what you want.

- **Support** There are literally thousands of Open Source advocates out there on newsgroups and e-mail lists who can answer your questions when you need help. Best of all, it's free. Contrast this with the big money you throw to the closed source vendors, who may or may not be able to help you. And if you really feel the need to pay for support, there are several companies out there now providing 7×24 technical support for Linux.
- **Freedom** With proprietary software, the primary goal is to make money. That the software may be useful to you is only a secondary concern. And, that software never truly belongs to you, but is instead licensed for your use. The software vendor has all the advantages; you have none of them. However, Free and Open Source software gives you the freedom to view, modify, and share the code with others.

R&D Processes and Practices

The traditional development process of software has always gone something like this: A software company decides to create a package. Specifications are drawn up, some prototyping is done, software designers write, rewrite, and refine it. It goes back and forth for review and bug testing. Finally, the decision is made to release the product; it gets stamped onto media and shrink-wrapped. Only when the consumer unpacks the box does the software truly ever see the light of day, because throughout the entire lifecycle of the development process, the software was tested and developed only by the software company. Even in a Beta testing program, the number of participants is nowhere near the number of people who will finally use the software.

The Free and Open Source model differs significantly. Usually the process begins because a programmer has an "itch" that needs to be scratched. In other words, the programmer thinks it would be a fun project to, say, write a mail client. Or perhaps she's been reading Usenet, hearing people lament how they wish X mail client had these features. In any case, the programmer whips out some code and posts it to the Internet, asking for participants, peer reviewers, or just comments. Perhaps a few people join in, and add features to this code. A new revision is posted for others to see. As people become more interested, the project takes on a life larger than perhaps the original author intended. A programmer in Colorado might be working on the user interface, while programmers in Spain and Iceland collaborate on some other area of code.

In May of 1997, Eric S. Raymond presented his paper, "The Cathedral and the Bazaar" at the 1997 Linux Kongress. You can find this essay at http://www.tuxedo.org/~esr/writings. Raymond likened traditional software companies to cathedral builders, skilled artisans who worked meticulously on their software projects within the hallowed walls of the giant software companies.

"I had been preaching the UNIX gospel of small tools, rapid prototyping, and evolutionary programming for years. But I also believed there was a certain critical complexity above which a more centralized, a priori approach was required. I believed that the most important software (operating systems and really large tools like Emacs) needed to be built like cathedrals, carefully crafted by individual wizards or small bands of mages working in splendid isolation, with no beta to be released before its time."

But Linux showed another type of development model, which Raymond calls "the Bazaar." This is an environment where anybody with a computer, a compiler, and the desire to write software, can join in. Raymond writes:

"Linus Torvalds' style of development—release early and often, delegate everything you can, be open to the point of promiscuity—came as a surprise. No quiet, reverent cathedral-building here—rather, the Linux community seemed to resemble a great babbling bazaar of differing agendas and approaches (aptly symbolized by the Linux archive sites, who'd take submissions from anyone) out of which a coherent and stable system could seemingly emerge only by a succession of miracles."

But Linux has succeeded, and continues to do so under the same bazaar-style development process it began under in 1991.

Future Development

The future of Linux is filled with uncertainty and excitement. Uncertainty because it's hard to predict just where the course of the Internet and technology will run. Exciting because Linux will be right there with it when it happens.

Even now, exciting things are happening in the Linux world. Kernel development continues at a brisk pace, and companies like Red Hat Software are showing that the world is taking Linux seriously. On the day of its Initial Public Offering, the price of Red Hat Software stock tripled. Entire companies make their livings on Free and Open Source software, such as Cygnus, SuSE, VA Research, and others.

CERTIFICATION OBJECTIVE 1.04

Starting Out

Compared to previous versions of Linux, Red Hat Linux is pretty straightforward as far as operating system installs go. Still, you'll want to make sure you're prepared beforehand. Before installing Red Hat Linux, make sure:

- **You have documentation** You'll want installation documentation and post-install documentation, so you'll know how to use your new system.
- **You have the correct hardware** While Red Hat Linux supports more and more hardware with each release, you still need to check to make sure your components are supported.
- **You know your hardware's specifications** You should know what interrupt your network card, for instance, operates on. If you're using SCSI peripherals, make sure you know all their SCSI IDs.

- **You know what installation method you will be using** Upgrade, server, workstation, or custom.
- **You know how you will be laying your file systems out**

Needs

Before you begin a Red Hat Linux installation, you need to know what the purpose of the machine will be. Will it be a development workstation? Or an FTP or Web server? Or will it be a database server? Each of these examples requires a different configuration.

Workstation Installation

If you're new to Linux, or just need a basic workstation, Red Hat makes it easy to get started. During the installation, you are given three choices:

- Workstation
- Server
- Custom

Selecting "Workstation" will give you an easy and fast way (with some loss of flexibility in configuration) to get started. The Workstation install does the following:

- It removes any preexisting Linux and Linux swap partitions. It will not remove DOS partitions.
- It uses all free space on the primary drive.
- The following partitions are created:
  - A 64MB swap partition.
  - On Intel systems, a 16MB partition (mounted as /boot) is created. The kernel and associated files reside here.
  - On Alpha systems, a 2MB partition (mounted as /dos) is created, where the MILO boot loader will reside.

    - The rest of the disk is mounted as /, where all other files are placed.
- If a DOS/Windows partition exists, Red Hat Linux will automatically configure your system to dual-boot.

Approximately 600MB of free disk space is required for a Workstation install. Remember that performing a Workstation install will automatically overwrite all of the existing Linux and Linux swap partitions on the disk.

Server Installation

The Server installation will give you a fast and easy way (with some loss of flexibility in configuration) to set up a Web, FTP, or other type of server class system. When presented with the three types of installs, select "Server." The Server install does the following:

- It removes all preexisting partitions (even DOS partitions).
- It uses all space on the primary drive.
- The following partitions are created:
    - A 64MB swap partition.
    - On Intel systems, a 16MB partition (mounted as /boot) is created. The kernel and associated files reside here.
    - On Alpha systems, a 2MB partition (mounted as /dos) is created, where the MILO boot loader will reside.
    - A 256MB partition (mounted as /).
    - A 512MB (or more) partition mounted as /usr.
    - A 512MB (or more) partition mounted as /home.
    - A 256MB partition mounted as /var.
- A hard disk of at least 1.6GB in size is required for a Server install.

Remember that performing a Server install will automatically overwrite all of the partitions on the disk, including DOS/Windows partitions.

Note that a Server installation, unlike a Workstation installation, will remove all existing partitions on the primary hard drive, even DOS partitions.

Custom Installation

The custom Install gives you the most flexibility to choose how you want your system installed, at some loss of ease and speed. You determine how the disk is laid out, what size each partition is, and which packages will be installed. The Custom install is recommended for veteran Linux users only.

CERTIFICATION OBJECTIVE 1.05

Hardware

Although Red Hat offers Linux for Intel, Sparc, and Alpha platforms, we will concentrate on the most common platform, Intel.

Intel and Clones

Installing on most Intel-based computers is pretty straightforward. But you'll save yourself a lot of time and frustration by knowing exactly what hardware you have. You should know the following information about your system:

- **Drives** Check to see if you are using SCSI or IDE drives. You should know the manufacturer, model number, and capacity of the drive. If it's a SCSI drive, make sure you know its SCSI ID.
- **Hard drive controller** You should know the manufacturer and model number of the drive controller. Oftentimes this information is hard to obtain, so at the very least try to identify the chipset of the controller.

- **CD-ROM** If you're using a SCSI or IDE CD-ROM, you probably won't have to worry about what type it is. However, if you're using a CD-ROM with a proprietary interface (common with older models), you should know the manufacturer and the model number of the drive and controller. Also, for proprietary interfaces, you should also know what IRQ it uses.
- **Mouse** You should know what type of mouse you are using—PS/2, serial, or other type.
- **Display adaptor** If you will be running X, you will need the manufacturer, the model number, and how much memory is on the adaptor.
- **Sound, video, and game adaptors** If you want to set up sound on your system, you should know the manufacturer and the model number of the sound card. You should also know what IRQ it uses, if any.
- **Network adaptors** If you'll be networking your Linux system, you should know the manufacturer and the model number of the network adaptor. You should also know what IRQ it uses, if any.
- **Monitor** If you will be running X, you will need the manufacturer, the model number, the resolutions, and the frequencies of the monitor.

Not all hardware will work with Linux. After you've collected information about your system, you should consult the Intel Hardware Compatibility List in the next section to determine if your components are compatible with Red Hat Linux.

Intel Hardware Compatibility List

The complete Hardware Compatibility List is available on the Red Hat Linux CD-ROM, or in /usr/doc/HOWTO/Hardware-HOWTO on an installed Red Hat Linux system, or online at http://sunsite.unc.edu/pub/Linux/docs/HOWTO/Hardware-HOWTO. The list has had Chapters 3, 6, 7, 10–12, 14, 16, 17,19, 20–22, 26, 27, and 29 removed to conserve space.

Linux Hardware Compatibility HOWTO

Patrick Reijnen, <antispam.patrickr@antispam.bart.nl (remove "antispam")>

v98.3, 30 July 1998

This document lists most of the hardware supported by Linux and helps you locate any necessary drivers.

Table of Contents

```
7. Controllers (hard drive)

8. Controllers (SCSI)

   8.1 Supported
   8.2 Others
   8.3 Unsupported

9. Controllers (I/O)

10. Controllers (multiport)

   10.1 Non-intelligent cards
      10.1.1 Supported
   10.2 Intelligent cards
      10.2.1 Supported
      10.2.2 Others

11. Network adapters

   11.1 Supported
      11.1.1 Ethernet
      11.1.2 ISDN
      11.1.3 Pocket and portable adapters
      11.1.4 Slotless
      11.1.5 ARCnet
      11.1.6 TokenRing
      11.1.7 FDDI
      11.1.8 Amateur radio (AX.25)
      11.1.9 PCMCIA cards
   11.2 Others
      11.2.1 Ethernet
      11.2.2 ISDN
      11.2.3 ATM
      11.2.4 Frame Relay
      11.2.5 Wireless
   11.3 Unsupported

12. Sound cards

   12.1 Supported
   12.2 Others
   12.3 Unsupported
```

```
13. Hard drives

   13.1 Unsupported

14. Tape drives

   14.1 Supported
   14.2 Others
   14.3 Unsupported

15. CD-ROM drives

   15.1 Supported
   15.2 Others
   15.3 Notes

16. CD-Writers

17. Removable drives

18. Mice

   18.1 Supported
   18.2 Others
   18.3 Notes

19. Modems

20. Printers/Plotters

   20.1 Ghostscript
      20.1.1 Ghostscript supported printers
      20.1.2 Others

21. Scanners

   21.1 Supported
   21.2 Others
   21.3 Unsupported

22. Other hardware

   22.1 Amateur Radio
   22.2 VESA Power Savings Protocol (DPMS) monitors
   22.3 Touch screens
   22.4 Terminals on serial port
   22.5 Joysticks
```

---

1. Introduction

NOTE: Great news: HP Deskjet 720, 820 and 1000 series printers are supported under Linux. Have a look at

<http://www.rpi.edu/~normat/technical/ppa>

1.1. Welcome

Welcome to the Linux Hardware Compatibility HOWTO. This document lists most of the hardware components (not computers with components build in) supported by Linux, so reading through this document you can choose the components for your own Linux computer. As the list of components supported by Linux is growing rapidly, this document will never be complete. So, when components are not mentioned in this HOWTO, the only reason will be that I don't know they are supported. I simply have not found support for the component and/or nobody has told me about support.

Subsections titled Others list hardware with alpha or beta drivers in varying degrees of usability or other drivers that aren't included in standard kernels. Note that some drivers only exist in alpha kernels, so if you see something listed as supported but isn't in your version of the Linux kernel, upgrade.

The latest version of this document can be found on <http://users.bart.nl/~patrickr/hardware-howto/Hardware-HOWTO.html>, SunSite and all the usual mirror sites. Translations of this and other Linux HOWTO's can be found at <http://sunsite.unc.edu/pub/Linux/docs/HOWTO/translations> and <ftp://sunsite.unc.edu/pub/Linux/docs/HOWTO/translations>.
If you know of any Linux hardware (in)compatibilities not listed here please let me know, just send mail.

Still need some help selecting components after reading this document? Check the "Build Your Own PC" site at <http://www.verinet.com/pc/>.

1.2. Copyright

Copyright 1997, 1998 Patrick Reijnen

This HOWTO is free documentation; you can redistribute it and/or modify it under the terms of the GNU General Public License as published by the Free software Foundation; either version 2 of the license, or (at your option) any later version.

This document is distributed in the hope that it will be useful, but without any warranty; without even the implied warranty of

If you use this or any other Linux HOWTO's in a commercial distribution, it would be nice to send the authors a complimentary copy of your product.

1.3. System architectures

This document only deals with Linux for Intel platforms, for other platforms check the following:

ARM Linux
<http://www.arm.uk.linux.org/~rmk92/armlinux.html>

Linux/68k

Linux/8086
<http://www.linux.org.uk/Linux8086.html>

Linux/Alpha
<http://www.azstarnet.com/~axplinux/>

Linux/MIPS
<http://www.fnet.fr/linux-mips/>

Linux/PowerPC
<http://www.linuxppc.org/>

Linux for Acorn
<http://www.ph.kcl.ac.uk/~amb/linux.html>

Linux for PowerMac
<http://ftp.sunet.se/pub/os/Linux/mklinux/mkarchive/info/index.html>

2. Computers/Motherboards/BIOS

ISA, VLB, EISA, and PCI buses are all supported.

PS/2 and Microchannel (MCA) is supported in the standard kernel 2.0.7. There is support for MCA in kernel 2.1.16 and newer, but this code is

```
still a little buggy. For more information you can always look at the
Micro Channel Linux Home Page ( <http://glycerine.itsmm.uni.edu/mca/>)
2.1.  Specific systems


   IBM PS/2 MCA systems
   <ftp://ftp.dcrl.nd.edu/pub/misc/linux/>

   EFA E5TX-AT motherboard has a solvable problem with RedHat Linux
   5.0 and possibly other versions of Linux. It spontaneously reboots
   while probing hardware. To solve, update BIOS to version 1.01. Get
   the BIOS update at
   <http://www.efacorp.com/download/Motherboard/e5tx101.exe>.

Many new PCI boards are causing a couple of failure messages during
boot time when "Probing PCI Hardware". The procedure presents the
following message


    Warning : Unknown PCI device (8086:7100).  Please read include/linux/pci.h


It tells you to read the pci.h file. From this file is the following
quote


          PROCEDURE TO REPORT NEW PCI DEVICES
    We are trying to collect information on new PCI devices, using
    the standard PCI identification procedure. If some warning is
    displayed at boot time, please report
          - /proc/pci
          - your exact hardware description. Try to find out
            which device is unknown. It may be you mainboard chipset.
            PCI-CPU bridge or PCI-ISA bridge.
          - If you can't find the actual information in your hardware
            booklet, try to read the references of the chip on the board.
          - Send all that to linux-pcisupport@cao-vlsi.ibp.fr,
            and I'll add your device to the list as soon as possible

    BEFORE you send a mail, please check the latest linux releases
    to be sure it has not been recently added.

           Thanks
                Frederic Potter.
```

Normally spoken you motherboard and the unknown PCI devices will function correctly.

2.2. Unsupported

Supermicro P5MMA with BIOS versions 1.36, 1.37 and 1.4. Linux will not boot on this motherboard. A new (beta) release of the BIOS which makes Linux boot, is available at <ftp.supermicro.com/mma9051.zip>

Supermicro P5MMA98. Linux will not boot on this motherboard. A new (beta) release of the BIOS which makes Linux boot, is available at <ftp.supermicro.com/a98905.zip>?

DataExpert Corp. ExpertColor TX531 V1.0 motherboard with chipset ACER M1531 (Date: 9729, TS6) and ACER M1543 (Date: 9732 TS6) seems not reproducible segmentations faults, kernel oops and kernel hangs under heavy load and tape access. The problem seems to be the PCI-bus, respectively the ACER chipset.

3. Laptops

4. CPU/FPU

Intel/AMD/Cyrix 386SX/DX/SL/DXL/SLC, 486SX/DX/SL/SX2/DX2/DX4 are supported. Intel Pentium, Pentium Pro and Pentium II (basically it's a Pentium Pro with MMX) also work. AMD K5 and K6 work good, although older versions of K6 should be avoided as they are buggy. Setting "internal cache" disabled in bios setup can be a workaround.

Also IDT Winchip C6-PSME2006A processors are supported under Linux.

Linux has built-in FPU emulation if you don't have a math coprocessor.

Experimental SMP (multiple CPU) support is included in kernel 1.3.31 and newer. Check the Linux/SMP Project page for details and updates.

Linux/SMP Project
<http://www.linux.org.uk/SMP/title.html>

A few very early AMD 486DX's may hang in some special situations. All current chips should be okay and getting a chip swap for old CPU's should not be a problem.

ULSI Math*Co series has a bug in the FSAVE and FRSTOR instructions that causes problems with all protected mode operating systems. Some older IIT and Cyrix chips may also have this problem.

There are problems with TLB flushing in UMC U5S chips in very old kernels. (1.1.x)

enable cache on Cyrix processors
<ftp://sunsite.unc.edu/pub/Linux/kernel/patches/CxPatch030.tar.z>

Cyrix software cache control
<ftp://sunsite.unc.edu/pub/Linux/kernel/patches/linux.cxpatch>

Cyrix 5x86 CPU register settings
<ftp://sunsite.unc.edu/pub/Linux/kernel/patches/cx5x86mod_1.0c.tgz>

5. Memory

All memory like DRAM, EDO and SDRAM can be used with Linux. There is one thing you have to look at: normally the kernel is not supporting more than 64 Mb of memory. When you add more than 64 Mb of memory you have to add the following line to your LILO configuration file.

```
append="mem=<number of Mb>M"
```

So, when you have 96 Mb of memory this should become

```
append="mem=96M"
```

Don't type a number higher than the number Mb you really have. This can present unpredictable crashes.

6. Video cards

7. Controllers (hard drive)

8. Controllers (SCSI)

It is important to pick a SCSI controller carefully. Many cheap ISA SCSI controllers are designed to drive CD-ROM's rather than anything else. Such low end SCSI controllers are no better than IDE. See the SCSI HOWTO and look at performance figures before buying a SCSI card.

8.1. Supported

AMI Fast Disk VLB/EISA (BusLogic compatible)

Adaptec AVA-1502E (ISA/VLB) (AIC-6360). Use the AHA-152x driver

Adaptec AVA-1505/1515 (ISA) (Adaptec AHA-152x compatible)

Adaptec AHA-1510/152x (ISA/VLB) (AIC-6260/6360)

Adaptec AHA-154x (ISA) (all models)

Adaptec AHA-174x (EISA) (in enhanced mode)

Adaptec AHA-274x (EISA) (AIC-7771)

Adaptec AHA-284x (VLB) (AIC-7770)

Adaptec AHA-2920 (PCI). Use the Future Domain driver. LILO parameters are needed when used for hard disks.

Adaptec AHA-2940AU (PCI) (AIC-7861)

Adaptec AHA-294x/U/W/UW/D/WD (AIC-7871, AIC-7844, AIC-7881, AIC-7884)

Adaptec AHA-3940/U/W (PCI) (AIC-7872, AIC-7882) (since 1.3.6)

Adaptec AHA-398x/U/W (PCI) (AIC-7873, AIC-7883)

Adaptec PCI controllers with AIC-7850, AIC-7855, AIC-7860

Adaptec on board controllers with AIC-777x (EISA), AIC-785x, AIC-787x (PCI), AIC-788x (PCI)

Advansys 5140 (ISA)

<http://advansys.com/5140o.htm> for information.

Always IN2000

BusLogic (ISA/EISA/VLB/PCI) (all models)

DPT PM2001, PM2012A (EATA-PIO)

DPT Smartcache/SmartRAID Plus,III,IV families (ISA/EISA/PCI)
Take a look at <http://www.uni-mainz.de/~neuffer/scsi/dpt/>(EATA-DMA)
Cards in these families are PM2011, PM2021, PM2041, PM3021, PM2012B, PM2022, PM2122, PM2322, PM2042, PM3122, PM3222, PM3332, PM2024, PM2124, PM2044, PM2144, PM3224, PM3334

DTC 329x (EISA) (Adaptec 154x compatible)

Future Domain TMC-16x0, TMC-3260 (PCI)

Future Domain TMC-8xx, TMC-950

Future Domain chips TMC-1800, TMC-18C50, TMC-18C30, TMC-36C70

ICP-Vortex PCI-SCSI Disk Array Controllers (many RAID levels supported)
Patches for Linux 1.2.13 and 2.0.29 are available at <ftp://icp-vortex.com/download/linux/>. The controllers GDT6111RP, GDT6121RP, GDT6117RP, GDT6127RP, GDT6511RP, GDT6521RP, GDT6517RP, GDT6527RP, GDT6537RP and GDT6557RP are supported. You can also use pre-patch-2.0.31-4 to pre-patch-2.0.31-9.

ICP-Vortex EISA-SCSI Controllers (many RAID levels supported)
Patches for Linux 1.2.13 and 2.0.29 are available at <ftp://icp-vortex.com/download/linux/>. The controllers GDT3000B, GDT3000A, GDT3010A, GDT3020A and GDT3050A are supported. You can also use pre-patch-2.0.31-4 to pre-patch-2.0.31-9.

Media Vision Pro Audio Spectrum 16 SCSI (ISA)

NCR 5380 generic cards

NCR 53C400 (Trantor T130B) (use generic NCR 5380 SCSI support)

NCR 53C406a (Acculogic ISApport / Media Vision Premium 3D SCSI)

NCR chips 53C7x0

NCR chips 53C810, 53C815, 53C820, 53C825, 53C860, 53C875, 53C895

Qlogic / Control Concepts SCSI/IDE (FAS408) (ISA/VLB)

Quantum ISA-200S, ISA-250MG

Seagate ST-01/ST-02 (ISA)

SoundBlaster 16 SCSI-2 (Adaptec 152x compatible) (ISA)

Tekram DC-390, DC-390W/U/F

Trantor T128/T128F/T228 (ISA)

UltraStor 14F (ISA), 24F (EISA), 34F (VLB)

Western Digital WD7000 SCSI

8.2. Others

AMD AM53C974, AM79C974 (PCI) (Compaq, HP, Zeos onboard SCSI)
<ftp://sunsite.unc.edu/pub/Linux/kernel/patches/scsi/AM53C974-0.3.tgz>

Adaptec ACB-40xx SCSI-MFM/RLL bridgeboard
<ftp://sunsite.unc.edu/pub/Linux/kernel/patches/scsi/adaptec-40XX.tar.gz>

Always Technologies AL-500
<ftp://sunsite.unc.edu/pub/Linux/kernel/patches/scsi/al500-0.2.tar.gz>

BusLogic (ISA/EISA/VLB/PCI) (new beta driver)
<ftp://sunsite.unc.edu/pub/Linux/kernel/patches/scsi/BusLogic-1.3.0.tar.gz>

Iomega PC2/2B

<ftp://sunsite.unc.edu/pub/Linux/kernel/patches/scsi/iomega_pc2-1.1.x.tar.gz>

Qlogic (ISP1020) (PCI)
<ftp://sunsite.unc.edu/pub/Linux/kernel/patches/scsi/isp1020-0.5.gz>

Ricoh GSI-8

<ftp://tsx-11.mit.edu/pub/linux/ALPHA/scsi/gsi8.tar.gz>

8.3. Unsupported

Parallel port SCSI adapters

Non Adaptec compatible DTC boards (327x, 328x)

9. Controllers (I/O)

Any standard serial/parallel/joystick/combo cards. Linux supports 8250, 16450, 16550, and 16550A UART's. Cards that support non-standard IRQ's (IRQ > 9) can be used.

See National Semiconductor's ``Application Note AN-493'' by Martin S. Michael. Section 5.0 describes in detail the differences between the NS16550 and NS16550A. Briefly, the NS16550 had bugs in the FIFO circuits, but the NS16550A (and later) chips fixed those. However, there were very few NS16550's produced by National, long ago, so these should be very rare. And many of the ``16550'' parts in actual modern boards are from the many manufacturers of compatible parts, which may not use the National ``A'' suffix. Also, some multiport boards will use 16552 or 16554 or various other multiport or multifunction chips from National or other suppliers (generally in a dense package soldered to the board, not a 40 pin DIP). Mostly, don't worry about it unless you encounter a very old 40 pin DIP National ``NS16550'' (no A) chip loose or in an old board, in which case treat it as a 16450 (no FIFO) rather than a 16550A. - Zhahai Stewart <zstewart@hisys.com>

10. Controllers (multiport)

11. Network adapters

12. Sound cards

13. Hard drives

All hard drives should work if the controller is supported.

(From the SCSI HOWTO) All direct access SCSI devices with a block size of 256, 512, or 1024 bytes should work. Other block sizes will not work (Note that this can often be fixed by changing the block and/or sector sizes using the MODE SELECT SCSI command).

Large IDE (EIDE) drives work fine with newer kernels. The boot partition must lie in the first 1024 cylinders due to PC BIOS limitations.

Some Conner CFP1060S drives may have problems with Linux and ext2fs. The symptoms are inode errors during e2fsck and corrupt file systems. Conner has released a firmware upgrade to fix this problem, contact Conner at 1-800-4CONNER (US) or +44-1294-315333 (Europe). Have the microcode version (found on the drive label, 9WA1.6x) handy when you call.

Certain Micropolis drives have problems with Adaptec and BusLogic cards, contact the drive manufacturers for firmware upgrades if you suspect problems.

Multiple device driver (RAID-0, RAID-1)
<ftp://sweet-smoke.ufr-info-p7.ibp.fr/public/Linux/>

13.1. Unsupported

The following hard drives are mentioned as not supported by Linux. Read the bug report available.

NEC D3817, D3827, D3847
"These drives are slightly non-SCSI-2 compliant in the values reported in Mode Sense Page 3. In Mode Sense Page 3 all NEC D38x7 drives report their sector size as zero. The NEC drives are the first brand of drive we have ever encountered that reported the sector size as zero. Unfortunately, that field in Mode Sense Page 3 is not modifiable and there is no way to update the firmware on the D38x7 drives to correct this problem."

14. Tape drives

15. CD-ROM drives

For more information on CD-ROM drives check the CDROM-HOWTO at <http://sunsite.unc.edu/LDP/HOWTO/>.

```
15.1.  Supported


Common CD-ROM drives

    SCSI CD-ROM drives
    (From the CD-ROM HOWTO) Any SCSI CD-ROM drive with a block size of
    512 or 2048 bytes should work under Linux; this includes the vast
    majority of CD-ROM drives on the market.
    EIDE (ATAPI) CD-ROM drives (IDECD)
    Almost all double, quad and six speed drives are supported,
    including

    Mitsumi FX400

    Nec-260

    Sony 55E

Proprietary CD-ROM drives

    Aztech CDA268-01A, Orchid CDS-3110, Okano/Wearnes CDD-110, Conrad
    TXC, CyCDROM CR520ie/CR540ie/CR940ie (AZTCD)

    Creative Labs CD-200(F) (SBPCD)

    Funai E2550UA/MK4015 (SBPCD)

    GoldStar R420 (GSCD)

    IBM External ISA (SBPCD)

    Kotobuki (SBPCD)

    Lasermate CR328A (OPTCD)

    LMS Philips CM 206 (CM206)

    Longshine LCS-7260 (SBPCD)

    Matsushita/Panasonic CR-521/522/523/562/563 (SBPCD)

    MicroSolutions Backpack parallel portdrive (BPCD)

    Mitsumi CR DC LU05S (MCD/MCDX)
```

Mitsumi FX001D/F (MCD/MCDX)

Optics Storage Dolphin 8000AT (OPTCD)

Sanyo CDR-H94A (SJCD)

Sony CDU31A/CDU33A (CDU31A)

Sony CDU-510/CDU-515 (SOMYCD535)

Sony CDU-535/CDU-531 (SONYCD535)

Teac CD-55A SuperQuad (SBPCD)

15.2. Others

LMS/Philips CM 205/225/202
<ftp://sunsite.unc.edu/pub/Linux/kernel/patches/cdrom/lmscd0.4.tar.gz>

NEC CDR-35D (old)
<ftp://sunsite.unc.edu/pub/Linux/kernel/patches/cdrom/linux-neccdr35d.patch>

Sony SCSI multisession CD-XA
<ftp://tsx-11.mit.edu/pub/linux/patches/sony-multi-0.00.tar.gz>

Parallel Port Driver
<http://www.torque.net/linux-pp.html>

15.3. Notes

All CD-ROM drives should work similarly for reading data. There are various compatibility problems with audio CD playing utilities. (Especially with newer low-end NEC drives.) Some alpha drivers may not have audio support yet.

Early (single speed) NEC CD-ROM drives may have trouble with currently available SCSI controllers.

PhotoCD (XA) is supported. The hpcdtoppm program by Hadmut Danisch converts PhotoCD files to the portable pixmap format. The program can be obtained from <ftp://ftp.gwdg.de/pub/linux/hpcdtoppm> or as part of the PBM utilities.

Also, reading video CD is supported in kernel series 2.1.3x and later. A patch is available for kernel 2.0.30.

Finally, most IDE CD-ROM Changers are supported.

16. CD-Writers

17. Removable drives

18. Mice

18.1. Supported

- Microsoft serial mouse
- Mouse Systems serial mouse
- Logitech Mouseman serial mouse
- Logitech serial mouse
- ATI XL Inport busmouse
- C&T 82C710 (QuickPort) (Toshiba, TI Travelmate)
- Microsoft busmouse
- Logitech busmouse
- PS/2 (auxiliary device) mouse

18.2. Others

- Sejin J-mouse

<ftp://sunsite.unc.edu/pub/Linux/kernel/patches/console/jmouse.1.1.70-jmouse.tar.gz>

MultiMouse - use multiple mouse devices as single mouse
<ftp://sunsite.unc.edu/pub/Linux/system/misc/MultiMouse-1.0.tgz>

Microsoft Intellimouse

18.3. Notes

Touchpad devices like Alps Glidepoint also work, so long they're compatible with another mouse protocol.

Newer Logitech mice (except the Mouseman) use the Microsoft protocol and all three buttons do work. Even though Microsoft's mice have only two buttons, the protocol allows three buttons.

The mouse port on the ATI Graphics Ultra and Ultra Pro use the Logitech busmouse protocol. (See the Busmouse HOWTO for details.)

19. Modems

All internal modems or external modems connected to the serial port should work. Alas, some manufactures have created Windows 95 only modems. Check Appendix D for Linux incompatible hardware.

A small number of modems come with DOS software that downloads the control program at runtime. These can normally be used by loading the program under DOS and doing a warm boot. Such modems are probably best avoided as you won't be able to use them with non PC hardware in the future.

All PCMCIA modems should work with the PCMCIA drivers.

Fax modems need appropriated fax software to operate. Also be sure that the fax part of the modem supports Class 2 or Class 2.0. It seems to be generally true for any fax software on unix that support for Class 1.0 is not available.

Digicom Connection 96+/14.4+ - DSP code downloading program
<ftp://sunsite.unc.edu/pub/Linux/apps/serialcomm/smdl-

linux.1.02.tar.gz>

Motorola ModemSURFR internal 56K. Add a couple of line to RC.SERIAL to account for IRQ and ports if they are non-standard.

ZyXEL U-1496 series - ZyXEL 1.4, modem/fax/voice control program <http://www.pe1chl.demon.nl/ZyXEL/ZyXEL-1.6.tar.gz>

ZyXEL Elite 2864 series - modem/fax/voice control program <http://www.pe1chl.demon.nl/ZyXEL/ZyXEL-1.6.tar.gz>

ZyXEL Omni TA 128 - modem/fax/voice control program <http://www.pe1chl.demon.nl/ZyXEL/ZyXEL-1.6.tar.gz>

Also multimodem cards are supported by Linux.

Moreton Bay RAStel multimodem card
Check <http://www.moreton.com.au/linux.htm> for Linux drivers.

20. Printers/Plotters

21. Scanners

22. Other hardware

23. Related sources of information

Cameron Spitzer's hardware FAQ archive (??) <ftp://ftp.rahul.net/pub/cameron/PC-info/>

Guide to Computer Vendors <http://guide.sbanetweb.com/>

System Optimization Information <http://www.dfw.net/~sdw/>

24. Acknowledgments

Thanks to all the authors and contributors of other HOWTO's; many things here are shamelessly stolen from their works; to FRiC, Zane Healy and Ed Carp, the original authors of this HOWTO; and to everyone else who sent in updates and feedbacks. Special thanks to Eric Boerner and lilo (the person, not the program) for the sanity checks. And thanks to Dan Quinlan for the original SGML conversion.

25. Appendix A. S3 cards supported by XFree86 3.3.1.

NOTE: for the ViRGE/VX,DX,GX,GX2 chipsets you need XFree86 3.3.1. You should use the XF86_SVGA server.

26. Appendix B. Supported PCMCIA cards

27. Appendix C. Plug and Play devices

28. Appendix D. Linux incompatible Hardware

29. Glossary

Keep in Mind...

If you're going out specifically to purchase hardware for a Linux system, there are a few things to keep in mind:

- Avoid proprietary products, such as non-SCSI or non-IDE CD-ROM drives.
- Hardware that says on the package, "Requires Windows."
- Winmodems. Winmodems are modems that handle processing on the system through proprietary interfaces. Because these interfaces are generally not published, Linux has no support for these devices.
- Hardware not listed on the Hardware Compatibility List. Although some hardware not specifically mentioned on the Hardware Compatibility List will work with Linux, you should research before you buy. Ask the manufacturer or others running Linux.
- Intel and Clones.

- Hardware Compatibility Lists.
- What to Avoid.
- Reference Sources.
- Installation and Configuration.

Reference Sources

One of the often-cited reasons to use Linux is the incredible support base. If you're having problems, want to ask if a certain piece of hardware is supported, or just need Linux information, here are some resources.

- **The man pages** Using the *man* command at a Linux prompt will give you help on Linux commands and libraries. For example, to get usage on the *ls* command, type **man ls** at a command prompt. For help using the *man* command, type **man man**.
- **Package documentation** Many Red Hat Linux packages store their documentation in /usr/doc/*packagename*.
- **HOWTOs and FAQs** These are located in /usr/doc/HOWTO and /usr/doc/FAQ, respectively.
- The ***info* command** will give hypertext information on many commands on your system.
- **The Linux Documentation Project** (**LDP**) located on the Web at http://www.linuxdoc.org.
- **The Red Hat Knowledge Base** at http://www.redhat.com/knowledgebase.
- **Usenet newsgroups**
- **Red Hat mailing lists** at http://www.redhat.com/community/list_subscribe.html
- **The Free Software Foundation** at http://www.gnu.org.
- **The Open Source Community** at http://www.opensource.org.

CERTIFICATION SUMMARY

This chapter covered the differences and similarities between Open Source and Free Software, which make up most Linux distributions. We covered the traits that make Linux a viable operating environment, such as preemptive multitasking and memory management. We also covered the history behind UNIX, and the community that has driven it. The two major licenses, the General Public License and the Open Source Definition, were covered and compared.

Also covered were networking support and hardware compatibility. Finally, we covered the different types of Red Hat Linux installations and the advantages and disadvantages of each.

TWO-MINUTE DRILL

- ❑ Red Hat Linux is a modern, flexible, and mature operating system. Although it started life on the Intel platform, it has since been ported to many other platforms such as Amiga, DEC Alpha, Apple Power PC, Sun workstations, and others.
- ❑ All Linux distributions are based on the same idea: Take the Linux kernel and surround it with freely available software, to create a usable operating system. Red Hat Linux is Red Hat Software's latest distribution and is no exception.
- ❑ Although Linux traces its history back to 1991, it traces its heritage much further back. In 1969, a Bell Labs programmer named Ken Thompson invented the UNIX operating system. Around the same time, another programmer, Dennis Ritchie, was working on a new computer language called C. By 1974, the two had rewritten UNIX in the C language and ported it to several different machines. Linux owes its heritage to this combination of UNIX and C.
- ❑ "Free software" is the term typically used to refer to software that has been released under the GNU Public License, or GPL.

The GPL (also called "Copyleft") was designed with the philosophy that all software should be free.

- Open Source software, like Free software, requires that software source code be provided and readable. What Open Source does not promote, however, are the philosophical reasons behind Free software. Where the GPL makes freedom a central point, Open Source sidesteps the philosophy and sets only the guidelines for software to fit the Open Source definition.
- The obvious meaning for 'open source software' is 'You can look at the source code.'
- Most of the Internet runs on Free or Open Source software.
- In the development space, languages such as C, C++, Perl, Python, Tcl/Tk, Pascal, Cobol, Fortran, and many others are freely available. And, if you're curious as to how these compilers are built, the source code is available for every one of them.
- Exciting things are happening in the Linux world. Kernel development continues at a brisk pace, and companies like Red Hat Software are showing that the world is taking Linux seriously. On the day of its Initial Public Offering, the price of Red Hat Software stock tripled. Entire companies make their livings on Free and Open Source software, such as Cygnus, SuSE, VA Research, and others.
- Before you begin a Red Hat Linux installation, you need to know what the purpose of the machine will be. Will it be a development workstation? Or an FTP or Web server? Or will it be a database server? Each of these examples requires a different configuration.
- Installing on most Intel-based computers is pretty straightforward. But you'll save yourself a lot of time and frustration by knowing exactly what hardware you have.
- The complete Hardware Compatibility List is available on the Red Hat Linux CD-ROM, or in /usr/doc/HOWTO/Hardware-HOWTO on an Installed Red Hat Linux system, or online at http://sunsite.unc.edu/pub/Linux/docs/HOWTO/Hardware-HOWTO.

SELF TEST

The following Self Test questions will help you measure your understanding of the material presented in this chapter. Read all the choices carefully, as there may be more than one correct answer. Choose all correct answers for each question.

1. Although originally intended to run on the Intel platform, Linux has been ported to which other platform?

   A. Sparc

   B. Alpha

   C. Power PC

   D. All of the above

2. Currently, Linux scales up to how many processors?

   A. 2

   B. 8

   C. 16

   D. 32

3. The memory management system Linux uses is:

   A. Swapping

   B. Paging

   C. Preemptive multitasking

   D. Byte-swapping

4. Although Linux is a direct descendent of UNIX, it was originally modeled around what operating system?

   A. MS-DOS

   B. Minix

   C. POSIX

   D. OSF/1

5. Linux uses what type of kernel architecture?

   A. Static

   B. Microkernel

   C. Distributed

   D. Monolithic

6. Linux was the first real free operating system and spawned further free efforts such as the HURD kernel and BSD ports.

   A. True

   B. False

7. The term "Free Software" implies that:

   A. The software is free of cost.

   B. The distributor cannot charge you for the software.

   C. The software is freely modifiable and distributable.

   D. Only the software's author can charge a fee for using it.

8. Most of the software and utilities in distributions such as Red Hat Linux are:

   A. GNU utilities

   B. Red Hat RPMs

   C. Proprietary

   D. Linux kernel utilities

9. Most e-mail on the Internet passes through what free/open source mail transport software?

A. Microsoft Exchange
B. Netscape
C. Open Mail
D. Sendmail

10. Although there are many Linux distributions, the term "Linux" refers to:
A. Red Hat Linux
B. The Linux kernel
C. Linus Torvalds
D. Free operating systems

11. The protocol used by the Internet is:
A. TCP/IP
B. Ethernet
C. IPX
D. AppleTalk

12. Advantages of Free/Open Source software are:
A. Stability
B. Support
C. Freedom
D. All of the above

13. A Workstation installation of Red Hat Linux gives you:
A. An easy and fast install with maximum flexibility in configuration
B. A somewhat more complicated install with maximum flexibility in configuration
C. An easy and fast install with minimum flexibility in configuration
D. A somewhat more complicated install with minimum flexibility in configuration

14. DOS partitions are removed on what types of Red Hat Linux installations?
A. Workstation
B. Server
C. Workstation and Server
D. None of the above

15. What type of install gives you the most flexibility in configuration?
A. Workstation
B. Server
C. Custom
D. Server and Custom

16. Approximately how much disk space is needed for a Red Hat Linux Workstation install?
A. 250MB
B. 500MB
C. 600MB
D. 700MB

17. The kernel and associated files reside on which partition?
A. /boot
B. /etc
C. /usr
D. /var

18. In his paper, "The Cathedral and the Bazaar," Eric S. Raymond likened traditional software companies to:

A. Linux kernel developers
B. A bazaar
C. Cathedral builders
D. UNIX developers

19. Hardware to avoid using with Linux would be:

A. SCSI drives
B. Intel 486 systems
C. IDE CD-ROMs
D. Winmodems

20. When selecting disk drives for a Linux install, the following information should be documented:

A. Capacity
B. Drive type (SCSI or IDE)
C. Manufacturer
D. All of the above

2

Installation Preparation

CERTIFICATION OBJECTIVES

2.01 Planning the Installation

2.02 Intel CPU Hardware Selection and Configuration

One of the strong points of Red Hat Linux is its easy installation. There are several different methods of installation, and each of them is automated to a considerable degree. However, before the actual installation, some preparation is necessary.

CERTIFICATION OBJECTIVE 2.01

Planning the Installation

Before any software can be installed, the computer has to be able to recognize the hardware that it will be using. The installation process will ask you about your hardware; have this data ready before you start.

You should know the make and model number for each of the following pieces of hardware, if you have them:

- SCSI controllers
- Network Interface Cards (NIC)
- Video cards
- Sound cards

You might also need other information, such as base I/O address and interrupt that each piece of hardware uses. Hardware compatibility for Linux is discussed later in this chapter.

Packages to Be Installed

Red Hat Linux comes conveniently bundled with an array of preconfigured software packages. It is most likely that you will not need to install all of them, and for security reasons (or office policy) it is a good idea not to. Your boss might not appreciate the office network being used to serve personal Web pages from each employee's installation of an Apache Web server. Also, every computer on your network doesn't need to run a sendmail daemon.

Limit the packages you install to only the ones that you need. If other packages are required later, they can be installed easily enough with the rpm tool.

Partitioning the Drive

It is recommended that you make several partitions when preparing your hard drive to install Linux. It is a good idea for various reasons: First, Red Hat Linux uses two filesystems to run, a Linux native filesystem, and Linux swap space. Second, if you want to install Red Hat Linux and another operating system on the same computer, you will have to create separate partitions for each. The following section discusses more advantages of making partitions.

Stability and Security

The Linux native filesystem is usually divided among many hard drive partitions. The recommended configuration is a separate partition for each of these directories: /, /usr, /usr/local, /var, and /home.

Partitioning the hard drive in this manner keeps system, application, and user files isolated from each other. This aids in protecting the file space that the Linux kernel and the rest of your applications use. Files cannot grow across partitions. Therefore, an application that uses huge amounts of disk space, such as a newsgroup server, will not be able to use up all of the disk space needed by the Linux kernel. Another advantage is that if a bad spot develops on the hard drive, it will be easier to restore a single partition than the entire system. Stability is improved.

Security is also improved. Multiple partitions give you the ability to mount some filesystems as read-only. For example, if there is no reason for any user (even root) to write to the /usr directory, then mounting that partition as read-only will help protect the files in that filesystem from being tampered with.

While there are many incentives to partitioning your disk space, it might not be desirable for you. For single-user systems, or where disk space is scarce, a simpler system would be called for. For example, if the /var directory is on its own partition of 30MB, only 10MB might be used. That makes 20MB of wasted disk space .

Currently, there is no easy way to resize Linux partitions. Therefore, a lot of careful consideration should be put into if and how you want to partition your disk space.

How Much Space Is Required?

You should size your Linux partitions according to your needs and the function of the computer. For example, a mail server will require more space for the /var directory because the mail spool resides in /var/spool/mail. You may even want to create a separate partition just to accommodate /var/spool/mail. Generally, the root partition is a relatively modest size, and the rest is split up depending on system use.

EXAMPLE: FILE SERVER If the Linux system you are installing is to be a file server, then your filesystem could look something like Table 2-1.

The /usr filesystem is large enough to have Samba installed, as well as X11, if that is desired. Most of the disk space has been allocated to /home, for users' own files, and to /home/shared, for common files. Of course, this is only an example. The amount of disk space you allocate for file sharing will depend on factors such as the number of users and the type of files they work on.

TABLE 2-1

Example Disk Partition Scheme for a Linux File Server

Filesystem	Size (MB)	Mounted on
/dev/sda1	40	/
/dev/sda5	20	/var
/dev/sda6	300	/usr
/dev/sda7	60	swap space
/dev/sda8	1000	/home
/dev/sda9	6000	/home/shared

Linux Swap Space

Normally, Linux can use up to 4GB of Swap space in up to 8 separate partitions of swap space. There is no authoritative formula for deciding how much swap space should be made, but 2 to 3 times physical RAM size is common.

You should at least have some swap space, even if your estimate tells you that you don't need any. Linux will actively use swap space—not just when physical memory is full. Pages of memory that haven't been used will be swapped in an attempt to have as much physical memory available as possible. Instead of waiting for the operating system when swapping is needed, the system can do it earlier, when the disk is not being used.

Another way to speed up swapping is to place swap partitions strategically. You are not limited by only having one swap partition in one place. This is especially useful if you are using more than one hard disk on more than one controller. You could put some swap space on a hard disk on each controller. If one controller is busy, then another can be used for swapping. Also, where you put the swap space on the hard disk can affect performance. If the data that is being used most often is at the beginning of the disk, but your swap space exists at the end, the drive has to work harder to move between the data and swap space. Keeping your swap space close to your "busy" data will result in more efficient use of your hard drive.

BIOS Limits

Be aware that some computers have a BIOS (Basic Input/Output System) limitation that prevents access to hard disks beyond their 1024 cylinder. A common effect of this problem is your computer's inability to see any partitions past the first 512MB of disk space at boot time. If this limitation affects your computer, do not place any bootable partitions after this barrier, or the BIOS will not be able to access them and your operating system will not be able to load.

Partitioning Utilities

There are many disk-partitioning utilities for Linux—even utilities that do not run under Linux. Two of the main utilities that come packaged with Red Hat 6.0 are fdisk/cfdisk and Disk Druid. (Note: cfdisk is similar to fdisk, but with a full screen interface). They all work towards the same end, but Red Hat recommends that you use Disk Druid. It is safer to use than fdisk, and it has a graphical interface that makes its use easier.

EXERCISE 2-1

Partitioning Exercise

1. On a piece of paper, draw a rectangle to represent each hard drive on your computer.
2. Label them in order as Linux would (e.g., Hard Drive 1: /dev/hda, Hard Drive 2: /dev/sda, Hard Drive 3: /dev/sdb).
3. Use this diagram to plan your Linux partitions visually.

Using this method, you can organize your data, keeping system or users' files together, as well as strategically plan where to place your swap partition(s).

CERTIFICATION OBJECTIVE 2.02

Intel CPU Hardware Selection and Configuration

You have to be very careful not to choose any hardware that Linux does not yet support. It is up to the user to find out what is currently supported by Linux. Unfortunately for Linux, hardware manufacturers are still targeting the Microsoft Windows market. In order for hardware drivers to come available for Linux, either the manufacturers have to recognize the Linux market and produce drivers, or a third party has to do it. The latter brings up one of Linux's strong points. There is a vast community of Linux users, many of whom produce drivers for Linux and distribute them freely on the Internet. If a certain piece of hardware is popular, you can be certain that

Linux support for that piece of hardware will pop up somewhere on the Internet and will be incorporated into Linux distributions, such as Red Hat Linux.

Be careful when purchasing a new computer to run Linux on. Do not assume that Linux will run on it. The latest and greatest existing technology may not be supported under Linux (not yet, anyway). The hardware may also be targeted for specific operating systems and configurations. Winmodems and winprinters are examples of hardware that will not work with Linux because they are targeted for MS Windows. Integrated hardware (e.g., video chips that share system RAM) and parallel port devices (other than printers) are other pieces of hardware you should be wary of. While there may be ways to make these types of hardware work, the process of actually making them work may cause more frustration than they're worth.

Unless it has been proven that Linux will run on a newer machine, choosing an older model might be a better choice. Linux will run very well on lower-end computers. This is one of Linux's strong points over other operating systems, such as Microsoft's Windows NT.

Hardware Compatibility

You are not left without help or resources when choosing the right hardware for Linux. There are many places you can turn to for help, including mailing lists and newsgroups. Perhaps the best places to look are the LDP (Linux Documentation Project) or the Red Hat Hardware List. The LDP is a global effort to produce reliable documentation for all aspects of the Linux operating system, including hardware compatibility. Within the LDP, you can find the Linux Hardware HOWTO.

Linux Hardware HOWTO

The Linux Hardware HOWTO is a document that lists most of the hardware components supported by Linux. The list is updated regularly with added hardware support, so it is an up-to-date source of information. The latest version of the Linux Hardware HOWTO can be found at http://users.bart.nl/~patrickr/hardware-howto/Hardware-HOWTO.html, or within the LDP, which can be found at Sun Microsystems' Sunsite at http://metalab.unc.edu/LDP/HOWTO/Hardware-HOWTO.html or any mirror sites of Sunsite.

The Red Hat Hardware List

The Red Hat Hardware List is specific to all hardware that has been tested on systems running Red Hat Linux. Red Hat will provide installation support for any hardware that is listed as "supported." There is also an "unsupported" list. This list does not necessarily mean that the specified hardware will not run Linux; it just means that Red Hat will not provide installation support for that hardware. There is a list for Intel, Alpha, and SPARC architectures.

Like the LDP, the Red Hat Hardware List is kept up to date. If you want to check if any of the "latest" hardware (such as USB, for example) will run Linux, it's probably best to consult the LDP's Linux Hardware HOWTO. However, if you want the option of being able to contact Red Hat for support, stay within the "supported" list of the Red Hat Hardware List.

EXERCISE 2-2

Hardware Compatibility

1. On the Web, visit http://metalab.unc.edu/Linux. On the site, find the Linux Hardware Compatibility HOWTO. Take note of its date (it should be posted near the top). How current is it?
2. Research the topology of the network you are on and try to find a mirror of the Linux Documentation Project that is closest to you on the Internet.

RAM Sizing and Cache Issues

Because accessing a disk is relatively slow when compared to accessing memory, Linux uses *disk buffering*. Disk buffering is what happens when information from a disk is stored in memory until it is no longer needed. The memory that is used for disk buffering is called the *buffer cache*. For example, when a command such as ls is called, the directory information from that command is copied into memory. If ls is called again, the information is retrieved from memory instead of performing another "slow" disk read.

Write-Through Versus Write-Back Buffer Cache

There are two types of buffer caches. One type is *write-through*. With write-through buffer cache, any changes to blocks of data in the cache are written to disk at once. The second type is *write-back* buffer cache, in which writes are done at a later time, usually in the background, so as not to slow down other programs. While write-through cache is less efficient, write-back cache is more susceptible to errors. If the operating system crashes, or if power is suddenly cut, and any changes to the write-back buffer cache were not written back to disk, the data that was there will be lost. As long as proper procedure is followed to allow Linux to sync buffer cache to disk (e.g., shutting down and removing floppy disks), Linux takes care of the cache automatically.

Buffer Cache Size and Available Memory

Buffer cache uses physical memory (RAM). Since memory is a finite resource, there is an issue of how much the buffer cache should use. Usually, there can never be enough to hold all of the data that anyone ever wants to use. When the cache is full, the data that hasn't been accessed for the longest time will be flushed. Too small a cache will result in flushing data before it can be used again, while too large a cache uses up valuable memory that could be used for other processes.

In Linux, disk buffering is taken care of automatically. Linux dynamically resizes the buffer cache in order to use all the free memory in RAM. Also, there are several programs that are run in Linux to manage disk buffering. The program bdflush is used to flush any dirty buffers (buffers where data has changed) back to disk. Also, there is a sync command that forces all unwritten data to be written to disk. When Linux boots, a daemon named update is started in the background. Update runs bdflush and performs a sync command every 30 seconds.

Disk Subsystems (IDE, EIDE, and SCSI)

These systems are set up end initialized before the operating system is loaded. After Linux has loaded, the settings for the disk subsystems can be modified or dealt with through software. However, in order for Linux to be loaded in the first place, the computer's BIOS has to be able to recognize the hardware that makes up these subsystems.

IDE and EIDE

IDE stands for Integrated Drive Electronics. It is on the IBM PC ISA 16-bit bus standard, and it was adopted as a standard by ANSI in 1990 as Advanced Technology Attachment (ATA). A setback to IDE was that it could only access 504MB of disk space. To work around this, Enhanced IDE (EIDE) was created. As well as being able to support hard disks larger that 504MB, EIDE also improved access speeds to hard drives. Support was added for additional hard disks and Direct Memory Access (DMA) and ATA Packet Interface (ATAPI) devices, such as CD-ROMs and tape drives. ANSI adopted EIDE as a standard in 1994 as Advanced Technology Attachment-2 (ATA-2 or Fast ATA).

exam Watch

Problems due to hardware limitations are common and difficult to troubleshoot if you don't know about them. Be very familiar with as many hardware limitations as you can.

SCSI

The Small Computer System Interface (SCSI), developed by Apple Computer, allows your computer to interface to disk drives, CD-ROMs, tape drives, printers, and scanners. SCSI is faster and more flexible than (E)IDE, with support for up to 7 or 15 devices, depending on the bus width. Data transfer speeds for SCSI range from 5 to 80MB per second.

Primary, Extended, and Logical Partitions

You are limited to making only four primary partitions on each hard disk. To work around this, the extended partition was developed. Within an extended partition, logical partitions can be created. IDE disks can have up to 16 partitions, and SCSI disks up to 15.

Cylinder/Head/Sector Geometry and Remapping

The size of a hard drive is determined by its geometry. The geometry includes the number of cylinders, heads, and sectors available on the hard disk. Together, these numbers make up an address on the hard disk. Normally, the geometry that your BIOS will support is limited to 1024 cylinders, 256 heads, and 63 sectors. Using the numbers, 1024 cylinders × 256 heads × 63 sectors × 512 bytes per sector, provides 8 gigabytes maximum. But 256 heads would be a very large drive. Instead, as disks have evolved usually more cylinders are added so if the real mode cylinder count exceeds 1024 then your computer will not be able to address the entire hard disk. However, you can bypass this problem by using Logical Block Addressing (LBA) for your hard disks.

exam Watch

Since SCSI devices have their own BIOS, this limitation does not affect SCSI hard disks.

Logical Block Addressing (LBA)

If your computer was manufactured after 1994, then you will likely be able to select LBA mode for your hard disks in your computer's CMOS. LBA involves a special way of addressing sectors. Instead of referring to a cylinder, head, and sector for a location on the hard disk, each sector is assigned a unique number from 0 to N-1, where N is the number of sectors on the disk. LBA mode allows geometry translation, which means that the BIOS can be fooled into believing that the hard disk's geometry is acceptable.

EXAMPLE A hard disk with 2048 cylinders, 16 heads, and 63 sectors is installed in a machine. Without using LBA, the 1024 cylinder limit has been exceeded, so your BIOS will not be able to handle the hard disk. If your system uses LBA mode, it will "lie" to the BIOS and say that the hard disk has 32 heads instead of 16. This changes the geometry to 1024 cylinders, 32 heads, and 63 sectors—within the BIOS limits. The new geometry has the same storage capacity as before, and it can be accessed entirely through LBA mode translation.

Multiple Controllers

It is possible to use more than one disk controller at the same time. In fact, doing so can increase throughput on your system by reducing bottlenecks.

You can use both SCSI and (E)IDE controllers in the same machine, but there are a few snags you should be aware of. The BIOS can only access the first two (E)IDE hard drives at boot time. Also, SCSI disks may not be accessible if (E)IDE drives are installed. The BIOS might have a setting to allow you to boot from SCSI hard disks. Make sure you understand which drives the BIOS will be able to access at boot time, because if you install the boot sector to a drive that cannot be accessed, Linux will not be able to boot.

When your computer boots, the BIOS assigns a number to each drive letter it sees. The order in which the BIOS assigns them might not be the same order that Linux does. This can confuse LILO and cause it to fail.

EXAMPLE Your computer is set up to boot Linux from a SCSI disk, and the BIOS assigns the number 0x80 to /dev/sda (the SCSI disk) and 0x81 to /dev/hda (the first (E)IDE drive). Linux, however, assigns 0x80 to /dev/hda, 0x81 to /dev/hdb (the second (E)IDE disk), and 0x82 to the SCSI disk. There is a disagreement between the BIOS and LILO. LILO will not find the boot sector on /dev/sda and, therefore, will not be able to boot Linux. When you run /sbin/lilo in Linux, you will get the message "BIOS-Drive 0x82 may not be accessible." (See the section on configuring LILO in Chapter 4, "Basic Configuration and Administration," for more information; look up the 'bios=' option for /etc/lilo.conf.)

RAID and MD Systems

RAID (Redundant Array of Independent (or Inexpensive) Disks) can be set up in Linux using either hardware or software. The tradeoffs between them are performance versus price. Hardware implementations are faster and more expensive.

The hardware implementation of RAID uses a RAID controller connected to an array of several hard disks. A hardware RAID system would not require any internal Linux support as it appears as just another disk or set of disks. An alternate solution is through a software program that assembles multiple drive partitions into a RAID set. Linux offers a software solution to RAID with the md kernel patch. You should use Linux kernel 2.0.36 or a recent 2.2.*x* version. Once RAID is configured on your system, Linux can use it just as it would any other block device.

RAID can be set up with many different configurations, called *levels*. The following are a few basic RAID levels that the RAID patches for Linux support:

RAID-0 Reads and writes to the hard disks are done in parallel, increasing performance, but filling up all hard drives equally with the same data. There is no redundancy in this level, since a failure of any one of the drives will result in data loss. This level is used for speed increases. If one disk is busy, the data can be accessed from another. The limit to the speed of a RAID-0 system is the bus speed that connects to the disks. RAID-0 is also called "stripe mode."

RAID-1 This level mirrors information from one disk to one or more other disks. If one disk is damaged/removed, all data will still be intact and accessible from the other disk(s) available. Also, if any spare disks exist in the system, it will be used as another mirror to replace a missing or damaged drive. While performance may actually be decreased in this level, reliability is increased.

RAID-4 This level requires three or more disks. Like RAID-0, data reads and writes are done in parallel, except that there must be one extra disk that keeps parity information of all the data. If one drive fails, then the parity information can be used to reconstruct the data. Reliability is improved, but since parity information is updated with every write operation, the parity disk can be a bottleneck on the system.

RAID-5 RAID-5 works on three or more disks, with optional spare disks. With this level, several disks can be combined with both performance and reliability increases. Like RAID-4, parity information of the data is recorded. However, instead of dedicating one disk to store the parity information, it is distributed evenly across all disks. If one disk fails, the data can be reconstructed onto a spare disk.

LINEAR MODE Linear mode is combining one or more disks to work as one larger device. There is no redundancy in linear mode—the disks are simply filled up in the order they appear (e.g., disk 1, disk 2, etc.). The only performance gain linear mode will experience is when several users access data that reside on different disks.

The exam may use examples from any level of RAID, including a combination of several different levels into one solution.

IRQ Settings

An interrupt request (IRQ) is a signal that is sent to the computer to request some processing time. Each device that you attach to your computer will need its own IRQ value. This value is unique to each device so as not to confuse the computer, except for possibly PCI devices (which is explained later). The Intel architecture is limited to using only 16 IRQs (0–15).

Planning the IRQ Layout—Standard IRQs

Some IRQs are reserved by the motherboard to control devices such as the hard disk controller and real-time clock. Do not use these interrupts, or there will be conflicts! In Linux, you can check /proc/interrupts to see which interrupts are being used. Any interrupt that is not assigned is a valid candidate for a new device to use. However, there is a standard IRQ layout that you can follow, shown in Table 2-2.

IRQs and the PCI Architecture

A common problem with PCs today is having more devices than available interrupts. PCI devices can get around this predicament by sharing an IRQ. This is accomplished using the PCI bus. The PCI bus is independent of the processor, so PCI devices can have their own internal interrupts that

TABLE 2-2

Standard IRQ Layout for PCs

IRQ	Assigned to
0	Nonmaskable interrupt (NMI)—detects parity errors
1	System timer
2	Cascade for controller 2
3	Serial port 2 and 4 (shared is both exist)
4	Serial port 1 and 3 (shared is both exist)
5	Parallel port 2
6	Floppy diskette controller
7	Parallel port 1
8	Real-time clock
9	Redirected to IRQ2
10	Not assigned (usually used for a network card)
11	Not assigned
12	PS/2 mouse, if installed
13	Coprocessor
14	Hard disk controller 1
15	Hard disk controller 2

determine which device will send an IRQ to the processor. However, your BIOS must support PCI sharing for it to work. If it does, you should be able to turn it on through your computer's CMOS.

Plug and Play

With plug-and-play devices, computer users do not have to tell the computer that the device is there. The operating system should be able to recognize the device and set it up automatically. Plug and play has been available for Macintosh computers for quite some time, and has been incorporated into Microsoft's Windows operating systems. However, Linux, as well as other unix variants, are behind on this technology. Linux is trying to catch up, but it is difficult to cope with a technology that is mainly driven by non-Unix operating systems (Microsoft Windows and MacOS).

Plug-and-Play Support in Linux

The unfortunate truth is that Linux doesn't handle plug and play very well. The main problem lies with plug-and-play support for devices that run on an ISA bus. ISA is an old technology from older IBM PCs. ISA was created without plug and play in mind, so support for it is very complicated. Red Hat includes some utilities to help handle ISA plug-and-play devices. These utilities (e.g., isapnp and pnpdump) are kept in a package named isapnptools. You should be able to find this package in rpm format with your Red Hat installation.

The newer, faster bus technology, PCI, is a different story. As Linux loads, device drivers can easily find their devices if they are PCI. This makes plug and play much easier for hardware that runs on a PCI bus. However, there still may be conflicts with the ISA bus.

All in all, when it comes to plug and play, Linux needs to cope better. Support is improving, so the outlook is hopeful. Just keep in mind that you will probably have more trouble configuring an ISA device than a PCI device.

Handling Jumperless Cards

Some cards have no jumpers; instead, information on which port, IRQ, and address it uses is stored in a ROM chip on the card. With these cards is usually shipped a program that will allow you to change these settings. Alas, it is a Microsoft world, and these utilities usually need DOS to run. If you have a card that works like this, you'll need a DOS boot disk or partition to be able to configure them.

If you are not licensed to use MS DOS or Windows, there are some possible alternatives. The FreeDOS Project (http://freedos.org) is an effort to create a free version of DOS that is compatible with MS DOS. Within Linux, there is an MS Windows Emulator called WINE that is capable of running some Windows programs with varying degrees of success. All in all, a better solution is to try and use hardware that does not need to be configured this way.

IRQs and Standard Serial Ports

The standard serial ports in Linux are /dev/ttyS0, /dev/ttyS1, /dev/ttyS2, and /dev/ttyS3 (COM1 through COM4, respectively). In your BIOS the serial ports tpyS0 and ttyS2 are normally set to IRQ4, serial port ttyS1 and ttyS3 are normally set to IRQ3. With Linux kernel 2.2, there is the ability to share these interrupts. For kernel versions earlier than 2.2, you will need to assign unique IRQs to each serial port that you use. This can be done at boot time by using the setserial utility and modifying the /etc/rc.d/rc.serial file similar to the following (assuming, of course, that all of these interrupts are available):

```
/sbin/setserial  /dev/ttyS0   irq 3  # dumb terminal
/sbin/setserial  /dev/ttyS1   irq 4  # serial mouse
/sbin/setserial  /dev/ttyS2   irq 5  # first modem
/sbin/setserial  /dev/ttyS3   irq 9  # second modem
```

Serial and Other Interface Mice

For your mouse to work, you will need to know what interface and which protocol it uses. Serial mice interface to a serial port, while PS/2 mice have a port and IRQ set aside. There is also another type of interface called a *busmouse.* Of these, Linux has support for these three: Inport (Microsoft), Logitech, and ATI-XL. In order for a PS/2 mouse to work, support has to be compiled into Linux. The same goes for a busmouse, except that it can also be compiled as modules.

Serial Mice

To use a serial mouse, you might need to assign it an IRQ if you are using more than three serial devices. Otherwise, it's just a matter of selecting the correct protocol for the mouse to use. Common protocols are Microsoft, for Microsoft mice, and Logitech, for Logitech mice. The connector for a serial mouse is rectangular with 9 or 25 pins, and plugs into a serial port. The device file for serial mice is a linked file from /dev/mouse to whatever serial port it is using (e.g., /dev/ttyS0).

PS/2 Mice

A PS/2 mouse (used on newer PCs and on most laptops) has its own port and uses IRQ 12. A PS/2 mouse uses a 6-pin mini DIN connector and communicates using the PS/2 protocol. The device file for PS/2 mice is /dev/psaux.

Busmouse

You can usually identify a busmouse from its round 9-pin connector. The mice usually plug into a card, which might have jumper settings or some with software (for DOS) to set IRQs and base I/O addresses. While most busmice use the BusMouse protocol, there are some older mice that use other protocols such as MouseSystems or Logitech. The device files for Inport, Logitech, and ATI-XL busmice are /dev/inportbm, /dev/logibm, and /dev/atibm, respectively.

The Red Hat installation process will ask you for information about your mouse. Know what kind of mouse you have! Later, you can modify your mouse settings by using the XF86Setup tool for X11, or the mouseconfig tool for using the mouse in console mode.

EXERCISE 2-3

Your Computer's BIOS

Look through your computer's BIOS. To get into the BIOS, you normally have to press a key soon after you power on your computer. This key is commonly the DELETE, or F1, key on your keyboard. Browse through the menus and try to locate the areas where the following information is kept:

- Your hard drive information: Take note of the "translation mode" that your hard drive is using (e.g., CHS, Large, or LBA).
- Locate the IRQ settings that your BIOS assigns to your serial and parallel ports, real-time clock, and hard disk controllers. Can you change any of these settings? (Be careful that you don't save your changes!)
- Find out if your BIOS supports PCI sharing (for IRQs). If it does, is it turned on or off on your computer?

PC Card (PCMCIA)

Linux has one package that deals exclusively with PC Cards called "Card Services." This package includes all of the kernel modules you'll need to manage PCMCIA cards and a set of drivers for specific cards. The package also includes a daemon that handles hot swapping of most types of cards.

While development of the Card Services package is ongoing, there is often a period where there is no support for new technologies. For this reason, the latest laptop on the market is often not a good choice for a Linux installation. Furthermore, there are some laptop manufacturers that have little to no Linux support at all, and future support is uncertain.

Supported Chip Sets

This list is frequently updated. An up-to-date list of supported chip sets can be obtained from the LDP's PCMCIA-HOWTO.

Supported Cards

The Card Services package comes bundled with a file named SUPPORTED.CARDS. Also, you can check the LDP's PCMCICA-HOWTO or the Red Hat Hardware Compatibility List for supported cards.

on the Job

During your career as a computer professional, there will be times that you will be asked to research a specific product or technology. To get an idea of how hard or easy this can be, call a local or international computer reseller or manufacturer and inquire about their latest laptop. Ask them if it will support Linux. What kind of answer do you get? Ask them if they have any earlier model that will. Do you believe that the answers you receive are reliable? Check out the company's Web page, if you can, and find out if they provide any information about the product on the Internet. Doing this kind of research can be very trying, with or without success. Before deciding what kind of hardware you want to

install Linux on, you should have a good understanding of what will and will not work. Start early and build a good base of reliable references you can use to find out new computer information. There are Web sites, such as Sunsite's Metalab (and mirrors), and magazines such as "Sys Admin Magazine" or "PC Magazine," that will help you stay informed.

Here are a couple of scenario questions and answers:

QUESTIONS AND ANSWERS

You are using Linux and Apache to run a Web server on a LAN for a small office. Several of the employees who work in that office are responsible for updating various parts of the Web site. However, all of these people are Windows users, and are not experienced at using shell accounts. What package could you install to give these employees the easiest access to the files they need on the Web server?	One possibility is to install an ftp daemon, but for Windows connectivity, the Samba package would make the employees' work easier and more transparent. Users do not have to know how to use a shell account (and an editor such as emacs or vi) or an ftp client. The directories that contain the files they need could be mounted directly to their Windows desktop or separate drive letter.
You have run out of disk space for your /home directory! What are the steps you should take to move this data to the new hard drive you just installed?	First, you will have to prepare the new drive to accommodate the new /home filesystem. Use fdisk to create a partition with enough space for your /home directory. Use mkfs to create the filesystem and mount the partition somewhere temporarily (e.g., /mnt/tmp). Copy all of your data from /home to the new partition (e.g., cp /a /home/* /mnt/tmp). Unmount both filesystems, then remount /home to the new partition. Edit /etc/fstab to reflect the new /home location as well. You should probably do all of this in single user mode. To get to single user mode, at the lilo prompt enter lilo: Linux single. To exit single user mode, press CTRL-ALT-DEL

CERTIFICATION SUMMARY

Planning your Linux installation makes the process an easier one. You can imagine how frustrating it would be to begin the installation, and then discover something wrong; for example, a piece of hardware isn't supported, or you installed LILO in the wrong place and now Linux will not boot. Being prepared for this will help prevent it.

You should now know enough to be able to plan which hardware you will need to fit your needs. Moreover, you should be able to find resources that will help you make well-informed decisions about what hardware will work with Linux. Organization is the key to experiencing success with Linux. Plus, it makes you look good.

TWO-MINUTE DRILL

- ❑ One of the strong points of Red Hat Linux is its easy installation. There are several different methods of installation, and each of them is automated to a considerable degree.
- ❑ Before any software can be installed, the computer has to be able to recognize the hardware that it will be using. The installation process will ask you about your hardware; have this data ready before you start.
- ❑ Red Hat Linux comes conveniently bundled with an array of preconfigured software packages. Limit the packages you install to only the ones that you need. If other packages are required later, they can be installed easily enough with the rpm tool.
- ❑ It is recommended that you make several partitions when preparing your hard drive to install Linux.
- ❑ The Linux native filesystem is usually divided among many hard drive partitions. The recommended configuration is a separate partition for each of these directories: /, /usr, /usr/local, /var, and /home.

- ❑ Security is improved with multiple partitions, which give you the ability to mount some filesystems as read-only.
- ❑ You should size your Linux partitions according to your needs and the function of the computer.
- ❑ Be aware that some computers have a BIOS (Basic Input/Output System) limitation that prevents access to hard disks beyond their 1024 cylinder. Look for a PC that uses LBA mode.
- ❑ You have to be very careful not to choose any hardware that Linux does not yet support. It is up to the user to find out what is currently supported by Linux. Unfortunately for Linux, hardware manufacturers are still targeting the Microsoft Windows market. In order for hardware drivers to come available for Linux, either the manufacturers have to recognize the Linux market and produce drivers, or a third party has to do it.
- ❑ You are not left without help or resources when choosing the right hardware for Linux. There are many places you can turn to for help, including mailing lists and newsgroups. Perhaps the best places to look are the LDP (Linux Documentation Project) or the Red Hat Hardware List.
- ❑ The Linux Hardware HOWTO is a document that lists most of the hardware components supported by Linux. The list is updated regularly with added hardware support, so it is an up-to-date source of information. The latest version of the Linux Hardware HOWTO can be found at http://users.bart.nl/~patrickr/hardware-howto/Hardware-HOWTO.html, or within the LDP, which can be found at Sun Microsystems' Sunsite at http://metalab.unc.edu/LDP/HOWTO/Hardware-HOWTO.html or any mirror sites of Sunsite.
- ❑ Because accessing a disk is relatively slow when compared to accessing memory, Linux uses *disk buffering*. Disk buffering is what happens when information from a disk is stored in memory until it is no longer needed. The memory that is used for disk buffering is called the *buffer cache*.

- There are two types of buffer caches. One type is *write-through*. With a write-through buffer cache, any changes to blocks of data in the cache are written to disk at once. The second type is the *write-back* buffer cache, in which writes are done at a later time, usually in the background, so as not to slow down other programs.
- IDE stands for Integrated Drive Electronics. It is on the IBM PC ISA 16-bit bus standard, and it was adopted as a standard by ANSI in 1990 as Advanced Technology Attachment (ATA). A setback to IDE was that it could only access 504MB of disk space. To work around this, Enhanced IDE (EIDE) was created. As well as being able to support hard disks larger than 504MB, EIDE also improved access speeds to hard drives. Support was added for additional hard disks and Direct Memory Access (DMA) and ATA Packet Interface (ATAPI) devices, such as CD-ROMs and tape drives.
- The Small Computer System Interface (SCSI), developed by Apple Computer, allows your computer to interface to disk drives, CD-ROMs, tape drives, printers, and scanners. SCSI is faster and more flexible than (E)IDE, with support for up to 7 or 15 devices, depending on the bus width. Data transfer speeds for SCSI range from 5 to 80MB per second.
- The size of a hard drive is determined by its geometry. The geometry includes the number of cylinders, heads, and sectors available on the hard disk. Together, these numbers make up an address on the hard disk. Normally, the geometry that your BIOS will support is limited to 1024 cylinders, 256 heads, and 63 sectors.
- RAID (Redundant Array of Independent (or Inexpensive) Disks) can be set up in Linux using either hardware or software. The tradeoffs between them are performance versus price. Hardware implementations are faster and more expensive. RAID can be set up with many different configurations, called *levels*.
- An interrupt request (IRQ) is a signal that is sent to the computer to request some processing time. Each device that you attach to your computer will need its own IRQ value.

- With plug-and-play devices, computer users do not have to tell the computer that the device is there. The operating system should be able to recognize the device and set it up automatically.
- The unfortunate truth is that Linux doesn't handle plug and play very well. The main problem lies with plug-and-play support for devices that run on an ISA bus. ISA is an old technology from older IBM PCs.
- The standard serial ports in Linux are /dev/ttyS0, /dev/ttyS1, /dev/ttyS2, and /dev/ttyS3 (COM1 through COM4, respectively). Use fixed line from notes. With Linux kernel 2.2, there is the ability to share these interrupts.
- For your mouse to work, you will need to know what interface and which protocol it uses. Serial mice interface to a serial port, while PS/2 mice have a port and IRQ set aside. There is also another type of interface called a *busmouse*. Of these, Linux has support for these three: Inport (Microsoft), Logitech, and ATI-XL. In order for a PS/2 mouse to work, support has to be compiled into the Linux. The same goes for a busmouse, except that it can also be compiled as modules.
- Linux has one package that deals exclusively with PC Cards called "Card Services." This package includes all of the kernel modules you'll need to manage PCMCIA cards and a set of drivers for specific cards. The package also includes a daemon that handles hot swapping of most types of cards.
- The Card Services package comes bundled with a file named SUPPORTED.CARDS.

SELF TEST

The following Self Test questions will help you measure your understanding of the material presented in this chapter. Read all the choices carefully, as there may be more than one correct answer. Choose all correct answers for each question.

1. You install Linux onto a laptop and discover that there are two PCMCIA cards that you will need to install drivers for: an Ethernet card and a modem. What do you need to do in order to get these cards working?

   A. Recompile the Linux kernel to support Ethernet. Setting up the modem should be as easy as configuring the serial port it uses.

   B. Install the Card Services package to get the needed kernel modules and utilities to manage PCMCIA.

   C. Run the route utility to configure the cards.

   D. Edit the file /proc/devices to reflect the new hardware, then configure the files in /etc/sysconfig to get them up and running.

2. A coworker bought a brand new mouse to use on his Linux workstation. He tells you that the person he bought it from said it would work, but he is very frustrated because it doesn't. The old mouse had a rectangular 9-pin connector, and the new mouse has a round 6-pin mini DIN connector. What is most likely the reason why your coworker's new mouse doesn't work?

   A. The person who sold him the mouse sold him the wrong type. Your coworker should take it back and get a refund.

   B. The new mouse must have an adapter to change the round 6-pin mini DIN connector to the rectangular 9-pin connector.

   C. Your coworker's Linux workstation isn't set up to use a PS/2 mouse.

   D. Your coworker's Linux workstation isn't configured to use a busmouse.

3. How do you set up a third or fourth serial port in Linux? (Choose all that apply.)

   A. Use the addserial utility with the appropriate flags for the new serial port.

   B. Linux kernel 2.2 automatically handles this for you.

   C. Linux will not support more than two serial ports.

   D. Use the setserial utility to assign resources to the new serial port.

4. After installing an ISA plug-and-play device into a computer running Linux, what needs to be done in order to get the card working?

   A. Install and configure the isapnptools package for Linux.

B. Nothing. Since it's a plug-and-play card, Linux will be able to install the device drivers and kernel modules automatically.

C. The card will not work. Plug-and-play ISA cards are not supported in Linux.

D. Run the pnpprobe utility, then set the resources that the card should use.

5. You installed a printer onto a Linux workstation. After experiencing a lot of trouble trying to make it print, you're finally successful. However, now the sound card has stopped working. What most likely went wrong?

   A. The sound card was probably a plug-and-play device, and since Linux doesn't handle plug and play well, it couldn't detect the card after the new printer was installed.

   B. There is an IRQ conflict between the printer and the sound card.

   C. The sound card and printer are using the same device file in the /dev directory. You need to create a new device in the /dev directory to use both devices.

   D. None of the above.

6. Which of the following RAID levels provides both redundancy and performance increases?

   A. RAID-5

   B. RAID-4

   C. RAID-1

   D. RAID-0

7. What problems could you come across when using systems that mix (E)IDE and SCSI technologies?

   A. You can't mix them together.

   B. There are potential IRQ conflicts between the controllers for each device.

   C. The computer's BIOS may not be able to access SCSI devices.

   D. SCSI disks cannot use LBA translation as (E)IDE devices can.

8. How would an EIDE drive's geometry be changed, using LBA translation, if the drive had 1136 cylinders, 16 heads, and 63 sectors?

   A. 1024 cylinders, 128 heads, 63 sectors

   B. 1024 cylinders, 16 heads, 175 sectors

   C. 284 cylinders, 64 heads, 63 sectors

   D. 568 cylinders, 32 heads, 63 sectors

9. You are setting up a Linux Server to be a file server for an office of 30 people. The server has 64MB of memory. How much of that memory should you reserve to be used as buffer cache?

   A. Find out the maximum memory requirements of the system, then subtract the amount of RAM (64MB). The remaining value should be used to buffer cache.

   B. You don't need to. Linux handles the buffer cache automatically.

   C. About 1MB per user should be sufficient; therefore, use 30MB.

   D. Always use double the amount of available RAM.

10. What does LDP stand for?
    A. Linux Development Project
    B. Linux Development and Planning
    C. Linux Documentation Project
    D. None of the above
11. Of the following hardware, which would be the easiest to install Red Hat Linux on?
    A. A Toshiba laptop with an Intel Pentium II 266MHz CPU
    B. An IBM PC XT
    C. A 486DX/100 IBM Clone
    D. A PowerMac G3
12. What downside is there to extensive partitioning?
    A. Slower disk access.
    B. Unused disk space is wasted.
    C. Data fragmentation.
    D. The root partition might not be able to be accessed at boot time.
13. You attempt to install Linux on an old 80386 computer. You manage to scavenge an 800MB hard drive to use. However, when you boot the computer, it reports the hard drive to be only 504MB. Why?
    A. The BIOS can access only the first partition, which must be 504MB.
    B. The hard drive must have bad sectors.
    C. The BIOS only supports IDE, not EIDE.
    D. An 80386 CPU can only address 504MB of data.
14. What do you need to do in order to get past the 504MB barrier with an EIDE hard disk controller?
    A. Add a SCSI controller.
    B. Upgrade to an ATA-2 controller.
    C. Set jumpers on the hard disks to support EIDE.
    D. Set the hard drive translation mode to LBA in the BIOS.
15. You get a phone call from a frustrated user who just bought a new modem. The modem is a Lucent 56k Winmodem, and the user is having trouble making it work in Linux. Which of the following is most likely the source of his trouble?
    A. An IRQ conflict is preventing Linux from using the modem.
    B. Winmodems are specific to Windows operating systems. Linux cannot use them.
    C. The modem is a plug-and-play device, and the user does not have the isapnptools package installed/configured.
    D. Linux does not support 56k modems.
16. When planning your Red Hat Linux installation, which of the following information is the least important to take note of?
    A. The speed of your CD-ROM.
    B. What type of mouse you will be using.
    C. The frequency specifications of your monitor.
    D. The model of your network card.

17. RAID is an acronym for:
    A. Redundant Array of Independent Disks
    B. Redundant Array of Inexpensive Disks
    C. Reliable Array of Independent Disks
    D. Redundant Assortment of Inexpensive Disks

18. What is the maximum number of partitions that you can create for (E)IDE and SCSI disks?
    A. There is no maximum.
    B. 16 for (E)IDE and 15 for SCSI.
    C. 24 for (E)IDE and 16 for SCSI.
    D. Linux only supports a total of 64 partitions of all disks together.

3

Installation

CERTIFICATION OBJECTIVES

3.01	Disk Partitioning Strategies for Server and Workstation Installations
3.02	Choosing an Installation Class: Workstation, Server, or Custom
3.03	The Installation Process
3.04	The LILO Boot Process and Intel Hardware/BIOS Issues
3.05	Using loadlin
3.06	Additional Installation Details
3.07	Creating Partitions: Details
3.08	Additional Notes on Access Media Options
3.09	Viewing Boot Time Information
3.10	The Boot Up Messages in dmesg
3.11	Understanding the Standard Boot Process
3.12	Validating the Installation
3.13	Login as root
3.14	How Do You Know When Your Hardware Is Not Supported?
3.15	Sample Installation Exercises

There is a perception that a Workstation and a Server are two distinct things. In the Linux environment, this is more an optimization for usage than a type of platform. Both Workstation and Server installations use the exact same installation disk, the difference being the software sets, also called *packages*, loaded by each option.

The Workstation installation is designed mainly for inbound traffic to the host. The workstation uses network services from the network servers. The workstation usage concept is one where the user sits at the machine and performs day-to-day activities.

The Server installation includes all the common network services like Web, FTP, NFS, Samba, and many more. You can add any combination of these network services to any machine. You can at any time upgrade a workstation to be a server by installing these services. A server designation conceptually is a machine that is centrally located and centrally managed, offering network services to many other hosts, usually the workstations.

The Workstation and Server designations are oriented more for perceived use; there are no actual limitations as in some operating systems.

The next section is an overview of the installation program to point out aspects of the installation that you need to be aware of. This chapter will attempt to provide a bigger picture for most of the more difficult concepts.

After stepping through the overview, the first preinstallation topic of utmost importance is the disk partitions, their layout, and what is needed for the various installation options. Since there are unlimited possibilities when installing an operating system, you are introduced to various scenarios such as when the target system is new, and when the target system already has an operating system that you may or may not want to keep.

CERTIFICATION OBJECTIVE 3.01

Disk Partitioning Strategies for Server and Workstation Installations

By the very nature of the usage, the Workstation installation is usually much simpler in design than the Server installation. The workstation is usually optimized for local user applications centered around the X Window system and using services from the network.

The server system needs to be designed for optimal management and flexibility of use. This normally means that the server has many more distinct partitions that make up the file system. This allows for more selective management of these sections, like the user home directories. By separating the user home directories to one partition, disk quotas can be maintained on just that file system, and backups and restores are more specific. With the smaller file systems, failures are easier to rebuild, and expansion of any one file system is made easier.

The Red Hat installation program has preconfigured options that build a generic workstation and a generic server. Although these are not perfect, they are excellent starting points for new systems. The Custom option allows you to create any combination of partitions and software services for either a workstation or a server usage. The Custom option can be used to create any installation design, including a server or workstation type of installation.

CERTIFICATION OBJECTIVE 3.02

Choosing an Installation Class: Workstation, Server, or Custom

This section will introduce you to the three installation options that you will encounter during installation. The next sections will try to demystify the reasons behind why there are many partitions, the differences between the three installation choices, and why you would choose one over the other.

Three Installation Options

There is a Custom option that allows selection of any combination of software, and there are two installation options with preconfigured product sets. All three options are presented during an interactive installation.

The Custom option can actually be used to create either a Server or a Workstation installation, but offers the added benefit that you can make changes to the defaults.

The Custom installation requires that you be aware of how to configure disk drives and their partitions, what the swap partition is, how to create a swap partition, how to create separate file systems for important directory structures, and why you need to plan this all beforehand.

Base Packages Installed

On the Red Hat CD-ROM in the /RedHat/base/ directory, the comps text file lists all the packages associated with each group. A "package" is just one set of files related to a given application. For example, there is a Perl (another more advanced shell) package named perl-5.00503-2.i386.rpm. This Perl package, at about 4.3MB, is in the /RedHat/RPMS directory on the CD-ROM and contains all the required executables, library, help files, and the installation requirements. You can install this package, or any other, on any Red Hat Linux host as needed at any time using the rpm (Red Hat Package Manager) utility.

Workstation Installation Details

The Workstation installation option first deletes all ext2 (Linux) partitions. Then the Workstation installation uses *all* the remaining free space, whether it was ext2 type before or not, and creates three partitions as follows:

1. 64MB swap partition
2. 16MB /boot partition for all Intel platforms (a 2MB partition mounted as /dos and used for the Milo boot loader for an Alpha platform)
3. A variable-sized partition for the root, denoted as "/", that consumes all available remaining free space

Any previous operating system that existed on the machine is left intact. This may be good or bad. It is good if this is a test or development system and you want to be able to boot into any one of the operating systems on the machine. It is bad if this machine will only be running Linux. The other operating systems will take up space that may not ever be available to the Linux operating system for use. You must decide whether you want to keep the previous operating system or not before you do your installation.

Note that the Apache Web Server package is NOT installed with a Workstation installation. You can add this package at any time as indicated earlier using the rpm utility.

Custom Partition Strategy—Workstation

A workstation machine will be one used interactively by one or more users. It is not normally intended as a server, although it can provide network services if desired.

The easiest partition setup for a basic workstation would be to create a single swap partition and then a single root partition. Technically speaking, you could start from this and change it at any time by adding more disk space, reconfiguring the system as needed, backing up directory trees and mounting new disk space and restoring the backed up trees, and so forth.

WORKSTATION OPTION PACKAGES INSTALLED The list of file packages installed by a default Workstation installation is on the

CD-ROM in /RedHat/base/comps. This list contains over 250 packages that are installed. Each package contains at least one and usually several files. There are several hundred files installed during an installation, and this is only the beginning.

Server Installation Details

If you are intending to run this machine as a server of common network services and do not want to have to go through the selection of packages during the installation, then the Server installation option is your best choice.

Be careful! This installation will remove all partitions on all disks.

If you already have an operating system on this machine, it will be overwritten, and no opportunity is given to back up anything during the installation. This installation assumes you are creating a full-time server, and any other operating system would just waste disk space.

Server Partitions

You need at least 1600MB, or 1.6GB, of total disk space. There are six partitions created, four with a fixed size and two that share the remainder of the disk or disks. The four fixed-size partitions created are a 64MB swap partition, a root partition of 256MB, a /boot partition of 16MB, and a /var partition of 256MB. The two variable-sized partitions created are a /usr partition of at least 512MB and a /home partition of at least 512MB.

The following list provides an overview of the partitions created automatically by a Server installation:

1. 64MB swap partition
2. 16MB /boot partition for all Intel platforms (a 2MB partition mounted as /dos and used for the Milo boot loader for an Alpha platform)
3. A root (/) partition of 256MB
4. A /var partition of 256MB
5. A /home partition of at least 512MB
6. A /usr partition of at least 512MB

Note that the variable-sized partitions, /home and /usr, split the remainder of space and hence consume the rest of up to two additional disks if needed. If more than three disks are present, some of the disks will not be used.

Server Option Network Packages Installed

Table 3-1 is a sublist of the application packages loaded by the Server installation that are network related. (The order matches the sequence in the /RedHat/base/comps installation file.)

Custom Installation Option

The Custom installation option provides the most flexibility for an experienced Linux or UNIX administrator. During this installation option, you can select more or fewer groups and even individual packages within each group, and configure the partitions to suit your needs more explicitly.

TABLE 3-1

Network-related packages specific to server installation

metamail	modemtool	netcfg	printtool
yp-tools	ypbind	traceroute	
tcp_wrappers	rdist	rdate	portmap
knfsd	ncftp	timed	bind-utils
telnet	rwho	rusers	tftp
routed	talk	netkit-base	fwhois
ftp	finger	uucp	rsh
minicom	lrzsz	dip	statserial
perl-MD5	cleanfeed	inn	ppp
ncpfs	anonftp	mars-new	samba
wu-ftpd	apache	caching-nameserver	ipxutils
bind	tcpdump	pidentd	ipchains
ucd-snmp	ucd-snmp-utils		

Selecting Package Sets

There are many package sets available, as listed in Figure 3-1. Each package set that is selected during installation has a list of associated modules. In many cases, the associated module names are required for more than one group and hence appear duplicated in many of the package options. This ensures that all required dependencies are installed if only one or two optional packages are picked.

After all package group options have been selected, the system checks for duplicate name requests and then installs all required packages just once. For full details on these package sets, see the /RedHat/base/comps text file.

Figure 3-1 shows all the various package set names that are available during a Custom installation. Some packages will already be selected for you and will have an asterisk (*) in the selection box. During installation, you only see the first few names in this list. There are more than can fit on one screen. During installation, you can use the arrow keys to scroll up and down. Press the SPACE BAR to toggle the selection on or off. An asterisk means "selected." The base Linux system is included automatically in all cases.

In Figure 3-1, the choices are many and the combinations are numerous. You should only pick packages you need. For instance, if you want to write C language programs, you would want the C Development packages and possibly the C Development libraries. The Extra Documentation package is usually a good idea for at least one machine in your network.

How Much More Space Is Needed?

The question of disk space needed is always relevant. You need as much as it takes, and probably more. The minimum is around 200MB of disk space if you install Linux without X and few server services. With 300MB, you could probably get in X, but few server services and few games.

The 600+MB for a Workstation installation, or at least 1600MB (1.6+ GB) for the Server installation, are just starting points. You will also have to factor in disk space for applications and user data. As of 1999, you probably cannot even get a PC with less than 2000MB (2GB) of disk space. For a

FIGURE 3-1

List of software group options

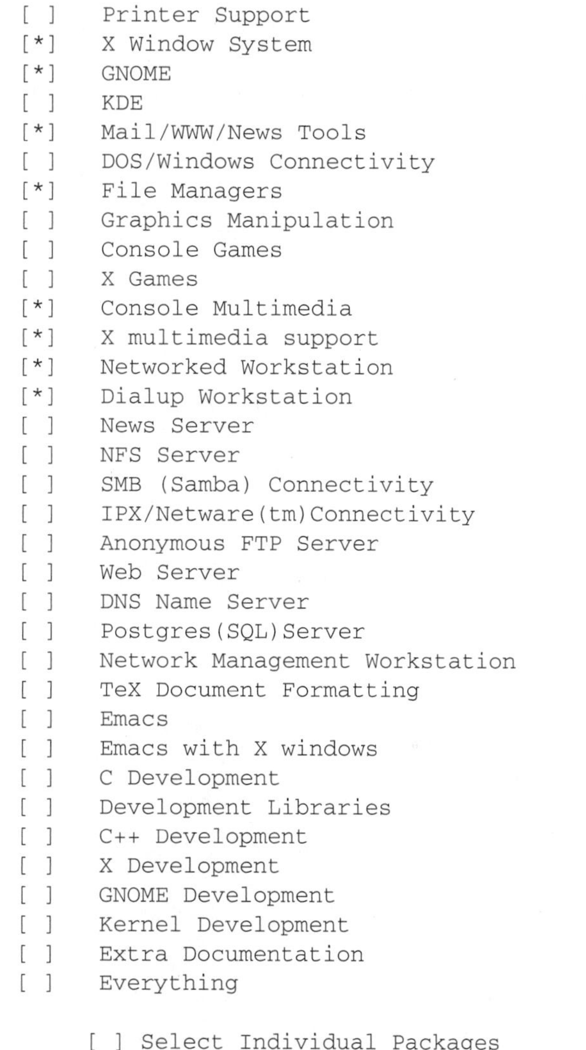

```
[ ]   Printer Support
[*]   X Window System
[*]   GNOME
[ ]   KDE
[*]   Mail/WWW/News Tools
[ ]   DOS/Windows Connectivity
[*]   File Managers
[ ]   Graphics Manipulation
[ ]   Console Games
[ ]   X Games
[*]   Console Multimedia
[*]   X multimedia support
[*]   Networked Workstation
[*]   Dialup Workstation
[ ]   News Server
[ ]   NFS Server
[ ]   SMB (Samba) Connectivity
[ ]   IPX/Netware(tm)Connectivity
[ ]   Anonymous FTP Server
[ ]   Web Server
[ ]   DNS Name Server
[ ]   Postgres(SQL)Server
[ ]   Network Management Workstation
[ ]   TeX Document Formatting
[ ]   Emacs
[ ]   Emacs with X windows
[ ]   C Development
[ ]   Development Libraries
[ ]   C++ Development
[ ]   X Development
[ ]   GNOME Development
[ ]   Kernel Development
[ ]   Extra Documentation
[ ]   Everything

     [ ] Select Individual Packages
```

single-user workstation, this is plenty. For a server, this may be too small. If it is too small, you will know soon enough. However, it is easy to add disks to Linux and expand your file system at any time, so this should not be a big concern. Get the biggest disk you can afford as a starting point.

Then select either Workstation for a single dedicated user or the Server option for Web, FTP, File and Print, DNS services.

Although it is not necessary to have extra space, the benefit of having it for the next upgrade will be understood by all concerned. Having an extra partition allows you to install the next version upgrade into the spare partition, thus preserving your current root partition just in case you need to go back to the previous version. If you are lucky, you may have or get a new machine when the next upgrade comes by and this scenario will not be a problem. However, when you have invested in a laptop, upgrades become a terrifying experience. Losing something that is already working may make you hesitate longer than you need to. An extra partition to test the new version becomes very handy then.

CERTIFICATION OBJECTIVE 3.03

The Installation Process

There are many interrelated questions you need to answer during installation. There are many ways to access the installation files and there are many options on how to install the operating system. The installation outline here is designed to get you through it in an easy-to-understand flow, in as simple a fashion as possible, with just enough detail to keep going. There are many details spread throughout the rest of the text to answer most of the other questions you might encounter.

Pre-Installation Preparation

Red Hat Linux has been specifically crafted to work on almost any "old" PC hardware. It can also be installed to Alpha and PowerPC based computers, to name two. There are not many manufacturers currently providing Linux driver support, but this is growing quickly. You are better off with hardware that was around before the summer of 1999; drivers are more likely to be available from either the installation disk or the Internet.

Brand new hardware, like new video hardware, may be troublesome to get working with older drivers; new driver files may be hard or impossible to find. Most of the major manufacturers, such as Compaq, Dell, and HP, offer their hardware preinstalled with Red Hat Linux. This is one way to get the latest hardware with all the correct drivers, direct from the manufacturer.

You can check the Red Hat Web site (http://www.redhat.com/hardware) for current hardware drivers and pointers to other resources at any time.

Pre-Install Hardware Information

There is certain hardware configuration information you should know before you begin:

- Hard drive(s), their geometry and size (and SCSI ID if using SCSI)
- Physical RAM (Random Access Memory) of the machine
- CD-ROM and its interface type: IDE or SCSI
- Mouse type and the port it is attached to
- NIC (Network Interface Card) make, model, and parameters
- SCSI adapter and settings if one is present

Additional information you should note:

- If you plan on installing the X Windows system, you also need
  - Video adapter card type and local memory size
  - Monitor brand name or its specifications
- Whether you plan on keeping your old operating system or not
- Primary use of this machine: user or server based

Installation Diskette(s) Needed

You should have the installation diskette already created, as indicated next. There are a few options here, depending on where the installation files will be retrieved from.

If your system does not boot from the CD-ROM, you need at least one of these two images on a diskette:

- **boot.img** Installations using local hard disk or local CD-ROM
- **bootnet.img** Installations using HTTP, FTP, or NFS primarily

You may need this image on a diskette too:

- **pcmcia.img** Installations on laptops that need to start the PC Card manager service, originally known as the PCMCIA manager service

This is a secondary support disk asked for if needed only.

- **Special Note:**
  rescue.img Used for recovery of a failed system. You should always keep one handy for emergency purposes. It will boot the system with a minimal Linux kernel and its file system in a virtual RAM drive. This allows you to run various programs from the diskette and any mountable partition.

To Use rescue.img

You must boot your machine with the BOOT.IMG diskette. When you get to the first screen prompt showing lilo, you must type **rescue**, and press ENTER. The boot disk will continue to load and you will eventually be asked for the next disk. Replace the BOOT.IMG disk with the RESCUE.IMG diskette. Press ENTER and the bootup should continue. The rescue disk will load a virtual file system into memory and supply a few very basic but essential binary files for you to try to recover your system. You can mount any partitions onto any directories that exist or that you create to access any files on them. If the file system is corrupt, you can run the File System Check program, fsck, to repair the disk if possible. You can edit files that need to be changed. You can rebuild the lilo boot block. You can do whatever you need to fix the system.

The following is an illustration of what to expect when booting up with the rescue disk:

```
Lilo:  rescue <ENTER>
… (installation of kernel and processes proceed)
Insert root file system disk: (replace BOOT.IMG disk with RESCUE.IMG
```

```
                                  disk) <ENTER>
... (boot up continues until you get a shell prompt)
```

These boot diskette image files are supplied on the CDROM and can be created in two ways:

- From any Windows based system by using the supplied RAWRITE.COM utility (in \DOSUTILS on the installation CD-ROM)
- By using the dd command from any running UNIX or Linux computer and these image files on the CD-ROM

Almost Ready to Install

With one of the two boot image disks (BOOT.IMG or BOOTNET.IMG) in the floppy drive and your Red Hat Linux (marked with the number 1) CD-ROM in the CD-ROM drive, reboot your machine or power cycle your machine.

Laptop Reboot

If you have a laptop that does not really power down, then you will need to use the SHUTDOWN and RESTART option of that operating system.

on the job

This inability to really shut down is a huge frustration for laptop users. You might want to set the hardware to power down with the POWER button if this is configurable—check the manual for the laptop. If the laptop does not do this and power management (finally built-in as of RH6) doesn't work, you may have trouble turning off the computer (especially if you have removed Windows entirely from the laptop).

Win9x / NT Reboot Procedure

For Windows 9*x* / NT, click START, and then click the first option above START, Shut Down. You will be prompted with a box offering a few options, one of which should be Restart. Select the Restart option if it is not already selected, and then click OK. You may have to wait a few moments before the system screen goes blank and the system BIOS starts rebooting.

Bootable CD-ROM

On some of the newer systems, the system can boot an operating system from the CD-ROM. This is fine for what you want. You could also go into the system CMOS settings (this varies, but the option may be as simple as pressing the DEL key before the memory test is finished), changing the boot order to be the A: (floppy) first, using one of the boot diskettes. Technically speaking, the Red Hat Linux CD-ROM is bootable.

Booting from DOS and Win9x, Not NT

If you already have MS-DOS 6.22, simply boot the machine until you get to a command prompt. If you have Win9*x* on your machine, reboot the machine into COMMAND MODE. You cannot do this from NT as this only works from a purely DOS-like command prompt, not from within a DOS PROMPT window of any MS Windows operating system.

Once in command mode, assuming you have access to your CD-ROM drive via an installed driver in the config.sys setup, you can run the file (assuming your CD-ROM drive is E:) E:\DOSUTILS\AUTOBOOT.BAT. This will get you to the Installation program.

CD-ROM or Boot Diskette Starts Installation

After the hardware tests, the PC should boot from the floppy or CD-ROM. After a few files are opened and decompressed, a "Welcome to Red Hat Linux" screen should appear.

You are finally at the first stage of the installation. This is a good time to point out a few things you need to know before you move on.

More Details You Should Know

The installation program uses an "almost graphical" interface. Although the mouse does not work specifically, you can move the cursor around using arrow keys, the TAB key, and special function keys as described next. The 6.0 installation is not like a real GUI interface, but it's better than just a text command line.

Screen Cursor Movement, Selection, and Text Entry

The screens or windows that will appear during the installation have a standardized look and feel. The first screen offers an option to display help. Press the ENTER key to continue to the next screen. There are some keys assigned that provide "movement" on these screens of the "cursor." The cursor appears as a blinking underline or as a reverse colored box over an item.

Figure 3-2 is just one of the many screens that will appear during installation. Not all screens will require cursor movement and allow you to select multiple options. This screen shows all these features and is used to illustrate how to move around and select or unselect an option.

If you press the arrow keys, you move up or down through the option selections at the top, in this case, the various mouse types. To get to the next field, press TAB to go forward or ALT-TAB to go backward. When not

FIGURE 3-2

An Install Screen example

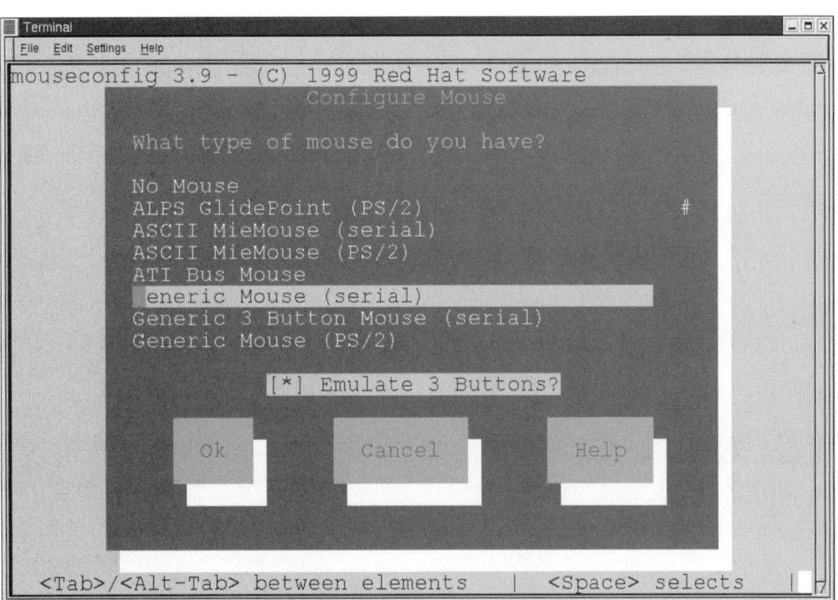

in a field of multiple selections, you can also use the up and down arrow keys to go between fields.

The keys described in Table 3-2 can be used for navigation:

Assuming you are at the screen depicted in Figure 3-2, and your cursor is on the same option, if you press TAB, the cursor will move to the line "[ ] Emulate 3 Buttons?" You could toggle this selection on with the SPACE BAR and toggle it off by pressing it again. If you press the TAB again, the cursor will move to the OK box as shown in Figure 3-3.

At this point, you could use the arrow keys to circle through OK to CANCEL to HELP and to <mouse option>. Once at the <mouse option>, the cursor keys select another <mouse option> line. Using ALT-TAB reverses the direction of the cursor movement. If you press ENTER or F12 at any time, it defaults to the OK option, unless you click CANCEL, along with all currently selected options. You can use the Space Bar to toggle an option, like Emulate 3 Button Mouse, on and off when it is the selected option.

Quick Overview of Installation

The installation starts after the initial bootup screen. Each "step" is given as a sequenced screen step in the following long section. This is a condensed overview of the titles and their basic "step." Each of these screen steps also contains OK, CANCEL, BACK, and sometimes other details. These are not shown, just the relevant options and some comments as to why or why not to choose one over another. The first installation is always the hardest; the next are much easier. Practice on a machine that is not important until you are sure of what you are doing.

TABLE 3-2

Navigation keys

Key	Function
TAB	Go to next element
ALT-TAB	Go back to previous element
(up/dn arrows)	Move up/down through selections or menu items
SPACE BAR	Toggle a selection ON or OFF
F12, ENTER	Accept entries on current screen

FIGURE 3-3

Install screen after cursor movement

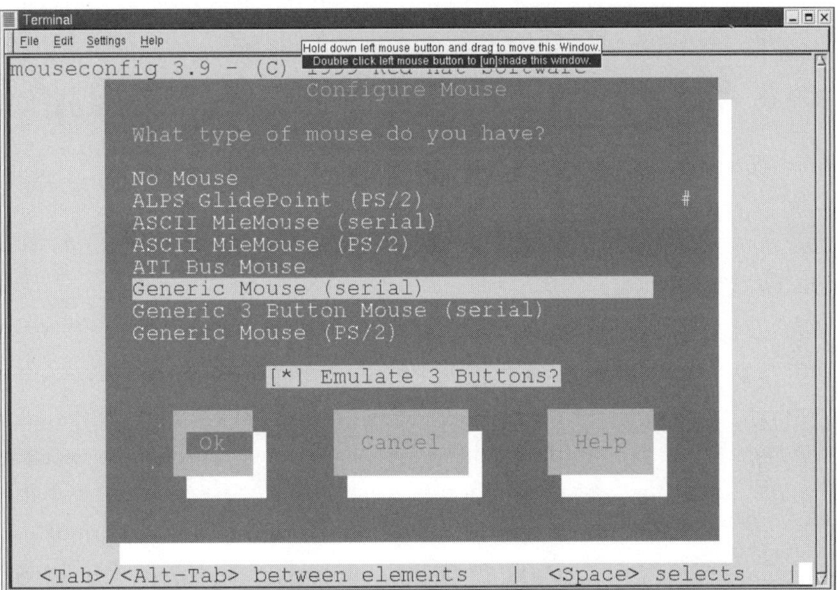

The installation has two distinct initial paths based on whether you use the BOOT.IMG diskette to install from local hardware or you use BOOTNET.IMG to install from a network-based resource like NFS, HTTP, or FTP. After the first three common steps, the specific steps for these two options are then presented separately. Then there is the choice of what type of installation: Workstation, Server, or Custom. Then you can either Upgrade or Install (new copy). There are many more optional screens, and most other steps are then common until the end.

How to Follow This Installation Guide

Each major screen has a base number. The first screen is 0.0, and the next topic is 1.0. If this topic 1.0 screen asks a question that is related to it, then the options on this screen are just numbered, and their corresponding steps are 1.1 for the first option, 1.2 for the second option. If substep 1.1 has options, then the first option to 1.1 is step 1.1.1, and so on. Every additional substep is another "dot number" addition. When the first number changes, you are on another topic altogether.

Part 1: Beginning Installation Steps

Step 0 is the Welcome screen. These are the next three screens, steps 1–3. Figure 3-4 shows the installation Welcome screen.

OPTION 3.1: NO TO PCMCIA If there is no need for PCMCIA, this is not on a laptop, and no further diskettes need to be loaded.

OPTION 3.2: YES TO PCMCIA You will be prompted to insert the diskette created from the PCMCIA.IMG file described earlier into the floppy drive. This diskette will contain the necessary additional software drivers needed to configure most common PCMCIA hardware.

Part 2: Media Access Options: Local or Remote

You only need to follow one of these next versions of the step 4 options, based on the installation diskette you chose to use. If you are using BOOT.IMG, then the next set of steps is 4.0. Step 4.0 asks to look for the installation files on local media: a CD-ROM or a hard drive. If you are using a BOOTNET.IMG startup diskette, then the next steps for you are marked 4.1. Step 4.1 asks which network access method should be used to get to the installation files: NFS, HTTP, or FTP.

FIGURE 3-4

First three screens after Welcome screen

Step	Title of screen	Option	Comments
1.0	Choose a Language	English	many languages available
2.0	Keyboard Type	us	for usa keyboard
3.0	PCMCIA Support	(3.1)No	All but laptops usually
		(3.2)Yes	if yes, need support diskette with PCMCIA.IMG on it. This can be for the network card or SCSI CDROM interface (laptops)

You will only need to follow one of these sets of steps, either 4.0 steps or 4.1 steps.

LOCAL MEDIA ACCESS—BOOT.IMG If you started out with the diskette created from the BOOT.IMG file, you will only be asked if the location of the installation files, media access, is from a local CD-ROM or a local hard disk. If it is from a CD-ROM, then the installation will have to try to mount the CD-ROM or the hard disk device so it can access the files from it directly. In either case, you must decide whether this secondary device is on a SCSI controller or not.

Note that if you started with BOOT.IMG, you can only do an installation from LOCAL MEDIA. You will not have an opportunity to get the install files from any network resource. Figure 3-5 shows the Installation Method screen.

In step 4.0, you must indicate whether the Red Hat installation files are on a local CD-ROM or on a local hard drive. In either case, the next step, 4.0.1, shown in Figure 3-6, requests information as to whether you are using a SCSI controller to connect to either of these two drives.

If you select SCSI in 4.0.1, your next step is 4.0.1.1. If you select Other in 4.0.1, your next step is 4.0.1.2.

Step 4.0.1.1. If SCSI was selected in 4.0.1, enter the following:

SCSI Driver ID
SCSI Parameters if needed

You will need to know something about the SCSI hardware setup to use the CD-ROM device. These choices are shown in Figure 3-7.

Note: Skip past all 4.1 steps if you used BOOT.IMG.

FIGURE 3-5

Step 4.0: The Installation Method screen

```
CDROM
Hard Drive
```

FIGURE 3-6

Step 4.0.1: Hardware Specifics Needed screen

```
Screen              Comment
SCSI                if on supported SCSI
Other               if non-SCSI CDROM
```

REMOTE MEDIA ACCESS—BOOTNET.IMG If you started with the BOOTNET.IMG diskette, then your choices are different for where to locate the installation files. In Figure 3-8 you will need to select the network access to use (NFS, HTTP, FTP), the name of the service to use, and then configure your own hardware to connect to it using DHCP, BOOTP, MANUAL (you enter IP setup info).

You are first asked what installation method to use in step 4.1. If you are not familiar with how to access NFS, FTP, or an HTTP resource, refer to the additional information supplied later in this chapter. This section assumes you know how to fill in the request.

Next, in Figure 3-9, you need to configure your local network interface before you can test whether you can access the resource.

For any network connection to work, the network card and network software must be able to establish a connection to the server in question. The details for each option in this step are given later in this chapter.

Part 3: Type of Installation

This next step is used to decide what type of installation to perform, whether an upgrade (no further options required) or a new installation (overwrites any current installation).

FIGURE 3-7

Step 4.0.1.2: "Other" type of CD-ROM

```
like a Sound Blaster card CDROM
- choose driver from list
- enter parameters if needed
```

FIGURE 3-8

Step 4.1.0: Installation method (network part)

Screen	Comment
NFS Image	Need nfs server IP, export name
FTP	Need ftp server IP, directory name
HTTP	Need http server IP, directory name

The installation screen, shown in Figure 3-10, offers two choices, to Upgrade an existing Linux or to Install a new copy over whatever is currently on your system.

In this case, if you pick Upgrade, then the next step for you is detailed in step 5.1. If you select Install, then your next step is 6.0, and you can skip the details about step 5.1.

OPTION 5.1: IF UPGRADE CHOSEN Note: Only if you are upgrading from a previous version of Linux would you select this option. You must already have a version of Linux installed for this installation to continue.

There are a few installation-related questions after this step. Then the installation will simply try to replace all existing packages with the current versions of the same packages, plus add any required new dependencies not already found on the system. Most of your system configuration files are left untouched. A log file is maintained about all changes in /tmp/upgrade.log. There is a small chance of a software upgrade failing: locked files, improper or modified rpm packages, and other errors. Just be aware that you should have a tested backup ready just in case.

FIGURE 3-9

Step 4.2: Your network setup screen

Screen
DHCP
BOOTP
MANUAL

FIGURE 3-10

Step 5.0: Installation Path screen

Screen	Comment
Upgrade	if Linux version 2.0 or later
Install	wipes out any previous version, make sure you have a backup

Part 4: Installation Type (Custom), Disk Partitioning

Here is an important fork in the installation roadway. If you choose Workstation or Server installation at this point, you will get a predetermined partition layout scheme created on your system, as well as a predetermined set of installation files installed on your machine. You still have to answer questions about setting up your network, printer, and so forth. Figure 3-11 shows you these installation options. The Workstation option deletes all Linux partitions, Server deletes all partitions first, and Custom will give you complete control of partitions and packages.

If you choose the Custom option, you will be allowed to configure the partitions using either fdisk or Disk Druid, or use the current ones, assuming they are sufficient. In all cases, you are asked for the controller type of the local disks in step 6.2, shown in Figure 3-12. Select Yes if needed for local disk access, and no if access is not required locally.

Note: The Workstation and Server class installations complete all further tasks except setting up your network card(s) and your X Server.

Only if you select the Custom option do you need to go through these next steps interactively. Step 6.3, shown in Figure 3-13, is a critical point in the installation. Disk Druid is only available at installation, and has some very interesting features. Fdisk has a text-based interface. Continue indicates that all partitions are ready to go.

FIGURE 3-11

Step 6.1: Installation Class screen

Screen	Comment
Workstation	only deletes Linux partitions
Server	deletes all partitions
Custom	you must configure all partitions

FIGURE 3-12

Step 6.2: Controller Type screen

Screen		Comment
SCSI Support	Yes	checks for controller
	No	

If you already have all the partitions ready to go, then you would select "continue," and your next step would be 7.0. If they are not ready, you can select either Disk Druid (next step is 6.3.1) or fdisk (next step is 6.3.2). When would they be ready? If you had a previous installation and you wanted to overwrite the partitions rather than upgrade the current version of Linux then these current partitions are ready.

You need to know what to do at this critical step. The installation will not continue unless the minimum number of partitions are available: a swap partition and a root partition. If these are not available, the installation will fail and will allow you to return to step 6.3 to try again. You have the option of creating the partitions at this point if you select either fdisk or Disk Druid options; then you can choose "Continue."

You should already have an idea of what size partitions you want for each of the desired file systems. You may want to look at Table 3-3, "Getting Started: Installation Worksheet," later in this chapter and the rest of that section before continuing at this point.

You must identify which partition is to be used with what file directory structure either within Disk Druid or after finishing with fdisk.

In step 6.3.1, if you select Disk Druid, you get a "graphical" disk partitioning utility in which you can assign the mount point to a partition

FIGURE 3-13

Step 6.3: Disk Setup screen

	Screen	Comments
Disk Setup	Disk Druid	Only available at installation, Has some very neat features
	fdisk	text based interface (used below in all examples)
	continue	all partitions are ready to go

of a specific or "growable" size. This is the easier utility to use at this point if you know what partitions you want to remove and create.

Disk Druid is the utility of choice for most advanced users. Disk Druid is easy to use and graphical in nature BUT is ONLY available during installation. (The fdisk utility is always available.) In an emergency situation, you will only have fdisk. There is an entire subsection in this chapter that explains how to use fdisk, as it is universal to most, if not all, versions of Linux.

In step 6.3.2, if you select fdisk to create partitions, you get a shell command line with the fdisk command prompt as illustrated in great detail later in this chapter. You can remove, add, or change the partition layout of any disk with this utility. You should become familiar with fdisk in case of an emergency.

Note: If you use fdisk at this point to create the partitions, the system may be forced to reboot. You then have to go through all the same installation screens as indicated earlier.

After using fdisk to create the raw partitions, you will be prompted to make the "partition to directory mount point" assignments as illustrated in Figure 3-14, step 6.4.

FIGURE 3-14

The displayed file system configuration

```
Mount Point    Device         Requested        Actual        Type
               hda1           16M              16M           Linux Native
               hda2           64M              64M           Linux Swap
               hda3           1604M            1604M         Linux Native
               hda5           1228M            1228M         Linux Native


Drive Summaries

Drive          Geom [C/H/S]        Total       Used          Free
had            [  1004/128/63]     4048M       2902M         1146M

Edit           Delete              Ok          Back
F2-Add NFS     F3-Edit             F4-Delete   F12-OK        vX.XX
```

Figure 3-14 shows you a sample of a prepartitioned drive with four partitions already configured on a single drive called hda. Each partition is then a numbered "piece" of this drive: hda1, hda2, and so on.

You need to select one partition, for example hda1, then TAB to EDIT, and press RETURN. You are prompted to enter the mount point for this partition. In this case, you would enter /boot. The second partition, hda2, will automatically be used for the swap partition. You could assign hda3 to / (root of file system). The last partition, hda5, can be used for whatever you want. For example, if you knew this was to be a Web server, you could mount hda5 as **/home/httpd**.

The overriding assumption for this entire section is that you already know what directories should be separated into separate partition space. A full discussion of why file systems are separated is provided later in this section.

ADDING AN NFS MOUNT In step 6.4.1, within Figure 3-14, the F2 key allows you to include any number of NFS mount points, and connections to file share services from any NFS server, usually UNIX or Linux. You can make these extra connections now so the installation will configure the file system table setup permanently this way, or you can manually do this later after the installation is complete. Figure 3-15 is just an example of an NFS mountable service that you could additionally mount into your file system at this point in the installation.

FIGURE 3-15

Step 6.4.1: Example setup for NFS service connection

```
Edit NFS Mount Point
NFS Server         :          Linux6.vaddac.com
NFS Path           :          /usr/man
Mount Point        :          /usr/man

          Ok          Cancel
```

Figure 3-15 illustrates using an NFS service called /usr/man from the host Linux6.vaddac.com to be mounted locally as /usr/man. The local connection can be any directory point you want.

COMPLETED MOUNT POINTS After you have finished configuring your partition mount points, your screen should look something like Figure 3-16 (which does not include the NFS share example in Figure 3-15).

Fantastic! This was the most difficult part so far. The rest will seem easy until you get to the last step, the X configuration.

Part 5: Actual File Systems Formatted, Packages to Install

For this step, you are presented with a screen showing only a few of the partitions that are available. You should select all that are new or being overwritten for formatting. There is a tendency to forget that there may be more partitions to be formatted than are displayed on the screen. Make sure to scroll down and select all partitions whether they appear on the first screen (shown in Figure 3-17) or not.

FIGURE 3-16

Completed example partition file system setup

```
Mount Point      Device    Requested    Actual    Type
/boot            hda1      16M          16M       Linux Native
                 hda2      64M          64M       Linux Swap
/                hda3      1604M        1604M     Linux Native
/home/httpd      hda5      1228M        1228M     Linux Native

Drive Summaries
Drive      Geom [C/H/S]        Total     Used     Free
hda3       [  1004/128/63]     4048M     2902M    1146M

           Edit       Delete     Ok       Back

F2-Add NFS   F3-Edit    F4-Delete   F12-OK   vX.XX
```

FIGURE 3-17

Step 7.0: Format Partitions screen (this screen will vary depending on the number of partitions to format)

```
Options presented         Comments
(partition 1)             press <SPACE> to force format
(partition 2 ...)         (format them all)

check for bad blocks      not absolutely necessary, adds time
```

Figure 3-18 shows the Initializing Swap screen. The contents of this screen will vary depending on your installation, but usually there will be just one swap file, and a maximum of eight swap files.

Wow! You are almost there. The installation now wants to get to the actual installation files. Depending on where they are, it may soon start installing (local CD-ROM) or ask how to get to the network connection if the first attempt failed. If the files are on the CD-ROM, the CD-ROM is initialized, and the installation formats all partitions on all disks that you selected in step 7.0.

Note: If the /RedHat files are on a local hard disk they must be in \RedHat or /RedHa!. You are asked what partition has them. If it is a Windows C: drive, then it is probably device hda1.

PACKAGES TO INSTALL The Workstation and Server Installation options already have a preset list of packages to install. The list of packages was discussed earlier.

For a custom installation, you are prompted for which packages of software to install. Step 8.0 (shown in Figure 3-19) displays a long list of product group "packages" that you can choose to install. There is a list of these product groups in Figure 3-1 if you need more detail. Note that the

FIGURE 3-18

Step 7.1: Initializing Swap

```
[ ]  (each swap partition)      press <SPACE>, force format as swap
```

FIGURE 3-19

Step 8.0: Selecting components (see list of groups in Figure 3-1)

```
[ ]     (Some Group)              Press <SPACE> to select/deselect
[*]     Everything                Requires about 1.6 GB.

        [ ] Select individual
        packages
```

system has prechosen some packages for you, similar to a basic Workstation installation.

This is an abbreviated display of the real screen you would see. Figure 3-1 has a complete list that is more than you will see on one screen. Make sure you scroll down through all the choices.

exam Watch

If you "Select individual packages," this requires you to go through many more screens to pick and choose each file of the many software product packages that make up each selected group.

PACKAGES START INSTALLING The long-awaited installation of the files has finally arrived. Step 8.1 (shown in Figure 3-20) will now show a sort-of-graphical display of each file being installed, an estimate of how much time remains, how long it has taken so far, and how many files are done and how many still remain.

Step 8.1 in Figure 3-20 shows current package, size, load time, and current and estimated finish times. At this point, you are about 75% finished with questions and about 90% of the time element will be behind

FIGURE 3-20

Step 8.1: Package Installation screen

```
Package Installation                          informational screen
```

you when all packages are finished installing. There are a few final screens to go through yet.

Part 6: Final Hardware Configuration Information

Figures 3-21 through 3-34 show the final stages of the installation process. In Step 9.1 in Figure 3-21, you will be asked if you want to configure a mouse.

In step 9.2, shown in Figure 3-22, you must know a valid IP address and Network Mask as a minimum to configure your network OR choose DHCP or BOOTP if either of these servers is available to configure your network settings.

In Figure 3-23, you will be asked to select your time zone. Use GMT (if not a dual boot with another Windows OS, otherwise do not select GMT) and then specify your time zone. In this example, use U.S. Eastern.

In Figure 3-24, you will be asked to configure services at bootup. For most configurations, this can be left with the default information.

The screen in Figure 3-25 will ask if you want to configure a printer. Selecting Yes will allow you to configure a local or remote printer along with the driver. If you select No, you may still configure the printer at a later time.

FIGURE 3-21

Step 9.1: Mouse Configuration screen

```
Configure a Mouse      yes/no     this is the software, not the manufacturer
```

FIGURE 3-22

Step 9.2: Networking Configuration screen

```
Configure Networking     yes/no
```

FIGURE 3-23

Step 9.3: Time Zone Configuration screen

```
Configure Time Zone      [  ] GMT
```

FIGURE 3-24

Step 9.4: Services at Bootup Configuration screen

```
Configure Services at Bootup
```

FIGURE 3-25

Step 9.5: Printer Configuration screen

```
Configure a Printer     yes
                        no
```

The screen in Figure 3-26 will ask you to specify a password. The password must be at least six characters long and a combination of digits and numerals. You must enter the password twice; nothing appears on the screen.

If you have NIS (Network Information Service) being supported locally, you must fill in the name of the NIS Domain and then the server DNS name, the server IP, or use the "Request via broadcast" option. This process is shown in Figure 3-27. NIS is a centrally managed authentication service that is shared out to all integrated hosts.

Step 9.8 in Figure 3-28 will ask you if you want a Custom Boot Disk. In most situations, you will select Yes.

Step 9.9 in Figure 3-29 will ask you to update the Lilo Boot Loader. The recommended configuration is to select MBR, which puts lilo as the first MBR. Select hdax is another boot loader already being used.

Step 9.10 shown in Figure 3-30 will ask you to Add Options to Lilo Boot. The only time you would ever select Yes would be for an older BIOS or for big disks. In this configuration, we will pick No. You would use liner mode if your machine used LBA mode.

FIGURE 3-26

Setting Root Password screen

```
Set a Root Password     enter password twice
                        nothing will display on screen
                        (i.e., no stars/asterisks like
                        a Windows password)
```

FIGURE 3-27

Step 9.7: Authentication Configuration

```
Authentification          Configuration
[  ] NIS
[*]  MD5
                          [*] Shadow Passwords
```

FIGURE 3-28

Step 9.8: Custom Boot Disk

```
          Yes       Custom boot disk
          no
```

FIGURE 3-29

Step 9.9: Update the Lilo Boot Loader

```
          MBR       update Lilo
          hdax
```

FIGURE 3-30

Step 9.10: Add options to Lilo Boot

```
Lilo options           yes
                       no
                              [ ]Use linear mode (SCSI)
```

Note: There are alternatives to lilo, notably LOADLIN, which is discussed in more detail later in this section.

Step 9.11.0 shown in Figure 3-31 is the screen where you will select bootable partitions. This will only appear if you have another operating system on your machine and you want to configure a boot option, which you probably do want to do. In our example, there was no other operating system, so Figure 3-31 would not appear.

The following is an example where the first partition has a Windows operating system (it does not matter which one), and a Workstation installation was performed creating three additional partitions in the free space that was available.

Cursor to the first entry, then press TAB twice to get to the Edit option, and press RETURN. You are prompted for a name, the label, that lilo can be

FIGURE 3-31

Step 9.11.0: Selecting bootable partitions

```
The boot manager Red Hat uses can boot other operating
systems as well. You need to tell me what partitions you
would like to be able to boot and what label you want to
use for each of them

Device          Partition Type          Default         Boot Label
/dev/hda1       DOS 16 bit >=32
/dev/hda2       Linux Native            *               Linux
/dev/hda5       Linux Native

                Ok            Edit            Back
```

prompted to present to you during the first stage of every bootup. If you had Win98 on that first partition, then enter the string 'Win98' or anything else you like. This is just a name that you can enter when promted to access that other operating system. You can press TAB at the lilo: prompt during a bootup to display these names. The first name is the default. The * under the word Default means that the system currently defaults to booting the operating system on partition hda2, your Linux installation that you are just about to complete.

Step 9.11.1 shown in Figure 3-32 shows the screen after adding the Win98 label. You would TAB to OK and press ENTER to continue with the installation.

FIGURE 3-32

Step 9.11.1 (after changes): Selecting bootable partitions

```
The boot manager Red Hat uses can boot other operating
systems as well. You need to tell me what partitions you
would like to be able to boot and what label you want to
use for each of them

Device          Partition Type          Default         Boot Label
/dev/hda1       DOS 16 bit >=32                         Win98
/dev/hda2       Linux Native            *               Linux
/dev/hda5       Linux Native

                Ok            Edit            Back
```

Remember during step 9.11.1 that whenever this system reboots from now on, the lilo prompt appears first on the screen for five seconds by default. You can press either a question mark or TAB to list the label options. You can then enter the other label name, like Win98, to boot the other operating system.

Figure 3-33 is the Install X Windows System screen. If you select Yes, the system should be able to discover your video card, but just in case, you should know your video card and monitor. The installation of X Windows System is covered in detail in Chapter 7. In general, if you have hardware that is on the compatibility list, the installation should be able to probe for your video control card hardware and set it up correctly. Your monitor will probably have to be selected from a list.

That's it. You are done! Step 10.0 in Figure 3-34 shows the completed installation screen.

You are now done with the installation. Press ENTER to reboot as indicated in Figure 3-34.

CAVEAT EMPTOR ON INSTALLATION Do not worry if you make a mistake the first time on test machine. Just redo the installation; it will be significantly faster and easier. There are so many options and possibilities in the overview just presented, it is not possible to name them all or take them all into account. In most cases, the default is sufficient if you do not understand the question posed. Move on and get it installed, then read the FAQs, HOWTOs, and other related docs once you are up and running. You can always reinstall; the second and third installs are always significantly easier.

Although you have finished the installation and have worked the concepts of partitioning and possibly multiple operating system boots, there

FIGURE 3-33

Step 9.12: Install X Window System

```
yes
no
```

FIGURE 3-34

Installation completed!

```
Congratulations, installation is complete.

Remove the boot media and press return to reboot. For
Information on fixes which are available for this
release of Red Hat Linux, consult the Errata available
from http://www.redhat.com.

Information on configuring your system is available in
the post install chapter of the Official Red Hat Linux
User's Guide.

                        Ok
```

are still a few more details to note, such as the lilo errors, BIOS issues, and more, all described in the following sections.

CERTIFICATION OBJECTIVE 3.04

The LILO Boot Process and Intel Hardware/BIOS Issues

The original Intel motherboard design provided a mechanism to start any operating system: It would load a bootup program, called the Master Boot Record, or MBR. This is the first program loaded by the BIOS. This program then loads the real operating system boot control program(s), which in turn starts the operating system.

The main issue with this bootup is that the MBR has to be found in the first 1024 cylinders of any disk. This is because the BIOS programs stored on the motherboard would not be able to "see" any value over 1024, a limitation of the original BIOS design. With newer motherboards, they use a mechanism called Logical Block Addressing, or LBA mode, on disks to alleviate this problem. The disk LBA mode reports back "logical" values for the cylinder, head, and sector so that the BIOS can then "see" a larger disk drive. Internally, the drive uses the LBA values to find the real cylinder, head, and sector. One way or another, you must ensure that the boot block for Linux is not past this magical boundary, or the boot will fail.

Usually, Linux opts for the /boot partition if it does not rewrite the MBR. You can put it on any partition that is available. The MBR is just the most convenient; the system can cascade to any previous OS. My laptop has lilo cascade to NT, which cascades to Win95. I can choose Linux first, or NT second, if I want, or just let it cascade to Win95.

Boot Control of Your System

Linux uses a set of files to boot your system referred to collectively as lilo, short for Linux Loader. During or after installation, you have two options:

- Create a boot disk
- Update a local disk partition with the lilo MBR

The boot disk is an excellent way to hide the Linux system for other users. For development or help desk systems with multiple operating systems, you can create a boot disk that specifically boots just Linux when inserted into the floppy drive.

One major danger with a floppy is the chance of damaging that boot disk. You may want to make multiple copies to make this a minor problem. You can use the dd command to make multiple copies of the disk. Here is an example of the commands needed to create a copy of the original diskette to a local file, and then how to create duplicates from this local file:

```
$ dd  if=/dev/fd0    of=diskettebootup.img # stores a copy of diskette
$ dd  if=/diskettebootup.img   of=/dev/fd0  # makes the copy
```

Updating /dev/hda MBR

The old MBR, if there was a previous operating system, is moved to a new location and Linux installs its own MBR. This is only the first part of the loading operation required to get Linux started. The second part of the bootup process is contained within the /boot directory structure. This assumes you installed the boot block to /dev/hda. If you installed the lilo boot into /boot (/dev/hdaX) or elsewhere, then this does not apply.

/etc/lilo.conf

You can update or change your bootup options with the lilo configuration file, **/etc/lilo.conf**, and with the boot loader install utility, **/sbin/lilo**.

The first part of the loading operation provides a prompt allowing you to enter any valid listed boot option along with any command options for that boot option. All lilo configuration is maintained in the system file, **/etc/lilo.conf.** The following listing shows the details of deciphering /etc/lilo.conf.

```
==========================================================

[root@linux6 /root]# cat /etc/lilo.conf
boot=/dev/hda
map=/boot/map
install=/boot/boot.b
prompt
timeout=50
default=Win95
image=/boot/vmlinuz-2.2.5-15
        label=linux
        root=/dev/hda8
        initrd=/boot/initrd-2.2.5-15.img
        read-only
other=/dev/hda1
        label=Win95
        table=/dev/hda
[root@linux6 /root]#
==========================================================
boot=/dev/hda
map=/boot/map
```

The system will look on the first hard disk for the bootup and map info.

```
install=/boot/boot.b
```

This is the location for the second part of the lilo program startup routine.

```
prompt
```

This forces the lilo: prompt on the console.

```
timeout=50
```

This is the default five seconds before the boot process continues automatically. You can adjust this to any number of tenths of a second.

```
default=Win95
```

Normally, the first boot listing (next section) is default; this line supercedes the default action and selects any boot choice via the identifying label.

```
image=/boot/vmlinuz-2.2.5-15
```

This is the actual virtual memory compressed kernel (version 2.2.5, with the -15 representing the Red Hat revision number) of Linux.

```
        label=linux
```

Identifying the "boot option" label that appears if you press TAB at the lilo prompt.

```
        root=/dev/hda8
```

Location of the root, /, directory file system partition.

```
        initrd=/boot/initrd-2.2.5-15.img
```

Location of the second part of the kernel load.

```
        read-only
```

During installation, the file system is started in read-only mode.

The next section is another boot option; in this case, to boot Windows 95 on the first partition, known as C: to Windows 95, but known as /dev/hda1 to Linux.

```
other=/dev/hda1
        label=Win95
        table=/dev/hda
```

The table is the location of the partition table to be used; in this case, the first physical IDE type disk on the system.

What to Do When You See LILO

When you restart the system, after the internal POST, Power On Self Test, the lilo boot block, MBR, is loaded and you get the following prompt:

```
lilo:
```

By default, you have five seconds to enter something; otherwise, the system will automatically continue with the first labeled boot (default) option.

If you press TAB (bolded text shown next is your inputs) before the five-second timeout, this program will list all known boot blocks by their given label name as illustrated in the following example:

```
lilo: <TAB>
linux          Win95
lilo:
```

The first named option is the default that will be chosen after the default time has expired and if no input is entered at the prompt.

By simply pressing ENTER, the default entry is selected; in this case, the one known as Linux. If you wanted to select the Win95 option, you would enter the specific label name (case should not matter).

```
lilo: win95<ENTER>
```

LILO Parameters

To pass a parameter to lilo, type the parameter after the label name. For example, if you wanted to start your system in rescue mode, you would type **rescue** at the prompt when booting with the BOOT.IMG or BOOTNET.IMG diskette. If you wanted to start your system in single-user mode, either of the two following commands would provide the same result:

```
lilo: linux  single<ENTER>
lilo: linux  1<ENTER>
```

Single-User Mode

A common option is the word "single," or, alternatively, the number 1. Both of these options change the default behavior of the startup such that the system boots into runlevel 1, also known as single-user mode.

Many more parameters can be added, including how much memory to use, and what device to load as the root device in the case of a broken mirror set. All of these are documented on the CD-ROM in the **/usr/doc/LILO** subdirectory.

Single-user mode is the most commonly used option. This is the system maintenance mode for experienced Linux superusers. In single-user mode, no file systems other than the root file system are loaded. You are then able to do clean backups and restores to any partitions in this mode. You also have the ability to run administration commands, recover or repair passwd and shadow password files, run file system checks, and so forth.

To get out of single-user mode, in some cases, you just have to type **exit** and your system will exit single-user mode and go into multiuser mode. Alternatively, if you have made changes or repairs to any partitions, you should reboot the machine. Press CTRL-ALT-DEL to reboot from within single-user mode.

LILO Errors

The lilo first stage will also indicate some common and not so common problems:

```
 (nothing)  did not get to lilo at all
L           first stage loaded and started
LI          second stage loaded from /boot
LILO        all of lilo is loaded correctly
```

Occasionally, there may be an error due to partition table changes, bad blocks, and so forth. On these rare occurrences, you will only get partial lilo prompts:

```
LIL             second stage boot loader is started
LIL?            Second stage loaded at an incorrect address
LIL-            the descriptor table is corrupt
```

What to Do If /etc/lilo.conf Changes?

If you want to add additional kernel options, you use a text editor such as vi, pico, joe, or any other to modify the /etc/lilo.conf file. Once modified, the changes must be added to the lilo boot process. This is done by running the /sbin/lilo utility at the prompt. This forces the update of the boot record to include the changed options.

exam Watch

If you have a dual boot system, you may want to change the default to another operating system for a short time of use. You update the /etc/lilo.conf file and then you must run /sbin/lilo to force the changes at bootup. This may also need to be done in some rescue situations; you will need to rebuild the boot record. In the case of a rescue, you should be aware that this boot record uses a relative offset to point to the files to be loaded. Make sure you mount any extra file systems, after the root file system, in similar locations to normal.

CERTIFICATION OBJECTIVE 3.05

Using loadlin

Although Red Hat Linux uses the lilo boot loader program to manage the initial bootup process, there are alternates that some of the other distributions of Linux use.

During installation, you will see another loader called Syslinux.n.m-x. This is an MS-DOS based loader and is used on all the installation images because it is small enough to fit on a floppy and boot a basic Linux kernel. You can get more information about Syslinux from http://metalab.unc.edu/pub/Linux/system/boot/loaders/.

Another popular option is called loadlin. The loadlin program is also MS-DOS based and requires a copy of the Linux kernel, and possibly an initial RAM disk if your drives are SCSI types, to be MS-DOS available. You can read the HOWTO and FAQs on loadlin if you want to use it instead of lilo. You can get more information for loadlin from http://metalab.unc.edu/pub/Linux/system/boot/dualboot/.

Essentially, the loadlin program relies on MS-DOS instead of your system BIOS to load Linux. The advantage is that loadlin can load a kernel beyond the 1023 cylinder boundary, from any file system that is accessible to MS-DOS. Note that loadlin cannot be used from any Win9*x* or NT DOS PROMPT environment; you must boot into MS-DOS mode.

There are also some commercial boot loaders available, like System Commander, that can create a multiple table entry set of optional boots for almost any other operating system that you can install on an Intel based PC. Some of these commercial products can update the NT boot loader system and provide a direct boot option to Linux from the NT boot prompt. More information on System Commander can be found at http://www.systemcommander.com/products/products.html.

There is a mini-Howto document for loadlin being used with Win95 on the CD-ROM at /doc/HOWTO/mini/Loadlin+Win95 if further details are needed.

CERTIFICATION OBJECTIVE 3.06

Additional Installation Details

Now that the basic screens from the install have been explained, here are the details about some of the more important concepts and aspects that you must know before you actually attempt any installation of Linux.

Partition Concepts

With either fdisk or Disk Druid utility, you must know what you are doing first. Figure 3-35 shows device names on the first IDE hard drive.

You do not have to create all 3 primary and all 12 logical; the combinations are many.

In Figure 3-35, there are 16 partitions displayed. Although 16 partitions are possible, unless you needed them, you would probably not break a disk into this many sections. It is totally up to you.

Preparation Details Before fdisk or Disk Druid

You will be introduced to using fdisk in full detail in the next section. There have been a few references during the installation about using fdisk and Disk Druid to create partitions, but you still need to know what all these partitions are actually for. This is the most challenging question to answer, as there is no one general answer.

You must decide what to do with the disk space before you begin to partition it. This is the first and probably the most important preinstall detail to know about any machine: what partitions will you need to create. If you have a new machine, you can have the Workstation or Server

FIGURE 3-35

A maximum of 16 devices for any one disk

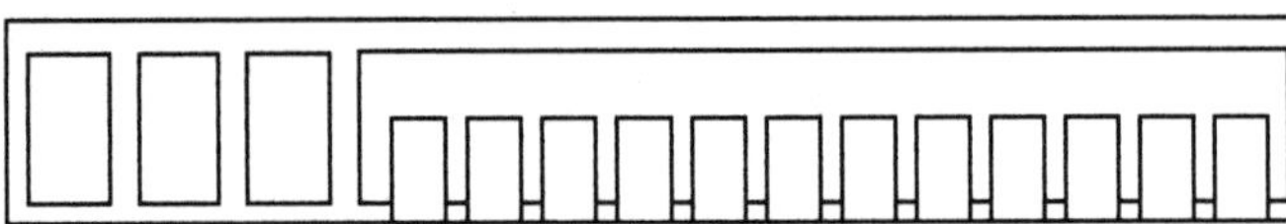

installation options do it for you. If you plan to use the Custom option, you need to be prepared with a clear idea of your partition scheme.

Getting Started: Sample Partition Table

As a preliminary step to getting started, you need to have a clear idea of how to separate your file system onto various disks. Table 3-3 can be used as a starting guide to decide how to create your partition scheme.

IMPROVED PERFORMANCE: SPREAD OUT THE LOAD

Performance improvements can be obtained for any system in two simple ways:

- With increased memory
- By spreading the load of read and write operations across multiple disks, and even better, across multiple controllers.

Keep this performance enhancement in mind when deciding what directory structure to put on which partition on what disk. You should try to keep the system files separate from the data files, and preferably on separate disks and controllers.

Another way to "spread the load" is to use software or hardware solutions that use various forms of RAID. On a big server, RAID can be an excellent way to provide better performance and better reliability. Hardware solutions are more expensive and provide better service in case of disasters than software based RAID solutions do. How to set up RAID is discussed in Chapter 5, or you can check the HOWTO documents for more information.

Table 3-3 lists some of the commonly separated file system directories in the left column, and in the right column, comments as to size and why to separate it. You can then fill in the second, third, and fourth columns with the actual information for your system and post it on the machine for easy reference.

TABLE 3-3 Getting Started: Installation Worksheet

Use	Disk	Partition	Size (MB)	Comments
Swap	hda / hdb / hdc / …			(required) Have to have at least 1, 2–3 times memory is typical (can split swap space across multiple disks and controllers for better performance) 64MB def.
/boot				Must be within first 1024 "seeable" cylinders on any disk 16MB default
/ (root)				Contains system, access to all other partitions (required) No default, 600+ workstation, 256MB server NOTE: recommend 1000+ MB if no other partitions
(unusable as a file system)	hda / hdb /hdc / hdd	4		"Extended" container partition for the logical drives (max 12)
/var				Variable area for system logs, spooling, email, etc. 256MB default server
/usr				Usually for "user" stuff: binaries, data, games, etc. 512+ MB default server
/home				Home directories, good idea to separate for backup and quota management. 512+ MB default server
/home/http				Separate if large Web system
/home/ftp				Separate if large FTP site
/yourdata				Your specific needs
/opt				Many software packages install to here

CERTIFICATION OBJECTIVE 3.07

Creating Partitions: Details

Now that you have the partition layout for your system, you need to actually create them. For this, you will probably use the fdisk utility, either from a boot diskette or from the running system. The next section details exactly how to use fdisk to create your system partitions.

Why Separate File Systems?

The UNIX, and hence Linux, file system has been historically split up into smaller, more manageable pieces for various reasons: everything started on small disks, small partitions are easier to dump and restore, partition limits can be used to restrict or control disk usage.

The Linux file system can also be broken up into smaller pieces or can be one big piece if so desired. When would you use one big partition? When you have a large RAID 5 disk farm providing your file system, or when you are creating a small test system.

Linux File Systems: /tmp /boot /usr/local /var /home

The historical separations have been blurred over time, but the following are the Red Hat Linux recommended file system breakouts for the base system of any server:

/tmp	Used by everyone, no need to back up, gets very fragmented, usually have a crontab entry for "cleanup"
/boot	Represents second-stage extras for lilo, must be within first 1024 "seeable" cylinders
/var	The variable area gets written to by memory very often used for mail and spooling, and system memory data becomes very fragmented

/home	Home directories of all users, good idea to keep them separate from system files if using quotas, restricts quota management "area"
/usr/local	Specific binaries, data, and setup files for this specific machine

Additional file systems can be created to meet specific needs of related groups of users; for example, /development, /dbms, /financials, /inventory, /home/httpd, /home/ftp, and so forth.

Possible Target File Systems for Separate File System Placement

Your Linux host may also be supporting a very specific set of applications, such as Web and FTP hosting; any one of the many file and print sharing services, such as NFS, Samba, NetWare, Macintosh; or a third-party application, such as a database management system, financials, Geographical Information System, video, software development, and so forth.

In many cases, you probably want to separate these files into separate, manageable units, possibly split over many partitions if they are very large. This spreads the load out across the file system, provides better disk management, backup, and recovery options, and allows for a more flexible overall system design.

Swap Space Partition Sizing and Placement

Although there is no hard-and-fast rule, a good rule of thumb is to create your swap partition to be two to three times the memory for small memory systems. This was typical in the early days of UNIX when RAM was very expensive and disk was cheap. Current systems can easily have large amounts of memory. Is there an upper limit? Not really, but you could have a smaller swap space if you had a huge amount of RAM.

One recommendation is to use two to three times memory for any system with less than 512MB of RAM. After this point, it might seem wasteful to create a 1GB swap file that is almost never used on a system with 512MB RAM. You might opt for a 512MB or even as low as 256MB swap partition.

The swap file is used sparingly for some system information, but is used heavily to page out user processes when more memory is needed. In essence, you *never* want to swap user processes. RAM is in nanoseconds of speed; disk is in milliseconds of speed—that is a million-fold difference in speed. The swap is just there in case you have a very sporadic need for lots more virtual memory. If your machine constantly uses swap space, this action will slow it down significantly. You should get more RAM for your system, or reduce the workload.

Technically speaking, you can have up to eight swap partitions, totaling a maximum of 4GB. Any single swap partition can be up to 2GB maximum. Swap partitions are only used for virtual memory, acting like additional RAM to your system. Swap partitions use a different file system from the other partitions. The other partitions may be used for raw data as opposed to an ext2fs.

Supported File System Types

Linux natively supports many other file systems, such as DOS, HPFS, FAT, VFAT, and NTFS. The native file system is called Second Extended File System, denoted by ext2fs or just ext2. The benefit is that if you have OS/2, Windows 9*x*, or a DOS operating system using some other partitions on the same machine as Linux is installed on, you can create directory access to them. The system will be able to "see" the native files.

In Figure 3-36, the first command, df, displays the total, used, and available free space on all currently mounted file systems. The second command, mount, shows the "type" of file system. In this case, the device /dev/hda1 is mounted using VFAT as /DosC and represents direct access to what would be the C: drive of the Windows operating system on this first partition. Linux can directly access many other native file systems.

Figure 3-36 shows a typical Workstation installation with two additional mount points for the C: and E: drives that are used by the Win9*x* and NT operating systems also resident on this machine. Why would you bother to do this? Test machine, help desk machine, development, only got one machine and need to practice, classroom, and many more possible scenarios. You would not do this for a typical single-user production machine.

FIGURE 3-36

Native support of FAT, VFAT file systems

```
==================================================================
[root@linux6 /root]# df
Filesystem           1k-blocks      Used Available Use% Mounted on
/dev/hda8               932833    502478    382162  57% /
/dev/hda7                23300      2588     19509  12% /boot
/dev/hda1              1052064    914784    137280  87% /dosC
/dev/hda6              1052064    111648    940416  11% /dosE
/dev/hdb                556054    556054         0 100% /mnt/cdrom
[root@linux6 /root]# mount
/dev/hda8 on /          type ext2 (rw)
none      on /proc      type proc (rw)
/dev/hda7 on /boot      type ext2 (rw)
/dev/hda1 on /dosC      type vfat (rw)
/dev/hda6 on /dosE      type vfat (rw)
none      on /dev/pts   type devpts (rw,mode=0622)
/dev/hdb  on /mnt/cdrom type iso9660 (ro)
[root@linux6 /root]# ls /dosC
CDsetup.bat      boot.ini       detlog.old     io.sys        sbide.sys
Exchange         bootlog.prv    detlog.txt     mscdex.exe    scandisk.log
My Documents     bootlog.txt    digipix        msdos.---     setuplog.old
Program Files    bootsect.dos   drvspace.bin   msdos.bak     setuplog.txt
RescuedDoc1.txt  ca_appsw       dswin          msdos.dos     suhdlog.---
RescuedDoc.txt   command.com    ffastun.ffa    msdos.sys     suhdlog.dat
acess            command.dos    ffastun.ffl    mskids        system.1st
autoexec.bat     config.dos     ffastun.ffo    netlog.txt    temp
autoexec.dos     config.sys     ffastun0.ffx   ntdetect.com  w95undo.dat
autoexec.old     config.win     himem.sys      ntldr         w95undo.ini
boot.---         dblspace.bin   io.dos         recycled      win95
[root@linux6 /root]#
==================================================================
```

One of the benefits is that you can move and copy files between the Linux partitions and the DOS partitions using standard Linux commands. You cannot run any Windows applications within Linux unless you run a DOS or Windows Emulation package.

The fdisk Utility

The fdisk utility is universally available and should be considered one of the first tools you should get familiar with. There are many commands, even an expert mode, but you only need to know a few as discussed here.

You can modify the physical disk partition layout using many programs, but in this case you will be introduced to fdisk. This program is supplied on the Linux installation disk, runs under DOS, and can be used to reconfigure any disk's partition table. FDISK.EXE from DOS 6.*xx* has the same name but is less powerful and can only create one Primary partition and one Extended partition. The version on the Linux BOOT.IMG or BOOTNET.IMG created diskette is a Linux-specific version and is syntactically identical to the utility that you can run on any Linux host to manage disk partitions once your system is up and running.

USING FDISK: STARTING, GETTING HELP, QUITTING

The following screen output shows how to start the fdisk program, how to get help, and how to quit the program.

```
==================================================
A:> fdisk
Using /dev/hda as default device!

Command (m for help): m
Command action
   a   toggle a bootable flag
   b   edit bsd disklabel
   c   toggle the dos compatibility flag
   d   delete a partition
   l   list known partition types
   m   print this menu
   n   add a new partition
   o   create a new empty DOS partition table
   p   print the partition table
   q   quit without saving changes
   s   create a new empty Sun disklabel
   t   change a partition's system id
   u   change display/entry units
   v   verify the partition table
   w   write table to disk and exit
   x   extra functionality (experts only)

Command (m for help): q

==================================================
```

The fdisk utility is all text based, and as such, it displays hard drive parameters at startup.

USING FDISK: IN A NUTSHELL You should print to screen (p) the current partition table entries. You then create a new (n) partition, either primary (p) or logical (l), partition number (1–16), starting one number after whatever is the current last-used cylinder number. The size of the partition will depend on disk geometry; do not worry about the exact size here. Normally, fdisk defaults to creating a Linux Native type (83) partition. For the swap partition, the partition "type" has to be toggled (t) to type 82 swap. Repeat these general steps for each required partition. Note that all other partitions should be type 83, Linux Native.

Note: fdisk is memory resident and makes all these changes in memory. You need to write (w) these changes to the disk as the last step; otherwise, no changes are made.

USING FDISK: DELETE, CREATE PARTITIONS In the following screen output sample, you will remove the only partition. The sample output screen first starts fdisk. Then you print (p) the current partition table. Delete (d) the partition by number (1 in this case). Write (w) the changes to the disk. Quit (q) from the program.

Warning: Last chance to change your mind before you delete the current partition.

```
===================================================
A:> fdisk
Using /dev/hda as default device!

Command (m for help): p
Disk /dev/hda: 255 heads, 63 sectors, 525 cylinders
Units = cylinders of 16065 * 512 bytes

Device      Boot     Start       End     Blocks    Id  System
/dev/hda1    *           1       525    4217031     6  FAT16
Command (m for help): d
Partition number (1-1): 1

Command (m for help): w

===================================================
```

You did it! Now you can create the partitions you need.

USING FDISK: A NEW PC WITH NO PARTITIONS Start fdisk from the boot floppy. To create a new partition, type Primary for the first three and then an Extended for the rest of the disk as partition 4 before creating logical drives, drives 5–16, within the extended partition. Create them in an appropriate order, making sure at least that the /boot partition is within the first 1024 cylinders; all others are up to you.

Using fdisk: Create Partition, Make Bootable, Write

The following screen output sample shows the steps used to create (n) the first (/boot) partition, make it bootable (a), and then finally write (w) the partition information to the disk. (Note: Although you may ask for a 16MB partition, the geometry of the disk may not allow that size as in the example.)

```
===================================================
A:> fdisk
Using /dev/hda as default device!

Command (m for help): n
Command action
   l   logical (5 or over)
   p   primary partition (1-4)
p
First cylinder (1-256, default 1): 1
Last cylinder or +size or +sizeM or +sizeK (2-256,def 256): 2

Command (m for help): p
Disk /dev/hda: 255 heads, 63 sectors, 256 cylinders
Units = cylinders of 16065 * 512 bytes
   Device Boot     Start        End     Blocks    Id  System
/dev/hda1              1          2      16044    83  Linux
Command (m for help): a
Partition number (1-1): 1

Command (m for help): p
Disk /dev/hda: 255 heads, 63 sectors, 256 cylinders
Units = cylinders of 16065 * 512 bytes
   Device Boot     Start        End     Blocks    Id  System
/dev/hda1   *          1          2      16044    83  Linux

===================================================
```

You only need to set one partition as "bootable." What the bootable partition means is the one marked "Active" in the DOS world. This is the partition that the hard disk has marked internally as having the boot block. When a motherboard loads the "boot" program, it assumes it is the first sector of the "Active" partition in DOS, or the "Bootable" one in Linux. This is usually the first partition but it does not have to be.

Repeat the commands to create the rest of the partitions. After all are created, you should end up with the final design as illustrated in the following output screen sample:

```
=====================================================
Command (m for help): p

Disk /dev/hda: 255 heads, 63 sectors, 256 cylinders
Units = cylinders of 16065 * 512 bytes
   Device Boot  Start     End   Blocks  Id  System
/dev/hda1   *       1       2    16044  83  Linux
/dev/hda2           3      18    64176  82  swap
/dev/hda3          19     169  1203300  83  Linux
/dev/hda4         170     250   649782   5  Extended
/dev/hda5         170     201   248682  83  Linux
/dev/hda6         202     257   449232  83  Linux

Command (m for help): w

=====================================================
```

FDISK WRITE OPTION The last option used in the preceding listing, the "w," is actually the most important! Up to this point, you have been changing things in program memory; you have not actually made any changes to the physical disk table at all. The write option, "w," actually updates the disk's internal partition table information. This always requires a reboot, as significant changes were just made. The alternate to this option is "q," to quit without saving these changes.

Disk Druid

One of the excellent additional programs supplied with the Red Hat Linux installation is the more graphical Disk Druid program that provides a more intuitive interface. The actions are similar, but the interface hides the need to know about the partition ID (it just uses a text name ID) and has an option called "Growable." This option allows the system to determine how much disk space a partition will take based on available free space.

Note: This "'Growable" option is very beneficial in the kickstart scripts (automated installation scripts) where the target hardware may have varying sized disks. All partition space can be allocated by allowing it to "Grow" to fill the disk during installation. This is something that fdisk cannot do.

Hardware Installation Scenarios

You may be given machines that already have operating systems that use all the available disk space, or machines with operating systems that can be completely replaced.

One Operating System Only

If you do not want to save the old OS, you can delete all old partitions and start with no partitions on the disk. If the machine will only be used for one operating system, Linux, then this is the best option. You then only need to decide whether the Workstation or the Server options will meet your needs. If they do not meet your needs, you can use the Custom Installation option to modify either the Workstation or the Server design to better suit your needs.

Already Got Windows *x.xx*

If you purchased a basic PC, chances are it was preconfigured with an MS Windows based operating system. Most likely, the entire disk has been formatted as one big partition, known as the C: drive. This is an unfortunate design for you at this point. If you want to keep the current operating system as is, you can find some software that will shrink the partition down for you.

There are commercial versions, such as Partition Magic from PowerQuest Inc. (http://www.powerquest.com), and free versions, such as the fips utility supplied on the installation images.

Note: Due to the variance of hardware and software available, neither of these products is guaranteed by Red Hat or the author to be without possible peril. You need to read the documentation and back up everything twice to be sure, then try this with the assumption something may go wrong but you can always rebuild (assuming you know how to do this). Many before you have successfully used these utilities, including the author, but things can still go wrong, so be prepared for the worst.

Note: If you use fips, it will create a second partition out of the available space you retrieved from any other partition. You should delete this new empty partition before starting the Linux installation. This will allow the installation script to create the Workstation, or Server, required partitions from the available space, or allow you to create the partition scheme yourself in the Custom installation.

REAL-WORLD APPLICATION—USING PARTITION MAGIC A preconfigured laptop came with 1.5GB of disk space on one IDE disk drive allocated as one Primary partition and had Windows 95 as the operating system. The first step was to make sure that the current set of files on the disk drive was reduced to less than the 1GB boundary. Unnecessary software and files were archived and removed so that there were only 800MB of used space on this primary disk. With the use of Partition Magic Software, the files were shifted to ensure they were within the first 800MB of the disk, then the first primary partition end cylinder value was changed so that it ended at 1.0GB. This freed up 500MB for the second OS to be loaded. All of this was done through the Partition Magic Software, and without loss of the original Windows 95 OS.

Changing a Partition Size—SIPS

You can magically move the partition table boundary without loss of data by using the supplied fips program or a commercial product, such as Partition Magic.

You start with a disk that has only one partition as shown in Figure 3-37.

All cylinders are used by the single partition table entry. Assuming the actual files on this partition do not use all the disk space, or you can remove

FIGURE 3-37

```
0  Cylinder        to         linder  n
```

Single partitioned disk before repartitioning

some to make unused space available, then you can shrink back the end cylinder for this first partition without affecting the files already contained on the disk.

Figure 3-38 shows what the disk might look like after you have changed the end wall of the first partition.

By using the fips program, you can shrink the first partition and make the extra space available for one or more partitions. You can then use fdisk to add additional partitions, as illustrated in Figure 3-39.

Primary and Extended Partitions

A partition on a disk is a logical set of cylinders that represents all or part of the entire disk. Each disk can be one big partition or can be separated into many. Due to a design in the early stages of the PC and the DOS operating system, you are restricted to a maximum of four primary partitions, one of which can be a special type of primary partition called an *Extended* partition. Each of the other three primary partitions can represent one logical drive. The extended partition is a special case that allows you to break it up into a maximum of 12 more "logical" partitions. This gives a total of 16 partitions, of which only 15 are usable on an IDE computer.

Note: A SCSI type disk is only capable of 14 partitions total, 11 logical partitions in the extended partition.

Partition File Names

All device files are located in the /dev directory. Linux has a standard naming convention for the different hard drive types (IDE or SCSI), the drive ID, and for each partition.

FIGURE 3-38

```
0                    a                    yl) n
```

Multiple partitioned disk after repartitioning

FIGURE 3-39

Multiple partitioned disk after basic Workstation installation

0		a	a+1	b	b+1	c	c+1	(cyl) n
	hda1				hda2		hda3	hda5

IDE PARTITION FILE NAME CONVENTION With IDE, a PC can have a maximum of four devices, two on each of the first and second controllers. The first controller would be denoted as hda, hard disk 'a' or first controller ID. Then the partition number follows as in hda1 for the first partition on the first drive on the first controller. Figure 3-40 shows a sample of a disk partition table with three partitions on a single disk.

The second drive, first partition would be hdb1. The full path name is /dev/hdb1.

The third drive, first partition would be hdc1. The full path name is /dev/hdc1.

SCSI Devices

SCSI is another type of interface device for disk drives. SCSI has more devices per controller: seven additional for early SCSI, and 15 additional for SCSI-2. SCSI is more expensive and has a higher throughput of data.

For SCSI devices, the file names begin with the letters sda, for SCSI disk on first controller. The partitions on this first drive are sda1, sda2, sda3, and so forth. The second drive partitions are sdb1, sdb2, and so forth. The partitions on the sixth drive are sdf1, sdf2, sdf3, and so forth. Figure 3-41 shows the names of the partitions for the third SCSI drive.

FIGURE 3-40

First three partition names on first IDE disk

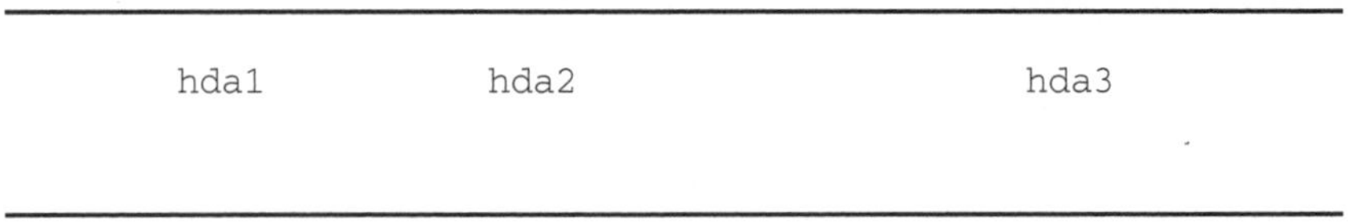

hda1	hda2	hda3

FIGURE 3-41

Third SCSI drive partition names

sdc1	sdc2	sdc3

CERTIFICATION OBJECTIVE 3.08

Additional Notes on Access Media Options

During the installation, you may be asked some very specific questions about the Access Media. This is in reference to accessing the installation files on the media, and how to access it. Even for something as simple as the local disk, the installation program must know a few things about the hardware before it can "connect" to it. Additionally, if the installation files are on some network service, you need to enter inputs to configure that service connection. The next few sections provide more details about these media access options.

Hard Disk Installation

The installation files on the CD-ROM can be copied to a directory on the local hard disk using any DOS or previous version of Linux, but the file system must be FAT for the boot loader to see it.

The files you need copied are all under the /RedHat directory on the CD-ROM. You can use any method you have to copy these files over to the hard disk. You need to create the same structure as on the CD-ROM, so the top-level directory should be \Redhat. You do not necessarily need every file from the CD-ROM, only those that are needed for installation. If you know what you are doing, you can trim the number of files down.

Note: The filenames under DOS will be truncated to 8.3 equivalents when viewed by DOS. The installation system does not actually care what the name of the product is, but you will have to figure out the name if you want to install any RPM packages later.

During the installation, you will be prompted for the location of the files; select "Hard Disk." The installation then shows all the hard disk partitions. You must select the one containing the \Redhat directory.

Source Files on the CD-ROM

By far the easiest, this installation assumes a standard ATAPI-type CD-ROM is locally attached. The CD-ROM installation can be selected from a standard BOOT.IMG installation startup disk, or when booting directly from the CD-ROM itself.

Source Files from Network Installations

Before you can get to any network source files, you need to configure your network card to be a part of the network. You will need to input a valid, unused IP address, the local network mask, the default gateway IP address (if network resource is on another network segment), and, optionally, the primary DNS IP, the Domain Name, and the hostname to use for this machine.

You are presented with three options for setting up your machine on the network:

Static IP Address	You fill it in, you know the numbers
BOOTP	Dynamically sent to you from a BOOTP server
DHCP	Dynamically sent to you from a DHCP server

The last two options are the easiest; your machine sends out a BOOTP or DHCP request and that service sends back all the IP information your machine needs to get on the network.

The first option allows you to enter the information directly. If you are on a local network, an IP address and the associated Network Mask are enough information to get you on to your local network and access a local server. If your network was 206.195.1.0, and your host was number 222, you could use the following information:

IP Address	206.195.1.222
Network Mask	255.255.255.0

You may also need or want to use advanced hostname resolution so you do not need to remember the IP address of the servers. DNS can provide this service if it is already configured on your network. DNS is what the Internet uses for hostname resolution. If DNS is not configured, you have to use the IP address of any network hosts you wish to get access to. DNS is just a convenience when there are many hosts; their names are usually easier to remember than their IP address.

IP Address	206.195.1.222
Network Mask	255.255.255.0
Default Gateway	206.195.1.254
Primary Name Server	192.168.15.1
Domain Name	vaddac.com
Hostname	linux56.vaddac.com

The Default Gateway IP is the portal to the rest of the network. In the preceding scenario, the DNS server is on another network somewhere and you will need the Gateway IP address to access it.

Source Files from FTP, HTTP

Any FTP or HTTP server running on your network can provide a convenient path to the Red Hat subdirectory either directly on the CD-ROM or from a copy of these files on a local file system.

To use either an FTP or HTTP server, you need to know the IP address and the name of the directory structure that contains the /RedHat directory tree.

IP Address	206.195.1.1	or use the full Domain Name
Directory	/pub/I386	directory containing RedHat/

Source Files from NFS

This installation option allows an NFS server on the network configured as an export server to provide the Red Hat subtree files via a network connection. The NFS share can be directly from the CD-ROM or from a copy on the local machine.

This assumes you have NFS running on another host accessible via a network connection on the target machine. You will be asked for the NFS server IP address and the export share name.

NFS Address	206.195.1.1	or use the full Domain Name
NFS export	/exports/I386	directory containing RedHat/

Creating an NFS Export Service

You can either just use the CD-ROM itself if it is fast enough, or you can copy the files to a directory on a partition with enough space. You can use the du command to see how much space is needed for the files on the CD-ROM.

EXPORT CD-ROM FILE SYSTEM DIRECTLY You can export the Red Hat directory structure directly from the CD-ROM if it is a relatively fast, 20x or more, device. Slower CD-ROMs, like 2x and 4x, will suffice if you are patient. With a good cache size on the host server, you may not even notice the slower-speed drives. The following screen output shows how to mount the CD-ROM device onto a local directory and then export it to the network.

```
=============================================================
#          # assuming NFS is already running
#          # if it does not already exist, create it
# mkdir /mnt/cdrom
#          # mount cdrom into file system
# mount  /dev/cdrom  /mnt/cdrom
#          # add the export request
# echo '/mnt/cdrom/Redhat  (ro)' >> /etc/exports
#         # stop and start the nfs service
# /etc/init.d/rc.d/nfs  stop
# /etc/init.d/rc.d/nfs  start
=============================================================
```

COPY FILES AND EXPORT LOCAL FILE SYSTEM Instead of using the files on the CD-ROM directly, if you have enough spare disk space, you can copy the files to a local disk to get better access performance usually.

The following output sample shows how to make a directory to hold the Red Hat file tree if you do not want to share out the CD-ROM itself and then export this directory. If your CD-ROM is not a high-speed type, or you have lots of hard disk space and this service will be used by many installations, you should copy the files to the hard disk.

```
===============================================================
# mkdir -p /nfs/exports
#          # assuming NFS is already running
#          # if it does not already exist, create it
# mkdir /mnt/cdrom
#          # copy to a local file system
# mount  /dev/cdrom  /mnt/cdrom
#          # add the export request
# cp -r /mnt/cdrom/Redhat    /nfs/exports
#          # add the export request
# echo '/mnt/cdrom/Redhat  (ro)' >> /etc/exports
#          # stop and start the nfs service
# /etc/init.d/rc.d/nfs  stop
# /etc/init.d/rc.d/nfs  start
===============================================================
```

At the Client

You need to know the IP address of your NFS server and the name of the NFS export service, and enter this when prompted. At an NT server, you can use the **IPCONFIG /ALL** command at a command prompt to see the IP information. At the UNIX or Linux NFS server, to display the IP information for your host, you can use the **ifconfig** command as root user as illustrated in the following screen output sample.

```
===============================================================
 [root@linux6 /root]# ifconfig
eth0 Link encap:Ethernet  HWaddr 00:00:C0:A8:16:BA
     inet addr:206.195.1.222  Bcast:206.195.1.255/
Mask:255.255.255.0
     UP BROADCAST RUNNING MULTICAST  MTU:1500  Metric:1
...
[root@linux6 /root]#
===============================================================
```

Source Files from Samba

At this writing, Red Hat 6.0 is not able to use Samba services for installation. Samba services represent the native Windows 9*x* and NT file-sharing protocol, SMB, Server Message Block. In previous incarnations, you could share the /RedHat directory from any Win9*x* or NT host as a local SMB share and access it through the network by knowing the name of the server and the share name. The next version of Red Hat, version 6.1, is expected to provide this installation media access method.

An example share from the server identified as NT4PDCNYC having a share named REDHAT (representing the CDROM /RedHat directory) would use the following reference to connect to this resource:

```
\\NT4PDCNYC\REDHAT
```

The Installation Log File

During every installation, a copy of the installation options and the related files are written to an installation log file called /tmp/install.log. This information is duplicated to the various console displays during the installation. Be sure to copy this file to a backup before the system or you inadvertently delete the file. You can view most of the information about your installation on one of the other virtual terminals maintained during the installation.

CERTIFICATION OBJECTIVE 3.09

Viewing Boot Time Information

There are actually many processes running and many parts to the installation. The system logs everything to an installation log file and separates related information between four of the five virtual console screens supported during the installation.

The Console Install Screens

When you start the installation, you are on the first virtual console. This console is accessed with ALT-F1. A bash shell is on the second, an installation message log is on the third, kernel messages are on the fourth, and the output of mke2fs on each file system is displayed. If you want to see the other screens, you can press the following key sequences in any order at any time:

Alt-f1	Installation display (this is what you normally see, all others are FYI)
Alt-f2	Bash shell gives you access to limited system information
Alt-f3	Installation message log displayed
Alt-f4	Displays all kernel messages
Alt-f5	Installation displays partition formatting

Note: The partition formatting display includes the alternate superblocks. In an emergency situation where a file system disk is corrupt and cannot be repaired by /sbin/fsck, the check program may want to try an alternate superblock. These are usually a multiple of some block size, like 8K; block 8192 ends the first 8K, so 8193 is the next block and is a duplicate copy of the primary superblock. This ALT-F5 virtual terminal will provide the list of alternate superblock numbers. Superblocks contain the inode information and used bit block map, amongst other things. You can also get a listing of the internal file system information using the dumpefs program as illustrated in the following sample screen output. The first command line lists the file system characteristics of the hda5 partition:

```
==============================================================
[root@rh6laptop /root]# dumpe2fs /dev/hda5 | head -5
dumpe2fs 1.14, 9-Jan-1999 for EXT2 FS 0.5b, 95/08/09
Filesystem volume name:   <none>
Last mounted on:          <not available>
Filesystem UUID:          57a1b50a-6f62-11d3-9656-c2da53691d05
Filesystem magic number:  0xEF53
[root@rh6laptop /root]#
==============================================================
```

Using *page up/page down* at the Virtual Consoles

Another nice feature of Linux virtual terminals is that you can go back and forth through previous pages that have scrolled off the screen by using SHIFT-PGUP and SHIFT-PGDN. Although only a few more lines are available, the added feature is still very useful and is available at any time during system operation.

CERTIFICATION OBJECTIVE 3.10

The Boot Up Messages in dmesg

The file /var/log/dmesg contains boot messages duplicated from the console output as seen during each bootup. These messages contain hardware information, process initialization, and sequencing information to name a few:

```
==============================================================
 [root@linux6 /root]# head -7 /var/log/dmesg
Linux version 2.2.5-15 (root@porky.devel.redhat.com) (gcc version egcs-2.91.66 1
9990314/Linux (egcs-1.1.2 release)) #1 Mon Apr 19 22:21:09 EDT 1999
Detected 199964089 Hz processor.
Console: colour VGA+ 80x25
Calibrating delay loop... 398.95 BogoMIPS
Memory: 62836k/65536k available (996k kernel code, 412k reserved, 928k data, 60k init)
VFS: Diskquotas version dquot_6.4.0 initialized
CPU: Intel Pentium MMX stepping 03
… (skipping many lines for brevity)
autorun ...
... autorun DONE.
VFS: Mounted root (ext2 filesystem) readonly.
change_root: old root has d_count=1
Trying to unmount old root ... okay
Freeing unused kernel memory: 60k freed
Adding Swap: 72256k swap-space (priority -1)
[root@linux6 /root]#
==============================================================
```

CERTIFICATION OBJECTIVE 3.11

Understanding the Standard Boot Process

The boot process starts from a DOS based boot loader and as such is restricted to finding the second part of lilo in the first 1024 cylinders of whichever disk is the boot disk.

The first sector of the first disk drive must have the MBR. This MBR is used to load an operating system. Each operating system has its own MBR, which may in fact start another program.

With Linux, the MBR provides a prompt that has a short time-out period (configured in /etc/lilo.conf) in which the console operator can select any boot selection or add options to any boot selection.

If the machine started with a DOS format, the first sector had a DOS MBR. This MBR program was loaded by the hardware boot CD-ROM at initialization. This MBR would point to the boot sequence for DOS, Win9*x*, or NT, whatever was last installed. After installation of the files, the installation copies the old MBR block to another block and adds a bootup reference for it. The system then adds the lilo MBR. This lilo MBR then points to the setup options available for this system. The Workstation and Server installations put the boot files into their own partition /boot.

The /boot directory and files

There are many files that are put into the /boot directory after the installation. They represent the compressed starting virtual memory kernel, vmlinuz-x.x.x, the loadable modules section, system map if needed, and more as shown in Figure 3-42.

FIGURE 3-42

Contents of /boot directory after installation

```
================================================================
[root@linux6 /root]# ls  -l  /boot
total 2587
lrwxrwxrwx  1 root  root      19 May 29 16:13 System.map ->
System.map-2.2.5-15
-rw-r--r--  1 root  root  186846 Apr 19 19:36 System.map-2.2.5-15
-rw-r--r--  1 root  root     512 May 29 16:37 boot.0300
-rw-r--r--  1 root  root    4544 Apr 12 21:19 boot.b
-rw-r--r--  1 root  root     612 Apr 12 21:19 chain.b
-rw-r--r--  1 root  root  308008 May 29 16:37 initrd-2.2.5-15.img
drwxr-xr-x  2 root  root   12288 May 29 16:09 lost+found
-rw-------  1 root  root   15872 May 30 00:24 map
lrwxrwxrwx  1 root  root      20 May 29 16:13 module-info ->
module-info-2.2.5-15
-rw-r--r--  1 root  root   11773 Apr 19 19:36 module-info-2.2.5-15
-rw-r--r--  1 root  root     620 Apr 12 21:19 os2_d.b
-rwxr-xr-x  1 root  root 1469449 Apr 19 19:36 vmlinux-2.2.5-15
lrwxrwxrwx  1 root  root      16 May 29 16:13 vmlinuz -> vmlinuz-2.2.5-15
-rw-r--r--  1 root  root  617431 Apr 19 19:36 vmlinuz-2.2.5-15
[root@linux6 /root]#
================================================================
```

All of the files shown in Figure 3-42 must be present for the system to boot normally. The actual starting point file of the Linux operating system is the vmlinuz-2.2.5-15, about 610K, as shown in Figure 3-42.

CERTIFICATION OBJECTIVE 3.12

Validating the Installation

After the installation is done, the installation script shuts down and reboots the machine. At this point, the system defaults to start in runlevel 3 (text mode) for server installations or run level 5 for Workstation on installs, which is the X Windows login screen.

If your X Windows server is not configured properly, then you can press CTRL-ALT-F1 to go back to a text-based login screen.

You must log in to the system as root. Then you can force the system to reinitialize back to runlevel 3, the text-based login level, where you can fix the X configuration and then go back to runlevel 5. All three steps are shown in the following screen output sample:

```
================================================================
[root@linux6 /root]# init 3# goes back to multi-user mode, no X

[root@linux6 /root]# Xconfigurator         # 'wizard' to set up X,
# NOTE: need video card type, memory and display type

[root@linux6 /root]# init 5                # multi-user mode with X on screen

[root@linux6 /root]#
================================================================
```

Your runlevel 5 initial screen will show the Red Hat logo and a login screen. Once validated, the Gnome system will initialize the Enlightenment desktop environment and display something like Figure 3-43.

FIGURE 3-43

X Windows system Gnome desktop

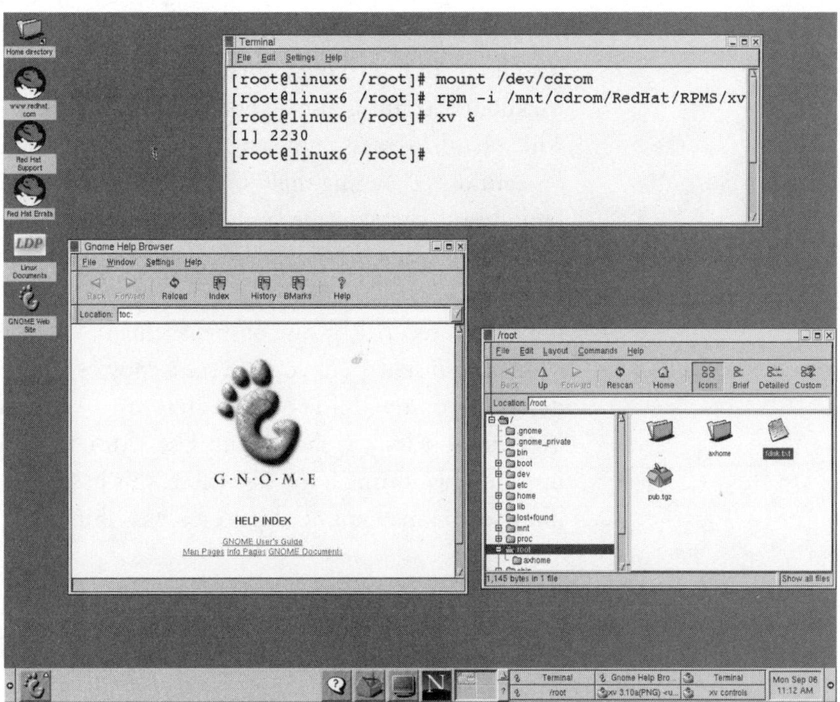

CERTIFICATION OBJECTIVE 3.13

Login as root

In any runlevel, you can log in using the default superuser account known as root. This is the only account on the system after installation and has full privileges to do anything to the system. This account should only be used for system administration. You should create alternate accounts for users to log in with. In Linux 6.1 you can add users during the install.

Part of the installation script included the setting of the root password. In Linux 6.1, this is when you can add additional nonprivileged users. The root user is the normal system administrator or superuser account within Linux and most UNIX systems. There is nothing special about this name; you can change it to anything. Changing it is one good security idea. A more devious security idea is to assign the root account a useless UID and GID, like 65535/65535, that has access to nothing. This provides hackers with hours of fun trying to break into a useless login account. Having a backdoor account is also a good idea. This is an alternate root type account with a hard-to-guess name and password combination.

Caution: Changing the root account name or the root home directory location may break some applications, administration scripts, or future installation scripts. This is part of the price of security—more work on your part to maintain a higher level of security. You must decide which is more important, security or ease of management.

During installation, you can see a copy of the messages going into the dmesg file on the third console. Press ALT-F3 to access this terminal session. You can only look at the output. Use SHIFT-PGUP and SHIFT-PGDN to page up and down through the text (note: this has a limited number of retained lines, so you may not be able to see everything).

CERTIFICATION OBJECTIVE 3.14

How Do You Know When Your Hardware Is Not Supported?

Chances are it is supported, somewhere, somehow. Assume it is, and if in doubt, try some of the generic options for the device. A generic option might be a US Robotics or Hayes compatible modem, generic VGA or SVGA video card, a general multisync monitor, and so forth.

When your hardware is just not supported directly from the Red Hat CD-ROM, you have a couple of options. You can search the Internet for some information, or you may need to get different hardware. Rarely does most general hardware not work, since Linux runs on almost every known CPU and with almost all hardware that is at least six months older than the release date of the software. Brand new technology is probably not supported, and non-name brand laptops are usually a nightmare.

This should not be a surprise. Most major brand name machines are directly supported, and most of their models from the last year or two should work. The operative word was *should*; nothing is guaranteed. However, the many laptops that have Red Hat Linux installed attest to the low chance of it not working on your hardware. If you really want to see if it has been tested, check the Red Hat Web site for the latest list of known tested hardware:

http://www.redhat.com/	keeps up-to-date compatibility list

Laptops are notoriously full of proprietary hardware. There is a special Web site that keeps track of X Windows setups for all kinds of laptops, new and old, top brands, and some not so well-known name brands:

http://www.XFree86.org/cardlist.html	more complete X information

With all that said, there are a few other locations on the Internet to look for the installation and distribution that has been tweaked for other funny, new, rare, or noncommercial hardware. There is even a special version of Linux for a Palm Pilot. You just have to do a little digging on the Internet to find it and retrieve it.

Installation Complete

The information in this chapter is all you really need to know to get started. It's not much, really, unless you have some bizarre equipment, want to really customize the installation, or have never partitioned a disk before. If you get past all that, congratulations—you are well on your way to being a guru!

CERTIFICATION OBJECTIVE 3.15

Sample Installation Exercises

The following exercises are meant to provide you with a step-by-step set of progressively more complex installation exercises that cover basic Workstation to very specific and advanced Server installations.

Warning: You should do these exercises on test machines only.

Introduction to Installation Exercises

All these exercises assume you have a basic PC available at your disposal to work with as a learning station. You do not need a network connection, nor do you need to know how to configure X for these exercises—you can select the default answers in most cases.

These exercises are designed to provide progressive development of your knowledge of installing Linux. Workstation and Server installations will do all the disk partitioning for you. In these exercises, you will be asked to configure the installation for a specific usage and customize the disk partition table to meet the needs of the intended usage. This will require that you do a Custom installation in all but one of the exercises.

These exercises also assume that your machine boots from the floppy during a normal reboot; that there is no pertinent information on these test machines; and you realize that all data will be overwritten on these machines.

EXERCISE 3-1

Disk Partitioning Strategies for a Workstation Installation

A typical Workstation installation uses only available unused disk space. In this exercise, you will remove all current partitions and install this sample host strictly as a Linux OS workstation. You will need to create the partitions on a 2GB or larger hard disk (see Table 3-4).

1. Create a BOOT.IMG diskette, then reboot the system with this disk in the floppy drive.
2. Press ENTER to move through the first few screens.
3. Choose Custom Installation when presented with Installation Options.
4. Continue pressing ENTER until you are presented with the Partitioning Options.
5. Select Disk Druid (easiest, graphical) or fdisk, whichever you are familiar with.
6. Delete all partitions.
7. Create the first partition with all but about 100MB of disk space.
8. Use the remaining disk space for swap; make sure the partition is Linux Swap (Disk Druid) or ID 0x83 (fdisk).
9. When asked to select packages, leave the default choices.
10. Select a root account password; e.g., redhat or linux.
11. Finish the Workstation installation normally (skip any network or X installation).
12. Reboot the machine when prompted.
13. Log in as root with your selected password.

TABLE 3-4

Customized Workstation installation

Custom Installation as a Workstation (No Other OS) 200 MHz Pentium II, 2GB single disk, 64MB memory			
Partition	**Size**	**Use**	**Comment**
hda1	1900MB	/	Plenty of room for the base and can still add lots more such as Web and print services
hda2	100MB	swap	More than adequate

For a more robust workstation, you could create the same partitions as per the Workstation or Server installation and just modify their size to match your needs.

EXERCISE 3-2

Advanced Workstation Installation

In this exercise, you will distribute your file system over more than just one partition. You will need to create the partitions on a 2GB or larger hard disk (see Table 3-5).

1. Create a BOOT.IMG diskette, then reboot the system.
2. Choose Custom Installation.
3. Use Disk Druid to reconfigure the partition table.
4. Delete all partitions.
5. Create the first partition with 16MB of disk space, Linux Native, assign to /boot.
6. Create the next primary partition, hda2, as Linux Swap, ID 0x83.
7. Create third partition with about 1200MB disk space, Linux Native, assign to / (root).
8. Create an extended partition containing all the rest of the disk space.
9. Create the first logical partition, fifth in number, with about 250MB, assign to /var.
10. Create the next logical partition, hda6, with remainder, about 450MB, Linux Native, assign to /home/httpd.
11. When asked to select packages, leave the default choices.

TABLE 3-5

Advanced Workstation configuration

Custom Installation as a Workstation (No Other OS) 200 MHz Pentium II, 2GB single disk, 64MB memory			
Partition	**Size**	**Use**	**Comment**
hda1	16 MB	/boot	Maintains bootup files
hda2	64 MB	swap	Plenty of space
hda3	1200 MB	/	The base with NFS, plus Web and print services
hda4	700 MB	Extended partition	CANNOT be used for any file system, can only contain logical partitions within it
hda5	250 MB (of 900 in hda4)	/var	Separate the spooling used by print services
hda6	450 MB (rest of hda4)	/home/httpd	Web services

12. Enter a root password such as password or system.
13. Finish the Workstation installation normally; do not configure the network or X.
14. Reboot the machine and log in as root.

EXERCISE 3-3

Disk Partitioning a Server Installation

In this exercise, you will use a Custom Installation option to create a basic server. You will need to create the partitions on a 2GB or larger hard disk (see Table 3-6).

1. Create a BOOT.IMG diskette, then reboot the system.
2. Choose Custom Installation.
3. When prompted, select Disk Druid to edit partitions.
4. Delete all partitions.
5. Create the first partition with 16MB of disk space, Linux Native, assign to /boot.
6. Create the next primary partition, hda2, as Linux Swap, ID 0x83.

TABLE 3-6

Custom Server configuration

Custom Installation as a Server (No Other OS) 200 MHz Pentium II, 2GB single disk, 128MB memory Main use is as Web and NFS server of files and print, no interactive users			
Partition	**Size**	**Use**	**Comment**
hda1	16MB	/boot	Maintains bootup files
hda2	64MB	swap	Probably plenty of space
hda3	320MB	/	The base with NFS, plus Web and print services
hda4	1600MB	Extended partition	CANNOT be used for any file system, can only contain logical partitions within it
hda5	350 /1600MB	/var	Separate the spooling used by print services
hda6	500 /1600MB	/home/httpd	Web services
hda7	50 /1600MB	/home	No interactive users
hda8	700 /1600MB	/usr	Additional network services such as DHCP, DNS, nw_mars, ...

7. Create third partition with about 320MB disk space, Linux Native, assign to / (root).
8. Create an extended partition containing all the rest of the disk space, 1600MB.
9. Create the first logical partition, hda5, with about 350MB, assign to /var.
10. Create the next logical partition, hda6, with remainder, about 500MB, Linux Native, assign to /home/httpd.
11. Create the next logical partition, hda7, with remainder, about 50MB, Linux Native, assign to /home.
12. Create the next logical partition, hda8, with remainder, about 700MB, Linux Native, assign to /usr.

13. When asked to select packages, include Apache Web service, Novell service, DHCP service, DNS service.
14. Enter a root password.
15. Finish the installation normally.
16. Reboot when prompted and log in as root.

EXERCISE 3-4

Disk Partitioning Strategy for Database Server Installation

In this exercise, you will use a Custom Installation option and configure the partitions for an imaginary database server. You will need to create the partitions on a 2GB or larger hard disk (see Table 3-7).

1. Create a BOOT.IMG diskette, then reboot the system.
2. Choose Custom Installation.
3. Select Disk Druid to make partition changes.
4. Delete all partitions.
5. Create the first partition with 16MB of disk space, Linux Native, assign to /boot.
6. Create the next primary partition, hda2, as Linux Swap, ID 0x83.
7. Create third partition with about 320MB disk space, Linux Native, assign to / (root).
8. Create an extended partition containing all the rest of the disk space, 1600MB.
9. Create the first logical partition, hda5, with about 350MB, assign to /var.
10. Create the next logical partition, hda6, with remainder, about 750MB, Linux Native, assign to /opt.
11. Create the next logical partition, hda7, with remainder, about 500MB, Linux Native, assign to /usr.
12. When asked to select packages, include Ingres Database services.
13. Enter a root password.
14. Finish the installation normally.
15. Reboot and log in as root.

TABLE 3-7

Custom Database Server installation

Custom Installation as a Server (No Other OS) 200 MHz Pentium II, 2GB single disk, 128MB memory Main use is as database, file and print server, few interactive users			
Partition	**Size**	**Use**	**Comment**
hda1	16MB	/boot	Maintains bootup files
hda2	64MB	swap	Probably plenty of space
hda3	320MB	/	The base with NFS, plus Web and print services, few users
hda4	1600MB	Extended partition	CANNOT be used for any file system, can only contain logical partitions within it
hda5	350 /1600MB	/var	Separate the spooling used by print services
hda6	750 /1600MB	/opt	Database system
hda7	500 /1600MB	/usr	File services

EXERCISE 3-5

Disk Partitioning Strategy Custom Web Server Installation

In this exercise, you will configure using a Custom Installation, a server that is primarily used as a Web service. You will need to create the following partitions on a 2GB or larger hard disk (see Table 3-8).

1. Create a BOOT.IMG diskette, then reboot the system.
2. Choose Custom Installation.
3. Select Disk Druid to make partition changes.
4. Delete all partitions.
5. Create the first partition with 16MB of disk space, Linux Native, assign to /boot.
6. Create the next primary partition, hda2, as Linux Swap, ID 0x83.
7. Create third partition with about 1200MB disk space, Linux Native, assign to / (root).

8. Create an extended partition containing all the rest of the disk space, 700MB.
9. Create the first logical partition, hda5, with about 250MB, assign to /var.
10. Create the next logical partition, hda6, with remainder, about 450MB, Linux Native, assign to /home/httpd.
11. When asked to select packages, include Apache Web Service.
12. Enter a password for the root account.
13. Finish the installation normally.
14. Reboot and log in as root.

END OF EXERCISES With all this new-found knowledge and practice with installing Linux, here are some questions containing some real-world scenarios for you to think about, and their answers.

TABLE 3-8

Custom Web Server configuration

Custom Installation as a Workstation (No Other OS) 200 MHz Pentium II, 2GB single disk, 64MB memory Web server mainly, few users			
Partition	**Size**	**Use**	**Comment**
hda1	16MB	/boot	Maintains bootup files
hda2	64MB	swap	Plenty of space
hda3	1200MB	/	The base with NFS, plus Web and print services
hda4	700MB	Extended partition	CANNOT be used for any file system, can only contain logical partitions within it
hda5	250MB (of 900 in hda4)	/var	Separate the spooling used by print services
hda6	450MB (rest of hda4)	/home/http	Web services

QUESTIONS AND ANSWERS

On your current PC with a CD-ROM, sound card and 2MB SVGA S3 video card, you have an unused 300MB partition on the first drive and 350MB on the second drive that you can use for a development and test platform of the X Windows system. What installation options are available?	Workstation Install Only if you wanted a simple system Server Install Get all the basic networking functions Custom Install Make anything you want
There is an older 90 MHz Pentium PC that will be retired soon with 32MB RAM and two hard disks of 800MB and 1200MB. What are your installation options? Why not the others?	There is enough space for any installation option. You may not want to use X on such a slow system, but you could run this as an interoffice Web, FTP, NFS, Samba, and/or print server even with the small amount of memory. Workstation Install Only if you wanted a simple system Server Install Get all the basic networking functions Custom Install Make anything you want
You want to dual boot the help desk machines (total of five) such that Linux is available as an option during reboot. You have a little money to spend on a hardware upgrade, but not enough to replace all machines. You will want to run X and some network services to connect to the main server for file and print services. What are your installation options? Why not the others?	Add a new disk to each machine and maybe add RAM if there is less then 48MB. Adding a new 2+GB disk and upgrading all machines to at least 64MB RAM will make the systems run better for all operating systems, and the added disk space can be shared with the other operating systems and provide enough to do a full install of Linux. Workstation Install (recommended) Only if you wanted a simple system Custom Install Make anything you want Cannot use Server install; does not create dual boot.

QUESTIONS AND ANSWERS	

You already have Red Hat Linux 5.2 installed on your machine in five partitions that cover 2GB. None of the information is absolutely critical. What are your installation options? Why not the others?	This is a scenario that allows you to be lazy and use either the Workstation or Server install, depending on use, or if you want to save some of the information, you can use the Upgrade option.
	Workstation Install
	    Only if you wanted a simple system
	Server Install (recommended)
	    Get all the basic networking functions
	Custom Install
	    Make anything you want

You already have Red Hat Linux 5.2 installed on your machine in five partitions that cover 2GB. Two of the partitions are absolutely critical. What are your installation options? Why not the others?	Use Custom Installation Cannot use Server Install; blows away all other partitions. Workstation install deletes all old Linux partitions; would require backup and restore of critical partition information.

CERTIFICATION SUMMARY

Installation is a very important aspect of the certification process. This chapter has dealt with the decisions you must make when installing Red Hat Linux on either a brand new machine or a machine that already has an OS.

Partitioning the disk into usefully assigned partitions is very important. The Custom installation option provides the most flexible choice for the experienced installer. You can manage and create any number of partitions and install any package combination you want. For a user with little experience installing operating systems, the other two options may fit your needs perfectly, the Workstation or Server installation options.

The Workstation installation creates three partitions from all unused disk space as /boot, swap, and the / (root), installs a preconfigured set of mostly user application-type packages, and it then sets up your machine to dual boot between the old OS and Linux.

The Server installation option deletes all old partitions, creates six partitions for the various system file structures, installs all the network services software packages, and installs the lilo boot loader to load this installation only.

There is no one set answer when it comes to installing another operating system. The Workstation and Server installation options contain the two most common and useful package sets for "usage" oriented machines.

The Custom installation option provides the most flexibility but also requires the most knowledge about all the details required for installation by the installer.

TWO-MINUTE DRILL

- On the Red Hat CD-ROM in the /RedHat/base/ directory, the comps text file lists all the packages associated with each group. A "package" is just one set of files related to a given application.
- The Apache Web Server package is NOT installed with a Workstation installation. You can add this package at any time using the rpm utility.
- For a Server Class installation you need at least 1600MB, or 1.6GB, of total disk space. There are six partitions created, four with a fixed size and two that share the remainder of the disk or disks.
- The variable-sized partitions, /home and /usr, split the remainder of space and hence consume the rest of up to two additional disks if needed. If more than three disks are present, some of the disks will not be used.
- The question of disk space needed is always relevant. You need as much as it takes, and probably more. The minimum is around 200MB of disk space if you install Linux without X and few server services. With 300MB, you could probably get in X, but few server services and few games.

- ❑ Red Hat Linux has been specifically crafted to work on almost any "old" PC hardware. It can also be installed to Alpha and PowerPC based computers, to name two.
- ❑ To Use rescue.img, you must boot your machine with the BOOT.IMG diskette. When you get to the first screen prompt showing lilo, you must type **rescue**, and press ENTER. The boot disk will continue to load and you will eventually be asked for the next disk. Replace the BOOT.IMG disk with the RESCUE.IMG diskette. Press ENTER and the bootup should continue. The rescue disk will load a virtual file system into memory and supply a few very basic but essential binary files for you to try to recover your system.
- ❑ On some of the newer systems, the system can boot an operating system from the CD-ROM.
- ❑ The installation has two distinct initial paths based on whether you use the BOOT.IMG diskette to install from local hardware or you used BOOTNET.IMG to install from a network-based resource like NFS, HTTP, or FTP.
- ❑ The original Intel motherboard design provided a mechanism to start any operating system: It would load a bootup program, called the Master Boot Record, or MBR. This is the first program loaded by the BIOS. This program then loads the real operating system boot control program(s), which in turn starts the operating system.
- ❑ If you have a dual boot system, you may want to change the default to another operating system for a short time of use. You update the /etc/lilo.conf file and then you must run /sbin/lilo to force the changes at bootup. This may also need to be done in some rescue situations; you will need to rebuild the boot record. In the case of a rescue, you should be aware that this boot record uses a relative offset to point to the files to be loaded. Make sure you mount any extra file systems, after the root file system, in similar locations to normal.

- Although there is no hard-and-fast rule, a good rule of thumb is to create your swap partition to be two to three times the memory for small memory systems.
- If your X Windows server is not configured properly, then you can press CTRL-ALT-F1 to go back to a text-based login screen.
- In any runlevel, you can log in using the default superuser account known as root. This is the only account on the system after installation and has full privileges to do anything to the system. This account should only be used for system administration. You should create alternate accounts for users to log in with.
- Changing the root account name or the root home directory location may break some applications, administration scripts, or future installation scripts. This is part of the price of security—more work on your part to maintain a higher level of security. You must decide which is more important, security or ease of management.

SELF TEST

The following Self Test questions will help you measure your understanding of the material presented in this chapter. Read all the choices carefully, as there may be more than one correct answer. Choose all correct answers for each question.

1. When you try to boot your newly created installation, with a root, /boot and swap partition, the system complains that there is no active boot drive. What should you do?
   A. Reboot with the installation diskette and redo the installation.
   B. Reboot with a DOS boot diskette and run FDISK /MBR.
   C. Reboot with the installation diskette and run fdisk to activate the proper boot partition.
   D. Reboot with the bootup diskette created during installation.
2. If you already have a PC with a previous version of Linux on it that you do not want to keep, which installation option will automatically delete only the Linux partitions and install a basic network and X-Windows-ready Linux system?
   A. Workstation
   B. Server
   C. Custom
   D. Dual Boot
3. After you have completed your installation, during bootup, the following appears on the console LI and then the system seems to hang. What appears to be the problem?
   A. Cannot find second part of boot loader. /boot may be beyond 1024 cylinder.
   B. Other operating system boot loader interfering with lilo.
   C. Did not configure an active (boot) partition.
   D. System is waiting for special options to the command line.
4. You have installed different versions of Linux before. During the installation, you are given a second option to create disk partitions, but you are only familiar with the text-based disk partition management program called:
   A. fixdisk
   B. rdisk
   C. fdisk
   D. druidisk
5. You are asked to install on a machine that has several versions of UNIX on it. There are many different partitions. You only want to use the same type of partitions that Linux already uses. What is the native file system format used by Linux?
   A. ufs
   B. ext2fs
   C. dos
   D. fat

6. You have configured a new Workstation installation so that it dual boots with Win95. However, you have forgotten the name you used. When you enter Win95, lilo complains it cannot find that installation. You need to display all possible boot choices.
   A. Press SPACE BAR-h ENTER
   B. Help ENTER
   C. TAB
   D. ESC1B ENTER
7. Your main Linux Web server has been diagnosed as having to use swap on a regular basis. You notice that there is only one big swap file on the same physical disk as the root file system. There are three other disks with space available. How many swap partitions can be utilized, what is the maximum size for any one, and what is the maximum overall swap space allowed per system?
   A. Eight partitions, max 2GB any one, 4GB total
   B. Six partitions, max 3GB any one, 4GB total
   C. Four partitions, max 4GB any one, 8GB total
   D. Two partitions, max 5GB any one, 8GB total
8. Your MIS manager is concerned about the installation of Linux on the hundreds of workstations in the company. She thinks it requires someone to install from a CD-ROM on every machine, and only a few machines have CD-ROM drives. You want to reassure her that there will not be any problem using currently running network services. (Select all that apply.)
   A. NFS
   B. Samba
   C. FTP
   D. HTTP
   E. DNS
   F. DHCP
9. Your current user of this workstation could not get Windows to run so she ran the DOS FDISK.EXE with /MBR to put the boot sector back in place. Now you cannot run Linux. You boot up with the emergency startup disk you created. You need to update the MBR with the Linux Loader program with:
   A. /etc/lilo.conf
   B. /bin/configlilo
   C. /sbin/lilo
   D. /bin/sys/liloconf
10. After you update the MBR, it only indicates one entry. You need to fix the setup file to include both options. What system file is used to set and create boot entries?
   A. /bin/sys/liloconf
   B. /sbin/liloconf
   C. /etc/lilo.conf
   D. /usr/sys/liloconf

11. Your MIS manager has heard that there is another boot loader capable of loading many different operating systems. What is an alternate boot loader available for Linux?

    A. syslinuz
    B. bootfs
    C. loadlin
    D. pmagic

12. You are told to check the Web server drive table after installation. There are eight partitions. Your MIS manager asks how that can be; DOS can only create one primary and one extended. How many primary partitions can any one disk drive contain?

    A. 4 primary, 1 extended, 16 total partitions
    B. 3 primary, 2 extended, 12 total partitions
    C. 12 primary, 1 extended partition
    D. 16 extended partitions

13. A new product you are to add to the server asks you to go into single-user mode to run a system check on the file system. How do you start your system in single-user mode?

    A. lilo : boot 1
    B. lilo : init 1
    C. lilo : single user
    D. lilo : linux single

14. The MIS manager wants a further explanation of the drive table on the server, specifically, the type of partition that can contain logical partitions.

    A. ext2fs
    B. nfs
    C. primary
    D. extended

15. During the installation, you are asked to configure your network card to access the installation source files from an NFS server. Assuming you have already input the IP address and netmask for this host, you need to have:

    A. DNS Server IP, BOOTP Server IP, NFS export name
    B. DNS export name, BOOTP Server IP, NFS Server IP
    C. DHCP Server IP, DHCP name, NFS export name
    D. NFS export name, NFS Server IP

16. Your MIS manager has asked you to put Linux on a laptop for a CEO. The laptop has about 1GB of free disk space, but there is one partition with all available space allocated to it. What free utility is supplied with the installation that allows you to resize a partition?

    A. fdisk
    B. fips
    C. bootp
    D. syslinux

17. What program allows you to manage a dual boot between Linux and Win98?

    A. lilo
    B. syslinux
    C. bootp
    D. fdisk

18. During installation, you create the first six partitions and then you allocate the file system directory to them sequentially. But there is one partition that you cannot assign as a file system:

    A. hda4
    B. hda1
    C. hda5
    D. had

19. You are in a rush to install a workstation with the minimum number of partitions. What partitions are absolutely required?

    A. /boot, swap, /system
    B. root (/), swap
    C. swap , /boot, /usr
    D. /boot, /root

20. A Windows administrator is puzzled by the amount of swap space configured and wants to know what is recommended for Linux.

    A. Same as RAM memory.
    B. 40–90MB.
    C. Same as the server uses.
    D. Two to three times the RAM.
    E. There is no recommended amount of swap space; you need to know exactly how much space will be required.

21. What partitions are created by a Workstation installation?

    A. /boot, swap, / root
    B. /, swap, /root
    C. swap, /boot, /usr
    D. /boot, /root, /usr

22. What partitions are created by a Server installation?

    A. /boot, swap, /, /usr
    B. /, swap, /var, /boot
    C. swap, /boot, /usr, /home
    D. /boot, /, /usr, /home, swap, /var

23. During your installation, you are not presented with any option to get to the NFS share where you provided access to the installation files. You do not have a CD-ROM available on this workstation. How do you remedy this?

    A. Create the RESCUE.IMG diskette, then reboot with this diskette in the floppy drive.
    B. Create the PCMCIA.IMG diskette, then reboot with this diskette in the floppy drive.
    C. Create the BOOTNET.IMG diskette, then reboot with this diskette in the floppy drive.
    D. Create the SCSI.IMG diskette; enter when prompted.

24. You have a PC that already contains a different version of Linux. During the installation, you are asked where to put the boot loader, lilo. You know there is already another loader called loadlin installed. Where should you put the installation boot record?

    A. In any partition except /boot
    B. In any partition except /
    C. In partition /boot
    D. You do not need to install the lilo boot loader

25. During the installation, the authentication screen provides three options. You remember what the shadow password is and MD5, but forget exactly what the third option NIS is.

    A. Network Inode Slave—Provides shared disk resources
    B. Network Information Service—Provides centralized authentication
    C. New Internet Standard—Centralized authentication of shared access
    D. Newton Interrupt Sequence—File sharing protocol

RHCE®

RED HAT CERTIFIED ENGINEER®

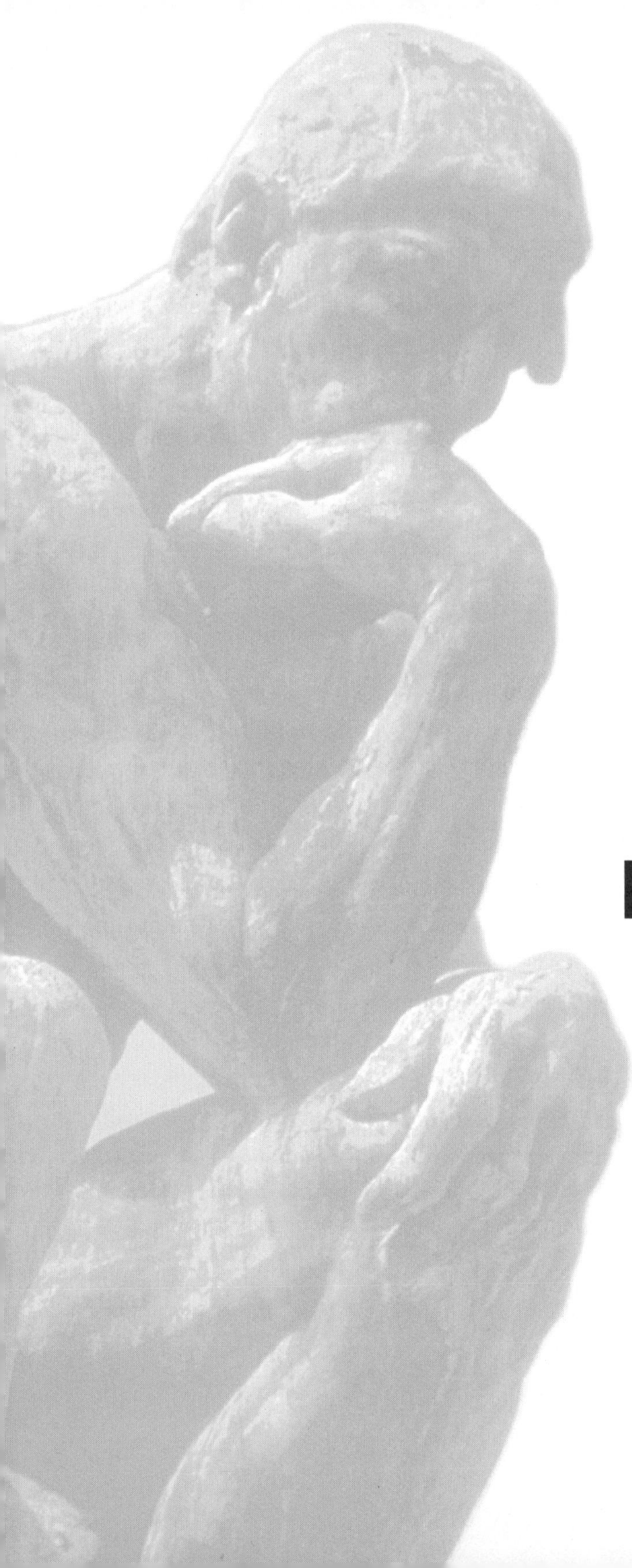

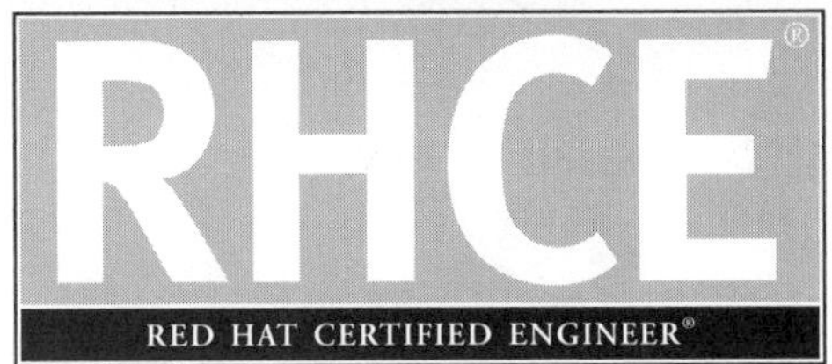

4

Basic Configuration and Administration

CERTIFICATION OBJECTIVES

4.01	Adding, Deleting, and Modifying User Accounts
4.02	The Basic User Environment
4.03	File System Configuration
4.04	Using the Red Hat Package Manager
4.05	Basic Networking
4.06	chkconfig and ntsysv
4.07	Virtual Consoles
4.08	kbdconfig, timeconfig, mouseconfig
4.09	Mounting Floppy Disks and Removable Media
4.10	Sound Cards, the sndconfig Utility

After installation is complete on your Red Hat Linux 6.0 system, you still have some work to do to make the system functional. User accounts need to be set up, filesystems configured, and some packages may need to be added or removed.

This chapter will get you started with the basics that every Red Hat Linux administrator should know about their system. At the end of this chapter you should know how to manage user accounts and environments, configure and mount filesystems, use RPM to manage and create packages, configure PCMCIA, manage system daemons, and configure virtual consoles, keyboards, and mice.

CERTIFICATION OBJECTIVE 4.01

Adding, Deleting, and Modifying User Accounts

After installation, your system has only a single login account, the root account. For most installations, you'll want to create more accounts. Even if you're going to be the only user on the system, it's a good idea to create a single, nonprivileged account to do your day-to-day work, and use the root account only for administering the system. Accounts are added to Red Hat Linux 6.0 systems using the *Linuxconf* utility.

Linuxconf

Linuxconf can be run in graphical or character mode. If you have already configured X, and are running a graphical desktop, Linuxconf will start in graphical mode. Otherwise, it will start in character mode. In either mode, the instructions are the same. Figure 4-1 shows Linuxconf in graphical mode.

FIGURE 4-1

Linuxconf main screen

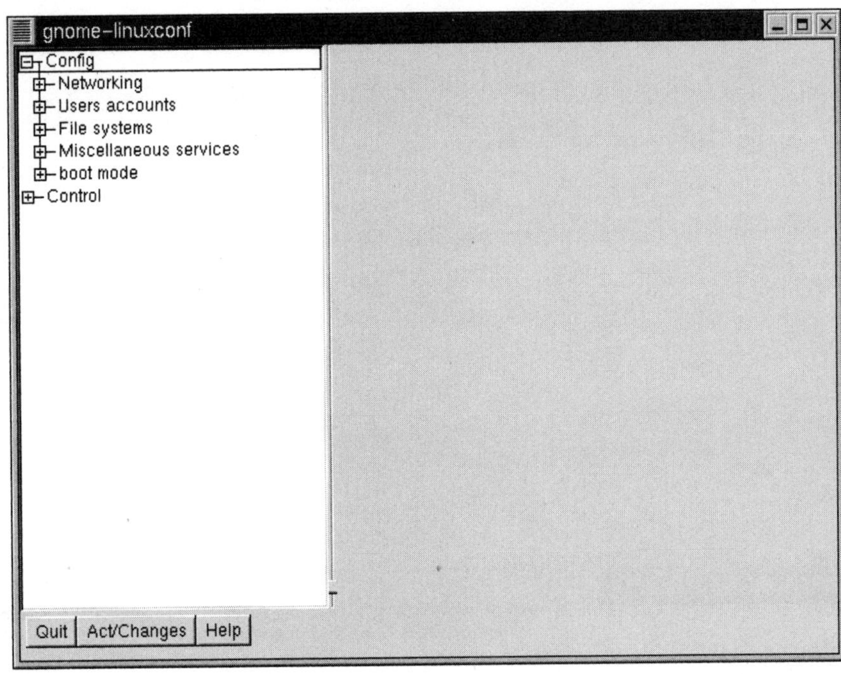

Adding a User with Linuxconf

To add a user with Linuxconf:

1. Run /bin/linuxconf.
2. Open Config | User accounts | Normal | User accounts. (This notation indicates that you should open the Config tab, followed by the User accounts tab, then the Normal tab, and, finally, the User accounts tab. This will open the User accounts form, as shown in Figure 4-2.) If you have more than 15 accounts on the system, Linuxconf will present a Filter control screen. You can use this screen to select a smaller range of accounts to view, or just press Accept to view all accounts.

3. Select the Add button.
4. Complete the form (Figure 4-3) and press the Accept button. The only required field is Login name, but you will most likely want to specify more information for each account. Table 4-1 describes each field.
5. You will be prompted to enter the user's password. The password should be at least six characters (you'll get an error message if it's less than six characters, but Linuxconf will allow you to use the password anyway), and should contain a mix of upper- and lowercase letters, numbers, and symbols to keep it from being easily guessed. Enter the password in the Confirmation field to ensure you haven't misspelled it, then press Accept.
6. When you have finished adding users, press Quit to exit Linuxconf.

FIGURE 4-2

User accounts

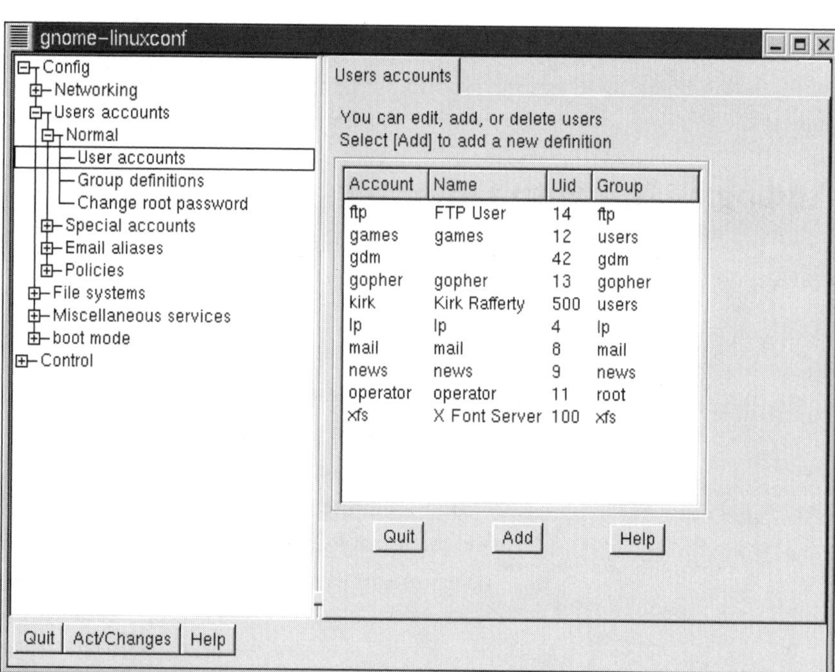

FIGURE 4-3

User account creation

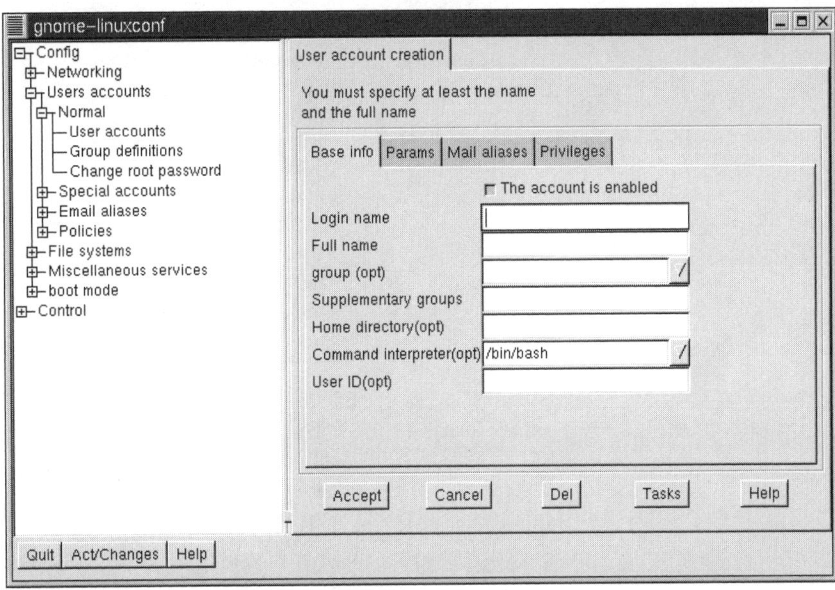

on the job

Although creating user accounts may seem to be a straightforward process, there are a few things to watch out for.

Linuxconf will let you get away with using invalid characters in usernames, such as %, &, *, and !. However, many Linux programs will fail to function with usernames containing these characters.

If your installation doesn't require each user having their own unique group ID (GID), assign your users to the group 'users.' There's rarely a need for each user to have an individual GID, and having most users assigned to the 'users' group makes system administration easier.

Ask your users to use passwords that are difficult to guess. Spouses' and dogs' names make bad passwords. Several words strung together with numbers or symbols make better passwords, such as 'toy+jobs' or 'rule%key.' These are easy to remember, yet difficult to guess.

Discourage the use of shared accounts, where several people use a single account. Shared accounts are almost always unnecessary, and are easily compromised.

TABLE 4-1

User Fields

Field	Instructions
The Account is enabled	Make sure this is checked if you want the user to be able to log in. If you're creating an administrative account that won't be used to log in, uncheck this box.
Login name	The user logs in with this name. The Login name should only contain alphanumeric characters, and the - and _ characters. In almost all cases, the Login name should not contain uppercase letters. Although a login name can be up to 256 characters, you typically want to keep it to 10 or less, for ease of account maintenance. Examples: nick, catherine, heather, willr.
Full name	The full name of the user. Example: Dana Gordon.
group (opt)	The numeric group ID (GID) the user will belong to. By default, Red Hat Linux 6.0 creates a new group for every new user. If you want all your users to be in the 'users' group, enter 'users' here.
Supplementary groups	Enter any additional groups you want this user to be a member of.
Home directory (opt)	By default, Red Hat Linux 6.0 places new home directories in /home/username.
Command interpreter (opt)	Enter the name of the shell program this user will use. Red Hat Linux 6.0 defaults to the Bourne Again Shell (bash).
User ID (opt)	The user will be assigned the next available User ID (UID) if left blank. In most cases it's best to leave this blank.
Must keep # days	If set to a positive number, the user must keep a new password this many days before being allowed to change it.
Must change after # days	If set to a positive number, the user must change their password after this many days.
Warn # days before expiration	If set to a positive number, the user will be warned when logging on this many days before their password expires.
Account expire after # days	If set to a positive number, the account will be locked after this many days. This is a good setting for temporary logins.

If you'll be using Network File System (NFS), make sure users maintain the same UID across systems.

Deleting a User Account with Linuxconf

Removing user accounts is as straightforward as adding them, with a few exceptions. When you remove a user from your system, you'll have to make some choices about how (or if) you will save the files in the user's home directory. Linuxconf gives you several choices regarding this decision.

1. Run /bin/linuxconf.
2. Select Config | User accounts | Normal | User accounts. This will open the User accounts form. If you have more than 15 accounts on the system, Linuxconf will present a Filter control screen. You can use this screen to select a smaller range of accounts to view, or just press Accept to view all accounts.
3. Select the account to be deleted.
4. Select the Del button.
5. Select the appropriate option for the account data (see Table 4-2).
6. Select the Accept button.

It is important to note that only files in the deleted user's home directory are processed. Any files owned by the deleted user stored outside the home directory still exist, under the UID of the deleted user. If a new user is created with the old user's UID, the new user owns those files.

Modifying a User Account Using Linuxconf

1. Run /sbin/linuxconf.
2. Select Config | User accounts | Normal | User accounts. This will open the User accounts form. If you have more than 15 accounts on the system, Linuxconf will present a Filter control screen. You can use this screen to select a smaller range of accounts to view, or just press Accept to view all accounts.

TABLE 4-2

Delete Account Options

Deleting Account Data Option	Action
Archive the account's data	Data stored in the user's home directory is archived in /home/oldaccounts, under the filename username-yyyy-mm-dd-pid.tar.gz, where username is the name of the deleted user; yyyy, mm, and dd are, respectively, the year, month, and day the account was deleted; pid is the process ID of the Linuxconf process that created this file; and .tar.gz indicates this file was tar'd and gzip'd. The user's home directory is then removed.
Delete the account's data	The user's home directory and all its contents are removed.
Leave the account's data in place	Nothing is done to the user's home directory and its contents.

3. Select the account to be modified.
4. Make the desired modifications to the account.
5. Select the Accept button.

CERTIFICATION OBJECTIVE 4.02

The Basic User Environment

Each user on your Red Hat Linux 6.0 system has an *environment* when logged on to the system. The environment defines where a user looks for programs to be executed, what the login prompt looks like, what terminal type is being used, and more. This section explains how default environments are set up.

Home Directories and /etc/skel

Red Hat Linux 6.0 makes it easy to run a set of standard templates to propagate to new users' home directories via files in /etc/skel.

Home Directories

The home directory is the initial directory in which users are placed when they first log on to a Red Hat Linux 6.0 system. For most normal users this will be /home/*username*, where *username* is the user's login name. Users typically have write permission in their own home directory, so they're free to read and write their own files there. In Chapter 5, you'll learn how to configure disk quotas, so users don't allocate more than their fair share of disk space.

/etc/skel

The /etc/skel directory contains default environment files for new accounts. Linuxconf copies these files to the home directory when a new account is created. The files included in /etc/skel and their purpose are listed in Table 4-3.

As the system administrator, you can edit these files, or place your own files in /etc/skel. When new users are created, these files will be propagated to the new users' home directories.

Window Manager Configuration File Locations

Red Hat Linux 6.0 comes with several window managers. You will at some point want to configure one or more of them for use on your system. Window manager configuration files are stored in /etc/X11/ <windowmanager>, where <windowmanager> is the name of the window manager. Within the window manager subdirectory, there is usually a file named system.<windowmanager>, which contains default behavior for the window manager.

TABLE 4-3

Files in /etc/skel and Their Purpose

Files	Purpose
.Xdefaults	Contains default settings for a few common X applications.
.bashrc	The individual per-interactive-shell startup file.
.bash_logout	Source the commands in this file upon logout.
.bash_profile	The personal initialization file, executed for login shells.

CERTIFICATION OBJECTIVE 4.03

File System Configuration

There are as many, if not more, filesystem types as there are operating systems. Red Hat Linux 6.0 can understand many of these formats.

Filesystem Types

At the heart of every Red Hat Linux 6.0 installation are the filesystems on which it relies. Linux supports a rich set of different filesystem types (see Table 4-4).

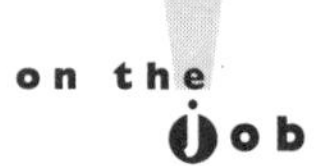

If you have the kernel source RPMs loaded on your system, you can see which filesystems any version or distribution of Linux currently supports. Look at the file /usr/src/linux/fs/filesystems.c.

The Filesystem Table

Information about your local and remotely mounted filesystems is stored in /etc/fstab. Each filesystem is described on a separate line. Each line is composed of multiple fields, each separated by spaces or tabs. When your system boots, it processes each filesystem in the order listed.

A sample /etc/fstab might look like the following:

```
/dev/hda1       /           ext2        defaults        1   1
/dev/hda2       swap        swap        defaults        0   0
/dev/hda5       /usr        ext2        defaults        1   2
/dev/hda7       /tmp        ext2        defaults        1   2
/dev/hda8       /var        ext2        defaults        1   2
/dev/hda9       /home       ext2        defaults        1   2
/dev/hdc        /cdrom      iso9660     ro,noauto,user 0   0
none            /proc       proc        defaults        0   0
```

Table 4-5 provides a description of each field.

TABLE 4-4

Linux Filesystem

Filesystem Type	Description
ADFS	The Acorn Disc Filing System. The standard filesystem of the Acorn's RISC-PC systems and the Archimedes line of machines. Currently, Linux supports ADFS as read-only.
Amiga FFS	The Fast File System is used by Amiga Systems computers.
Apple HFS	The Hierarchical File System used by the Apple Mac Plus and all later Macintosh computers.
MSDOS, VFAT, and UMSDOS	These filesystems allow you to read MS-DOS formatted filesystems. MSDOS allows you to read pre-Windows 95 partitions. VFAT allows you to read Windows 95 partitions, and UMSDOS allows you to run Linux from a DOS partition (not currently supported by Red Hat). Note that it is possible to read a Windows 95 partition with only MSDOS support enabled, but you will not be able to see the long filenames generated by Windows 95.
ISO 9660 CDROM	The standard filesystem used on CD-ROMs. It is also known as the "High Sierra filesystem," or HSFS on other UNIX systems.
Minix	The standard filesystem for the Minix operating system. This is the original default Linux filesystem, although the ext2 filesystem has since superceded it.
NTFS	NTFS is the filesystem for Microsoft Windows NT. Currently it is only supported as read-only.
OS/2 HPFS	The standard filesystem for IBM's OS/2 operating system. Currently it is only supported as read-only.
/proc	The /proc filesystem is the Linux *virtual* filesystem. *Virtual* means that it doesn't occupy real disk space. Instead, files are created on the fly when you access them. /proc is used to provide information on kernel configuration and device status.
/dev/pts	The /dev/pts filesystem is the Linux implementation of the Open Group's Unix98 PTY support.

TABLE 4-4 Linux Filesystem *(continued)*

Filesystem Type	Description
QNX	The standard filesystem for the QNX 4 operating system.
ROM	The ROM filesystem is a read-only filesystem, intended primarily for initial RAM disks.
Second Extended (ext2)	The standard filesystem for the Linux operating system.
System V and Coherent	The standard filesystem for Coherent, SCO, and Xenix.
UFS	The standard filesystem for BSD and BSD derivatives, SunOS, and NeXTstep.
Coda	Coda is a networked filesystem similar to NFS. Currently Linux supports Coda clients only.
NFS	The Network filesystem. This is the networked filesystem most commonly used among Linux and UNIX computers.
SMB	Server Message Block (SMB) is a protocol used by Windows for Workgroups, Windows 95, Windows NT, and OS/2 LAN Manager to share printers and files remotely. SMB allows Linux to use SMB as a client.
NCP	Netware Core Protocol (NCP) is the network filesystem used by Novell, over the IPX protocol. NCP allows Linux to use NCP as a client.

Mount Options

Although most filesystems in /etc/fstab are given the mount option of "default," there are other options you can use. Options are listed in /etc/fstab separated by commas (no spaces or tabs). The standard mount options are listed in Table 4-6.

Some filesystem types supported by Red Hat Linux 6.0 have additional options. If you are using non-ext2 filesystems on your system, consult the mount(8) man page for more information regarding special mount options for your filesystem types.

You can also access filesystem information via Linuxconf.

TABLE 4-5 Field Functions

Field Name	Description
fs_spec	Describes the block device or remote filesystem to be mounted.
fs_file	Describes the mount point (the directory the filesystem will be mounted as). For swap partitions, this should be "none."
fs_vfstype	Describes the filesystem type. Valid filesystem types are minix, ext, ext2, xiafs, msdos, hpfs, iso9660, nfs, and swap. This field can also be set to "ignore," which will cause the system to ignore the entry. Ignoring an entry is useful for marking unused partitions.
fs_mntops	Mount options. Specifies mounting options. Mount options are covered later in this section.
fs_freq	Used by the dump(8) command to determine which filesystems need to be dumped. A value of 0 indicates that the filesystem does not need to be dumped.
fs_passno	Used by the fsck(8) program to determine the order in which filesystems are checked upon boot. The root filesystem should have an fs_passno setting of 1, and other local filesystems should have an fs_passno of 2. Remote filesystems should have an fs_passno of 0, which indicates that they should not be checked on boot.

TABLE 4-6 Mount Options

Mount Option	Description
async	I/O is done asynchronously to this filesystem.
atime	Timestamps for each inode are updated when accessed.
auto	Can be mounted with the -a option of the mount(8) command.
defaults	Use the default mount options: rw, suid, dev, exec, auto, nouser, and async.
dev	Interpret character or block special devices on the filesystem.

TABLE 4-6

Mount Options *(continued)*

Mount Option	Description
exec	Allow binaries (programs) to be executed on this filesystem.
noatime	Timestamps for each inode are not updated when accessed.
noauto	Cannot be mounted with the -a option of the mount(8) command (it must be mounted explicitly).
nodev	Do not interpret character or block special devices on the filesystem.
noexec	Do not allow binaries (programs) to be executed on this filesystem.
nosuid	Do not allow setuid or setgid permissions on programs to take effect.
nouser	Do not allow nonroot users to mount this filesystem.
remount	Attempt to remount a filesystem that has already been mounted. This is typically used to change mount options, and is only used by the mount(8) command (never used in /etc/mnttab).
ro	Mount the filesystem as read-only.
rw	Mount the filesystem as read-write.
suid	Allow setuid or setgid permissions on programs to take effect.
sync	I/O is done synchronously to this filesystem.
user	Allow nonroot users to mount this filesystem. This option also sets the noexec, nosuid, and nodev options, unless overridden.

Run /sbin/linuxconf

Open Config | File systems | Access local drive. This opens the Local Volume display similar to Figure 4-4.

FIGURE 4-4

Filesystem information in Linuxconf

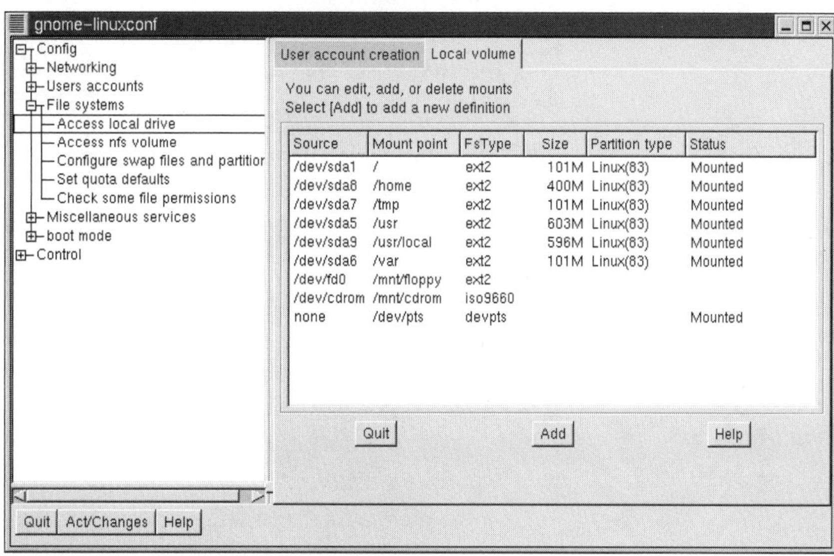

CERTIFICATION OBJECTIVE 4.04

Using the Red Hat Package Manager

One of the mundane yet necessary duties a Systems Administrator faces is software management. Applications and patches come and go. After months or years of adding, upgrading, and removing software applications, it's hard to tell just what's on a system, what version a software package is, and what other applications it depends on. Outdated files often wind up lying around because nobody's quite sure what they belong to. Worse, you may install a new software package only to find that it has overwritten a crucial file from a currently installed package. The Red Hat Package Manager (RPM) was designed to eliminate these problems. With RPM, software is managed in discrete "packages," each package being a collection of the files that make up the software, and instructions for adding, removing, and upgrading those files. RPM also makes sure that you never lose configuration files by backing up existing files before overwriting. RPM also tracks which version of an application is currently installed on your system.

A key feature of RPM is that filenames can be specified in Uniform Resource Locator (URL) format. For example, if you know that the package foo.rpm is on the FTP server ftp.rpmdownloads.com, in the /pub directory, you can specify that filename as ftp://ftp.rpmdownloads.com/pub/foo.rpm. RPM is smart enough to log on to the FTP server anonymously and pull down the file. You can also use the format ftp://<username>:<password>@host-name:<port>/path/to/remote/package/file.rpm, where <username> and <password> are the username and password you need to log on to this system non-anonymously, and <port> specifies a nonstandard port used on the remote machine. You may use these formats anywhere a filename is called for in RPM.

What Is a Package?

In the generic sense, a package is a container. It includes the files needed to accomplish a certain task, such as the binaries, configuration, and documentation files in a software application. It also includes instructions on how and where these files should be installed, and how the installation should be accomplished. A package also includes instructions on how to uninstall itself. RPM packages are often identified by filenames that usually consist of the package name, the version, the release, and the architecture for which they were built. For example, the package penguin-3.26.i386.rpm indicates that this is the (fictional) Penguin Utilities package, version 3, release 26. i386 indicates that it has been compiled for the Intel architecture. Note that although this is the conventional method of naming RPM packages, the actual package name, version, and architecture information are read from the contents of the file by RPM, not the filename. You could rename the file blag.rpm, but it would still install as penguin-3.26.i386.rpm.

What Is RPM?

At the heart of RPM is the RPM database. This database tracks where each file in a package is located, its version, and much more. The RPM also maintains an MD5 checksum of each file. Checksums are used to determine if a file has been modified, which comes in handy if you need to verify the integrity of one or more packages. The RPM database makes adding, removing, and upgrading packages easy, because RPM knows which files to handle, and where to put them. RPM also takes care of conflicts between packages. For example, if package X, which has already been installed, has a configuration file called /etc/someconfig, and you attempt to install a new package, Y, which wants to install the same file, RPM will manage this conflict by backing up your previous configuration file before the new file is written. The workhorse of the RPM system is the program rpm. rpm is the "driver" responsible for maintaining the RPM databases. Of rpm's 10 modes of operation, we will cover the four most common: query, install, upgrade, and remove.

Validating a Package Signature

RPM has two methods of checking the integrity of a package: MD5 checksum and PGP signature. Due to export restrictions, Red Hat Linux 6.0 does not include PGP, so if you want to check the PGP signature of a package, you will have to obtain a copy of PGP (available at http://www.pgpi.com). Once you have obtained and properly installed PGP, follow these steps to use PGP with RPM.

1. Make sure the pgp command is in your path.
2. Your public keyring must be available to PGP. You can either set the PGPPATH environmental variable to the directory containing your keyring, or set the pgp_path in the rpmrc file.

After you have configured PGP correctly for use with RPM, you need to start adding public keys to the public keyring used by RPM. Public keys are used by package builders to verify the authenticity of the package you're installing. You will need a public key for each builder's package you wish to authenticate. Once you have added a package builder's public key, you can verify a package.

```
# rpm --checksig rpm-3.0-6.0.i386.rpm
rpm-3.0-6.0.i386.rpm: size pgp md5 OK
```

To check the signature of a package without PGP, invoke RPM with the —checksig -option and the -nopgp option.

```
# rpm --checksig --nopgp zsh-3.0.5-10.i386.rpm
zsh-3.0.5-10.i386.rpm: size md5 OK
```

Adding and Removing Components

RPM makes it easy to add and remove software packages to your system. RPM keeps a database regarding the proper way to add, upgrade, and remove packages, making it as simple as running a single command to add and remove software packages.

Install Mode

The Install mode, as its name suggests, is used to install RPM packages on your system. Installing a package is accomplished with the -i option.

```
# rpm -i penguin-3.26.i386.rpm
```

Or, if the package were stored on a remote FTP server, you could use

```
# rpm -i ftp://ftp.rpmdownloads.com/pub/penguin-3.26.i386.rpm
```

Before installing the package, RPM performs several checks. First, it makes sure the package you're trying to install isn't already installed—RPM won't let you install a package on top of itself. It also checks to make sure you aren't installing an older version of the package. Next, RPM does a dependency check. Some packages depend on other packages being installed first. In this example, you've just downloaded the latest RPM version of Penguin utilities, and now want to install it.

```
# rpm -i penguin-3.26.i386.rpm
failed dependencies:
iceberg >= 7.1 is needed by penguin-3.26.i386.rpm
```

This error indicates that the penguin package failed to install because it requires the iceberg package version 7.1 or later. You'll have to find and install the iceberg package, and any packages iceberg may require.

Finally, RPM checks to see if any configuration files would be overwritten by the installation of this package. RPM tries to make intelligent decisions about what to do with conflicts. If RPM replaces an existing configuration file with one from the new package, a warning will appear on the screen.

```
# rpm -i penguin-3.26.i386.rpm
warning: /etc/someconfig saved as /etc/someconfig.rpmsave
```

It's up to you to look at both files and determine what, if any, modifications need to be made.

Upgrade Mode

The -u switch is used to upgrade existing packages. For example, if Penguin Utilities version 3.25 is already installed, issuing the command

```
# rpm -u penguin-3.26.i386.rpm
```

will replace the old version of the package with the new one. In fact, one of the quirks of RPM's Upgrade mode is that the older package doesn't even have to exist in the first place. -u works identically to -i in this case.

Remove Mode

The rpm -e command removes a package from your system. Like the Install mode, RPM does some housekeeping before it will let you remove a package. First, it does a dependency check to make sure no other packages depend on the package you are removing. If you have modified any of the configuration files, RPM makes a copy of the file, appends ".rpmsave" to the end of it, and then erases the original. Finally, after removing all files from your system and the RPM database, it removes the package name from the database.

Note: be very careful about which packages you remove from your system. Like most Linux utilities, RPM assumes omniscience, and will silently let you shoot yourself in the foot. Removing the passwd or kernel package would be devastating.

Adding Updates, Security Fixes, etc.

Red Hat Linux 6.0 is constantly being updated. As bugs or security problems are found, they are posted to Red Hat Corporation's Errata Web page, located at http://www.redhat.com/support/docs/errata.html. You should check this page regularly to ensure your system is up to date. Here's a good checklist to follow whenever you check the errata page:

- Select the Red Hat Linux 6.0 (Hedwig) General Errata link.
- Scroll down to the Overview section. Go through the lists, selecting each package listed.
- If you have an affected package loaded on your system, consider upgrading it with the recommended replacement.
- Before replacing an affected package, consider the ramifications. You may need to bring the system down to single-user, or perform a reboot.
- When performing the upgrade, watch for configuration file warnings. If your local configuration files are replaced with new files, you may need to change the new configuration files to reflect your current settings.
- Thoroughly test the new package. Make sure you have it configured correctly.
- If a package is listed in the errata but not installed on your system, chances are there's no reason to put it on your system now. Read the detailed errata entry for that package carefully, and only install it if you need it.

Verifying One or More Packages

Verifying an installed package compares information about that package with information from the RPM database on your system, or the original package. Verify does a check against the size, MD5 checksum, permissions, type, owner, and group of each file in the package. Here are a few examples of using the "verify" switch:

- Verify all packages

  ```
  # rpm --verify -a
  ```

- Verify all files within a package against an RPM file

  ```
  # rpm --verify -p fileutils-4.0-1.i386.rpm
  ```

- Verify a file belonging to a particular package

  ```
  # rpm --verify --file /bin/ls
  ```

If the files or packages you were verifying checked out okay, you will see no output; otherwise, you'll see what checks failed. The output will be a string of 8 characters, possibly a 'c' denoting configuration file, then the filename that failed. Each character in the 8-character field contains the result of a particular test. A "." (period) indicates that test passed. The following example indicates that /bin/vi has an incorrect group id assigned to it:

```
# rpm --Verify --file /bin/vi
......G.   /bin/vi
```

Table 4-7 lists the failure codes and their meanings.

TABLE 4-7 Failure Codes

Failure Code	Meaning
5	MD5 checksum
S	File size
L	Symbolic link
T	File modification time
D	Device
U	User
G	Group
M	Mode

Seeing What Packages Are Installed

Without RPM, you'd need to search around your filesystems to figure out if a particular software package is installed. RPM makes it easy for you to figure out what RPM packages are installed, and to get information about those packages.

Query Mode

One of the strengths of RPM is that, ideally, every system or application file on your system is accounted for. Using RPM's query mode, you can determine which packages are installed on your system, or what file belongs to a particular package. This can be a big help if you want to locate a file that belongs to a certain package. Query mode can also be used to identify what files are in an RPM file before you install it. This lets you see what files are going to be installed on your system before they're actually written.

The -q switch is used to query packages. By itself, -q will give you the version of a specified package. If you want to see which version of the tin newsreader you have on your system, you would issue the following command:

```
# rpm -q tin
tin-1.22-12
```

If you want to see which installed package owns a file, use the -f modifier. Here we want to see which package owns /etc/passwd.

```
# rpm -q -f /etc/passwd
setup-1.9.2-1
```

Likewise, if you want to generate a list of files belonging to a certain package, use the -l modifier.

```
# rpm -q -l tin
/usr/bin/rtin
/usr/bin/tin
/usr/doc/tin-1.22
/usr/doc/tin-1.22/CHANGES
/usr/doc/tin-1.22/FTP
```

```
/usr/doc/tin-1.22/HACKERS
/usr/doc/tin-1.22/INSTALL
/usr/doc/tin-1.22/INSTALL.NNTP
/usr/doc/tin-1.22/MANIFEST
/usr/doc/tin-1.22/README
/usr/doc/tin-1.22/TODO
/usr/man/man1/tin.1
```

One of the most common modifiers to -q is -a, query all packages on your system. My system has about 350 packages installed, but here's a truncated output:

```
# rpm -q -a
setup-1.9.2-1
filesystem-1.3.2-3
basesystem-4.9-3
ldconfig-1.9.5-8
...
code_crusader-1.1.0-1
lyx-0.11.53-1
xforms-0.86-1
```

For even more information about a package, use the -i (information) modifier.

```
# rpm -q -i passwd
Name        : passwd                      Relocations: (not relocateable)
Version     : 0.58                            Vendor: Red Hat Software
Release     : 1                           Build Date: Wed Apr 14 15:21:39 1999
Install date: Tue Jun 22 11:34:34 1999   Build Host: porky.devel.redhat.com
Group       : System Environment/Base     Source RPM: passwd-0.58-1.src.rpm
Size        : 15845                           License: BSD
Packager    : Red Hat Software <http://developer.redhat.com/bugzilla>
Summary     : The passwd utility for setting/changing passwords using PAM.
```

The passwd package contains a system utility (passwd) that sets and/or changes passwords, using PAM (Pluggable Authentication Modules). To use passwd, you should have PAM installed on your system. Table 4-8 lists some of the most important entries.

TABLE 4-8

Important Entries

Entry	Description
Name	The name of the package.
Version	The version of the package.
Release	The number of times this package has been released using the same version of the software.
Install date	When this package was installed on your system.
Group	Your RPM database is divided into groups, which describes the functionality of the software. Every time you install a package, it will be grouped accordingly.
Size	The total size in bytes of all the files in the package.
License	The license the original software has been released under.

Typically, the filename will indicate what's inside the package, but not always. You may receive a package simply named glibc.rpm, which isn't really helpful. You can use the -p modifier to find out what version and release this RPM contains (and perhaps rename it appropriately).

```
# rpm -q -p glibc.rpm
glibc-2.0.7-29
```

Creating and Using Custom RPMs

Source RPMs are, as the name indicates, the source codes used to build architecture-specific packages. Source RPMs are identified with the string "src" appearing where the architecture indicator normally appears, such as:

```
polarbear-2.07-2.src.rpm
```

Binary RPMs are built from source RPMs. The source RPM contains the source code and specifications necessary to create the binary RPM.

Installing Source RPMs

Like normal RPMs, a source RPM (SRPM) is installed using the -i option. This will place the contents of the SRPM within the /usr/src/redhat directory structure.

The /usr/src/redhat/... Directory Structure

There are five subdirectories within the /usr/src/redhat directory structure (see Table 4-9).

When you build an SRPM, you will build it within this structure. If you install an SRPM, it will be extracted into this structure.

Changing Compile Time Options for a Source RPM

While most precompiled time options will serve your needs, there are times when you will want to modify the source code.

THE SPEC FILE To change the compile time options in an SRPM, you must understand spec files. The spec file is stored in /usr/src/redhat/SPECS/<packagename>.spec. The spec file controls the way a package is built, and what actions are performed when it is installed or removed from a system. There are eight different sections in a spec file (see Table 4-10).

You would change the compile-time options for a package in the build section of the spec file. Here's a sample build section in a prep file:

```
%build
rm -rf $RPM_BUILD_ROOT
mkdir -p $RPM_BUILD_ROOT/usr/bin $RPM_BUILD_ROOT/etc
./configure --prefix=/usr --exec-prefix=/
make CFLAGS="$RPM_OPT_FLAGS" LDFLAGS=-s
```

This section, a shell script, begins with some housekeeping. The fourth line runs the configure script in the software package, then finally a "make." The make utility is commonly used to build software from sources. The

TABLE 4-9

Subdirectories with the /usr/src/redhat Directory Structure

Directory	Purpose
/usr/src/redhat/SOURCES	Contains the original program source code.
/usr/src/redhat/SPECS	Contains spec files, which control the RPM build process.
/usr/src/redhat/BUILD	Source code is unpacked and built here.
/usr/src/redhat/RPMS	Contains the resulting binary RPM.
/usr/src/redhat/SRPMS	Contains the SRPM created by the build process.

TABLE 4-10

Spec File Sections

Section	Description
preamble	Describes what information a user sees when he or she requests information about this package. It also contains a description of the package's function and the version, and information about the sources and patches used. It also may contain an icon to be used if the package is manipulated with a graphical RPM manager.
prep	This is where the real work begins. If work needs to be done to the source code before actually building it, it's described here. At a minimum, this usually means unpacking the source code. The contents of this section are a shell script.
build	Commands to actually compile the spec file and build the sources are in a shell script here.
install	Commands to install the software on a system.
install and uninstall scripts	This section contains scripts that will be run on the end user's system to install or remove the software. RPM can execute a script before the package is installed, after the package is installed, before the package is removed, and after the package is removed.
verify	Although RPM takes care of most verification tasks, a script can be inserted here to take care of extra tasks the package builder may want to do.
clean	A script can be specified here to perform any necessary cleanup tasks.
file list	This is a list of files in the package.

compile time options being passed in $RPM_OPT_FLAGS are defaults, set by RPM.

Building Custom Source and Binary RPMs

There's much more to customizing RPMs. Once you have modified the spec file, you need to tell RPM to build a new RPM and SRPM.

Starting a Build

You build an RPM with the build option of RPM, -b. You will normally modify the -b option with an "a," which means that all steps of the build operation must be performed. The RPM build operation is directed at a spec file. For example, the command

```
# rpm -ba foo-2.2.spec
```

directs RPM to create a binary and source RPM from this spec file.

Building an RPM from a Tar Archive

Now that you understand the basics of building an RPM from an SRPM, it's relatively easy to build an SRPM and RPM from a tar archive.

Obtain the Source Files

You'll need to obtain the source code for the package you want to create. You'll need to locate the FTP or Web site for the software you want, obtain the latest version (or whatever version you want to use), and download it. Once you have a copy, put it in the SOURCES directory.

Create the Spec File

Here's where you get to brew a spec file from scratch. Depending on how complicated your source software is, you may wind up with a pretty complicated spec file. However, for this run, we're going to just cover the basics you'll need to get a spec file running.

THE PREAMBLE You'll need to fire up your favorite text editor and start working on the spec file. Let's start with the preamble section. Here's the preamble (abridged) from fileutils-3.16.spec:

```
Summary: GNU File Utilities
Name: fileutils
Version: 3.16
Release: 10
Copyright: GPL
Group: Utilities/File
Source0: ftp://prep.ai.mit.edu/pub/gnu/fileutils-3.16.tar.gz
```

```
Source1: DIR_COLORS
Patch: fileutils-3.16-mktime.patch
Patch1: fileutils-3.16-glibc21.patch
Buildroot: /var/tmp/fileutils-root
Summary(de): GNU-Datei-Utilities
Summary(fr): Utilitaires fichier de GNU
Summary(tr): GNU dosya iþlemleri yardýmcý yazýlýmlarý
Prereq: /sbin/install-info
%description
These are the GNU file management utilities.  It includes programs
to copy, move, list, etc, files.
The ls program in this package now incorporates color ls!
```

Preamble entries consist of a tag, followed by a colon, followed by information. Some entries are language specific; these are denoted by a two-letter country code in parentheses just before the colon. The order of the lines is unimportant. Table 4-11 lists entries that may be included in the preamble.

THE PREP SECTION The prep section prepares the source files for packaging. Usually the prep section starts out by removing the leftovers from any previous builds, and unarchives the source files. A sample prep section might look like this:

```
%prep
/bin/rm -rf $RPM_BUILD_DIR/foo-2.2
/bin/tar xzf $RPM_SOURCE_DIR/foo-2.2.tar.gz
```

Note that the prep section is nothing more than a shell script. The environment variables RPM_BUILD_DIR and RPM_SOURCE_DIR are preset by RPM. They expand to /usr/src/redhat/BUILD and /usr/src/redhat/SOURCE, respectively. This prep script extracts the contents of foo-2.2.tar.gz into the SOURCE directory. If we needed to do any patching to the sources, it would be done here.

There is, by the way, a predefined macro that will handle both of the steps we coded in the previous example. The %setup macro removes any files left over from a previous build, and then extracts the contents of the source file. Now our prep script becomes

```
%prep
%setup
```

TABLE 4-11

Preamble Entries

Tag	Description
Name	The name of the package.
Version	The version of the software being packaged.
Release	The number of times this software has been packaged. This will become part of the package label and filename.
Buildroot	The directory this package was built in.
Copyright	Contains the software's copyright information.
Group	Which RPM group this software should be packaged in.
Patch	Patches applied to the software.
Source	There are two entries for this tag. The first indicates where the packaged software's source may be found. The second gives the name of the source file in the SOURCES subdirectory.
Summary	A short, one-line description of the software being packaged.
URL	This tag, if present, usually indicates the home page or where documentation for the software can be found.
Distribution	The product line this package was created for. This is normally used by Linux distribution companies such as Red Hat Software to indicate which release this package was part of.
Vendor	The group or organization that distributes the software being packaged.
Packager	The group or organization that packaged this software.
Description	This entry may take up more than one line. It is a detailed description of the packaged software.

THE BUILD SECTION Like the prep section, the build section is also a shell script. This script will handle building binary programs out of the source code. Depending on the software, this step may be very easy, or quite involved. A sample build script might be

```
%build
make clean
```

```
./configure -prefix=/usr -exec-prefix=/
make
```

These commands run "make clean" to ensure any old object and configuration files are removed. Then the software's configure script (with some additional options) is run, which configures the software for the platform you're compiling on. The make command with no arguments is then run to compile the software.

THE INSTALL SECTION Yet another shell script, the install section, allows you to build install targets within the source distribution. For uncomplicated software, this may be as simple as

```
%install
make install
```

THE FILES SECTION This is a list of files that will become part of the package. Any files that you want to distribute in the package must be listed here.

You may specify a %doc directive on a line, which indicates that the file listed on this line is documentation. That file will be placed in the /usr/doc/<package> subdirectory when the end user installs this package on the system. Here's an example of a files section from our fictional package foo-2.2:

```
%files
%doc README
%doc FAQ
/usr/bin/foo
/usr/man/man1/foo.1
```

The preceding example shows that the files README and FAQ will be placed in the /usr/doc/foo-2.2 subdirectory.

Build the RPM and SRPM

At this point, it's just a matter of running

```
# rpm -ba foo-2.2.spec
```

to build your RPM and SRPM. Some other modifiers that are handy to run with the -b option are listed in Table 4-12.

TABLE 4-12

Modifiers

Option	Description
-bp	Execute only the prep section.
-bl	Check the files section to make sure all of the files exist.
-bc	Execute only the build section.
-bi	Execute only the install section.
-bs	Build only the SRPM.
--test	Do not execute any build stages. Useful for testing the syntax of your spec file.

Test Your RPM

It's important that you test your RPM thoroughly before releasing it for general distribution. Install it, uninstall it, run the program through its paces. Make sure that the documentation and man pages were installed correctly, and that configuration files are present and have sane defaults.

Like many Linux tools, RPM has short options that have long option equivalents. For example, the -i option (a "short" option) can also be specified using the --install option (a "long" option). Learn which options have "long" equivalents.

CERTIFICATION OBJECTIVE 4.05

Basic Networking

The network is where the power of Red Hat Linux 6.0 really comes alive; however, getting there may not be trivial. As in all other things Linux, it's a learning experience.

The /etc/sysconfig/… Files Used in Network Setup

We'll start our tour in the /etc/sysconfig directory. This is where Red Hat Linux 6.0 stores and retrieves its networking information. With Linuxconf, you'll almost never have to touch these files, but it's good to know they're there (see Table 4-13).

TABLE 4-13

Files in the /etc/sysconfig Directory

Filename	Description
/etc/sysconfig/network	This file stores your system's host name, IPV4 forwarding information, your NIS domain, your gateway and gateway device, and whether or not your system uses any type of networking. Some of these values may not be present, depending on how your system is configured.
/etc/sysconfig/ network-scripts	This directory, as its name implies, stores the networking scripts necessary for your system to get itself up on the network.
/etc/sysconfig/ network-scripts/ifcfg-lo	The loopback device configuration script. If you're running TCP/IP, you will almost always have a loopback device configured. The loopback isn't a real device but a dummy interface designed to test your TCP/IP stack.
/etc/sysconfig/ network-scripts/ifcfg-*	Each network interface on your machine will, if it is configured, have an associated ifcfg-* script. For example, the first Ethernet card on your system, eth0, will have a corresponding ifcfg-eth0 script. This file contains information about the interface's IP address, netmask, what network it's on, its broadcast address, and whether it should be brought up at boot time. Depending on the type of interface (such as PPP or SLIP), it may contain other information.
/etc/sysconfig/ network-scripts/ifup /etc/sysconfig/ network-scripts/ifdown	These scripts take a network interface as an argument. The ifup script brings the specified interface up; ifdown takes it down.
/etc/sysconfig/network-scripts/network-functions	This script contains functions used by other network scripts to bring network interfaces up and down. This script should never be called directly.
/etc/sysconfig/ network-scripts/chat-*	Chat scripts for PPP and SLIP connections.

TABLE 4-13

Files in the /etc/sysconfig Directory *(continued)*

Filename	Description
/etc/sysconfig/network-scripts/ifup-post	This script is called whenever a network device (SLIP excluded) comes up. This script calls the ifup-routes script for static routes, configures aliases for the given device, sets the host name if it's not already set (and if it can resolve a name to the IP address), and sends a SIGIO to programs that have requested notification of network events.
/etc/sysconfig/network-scripts/ifdhcpc-done	The DHCP daemon, dhcpd, calls this script when DHCP configuration is complete. It then configures /etc/resolv.conf from /etc/dhcpc/resolv.conf.
/etc/sysconfig/network-scripts/ifup-* and /etc/sysconfig/network-scripts/ifdown-*	These scripts bring up or take down, respectively, their assigned protocols. For example, ifup-ipx brings up the IPX protocol.

/etc/sysconfig Files for Clock, Mouse, Static-Routes, Keyboard, and PCMCIA

While we're in /etc/sysconfig, let's take a little detour and discuss some of the other things in here that make your system run (see Table 4-14).

Setting Up a Network Interface

Using Linuxconf, you can modify your system name, and add, remove, and edit network interfaces.

Changing Your System Name with Linuxconf

To change your system name, run Linuxconf. Then open Config | Networking | Client tasks | Basic host information. You will see a display similar to Figure 4-5. The default host name is "localhost.localdomain."

TABLE 4-14

/etc/sysconfig Files for Clock, Mouse, Static-Routes, Keyboard, and PCMCIA

File	Description
/etc/sysconfig/clock	Contains defaults for the system clock. There are currently only two entries: UTC=true|false—Indicates that the clock is or is not set to UTC (Universal Time Code). ARC=true|false—On alpha platforms, indicates that the ARC console's 42-year time offset is in effect.
/etc/sysconfig/mouse	Contains mouse configuration information. Entries are MOUSETYPE=*type*, where *type* is one of microsoft, mouseman, mousesystems, ps/2, msbm, logibm, atibm, logitech, mmseries, and mmhittab. See the Hardware-HOWTO in /usr/doc/HOWTO for information on supported mice. XEMU3=yes|no Indicates whether a three-button mouse should be emulated on two-button mice. If you have a two-button mouse, you'll want to select three-button emulation to run X, which uses the third button extensively. The third button is simulated by pressing the first and second buttons simultaneously.
/etc/sysconfig/static-routes	Contains lines in the form of: *device* net *network* netmask *mask* gw *gateway* These values correspond to arguments in the route(8) command.
/etc/sysconfig/keyboard	Contains a single line, indicating which keyboard map to use: KEYTABLE="/usr/lib/kbd/keytables/us.map"
/etc/sysconfig/pcmcia	Contains PCMCIA configuration information. The most relevant value in here is: PCMCIA=yes|no Indicates whether PCMCIA modules should be loaded on boot. Setting this to "yes" would tell the kernel to load PCMCIA modules automatically at boot time. This setting is typically only needed for PCMCIA-enabled devices such as laptops.

FIGURE 4-5

Changing the hostname in Linuxconf

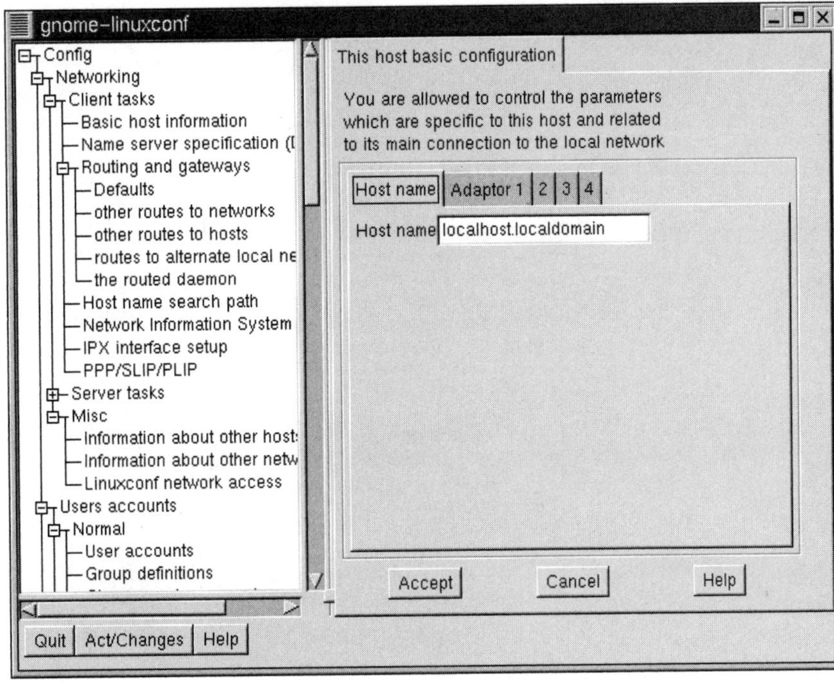

You can replace this with the host name, followed by the domain name your server is in. You may then select the Act/Changes button for your new host name to take effect.

Modifying Network Interfaces with Linuxconf

To modify network interfaces with Linuxconf, open Config | Networking | Client tasks | Basic host information. Then select the Adaptor 1 tab, or the tab corresponding to the interface you wish to modify. You will see a form similar to the one shown in Figure 4-6.

You may enter or modify any of the values in this form. Table 4-15 lists each field and its description.

You may then select the Act/Changes button for your new interface edits to take effect.

FIGURE 4-6

Modifying network interfaces with Linuxconf

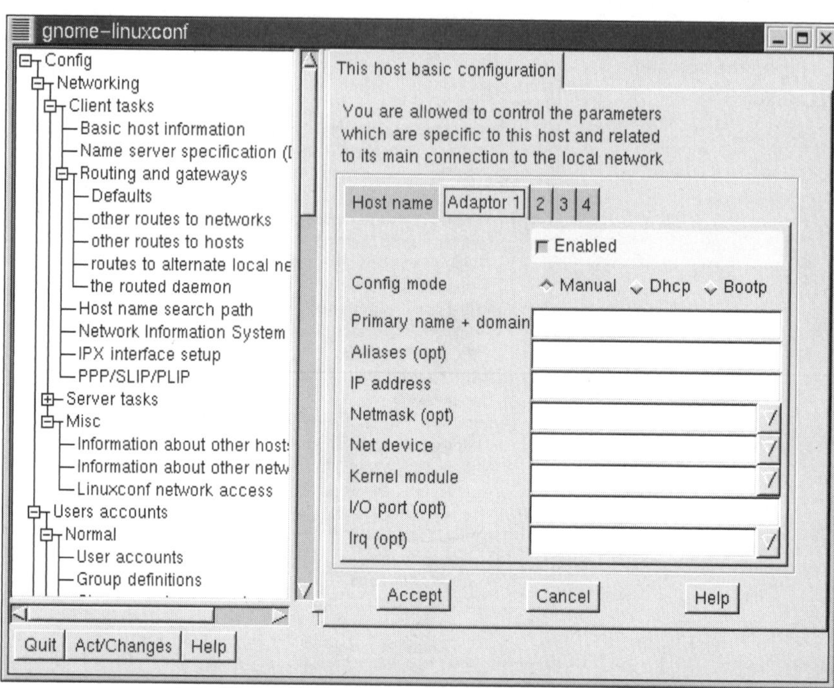

TABLE 4-15

Fields

Field	Description
Primary name + domain	The host name and domain name that will be bound to this interface.
Aliases	Any aliases you wish this interface to be known by.
IP Address	The IP address assigned to this interface.
Netmask	The netmask used by this subnet.
Net device	The device this interface uses.
Kernel module	If the driver for this module isn't loaded statically in the kernel, then the loadable module will need to be identified here.
I/O port	Only necessary if the driver requires that you specify an I/O port.
Irq	Only necessary if the driver requires that you specify an IRQ setting.

ifup/ifdown

Recall that for each network interface present on your system, there is a corresponding ifcfg-* file in /etc/sysconfig/network-scripts. You can bring an interface up, or take it down, using the ifup and ifdown commands. You can also use the device name directly with the ifup and ifdown commands. The following two commands do the same thing:

```
# ifup ifcfg-eth0
# ifup eth0
```

Either one of the preceding commands will bring up the eth0 network interface.

ifconfig

The ifconfig command is used to configure and display network devices. Here is some sample output of an ifconfig command:

```
# ifconfig eth0
eth0      Link encap:Ethernet  HWaddr 08:00:20:74:17:33
          inet addr:207.174.142.141  Bcast:207.174.142.143  Mask:255.255.255.240
          UP BROADCAST RUNNING MULTICAST  MTU:1500  Metric:1
          RX packets:1426914 errors:0 dropped:0 overruns:0
          TX packets:1199517 errors:1 dropped:0 overruns:0
```

The preceding command is querying the first Ethernet device on the system, eth0. With only the device as an argument, ifconfig only displays information about the specified interface. When invoked with no parameters, ifconfig shows all interfaces. Table 4-16 lists what the significant fields in the ifconfig output mean.

As indicated, ifconfig is also used to configure network interfaces. The following command would be used to change the IP address of the eth0 interface:

```
# ifconfig eth0 207.174.142.142
```

The first parameter, eth0, tells us which interface is being configured. The next argument, 207.174.142.142, indicates the new IP address being assigned to this interface. If we want to make sure our change worked, we issue the ifconfig command again, to view its current settings.

TABLE 4-16

Significant Fields in the ifconfig

Field	Description
RX and TX	Indicates how many error-free packets have been received and transmitted, respectively. It also shows how many errors occurred, how many packets were dropped, and how many overruns occurred. An overrun usually occurs when packets come in faster than the kernel can service the interrupt.
Inet addr	The IP address assigned to this interface.
Bcast	The network broadcast address.
Mask	The netmask used by this subnet.

```
# ifconfig eth0
eth0      Link encap:Ethernet  HWaddr 08:00:20:74:17:33
          inet addr:207.174.142.142  Bcast:207.174.142.143  Mask:255.255.255.240
          UP BROADCAST RUNNING MULTICAST  MTU:1500  Metric:1
          RX packets:1426914 errors:0 dropped:0 overruns:0
          TX packets:1199517 errors:1 dropped:0 overruns:0
```

Looking at the output of our command, we successfully changed the IP address on the eth0 interface to 207.174.142.142. There are a number of other parameters used with ifconfig for modifying interface information (see Table 4-17).

netstat -r

The netstat command is used to display a plethora of network connectivity information. The more commonly used option to netstat, -r, is used to display the kernel routing tables. Here's a sample netstat -r output:

```
# netstat -n -r
Kernel routing table
Destination     Gateway         Genmask         Flags Metric Ref Use
127.0.0.1       *               255.255.255.255 UH    1      0
191.72.1.0      *               255.255.255.0   U     1      0
191.72.2.0      191.72.1.1      255.255.255.0   UGN   1      0
```

Did you notice that we used a -n flag? -n tells netstat to display addresses as IP addresses, instead of as host names. This makes it a little easier for us to see what's going on.

TABLE 4-17 Parameters Used with ifconfig for Modifying Interface Information

Parameter	Description
Up	Marks the interface up to the IP stack.
Down	Marks the interface down to the IP stack.
Netmask *mask*	Assigns a subnet mask to the interface. The mask can be entered as a 32-bit hexadecimal number preceded by the string "0x", as a dotted quad of decimal numbers, or as a string of hexadecimal numbers.
Pointopoint	Used to configure PPP links that only involve two hosts.
Broadcast address	While ifconfig allows you to change the broadcast address, you'll almost never have to use this option, except in very old networking environments.
Metric *number*	Allows you to set a metric value for the routing table entry created for the interface. You will almost never need to set this.
Mtu *bytes*	Sets the maximum transmission unit.
Arp	Allows ARP, the Address Resolution Protocol, to detect the physical addresses of hosts on the network. This is on by default.
-arp	Turns ARP off.
Promisc	Puts the interface in "promiscuous" mode. This allows the interface to receive all packets on the network, whether they were destined for this host or not. This is most commonly used for analyzing the network for problems or bottlenecks.
-promisc	Turns off promiscuous mode.

The Destination column shows the different routes we set up for our network to access. The Gateway column indicates gateway addresses. A gateway, as its name implies, is a route a packet must take first to get to its destination. If no gateway is necessary, an asterisk is printed. The Genmask column shows the "generality" of the route. When attempting to determine a suitable route for an IP address, the kernel will go through the routing table and take a bitwise AND of the Genmask and the address, before comparing it to a route target. The Flags column describes the route. The values you may see present are listed in Table 4-18.

TABLE 4-18

The Ref column indicates how many other routes rely on this entry.

Flag	Description
G	The route uses a gateway.
U	The interface to be used is up.
H	Only a single host can be reached via this route.
D	This entry was created by an ICMP redirect message.
M	This entry was modified by an ICMP redirect message.

arp as a Diagnostic Tool

The arp command is used to view or modify the kernel's Address Resolution Protocol (ARP) table. Using arp, you can detect problems such as duplicate addresses on the network, or manually add arp entries when arp queries fail. Here's an example arp command, showing all arp entries known to the kernel:

```
# arp -a
IP address        HW type                 HW address
10.40.6.2         10Mbps Ethernet         00:00:C0:2C:33:CA
10.40.6.3         10Mbps Ethernet         00:00:C0:4A:B3:42
10.40.6.6         10Mbps Ethernet         00:00:C0:0C:A6:A2
```

The IP address column shows the IP addresses of the hosts it knows about. The HW type column shows the hardware type of the host, and the HW address column shows the Ethernet address of the device queried.

You can use the -H option to limit arp's output to the hardware specified. The hardware type can be a X25, ether, or pronet. The default is ether.

A common problem the arp command addresses is when a host on the network is configured with the IP address of a preexisting host on the network. Such cases happen by mistake but may also happen under circumstances that are more nefarious. In any case, you'll want to remove the offending machine's arp entry from your arp table and add the correct arp entry. To remove an arp entry, use the -d option.

```
# arp -d bugsy
```

This removes all arp information for the host bugsy. To add an arp entry, use the -s option.

```
# arp -s bugsy 00:00:c0:cf:a1:33
```

This entry will add the host bugsy to the arp table. Note that an Ethernet, not an IP address, must be specified. The Ethernet address is a physical address associated with the network card.

CERTIFICATION OBJECTIVE 4.06

chkconfig and ntsysv

Red Hat Linux 6.0 provides two utilities that assist the systems administrator in configuring and maintaining the startup and shutdown process. The ntsysv utility provides a screen-oriented interface, while chkconfig provides a command-line interface.

The Boot Process

Understanding how your system boots and shuts down will help you immensely as a Red Hat Systems Administrator. Red Hat Linux 6.0 uses a process called System V init. To understand the process better, let's go through the steps Red Hat Linux 6.0 takes to boot itself up to a usable system.

The init program is called by the kernel when it starts up. The init process in turn runs /etc/rc.d/rc.sysinit. rc.sysinit performs a number of tasks, including configuring the network, setting up the default keymapping, starting up swapping, and setting the host name. The init process then determines which runlevel it should be in by looking at the "initdefault" entry in /etc/inittab. For example, the entry

```
id:5:initdefault:
```

indicates that this system should start up in runlevel 5. After determining which runlevel it should be at, init runs the appropriate startup scripts. System V init scripts are stored in the directory /etc/rc.d. Within this directory are the following subdirectories:

```
init.d
rc0.d
rc1.d
rc2.d
rc3.d
rc4.d
rc5.d
```

If the default runlevel is 5, init will look in /etc/rc.d/rc5.d and run each script it finds there. However, if you run an ls -l command in this directory, you'll find that there are no real files here, only symbolic links to the scripts in /etc/rc.d/init.d.

```
# ls -l
total 0
lrwxrwxrwx   1 root     root          16 Jun 22 15:34 K20rstatd -> ../init.d/rstatd
lrwxrwxrwx   1 root     root          17 Jun 22 15:34 K20rusersd -> ../init.d/rusersd
lrwxrwxrwx   1 root     root          15 Jun 22 15:34 K20rwhod -> ../init.d/rwhod
lrwxrwxrwx   1 root     root          13 Jun 22 15:34 K35smb -> ../init.d/smb
lrwxrwxrwx   1 root     root          15 Jun 22 15:34 K50snmpd -> ../init.d/snmpd
lrwxrwxrwx   1 root     root          16 Jun 22 15:34 K55routed -> ../init.d/routed
lrwxrwxrwx   1 root     root          14 Jun 22 21:40 K92apmd -> ../init.d/apmd
lrwxrwxrwx   1 root     root          17 Jun 22 15:34 S10network -> ../init.d/network
lrwxrwxrwx   1 root     root          17 Jun 22 15:34 S11portmap -> ../init.d/portmap
lrwxrwxrwx   1 root     root          15 Jun 22 15:34 S15netfs -> ../init.d/netfs
lrwxrwxrwx   1 root     root          16 Jun 22 15:34 S20random -> ../init.d/random
lrwxrwxrwx   1 root     root          16 Jun 22 15:34 S30syslog -> ../init.d/syslog
lrwxrwxrwx   1 root     root          13 Jun 22 15:34 S40atd -> ../init.d/atd
lrwxrwxrwx   1 root     root          15 Jun 22 15:34 S40crond -> ../init.d/crond
lrwxrwxrwx   1 root     root          16 Jun 22 15:34 S45pcmcia -> ../init.d/pcmcia
lrwxrwxrwx   1 root     root          14 Jun 22 15:34 S50inet -> ../init.d/inet
lrwxrwxrwx   1 root     root          15 Jun 22 15:34 S55named -> ../init.d/named
lrwxrwxrwx   1 root     root          13 Jun 22 15:34 S60lpd -> ../init.d/lpd
lrwxrwxrwx   1 root     root          13 Jun 22 15:34 S60nfs -> ../init.d/nfs
lrwxrwxrwx   1 root     root          18 Jun 22 15:34 S75keytable -> ../init.d/keytable
lrwxrwxrwx   1 root     root          18 Jun 22 15:34 S80sendmail -> ../init.d/sendmail
```

```
lrwxrwxrwx   1 root     root           13 Jun 22 15:34 S85gpm -> ../init.d/gpm
lrwxrwxrwx   1 root     root           15 Jun 22 15:34 S85httpd -> ../init.d/httpd
lrwxrwxrwx   1 root     root           15 Jun 22 15:34 S85sound -> ../init.d/sound
lrwxrwxrwx   1 root     root           13 Jun 22 11:37 S90xfs -> ../init.d/xfs
lrwxrwxrwx   1 root     root           19 Jun 22 15:34 S99linuxconf -> ../init.d/linuxconf
lrwxrwxrwx   1 root     root           11 Jun 22 11:30 S99local -> ../rc.local
```

What's going on here? System V init knows that scripts starting with an "S" mean to run the script on startup/boot. Scripts that start with "K" are run on kill/shutdown or reboot. By using symbolic links, any changes that need to be done to the real init scripts only need to be done in one place, /etc/rc.d/init.d. In addition, the two numbers after the "S" or "K" indicate the order in which the script should be run. System V init runs the scripts alphanumerically, so the order you see them in an ls is the order in which they will be run.

Startup scripts can usually take one of two arguments, start and stop, which mean exactly what they say. So, on startup, all the scripts in the default runlevel directory will be run with a "start" option. Red Hat Linux 6.0 uses the definitions for System V init runlevels listed in Table 4-19.

It should go without saying that if you set your initdefault to 0, your system will immediately halt when it comes up. Likewise, if you set the initdefault to 6, your machine will exist in a perpetual state of rebooting. Neither of these situations is desirable.

TABLE 4-19

System V init Runlevels

Runlevel	Description
0	Halt
1	Single-user mode
2	Multiuser, without NFS
3	Multiuser mode
4	Unused
5	X11
6	Reboot

Make sure you go through the /etc/rc.d hierarchy and /etc/inittab, and /etc/rc.d/rc.sysinit files, and understand what's happening along the way. This is the key to understanding what's happening during the boot process.

The chkconfig Utility

The chkconfig command gives you a simple way to maintain the /etc/rc.d directory structure. With chkconfig, you can add, remove, and change services, list startup information, and check the state of a particular service. If you want to see which runlevels the Sendmail service are configured to run on, you should run

```
# chkconfig --list sendmail
sendmail 0:off 1:off 2:on 3:on 4:on 5:on 6:off
```

which indicates that the sendmail service is configured to run only on runlevels 2–5. If you want to turn the Sendmail service off for runlevel 4, you run

```
# chkconfig --level 4 sendmail off
```

Now Sendmail is configured to run only on runlevels 2, 3, and 5. To turn it back on, you run the same command, substituting "on" for "off." With chkconfig, you can also add or delete services. Adding a service sets up the appropriate links within the /etc/rc.d/ hierarchy. Deleting a service removes any symbolic links in the /etc/rc.d hierarchy.

The ntsysv Utility

The ntsysv command takes the functionality of chkconfig and wraps it into an easy-to-use screen interface. By default, ntsysv configures the current runlevel. You can specify a different runlevel with the --level flag.

The ntsysv interface is extremely easy to use. Select the service you want to modify using the arrow keys. You then toggle the service on or off using the space bar. Selecting Ok will commit the changes; selecting Cancel will cancel any changes you made (see Figure 4-7).

FIGURE 4-7

ntsysv

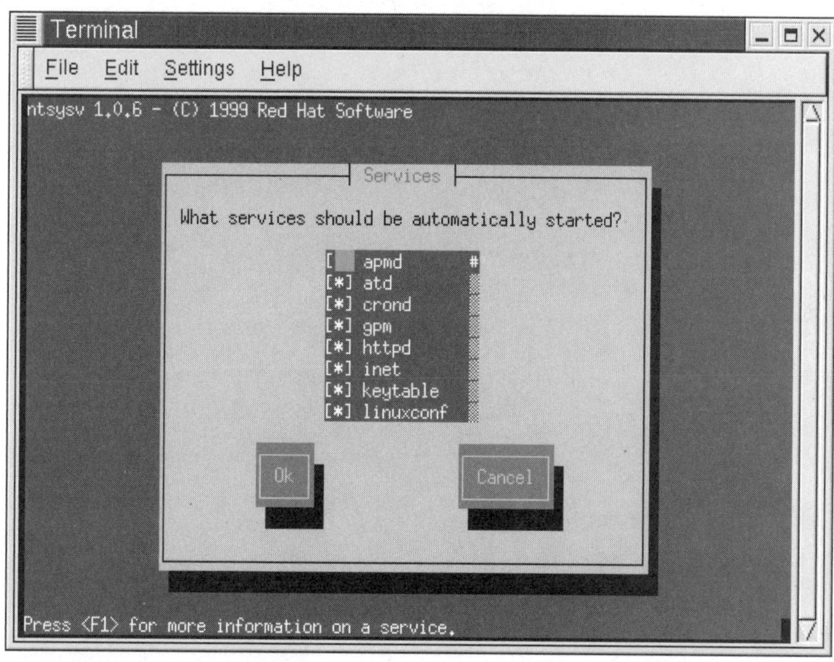

CERTIFICATION OBJECTIVE 4.07

Virtual Consoles

Because Red Hat Linux 6.0 is a multitasking operating system, it allows you to have more than one login session on the system console at a time. It supports this behavior through the virtual console system.

You switch between virtual consoles using ALT-Function-key sequences. For instance, to switch to virtual console 2, hold down the ALT key, and press F2. You can switch between adjacent virtual consoles by pressing ALT-right-arrow or ALT-left-arrow. For example, to move to virtual console 2 while on virtual console 3, press the ALT-left-arrow key (this does not work in X consoles). By default, Red Hat Linux comes with the first six virtual consoles configured. You can enable up to 12 virtual consoles by editing the appropriate /etc/inittab entries. Here are the default /etc/inittab entries for the first six virtual consoles:

```
1:2345:respawn:/sbin/mingetty tty1
2:2345:respawn:/sbin/mingetty tty2
3:2345:respawn:/sbin/mingetty tty3
4:2345:respawn:/sbin/mingetty tty4
5:2345:respawn:/sbin/mingetty tty5
6:2345:respawn:/sbin/mingetty tty6
```

Virtual consoles really bring the multiuser capabilities of Linux to life. You can be viewing a man page on one console, compiling a program in another, and editing a document in yet another virtual console.

CERTIFICATION OBJECTIVE 4.08

kbdconfig, timeconfig, mouseconfig

Three screen-oriented programs included with Red Hat Linux 6.0 make configuring your keyboard, system time, and mouse easier.

kbdconfig

The kbdconfig utility allows you to set the type of keyboard you have. Figure 4-8 shows the kbdconfig screen. You can use your arrow, PGUP, and PGDN keys to traverse the list of keyboards. Highlight the proper keyboard, then press the ENTER key to accept the new setting, or the ESC key to exit without saving. Changes made here are saved to the /etc/sysconfig/keyboard file.

timeconfig

The timeconfig utility allows you to set your time zone. Figure 4-9 shows the timeconfig screen. If your system clock is set to Greenwich Mean Time

FIGURE 4-8

kbdconfig

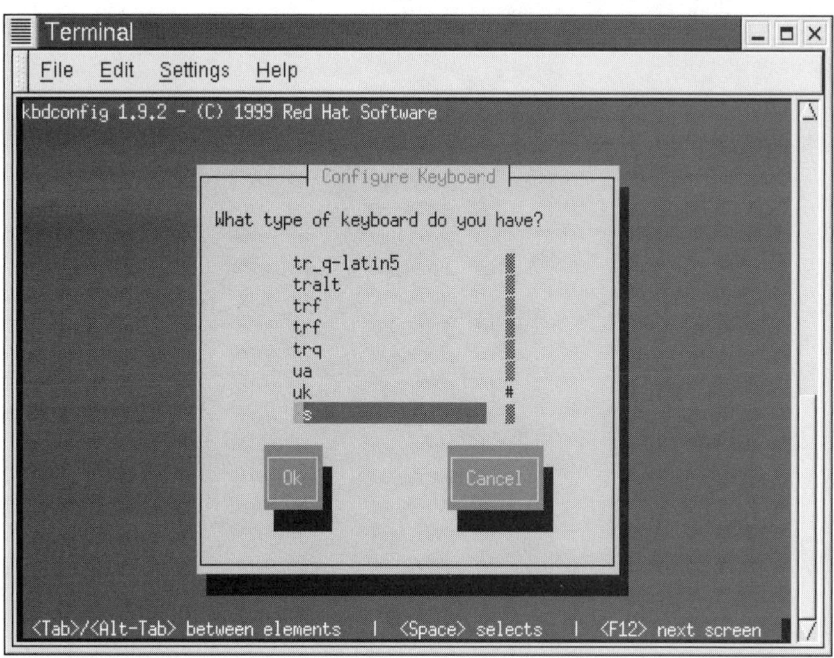

(GMT), select the "Hardware clock set to GMT" entry. You can use your arrow, PGUP, and PGDN keys to traverse the list of time zones. Highlight the proper time zone, then press the ENTER key to accept the new setting, or the ESC key to exit without saving. Changes made here are saved to the /etc/sysconfig/clock file.

mouseconfig

The mouseconfig utility allows you to set your mouse to the correct type. Figure 4-10 shows the mouseconfig screen. You can use your arrow, PGUP, and PGDN keys to traverse the list of mouse types. Highlight the proper mouse type, then press the ENTER key to accept the new setting, or the ESC key to exit without saving. If you are using a two-button mouse, and wish to emulate three

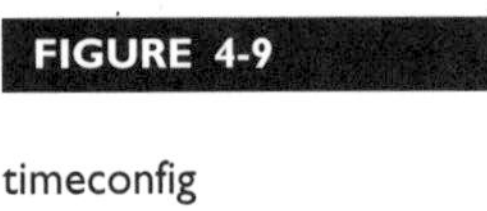

FIGURE 4-9

timeconfig

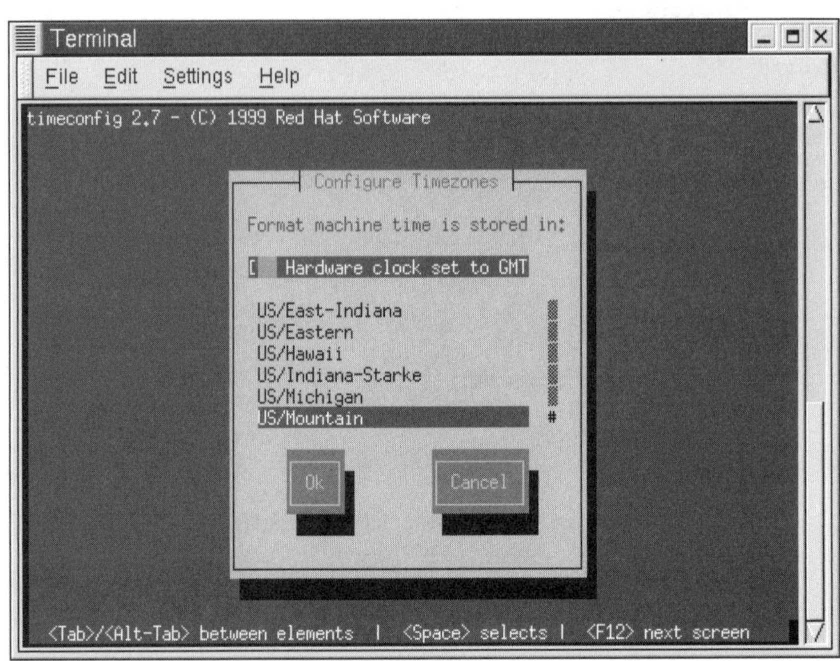

buttons (by clicking both buttons at the same time), select "Emulate 3 Buttons?" Changes made here are saved to the /etc/sysconfig/mouse file.

CERTIFICATION OBJECTIVE 4.09

Mounting Floppy Disks and Removable Media

To read floppy disks and other removable media with Red Hat Linux 6.0, you need to mount it, just as you would any other filesystem. Red Hat has created mount points in the /mnt directory for just this purpose. The subdirectory /mnt/floppy is for mounting floppy disks, and /mnt/cdrom is

FIGURE 4-10

mouseconfig

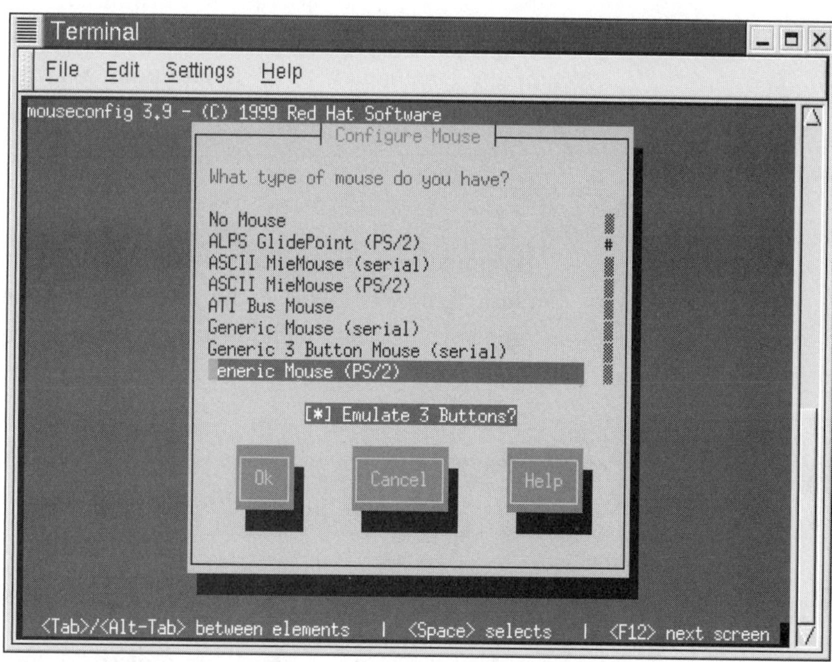

used to mount CD-ROMs. To mount an MS-DOS formatted floppy, you would run

```
# mount -t msdos /dev/fd0 /mnt/floppy
```

Recall that the -t option to the mount command specifies the type of filesystem we're mounting. The device, /dev/fd0, is the first floppy disk device. If you have a second floppy disk, the second device would be /dev/fd1. The final argument tells mount which mount point to use. After you have mounted the floppy disk, any reads or writes you perform in /mnt/floppy happen on the floppy disk. The device for your CD-ROM is normally /dev/cdrom. To mount an IS09660 CD-ROM, run

```
# mount -t iso9660 /dev/cdrom /mnt/cdrom
```

Now you can read the contents of /mnt/cdrom as if it were a normal filesystem on your system. To unmount a floppy or CD-ROM, use the 'umount' command with the mount point as an argument. The following commands unmount both our floppy and CD-ROM:

```
# umount /mnt/floppy
# umount /mnt/cdrom
```

It is important that you unmount floppy disks before removing them. Because of the way UNIX caches information before writing to disk, there is a good chance that you'll lose data by simply removing a floppy without unmounting it.

CERTIFICATION OBJECTIVE 4.10

Sound Cards, the sndconfig Utility

Red Hat Linux 6.0 provides a screen-oriented interface to make installing your sound card easier by setting up the necessary configuration files to run a sound card. If Plug-n-play (PnP) support is compiled in, sndconfig will probe for PnP sound cards. Sometimes, however, this probe causes the machine to lock up, so you can disable probing by running sndconfig with the --noprobe option.

If no cards are detected, or the --noprobe option was given, you'll be presented with a list of cards to choose from, shown in Figure 4-11. From there, you'll need to choose the I/O port, IRQ, and DMA settings for the sound card. These can be obtained by consulting your sound card documentation.

One other option, --noautoconfig, can be used when probing for PnP cards. Normally, sndconfig will determine the correct values to run the sound card. With --noautoconfig, you can set the settings yourself.

FIGURE 4-11

sndconfig

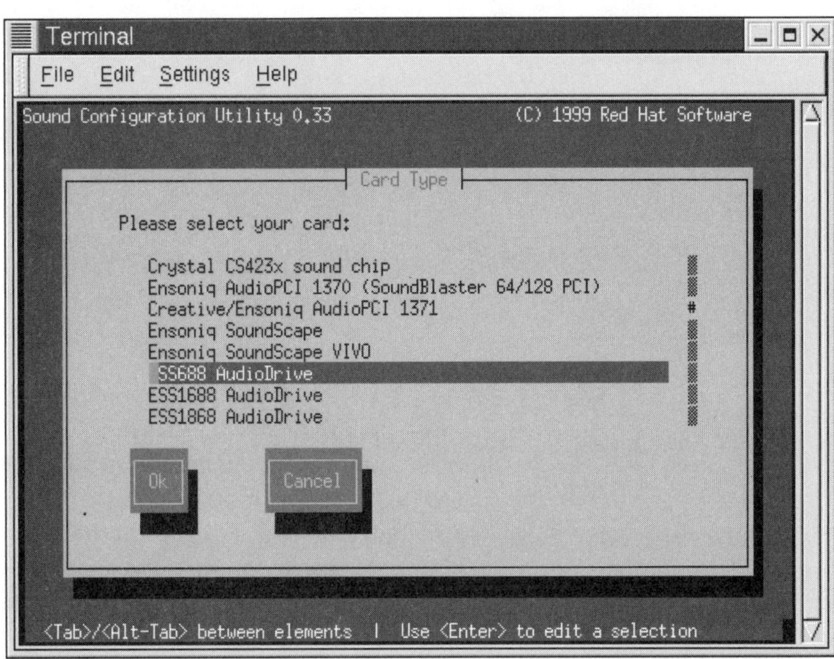

CERTIFICATION SUMMARY

This chapter covered basic configuration and administration of a Red Hat Linux 6.0 system. We learned the steps necessary to create a basic user, how to populate a user's home directory with the templates in /etc/skel, and found out where window manager configuration files are located. We also covered the different types of filesystems Linux uses, discussed how to mount them, and what mount options to use with them.

In "Using RPM," we learned the steps necessary to validate a package signature, how to add, remove, and upgrade packages, and how to add updates. We also talked about verifying packages, and how to see what package a file belongs to. We finished the topic with a discussion on installing SRPMs, and building RPMs from SRPMs and tar archives.

In "Basic Networking" we covered the configuration files in the /etc/sysconfig hierarchy, including files for the clock, mouse, static routes, keyboard, network, and pcmcia. We also discussed the ifup, ifdown, ifconfig, netstat, and arp commands.

We concluded the chapter by talking about virtual consoles, the kbdconfig, timeconfig, and mouseconfig screen utilities, how to mount floppy disks and removable media, and the sndconfig utility.

TWO-MINUTE DRILL

- After installation, your system has only a single login account, the root account. For most installations, you'll want to create more accounts. Even if you're going to be the only user on the system, it's a good idea to create a single, nonprivileged account to do your day-to-day work, and use the root account only for administering the system. Accounts are added to Red Hat Linux 6.0 systems using the *Linuxconf* utility.
- Linuxconf can be run in graphical or character mode.
- Linuxconf will let you get away with using invalid characters in usernames, such as %, &, *, and !. However, many Linux programs will fail to function with usernames containing these characters.
- If your installation doesn't require each user having their own unique group ID (GID), assign your users to the group 'users.' There's rarely a need for each user to have an individual GID, and having most users assigned to the 'users' group makes system administration easier.
- Several words strung together with numbers or symbols make good passwords, such as 'toy+jobs' or 'rule%key.' These are easy to remember, yet difficult to guess.

- ❑ Discourage the use of shared accounts, where several people use a single account. Shared accounts are almost always unnecessary, and are easily compromised.
- ❑ If you'll be using Network File System (NFS), make sure users maintain the same UID across systems.
- ❑ Each user on your Red Hat Linux 6.0 system has an *environment* when logged on to the system.
- ❑ The home directory is the initial directory in which users are placed when they first log on to a Red Hat Linux 6.0 system.
- ❑ Window manager configuration files are stored in /etc/X11/<windowmanager>, where <windowmanager> is the name of the window manager.
- ❑ If you have the kernel source RPMs loaded on your system, you can see which filesystems any version or distribution of Linux currently supports. Look at the file /usr/src/linux/fs/filesystems.c.
- ❑ The RPM database tracks where each file in a package is located, its version, and much more.
- ❑ The Install mode, as its name suggests, is used to install RPM packages on your system.
- ❑ The Upgrade mode will replace the old version of the package with the new one.
- ❑ The rpm -e command removes a package from your system.
- ❑ Verifying an installed package compares information about that package with information from the RPM database on your system, or the original package.
- ❑ Using RPM's query mode, you can determine which packages are installed on your system, or what file belongs to a particular package.
- ❑ Source RPMs are, as the name indicates, the source codes used to build architecture-specific packages.

- The spec file is stored in /usr/src/redhat/SPECS/<packagename>.spec. It controls the way a package is built, and what actions are performed when it is installed or removed from a system.
- Run "# rpm -ba foo-2.2.spec" to build your RPM and SRPM.
- Like many Linux tools, RPM has short options that have long option equivalents. For example, the -i option (a "short" option) can also be specified using the --install option (a "long" option). Learn which options have "long" equivalents.
- To change your system name, run Linuxconf.
- The ifconfig command is used to configure and display network devices.
- The netstat command is used to display a plethora of network connectivity information.
- The arp command is used to view or modify the kernel's Address Resolution Protocol (ARP) table.
- The ntsysv utility provides a screen-oriented interface, while chkconfig provides a command-line interface.
- Make sure you go through the /etc/rc.d hierarchy and /etc/inittab, and /etc/rc.d/rc.sysinit files, and understand what's happening along the way. This is the key to understanding what's happening during the boot process.
- The chkconfig command gives you a simple way to maintain the /etc/rc.d directory structure.
- The ntsysv command takes the functionality of chkconfig and wraps it into an easy-to-use screen interface. By default, ntsysv configures the current runlevel.
- Because Red Hat Linux 6.0 is a multitasking operating system, it allows you to have more than one login session on the system console at a time.
- The timeconfig utility allows you to set your time zone.

- The mouseconfig utility allows you to set your mouse to the correct type.
- To read floppy disks and other removable media with Red Hat Linux 6.0, you need to mount it, just as you would any other filesystem. Red Hat has created mount points in the /mnt directory for just this purpose.
- Red Hat Linux 6.0 provides a screen-oriented interface to make installing your sound card easier by setting up the necessary configuration files to run a sound card.

SELF TEST

The following Self Test questions will help you measure your understanding of the material presented in this chapter. Read all the choices carefully, as there may be more than one correct answer. Choose all correct answers for each question.

1. When adding a user using Linuxconf, what field is required to be filled in?
   A. Full name
   B. Login name
   C. Command interpreter
   D. Home directory
2. When deleting a user account using Linuxconf, if "Archive the account's data" is selected, where is the deleted user's data archived?
   A. /home/oldaccounts
   B. /root/oldaccounts
   C. /home/oldusers
   D. /root/oldusers
3. Window manager configuration files for the fvwm2 window manager are stored in which directory?
   A. /usr/lib/X11/fvwm2
   B. /etc/X11/wmconfig/fvwm2
   C. /etc/fvwm2/config
   D. /etc/X11/fvwm2
4. To change the mount options for a local filesystem, you would edit which file?
   A. /etc/filesystems
   B. /etc/fstab
   C. /etc/group
   D. /etc/mnttab
5. Which option would you mount a filesystem with, such that binaries cannot be executed on it?
   A. nouser
   B. nosuid
   C. noauto
   D. noexec
6. Which of the following commands correctly installs the package "penguin-3.26.i386.rpm"?
   A. rpm -I penguin-3.26.i386.rpm
   B. rpm -i penguin
   C. rpm -i penguin-3.26.i386.rpm
   D. rpm --install penguin.rpm
7. Checking the Red Hat Corporation's Errata Web page, you find a package listed that is currently on your system. A good strategy to update your system would be:
   A. Check to see the ramifications of upgrading the affected package.
   B. Watch for warnings when updating the package for config file replacements.
   C. Test the new package to ensure it's been configured correctly.
   D. All of the above.

8. Source RPMs are by default installed in which directory?

   A. /usr/lib/rpm

   B. /usr/src/rpm

   C. /usr/src/redhat

   D. /usr/src/redhat/rpm

9. What subdirectories are in the /usr/src/redhat directory?

   A. SOURCES, SPECS, BUILD, RPMS, SRPMS

   B. SOURCES, SPECS, LIBS, RPMS, DESC

   C. SOURCES, SPECS, BINS, RPMS, DESC

   D. SOURCES, SPECS, ETC, RPMS, SRPMS

10. Which section of an RPM spec file is used to compile the source code?

    A. clean

    B. prep

    C. build

    D. install

11. The prep section of an RPM spec file serves what purpose?

    A. Describes what information users see when they request information about this package.

    B. Contains commands to compile and build the binaries from source code.

    C. Takes care of extra tasks to be performed when a verify command is issued.

    D. Unpacks the source code and configures it for building.

12. When building an RPM from a tar archive, the tar file should be placed in what directory?

    A. /usr/src/redhat

    B. /usr/src/redhat/SOURCES

    C. /usr/src/redhat/TAR

    D. /usr/src/redhat/SRPMS

13. Issuing the command rpm -bc foo-2.2.spec causes what to happen?

    A. A binary and source RPM is created based on the spec file.

    B. Only the SRPM is built.

    C. Only the install section of the spec file is executed.

    D. Only the build section of the spec file is executed.

14. The /etc/sysconfig/network file contains information about:

    A. Your system's host name and NIS domain.

    B. The devices used for your network connections.

    C. Chat scripts for PPP and SLIP connections.

    D. The status of the network.

15. What command is used to configure and display network devices?

    A. netstat
    B. arp
    C. ifconfig
    D. ifup

16. The netstat -r command is used to:

    A. Display kernel routing tables.
    B. Display gateway metrics.
    C. Configure kernel routing tables.
    D. Configure gateway metrics.

17. The command arp -d rhino causes the following to happen:

    A. All ARP tables are removed on the host rhino.
    B. All ARP information for the host rhino is removed.
    C. All ARP tables on the host rhino are displayed.
    D. All ARP information pertaining to the host rhino is displayed.

18. Upon boot, the kernel invokes init, which in turn runs

    A. /etc/rc.d/init.d
    B. /etc/inittab
    C. /etc/rc.d/initdefault
    D. /etc/rc.d/rc.sysinit

19. If you want to see what runlevels crond is configured to start in, you issue which command?

    A. chkconfig -list -crond
    B. chkconfig -l crond
    C. chkconfig --list crond
    D. chkconfig crond

20. To switch from the current virtual console to virtual console 4, you press:

    A. ALT-4
    B. ALT-F4
    C. CTL-4
    D. CTL-F4

5

Advanced Installation

CERTIFICATION OBJECTIVES

5.01 Dual boots: Linux and Windows NT

5.02 Raid Configuration

5.03 Using Kickstart to Automate Installation

5.04 Hardware Conflicts and Plug and Play

5.05 PCMCIA

5.06 Advanced Power Management (APM) BIOS

5.07 Understanding /etc/inittab

5.08 System Start-up Script /etc/rc.d/rc.sysinit

5.09 Understanding Kernel Modules

5.10 The /lib/ modules/.../Directory Structure

In this chapter you will learn how to install and troubleshoot Linux in advanced scenarios. The installation topics cover booting multiple operating systems, troubleshooting and fixing hardware conflicts, and a firm understanding for the boot scripts that are used. You will learn how to set up a Redundant Array of Inexpensive Disks (RAID), and master the intricate details of the rc.sysinit startup script and modules.

CERTIFICATION OBJECTIVE 5.01

Dual Boots: Linux and Windows NT

A very common setup between Windows NT and Linux is dual booting. There are several different ways to accomplish dual booting. The first example covers the setup with NT installed first and Linux installed second. The example uses NT's loader to load both Linux and NT's loader installs to the Master Boot Record (MBR), and relies on three major files: ntdetect.com, ntldr and boot.ini. All three of these files are hidden system files in the root directory of your boot drive. The only file that really concerns us is the boot.ini file. Here is an example of a boot.ini file for an NT workstation install:

```
 [boot loader]
timeout=30
default=multi(0)disk(0)rdisk(2)partition(1)\WINNT
[operating systems]
multi(0)disk(0)rdisk(2)partition(1)\WINNT="Windows NT Workstation
Version 4.00"
multi(0)disk(0)rdisk(2)partition(1)\WINNT="Windows NT Workstation
Version 4.00 [VGA mode]? /basevideo /sos
C:\="Microsoft Windows 98"
```

This example is a simple boot.ini on a system that has NT installed on the second hard drive and Windows 98 installed on the first. The timeout=## line shows how long the loader will wait for you to choose an OS before it boots the default OS. The next line is the default OS. Here it is pointing to NT. If you wanted it to boot Windows 98 you could change the default OS to: default=C:\.

We can see from this example that NT is capable of loading other operating systems, but note that it handles non-NT systems differently. It is not inherently obvious from this example how to load the second OS. There is a copy of the boot sector of the other OS in the C: drive. As far as NT is concerned, the C: drive is the first drive (the boot drive). In the root of the C: drive there is a file called bootsect.dos. This file contains the original bootsector of an alternative OS. This file is created for you if MS-DOS or windows is installed before you install NT.

All we need to do is copy the Linux bootsector to the C: drive under a new name (ex: bootsect.ln1) and edit the boot.ini file. The following illustration shows a graphical display of our physical disk layout.

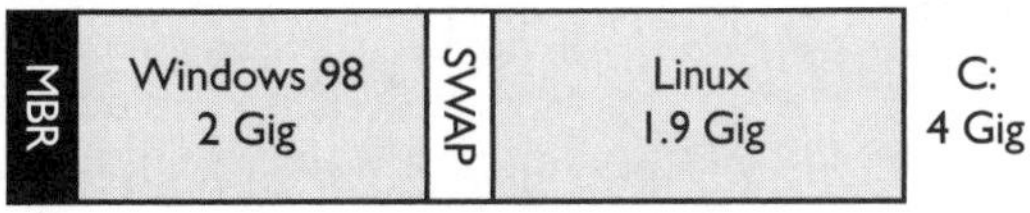

MBR	Windows 98 2 Gig	SWAP	Linux 1.9 Gig	C: 4 Gig

If there isn't any space left on your disk and you have DOS, Windows 95 or Windows 98 then you can shrink the partition by hand. First you must defrag the drive. This will force all of your data to the beginning of the drive. Then use the Linux boot disk to partition your disk. Linux has a non-destructive fdisk so you can make the old partition smaller than it originally was. Be careful not to make it smaller than the space you are using on your drive. For example: If you defrag a 2 Gig drive and have 1 Gig of space that is currently used, then you cannot shrink the partition less than 1 Gig. If you are using NT, or some other operating system that has a special filesystem, then it is best to use a third party utility that can repartition the disk.

Now we will place our Linux install at the end of drive C. First we will make a 32 Meg Linux Swap partition and then fill the rest of the drive with Linux. After our Linux installation we will do the rest of the work from within Linux. Linux will map out the layout as follows:

```
/dev/hda         (C:Drive )
/dev/hda1        (2 Gig VFAT)
/dev/hda2              (32 Meg Linux Swap)
/dev/hda3              (1.968 Gig Linux Native)
```

```
/dev/hdb            (D:Drive)
/dev/hdb1                 (4 Gig NTFS)
```

Here is a graphical look at the first disk.

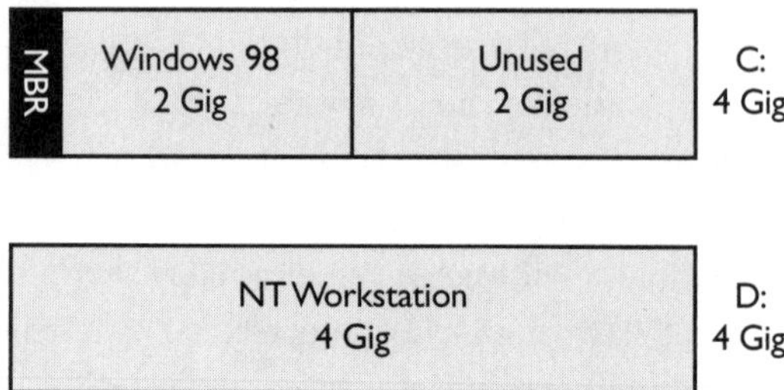

Now we need to edit the /etc/lilo.conf file to setup our bootsector. There are many ways to do this so make sure you have read Chapter 2 as well as studied the man pages for both lilo(8) and lilo.conf(5). There are also several different ways of placing your bootsector in the root of the boot drive. The quickest way is to install lilo to the SuperBlock of the Linux Native partition (hda3). This is the first sector of the partition and is used to boot when the partition is marked as active. Here is an example of the lilo.conf file:

```
boot=/dev/hda3
image=/boot/vmlinuz-2.2.5-15
         label=linux
         root=/dev/hda3
         read-only
```

This is a very simplified lilo.conf file but it should be sufficient to create a basic bootsector. You should not install LILO to the MBR on NT/Linux systems because NT likes its loader there and you would overwrite the loader if you changed boot to point to /dev/hda. To install this bootsector, just type **lilo**.

Now we need to copy the bootsector from /dev/hda3. Issue the following command from Linux:

```
dd if=/dev/hda3 of=/bootsect.ln1 bs=512 count=1
```

This command will dump the first 512 bytes from the beginning of /dev/hda3 to the file /bootsect.ln1. You can call the output file anything you like but it must match what we add to the boot.ini file.

Next we can copy the bootsect.ln1 to the C: drive. This can be accomplished simply by copying the file to a disk, rebooting and then copying the file over to the C: drive. With our example everything can be accomplished from within Linux. First mount /dev/hda1 as VFAT (if the install didn't do it for you). You may have to load the VFAT module first. For our example we will create a directory to mount our 98 partition.

```
mkdir /win98
modprobe vfat
mount -t vfat /dev/hda1 /win98
```

You could use the older msdos filesystem if you wanted to but VFAT is preferable. Next copy /bootsect.ln1 to the mounted directory cp bootsect.ln1 /win98 and simply edit the boot.ini file on the mounted filesystem. Add the following line to the bottom of the file:

```
C:\bootsect.ln1="Linux 2.2.5"
```

Now once you reboot, Linux 2.2.5 should be the last option. Simply select it and Linux should load. You can also place development kernels under different names in the root directory, like bootsect.ln2. This is very useful for testing out new kernels. You should keep your repair disk that you made during setup on hand in case you mess up the lilo.conf file or the boot.ini file.

If you are having problems you should try to make a LILO boot disk. Just modify the /etc/lilo.conf file's boot option to read: boot=/dev/fd0. Run LILO, reboot and test the disk. You should be able to boot with it. Once you have a working LILO boot disk you can simply copy the bootsector from the disk instead of the hard drive. The following command will copy the bootsector from your floppy:

```
dev/fd0 of=/bootsect.ln1 bs=512 count=1
```

If you are still not booting you should refer to the LILO man pages and check for updates to the LILO-HOWTO file on the internet.

Lilo Error Messages

There are two places where you may see error messages when using LILO. One is when you type **lilo** and the other when you try to boot with LILO. Errors you receive after running the lilo command are fairly self-explanatory but the LILO boot error codes are very cryptic. The following chart should help you figure out what your problem is with the boot process.

- **(nothing)** No part of LILO loaded.
- **L <error>** LILO started but there is either a media failure or a disk geometry mismatch. The <error> is a two-digit error code.
  - **0x00** Internal error. Usually corrupt LILO install.
  - **0x02** Address mark not found. Media problem.
  - **0x04** Sector not found. Usually a disk geometry mismatch.
  - **0x07** Invalid Initialization. BIOS failed, used BIOS overides for LILO.
  - **0x0C** Invalid media. Media error.
  - **0x10** CRC error. Media error, try re-running the map installer.
  - **0x20** Controller error.
  - **0x40** Seek failure. May be a media problem.
  - **0x80** Disk timeout. Media is bad or the disk isn't spinning.
  - **0xBB** BIOS error. First reboot; if problem persists, remove the COMPACT option.
- **LI** The second part of LILO loaded but could not execute. This is usually caused by a disk geometry mismatch. This can also mean that the /boot/boot.b file was moved and you did not run the map installer.
- **LIL** The second part of LILO loaded but the third did not. Again, this is typically caused by a media failure or a disk geometry mismatch.

- **LIL?** The second stage of LILO loaded but at an incorrect address. This is usually caused by a subtle geometry mismatch or by moving the /boot/boot.b file without running the map installer.
- **LILO** LILO loaded successfully.

You may also run into a problem if you have a SCSI and an IDE hard drive. LILO will not know which drive to attempt to boot with. If the SCSI disk is normally the drive your BIOS likes to boot from then consider it the first disk. You need to override the BIOS options with the following lilo.conf bios options:

- **Bios = 0x80** For the first disk
- **Bios = 0x81** For the second disk

Choose the disk that the Linux root partition is installed on.

For disk geometry errors try to use the *linear* option or specify the heads, cyliders and sectors within the lilo.conf.

CERTIFICATION OBJECTIVE 5.02

Raid Configuration

Linux RAID is still going through many changes. There are mainly two different types of RAID setups, software based and hardware based. Hardware based RAID systems are still in development with Linux. SCSI host based adapters from DPT are the only controllers with some Linux documentation. For more information on hardware and DPT based RAID you should refer to the DPT-Hardware-RAID-HOWTO document. The software based RAID is what we will focus on in this text although some of the principles apply to hardware as well.

This text assumes you already have some knowledge of the differences in RAID levels. Table 5-1 gives a quick overview.

RAID 0 and 1 require two or more drives, while RAID 5 requires three or more drives.

RAID levels 2, 3, and 4 are not used much any more and have mostly been made obsolete by RAID 5. If you have a spare disk that is NOT part of the RAID array, then when one disk fails it is marked bad and the data is immediately reconstructed on the first spare disk it can find, hopefully resulting in no down time. It should be noted that RAID 1 can also support spare disks.

We will demonstrate both RAID 1 and 5. Here is what our server looks like:

```
Drive 1:     Currently   Drive 2     Drive 3     Drive 4
hda1         /           hdb1        hdc1        hdd1 not used
hda2         swap        hdb2        hdc2        hdd2 not used
hda3         /home       hdb3        hdc3        hdd3
hda4         /var        hdb4        hdc4        hdd4
```

Assume that the three other drives are of the same relative size as Drive 1, have the same partition sizes and schemes, but are not currently using the third and fourth partitions for any file systems.

TABLE 5-1 RAID Level Quick Overview

RAID Level	Description
RAID Level 0: Striping	Any 2.x.x kernel will support this level of RAID. It is used primarily for increased speed and access to the disk but has no fault tolerance.
RAID Level 1: Mirroring	This will keep a complete duplicate of one partition on another. Provides good single disk fault tolerance, has the best *read* performance, requires two or more disks.
RAID Level 5: Mirror with parity striping	These levels will keep parity information about the partitions as well. The RAID unit can reconstruct a bad partition with the parity information. This method allows for good fault tolerance with the best *write* performance. This setup requires three or more drives.

Setting Up RAID1

In the first example below, you want to mirror (RAID 1) both the /home and the /var partitions to identical partitions on Drive 2 and Drive 3 and set the Drive 4 partition equivalents as the spare.

First, make a backup of any current file systems that are on the first hard disk, hda3 and hda4 partitions. You must unmount these file systems before continuing. You will restore these file systems after the RAID disks have been created, configured together, formatted, and remounted as these directories.

NOTE: you either must have these partitions ready or will need to create identically sized partitions on Drives 2 and 3.

In this example, these partitions are already created and ready to go. You must also mark these specific partitions on all drives as type: 0xFB, using fdisk, for autodetection of the RAID settings. You cannot change their type if they are mounted.

In the partition tables of these disks, we will have /dev/hda3, /dev/hda4, /dev/hdb3, /dev/hdb4, /dev/hdc3, /devhdc4 all with partition IDs of type 0xFB.

Configuration File — /etc/raidtab

You will now need to edit the /etc/raidtab to create the two multiple drive, md, devices for the two mirror sets. Within /etc/raidtab, you use raiddev to create these devices and then assign all the partitions in a sequenced order as follows:

```
raiddev /dev/md0
raid-level 1
nr-raid-disks 3
nr-spare-disks 1
persistent-superblock 1
chunk-size 4
device /dev/hda3
raid-disk 0
device /dev/hdb3
raid-disk 1
device /dev/hdc3
raid-disk 2
device /dev/hdd3
spare-disk 0
raiddev /dev/md1
```

```
raid-level 1
nr-raid-disks 3
nr-spare-disks 1
persistent-superblock 1
chunk-size 4
device /dev/hda4
raid-disk 0
device /dev/hdb4
raid-disk 1
device /dev/hdc4
raid-disk 2
device /dev/hdd4
spare-disk 0
```

Table 5-2 shows what some of the commands are and a brief description of what they do.

exam Watch

Take special note that raid-disks and spare-disks start counting at 0. Nr-raid-disks and nr-spare-disks are the correct number of drives. Example: If nr-raid-disks = 3, then the last raid-disk will be 2.

TABLE 5-2

Raid Commands

Command	Description
nr-raid-disks	Number of RAID disks to use
nr-spare-disks	Number of spare disks to use
persistent-superblock	Needed for autodetection
chunk-size	Amount of data to read/write
parity-algorithm	How RAID 5 should use parity

Now we have to initialize the md0 and md1 devices. To do this run:

```
mkraid /dev/md0; mkraid /dev/md1
```

The /proc/mdstat file will show you the status on your RAID configurations. You can now mount the device, format it and continue with your project.

To simplify the RAID 5 we are going to set up a raid on the /var partition to preserve mail, etc. The /etc/raidtab looks as follows:

```
raiddev /dev/md0
raid-level 5
nr-raid-disks 3
nr-spare-disks 1
persistent-superblock 1
chunksize 32
parity-algorithm right-symmetric
device /dev/hda4
raid-disk 0
device /dev/hdb4
raid-disk 1
device /dev/hdc4
raid-disk 2
device /dev/hdd4
spare-disk 0
```

Again, run **mkraid /dev/md0** to initialize the RAID 5. Before you run mke2fs to format the device you should use the special mke2fs stripe option. For instance if you have a chunk-size of 32 KB then write 32 KB consecutively. If you format using 4K block sizes then use 8 blocks per chunk. If you specify this when you format the RAID 5 device you will see a considerable increase in performance. For our example type:

```
mke2fs -b 4096 -R stride=8 /dev/md0
```

For autodetection to work properly you need to have the partitions set to type 0xFB as described earlier. You also must have autodetection turned on in the kernel, and you will need to use the persistent-superblock option. If all is well, when the kernel boots it will automatically detect RAID and fix any errors from crashes during bootup.

Having a RAID level root device is a bit trickier. It may be in your best interest to manually copy the contents of your root partition to other drives. After doing so you should use LILO to write the kernel to the root devices of those drives as well. This will allow for a static copy of your root device in case of failures. To do a true root RAID is possible but is beyond the scope of this text. I suggest you read the Root-RAID-HOWTO documentation for a detailed overview on how to accomplish this.

CERTIFICATION OBJECTIVE 5.03

Using Kickstart to Automate Installation

Kickstart is Red Hat's solution for an automated installation of Red Hat. All of the questions that are asked during set up can be automatically selected with one file. You can easily set up nearly identical systems very quickly. Kickstart files are very useful for quick deployment and distribution of Linux systems.

exam Watch

Kickstart installations can only be performed from a CD-ROM or NFS server. You cannot use FTP, HTTP or SMB to do your install.

You will need to copy and modify the kickstart sample file that is on the CD. It is located under the mnt/cdrom/doc/ directory as sample.ks. Place this file where the installation can read it. This is usually a boot disk or on a DHCP/BOOTP server. If you plan to put the file on the boot disk just mount the disk as an MS-DOS disk and copy it over. If you want to put it on a DHCP/BOOTP server you must specify the kickstart file (usually done with the filename: option). You can also specify a directory for kickstart. In this case the setup program will look in the directory for <client_ip>-kickstart (ex: 192.168.17.18-kickstart). By default it will use the DHCP/BOOTP server as the NFS server for the install but you may specify another server if you like. To do this, use the next-server option.

No matter where you choose to put the kickstart file you MUST boot with a floppy. You will use lilo's boot options to fire off the kickstart file. To boot, and do the install from a disk, type:

```
boot: linux ks=floppy
```

To boot from the network type:

```
boot: linux ks
```

Most of the options in the sample kickstart file are self-explanatory. Every option is in the sample file and is well commented. Here are some ground rules and guidelines to use when setting up a kickstart file:

- Do *not* change the order of the options.
- You do not need to use all the options.
- If you leave out a required option the user will be prompted for the answer.
- For Upgrades you *must* have the following options defined:

  1 language
  2 installation method
  3 device specification
  4 keyboard setup
  5 the upgrade keyword
  6 LILO configuration

There are a couple of key options that need further explanation.

Most options are obvious but static needs special attention. Here is an example of a static network configuration:

```
network --bootproto static --ip 172.16.16.5 --netmask 255.255.255.0
-gateway 172.16.15.254 --nameserver 172.16.16.1
```

Please note that all options *must* be on *one* line.

If there are SCSI, ethernet, or non-ATAPI cdrom devices on the client don't forget to specify them. For example:

```
device scsi aha154x
```

If you have modules that need special irq and io ports set, then you can also specify those. For example:

```
device ethernet 3c509 --opts "io=0x330, irq=7"
```

You can also specify other options such as io and irq information on this line. Add the --continue option if you have more than one device, such as two different SCSI adapters or ethernet cards.

To add Linux partitions, use the part command with the following syntax:

```
part <mount dir> --size <size> [--grow] [--maxsize <size>]
```

The <size> is in Megabytes. You can use the --grow option to allow the partition to expand. This will not expand on the fly but rather, when all fixed partitions are added, it will use the rest of the space. If you specify multiple partitions with the --grow option their space will be divided evenly. You can also specify a --maxsize which will allow the partition only to grow to the size specified in Megabytes.

Another important option is: when setting the root password, consider setting it up in your kickstart file encrypted instead of cleartext. To use an encrypted root password use the following options:

```
rootpw --iscrypted <Your_encrypted_password>
```

You will need to paste a copy of your encrypted password string from either /etc/shadow or /etc/passwd into this file for this to work.

You should review the sample.ks file to see all the different options and familiarize yourself with the setup before taking the test. Here is a small sample kickstart file. We will use this kickstart file to set up similar PCs with only Linux and wipe out anything that was previously installed.

```
# Select your language
lang en
#We will get our IP from a DHCP server
network --bootproto dhcp
# It will be a CD-ROM based install
cdrom
# We need to clear out the MBR just to be safe
zerombr yes
# Also wipe out all of the partitions
clearpart --all
# We want a minimum of 400 Meg root partition but it can grow to be
# the full size of the disk minus the 32 Megs used for swap space.
part / --size 400 --grow
part swap --size 32
# We need to do a fresh install (especially since we just wiped out
#the partitions)
Install
# The PCs have 2 button PS/2 Mice but we want to emulate 3 buttons
mouse genericps/2 --emulthree
# Set our timezone …
timezone --utc US/Eastern
```

```
# We are just using a generic SVGA driver and we can specify the
# monitors here.
xconfig --server "SVGA" --monitor "tatung cm14uhe"
# Our root password does not have to be encrypted since it will
#install locally from the CD-ROM
rootpw cleartext
# This will enable shadow password and encryption algorithm of MD5
auth --useshadow --enablemd5
# LILO will need to be installed in the Master Boot Record (MBR)
lilo --location mbr
# We plan on doing a typical Workstation install for our packages.
%packages
@ Workstation
```

CERTIFICATION OBJECTIVE 5.04

Hardware Conflicts and Plug and Play

Hardware conflicts are fairly simple to eliminate. There are three possible areas of conflict:

- A physical hardware jumper is conflicting with another card.
- You have ISA Plug and Play cards that are not properly configured.
- You are out of interrupts or resources to add your new device.

Physical hardware jumpers need to be set to nonconflicting values in order for them to work; this is typically a little jumper setting on the card somewhere. To check what interrupts you are using, issue the following command:

cat /proc/interrupts

```
           CPU0
  0:   86311180          XT-PIC  timer
  1:      25820          XT-PIC  keyboard
  2:          0          XT-PIC  cascade
  6:        507          XT-PIC  floppy
  7:          0          XT-PIC  soundblaster
  8:          2          XT-PIC  rtc
  9:     263584          XT-PIC  aic7xxx
 11:    4065120          XT-PIC  eth0
```

```
 12:     529582          XT-PIC  PS/2 Mouse
 13:          1          XT-PIC  fpu
 14:     352260          XT-PIC  ide0
NMI:          0
```

This is a list of devices that *are* loaded by the kernel. You can quickly scan over the left side to see what interrupts are available. In our example IRQ 5 is not used yet. To get a list of IO addresses, issue the following command:

cat /proc/ioports

```
0000-001f : dma1
0020-003f : pic1
0040-005f : timer
0060-006f : keyboard
0070-007f : rtc
0080-008f : dma page reg
00a0-00bf : pic2
00c0-00df : dma2
00f0-00ff : fpu
01f0-01f7 : ide0
0220-022f : soundblaster
02f8-02ff : serial(auto)
0388-038b : Yamaha OPL3
03c0-03df : vga+
03f0-03f5 : floppy
03f6-03f6 : ide0
03f7-03f7 : floppy DIR
03f8-03ff : serial(auto)
f800-f8be : aic7xxx
fc90-fc97 : ide0
fcc0-fcff : eth0
```

DMA resources:

cat /proc/dma

```
 1: SoundBlaster8
 2: floppy
 4: cascade
```

With a physical conflict you can simply check what is available and change the jumper. For an ISA PnP card it is a little bit harder. First, probe for PnP cards and dump the results to a file by typing:

pnpdump > isapnp.conf

Next edit the isapnp.conf file. You should see all of your ISA Plug and Play devices and all possible settings. This file is a configuration file, and almost all values are commented out with the # symbol. You need to uncomment all the valid IRQ, IO, DMA ports that you want your card to work on, and uncomment the ACT Y line at the bottom of your card's information. After you have set up your card to non-conflicting values you can run isapnp. The following is an excerpt from a pnpdump output:

```
# $Id: pnpdump.c,v 1.18 1999/02/14 22:47:18 fox Exp $
# This is free software, see the sources for details.
# This software has NO WARRANTY, use at your OWN RISK
#
# For details of this file format, see isapnp.conf(5)
#
# For latest information and FAQ on isapnp and pnpdump see:
# http://www.roestock.demon.co.uk/isapnptools/
#
# Compiler flags: -DREALTIME -DNEEDSETSCHEDULER -DABORT_ONRESERR
#
# Trying port address 0203
# Board 1 has serial identifier 6d ff ff ff ff f0 00 8c 0e
# (DEBUG)
(READPORT 0x0203)
(ISOLATE PRESERVE)
(IDENTIFY *)
(VERBOSITY 2)
(CONFLICT (IO FATAL)(IRQ FATAL)(DMA FATAL)(MEM FATAL)) # or WARNING
# Card 1: (serial identifier 6d ff ff ff ff f0 00 8c 0e)
# Vendor Id CTL00f0, No Serial Number (-1), checksum 0x6D.
# Version 1.0, Vendor version 1.0
# ANSI string -->Creative ViBRA16X PnPR<--
#
# Logical device id CTL0043
#     Device supports vendor reserved register @ 0x38
#     Device supports vendor reserved register @ 0x3a
#     Device supports vendor reserved register @ 0x3c
#
```

Edit the entries below to uncomment out the configuration required. Note that only the first value of any range is given; this may be changed if required. Don't forget to uncomment the activate (ACT Y) when you're happy.

```
(CONFIGURE CTL00f0/-1 (LD 0

#     ANSI string -->Audio<--
# Multiple choice time, choose one only !
#     Start dependent functions: priority preferred
#       IRQ 5.
#             High true, edge sensitive interrupt (by default)
# (INT 0 (IRQ 5 (MODE +E)))
#       First DMA channel 1.
#             8 bit DMA only
#             Logical device is not a bus master
#             DMA may execute in count by byte mode
#             DMA may not execute in count by word mode
#             DMA channel speed in compatible mode
# (DMA 0 (CHANNEL 1))
#       Next DMA channel 3.
#             8 bit DMA only
#             Logical device is not a bus master
#             DMA may execute in count by byte mode
#             DMA may not execute in count by word mode
#             DMA channel speed in compatible mode
# (DMA 1 (CHANNEL 3))
#       Logical device decodes 16 bit IO address lines
#             Minimum IO base address 0x0220
#             Maximum IO base address 0x0220
#             IO base alignment 1 bytes
#             Number of IO addresses required: 16
# (IO 0 (SIZE 16) (BASE 0x0220))
#       Logical device decodes 16 bit IO address lines
#             Minimum IO base address 0x0330
#             Maximum IO base address 0x0330
#             IO base alignment 1 bytes
#             Number of IO addresses required: 2
# (IO 1 (SIZE 2) (BASE 0x0330))
#       Logical device decodes 16 bit IO address lines
#             Minimum IO base address 0x0388
#             Maximum IO base address 0x0388
#             IO base alignment 1 bytes
#             Number of IO addresses required: 4
# (IO 2 (SIZE 4) (BASE 0x0388))
#       Start dependent functions: priority acceptable
#       IRQ 5, 7, 9 or 10.
#             High true, edge sensitive interrupt (by default)
[Many lines have been removed for clarity]
#     End dependent functions
 (NAME "CTL00f0/-1[0]{Audio                 }")
# (ACT Y)
```

```
))
#
# Logical device id CTL7005
#     Device supports vendor reserved register @ 0x38
#     Device supports vendor reserved register @ 0x3a
#     Device supports vendor reserved register @ 0x3c
#
```

Edit the entries below to uncomment out the configuration required. Note that only the first value of any range is given; this may be changed if required. Don't forget to uncomment the activate (ACT Y) when you're happy.

```
(CONFIGURE CTL00f0/-1 (LD 1

#     Compatible device id PNPb02f
#     ANS
I string -->Game<--
# Multiple choice time, choose one only !
#     Start dependent functions: priority preferred
#       Logical device decodes 16 bit IO address lines
#             Minimum IO base address 0x0201
#             Maximum IO base address 0x0201
#             IO base alignment 1 bytes
#             Number of IO addresses required: 1
# (IO 0 (SIZE 1) (BASE 0x0201))
#       Start dependent functions: priority acceptable
#       Logical device decodes 16 bit IO address lines
#             Minimum IO base address 0x0200
#             Maximum IO base address 0x020f
#             IO base alignment 1 bytes
#             Number of IO addresses required: 1
# (IO 0 (SIZE 1) (BASE 0x0200))
#     End dependent functions
 (NAME "CTL00f0/-1[1]{Game                }")
# (ACT Y)
))
# End tag... Checksum 0x00 (OK)
# Returns all cards to the "Wait for Key" state
(WAITFORKEY)
```

With this output you can see there is a SoundBlaster 16 ISA PnP card installed. This output also shows that there is a Game Port on the card that can be configured separately. As you can see all of the lines are commented out. You would have to check the /proc/interrupts and /proc/ioports to find available resources to configure your sound card. We will assume that IRQ 5, IO 0x220 and DMA 0 are not in use. To specify this we can simply uncomment the following lines:

```
# $Id: pnpdump.c,v 1.18 1999/02/14 22:47:18 fox Exp $
# This is free software, see the sources for details.
# This software has NO WARRANTY, use at your OWN RISK
#
# For details of this file format, see isapnp.conf(5)
#
# For latest information and FAQ on isapnp and pnpdump see:
# http://www.roestock.demon.co.uk/isapnptools/
#
# Compiler flags: -DREALTIME -DNEEDSETSCHEDULER -DABORT_ONRESERR
#
# Trying port address 0203
# Board 1 has serial identifier 6d ff ff ff ff f0 00 8c 0e
# Board 2 has serial identifier 31 a0 bc 8f b4 30 30 72 56
# (DEBUG)
(READPORT 0x0203)
(ISOLATE PRESERVE)
(IDENTIFY *)
(VERBOSITY 2)
(CONFLICT (IO FATAL)(IRQ FATAL)(DMA FATAL)(MEM FATAL)) # or
WARNING
# Card 1: (serial identifier 6d ff ff ff ff f0 00 8c 0e)
# Vendor Id CTL00f0, No Serial Number (-1), checksum 0x6D.
# Version 1.0, Vendor version 1.0
# ANSI string -->Creative ViBRA16X PnP<--
# Logical device id CTL0043
#     Device supports vendor reserved register @ 0x38
#     Device supports vendor reserved register @ 0x3a
#     Device supports vendor reserved register @ 0x3c
#
```

Edit the entries below to uncomment out the configuration required. Note that only the first value of any range is given; this may be changed if required. Don't forget to uncomment the activate (ACT Y) when you're happy.

```
(CONFIGURE CTL00f0/-1 (LD 0
#     ANSI string -->Audio<--
# Multiple choice time, choose one only !
#     Start dependent functions: priority preferred
#       IRQ 5.
#             High true, edge sensitive interrupt (by default)
 (INT 0 (IRQ 5 (MODE +E)))
#       First DMA channel 1.
#             8 bit DMA only
```

```
#               Logical device is not a bus master
#               DMA may execute in count by byte mode
#               DMA may not execute in count by word mode
#               DMA channel speed in compatible mode
 (DMA 0 (CHANNEL 1))
#         Logical device decodes 16 bit IO address lines
#               Minimum IO base address 0x0220
#               Maximum IO base address 0x0220
#               IO base alignment 1 bytes
#               Number of IO addresses required: 16
 (IO 0 (SIZE 16) (BASE 0x0220))
#       End dependent functions
 (NAME "CTL00f0/-1[0]{Audio                }")
 (ACT Y)
# Returns all cards to the "Wait for Key" state
(WAITFORKEY)
```

You have to uncomment the ACT Y for the card to actually be set. Once this card is properly set up you can load the soundblaster module with the following command:

modprobe sb irq=5 io=0x220 dma=0

If you don't have a joystick then there is no reason to enable it in the isapnp.conf file.

isapnp isapnp.conf

This will set up your card and the resources should show up in the appropriate /proc file. To have this setup whenever you boot you will need to copy the isapnp.conf file to the /etc directory.

PCI Plug and Play cards should set themselves up appropriately. If you cannot see what your PCI cards are set to, you can type: **cat / proc/pci**; otherwise you may have run out of resources. Your resources can vary depending on your architecture but on an i386 PC you typically have up to 15 interrupts: 0–14. If you run out of interrupts you may want to look into alternatives such as combo cards that have two devices on one card or Universal Serail Bus (USB) devices.

CERTIFICATION OBJECTIVE 5.05

PCMCIA

PCMCIA devices can be very frustrating. Typically the problem is having newer devices than drivers, which can usually be fixed by merely downloading the newest pcmcia drivers and compiling them.

PCMCIA works on Intel and Alpha based laptops. There is limited support for Macintosh laptops as well. The following is a list of supported PCMCIA controllers that are detected:

- Cirrus Logic PD6710, PD6720, PD6722, PD6729, PD6730, PD6732, PD6832
- Intel i82365sl B, C, and DF steps, 82092AA
- O2Micro OZ6729, OZ6730, OZ6832, OZ6833, OZ6836, OZ6860
- Omega Micro 82C092G
- Ricoh RF5C296, RF5C396, RL5C465, RL5C466, RL5C475, RL5C476, RL5C478
- SMC 34C90
- Texas Instruments PCI1130, PCI1131, PCI1210, PCI1220, PCI1221, PCI1250A, PCI1251A, PCI1251B, PCI1450
- Toshiba ToPIC95, ToPIC97 (experimental)
- Vadem VG465, VG468, VG469
- VLSI Technologies 82C146, VCF94365
- VIA VT83C469
- Databook DB86082, DB86082A, DB86084, DB86084A, DB86072, DB86082B

The PCMCIA driver will automatically load the devices and set up the IO ports to nonconflicting ports. However, if you do not want certain ports scanned or used then you may specify them in the /etc/pcmcia/config.opts file. You may need to edit the file /etc/sysconfig/pcmcia and set PCMCIA=yes. If you need the original source you can install it off of the Red Hat CD-ROM under the SRPM directory. This is a slightly modified version of the original source.

The cardmgr daemon actually takes care of the PCMCIA device, type **ps x** to see if it is running. Whenever a card is loaded you can check the /var/run/stab file.

cat / var/run/fstab

```
Socket 0: empty
Socket 1: 3Com 3c589D Ethernet
1       network 3c589_cs        0       eth0
```

Here we see that Socket 0 does not have a card while Socket 1 contains a network card. There are five columns displayed for loaded devices. The first is the socket number. Second is the device class. Third is the actual driver that was loaded. Fourth is the device number; some devices support multiple devices per socket. Finally the fifth column contains the actual device name.

When you insert a card you should hear two beeps; one for successfully identifying the card and another for properly configuring the card. If it fails you should hear a lower pitch beep. You will also hear a beep if you remove a card.

To see what settings your card is set to you can issue the **cardctl** command as follows:

[root] cardctl config

```
Socket 0:
  not configured
Socket 1:
  Vcc = 5.0, Vpp1 = 0.0, Vpp2 = 0.0
  Interface type is memory and I/O
  IRQ 9 is exclusive, level mode, enabled
  Function 0:
    Config register base = 0x10000
      Option = 0x41, status = 0000
    I/O window 1: 0x0300 to 0x030f, 16 bit
```

You can specify what ranges cardmgr will use to configure the card, as well as IO and IRQ settings it should avoid. These settings are stored in the /etc/pcmcia/config.opts file. You will need to include lines that limit the boundaries cardmgr is allowed to use and exclude lines for the settings it should avoid. For example:

cat /etc/pcmcia/config.opts

```
include memory 0xc0000-0xfffff, memory 0xa0000000-0xa0ffffff
exclude irq 4
```

You may also specify extra pcmcia options in the /etc/sysconfig/pcmcia file.

```
PCIC=i82365|tcic
PCIC_OPTS=<socket driver (i82365 or tcic) timing parameters>
CORE_OPTS=<pcmcia_core options>
CARDMGR_OPTS=<cardmgr options>
```

These options will be run at boot time.

CERTIFICATION OBJECTIVE 5.06

Advanced Power Management (APM) BIOS

The Advanced Power Management (APM) BIOS primarily monitors and controls the system battery. This option is typically found in laptops. You can also use it on workstations and servers if you want to implement the BIOS standby and suspend modes that are available on newer PCs.

The daemon that needs to be running is apmd. If the apmd daemon is running on your system there will be a file created that contains the battery information in the proc directory.

cat /proc/apm

```
1.9 1.2 0x07 0x01 0xff 0x80 -1% -1 ?
```

As you can see this format is not very readable. To have this information printed in a more readable format simply issue the **apm** command.

apm

```
AC on-line, battery status high: 100% (2:31)
```

This command reads the information created by apmd in the /proc/apm file and prints it in a much easier to read format.

The apmd daemon can be configured to do a variety of different things based on what BIOS reports back on the status of the battery. You can set apmd to log error messages to syslog when the battery life drops below a certain percentage level. You can also have it send a system-wide message to all logged in users when this warning level is reached. All changes in battery information are logged via syslog. To set up options for apmd you will need to edit the /etc/sysconfig/apmd file.

cat /etc/sysconfig/apmd

```
APMD_OPTIONS="-p 10 -w 5 -W
```

In this example apmd is instructed to log changes to the syslog file with every 10% of battery loss (-p 10). If the battery drops below 5%, apmd will send an alert to syslog (-w 5). Also, all logged in users will be notified that the system is about to die (-W).

The apm log is broken down into four parts of information.

- Percentage of discharge (percentage/minute). It will be a negative amount if it is charging.
- Time since total charge or time since last logged depending if the battery is fully charged or not.
- Estimate of battery time left.
- Percentage of battery life left.

When the BIOS tells the apmd daemon about a pending suspend or a standby call it immediately calls sync(2). It will then sleep for two seconds and tell BIOS to continue. If a critical resume occurs then apmd will attempt to reset the clock.

CERTIFICATION OBJECTIVE 5.07

Understanding /etc/inittab

The inittab describes what process should be started when booting as well as what should be running at normal operations levels. Init(8) reads in the inittab to determine what is to run at what runlevel. The valid runlevels range from 0 to 6 as well as A to C. Runlevels A to C are considered ondemand runlevels. The format for inittab is as follows:

```
id_number:runlevel:action:process
```

The *id_number* is a unique 1–4 alphanumeric character. The *runlevel* is a list of runlevels that the action should occur on. The *action* is what action should be taken. The *process* is what process should be executed. If the process begins with a + then no accounting information will be done for that process. To list multiple runlevels, list them without commas or spaces.

Example 1: 2345:respawn:/sbin/mingetty tty

This line will run at runlevels 2–5 but not 1 or 6. For a complete description of runlevels please refer to the following section. If init(8) switches to a runlevel that is not listed by a process then that process is killed.

The following is a list of the valid actions that can be used by inittab:

- **respawn** If the process is killed it will be automatically restarted.
- **wait** Will wait for the process to terminate before continuing.
- **once** Only run the process once.
- **boot** Run when booting and ignore the runlevel field.

- **bootwait** A combination of both boot and wait.
- **ondemand** Execute when an ondemand run level is called (A–C).
- **initdefault** This specifies the default runlevel after system boot. If this entry does not exist then init(8) will prompt the console for the runlevel. Process entries are ignored.
- **sysinit** Executes during system boot but before any boot or bootwait entries. The runlevel entries are ignored.
- **powerfail** This will run when init(8) recieves a power failure message from the kernel (SIGPWR). This usually is generated from a UPS battery backup. The runlevel entries are ignored.
- **powerwait** Same as above but it will wait for the process to finish. powerokwait - If init(8) receives a SIGPWR signal and there is an "OK" in the /etc/powerstatus file, then this process will run.
- **ctrlaltdel** This process is run when a user presses CTRL-ALT-DEL keys. This process is usually used to shut down the system into single user mode or to reboot the server.
- **kbrequest** You can map specific keyboard combinations to fire a process. You have to specify these in your keymaps file and map them to KeyboardSignal.

Table 5-3 shows default runlevels for Red Hat:

TABLE 5-3

Default Runlevels for Red Hat

0	Halt the system
1	Single user mode
2	Multiuser, without NFS
3	Full multiuser mode
4	Unused
5	X11
6	Reboot the system

The following code is an example of an inittab.

```
# Default runlevel
id:5:initdefault:
# System initialization.
si::sysinit:/etc/rc.d/rc.sysinit
l0:0:wait:/etc/rc.d/rc 0
l1:1:wait:/etc/rc.d/rc 1
l2:2:wait:/etc/rc.d/rc 2
l3:3:wait:/etc/rc.d/rc 3
l4:4:wait:/etc/rc.d/rc 4
l5:5:wait:/etc/rc.d/rc 5
l6:6:wait:/etc/rc.d/rc 6
# Things to run in every runlevel.
ud::once:/sbin/update
# Trap CTRL-ALT-DELETE
ca::ctrlaltdel:/sbin/shutdown -t3 -r now
# Power failures
pf::powerfail:/sbin/shutdown -f -h +2 "Power Failure; SystemShutting Down"
# Power restored
pr:12345:powerokwait:/sbin/shutdown -c "Power Restored;Shutdown Cancelled"
# Run gettys in standard runlevels
1:2345:respawn:/sbin/mingetty tty1
2:2345:respawn:/sbin/mingetty tty2
3:2345:respawn:/sbin/mingetty tty3
4:2345:respawn:/sbin/mingetty tty4
5:2345:respawn:/sbin/mingetty tty5
6:2345:respawn:/sbin/mingetty tty6
# Run X11 (xdm or other display manager)
# xdm is a separate service in Red Hat 6.0
x:5:respawn:/etc/X11/prefdm -nodaemon
```

The syntax is a SystemV syntax and appears difficult to read; once you get used to it, however, you can read the entire file at a glance. Here is a breakdown of each line in the file.

```
id:5:initdefault
```

This command sets the default to X11 after the system has finished running its boot scripts. The actual process to start X11 is listed later.

```
si::sysinit:/etc/rc.d/rc.sysinit
l0:0:wait:/etc/rc.d/rc 0
l1:1:wait:/etc/rc.d/rc 1
l2:2:wait:/etc/rc.d/rc 2
l3:3:wait:/etc/rc.d/rc 3
l4:4:wait:/etc/rc.d/rc 4
```

```
l5:5:wait:/etc/rc.d/rc 5
l6:6:wait:/etc/rc.d/rc 6
```

The first line (si) is the system initialization file. This is discussed in more detail in the next section. Lines l0–l6 are also initialization scripts that run at each runlevel. Notice that init(8) will not continue until each RC script has completed running.

```
ud::once:/sbin/update
```

This command gets run once every time we change runlevels. Notice that when you do not specify a runlevel then it will run for every runlevel.

```
ca::ctrlaltdel:/sbin/shutdown -t3 -r now
pf::powerfail:/sbin/shutdown -f -h +2 "Power Failure; SystemShutting Down"
pr:12345:powerokwait:/sbin/shutdown -c "Power Restored;Shutdown Cancelled"
```

These are all special actions. The first (ca) will shut down the system in 3 seconds and then reboot. The second line (pf) will halt the system 2 minutes after receiving the SIGPWR signal. The third line (pr) states that if the power resumes within two minutes (above line) then cancel the shutdown. Notice the runlevels list all relevant runlevels to cancel shutdown.

```
1:2345:respawn:/sbin/mingetty tty1
2:2345:respawn:/sbin/mingetty tty2
3:2345:respawn:/sbin/mingetty tty3
4:2345:respawn:/sbin/mingetty tty4
5:2345:respawn:/sbin/mingetty tty5
6:2345:respawn:/sbin/mingetty tty6
```

These lines set up 6 virtual consoles. Notice that no virtual consoles are loaded for runlevel 1 (Single user mode)

```
x:5:respawn:/etc/X11/prefdm -nodaemon
```

This line will run our X11 Display Manager (XDM). When the first line of the file is called (id) it runs this line. This line in turn runs the preferred XDM, which presents the user with a graphical X11 login. Again it is important to realize that initdefault does not actually run anything; it merely sets the runlevel. Later in the inittab you specify what you want that runlevel to do.

CERTIFICATION OBJECTIVE 5.08

System Start-up Script /etc/rc.d/rc.sysinit

This script does all of the major system setup and initialization. Here is a step-by-step rundown of the process that occurs when the script is run.

1. Checks for a /etc/sysconfig/network script. If it is there, then the system runs it, otherwise it turns networking off and sets your hostname to "localhost."
2. Executes /etc/rc.d/init.d/functions. This file sets up some basic functions that the rest of the scripts use (example: the boot daemon failure/success messages).
3. Sets the loglevel.
4. Loads the keymap. If you have specified a default keymap file in /etc/sysconfig/console/default.kmap it will use that, otherwise it will use /etc/sysconfig/keyboard.
5. Loads the system fonts.
6. Activates all swap partitions that are specified in the /etc/fstab file.
7. Sets up your hostname and your NIS domain name.
8. Runs fsck to check your filesystem if necessary. If fsck fails it will drop you to a shell and unmount the drives so you can work on repairing them.
9. Sets up ISA Plug and Play devices.
10. Remounts the root file system as read-write.
11. Check quotas on the root partition.

    All modules will now be loaded. Note that the sound and midi modules are loaded if there is an alias listed as sound or midi in the /etc/conf.modules. If your system requires a different module than sound, you will need to edit the /etc/conf.modules file. See Certification Objective 5.09 on kernel modules.

12. Then checks for a /etc/raidtab file and loads all raid devices.
13. Checks your filesystems with fsck again.
14. Mounts the rest of the filesystems listed in the /etc/fstab.
15. Turns quota support on if /sbin/quotaon exists and is executable.
16. Sets the system clock. It will run /etc/sysconfig/clock if it exists.
17. Initializes swap space.
18. Initializes serial ports.
19. Loads SCSI tape module if a SCSI tape was detected.
20. Reads the /etc/sysconfig/desktop file for a preferred X11 Display Manager and sets a link file as /etc/X11/prefdm.
21. Finally it dumps the kernel ring buffer (boot messages) to /var/log/dmesg.

This list is hard to remember. Once you familiarize yourself with the rc.sysinit bootup sequence you can use the short summary cheat sheet below as a quick reference.

1. Runs network script
2. Loads script functions
3. Loglevel
4. Keymap
5. Fonts
6. Swap space
7. Hostname/NIS domain
8. fsck root partition
9. ISA Plug and Play
10. Remounts root read-write
11. Checks root quotas
12. Loads modules

13. Initializes RAID
14. fsck filesystem
15. Mounts all filesystems
16. Turns on quotas
17. Sets clock
18. Reinitializes swap
19. Serial ports
20. SCSI tape drivers
21. Sets up XDM
22. Dumps dmesg

CERTIFICATION OBJECTIVE 5.09

Understanding Kernel Modules

When you compile your kernel you have the option to have components compiled as modules. A kernel module is not compiled directly into the kernel but as a plugable driver that can be loaded and unloaded into the kernel as needed. It is a good idea to make modules instead of directly compiling them into the kernel for the following reasons:

- It makes the kernel size smaller.
- Which in turn increases your kernel speed.
- As modules become unnecessary, they can be dynamically unloaded to take up less memory.

To have the kernel dynamically load and unload kernel modules as needed, a special daemon needs to be called, kerneld. Once kerneld is loaded it will take care of unloading the modules as needed. For special parameters and options you should edit the /etc/conf.modules file (NOTE: This file can be used interchangeably with modules.conf).

To load modules on the command line you should first issue:

```
depmod -a
```

This will scan through your modules and find out what the different dependencies for all of your modules are and map them out to a file (modules.dep). This file has a makefile styled structure to list dependencies and is located under the /lib/modules/x.x.x/ directory, where *x.x.x* is your kernel version. This command is usually run during execution of the boot scripts. Once this command is completed, you can load a module. If it has dependencies then all the modules that are needed will automatically load first. To load a module use modprobe.

```
modprobe 3c503
```

In this example the Ethernet module for a 3com 503 network card requires the 8390 module to work properly. If depmod was run first then 8390 would have loaded automatically before the 3c503 driver. If a dependency in the list fails during loading then all modules will be automatically unloaded.

You can do a lot of the tedious work with the /etc/conf.modules file. There are several commands that are accepted in this file.

```
alias - Allows you to bind a name to a module.
options - Allows you to specify options for a module.
install
pre-install
post-install
remove
pre-remove
post-remove - Allows you to install a module every time a module
is inserted or removed.
```

Here is an example of what a common conf.modules may look like.

```
alias eth0 3c59x
options sb irq=5 io=0x220 dma=1
alias midi awe_wave
alias parport_lowlevel parport_pc
```

Here the eth0 name is bound to the 3c59x module. To load the network card you can simply type **modprobe eth0** without knowing what card is in the machine. The next two lines show that the sound blaster module is desired for the default sound module. The sound blaster module (sb) requires that you specify the IRQ, IO address and DMA on the command line when you load the module. The option line specifies these options and binds them to the alias's name of sound. The sound card happens to be an AWE 32 so the alias's name midi is bound to the awe_wave module. Finally a parallel port module is bound to the parport_lowlevel alias.

The rc.sysinit script recognizes certain aliases and will load them if it finds them in this file. You need to specify the sound modules in conf.modules to have them automatically loaded. To have the sound modules automatically loaded during bootup without having to edit the /etc/rc.d/rc.sysinit file you can simply create an alias to sound and or midi in the conf.modules file.

To see what modules are loaded you can either type:

```
cat /proc/modules
```

or

```
lsmod
```

Both will reveal similar output to the following.

```
Module                  Size  Used by
awe_wave              157804    0  (unused)
3c59x                  18920    1  (autoclean)
nls_iso8859-1           2020    3  (autoclean)
nls_cp437               3548    3  (autoclean)
vfat                   11516    3  (autoclean)
fat                    25664    3  (autoclean) [vfat]
sb                     33204    0
uart401                 5968    0  [sb]
sound                  57208    0  [sb uart401]
soundlow                 300    0  [sound]
soundcore               2372    5  [sb sound]
```

The module name is listed on the left and its size is in the following column. The Used by column shows more detail on how the module is being handled. An (autoclean) message means that kerneld is taking care of the module and will handle removing it. If a module name is listed in brackets (example: [vfat]), then the module is a dependent of the module in brackets. In our example vfat is dependent on the fat module.

CERTIFICATION OBJECTIVE 5.10

The /lib/modules/.../ Directory Structure

All of your kernel modules are kept under /lib/modules/.../ directory, where ... is your kernel version. For example, if you are running version 2.2.5 of a Linux kernel, then your modules will be kept under /lib/modules/2.2.5/. If you have recently compiled a kernel and your modules are not loading properly, then you have probably forgotten to compile and install the modules. In the Linux source directory you will need to issue the following commands:

```
make modules
make modules_install
```

The first line compiles the modules, while the second places them under the proper directory tree. In this directory tree there are different subdirectories that represent different groupings. The following is a sample of a module directory:

ls -l /lib/modules/2.2.5/

```
total 36

drwxr-xr-x   2 root     root         1024 May 15 14:54 block
drwxr-xr-x   2 root     root         1024 May 15 14:54 cdrom
drwxr-xr-x   2 root     root         1024 May 15 14:54 fs
drwxr-xr-x   2 root     root         1024 May 15 14:54 ipv4
drwxr-xr-x   2 root     root         3072 May 15 14:54 misc
-rw-r--r--   1 root     root        23312 May 30 10:04 modules.dep
drwxr-xr-x   2 root     root         2048 May 15 14:54 net
drwxr-xr-x   2 root     root         1024 May 15 14:54 pcmcia
drwxr-xr-x   2 root     root         1024 May 15 14:54 scsi
drwxr-xr-x   2 root     root         1024 May 15 14:54 video
```

Notice there is a modules.dep file that lists all the dependencies for all the modules within the directories. Inside of the directories are different kernel modules for each grouping. You should become familiar with where to find certain modules when needed. Here are some of the types of modules you will find under each directory:

- **block** Block devices: ide-floppies, raid device levels
- **cdrom** non-ATAPI carom drivers: Mitshumi, Sony
- **fs** Filesystem modules, vfat, ntfs, smbfs, minix
- **ipv4** IP version 4 modules, masquerading modules
- **ipv6** Same as above but for IP version 6
- **misc** Misc. modules: joysticks, mouse, radio modules
- **net** Network modules, drivers, ppp, slip
- **pcmcia** Drivers used by the pcmcia cardmgr daemon
- **scsi** SCSI tape and hard drive modules
- **video** Special video modules for Linux, MGA consoles

All modules have an .o for an extension (example vfat.o). You do not need to specify the full name, just the first part (vfat). Once you know the directory structure you can have modprobe load all modules for a certain category. For instance if you are on a PC and you don't know the network card you can simply type:

```
modprobe -t net
```

This will try to load all modules in /lib/modules/.../net. It stops when one module has successfully loaded. To remove a module and all of its dependencies you can type either:

```
modprobe -r 3c503
```

or

```
rmmod -r 3c503
```

Both of these commands will remove the modules and all of their dependencies provided they are not in use by another module. If you want to remove only the module and leave the dependencies loaded, you can omit the -r option for the rmmod command.

CERTIFICATION SUMMARY

The Linux installation is extremely flexible. It can easily allow you to dual boot multiple operating systems with LILO, and incorporate them with NT's NTLDR boot program. You can also set up RAID level devices to mirror and stripe your drives. RAID level 1 and 0 require that you have two or more drives, while RAID 5 needs three or more. You can automate your entire installation of Red Hat Linux by using kickstart.

Kickstart installation files can reside on the boot floppy or on a DHCP/BOOTP server. If the file resides on the floppy you can initialize it with **linux ks=floppy**. To get the file from a BOOTP server you can type **linux ks**.

A kickstart installation can only install from a local CD-ROM or over NFS. When you are doing an upgrade you must be sure to define the language, installation method, device specifications, keyboard setup, LILO configurations and use the upgrade keyword.

When booting, the /etc/inittab file dictates the rest of the boot process as well as everything that runs during each runlevel. You use the initdefault keyword to specify your default runlevel. Some common default runlevels are runlevel 1 – single user, 2 – multiuser without NFS, 3 – Full multiuser and 5 – X11. The initial boot script is called by the sysinit keyword. This script is rc.sysinit per default.

The rc.sysinit script runs almost all crucial system dependent bootup operations. This script will check your Linux partitions for filesystem errors, load kernel modules, and set up initial swap space. It will also initialize RAID devices and set up all ISA Plug and Play devices, and if quotas are enabled on a partition then those will be turned on at this time.

TWO-MINUTE DRILL

- A very common setup between Windows NT and Linux is dual booting. There are several different ways to accomplish dual booting.
- There are mainly two different types of RAID setups, software based and hardware based. Hardware based RAID systems are still in development and SCSI host based adapters from DPT are the only controllers with some Linux documentation. For more information on hardware and DPT based RAID you should refer to the DPT-Hardware-RAID-HOWTO document. The software-based RAID is what we will focus on in this text although some of the principles apply to hardware as well.
- RAID 0 and 1 require two or more drives, while RAID 5 requires 3 or more drives.
    - Take special note that raid-disks and spare-disks start counting at 0. Nr-raid-disks and nr-spare-disks are the correct number of drives. Example: If nr-raid-disks = 3, then the last raid-disk will be 2.
- Kickstart is Red Hat's solution for an automated installation of Red Hat.
- Kickstart installations can only be performed from a CD-ROM, HTTP, FTP, or NFS server. You *cannot* use SMB to do your install. Hardware conflicts are fairly simple to eliminate. There are three possible areas of conflict:

1. A physical hardware jumper is conflicting with another card.
2. You have ISA Plug and Play cards that are not properly configured.
3. You are out of interrupts or resources to add your new device.

- PCMCIA works on Intel and Alpha based laptops.
- The Advanced Power Management (APM) BIOS primarily monitors and controls the system battery. This option is typically found in laptops. You can also use it on workstations and servers if you want to implement the BIOS standby and suspend modes that are available on newer PCs.

- ❑ The inittab describes what process should be started when booting as well as what should be running at normal operations levels. init(8) reads in the inittab to determine what is to run at what runlevel. The valid runlevels range from 0 to 6 as well as A to C. Runlevels A to C are considered ondemand runlevels.
- ❑ Script /etc/rc.d/rc.sysinit does all of the major system setup and initialization.
- ❑ When you compile your kernel (See Chapter 6) you have the option to have components compiled as modules. A kernel module is not compiled directly into the kernel but as a plugable driver that can be loaded and unloaded into the kernel as needed.
- ❑ To have the kernel dynamically load and unload kernel modules as needed, a special daemon needs to be called, kerneld. Once kerneld is loaded it will take care of unloading the modules as needed. For special parameters and options you should edit the /etc/conf.modules file.
- ❑ All of your kernel modules are kept under /lib/modules/.../ directory, where ... is your kernel version.

SELF TEST

The following Self Test questions will help you measure your understanding of the material presented in this chapter. Read all the choices carefully, as there may be more than one correct answer. Choose all correct answers for each question.

1. You are creating a dual boot NT/Linux system. You already have NT installed and plan to use the NTLDR to load Linux on the second drive. Linux is installed and you have made a bootdisk that properly boots Linux. What command would you issue from Linux to copy the bootsector from the floppy?

   A. dd if=bootsect.lnx of=/dev/fd0 bs=512 count=1

   B. dd if=/dev/fd0 of=bootsect.lnx bs=512 count=1

   C. dd if=bootsect.lnx of=/dev/fd0 bs=512

   D. dd if=/dev/fd0 of=bootsect.lnx count=512

2. You are dual booting an NT/Linux system. You have successfully copied a working bootsector over the NT boot partition and named it bootsect.lnx. What do you need to do so that the NTLDR loads Linux as an operating system?

   A. Edit the NTLDR file with C:\bootsect.lnx="Linux".

   B. Edit the BOOT.INI file with "Linux"=C:\bootsect.lnx.

   C. Edit the BOOT.INI file with C:\bootsect.lnx="Linux"

   D. Do nothing; NTLDR will detect any bootsector file that has the bootsect.xxx syntax.

3. You have a mirrored RAID system with 3 drives. The first two are mirrored and the third is supposed to be a spare. When you look at the /etc/raidtab file you see that it says spare-disks 0. What does this entry tell you?

   A. The raidtab entry is set up correctly.

   B. Spare-disks support is turned off. To turn it on change spare-disks to 1.

   C. Currently no spare disks are loaded.

   D. The mirror failed and had to use the spare disk.

4. You need to set up multiple Red Hat Linux systems over the network. You decided to have a bootdisk connect to your DHCP/BOOTP server and load a kickstart file. The kickstart file resides on the DHCP/BOOTP server with the following syntax: <client_ip-kickstart>. You plan to have the kickstart install Linux from an FTP server that does not reside on the DHCP/BOOTP server. What is the problem with this plan?

   A. You cannot have the FTP server on a different server than your DHCP/BOOTP servers.

B. The kickstart file name is wrong.

C. A BOOTP server can only be used to load kernels and will not load a kickstart file.

D. You cannot install from an FTP server.

5. You have several remote branches that you need to have Linux installed on. You decide the best way to do this is to have all the answers preconfigured on a kickstart file on a DHCP/BOOTP server and have it set up to install off an NFS server at the main branch. You plan to ship a bootdisk that has the kickstart file but are concerned that somebody on the network will see the root password in the file. What can you do?

   A. Encrypt the kickstart file that resides on the DHCP/BOOTP server.

   B. Boot the disk with **linux ks=encrypted**

   C. Use rootpw --iscrypted in the kickstart file.

   D. There is nothing you can do.

6. When trying to load a sound module you get a device busy error message. You feel that it is your ISA Plug and Play sound card. You would like to view its Plug and Play configuration options so you can edit them to nonconflicting values. What command would you use to create a file of all your ISA Plug and Play device options?

   A. dumppnp > isapnp.conf

   B. pnpdump > isapnp.conf

   C. displaypnp > isapnp.conf

   D. showpnp > isapnp.conf

7. You run Linux on a laptop. The cardmgr daemon for your PCMCIA cards is stomping on an IRQ that you want reserved. What file do you use to tell the cardmgr to exclude this IRQ from its list?

   A. /etc/pcmcia/config.opts

   B. /etc/sysconfig/pcmcia

   C. /etc/pcmcia/config.exclude

   D. /etc/rc.d/rc.sysinit

8. You frequently use your laptop as a server during work hours. Many users come in and work on special project files throughout the day. You are concerned that there could be a loss of power and would like to warn the other users when the battery is about to run out. What would be the best way to handle this?

   A. Tell each user to run **apm** as often as possible to check battery life.

   B. Set up a user policy that instructs all users to save every five minutes.

   C. Use the wall option in the /etc/sysconfig/apmd file.

   D. Edit the shutdown script that runs at runlevel 0.

9. What runlevel should you switch to in order to run X11 automatically at startup?

   A. 1

   B. 2

   C. 3

   D. 5

10. Which runlevel would you need to load single user mode?

    A. 1

    B. 2

    C. 3

    D. 5

11. What would happen if you modified the initdefault entry in the /etc/inittab file to look like this: id:5:initdefault:/usr/games/fortune?

    A. It would display a fortune every time you logged on.

    B. It would boot into X11 and display a fortune.

    C. It would display a fortune only when it booted.

    D. The fortune line would be ignored.

12. What startup file loads the modules?

    A. /etc/rc.d/rc.modules

    B. /etc/init.d/S10modules

    C. /etc/rc.d/rc.sysinit

    D. none of the above

13. Which of the following does NOT describe kernel modules?

    A. They makes the kernel size smaller.

    B. They increase your kernel speed.

    C. You can dynamically unload modules from memory.

    D. Modules have .dll extensions.

14. You have a network card that needs to have options specified at the command line when loading the module. You only need this network card on occasion so you want to leave it as a module. What can you do to simplify the loading of the module?

    A. Add a bind command to the conf.modules file.

    B. Add an options command to the conf.modules file.

    C. Add the options to the end of the alias command in the conf.modules.file.

    D. None of the above.

15. When you type in **lsmod** and see a list of running modules, you notice that some of them say (autoclean). What does this mean?

    A. The module will automatically remove its own files in the /tmp directory.

    B. The module is not in use and should be removed.

    C. The kerneld will automatically take care of removing it from memory.

    D. The modprobe command has set the module to autoclean.

16. You are on a foreign computer and are not sure what network card is inside of it. You have checked dmesg and no network cards are listed. You have a bunch of compiled network modules but none are currently loaded. What could you do to quickly load the unknown network device?

    A. Try loading each module manually.

    B. modprobe *

C. Kerneld will load the module when the network card is accessed.

D. modprobe -t net

17. You want to conserve as much memory as possible. When doing some checking you notice that there are some modules that are loaded but unused. What command could you use to remove these modules? (Choose all that apply)

A. rmmod

B. rmmod -r

C. modprobe -r

D. modprobe -d

18. You notice that a module you want to load will not load because its dependencies fail. When you examine the /lib/modules/…/ directory closer you notice that the modules.dep file does not exist. What would be the easiest way to recreate this file?

A. Add the dependencies by hand.

B. In the /usr/src/linux directory, type **make modules_install.**

C. depmod -a

D. None of the above.

19. With a default Red Hat install what is the name of the first script that runs on a system?

A. /etc/rc.d/rc.sysinit

B. /etc/init.d/rc.sysinit

C. /etc/rc.d/rc.0

D. /etc/rc.d/rc.1

20. If you wanted to change the initial boot script, what entry in the /etc/inittab file would you modify?

A. boot

B. bootwait

C. sysinit

D. initdefault

6

Advanced User Administration

CERTIFICATION OBJECTIVES

6.01	Setting Up and Managing Disk Quotas
6.02	System Initialization Scripts
6.03	Kernel Recompilation and Installation
6.04	PAM
6.05	The Cron System
6.06	System-Wide Shell Configuration for Bourne and Bash Shells

In this chapter, you will learn how to configure and tweak your system to give you complete control of how it operates. You will learn how to set up user and group quotas, and run reports on the system quotas and all of its users. There will also be a review of the system's initialization scripts.

You will also learn how to configure, compile, and install your own custom kernel. You will learn how to set up monolithic and modular kernels, and see the benefits and disadvantages of using each style. You will learn the details of the Linux kernel and how to optimize and control it with kernel variables. You will also learn multiple techniques for configuring and installing the kernel.

This chapter will also discuss the Pluggable Authentication Modules (PAM) used by Red Hat to provide a detailed and powerful security advantage. You will also learn how to set up the system's shell configuration scripts, and how to schedule jobs to run at any given time.

CERTIFICATION OBJECTIVE 6.01

Setting Up and Managing Disk Quotas

Quotas are used to limit a user's or a group of users' ability to consume disk space. There are two limitations that you can set up. You can limit the inodes and the block space a user can have. Inodes are the number of files a user has and blocks are the amount of hard drive blocks (in kilobytes) a user is using. There are two main methods used to configure a quota system, command line and through Linuxconf. The command line method will be discussed first, followed by the Linuxconf method.

exam Watch

Quota support can only be installed on an ext2partitoin.

Kernel Configuration

The kernel has to be setup to support Quotas on your partitions. By default this is typically enabled. If not you will need to install the kernel source and re-compile your kernel. For more information, see the following section on kernel re-compilation and installation. You have to set CONFIG_QUOTA=y in the kernel configuration. With menuconfig or xconfig, it is under the Filesystem section. Simply enable Quota support and re-compile your kernel. Once you have a kernel that supports quotas, you have to install quota software.

Installing the Quota RPM

There are several ways you can get the quota RPM (Red Hat Package Manager) and install it. One would be to mount your Red Hat CD-ROM and change to the RPMS directory.

```
cd /mnt/cdrom/RedHat/RPMS
```

Load the quota RPM with the following command:

```
rpm -ivh quota-1.66-6
```

This will tell the (rpm) to install (-I) verbosely (-v) with a percentage hash (-h) the quota package. You can also get the package via FTP or HTTP, or use GnomeRPM that is shipped with Red Hat 6.0 and click on Web find. This will search the Internet for the quota package and install it.

Once the package is installed, you will have the following files:

```
/sbin/quotacheck
/sbin/quotaoff
/sbin/quotaon
/usr/bin/quota

/usr/man/man1/quota.1
/usr/man/man2/quotactl.2
/usr/man/man3/rquota.3
/usr/man/man8/edquota.8
/usr/man/man8/quotacheck.8
/usr/man/man8/quotaon.8
/usr/man/man8/repquota.8
/usr/sbin/edquota
/usr/sbin/quotastats
/usr/sbin/repquota
/usr/sbin/warnquota
```

Notice that the man pages are also installed if you want more specific information than this text provides. The next step is to ensure the quotas are turned on and checked during boot up.

/etc/rc.d/rc.sysinit Quota Handling

The rc.sysinit script, as described in Chapter 4, handles your quotas during boot up. At minimum, your startup script should contain:

```
if [ -x /usr/sbin/quotacheck ]
          then
                 echo "Checking quotas. This may take a while."
                 /usr/sbin/quotacheck -avug
                 echo " Done."
          fi
           if [ -x /usr/sbin/quotaon ]
          then
                  echo "Turning on quota support."
                  /usr/sbin/quotaon -avug
          fi
```

Red Hat's rc.sysinit is a bit more complex, but it essentially accomplishes the same thing. First, it checks the root partition for quotas.

```
# Update quotas if fsck was run on /.
if [ X"$_RUN_QUOTACHECK" = X1 -a -x /sbin/quotacheck ]; then
        action "Checking root filesystem quotas"  /sbin/quotacheck
-v /
fi
```

Then it checks the remaining partitions that have quota support action "Checking filesystem quotas" /sbin/quotacheck -v -R -a. The next section just announces to the system that quotas are enabled with the quotaon command.

```
if [ -x /sbin/quotaon ]; then
    action "Turning on user and group quotas for local filesystems"
/sbin/quotaon -a
fi
```

That's it. If the quotas are not already in your startup script, you can quickly add them. You may be wondering how the quota programs know which partitions have quotas enabled and which do not. The answer lies in the fstab.

Modifications to /etc/fstab

You have to modify the fstab file to tell it which partitions to enable quotas on, and whether they are quotas for users, groups, or both. Quotas are enabled on a per-partition basis, not a per-directory basis. Here is a sample fstab before it's been edited.

```
#device     Mountpoint filesystem options       dump fsck
/dev/hdc5   /           ext2      exec,dev,suid,rw     1 1
/dev/hda1   /dos/c      vfat      defaults              0 0
/dev/hdb1   /dos/d      vfat      defaults              0 0
/dev/hdc1   /dos/e      vfat      defaults              0 0
/dev/hdc6   swap        swap      defaults              0 0
/dev/fd0    /mnt/floppy vfat      noauto,users          0 0
/dev/cdrom  /mnt/cdrom  iso9660   noauto,ro,users       0 0
none        /proc       proc      defaults              0 0
none        /dev/pts    devpts    mode=0622             0 0
```

The only entry we care about is the first one—our only ext2 file system partition and our root partition. To enable quotas on a partition, simply add usrquota, grpquota, or both. In our example, we will add both user and group quotas to the root file system.

```
#device     Mountpoint filesystem options       dump fsck
/dev/hdc5   /           ext2
exec,dev,suid,rw,usrquota,grpquota      1
1
/dev/hda1   /dos/c      vfat      defaults              0 0
/dev/hdb1   /dos/d      vfat      defaults              0 0
/dev/hdc1   /dos/e      vfat      defaults              0 0
/dev/hdc6   swap        swap      defaults              0 0
/dev/fd0    /mnt/floppy vfat      noauto,users          0 0
/dev/cdrom  /mnt/cdrom  iso9660   noauto,ro,users       0 0
none        /proc       proc      defaults              0 0
none        /dev/pts    devpts    mode=0622             0 0
```

Please note that there are so many options enabled for /dev/hdc5 that the entry is continued to the next line in the text, but should remain on one line in the fstab file. Linuxconf can make these changes for you. You will need to enter the File Systems | Access Local Drive menu and edit the ext2partitions that you want to enable quotas on. When editing, there is an Options section that has check boxes for both User and Group quotas. Check these two boxes and activate changes. Linuxconf will then edit the fstab file for you.

First, you will have to select an ext2 file system in order to turn on quota support. This is shown in Figure 6-1.

Next, you will need to select the Options tab, as shown in Figure 6-2.

FIGURE 6-1 Linuxconf—Access Local Drive menu

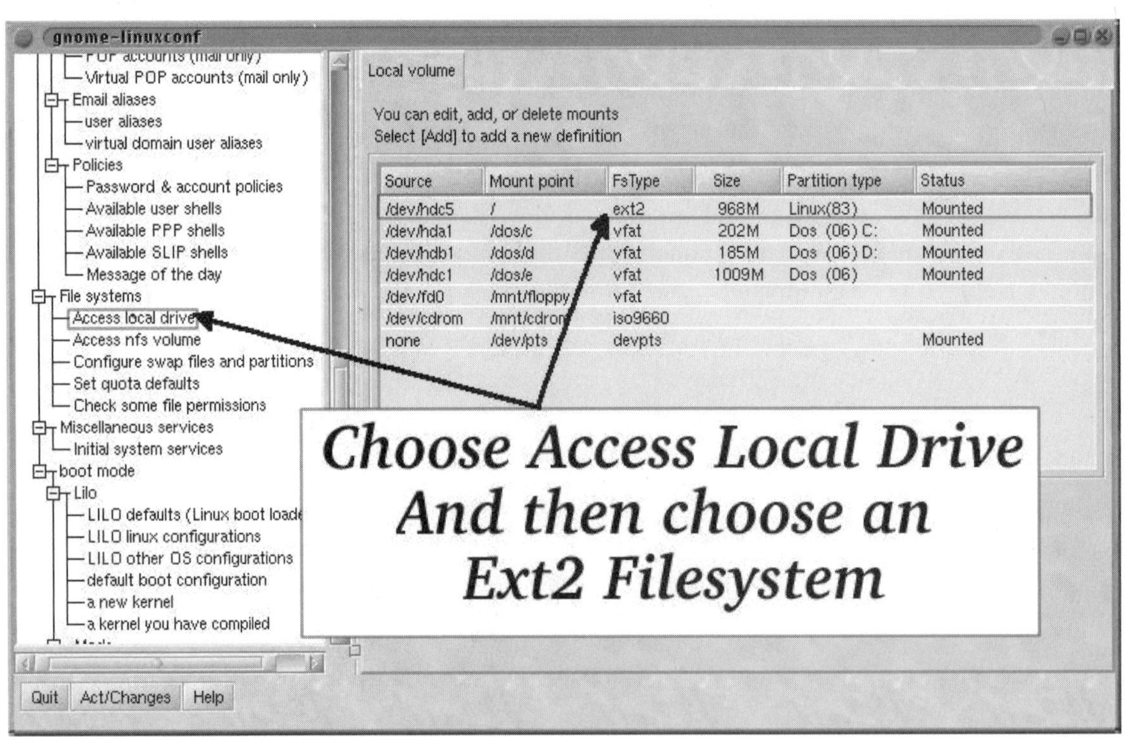

FIGURE 6-2 Linuxconf—Volume Specifications tab

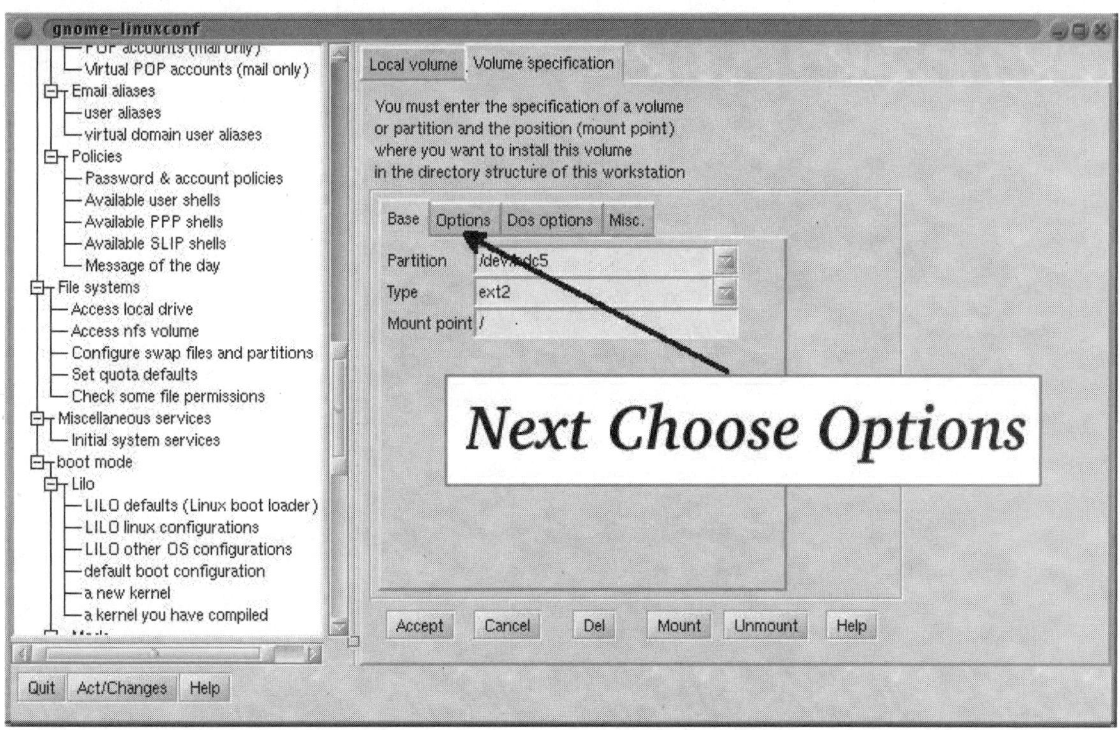

Finally, check both the User and Group check boxes at the bottom of the menu, as shown in Figure 6-3.

Once you have made these changes, the quota utilities will know which partitions to enable quotas on. Now that you have quota support enabled, you need to specify the limits for your users.

Creating the quota.user and quota.group for Each Partition

There are two ways to create the quota.user and quota.group for each partition: One is by hand, and the other is using the quotacheck utility. To do it by hand, you need to create an empty file in the root of your partition

FIGURE 6-3 User and Group Quota's check boxes on the Options tab

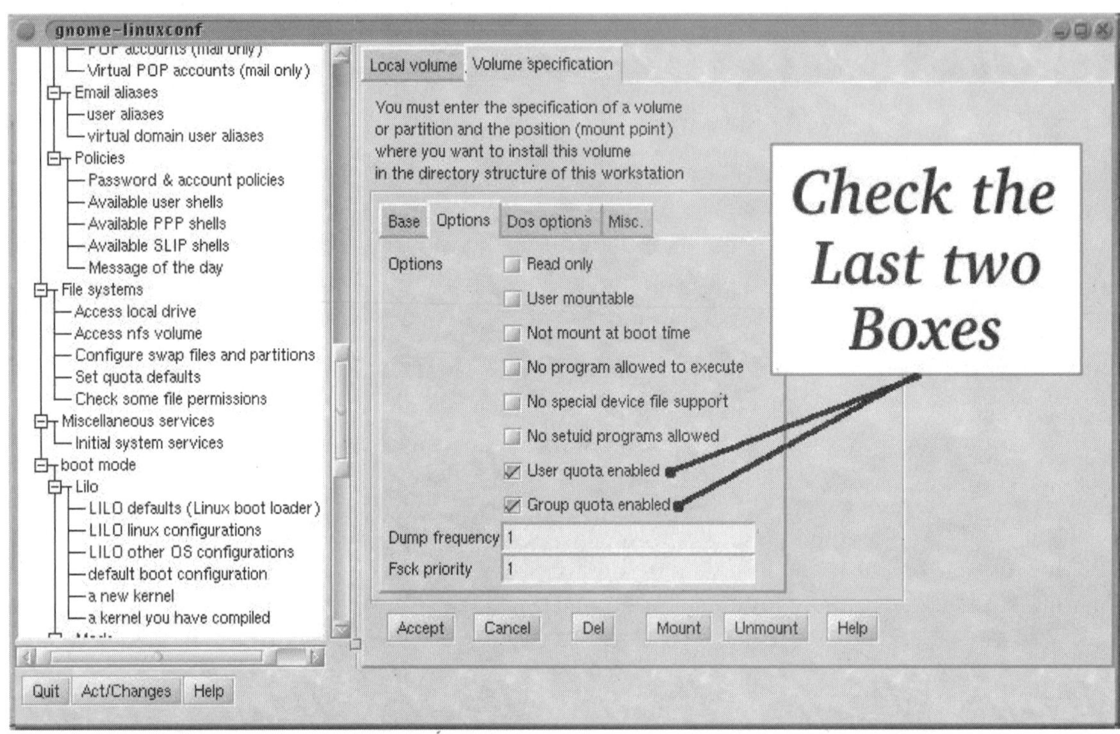

and set the security so that only root has read and write permissions. For example:

```
touch /quota.user
touch /quota.group
chmod 600 /quota.user
chmod 600 /quota.group
```

This step will be done automatically for you when you run quotacheck with the avug arguments. This will check the current quota information for all users, groups, and partitions. It stores this information in the root of your quota partitions:

```
quotacheck -avug
Scanning /dev/hdc5 [/] done
Checked 3253 directories and 54212 files
Using quotafile /quota.user
Using quotafile /quota.group
```

If you did not create these files by hand, they will be created now and should have the appropriate security already set, but you should double-check just to be safe.

If you used Linuxconf to enable quotas, when you activate changes it will ask if you want to run quotacheck; simply say yes and this step will be taken care of.

No matter which way you create the file, you need to run quotacheck to get initial information on your users. This can be accomplished by rebooting or by issuing quotacheck (if you haven't used it already).

Using edquota to Set Up Disk Quotas

To specify disk quotas, you need to run edquota. Edquota will edit the quota.user or quota.group file with the vi editor. You can change the editor by specifying a different one with the $EDITOR variable. In our example, we will pretend we have a user named Craig and that we want to restrict how much disk space he is allowed to use. We issue the following command to edit his quota record:

```
edquota -u Craig
```

This will launch vi and show us the following:

```
Quotas for user Craig:
/dev/hdc5: blocks in use: 12667, limits (soft = 0, hard = 0)
        inodes in use: 1749, limits (soft = 0, hard = 0)
```

If you run this command and only see the first line, then you probably forgot to run quotacheck.

In this example, our soft and hard limits are set to 0, which is the default. We can see that Craig is currently using 12MB of disk space and has almost 2000 files on our partition. We want to set a limit so that he does not exceed the 20MB usage policy. First, we need to elaborate on the meaning of soft and hard limits and grace periods.

- **Soft Limit** This is the maximum amount of space a user can have on that partition. If you have set a grace period, then this will act as the borderline threshold. The user will be notified when he is in quota violation. If you have set a grace period, then you will also need to set a Hard Limit.
- **Hard Limit** Hard Limits are only necessary when you are using grace periods. If grace periods are enabled, this will be the absolute limit that a person can use. If you are not using grace periods, the Soft Limit is the absolute space the user can use.

In our example, we will set our user to a 18MB Soft Limit and a 20MB Hard Limit. We will give Craig a seven-day grace period to get his stuff cleaned up.

```
Quotas for user Craig:
/dev/hdc5: blocks in use: 12667, limits (soft = 18000, hard = 20000)
        inodes in use: 1749, limits (soft = 0, hard = 0)
```

Now we can save this file. We still need to set the grace period. To do this, you again use the edquota command, but provide a -t as an argument.

edquota -t

vi will load and you will see something similar to the following:

```
Time units may be: days, hours, minutes, or seconds
Grace period before enforcing soft limits for users:
/dev/hdc5: block grace period: 7 days, file grace period: 7 days
```

Here we set the grace period to be seven days for both blocks and files. Now we just save the file, and the user is limited to 20MB of disk consumption.

Edquota allows you to use an already configured users quota as a template for new users. To use this feature, you need to use the -p <configured_user> argument.

edquota -u -p Craig Bob Sue

This command will not provide any output, but it will take the configuration settings of Craig and apply them to both Bob and Sue. You can list as many users as you want to edit or apply templates to.

You can also set up quotas on a per-group basis. To do this, simply run edquota with the -g <group_name> argument.

edquota -g games

```
Quotas for group games:
/dev/hdc5: blocks in use: 722, limits (soft = 0, hard = 0)
        inodes in use: 59, limits (soft = 0, hard = 0)
```

To use Linuxconf, choose User accounts | Normal | User accounts, and select the desired user. When editing the user's information, there is a section for quotas. You can add the hard and soft limits in this file.

First, select the user that you wish to add a quota for, as shown in Figure 6-4. Next, you will need to choose the Disk Quotas tab, as shown in Figure 6-5.

As shown in Figure 6-6, you can now specify the disk and file Hard and Soft Limits. You can also choose a grace period for this user. If you don't choose a grace period, the Hard Limits will be ignored.

Once you are satisfied, click ACCEPT. When you quit linuxconf, it will ask you to activate changes. After activating the changes, they will immediately become in effect.

Creating Default Quota Settings

You can set up system-wide defaults for your quotas, as shown in Figure 6-7. This is a nice feature that will save you some time if you have a system-wide policy. The easiest way to do this is with linuxconf. You need to access the Quota Defaults menu through File Systems | Set quota defaults. In this menu, you can add the Soft and Hard Limits, and the grace periods.

FIGURE 6-4 Linuxconf—User Accounts menu

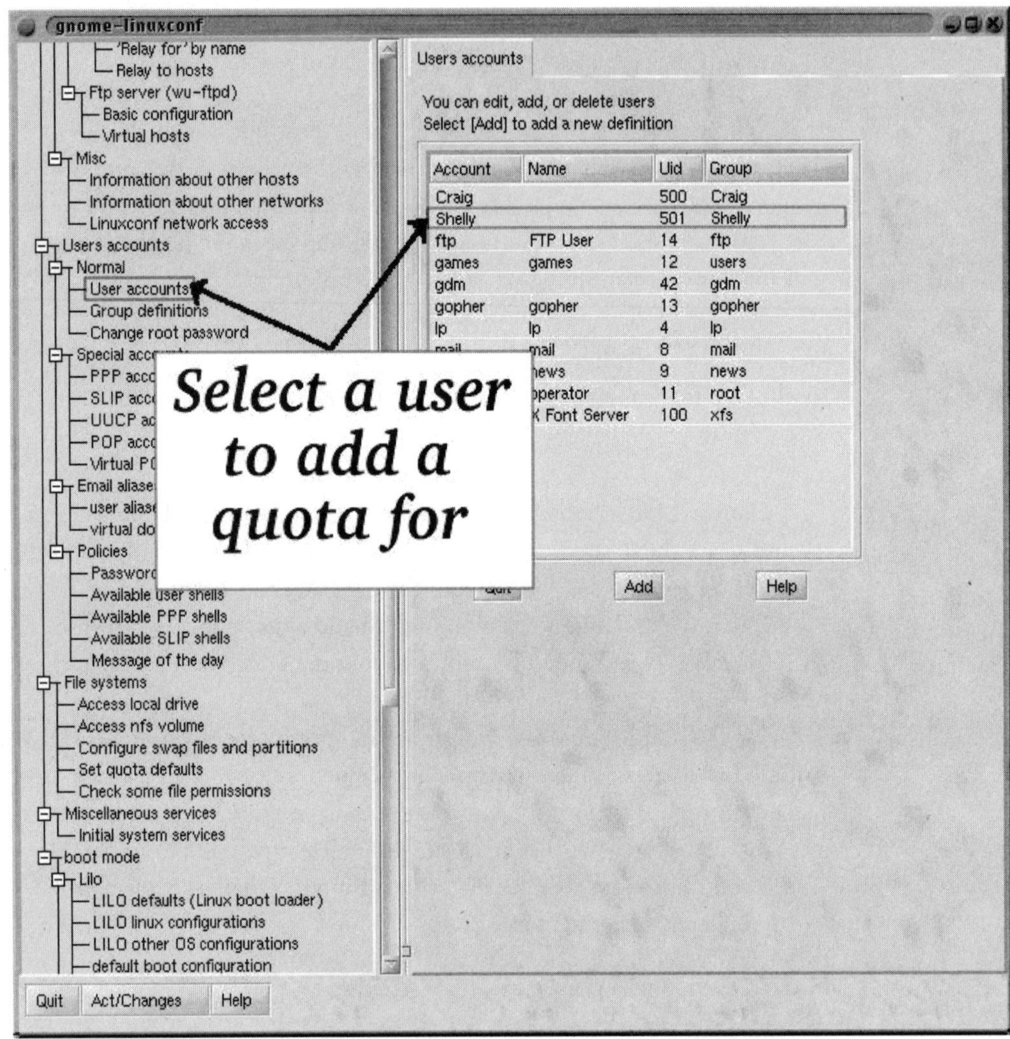

FIGURE 6-5 Linuxconf—User Information menu for user Shelly

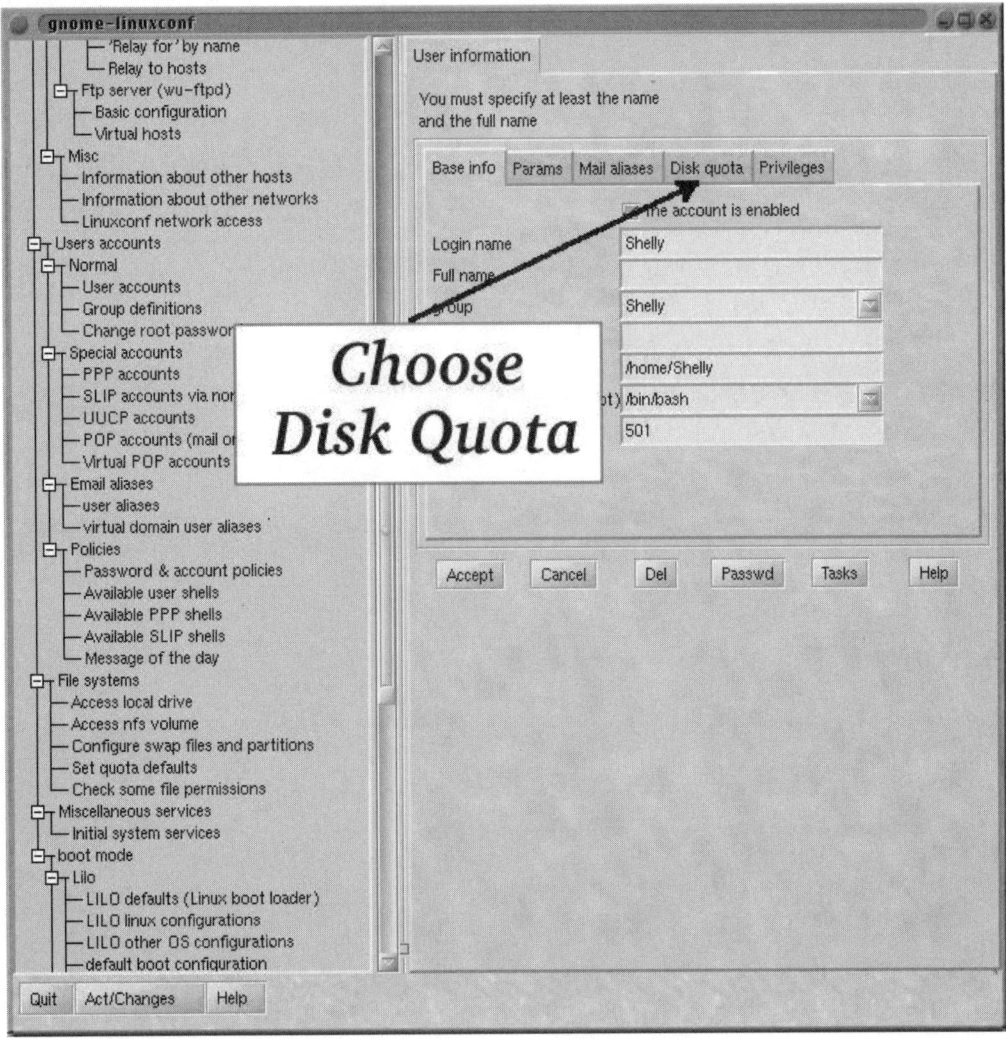

FIGURE 6-6 Linuxconf—Disk Quota tab under User Information

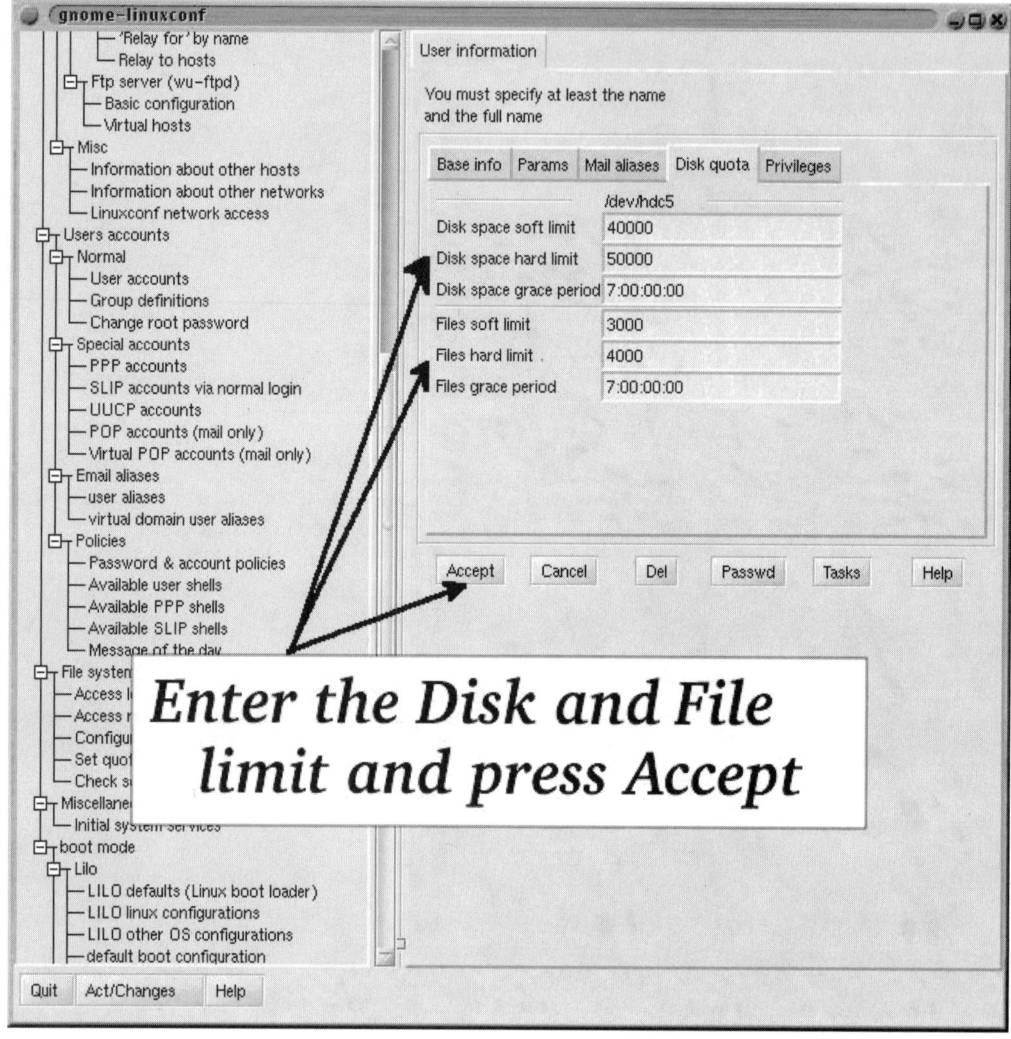

FIGURE 6-7 Linuxconf—File System Set Quota Defaults menu

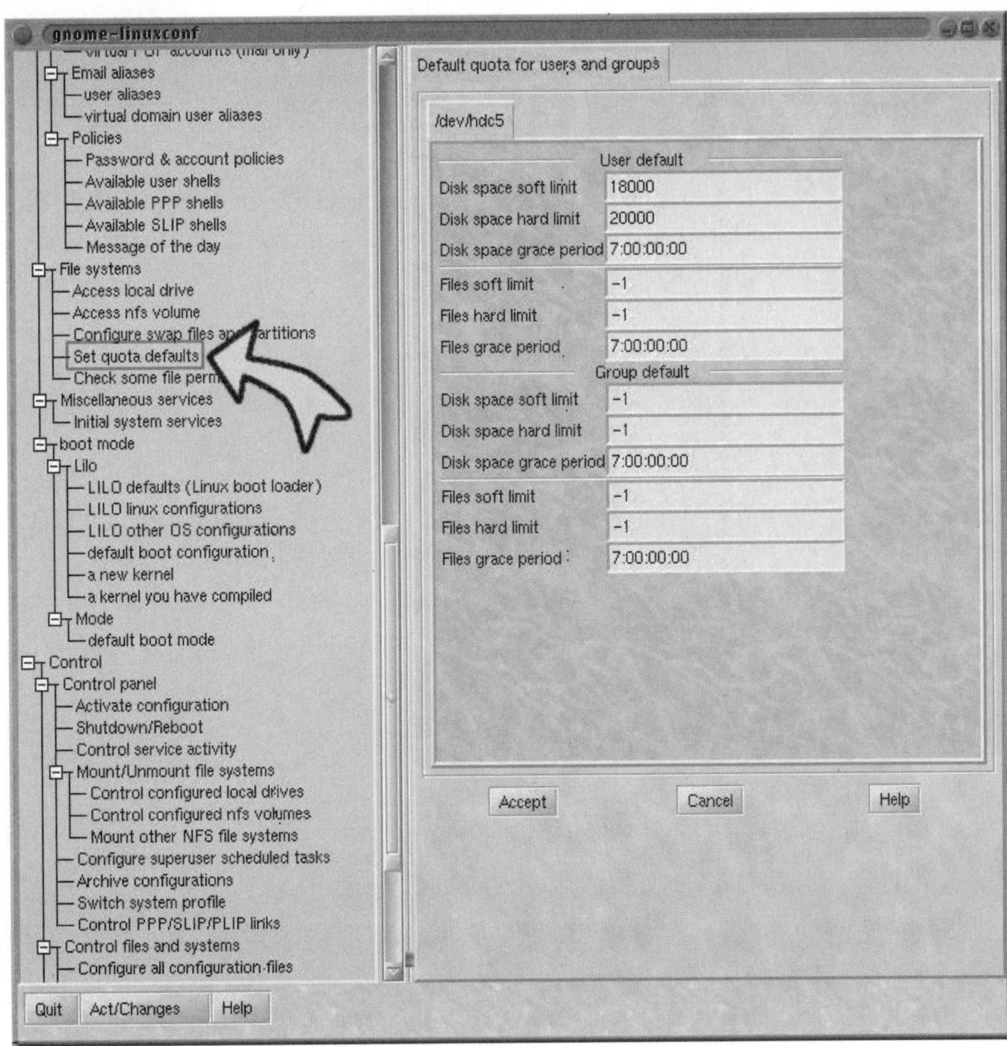

Note: When you change this setting, all of your other quota settings will be replaced with the system defaults. It's best to use this first and then set your users individually as needed.

Quota Reports

It is always nice to see reports on who is using the most disk space. You can generate reports on users, groups, or everybody on every partition. To view a report that shows you all the quota information, you can run the repquota -a command.

repquota -a

```
                        Block limits                  File limits
User            used    soft      hard  grace    used  soft  hard  grace
root      --  748092       0         0          48592     0     0
bin       --     135       0         0              5     0     0
daemon    --      22       0         0             18     0     0
sys       --       0       0         0            282     0     0
tty       --      16       0         0            650     0     0
disk      --       0       0         0           3489     0     0
lp        --      78       0         0              6     0     0
kmem      --       6       0         0              4     0     0
mail      --     143       0         0              5     0     0
uucp      --     995       0         0            458     0     0
man       --    2546       0         0            798     0     0
floppy    --      27       0         0             21     0     0

games     --     722       0         0             59     0     0
slocate   --     682       0         0              5     0     0
23        --     227       0         0             19     0     0
gdm       --     640       0         0             10     0     0
ftp       --    1524       0         0            145     0     0
nobody    --       1       0         0              1     0     0
users     --    4981       0         0            213     0     0
utmp      --     512       0         0              4     0     0
110       --    3366       0         0            352     0     0
xfs       --       1       0         0              2     0     0
Craig     --   10124       0         0           1396     0     0
Bob       --      42       0         0             41     0     0
Sue       --      42       0         0             41     0     0
2133      --    7416       0         0            811     0     0
5000      --    1018       0         0            120     0     0
```

```
                           Block limits                  File limits
User              used     soft     hard   grace     used   soft   hard   grace
root        --  750438        0        0             53969     0      0
daemon      --       2        0        0                 3     0      0
uucp        --     924        0        0                17     0      0
games       --       2    18000    20000                39     0      0
gdm         --     629    18000    20000                 2     0      0
xfs         --       1    18000    20000                 2     0      0
101         --    3366        0        0               352     0      0
112         --     790        0        0                94     0      0
204         --    3246        0        0                 1     0      0
405         --     227        0        0                19     0      0


Craig       --   12684    18000    20000              1749     0      0
Bob         --    2573    17000    20000               328     0      0
Sue         --    2573    17000    20000               328     0      0
2133        --    7416        0        0               811     0      0
5064        --    1018        0        0               120     0      0
```

You can use repquota to show you specific reports on all the users on a certain partition with the following command:

repquota -u /

To see specific information on just one user, use the quota command.

quota -u Craig

```
Disk quotas for user Craig (uid 500):
     Filesystem  blocks    quota    limit    grace    files    quota    limit
grace
      /dev/hdc5    12690    18000    20000              1749        0        0
```

An individual user can check his or her own usage with the quota command, but only root can use the -u option to look at other users.

Quotas on NFS File Systems

Setting quotas on an NFS file system is similar. NFS translates the remote users to local users. You specify how this translation works with the nfsd configuration. See Chapter 7 for more about NFS drives and related information. You need to set the disk quotas to the user that you plan on mapping outside users to. So, if you create a local user called nfsuser and you translate all remote requests to this user, then you need to set up quota restrictions for nfsuser on the mounted partition. This will limit the disk consumption of all incoming NFS users.

CERTIFICATION OBJECTIVE 6.02

System Initialization Scripts

After the /etc/rc.d/rc.sysinit script described in Chapter 4 runs, there are a few other scripts that run after it. These scripts include rc.serial, rc.local, and rc. The first two scripts are used for system-specific initialization, and the rc script is a general script that determines what demons run on what runlevel.

/etc/rc.d/rc.serial

This script is used for special setups for serial devices. It is not usually installed with a default Red Hat installation. You will typically find setserial commands in this script.

/etc/rc.d/rc.local

By default, rc.local sets up your issue and issue.net files. This script is the last script to run. You can put any specific programs you want to run in this script. Here is a default /etc/rc.d/rc.local script that is installed with Red Hat 6.0:

```
#!/bin/sh

# This script will be executed *after* all the other init scripts.
# You can put your own initialization stuff in here if you don't
# want to do the full Sys V style init stuff.
```

```
if [ -f /etc/redhat-release ]; then
    R=$(cat /etc/redhat-release)

    arch=$(uname -m)
    a="a"
    case "_$arch" in
         _a*) a="an";;
         _i*) a="an";;
    esac

    # This will overwrite /etc/issue at every boot.  So, make any
       changes you
    # want to make to /etc/issue here or you will lose them when you
      reboot.
    echo "" > /etc/issue
    echo "$R" >> /etc/issue
    echo "Kernel $(uname -r) on $a $(uname -m)" >> /etc/issue

    cp -f /etc/issue /etc/issue.net
    echo >> /etc/issue
fi
```

/etc/issue and /etc/issue.net

These two files are set up by rc.local. The /etc/issue is the message you see when you boot your PC into text mode. While the /etc/issue.net is almost identical, it is the logon banner you see when coming into your PC over the network using a program such as telnet.

Here is a typical /etc/issue file:

```
Red Hat Linux release 6.0 (Hedwig)
Kernel 2.2.5-15 on an i686
```

This is the default issue file for a Red Hat 6.0 Intel install. You should consider changing this file for security reasons. As you can see, these two lines usually contain more information about your setup than you'd want an outsider to see. You should also consider adding an Unauthorized Access Prohibited warning message. In order to do this, you must take out or change the rc.local file, or the next time you reboot, your issue file will be erased.

/etc/rc.d,/etc/rc0.d ... /etc/rc6.d

In the /etc/inittab file, the /etc/rc script is called and the desired runlevel is passed as a parameter. Here is an excerpt from /etc/inittab:

```
l0:0:wait:/etc/rc.d/rc 0
l1:1:wait:/etc/rc.d/rc 1
l2:2:wait:/etc/rc.d/rc 2
l3:3:wait:/etc/rc.d/rc 3
l4:4:wait:/etc/rc.d/rc 4
l5:5:wait:/etc/rc.d/rc 5
l6:6:wait:/etc/rc.d/rc 6
```

For more information on how /etc/inittab works, see Chapter 4. Here, you can see that for each runlevel, /etc/rc.d/rc is called and the runlevel is passed.

It then changes to the specific runlevels directory rc#.d. In this directory, you will see a bunch of link files, some that begin with a K and others with an S. There is a two-digit number after the first letter and then the daemon's name. Here is an example directory from an /etc/rc3.d directory:

```
K20nfs       K55routed    S15netfs    S50inet       S85sound
K20rstatd    K96pcmcia    S20random   S60lpd        S90xfs
K20rusersd   S05apmd      S30syslog   S75keytable   S91smb
K20rwhod     S10network   S40atd      S80sendmail   S99linuxconf
K50snmpd     S11portmap   S40crond    S85gpm        S99local
```

The links that begin with a K signal a Kill, and the S signals a start. The two-digit numbers are priority numbers; they determine which daemon loads first. When entering a runlevel, all the links that begin with an S are loaded, and when you exit that runlevel, all the links that begin with a K are killed.

These are not files, but links to the actual program. The actual daemon sits in /etc/rc.d/init.d. If we take a closer look at one of the links, we will see it pointing to the init.d directory.

```
lrwxrwxrwx   1 root root   13 May 15 15:05 S85gpm-> ../init.d/gpm
```

This program will start with a priority of 85 and execute ../init.d/gpm, and because this link is in the rc3.d directory, it will start when runlevel 3 is activated. This priority number is not the same as process priority; it is simply the sequence by which the services will load. This method may seem confusing at first, but it is quickly becoming a standard among other Linux distributions. This method is fast and takes up very little disk space because almost all the files are links to the real files.

Starting X Windows Automatically

This was discussed briefly in Chapter 4, and now we'll take a closer look at some of the other scripts that run. In Chapter 4 you noticed that runlevel 5 was the default level in the inittab file to load X Windows during bootup. Here are two lines that show how X boots:

```
l5:5:wait:/etc/rc.d/rc 5
x:5:respawn:/etc/X11/prefdm -nodaemon
```

You can see the first thing that runs is the rc5.d links, and then it runs prefdm. If you look at the rc5.d links, you will see that most if not all of the daemons are the same and are not X specific. The real magic happens when prefdm runs.

Prefdm is a link that points to the proffered display manager. This is typically xdm, kdm, or gdm. Xdm is X Windows' default window manager, Kdm is KDE's window manager, and gdm isGnome's window manager. The window managers actually provide you with the X logon box and start an X session for you.

You may be thinking, "that is really fascinating, but I still don't know how to start X automatically." To start X automatically, you simply change one number in the inittab file.

```
id:5:initdefault:
```

If this number isn't 5, change it to 5 and reboot. You will now boot in X Windows with your proffered window manager. You can also change your default runlevel with linuxconf, as shown in Figure 6-8. You should test your X configuration before setting this value to 5. If you set it to 5 and X windows fails to load properly, you can switch to a text-based terminal by pressing CTRL-ALT-F1.

FIGURE 6-8 Linuxconf—Initial System Services menu

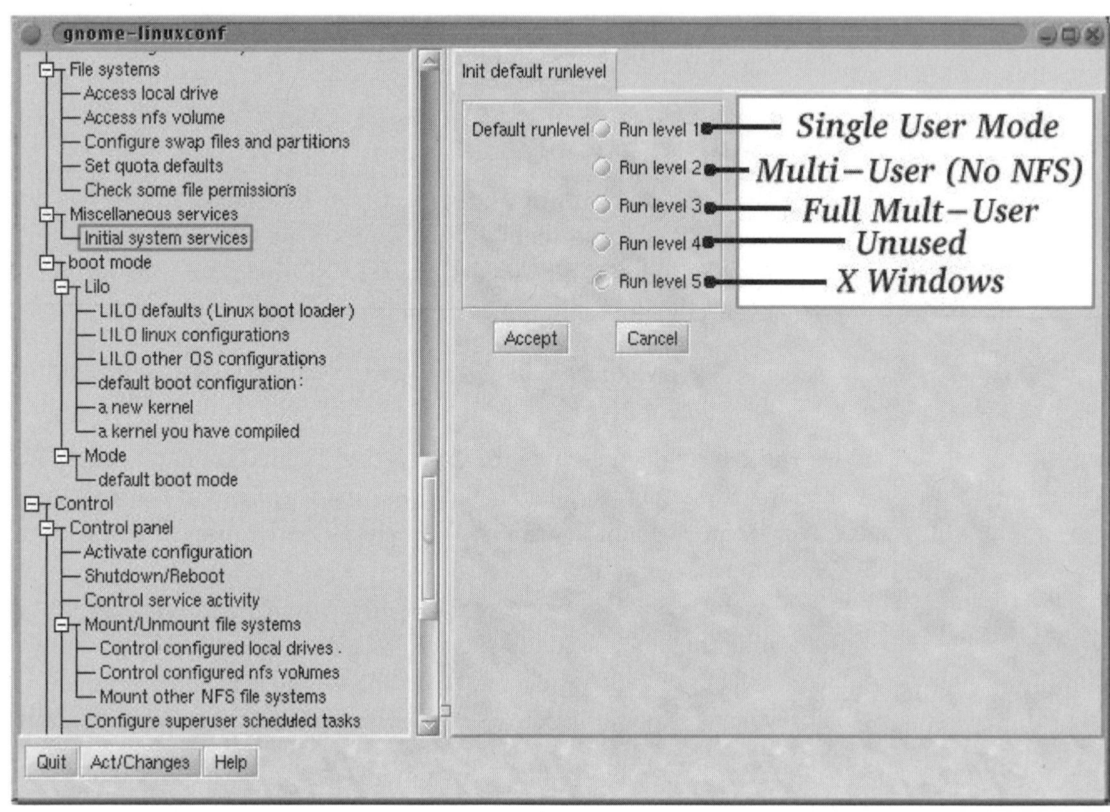

CERTIFICATION OBJECTIVE 6.03

Kernel Recompilation and Installation

One of Linux's strong features is the ability to recompile your kernel. The kernel is the heart of the whole operating system. It's what boots and loads up your different system-level device drivers. With the ability to recompile your kernel, you can greatly improve the speed and lower the memory consumption of your kernel. In essence, you can build a specific kernel for your architecture.

Best Practices

Your kernel should be compiled with only the things you need. The less stuff you add to the kernel that you probably won't use, the faster your whole system will run. For instance, if you are building a server that has a sound card, then there is probably no reason for you to compile sound support into your kernel (or to leave the sound card installed). By removing devices that you don't need, you will decrease the size of the kernel, which will increase its speed, lower memory consumption, and increase device recognition during booting.

It is also a good idea to have device modules compiled for extra equipment you may have lying around. Modules are not compiled directly into the kernel, but can be plugged in and removed as needed. They will be explained in more detail later in this chapter. The reason you would do this is so you do not have to recompile the kernel in the event of hardware failure. For example, if you have a 3c59x network card installed but also have some 3c905 cards in storage, then it may be a good idea to make the 3c905 module. In the case of a failure, you just have to slap in the new card and load the module—with minimum downtime.

Kernel Concepts

There are some basic kernel concepts you will need to understand before you can compile your own kernel. Most of these concepts were briefly discussed previously.

Monolithic Versus Modular

A *monolithic* kernel is a kernel that has all of the device modules built directly into it. A *modular* kernal has devices that are separate, loadable modules. A monolithic kernel can talk directly to its devices faster than a module. However, it will increase the size of your kernel. Increasing the size of your kernel decreases you system-wide available memory, and some systems need to have the kernel smaller than a certain size in order to boot. You can add more than one device in a monolithic kernel and it will load the right one for your architecture. Although this will slow down boot time and also unnecessarily increase the kernel size, there is a benefit to this. If you are working in an environment with people who don't understand

Linux, then you could load other possible drivers that may eventually be used in the system. For example, if your network card failed and you only had a different brand available in storage but it was compiled into the kernel, then you could just instruct someone over the phone to put the card in and turn the server back on. That's it! The server would boot up, load the different network card, and appropriately assign it the old IP.

A modular kernel has greater flexibility. You can compile almost all of your drivers as modules. A module can be inserted into the kernel whenever you need it. Modules keep the initial kernel size low, which increases the boot time and overall performance. You can use kerneld(8) to load modules when necessary, or modprobe(1) to load modules during bootup or at the command line. It should be noted that kerneld(8) is mainly used in older kernels because the newer kernels have this functionality built in.

One drawback to modules is that you may have to do some upkeep yourself. If you change to a different type of network card, then you will have to specify this in your boot scripts (modules.conf). There are a few tricks to have the modules load the appropriate driver that are discussed in Chapter 4.

As you can imagine, a typical system is usually a mix of both modular and monolithic kernels. Essential drivers may be built directly in while other parts remain modules. For example, a router may have its network cards built directly in while leaving all the IP masquerading abilities as modules.

The Kernel in Relation to the Rest of the System

A monolithic kernel will use the most memory and will probably waste space with unused drivers. It will talk faster to the devices than a modular kernel. A modular kernel will keep the kernel small and will load fast, but will take a performance hit when loading modules. Direct communication to the devices will be slightly slower, and there is more upkeep.

It should also be noted that the kernel reserves around 5MB of hard drive space that it doesn't show you—if the server runs out of hard drive space, you would still be able to boot and clean up the system. This shouldn't affect you as an administrator unless your partition fills.

Updating the Kernel

Updating the kernel is a relatively easy process. You should always keep a copy of your old kernel around in case you make a mistake. This can easily be done with lilo(8) by adding another image section in the /etc/lilo.conf file. The new section should point to your new kernel, then modify the old section to point to your old kernel, and change the label to "old" or something similar. If you do make a drastic mistake and the kernel doesn't boot, then you can simply reboot the server and type **old** at the LILO prompt. You should also save your kernel configuration files so you can easily copy them to the newer kernels and use them as a guideline. This will be discussed in more detail a little later. You should also be aware that the PCMCIA devices are not kept in the kernel; they need to be downloaded and installed separately.

/boot Partitions

It is a good idea to copy all of your kernels to the /boot directory. This boot directory can be made into a separate partition. When you set up a Linux box, you can set the first partition to a small (10MB) partition and mount it as /boot. By doing this, you can then move your hard drive to a machine that has an older BIOS and still boot without any changes. Older BIOSs have a hard drive limitation of around 500MB. If you take a bigger drive and set it up in the aforementioned way, Linux will still boot on an older system just like it would on a new system.

The reason for this is that Linux doesn't have drive limitation and is not reliant on the BIOS to provide information on the drive. However, lilo(8) is booted by the BIOS and needs to have the kernel where the BIOS can see it. Once the kernel starts to load, Linux will take over and you will not have any more limitations. In some installs where you are using an old BIOS or are installing to a third drive, you may need to reserve a small partition on the first drive for the /boot directory.

/proc directory

Proc is a directory that is virtual; it doesn't actually exist on the hard drive. All of its information is maintained by the kernel. This is a great source of information about what your kernel is doing. It also has many kernel variables that you can adjust to instantly change how the kernel is acting. You should spend some time looking at the files in the proc directory. Following are some examples of the types of information files present.

cat /proc/meminfo

```
        total:    used:    free:  shared: buffers:  cached:
Mem:  64651264 62717952  1933312 50225152  1527808 31232000
Swap: 37122048  1273856 35848192
MemTotal:      63136 kB
MemFree:        1888 kB
MemShared:     49048 kB
Buffers:        1492 kB
Cached:        30500 kB
SwapTotal:     36252 kB
SwapFree:      35008 kB
```

cat /proc/cpuinfo

```
processor       : 0
vendor_id       : GenuineIntel
cpu family      : 6
model           : 6
model name      : Celeron (Mendocino)
stepping        : 5
cpu MHz         : 400.924148
cache size      : 128 KB
fdiv_bug        : no
hlt_bug         : no
sep_bug         : no
f00f_bug        : no
fpu             : yes
fpu_exception   : yes
cpuid level     : 2
wp              : yes
flags           : fpu vme de pse tsc msr pae mce cx8 sep mtrr pge mca cmov pat pse36
mmx osfxsr
bogomips        : 399.77
```

There are many programs that simply look at the information and report it in a more readable format. More importantly, there are kernel variables that you can alter to change the way the kernel behaves. Here are some examples:

echo 1 > /proc/sys/net/ipv4/ip_forward

This will turn on forwarding on the system, essentially making it a router.

echo 1 > /proc/sys/net/ipv4/tcp_syncookies

This will enable the use of TCP SYN packet cookies, which prevents SYN flood attacks on your system.

echo "/sbin/modprobe" > /proc/sys/kernel/modprobe

This will allow the kernel to find modprobe if kmod is installed into the kernel. Kmod is a replacement for kerneld, and the kernel directly loads the modules. You can set these echo statements in your rc.local file for quick and easy modification of kernel variables.

The Kernel Source Tree and Documentation

The source code for the kernel is kept in the /usr/src/linux directory. The /usr/src directory usually looks as follows:

```
lrwxrwxrwx    1 root      root          11 May 15 14:55 linux -> linux-2.2.5
drwxr-xr-x   17 root      root        1024 May 17 19:48 linux-2.2.5
drwxr-xr-x    7 root      root        1024 May 15 14:58 redhat
```

The physical directory is linux-2.2.5, and there is a soft link called linux that points to this directory. Using this method, you can create a directory for a new kernel, change the link to point to the new directory, and still keep your old source for reference. The /usr/src/linux directory is laid out as follows:

```
COPYING          README                  drivers/ ipc/     net/
CREDITS          README.kernel-sources   fs/      kernel/  pcmcia-cs-3.0.9/
Documentation/   REPORTING-BUGS          ibcs/    lib/     scripts/
MAINTAINERS      Rules.make              include/ mm/
Makefile         arch/                   init/    modules/
```

You will really want to read the README file. Also, check out the Documentation directory. Everything is in there, from setting up Symmetrical Multiprocessors to serial consoles. The other directories are mainly source and you probably won't need to mess with those. There is also a hidden file in this directory named .config. This file will be described in more detail later in this chapter.

The Kernel rpms and the Linux Kernel Tar File

If you don't see the directories mentioned in the preceding section, then you haven't installed the kernel's source code. To install the source that was provided with your Red Hat installation, you simply need to mount the CD-ROM drive and install the kernel rpm.

```
mount /dev/cdrom
cd /mnt/cdrom/redhat/RPMS/
rpm -ivh kernel-2.2.5-15.src.rpm
```

Or, you can download the newest kernel from http://www.kernel.org. The version numbers are discussed in the next section. Once you have downloaded the kernel source, you will need to properly install it. For our example, we will assume you downloaded linux-2.2.10.tar.gz into the /usr/src/ directory.

```
cd /usr/src
mkdir linux-2.2.10
rm linux
ln -s linux-2.2.10 linux
tar xvfz linux-2.2.10.tar.gz
```

Here we manually created a new directory for the kernel. Then we removed the old link and made a new one that pointed to the new directory. When we uncompress the tar.gz file, it will uncompress to the Linux link.

Understanding Kernel Version Numbers

The version number may look a little confusing, but it is actually really useful. For our example, we will use kernel version 2.0.36 because each section has a different number.

The first number (2) is the major version number. These indicate drastic changes to the kernel. Typically, older version stuff will *not* work in the newer version when this number changes.

The second number (0) actually has two meanings. If the number is an even number, it is a stable release version. If it is an odd number, it is a developmental version. Version number changes here are very significant, and some major changes have typically been made.

The third number (36) is the minor version number for the kernel. These indicate changes that are typically small changes, bug fixes, and enhancements.

Usually, software that has kernel version requirements will only refer to the first two major numbers. For example, if you install software that will only work with version 2.2 and later kernels. This would mean that all 2.2.*x* and later kernels would be required for this software.

The Kernel Configuration Scripts

There is a hidden file that contains all the kernel configuration information, /usr/src/linux/.config. It is structured as a listing of variables. Here are some entries from the .config file:

```
CONFIG_IP_MASQUERADE=y
CONFIG_IP_MASQUERADE_IPAUTOFW=m
# CONFIG_IP_ROUTER is not set
```

There are three main types of variables you'll see in this file. The first will compile in direct support, the second will compile a module, and the third is commented out and will not compile anything. You should never have to edit this file directly; there are many nicer ways to configure your kernel.

The bare minimum script can be executed by running:

make config

This script will prompt you through your different options. Here is a snippet of some output:

```
Processor family (386, 486/Cx486, 586/K5/5x86/6x86, Pentium/K6/TSC, PPro/6x86MX)
[386] 586
  defined CONFIG_M586
```

```
Math emulation (CONFIG_MATH_EMULATION) [Y/n/?] n
MTRR (Memory Type Range Register) support (CONFIG_MTRR) [Y/n/?] n
Symmetric multi-processing support (CONFIG_SMP) [N/y/?] n
*
* Loadable module support
*
Enable loadable module support (CONFIG_MODULES) [Y/n/?] y
```

Here, your variables are listed in parentheses and your answers are in brackets. The default answer is in capital letters. If you answer with a ?, then you will see a help page explaining what this option does. If you just press ENTER, the defaults will be accepted.

A nicer way to create the .config file is to use menuconfig. This requires that you have ncurses installed. This is a text-based menu-driven system makes changes to a kernel easier. To load this, simply issue the following command:

make menuconfig

Here is what the screen looks like:

```
Linux Kernel v2.2.5 Configuration

--------------------------------------------------------------------------
 +------------------------------ Main Menu ----------------------------+
 |  Arrow keys navigate the menu.  <Enter> selects submenus --->.      |
 |  Highlighted letters are hotkeys.  Pressing <Y> includes, <N> excludes, |
 |  <M> modularizes features.  Press <Esc><Esc> to exit, <?> for Help. |
 |  Legend: [*] built-in  [ ] excluded  <M> module  < > module capable |
 | +-----------------------------------------------------------------+ |
 | |           Code maturity level options  --->                     | |
 | |           Processor type and features  --->                     | |
 | |           Loadable module support  --->                         | |
 | |           General setup  --->                                   | |
 | |           Plug and Play support  --->                           | |
 | |           Block devices  --->                                   | |
 | |           Networking options  --->                              | |
 | |           SCSI support  --->                                    | |
 | |           Network device support  --->                          | |
 | |           Amateur Radio support  --->                           | |
 | +----------v(+)---------------------------------------------------+ |
 +---------------------------------------------------------------------+
 |                  <Select>    < Exit >    < Help >                   |
 +---------------------------------------------------------------------+
```

The nice thing about menuconfig is that it works well over a telnet connection. Also, there are options at the bottom of the menu for saving the .config file with an alternate name which you can then use when you upgrade your kernel.

The last way to make changes to the kernel is to use X Windows. You can have a graphical menu system to configure your kernel by running xconfig. Figure 6-9 shows the Xconfig main menu.

You also have the ability to save to an alternate file. We will show some of the options for the submenus in the following sections.

Understanding Kernel Configuration Options

You will need to understand some of the main kernel configuration options. To learn more, you can almost always choose help from one of the aforementioned configuration scripts for a more elaborate description on specific options.

FIGURE 6-9 xconfig Main menu

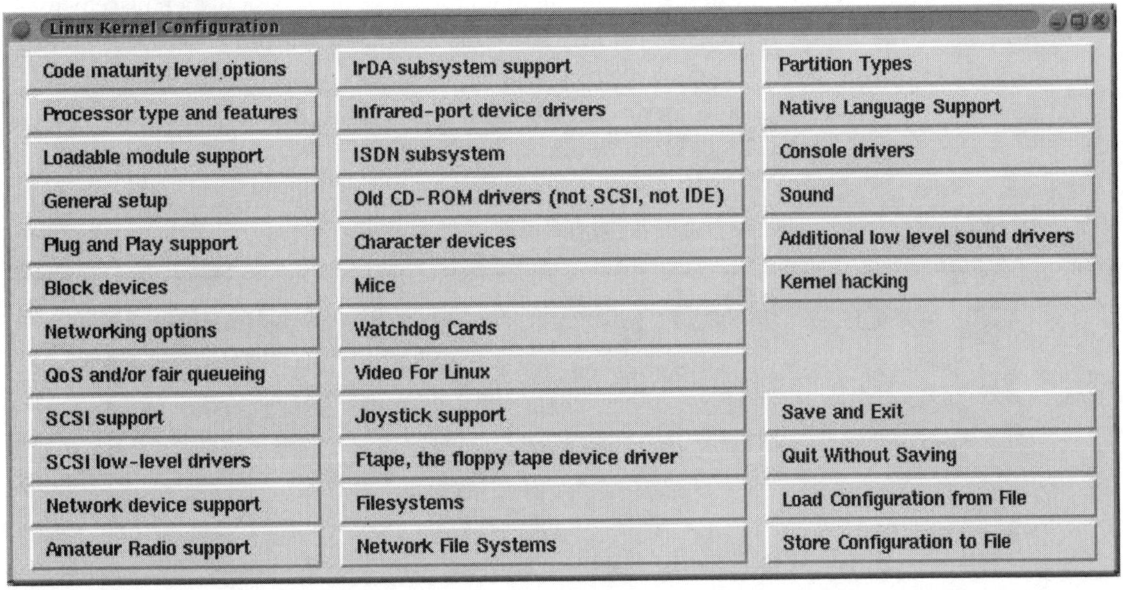

Linux Kernel Configuration

Code maturity level options	IrDA subsystem support	Partition Types
Processor type and features	Infrared-port device drivers	Native Language Support
Loadable module support	ISDN subsystem	Console drivers
General setup	Old CD-ROM drivers (not SCSI, not IDE)	Sound
Plug and Play support	Character devices	Additional low level sound drivers
Block devices	Mice	Kernel hacking
Networking options	Watchdog Cards	
QoS and/or fair queueing	Video For Linux	
SCSI support	Joystick support	Save and Exit
SCSI low-level drivers	Ftape, the floppy tape device driver	Quit Without Saving
Network device support	Filesystems	Load Configuration from File
Amateur Radio support	Network File Systems	Store Configuration to File

The Standard Red Hat Kernel Configuration

The standard distribution kernel has support for just about everything. Almost every module that can be made is made. This is a big kernel and there are a ton of modules for it with the standard installation. This is not a problem when installing, but it is highly recommended that you streamline the distribution kernel and remove unwanted modules. All xconfig images displayed in this chapter are from the default Red Hat configuration.

Code Maturity Level Options

The Code maturity level option, shown in Figure 6-10 is used to enable prompting for kernel source code drivers that are not fully developed yet. These can be considered alpha released drivers. These drivers are usually not ready for widespread use by uniformed administrators—The developers basically are trying not to get e-mail saying that there are still things that don't work.

Loadable Modules Support Options

The Loadable module support screen, shown in Figure 6-11, is where you enable the use of modules with your kernel. You also have the ability to enable the kernel to load modules for you. This is basically a replacement for kerneld. Here the kernel will load a module when the module is needed. To remove unused kernel modules with this option, you have to setup rmmod -a in root's crontab file. To read more about kmod, see /usr/src/linux/Documentation/kmod.txt.

FIGURE 6-10 xconfig—Code Maturity Level submenu

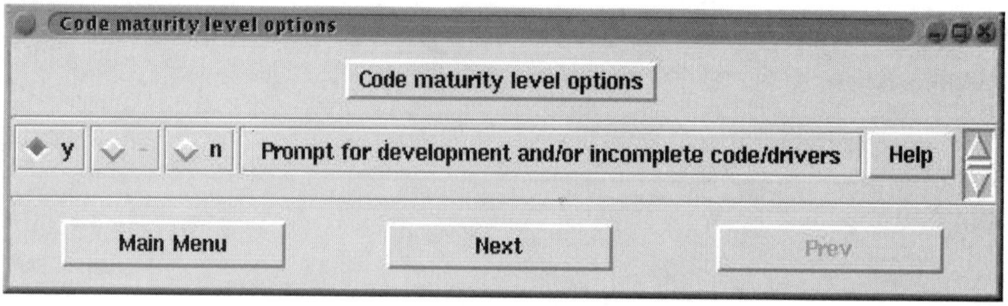

FIGURE 6-11 xconfig—Loadable Module Support submenu

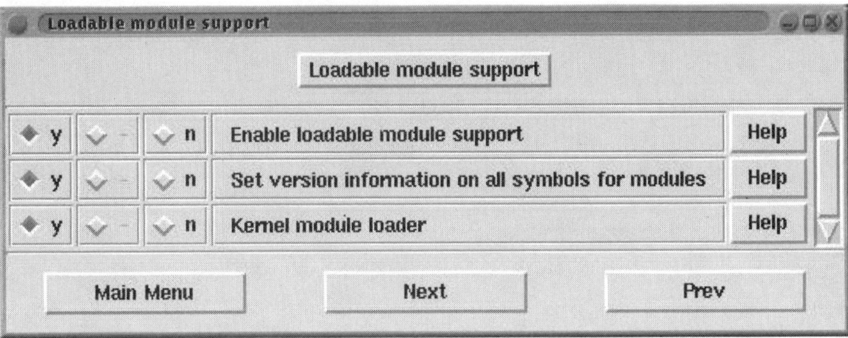

General Setup Options

Here are your general low-level options. Under General setup options, shown in Figure 6-12, you can turn support on or off for PCI, MicroChannel, and even SGI Visual Workstation. You can also specify your binary support. This is the type of executable you support.

a.out	Older format of Linux executable
ELF	Newest format for Linux
JAVA	Java binary support
MISC	Can run just about any binary

The MISC support makes ELF and JAVA support obsolete. It allows the kernel to run a binary based on either a magic byte code in the beginning of the file (see /usr/src/linux/Documentation/binfmt_misc.txt), or by the extension. For example, if you have the DOS emulator installed (DOSEMU) you could execute DOS programs from the command line. It will recognize the executable either by the magic number or the extension (ex: exe or com).

In the Advanced Power Management (APM) options, you can specify exactly how the BIOS APM will work with Linux. If you want the PC to turn off when booting, you could specify that here.

FIGURE 6-12 xconfig—General Setup submenu

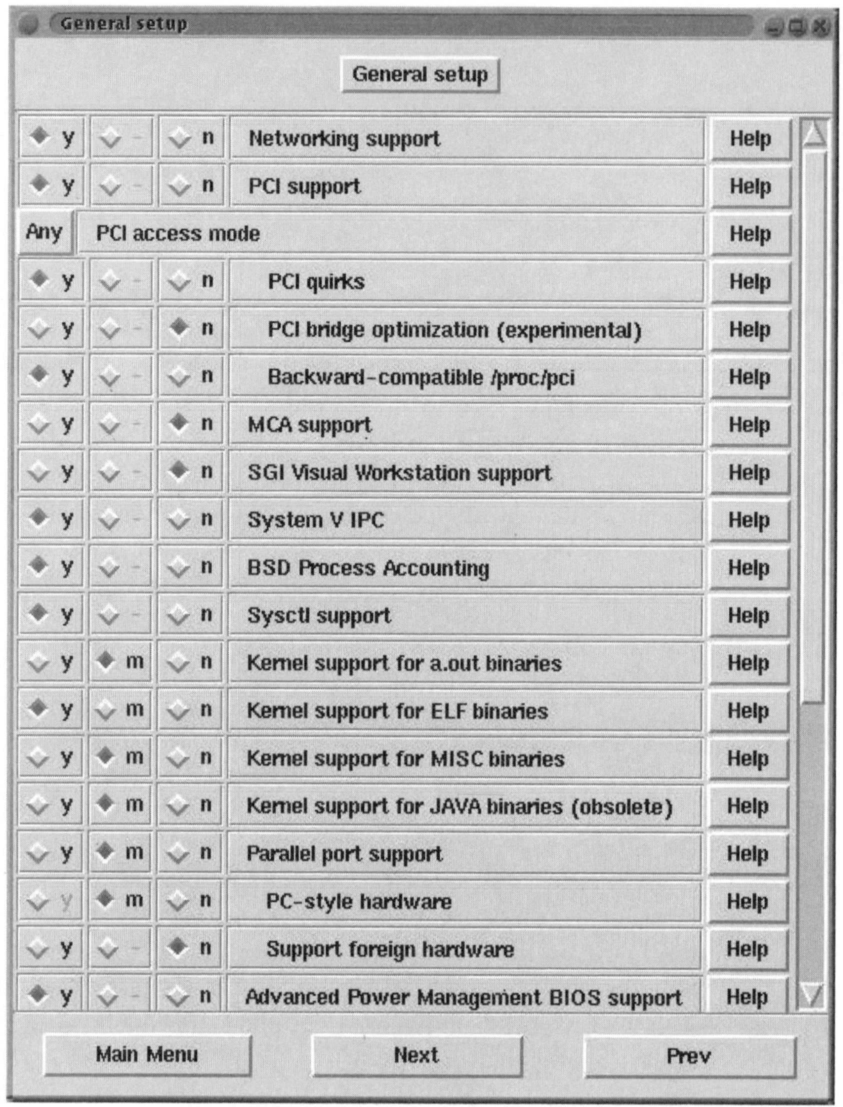

Floppy, IDE, and Other Block Device Options

You need to specify your floppy and hard drives, ATAPI devices, RAID, and several other block devices, as shown in Figure 6-13. You can specify support for ATAPI CD-ROMS, tape drives, and even ATAPI floppy drives. You can also enable loopback support and network block support (which lets you use a physical disk on the network as if it is a local disk). All of your RAID options are located in this section as well. If you have any parallel port devices such as external CD-ROMs or hard drives, you can enable support for those here. RAM disk support is also in this section.

FIGURE 6-13 xconfig—Block Devices submenu

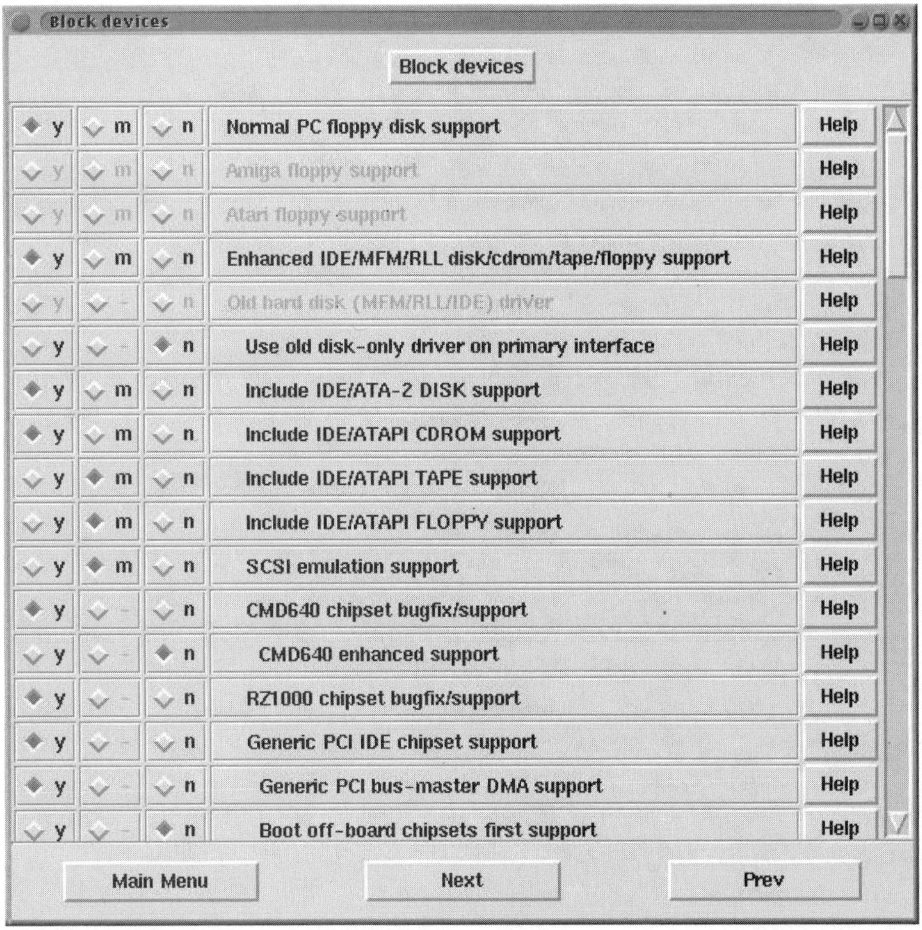

Block devices

y	m	n	Option	
y	m	n	Normal PC floppy disk support	Help
y	m	n	Amiga floppy support	Help
y	m	n	Atari floppy support	Help
y	m	n	Enhanced IDE/MFM/RLL disk/cdrom/tape/floppy support	Help
y	-	n	Old hard disk (MFM/RLL/IDE) driver	Help
y	-	n	Use old disk-only driver on primary interface	Help
y	m	n	Include IDE/ATA-2 DISK support	Help
y	m	n	Include IDE/ATAPI CDROM support	Help
y	m	n	Include IDE/ATAPI TAPE support	Help
y	m	n	Include IDE/ATAPI FLOPPY support	Help
y	m	n	SCSI emulation support	Help
y	-	n	CMD640 chipset bugfix/support	Help
y	-	n	CMD640 enhanced support	Help
y	-	n	RZ1000 chipset bugfix/support	Help
y	-	n	Generic PCI IDE chipset support	Help
y	-	n	Generic PCI bus-master DMA support	Help
y	-	n	Boot off-board chipsets first support	Help

Main Menu | Next | Prev

Non-IDE/SCSI CD-ROM Support Options

If you have an older CD-ROM that is not an IDE or SCSI CD-ROM, then you need to enable special support for it, as shown in Figure 6-14. This submenu has drivers for Mitsumi, Goldstar, Philips, Sony, and several others. All of these drivers can be loaded as modules.

FIGURE 6-14 xconfig—Old CD-ROM Drivers submenu

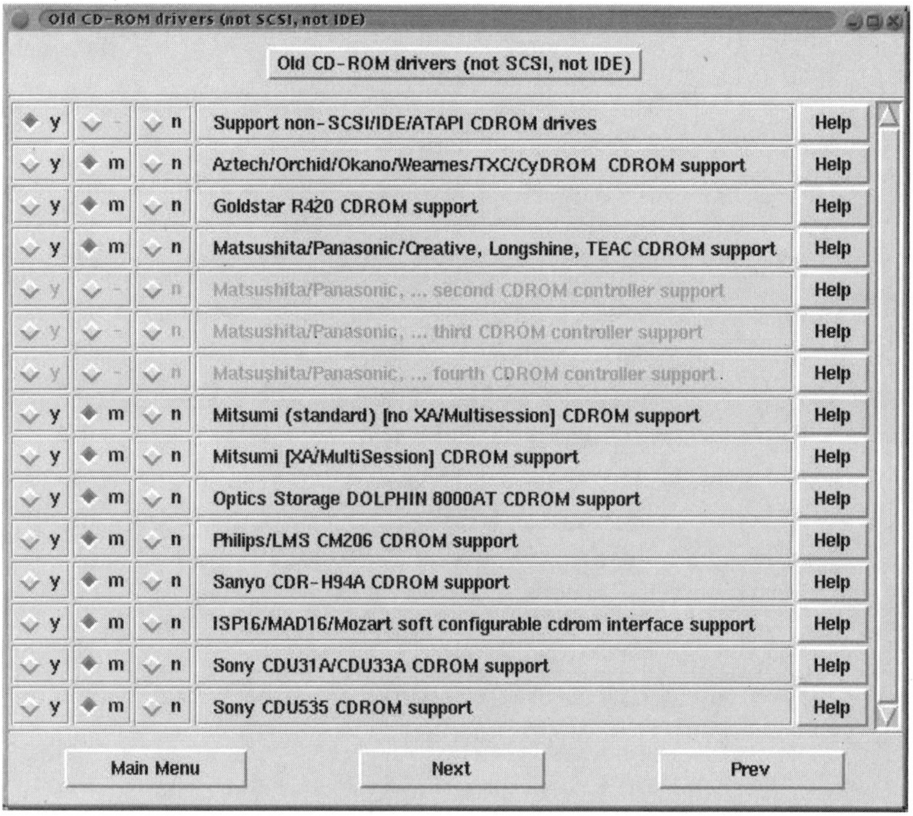

Old CD-ROM drivers (not SCSI, not IDE)

Old CD-ROM drivers (not SCSI, not IDE)

y	-	n	Support non-SCSI/IDE/ATAPI CDROM drives	Help
y	m	n	Aztech/Orchid/Okano/Wearnes/TXC/CyDROM CDROM support	Help
y	m	n	Goldstar R420 CDROM support	Help
y	m	n	Matsushita/Panasonic/Creative, Longshine, TEAC CDROM support	Help
y	-	n	Matsushita/Panasonic, ... second CDROM controller support	Help
y	-	n	Matsushita/Panasonic, ... third CDROM controller support	Help
y	-	n	Matsushita/Panasonic, ... fourth CDROM controller support	Help
y	m	n	Mitsumi (standard) [no XA/Multisession] CDROM support	Help
y	m	n	Mitsumi [XA/MultiSession] CDROM support	Help
y	m	n	Optics Storage DOLPHIN 8000AT CDROM support	Help
y	m	n	Philips/LMS CM206 CDROM support	Help
y	m	n	Sanyo CDR-H94A CDROM support	Help
y	m	n	ISP16/MAD16/Mozart soft configurable cdrom interface support	Help
y	m	n	Sony CDU31A/CDU33A CDROM support	Help
y	m	n	Sony CDU535 CDROM support	Help

Main Menu Next Prev

Networking and Network Device Options

There are many options for networking in the Linux kernel, which we will now discuss in more detail.

- **Packet Sockets and Kernel/User netlinks** Can be enabled to use low-level network programs. These programs typically do not use a network protocol and are usually packet sniffer applications. The Kernel/User netlink allows any user to read and write low-level packets to the network.
- **Network firewalls** Allow you to set up a packet-level firewall. You will also need to enable IP Firewalling to use packet filtering. The IP Masquerading option also requires this to be enabled. It should be noted that you cannot use fast switching with this option.
- **Linux Socket Filtering** Allows user programs to attach to a socket and filter their specific socket. This is based on the BSD styled socket filtering, but is much simpler.
- **IP Multicasting** Allows you to set up a multicast server that is capable of participating on an MBONE. An MBONE is a high-bandwidth network that carries voice and video streams. You can also enable IP Multicast Routing if your server is a router.
- **IP Kernel-Level Autoconfiguration** Allows you to set up your IP address from the command line when booting, or with BOOTP or RARP. You would also want this option if you want to boot your root file system with NFS.
- **IP Firewalling** Is used with the Network Firewalls option. You will need either ipchains(8) for version 2.2 and later, or ipfwadm(8) for older kernels. These programs usually come with the distribution of Linux.
- **IP Firewall Packet Netlink Device** Will create a user space device with rejected packets copied to it. By doing this, you could use a program to monitor this netlink device for attacks and respond appropriately.

- **IP Transparent Proxy Support** Allows the router to secretly forward packets to a proxy server. This requires no additional setup for the clients since they just use the router as their gateway and the router forwards the packets. It also has the nice feature of using ipchains(8) to set up the forwarding rules. This would allow you to send only certain ports (port 80) to the proxy, and allow others to do the same without the proxy if you so desired.
- **IP masquerading** Is very similar to the NAT routers. Masquerading allows one computer to masquerade as another computer. Typically, this is used by giving the router one valid IP address and using nonroutable internal IPs and masquerading the whole subnet out. This way, a private intranet could run with bogus IPs but appear to be fully connected to the Internet. You can also enable ICMP masquerading support, which will masquerade pings as well. You should also enable the special modules support. These additional modules will allow for special communications to be masqueraded; for example, IRC, FTP passive connections, VDO live, and quake.
- **IP ipautofw masq support** This is still experimental as of this writing, but is worth mentioning. This will allow for masquerading of protocols for which it does not yet have special support.
- **IP ipportfw masq support** Allows you to redirect ports. For instance, say you have a masquerade server acting as a router for your company, but somebody wants to use their PC that is on the intranet side of the network for a Web server. You can redirect incoming packets on port 80 (Web port) transparently to the user's Web server. From the outside, it will appear as though the router is hosting the Web page instead of the internal user.
- **IP optimize as router not host** Should be enabled whenever you build a router. It will speed up routing by removing unnecessary packet checking.
- **IP aliasing support** Allows you to have multiple IPs on one network card. This can be used to host multiple Web servers on one PC or to link two logical networks on your Ethernet. There is a mini-HOWTO on aliasing if you want to read more.

- **IP TCP syncookie support** Will protect you from SYNflooding attacks. These attacks are Denial-of-Service attacks that can severely slow down your server's network performance. Enabling syncookies will prevent this type of attack from occurring. After compiling this option, you will also need to issue the following command:

  ```
  echo 1 >/proc/sys/net/ipv4/tcp_syncookies
  ```

- **IP Reverse ARP** Will allow your server to answer RARP request by diskless workstations. These are typical Sun 3 machines and diskless Linux boxes.
- You can also use additional protocols such as Ipv6, IPX, AppleTalk, X.25, and LAPD.
- **You can also compile in WAN router support** This will cut the cost of a typically high-priced WAN router in half. All you'll need is a WAN interface card, the WAN-tools package, and to enable this option to build a WAN router.
- **Fast switching** Is an option that allows you to connect two computers directly together with a network cable. This is an extremely fast way for two computers to communicate. This option is not compatible with IP FIREWALL, but it will work with the IP ADVANCED ROUTER options.
- **QoS and/or fair queuing** Allows you to set up decision rules for which packet to route. Enabling this option can give you many different ways of determining which packets you'll route and which you will queue or drop. This can allow for priority IPs to always get certain bandwidth, while at the same time forcing other IPs to bandwidth consumption limits. QoS stands for Quality of Service and is currently being used; people who pay more, get more. In the network device section, you can enable traffic shaping to limit outbound bandwidth.
- **A wide range of network cards are supported** You should typically only choose the network card that is in your machine. It would be a wise idea to also include module support for other network cards that you have in stock. These options are shown in Figure 6-15.

- **Other network devices are also supported** such as T-1 cards, pocket network adapters, FDDI adapters, HIPPI adapters, Frame Relay DLCI, and wireless LAN cards. These device options are shown in Figre 6-16.
- **You can also encapsulate AppleTalk into IP, or vice versa** This can allow your Linux box to be a gateway on a MAC-only network. Note: You can only choose one type of encapsulation.
- **SLIPP, PLIP, and PPP support** Are all chosen under network device support section.

SCSI Support Options and Low-Level Drivers

You can enable SCSI hard disks, tape drivers, and CD-ROM support in this submenu, as shown in Figure 6-17. If you have a SCSI CD-ROM jukebox, you may have to enable probing all LUNs to force the controller to probe for multiple LUNs. There is a section for verbose SCSI error reporting. This section adds 12k to the kernel, but it makes debugging SCSI errors easier. You may want to enable specific low-level SCSI support for your controller and disable all others, as shown in Figure 6-18. This will save a lot of room and improve your loading. If you have an ADAPTEC controller, you should disable all other controllers in your config file.

ISDN Options

Integrated Services Digital Networks (ISDN) lines are fairly popular and inexpensive high-speed digital lines. Adding ISDN support will allow you to use an ISDN card for inbound or outbound dialing connections. The ISDN device has a built-in AT compatible modem emulator, autodial, channel-bundling, callback, and caller-authentication without the need for an external daemon to be running.

As shown in Figure 6-19, you can enable synchronous Point-to-Point Protocol (PPP) connections. You will need to download IPPPD to take advantage of this feature. With synchronous PPP and support for generic MP, you can bundle multiple ISDN lines together to increase your bandwidth.

FIGURE 6-15 xconfig—Network Options submenu

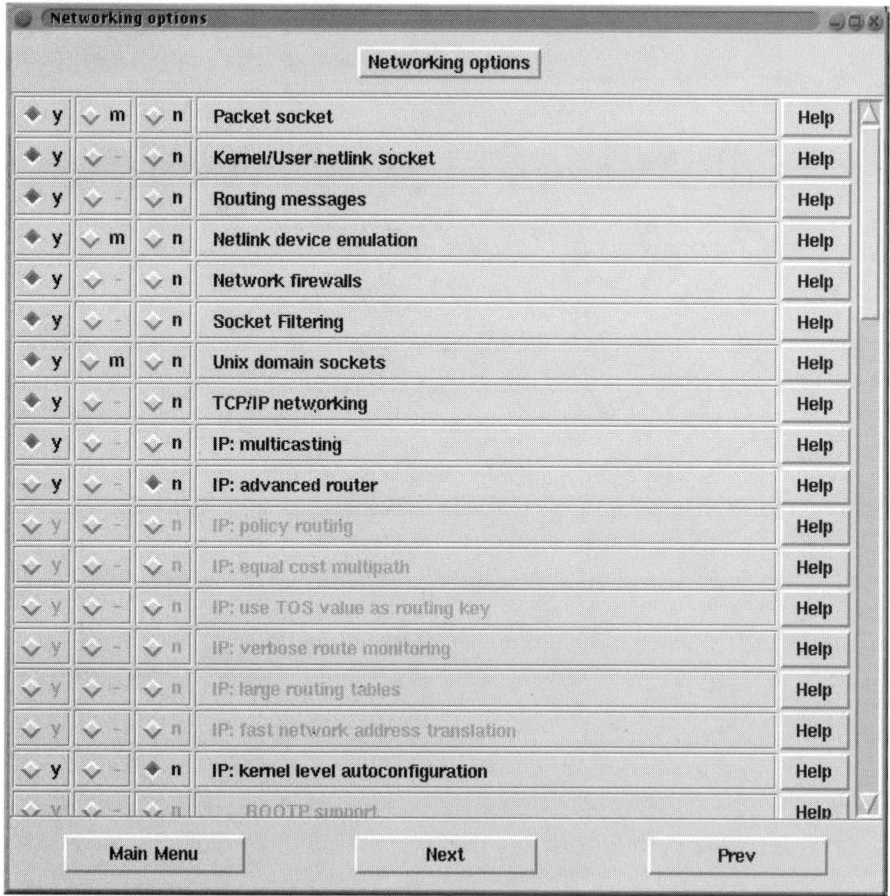

File System Options

The file system subsection is a list of all the different types of files systems that Linux supports. Here is where you would check if you feel that your kernel does not support quotas. You can also compile in the kernel automounter here.

FIGURE 6-16 Network Device support submenu

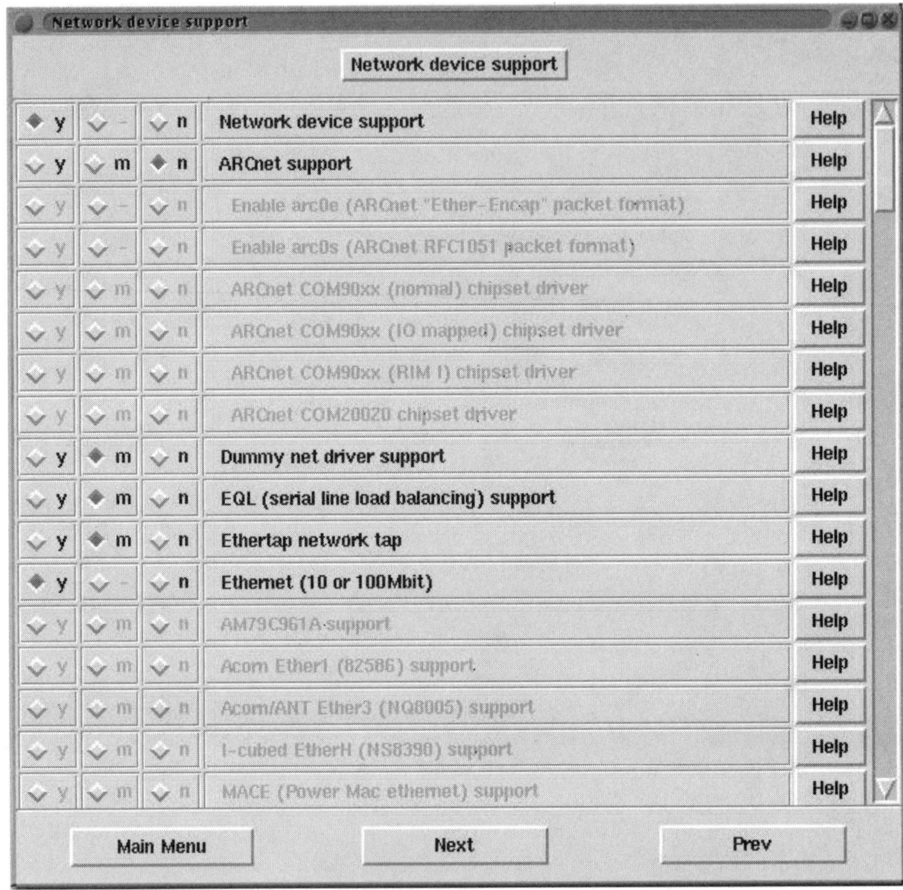

Table 6-1 lists some of the different file systems.
Figure 6-20 shows what the screen would look like.

Character Device Options

Character devices, shown in Figure 6-21, are where you specify support for a wide variety of devices, including virtual terminals, serial ports, parallel ports, mice, joysticks, Non-SCSI tape drives, and others.

FIGURE 6-17 xconfig—SCSI Support Options submenu

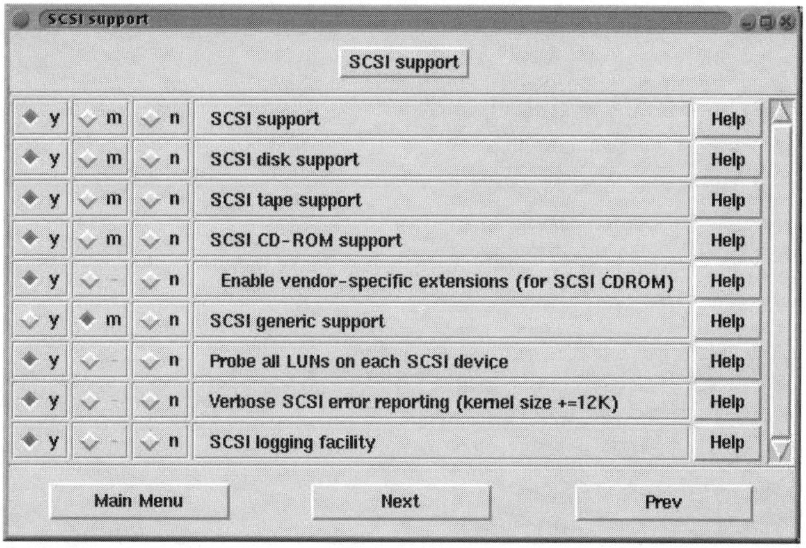

TABLE 6-1 Supported File System Reference

ADFS	(read-only) RiscOS file system
Amiga FFS	AmigaOS
Apple Macintosh	Macintosh file system
MSDOS	Old-styled DOS file system
VFAT	Windows 95/98 file system
UMSDOS	UNIX file system on top of an MSDOS file system
ISO 9660/Microsoft Joliet CDROM	CDROM file systems
Minix	Old Linux file system, usually found on old floppies
NTFS	(read-only or read/write) NT's file system
OS/2 HPFS	(read-only) OS/2's file system
QNX	(read-only or read/write) QNX 4 file system
ROM	(read-only) small read-only file system
Second extended file system	(Ext2) Linux Standard file system
UFS	(read-only or read/write) *BSD and NextStep file system

FIGURE 6-18 xconfig—SCSI Low-Level Drivers submenu

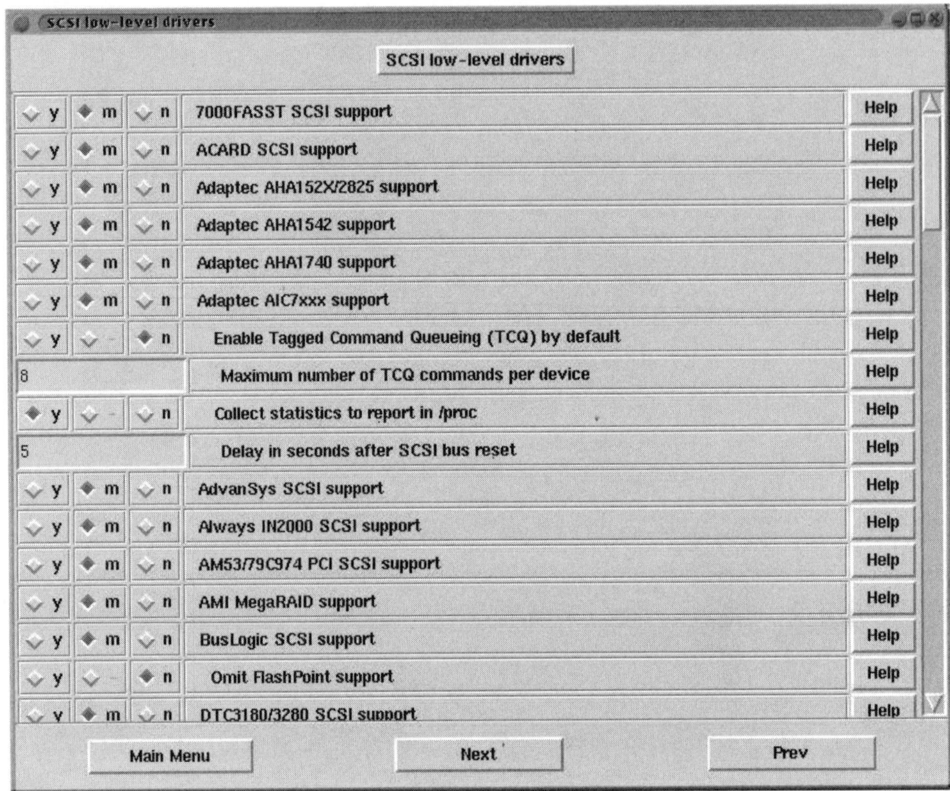

You can enable serial port support and reroute all system-level messages to it by disabling the console on virtual terminal support and enabling the console on serial port support. This will send all system-level messages to your serial port and your active terminal (use console=ttyS1 at bootup to turn this off). This section also has a wide range of support for multiport serial boards.

FIGURE 6-19 xconfig—ISDN subsystem

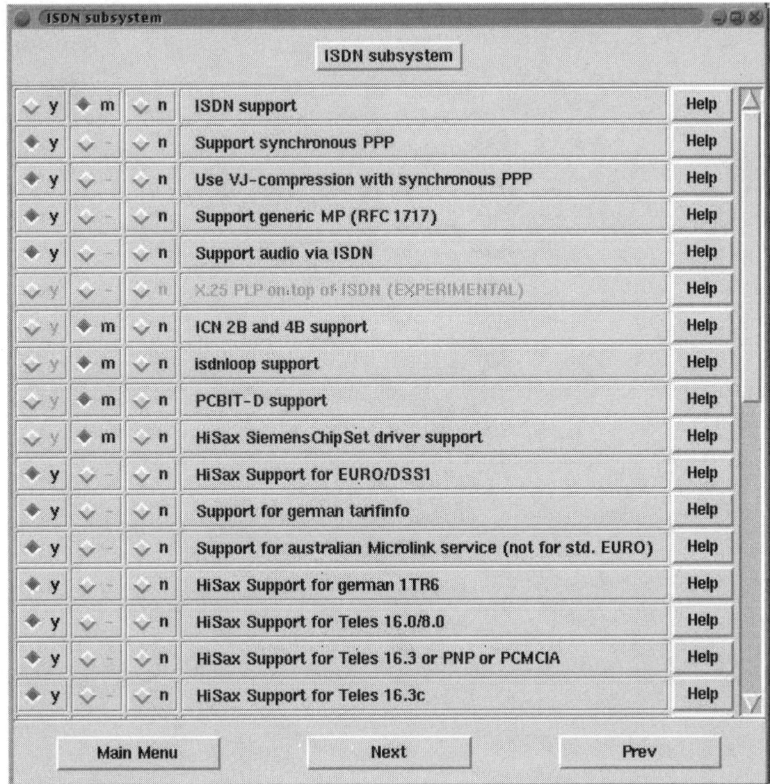

You can also enable Unix98 PTY support. This will allow you to leave the traditional pseudo-terminal naming convention of ptyXX and use a more elaborate naming convention. The Unix98 naming convention has a directory (/dev/pts/) where all of the devices are stored. You will need to answer yes to the /dev/pts filesystem for Unix98 option as well. The new pseudo terminals will now be created on-the-fly as pts/XXX; /dev/ttyp3

FIGURE 6-20 xconfig—File Systems submenu

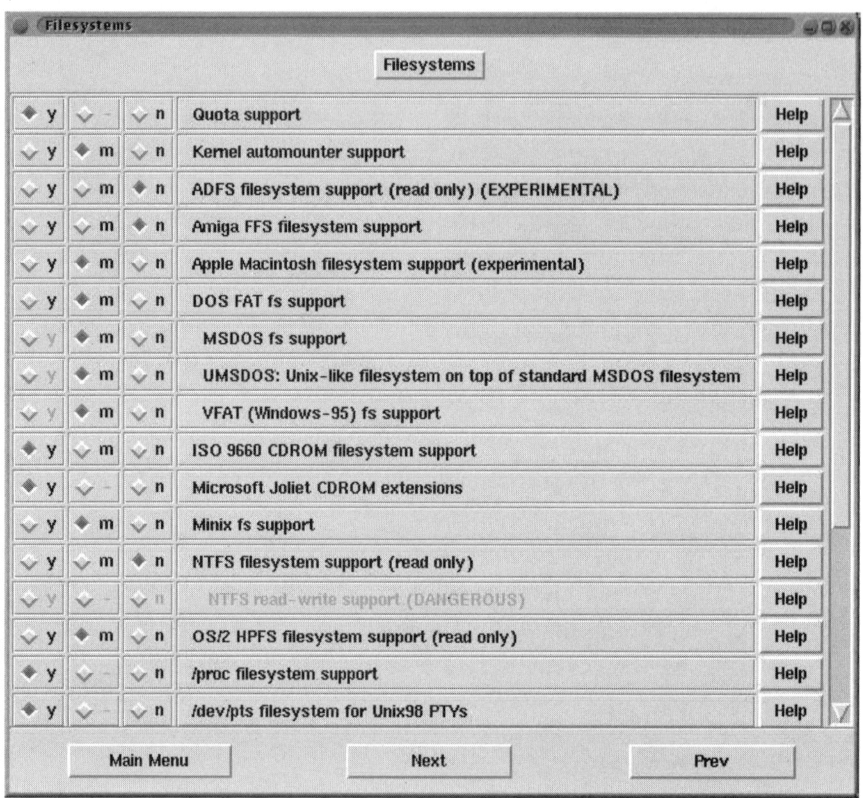

becomes pts/3. You can specify the maximum number of Unix98 PTYs; the default is 256. Each additional set of 256 will use around 8Kb of kernel memory on a 32-bit architecture.

You can also enable Watchdog timer support. This option forces the kernel to write to the /dev/watchdog file. If it fails to do this every minute, the server will reboot. You can enable software support for Watchdog timers or use a Watchdog hardware card. The Watchdog cards are much more reliable. This option could be useful for a network server, such as a router,

FIGURE 6-21 xconfig—Character Devices submenu

that needs to be online as much as possible. This way, if a flood of packets has caused the kernel to lock up, the router will simply reboot itself.

If you have a video card or a TV card, there is a whole section in the 2.2 kernels for you. You can even directly compile in support for basic QuickCams and Mediavision Pro Movie Studio cards.

If you have a floppy tape drive (QIC drive), then you will need to enable Ftape support. If you forget to add this option, you will not be able to use your tape drive.

Sound System Support Options

The following sound cards are supported with version 2.2.5. Figure 6-22 shows the configuration screen for the Sound submenu.

- Ensoniq QudioPCI
- S3 SonicVibes
- Turtle Beach MultiSound Classic and Pinnacle
- ProAudioSpectrum 16
- Sound Blaster and 100% compatible
- Generic OPL2/OPL3 FM synthesizer
- Gravis Untrasound
- PSS
- Microsoft Sound System
- Ensoniq SoundScape
- MediaTrix AudioTrix Pro
- OPTi MAD16 (Mozart)
- Crystal CS4232 based PnP cards
- Yamaha OPL3-SAx based PnP cards
- Aztech Sound Galaxy (non-PnP)
- Support for AD1816 cards
- Loopback MIDI
- 6850 UART
- ACI mixer
- AWE32 synch

You can also specify some specific low-level options for certain audio cards under the low-level sound drivers submenu. Additional low level sound drivers are shown in Figure 6-23.

FIGURE 6-22 Linuxconf—Sound submenu

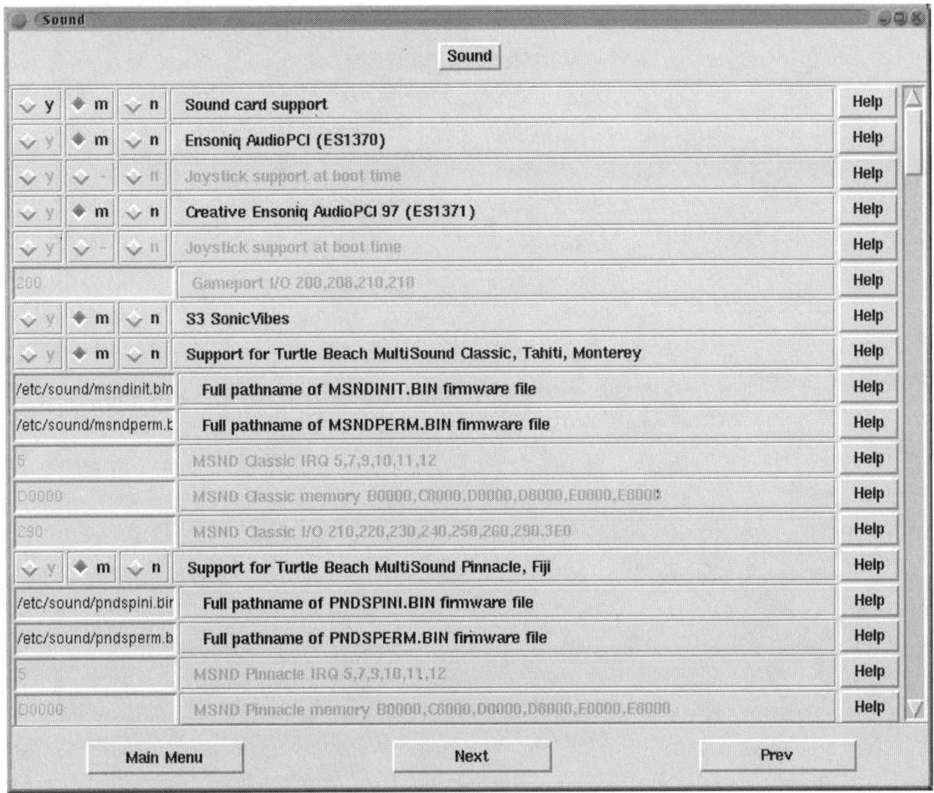

Compiling and Installing a Custom Kernel

After setting up all the options you want, you will need to compile your kernel. Here is a list of the commands you should give to successfully compile your kernel.

1. **cd /usr/src/linux** This command will bring you to the proper directory. All of your commands should be issued from here.
2. **make mrproper** This command will ensure that your source is properly installed and that your .o files and dependencies are stable.

FIGURE 6-23 xconfig—Low-Level Sound Drivers submenu

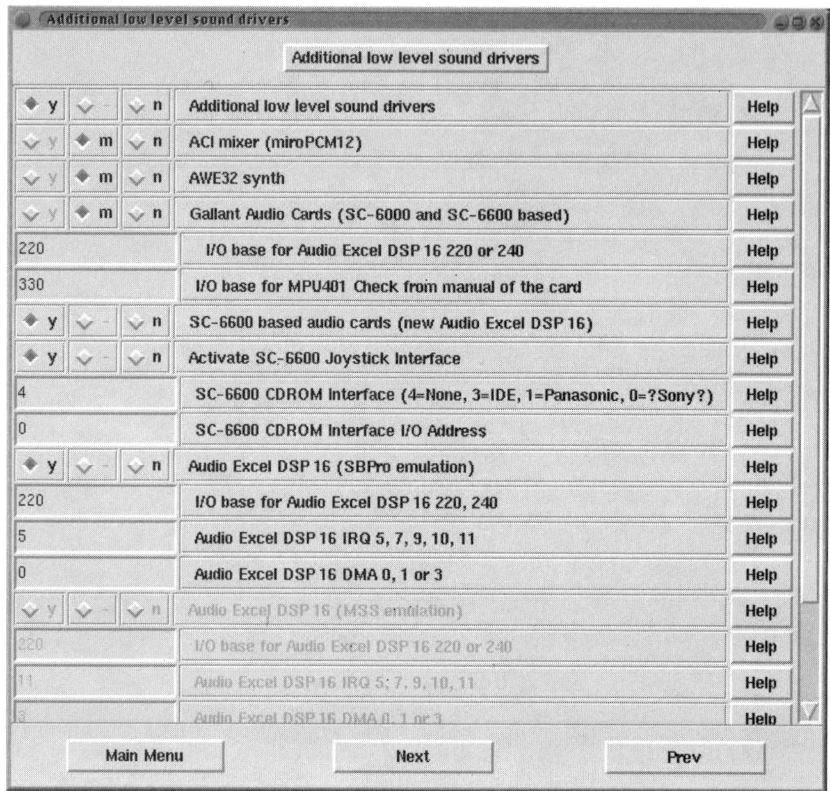

3. **make config** This command will run the text-based configuration script. You can also issue make menuconfig for an ncurses menu configuration script. Or, you can run make xconfig to use the X Windows configuration tool.
4. **make dep** This command will set up all of your dependencies correctly.

5. **make clean** This command will remove any old files left behind from a previous kernel compile
6. **make zImage** This command will create a compressed kernel image file. There are a few other options besides zImage you can use here. These will be discussed soon.

The kernel compilation actually doesn't take place until the last command is given. This can be a fairly time-consuming process. On a 386 or a 486, you will probably have to let it compile all night. On a Pentium 166 it will take approximately 30 to 45 minutes. If you have a Pention II or above, it will probably take less than 5 minutes to compile. If you want to build a kernel for a 486 machine but you don't want to wait all day, then you can compile the kernel on a faster machine (with the 486 settings) and simply copy the kernel to the 486 via floppy or FTP.

Both menuconfig and xconfig will remind you to run make dep after you save your settings. Xconfigs messages are shown in Figure 6-24.

If you want to use this step to make a bootdisk, you can issue make zdisk instead of zImage. If your lilo.conf file is set up properly, you can issue make zlilo. Often with the newer kernels you will find that your kernel is too big to compile with the make zImage command. If that is the case, then try make bzImage image instead.

FIGURE 6-24 xconfig—Exit Message box

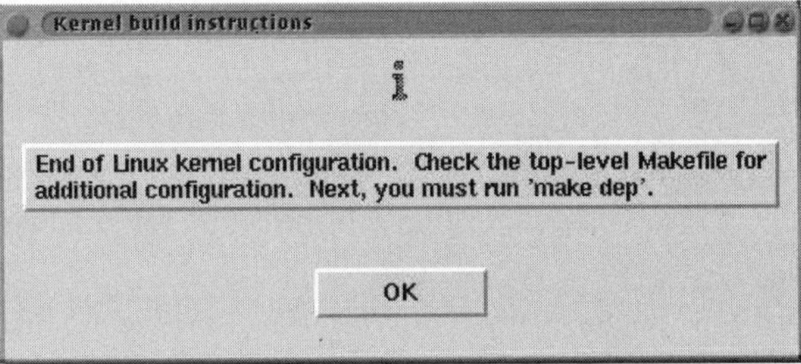
Kernel build instructions
i
End of Linux kernel configuration. Check the top-level Makefile for additional configuration. Next, you must run 'make dep'.
OK

Compiling and Installing Kernel Modules

If you enabled modules in your kernel configuration (by choosing M), then you will need to compile and install those modules at this time. To do so, simply issue the following two commands form the /usr/src/linux directory.

```
make modules
make modules_install
```

The first command will compile your different modules. After they finish compiling, issue make modules_install to put all the modules in their proper directories. This directory tree is discussed in Chapter 4.

If you already have a kernel set up and running, and you want to add support for another device but you didn't create the module for it, you can simply go into your configurator of choice and choose M for the device. After that, you can simply run make modules then make modules_install. After that, you can immediately load the modules with modprobe. This will save a lot of time by only compiling the missing module. If the module fails, it is probably because of a dependency; try running make dep and reissue the make modules command.

QUESTIONS AND ANSWERS

"I looked under /usr/src/ and did not see the Linux kernel source code. What did I do wrong?"	You did not install the kernel source code. Install the kernel-source RPM or download a new kernel from www.kernel.org.
"I configured the kernel as a monolithic kernel, but when I run make zImage it fails, saying that the kernel is too big."	You can either use make bzImage or reconfigure your kernel to use modules.
"I have a sound blaster card and I compiled my kernel so that it makes a module for the sound blaster, but I still don't have sound."	You didn't compile module autoloading and you haven't manually loaded your module. Use modprobe to load the desired module.

mkinitrd

The mkinitrd(8) command can create an initial ramdisk image for you. This image is reloaded when the kernel first boots. The initial ramdisk (initrd) is usually used to load essential block devices such as SCSI modules during boot time. This way it would be possible to have your root file system on a SCSI device that you wanted loaded into the kernel as a module. This command automatically loads all SCSI devices found in the /etc/conf.modules, as well as all other modules specified by /etc/conf.modules.

Some important mkinitrd(8) options are listed in Table 6-2.

Both preload and with can be used as many times as necessary in the command line. You will also need to specify the initrd image and the kernel version number on the command line. A simple example is as follows:

mkinitrd /boot/initrd 2.2.5

Depending on your system, you may or may not need to run this command.

Updating LILO

After you have compiled your kernel, you will need to make sure that when your system boots it will use your new kernel. To do this, you will first need to copy the kernel image to the /boot directory.

cp /usr/src/linux/arch/i386/boot/zImage /boot/mykernel-2.2.5

Your kernel file may be called bzImage if you compiled with make bzImage instead of zImage. For the rest of this example, our new kernel will

TABLE 6-2

mkinitrd Options Reference

–ifneeded	Only build image with needed modules
–omit-scsi-module	Will not load any SCSI modules
–preload=<module>	Will load a module before the SCSI modules
–with=<module>	Will load a module after the SCSI modules

be called mykernel-2.2.5. Now we need to edit the /etc/lilo.conf file. We want to have the ability to boot the old kernel if the new one fails. Here is the original liloconf file before we edit it.

```
boot=/dev/had
map=/boot/map
install=/boot/boot.b
prompt
timeout=50
image=/boot/vmlinuz-2.2.5-15
        label=linux
        root=/dev/hda1
        read-only
```

From this information you can see that the original kernel is called vmlinuz-2.2.5-15 and it resides on the first partition. LILO resides on the MBR of the first disk. The label when booting is linux. We now need to add another image section to point to the new kernel. The changes are in bold.

```
boot=/dev/hdc5
map=/boot/map
install=/boot/boot.b
prompt
timeout=50
image=/boot/mykernel-2.2.5
       label=linux
       root=/dev/hdc5
       read-only
image=/boot/vmlinuz-2.2.5-15
        label=old
root=/dev/hdc5
        read-only
```

Save this file then run lilo(8). The output should look like the following:

```
Added linux *
Added old
```

When you reboot, LILO will wait for you to enter a label. If you don't enter anything, or you just press ENTER, Linux will load. If the new kernel doesn't work, then all you will have to do is reboot the system and type **old** at the LILO prompt.

These steps can also be accomplished by using linuxconf. You can add a new kernel image that you have copied to the system, or you can have linuxconf try to detect a kernel that you have recently compiled. You have to go under Boot Mode | Lilo | A new kernel that you have compiled.

If you copied a kernel over you could choose the option Boot mode | Lilo | A new kernel, you could then specify the new kernel you wanted to add to the lilo.conf file.

mkbootdisk

mkbootdisk is a utility that can create a bootdisk for you. This is basically a rescue disk. Once created, this disk it can be used to simply boot your system, or you can type **rescue** at the LILO prompt. The only option you need to specify when using this command is the kernel version. Table 6-3 lists a few other options that may come in handy when creating a bootdisk with this command.

Here is an example of the mkbootdisk command:

mkbootdisk –device /dev/fd1 –verbose –noprompt 2.2.5

This will tell mkbootdisk to create a bootdisk on the second floppy drive. It will not suppress output and it will not prompt for a disk to be inserted. It will use kernel version 2.2.5.

When using this disk, you can also type **rescue** at the LILO prompt to use the disk as a rescue disk.

TABLE 6-3

mkbootdisk Options Reference

–device <device file>	Specifies where to put the image
–mkinitrdargs <args>	This can pass arguments to mkinitrd
–noprompt	Won't prompt to insert a disk
–verbose	Normally mkbootdisk has no output; this will turn the output on

CERTIFICATION OBJECTIVE 6.04

PAM

PAM stands for Pluggable Authentication Modules. PAM is not very useful in a single-user environment or where the users are trusted, but it is perfect for a multiuser system where users are not trusted. PAM allows for more granularity in defining security. You can use PAM to control access to certain resources with means that are not actually coded into the program. For example, you can have pppd authenticate users with a Novell or NT user database instead of the /etc/password or /etc/shadow file provided by Linux.

To check to see if a program supports PAM authentication, you can run **ldd <program>** to print out its shared libraries. Then look for two entries: libpam and libpam_misc.

The PAM configuration files are kept in /etc/pam.d/. In older versions this was one file named /etc/pam.conf. Here is a sample /etc/pam.d directory listing:

```
chfn   gdm    linuxconf other ppp       rlogin  shutdown    xscreensaver
chsh   halt   linuxconf-pair  passwd    reboot  rsh   su    xserver
ftp    kde    login           poweroff  rexec   samba       xdm
```

Each one of these files contain script files that tell PAM how to act with different applications. The syntax for these scripts is as follows:

```
module-type control-flag module-path arguments
```

See Table 6-4 for a description of each section.

TABLE 6-4

mkbootdisk Options Reference

Service-name	The name of the program
Module-type	Auth, account, session, or password
Control-flag	Required, requisite, sufficient, and optional
Module-path	The path of the PAM module
Arguments	The arguments for the module

The older way of configuring the PAM modules was with the /etc/pam.conf file. The syntax of this file has the following form:

```
service-name   module-type control-flag   module-path arguments
```

As you can see, it is almost identical except that you need to specify a service name. This is because there is only one file that contains all of the different services, while the directory system's filename tells the system which service the rules will apply to. Tables 6-5 and 6-6 give a brief description of the different columns.

The default system configuration module is called OTHER. You can use the OTHER service-name keyword in the /etc/pam.conf file or in the /etc/pam.d/other file. Here are some example scripts; don't worry about what they do just yet.

```
# Sample /etc/pam.conf, OTHER section
OTHER   auth     required      /usr/lib/security/pam_deny.so
OTHER   account  required      /usr/lib/security/pam_deny.so
OTHER   password required      /usr/lib/security/pam_deny.so
OTHER   session  required      /usr/lib/security/pam_deny.so

# Sample /etc/pam.d/other
       auth     required      /usr/lib/security/pam_warn.so
       auth     required      /usr/lib/security/pam_deny.so
       account  required      /usr/lib/security/pam_deny.so
       password required      /usr/lib/security/pam_warn.so
       password required      /usr/lib/security/pam_deny.so
       session  required      /usr/lib/security/pam_deny.so
```

TABLE 6-5

Module Type Reference

Auth	Prompts user for identification
Account	Account-based restriction (time, location, etc.)
Session	Session-oriented commands such as logging
Password	Updates authentication tokens

TABLE 6-6

Control Flag Reference

Required	User must authenticate but will not be notified immediately on failure
Requisite	User must authenticate and PAM will immediately return a failure
Sufficient	PAM will return success if they authenticate
Optional	This option does not determine success or failure but is optional

Table 6-7 is a quick reference list of the modules you can use with PAM along with a brief description on how to use them.

TABLE 6-7

PAM Library Reference

Pam_cheroot	Changes a root directory
Pam_cracklib	Checks for easy-to-crack passwords
Pam_deny	Returns a failure and denies access
Pam_env	Can unsend environmental variables
pam_filter	Can invoke a terminal filter program
pam_ftp	Allows for anonymous FTP mode access
pam_group	Grants group access to the user
pam_krb4	Kerberos 4 Authentication
pam_lastlog	Displays where the user lasted logged in from
pam_limits	Limits the system resources that can be obtained
pam_listfile	Allows access based on names in a file
pam_mail	Checks for new mail
pam_nologin	Denies access if /etc/nologin exists
pam_permit	Always permits access
pam_pwdb	Authenticates via the pwdb instead of the old UNIX style

TABLE 6-7

PAM Library Reference *(continued)*

pam_radius	Authenticates via a RADIUS server
pam_rhost_auth	Authenticates via traditional rlogin styles
Pam_rootok	Permits root access without a password
pam_securetty	Checks the /etc/securetty file first
pam_time	Restricts access based on time
pam_warn	Logs information about the session
pam_wheel	Provides root access if user is a member of the wheel group

CERTIFICATION OBJECTIVE 6.05

The Cron System

The cron(8) system will allow the administrator or any user to schedule jobs to run at given intervals. There is a daemon that runs named crond. The cron daemon searches the /var/spool/cron directory under each user's name every minute. It also searches the /etc/crontab file and the files in /etc/cron.d. These files are not intended to be edited in the directory. You should use the crontab(1) command to edit these files. You can allow or deny users the use of crontab. If the /etc/cron.allow file exists, then only users who are in this file can use crontab. If cron.allow does not exist but cron.deny exists, then the users listed in cron.deny *cannot* use crontab. If neither file exists, then anyone can use cron.

The cron daemon checks the crontab files every minute to see if they have been changed. If they have been changed then it will reread all the cron entries.

exam Watch

Because cron always checks for changes you do NOT have to restart cron every time you make a change.

The System crontab and Components

The crontab command is used to edit the cron files. There are several options you can use with crontab:

- -u <user> will specify a user's crontab to edit. If you are using su(8) to switch users, then you should always use the -u option
- -l will list the current entries in the crontab file
- -r will remove the cron entries
- -e will edit an existing crontab entry using the editor specified in the VISUAL or EDITOR variables

The crontab file has a certain format. Each line can be blank, a comment (#), a variable, or a command. Blank lines and comment lines (those that begin with #) are ignored. You cannot have a comment in a command line.

You can set environmental variables with the following syntax:

Variable=Value

Some variables are already set for you: HOME is your home directory, SHELL is the user's default shell, and LOGNAME is your username. HOME and SHELL can be overwritten; LOGNAME can not.

on the job

A handy variable to set is the MAILTO variable. If the MAILTO variable is set and is not a NULL value, then the cron daemon will send output via mail to the intended target. This can be useful if you are scheduling jobs for a services such as UUCP or have another mail account you check more frequently. You could easily add the line: MAILTO=me@somewhere.com to reroute all cron messages for that user to another mail account. If this variable is not set, then mail will be sent to the user running the command.

Here is the format of a line in the crontab:

```
#minute, hour, day of month, month, day of week, command

*         *     *              *         *              command
```

Commands are the heart of what cron does. Table 6-8 is a list of valid values for the specified fields.

All fields can also use an asterisk (*), which will mean every valid value. You can also specify ranges; for example, 7–10 would mean 7, 8, 9, and 10. Lists are also valid entries: 1, 2, 3–4, 6, 7–10. Another advanced feature is using steps. You can use the value 0-23/2 to mean every other value. It is also valid to use */2 for every other value.

You can use names for both the month and the day-of-week fields. You cannot have a list of names or a specified range of names. These names are typically abbreviated as Jan, Mar, Sat, Sun, and so forth.

The actual command is the sixth field. This command will be the rest of the line or until it reaches a percent (%) symbol. If it reaches a % symbol, it will be treated as a new line, and all of the following text will be used as standard input. Here is an example cron file:

```
# Sample crontab file
#
# Force /bin/sh to be my shell for all of my scripts.
SHELL=/bin/sh
# Run 15 minutes past Midnight every Saturday
15 0 * * sat      $HOME/scripts/scary.script
# Do routine cleanup on the first of every Month at 4:30 AM
30 4 1 * *  /usr/scripts/removecores > /tmp/core.tmp 2>&1
# Mail a message at 10:45 AM every Friday
45 10 * * fri    mail -s "Project Update employees%Can I have a status
update on your project?%%Your Boss.%
# Every other hour check for alert messages
0 */2 * * * /usr/scripts/check.alerts
# At 9:00 AM on January 1st remind me about the auditors.
0 9 1 jan *        echo The Auditors are coming!!!
```

TABLE 6-8

Cron Configuration Reference

minute	0–59
hour	0–23
day of month	0–31
month	0–12 (or names)
day of week	0–7 (or names)

EXERCISE 6-1

Create a Cron Job

In this exercise, we will create a cron job that will update the local database at 4:00 A.M. every night and mail a disk usage report every Friday.

1. Log in as root.
2. Run **crontab –e**.
3. Add the following line to update the locate database:

```
00 4 * * * updatedb &2>/dev/null
```

4. Add the following line to mail a disk usage report to your account. The remote admin account is admin@remote.site.com.

```
00 9 * * 5 df | mail admin@remote.site.com -s
DiskUsage &2>/dev/null
```

5. Save and exit.

CERTIFICATION OBJECTIVE 6.06

System-Wide Shell Configuration for Bourne and Bash Shells

All system-wide shell configuration files are kept in the etc directory. These files are bashrc, profile, and there is also a profile.d directory that contains special shell configuration scripts. Only a small amount of Bash shell programming will be discussed in this book, but the basics will be covered here. If you want more information, please read the man pages for bash(1).

/etc/bashrc

/etc/bashrc is used for system-wide aliases and functions. You can bypass this script with the -norc argument when invoking bash. Here is a short example of a /etc/bashrc file:

```
#/etc/bashrc
# System wide aliases and functions
# Setup the prompt
PS1="[\u@\h \W]\\$ "
# This alias shows colors with ls(1)
alias ls='ls -color'
```

/etc/profile

/etc/profile is used for system-wide environment and startup files. This script can be bypassed by invoking bash with the -noprifile argument. Here is an example profile script:

```
PATH="$PATH:/usr/X11R6/bin"
PS1="[\u@\h \W]\\$ "
ulimit -c 1000000
if [ `id -gn` = `id -un` -a `id -u` -gt 14 ]; then
        umask 002
else
        umask 022
fi

USER=`id -un`
LOGNAME=$USER
MAIL="/var/spool/mail/$USER"
HOSTNAME=`/bin/hostname`
HISTSIZE=1000
HISTFILESIZE=1000
INPUTRC=/etc/inputrc
export PATH PS1 HOSTNAME HISTSIZE HISTFILESIZE USER LOGNAME MAIL INPUTRC
for i in /etc/profile.d/*.sh ; do
        if [ -x $i ]; then
                . $I
        fi
done
unset i
```

/etc/profile.d/

Profile.d is not a script, but a directory of little scripts. If you were paying close attention you may have noticed that the /etc/profile script is actually the script in charge of handling this directory. Here is a sample directory listing:

```
-rwxr-xr-x    1 root      root            184 Apr 19 02:47 kde.csh
-rwxr-xr-x    1 root      root            149 Apr 19 02:47 kde.sh
-rwxr-xr-x    1 root      root           1444 Apr 19 15:39 lang.sh
-rwxr-xr-x    1 root      root             64 Apr 19 15:03 mc.csh
-rwxr-xr-x    1 root      root            107 Apr 19 15:03 mc.sh
```

By looking at the /etc/profile script you can see that any script in this directory that ends with a "sh" and is set as an executable that will be run when /etc/profile is executed. In this case, it will run kde.sh, lang.sh, and mc.sh. The .csh files do not actually match the *.sh requirement in the /etc/profile (these are called by /etc/csh.cshrc which is used by other shells).

CERTIFICATION SUMMARY

You can have great control over how your Linux installation is set up and configured. You can control almost all aspects of user security, as well has the details of your kernel. You can set up quotas to limit the user's disk usage. You can set up one quota per partition. You can set a Soft Limit and a Hard Limit. If a grace period is set, then the Soft Limit will warn users that they are over their limit and it will not allow them to exceed their Hard Limit. If a grace period is not set, then the Soft Limit will be the users' maximum amount of storage space.

The /etc/rc.d directory controls what daemons load at which runlevel. Each /etc/rc.d/rc#.d/ directory contains a link to the daemon that is located in the /etc/rc.d/init.d/ directory. Links that begin with an "S" will start daemon links, and links that begin with a "K" will kill the daemon when exiting a runlevel.

The kernel can be optimized for your particular installation and hardware; you have detailed control of every aspect of the kernel. To make a monolithic kernel you will run six commands: make mrproper, make config, make dep, make clean, make modules, and make modules_install. If you are compiling a monolithic kernel, you will *not* need to run make modules or make modules_install.

System security and maintenance can be controlled with PAM and cron. The Pluggable Authentication Module (PAM) can give you extra security, as well as extra control over how applications work and authenticate. Cron will allow you to schedule jobs to run at any given time. Any variables or system-wide function you may need to run can be kept in the /etc/bashrc or the /etc/profile script.

TWO-MINUTE DRILL

- Quotas are used to limit a user's or a group of users' ability to consume disk space.
- The kernel has to be setup to support Quotas on your partitions. By default this is typically enabled.
- A *monolithic* kernel is a kernel where all of the device modules are built directly into the kernel.
- A monolithic kernel will use the most memory and will probably waste space with unused drivers. It will talk faster to the devices than a modular kernel.
- Proc is a directory that is virtual; it doesn't actually exist on the hard drive. All of its information is maintained by the kernel.
- The Code maturity level option is used to enable prompting for kernel source code drivers that are not fully developed yet.
- The Loadable module support screen is where you enable the use of modules with your kernel.
- If you have an older CD-ROM that is not an IDE or SCSI CD-ROM, then you need to enable special support for it.
- mkbootdisk is a utility that can create a bootdisk.
- PAM stands for Pluggable Authentication Modules. PAM is not very useful in a single-user environment or where the users are trusted, but it is perfect for a multiuser system where users are not trusted.
- The cron(8) system will allow the administrator or any user to schedule jobs to run at given intervals.
- All system-wide shell configuration files are kept in the etc directory.

SELF TEST

The following Self Test questions will help you measure your understanding of the material presented in this chapter. Read all the choices carefully, as there may be more than one correct answer. Choose all correct answers for each question.

1. You have several users on your system. You want to restrict their disk space in their home directory, but because of the complexity of some of their programs, they need large temporary space. How could you restrict their disk usage in their home directories, but allow them unlimited access to the /tmp directory?
   A. Use edquota /home to edit the users' quota for their home directory.
   B. Use edquota and specify only the home directories in the text file.
   C. Mount the /tmp directory to a separate partition and use edquota on the partition that contains the home directory.
   D. None of these options will work.
2. You are running an ISP service and provide space for user Web pages. You only want them to use 40MB, but will allow up to 50MB until they can clean up their stuff. How could you use quotas to enforce this policy?
   A. Enable grace periods, set the Hard Limit to 40MB, and the Soft Limit to 50MB.
   B. Enable grace periods, set the Soft Limit to 50MB, and the Hard Limit to 40MB.
   C. Enable grace periods, set the Soft Limit to 40MB, and the Hard Limit to 50MB.
   D. None of the above.
3. The CIO of your company wants to see a full report on how much disk space each user on the system is using up. What command would you use to display this information?
   A. repquota -a
   B. quotareport -a
   C. quotareport -all
   D. quotashow -a
4. You recently received a notice from your legal department. They want all servers to have a message to thwart off unauthorized access at the login prompt. How would you go about doing this? (Choose all that apply.)
   A. Modify /etc/banner.net
   B. Modify /etc/issue
   C. Modify /etc/issue.net
   D. Modify /etc/login.msg

5. Your system currently boots into runlevel 3. After looking into the /etc/rc.d/rc3.d/ directory, you want to know what script will run first. Of the following links, what script will be the first to run when entering runlevel 3?

   A. K20rwhod

   B. S30syslog

   C. K96pcmcia

   D. S99linuxconf

6. How would you set the runlevel so that your server boots into X Windows when you boot?

   A. Modify the /etc/inetd.conf file and uncomment startx.

   B. Modify the /etc/inittab file and set the initdefault to 5.

   C. Modify the /etc/inittab file and set the initdefault to 6.

   D. Modify the /etc/inittab.conf file and set the initdefault to 5.

7. Which commands would you NOT execute when building a monolithic kernel? (Choose all that apply.)

   A. make bzImage

   B. make lilo

   C. make modules

   D. make modules_install

8. You are compiling a new kernel for a machine with an older BIOS that does not support large hard drives. The hard drive you plan to use is 4GB. Below is a simple description of your partitions:

   /boot(15 Meg)

   /usr(1 Gig)

   /home(1.9 Gig)

   /(1 Gig)

   Where could you place the kernel to avoid problems with the older BIOS?

   A. /usr/src/linux/arch/i386/boot

   B. /usr/src/linux

   C. /

   D. /boot

9. You are almost finished building a new router for your company. You have both network cards properly set up to two different networks. Each side can successfully ping its network card, but neither side can ping the other network. After checking your firewall and forwarding rules, you feel they are set up correctly. All the kernel configuration settings such as IP Firewalling are enabled. What is most likely the problem?

   A. You didn't load the router module.

   B. You need to enable the environmental variable, ENABLE_ROUTING=1.

   C. You need to add a "1" to the kernel variables file /proc/sys/net/ipv4/ip_forward.

   D. None of the above.

10. Which one of these kernels is a developer's kernel?

    A. 2.0.0
    B. 1.2.25
    C. 2.3.4
    D. 3.0.13

11. When compiling a kernel, what are the valid configuration options used by make? (Choose all that apply.)

    A. config
    B. menuconfig
    C. windowconfig
    D. xconfig

12. After specifying all of your options for your kernel, you type in your final command, make zImage. The kernel goes through all of its final stages of compiling, but at the end it complains that the kernel is too large. What steps could you use to fix this problem? (Choose all that apply.)

    A. Edit your kernel configurations and make as many options as you can modules.
    B. Compile the kernel on a bigger system, then copy it to your new system.
    C. Use make bzImage instead.
    D. Use make zImage -compress.

13. What does the command **mkinitrd /boot/initrd 2.0.35** do?

    A. Creates a list of kernel modules for kernel 2.0.35.
    B. Appends the system's /boot/initrd to kernel 2.0.35.
    C. Nothing, because the /boot directory is only referenced by the kernel during boot time.
    D. Creates an initial ramdisk to load necessary modules during boot time.

14. You have just compiled a new kernel and now you want to upgrade your old kernel using LILO. You compiled the kernel with the command make zImage. You need to copy the kernel to the /boot directory. Where is the kernel currently located?

    A. /usr/src/linux/
    B. /boot/
    C. /usr/src/linux/kernel/zImage/
    D. /usr/src/linux/arch/i386/boot/

15. You have just compiled a new kernel and you want to set up LILO to boot your new kernel by default but still have the option to boot the old kernel if necessary. You have already copied your kernel to the /boot directory. What section do you need to add to the /etc/lilo.conf file?

    A. boot=
    B. image=
    C. install=
    D. map=

16. What command could you use to easily create a rescue disk for your system?

    A. Fdrescue

    B. Mkrescuedisk

    C. Mkbootdisk

    D. None of the above

17. Where could you look to find out how Pluggable Authentication Modules (PAM) are installed on your system? (Choose all that apply.)

    A. /etc/pamd.conf

    B. /etc/pam.conf

    C. /etc/pam.d/

    D. /etc/pamd.conf/

18. The directory system for PAM and the older PAM configuration file are almost the same format. The older configuration file contains an additional column of information that is not in the directory-style PAM setup. What is the additional column?

    A. module-type

    B. module-path

    C. service-name

    D. service-path

19. What is the difference between a required PAM module and a module that is a requisite?

    A. If a user fails to authenticate a required section, then he will be immediately rejected.

    B. If a user fails to authenticate at a requisite section, then he will be immediately rejected.

    C. Requisite sections are accumulated, and after all the requisites are checked, if one fails then access is denied.

    D. None of the above.

20. You want to schedule a maintenance job to run on the first of every month at 4:00 A.M. Which of the following cron entries are correct?

    A. 00 4 1 * * ~/maintenance.pl

    B. 4 1 * * ~/maintenance.pl

    C. 0 4 31/1 * * ~/maintenance.pl

    D. 1 4 00 ~/maintenance.pl

RHCE®
RED HAT CERTIFIED ENGINEER®

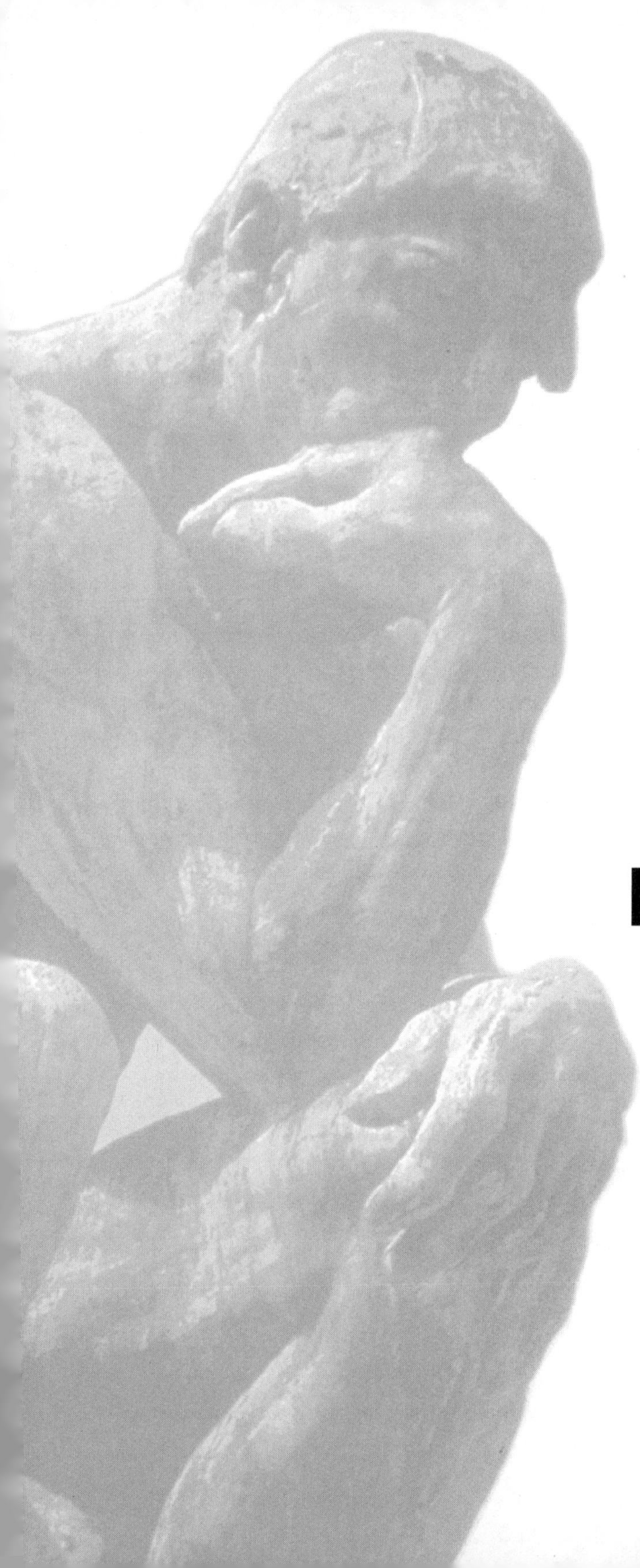

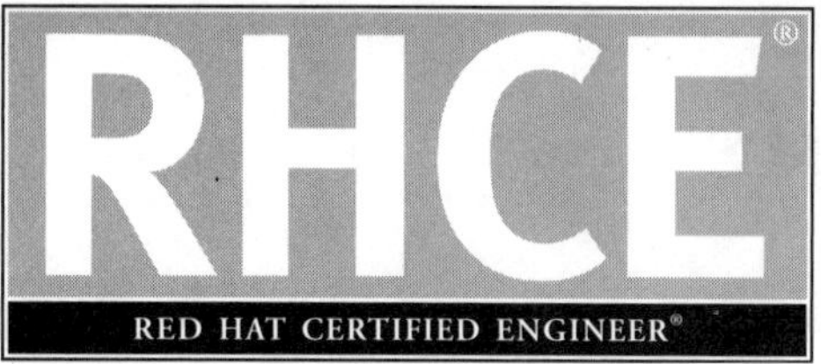

7

X-Windowing System

CERTIFICATION OBJECTIVES

7.01	X-Server
7.02	X-Clients
7.03	Startup
7.04	Remote display of X-apps

One of the most important aspects of getting a Red Hat Linux system up and running is configuring the user interface. On most systems, this means configuring the *X-Window* interface. The *X-Window system* is the graphical user interface (GUI) for Linux. Unlike other operating systems, in which the GUI interface is an integral part of the operating system itself, the X-Window system is not a part of Red Hat Linux but is a layered application. Thus you can have a fully functioning Linux system without running the X-Window interface.

Although it is quite possible to run Linux without using the X-Window GUI, most users who are using Linux for a workstation will benefit from the increased productivity provided by a graphical work environment and from the multitude of X-Window-based applications. If you are migrating users from Microsoft Windows to Linux, the X-Window system enables you to provide them with a familiar environment.

If you are running a dedicated system such as a DHCP server or a SAMBA server, you may elect not to configure the X-Window GUI. Or you may be a dyed-in-the-wool command line hacker and system administrator and decide an X-Window interface isn't necessary. If this is the case, you may want to reconsider your decision; one of the strengths of Red Hat Linux is in the number of X-Window-based system configuration and administration tools that are provided.

Because the X-Window system is such an important part of almost any Red Hat Linux system that you will encounter, it is essential that as a RHCE you are able to install, configure, and troubleshoot an X-Window system. This chapter will introduce you to the X-Window system and guide you through the process of installing and starting it on a Linux system. In addition you'll also take a look at using X-Window applications.

CERTIFICATION OBJECTIVE 7.01

X-Server

The X-Window system is designed as a flexible, powerful, client-server architecture. In order to configure and troubleshoot the X-Window interface it is important that you understand the client-server nature of the X-Window system.

As you might have guessed from the terms *client* and *server,* the X-Window system is designed to work in a networked environment. This does not mean your Linux system must be connected to a network in order to use X-Window applications; the X-Window system will work on a *stand-alone* system as well as a networked system. If your system is part of a network, not only can you run X-applications on your system, you can employ the powerful network capabilities of the X-Window system to run X-applications on other computers on your network and have the graphical displays from those applications display on your monitor. In fact, X-Window applications handle this task so well that, providing the network doesn't go down, you really can't tell which applications are running *locally* and which applications are running *remotely.*

Different Meanings for Client and Server

One small hurdle that you must overcome when working with the X-Window system is coming to an understanding that, in the X-Window world, the meanings of the terms *client* and *server* have been somewhat reversed. If you have experience in the world of personal computer networking, the term *server* brings to mind a dual processor monster with multiple gigabytes of RAM and multiple gigabytes of disk storage that sits behind glass walls in an air-conditioned machine room and holds all of your company's vital data. A *client* is a computer, such as the workstation on your desk, that you use to access and process the information that is stored on the server.

In the X-Window environment, these roles have been reversed. The *X-server* is the component of the X-Window system that you run on your desktop. The X-server is responsible for drawing images on your screen, getting input from your keyboard and mouse, and controlling access to your *display.* The X-Window applications that you run make use of these services that are provided by the X-server to display their output; hence they are referred to as clients or X-clients. X-clients can run *locally* or *remotely. Local* X-clients run on your workstation; *remote* X-clients run on other systems on the network. When you run an X-Window application remotely, you start the program on another system on the network and tell it to use the X-server running on your system for its console. The X-client sends its output to your X-server and gets keyboard and mouse input from your X-server. Figure 7-1 shows a local and a remote

FIGURE 7-1 You can run X-Window client applications on more than one system

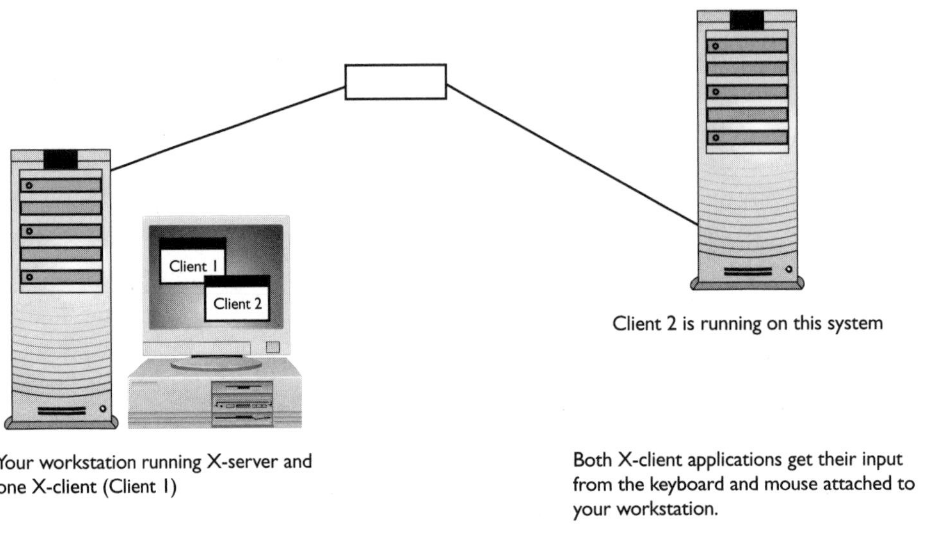
Client 1
Client 2
Client 2 is running on this system
Your workstation running X-server and one X-client (Client 1)
Both X-client applications get their input from the keyboard and mouse attached to your workstation.

X-client accessing the X-server on a workstation. X-clients and X-servers communicate using the X-protocol. We will look at running local and remote X-Window applications later in this chapter. Before we can talk about running client applications, we need to look first at getting an X-server running on our system.

Supported Hardware

Getting the X-Window system configured and working can be one of the most difficult tasks in setting up a Linux system. Fortunately, Red Hat Linux comes with tools that make this job relatively painless and easy.

One of the most important steps you can take to ensure that you wind up with a working X-Window configuration is selecting the proper hardware. Ironically, in the case of running the X-Window system under Linux, having the latest and greatest video card or monitor is not always the best situation to be in. When selecting video hardware, you should look for video cards and monitors that have been in production for a while. The more popular a given type of card or a given type of monitor, the better your chances are that the chipset for your video card and monitor will be supported.

Hardware: X-Server Selection

Red Hat Linux has support for hundreds of video cards and monitors. The best place to check to see whether your video card and monitor are supported is the Red Hat support site at http://www.Red Hat.com/corp/support/hardware/index.html.

If you don't find your video card or monitor among the list of Red Hat–supported hardware, you can also check http://www.XFree86.org/cardlist.html.

The X-Window server program that is shipped with Red Hat Linux is an open-source program called XFree86. The version of XFree86 that you install depends on the type of video hardware and monitor you have. When you install the X-Window system, you need to install an X-server program that contains the correct video drivers and settings for your particular video card.

Different Servers of XFree86.org

The Red Hat Linux distribution includes precompiled versions of the XFree86 server for the most common types of video cards. These images are stored in Red Hat package files (RPMS). For example, if your video card uses the S3 video chipset and you are manually configuring the X-Window system, although I wouldn't recommend this, as you will see shortly, you need to install the XFree86-S3-3.3.3.1-49 package from the Red Hat/RPMS directory on your Red Hat distribution CD-ROM.

If you are using an unsupported video card, support is also included for simple SVGA and VGA devices. Most video cards and monitors will work with these X-servers. Appendix D, Section 7.2, of the *Red Hat Linux 6.0 Installation Guide* provides a list of the X-server packages that are included with Red Hat Linux.

Tools for X-Configuration

The configuration file for XFree86 is /etc/X11/XF86Config. On earlier implementations of Linux, you had to manually edit this file to get the X-Window system working. This can be a time-consuming and frustrating process. One of the advantages of using Red Hat Linux is that it comes with tools that make it easy for you to configure the X-Window system and get it working. Although you can still edit the XF86Config file manually, using a text editor, using these tools for the task is much easier.

You can install the X-Window system at the same time you install Linux, or you can choose to install the X-Window system later. After the X-Window system is installed, you can reconfigure it at any time. One nice change that Red Hat has made from earlier versions of Red Hat Linux is that, if you do choose to install the X-Window system as part of your initial system install, it is the last thing that gets installed. The reason for this change is that installing the X-Window system is the most likely point of failure in any installation. Making the installation of the X-Window system optional and positioning it at the end of the install process ensures that if your X-Window installation bombs out, the rest of your install won't be affected.

Xconfigurator

The first tool we're going to take a look at is the Red Hat Xconfigurator program. If you chose to configure the X-Window system when you installed Red Hat Linux on your system, you have already encountered this program. In addition to being a stand-alone program that you can run at any time from the command line, the Xconfigurator program is also called by the installation program when you choose to install and configure the X-Window system.

The Xconfigurator program is a character-based GUI that leads you through a series of menus aiding you in configuring your video hardware. The Xconfigurator program will automatically probe your video card and try to pick the appropriate X-server image for it. If Xconfigurator cannot determine what make of card you have, then you must select your video card from the list of video cards supported under Red Hat Linux.

Running Xconfigurator

You start the Xconfigurator program by typing

```
Xconfigurator
```

at a command prompt. You can do this either from a console screen or from an X-terminal client.

You maneuver through the Xconfigurator screens using the TAB key and the up and down arrow keys. To toggle a selection, use the SPACE BAR. To click on OK or Cancel, tab to the item and press ENTER. When you start Xconfigurator, the first screen you see is a welcome screen with an OK button and a Cancel button at the bottom. The OK button is highlighted, which indicates that this is the default action that will happen when you press the ENTER key.

If Xconfigurator is unable to determine what type of video card you are using, pressing ENTER from the startup screen places you in the video card selection screen shown in Figure 7-2. Use the up and down arrow keys to select the video card for your system. If you do not see your card listed, it may not be supported. If this is the case, there are several options you can try:

- Select a video card that is similar to your model and then edit /etc/X11/XF86Config.
- Check the Web for others who are running the X-Window system with the same type of hardware.
- Use either the SVGA or VGA X-Window servers.
- After you have selected your monitor, you can either press TAB to move to the OK button and then press ENTER, or simply press ENTER, to move on to the monitor selection screen.

After you have selected a monitor, Xconfigurator will ask whether it can probe your video card to determine the resolutions it is capable of displaying. The default response is Don't Probe, but since this is generally a safe thing to allow, use the TAB key to highlight the Probe button and press ENTER.

During the probing process, your screen will blink several times and your monitor may click as different video modes and resolutions are tried. After the probing process finishes you may be asked to specify the amount of

FIGURE 7-2

Selecting a video card using Xconfigurator. Use your keyboard's arrow keys to highlight your card; use the TAB key to move between buttons

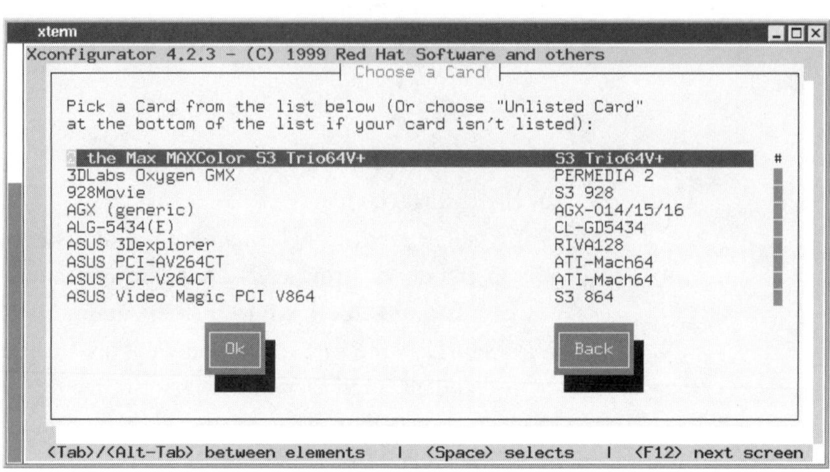

video RAM and the type of clockchip you have. If you are not sure, consult the documentation for your video card. The recommended setting for the clockchip is No Clockchip Setting.

At this point you are given a chance to select the video modes you wish to use. You probably want to select multiple video modes; you control the size and *color depth* of your display by switching video modes. Configuring multiple video modes is a good way to ensure that your X-Window installation is successful. Your video card may have difficulty displaying at a higher resolution video mode such as 1024x768 pixels but may do fine at a lower resolution such as 800x600 pixels. If you have configured your X-server to support multiple video modes, you switch between different modes (by pressing the CTRL-ALT-+ keys simultaneously) until you find a mode that displays properly on your hardware. A higher resolution equates to being able to fit more on your screen. The price you pay is that the fonts in your application will be smaller. Another advantage to configuring multiple video modes is that you can toggle between different resolutions depending on whether you're concentrating on one application or are trying to fit as many windows as possible on your display.

After you select the video modes you want to use, Xconfigurator will ask whether it can start the X-Window system to test your configuration. Select OK and your display will go blank while the X-Window server starts. After a short interval, your X-server should start and you should see a dialog box with a message asking whether you can read the display and with two buttons labeled Yes and No. If you can read the display and it looks like everything is working correctly, use your mouse to click Yes. This will tell Xconfigurator that everything is working correctly. If your display isn't working properly or you can't see the dialog box, don't worry. If you click the No button, or simply wait ten seconds, Xconfigurator switches back to the original video mode you were using and gives you the chance to retry your configuration or quit.

As the final step in configuring the X-Window system, you are asked whether you want to automatically start the X-server when the system boots. For most systems, the answer to this is Yes. If you decide not to configure the X-Window system for automatic startup, it is very easy to change this setting later.

If Xconfigurator is unable to determine what type of video card you have installed in your system and you are missing the documentation for your video card, you can use the XFree86 *SuperProbe* utility to obtain information about your video card. From a command prompt, type:

```
SuperProbe
```

The SuperProbe program issues a warning about possibly locking up your system and gives you a short time to cancel the program by typing CTRL-C. As the program runs, you will see your screen flash much as it does during the setup of the X-Window system. When SuperProbe finishes it displays the information it found for your video card. Here is the output the SuperProbe utility generated when run on an ancient 486:

```
First Video: Super-VGA
   Chipset: Cirrus CL-GD5428 (Port Probed)
   Memory:  1024 Kbytes
   RAMDAC:  Cirrus Logic Built-in 15/16/24-bit DAC
            (with 6-bit wide lookup tables(or in 6-bit mode))
```

Laptops

Configuring the X-Window system to run on a laptop can be more challenging than configuring the X-Window system to run on a desktop system. If you are planning to install Red Hat Linux on a laptop, in addition to consulting the Red Hat support site, you should also check the Linux laptop page at http://www.cs.utexas.edu/users/kharker/linux-laptop.

FROM THE CLASSROOM

Configuring the X-Window system is one of the few places in the process of setting up a Linux system in which the choices you make could potentially damage your hardware. The reason for this has to do with something called the *refresh rate* for your monitor. This is the rate at which the image you see on your screen is redrawn. The refresh rate is expressed in terms of Hertz (Hz). A refresh rate of 60 Hz means that an image is redrawn 60 times in one second. Computer monitors have both a vertical and a horizontal refresh rate. Some monitors, known as multisync monitors, support multiple vertical and horizontal refresh rates. Whether fixed frequency or multisync, these refresh rates vary from one model of monitor to another. When you specify the type of monitor you are using, what you are really doing is telling the video card what frequencies it can use to **drive** the monitor. If your monitor is a fixed frequency monitor and the type of monitor you select does not match the type of hardware you actually have, it is possible for your video card to overdrive your monitor, resulting in a blown monitor. Most modern monitors are of the multisync type, so this is less of a worry, but if you are installing Linux on older hardware you may want to make sure you have the specifications for the monitor's refresh frequencies available before you configure XFree86.

XF86Setup

As an alternate to using Xconfigurator, you may wish to use the XFree86 XF86Setup program. This program is not installed by default on Red Hat Linux version 6.0. To run XF86Setup you will need to mount the Red Hat Linux installation CD-ROM and install the XFree86-VGA16 and XF86Setup packages as follows:

```
mount /dev/cdrom
cd /mnt/cdrom/Red Hat/RPMS
rpm -i XFree86-VGA16-3.3.3.1-49.i386.rpm
rpm -i XFRee86-XF86Setup-3.3.3.1-49.i386.rpm
```

You run XF86Setup by typing **XF86Setup** at a command prompt. Unlike Xconfigurator, XF86Setup is an X-Window program. You do not have to have the X-Window system running in order to use it, however. If you are trying to set up an initial X-Window configuration, XF86Setup starts up a basic VGA X-server so that you can run the program. Once you have finished configuring your X-Window server, XF86Setup saves your configuration settings and starts up the X-server for the hardware you have chosen. Of course, if you already have the X-Window system running, you can run XF86Setup to make changes to your current X-server configuration. Note that in order to run XF86Setup, you must install the XFree86-VGA16 server.

Using a Two-Button Mouse

The X-Window system was designed to work with a three-button mouse. Most personal computers come with a two-button mouse. Although you might choose to purchase a three-button mouse, you don't need to do so in order to use the X-Window system. If you have a two-button mouse, the "missing" button is the middle button. You can emulate the middle button of a three-button mouse by simultaneously clicking both the left and right buttons on a two-button mouse.

The Red Hat Certified Engineer exam is primarily a performance-based exam. It is very important, therefore, that you try out the concepts presented in this chapter and experiment with them. Don't just read about them.

/etc/X11

Information about your X-Window configuration is stored in the /etc/X11 directory (Figure 7-3). One of the most important of these files is XF86Config. XF86Config is read by the XFree86 X-server when it starts. This file is where the X-server obtains its configuration information and is where the changes you make when you run Xconfigurator or XF86Setup are written. Although normally you should use one of these utilities to modify XF86Config, it is a text file and can be edited with any standard text editor. If you plan to modify this file manually, consult the XF86Config manual page.

Another thing you should notice in the listing of the /etc/X11 directory is that there is an entry for a file called *X*. This file is actually a symbolic link

FIGURE 7-3

Configuration information for the X-Window system is in /etc/X11

```
xterm
[root@localhost /root]# ls -l /etc/X11
total 29
drwxr-xr-x   4 root     root         1024 Aug 20 05:55 AnotherLevel
drwxr-xr-x   2 root     root         1024 Aug 20 05:55 TheNextLevel
drwxr-xr-x   2 root     root         1024 Aug 21 20:20 WindowMaker
lrwxrwxrwx   1 root     root           29 Sep  3 22:21 X -> ../../usr/X11R6/bin/
XF86_SVGA
-rw-r--r--   1 root     root        14473 Sep  3 22:21 XF86Config
drwxr-xr-x   5 root     root         1024 Aug 20 07:14 applnk
drwxr-xr-x   2 root     root         1024 Aug 20 07:20 fs
drwxr-xr-x   2 root     root         1024 Aug 20 06:17 fvwm
drwxr-xr-x   2 root     root         1024 Aug 20 06:17 fvwm2
drwxr-xr-x   4 root     root         1024 Aug 20 06:18 gdm
lrwxrwxrwx   1 root     root           12 Aug 29 15:38 prefdm -> /usr/bin/gdm
drwxr-xr-x   2 root     root         1024 Aug 20 07:16 twm
drwxr-xr-x   2 root     root         1024 Aug 20 07:22 wmconfig
drwxr-xr-x   3 root     root         1024 Aug 21 15:14 xdm
drwxr-xr-x   2 root     root         1024 Aug 20 07:21 xinit
drwxr-xr-x   2 root     root         1024 Aug 20 07:16 xsm
[root@localhost /root]#
```

that points to /usr/X11R6/bin/XF86_SVGA. This is the hardware-specific X-server that will be started when the X-Window system is started on this system. The file this link points to on your system will vary depending on the display hardware you use.

You need to be familiar with both the /etc/X11 directory and the /usr/X11R6 directory. This is the directory where the X-Window software is stored. Of particular importance is the /usr/X11R6/bin directory, where the X-Window executable images are stored. This directory must be in your PATH environment variable if you want to use the X-Window system. If you have run Xconfigurator, your PATH should be set correctly. You can check the value of the PATH variable with the command:

```
echo $PATH
```

If your PATH environment variable isn't set correctly, you can add the X-Window image directory to your PATH with the command:

```
PATH=$PATH:/usr/X11R6/bin
```

EXERCISE 7-1

X-Server

In this exercise, you will start your X-server without running any window manager and start an xterm X-client application. Some of the commands used in this exercise are covered later in the chapter. If the X-Window system is not running, you can skip steps 1 and 3.

1. If the X-Window system is running, change to a text console by pressing CTRL-ALT-F1.
2. Log in on the text console as root.
3. Stop the current X-Window server by typing:

   ```
   init 3
   ```

   (You must be root or another privileged user.)
4. Start the XFree86 X-server by typing the command:

   ```
   X &
   ```

   Note the capital X.

   Your X-server will start but all you will see is a blank gray screen.
5. Switch back to your text console session by pressing CTRL-ALT-F1.

6. Type the following command:

   ```
   xterm  -display localhost:0.0  &.
   ```

   Note that xterm starts with a lowercase x.
7. Switch back to your X-Window display by typing CTRL-ALT-F7.

You should now have an xterm terminal window. Select the window and try to enter commands from the xterm command line. Check out the contents of /usr/X11R6/bin. Try starting other X-client applications from the xterm command line. Reboot your system to return things to normal.

CERTIFICATION OBJECTIVE 7.02

X-Clients

Once you have your X-server working, you are (almost) ready to start connecting to it with X-Window clients. X-Window clients, or X-clients, are the application programs you run that use the windowing services provided by your X-server to display their output. You run one X-server process to control your display. In contrast, you can run as many X-clients as your hardware resources, primarily RAM, will support. If your Linux system is part of a network, you may also start X-clients on other systems on the network and have those clients send their displays to your X-server.

There are X-clients for almost any application you wish to name. There are X-clients for word processing, spreadsheets, games, and more. Most command line utilities, including many system administration utilities, come in an X-client version. There are even X-client versions of popular utilities such as the emacs program editor.

Starting X-Clients and Command Line Options

Starting an X-client is very easy. When you start the X-Window system for the first time on Red Hat Linux, several X-clients will already be started for you. You can start additional X-clients by using the mouse and selecting a program to start from a menu, or you can start an X-client from a command line.

X-client applications are standard Linux applications. If you choose to start an X-client from a command line, you can follow the command name with any number of options. Most X-clients understand a common set of options. These options are used to control things such as the size and location of the X-client's window, the font the application uses to display the text, and even the display on which the application should display its output. Table 7-1 lists some of the more useful options you can supply when you start an X-client from the command line.

The behavior of most of the command line options in Table 7-1 is self-descriptive, but we need to take a more detailed look at how some of the options work. We will look at the -display option later on in this chapter when we look at running remote X-clients.

The -geometry option is used to specify both the size of the window that the X-client starts up in and the location of the window. Notice that the first two numbers, the XSIZE and YSIZE, are separated by a lowercase "x." These two numbers specify the size of the client window in either pixels or characters, depending on the application. If you are starting an *xterm* window, for example, the size represents a terminal screen with XSIZE columns and YSIZE lines. If

TABLE 7-1

Commonly used X-client command line options

N	Example	Result
-display server:0.0	-display frodo:0.0	Send output to the X-server running on frodo.
-geometry XSIZExYSIZE+XOFF+YOFF	-geometry 100x100+10+20	Specify size and location of window.
-font fontname	-font lucidasans-14	Display text for this client using specified font.
-background color	-background blue	Set window background to blue.
-foreground color	-foreground white	Set window foreground to white.
-title string	-title "My Window"	Place a title on the client window's title bar.
-bordercolor color	-bordercolor green	Make the window border green.
-borderwidth pixels	-borderwidth 5	Make the window border 5 pixels wide.

you are starting an xclock, the size represents a window XSIZExYSIZE pixels in size. The next two numbers specify where you want the client window to appear on your display. The upper-left corner of your display is always "+0+0." You can specify these two numbers using any combination of plus and minus signs. A specification of "+10+10" says "position the client window so that the left edge is 10 pixels from the left edge of the screen and the top edge is 10 pixels from the top edge of the screen." A specification of "-10-10" says "position the window so that the right edge of the window is 10 pixels from the right edge of the display and the bottom edge of the window is 10 pixels from the bottom of the screen."

The -font option specifies the font that the X-client should use to display text. The X-Window system comes with a wide variety of both fixed and proportionally spaced fonts and you can add to these. In order to use a specific font, the files that contain the font definition must either be installed on your system or available from a network font server. The default path for X-Window fonts is /usr/X11R6/lib/X11/fonts. This directory contains a number of subdirectories, each of which contains font files for the various types of fonts installed on your system.

X-Window font names are usually very long. A typical font specification is:

-b&h-lucida-medium-i-normal-sans-14-140-75-75-p-82-iso8859-1.

This font specification contains all the information necessary to fully identify the font. Most fonts usually have an associated abbreviation. To use the font listed above, you can also use the abbreviated name lucidasans-14.

Many of the X-client command line options allow you to specify a color for different parts of the client window. You can specify a simple color such as red, green, white, black, and so on, or you can specify a color by indicating the red, green, and blue components of the color:

```
xclock -background RGB:FF/00/FF
```

xterm

One of the most useful X-clients is a program called xterm. As its name implies, xterm is an X-client application that creates a terminal window on your X-display. So, after all the hard work you've gone through to get a nice windowing display, you're right back where you started, with a command line interface. The difference is that now you can start up as many of these command line interfaces as you like, and you can switch between them with the click of a mouse. Since xterm is an X-client, you can even open up terminal windows on other computers on your network and have them display to your desktop. You can start xterm either from a menu or from a command line prompt.

Window Managers

As mentioned above, once you have your X-server running you're almost ready to start running X-applications. Before you get to that point, however, we need to look at a special type of X-client known as a *window manager.*

When you start the XFree86 X-server, it turns your display into a blank electronic canvas. If you are running Linux on a slow machine, you may even glimpse this canvas as your system goes through the process of starting the X-Window system. What you are seeing is the default desktop display for XFree86, which is an uninteresting gray background. The default mouse pointer for the X-Window display is a graphic representation of an "X." Once XFree86 starts and you have this canvas on your screen, the X-server is ready to start serving X-clients. In fact, you can start X-clients up at this point, and your X-server will open up windows to display their output. You will notice, however, that the windows seem to be missing something. You don't have any of the useful features such as borders, title bars, menu bars, and minimize–maximize buttons that you've come to expect from a graphical user interface. Figure 7-4 shows an example of what the default XFree86 display appears like with three different X-client applications started.

What you are seeing is the X-Window system in its natural state. To display your windows with all of the standard features you've come to expect from a graphical user interface, you need the services of a window manager. A window manager is a special type of X-client. A window manager cannot run on its own; it needs the services of an X-server to do its job. It is the job of the window manager to control how other X-clients appear on your display. This includes everything from placing title bars and drawing borders around

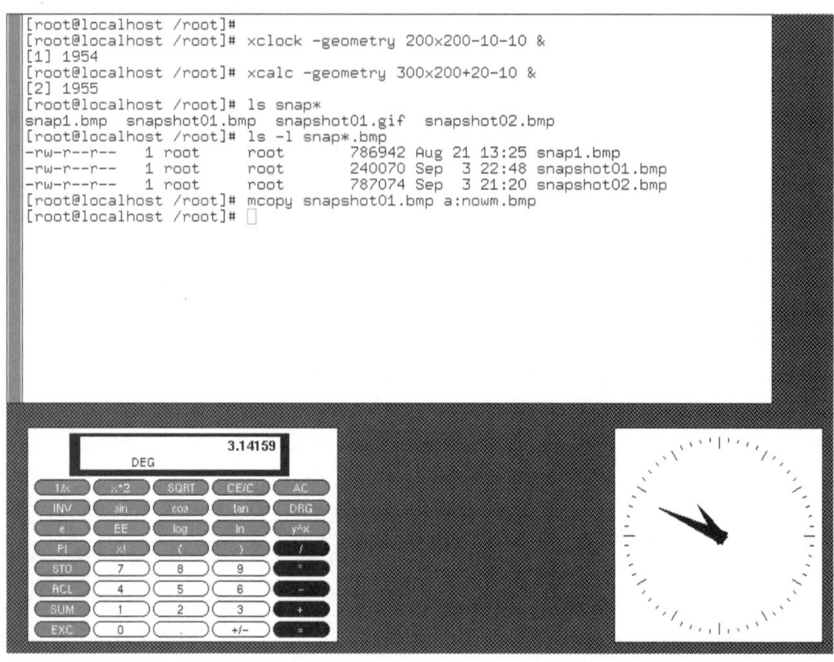

FIGURE 7-4

Running XFree86 without a window manager. The applications running are xterm, xclock, and xcalc

the window for each X-client application you start to determining the size of your desktop.

As is usually the case with all things Linux, there are multiple ways to accomplish the same task. Red Hat Linux comes with several window managers for you to choose from. Your choice of window manager will determine how the X-Window system appears and to some extent how it functions. The window manager is sometimes said to control the look and feel of your X-Window session.

fvwm, WindowMaker

One of the most popular window managers available for Linux is the *fvwm* window manager. The fvwm window manager was developed specifically for Linux and can be configured to emulate other window environments such as the commercial Motif window manager or even Windows 95. This can make fvwm a good choice if you are migrating users from a Microsoft Windows platform to Linux.

When you are running the X-Window system, your display is referred to as the desktop. The desktop is a workspace where the X-server places all of your windows and icons. The desktop itself is a special window called the root window. Some window managers limit the size of your desktop to be that of your actual hardware; if your hardware supports a video resolution of only 800x600 pixels, your desktop is limited to that size as well. Other window managers implement a virtual desktop that allows the area where you can place windows to be larger than the area of your display hardware.

The fvwm window manager uses a virtual desktop; the vwm in the name stands for virtual window manager. With fvwm's virtual desktop, your desktop is many times larger than your display. What you see displayed is only a portion of your desktop. To move to another area of your desktop, you drag the mouse in the direction you want to move and your display scrolls so that a new portion of the desktop is visible. The advantage of a virtual desktop is that you can have many X-client windows open on your desktop without having to try to squeeze them into the tiny area bounded by your display. To help you navigate your desktop, fvwm starts a pager program that displays a small window with a miniature map of your virtual desktop that shows you what areas have open windows. To move to a particular area of your desktop, you simply click on that portion of your desktop you want to bring into view with your mouse. The fvwm95 interface is shown in Figure 7-5.

WindowMaker is another very well done window manager that comes with Red Hat Linux. The WindowMaker interface is designed to resemble the commercial NEXTSTEP interface. We will see how to start the WindowMaker GUI later.

EXERCISE 7-2

Window Managers

Use the switchdesk utility and change your desktop environment to KDE. Try the AnotherLevel desktop. Follow the steps listed earlier to switch your desktop environment to WindowMaker. To switch back to the default GNOME desktop environment, delete the files .Xclients and .Xclients-default in your home directory.

FIGURE 7-5

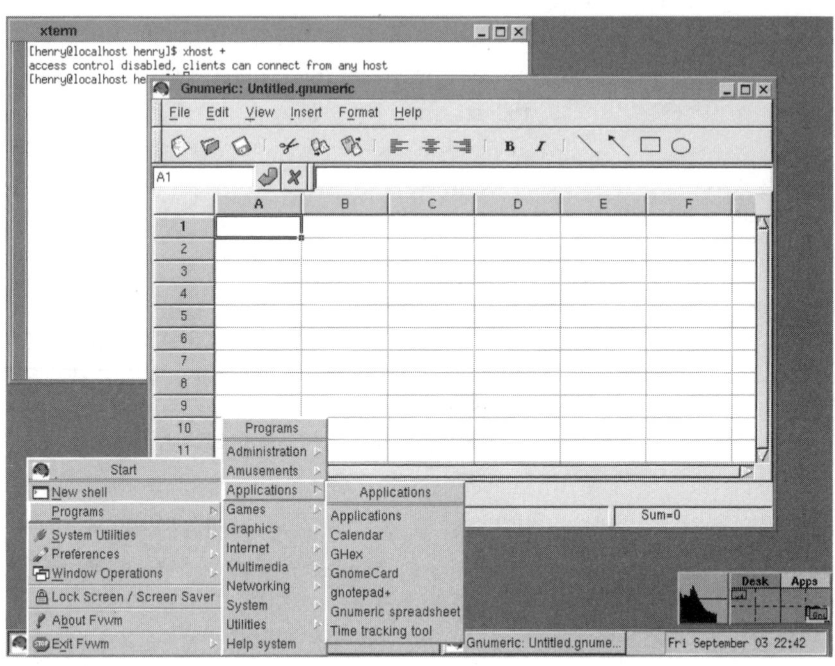

The fvwm95 interface. The pager applet is in the lower left corner

Desktops, GNOME, KDE

Two other powerful virtual desktop environments that come with Red Hat Linux are the GNOME (GNU Network Object Model Environment) desktop environment and the KDE desktop environment. Both GNOME and KDE are designed to emulate the look and feel of the Common Desktop Environment (CDE). The GNOME desktop, shown in Figure 7-6, is the default desktop for Red Hat Linux and is the desktop you first see after you install the X-Window system.

GNOME Features

The GNOME desktop includes support for the Common Object Request Broker Architecture (CORBA), which allows GNOME software components written in any language and running on different systems to work together. In addition, the GNOME developer community is also working on an architecture similar to Microsoft's Object Linking and Embedding (OLE) architecture that will allow one GNOME application to call and control another GNOME application. One very nice feature of GNOME-compliant applications is that they are *session aware*; that is, when you quit an application, the application "remembers" the location in the document where you were last working and will reposition your cursor to that point when you restart the application.

Enlightenment

Even though you may be using GNOME as your desktop environment, you still need the services of a window manager. The best way to think of the relationship between the window manager and GNOME is that they work together to control what you see on your display. The GNOME desktop will work with any window manager, but it works best with a GNOME-compliant window manager. Under Red Hat Linux, the default GNOME window manager is the Enlightenment window manager. IceWM is another GNOME-compliant window manager that you can use. Work is under way to make fvwm and other window managers GNOME-compliant. You can find more information about GNOME at http://www.gnome.org.

Using GNOME

Many of the features of the GNOME interface will be familiar to you from other desktop environments. On the left side of the screen are icons representing files and applications that can be opened by double-clicking on them with the mouse. The GNOME desktop environment also provides you with a virtual desktop. Next to the application buttons in the center of the panel is a pager that you can use to move from one area of the desktop to another.

One of the key features of GNOME is the panel, which you can see at the bottom of the screen in Figure 7-6. The panel is the control center for most of your activities while you use GNOME. The button at the far left of the panel with the imprint of a foot is the main menu button. Use your mouse to click this button and you will see a list of applications that you can run. You can also launch applications from the panel by clicking the appropriate icon. In the center of the panel at the bottom of the screen in

FIGURE 7-6

The GNOME desktop. This is the default desktop for Red Hat Linux

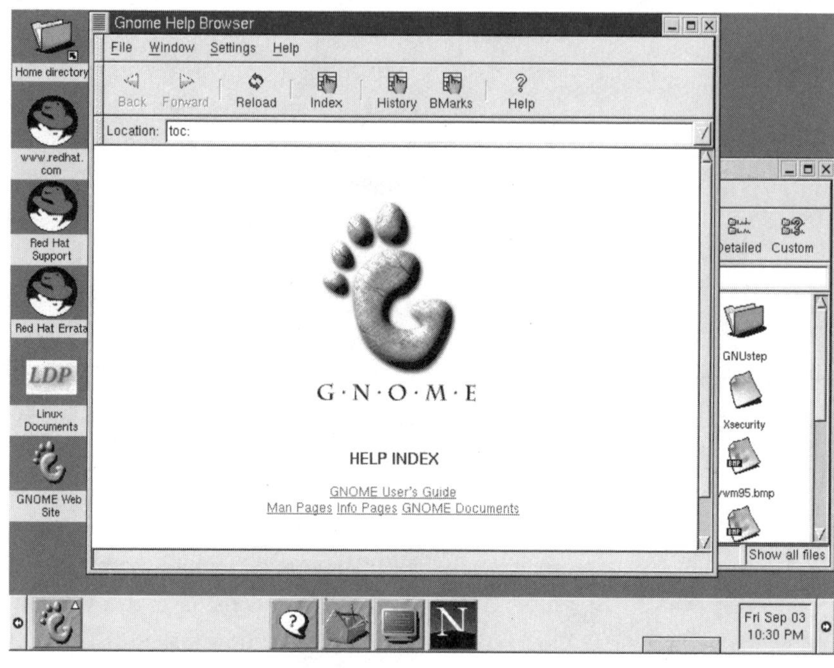

Figure 7-6 are buttons to launch the GNOME help utility, the GNOME configuration utility, a terminal emulator, and a Web browser. You can add applications and menus to the panel. You can also place additional panels on your desktop. Next to the main menu button is a narrow hide panel button. Click this button to store the panel out of sight. If a panel is hidden, click the hide panel button to make it reappear. Notice that there are hide buttons on both ends of the panel.

Choosing Desktop Environments

You can use the Red Hat Linux switchdesk utility to easily switch your default desktop from one environment to another. In order to switch from GNOME to another desktop environment, you must have the target environment installed.

As an example of switching desktops, here is the way to switch from GNOME to the KDE environment. Bring up an xterm window and enter the command:

```
switchdesk
```

This will display an X-client window on your display, as shown in Figure 7-7. Click the KDE option button and then click the OK button. As the final step in changing to your desktop, log out. When you log back in, you will be using the KDE environment. If you want to use the Windows 95 lookalike GUI, select the AnotherLevel desktop.

You can also use the switchdesk utility to switch to the other desktop environments that are not displayed as selectable options. The switchdesk program creates two hidden files in your home directory, ~/.Xclients and ~/.Xclients-default, that are used to start your alternate desktop. If you have an existing ~.Xclients file, it will be saved as ~.Xclients.switchdesk. To switch to an alternate desktop, you simply need to modify ~/.Xclients-default.

FIGURE 7-7

Use the Switchdesk menu window to change your desktop environment

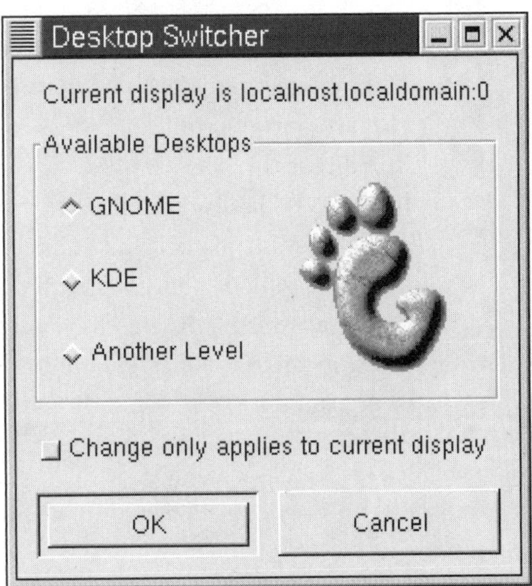

As an example, suppose you want to use WindowMaker as your default desktop environment. Run switchdesk and select the KDE desktop environment, but do not log out after exiting switchdesk. Use your favorite text editor to edit the .Xclients-default file and change the line that reads:

```
exec startkde.
```

to read:

```
exec wmaker.
```

Save your changes and log out. When you next log in, you will be running the WindowMaker desktop. To revert back to your original desk top, simply delete the ~.Xclients and ~.Xclients-default files and log out and log in again.

CERTIFICATION OBJECTIVE 7.03

Startup

You can configure the X-Window interface to start automatically when your system boots, or you can choose to start the X-Window system manually. Recall that this is the last decision you make when running Xconfigurator. If your X-Window configuration appears to be working correctly, you will probably want to go ahead and tell Xconfigurator to make the changes necessary to boot your system directly into the X-Window system. You should answer No if your X-Window configuration doesn't appear to be working correctly or if you are setting up your X-server to run with a new or nonstandard video card. If you choose not to boot into the X-Window system, Linux Red Hat will boot up with a text-based console screen and you can start the X-Window system manually.

startx

You use the *startx* command to start the X-Window interface manually from a command line prompt. Simply type the command:

```
startx
```

at the Linux command prompt. This starts XFree86 and switches your display into graphics mode. If you run startx and the X-Window system is already started, you will receive an error message telling you that an X-server is already running on your display.

When you exit an X-Window session that was started by running startx, your display resets to text console mode and you are placed back at the Linux command prompt level. You may decide to start the X-Window interface this way if you are debugging a new X-Window setup. Once you have your configuration working to your satisfaction, you can then configure Linux to automatically boot into the X-Window system.

on the job

The startx command is actually a customizable shell script that serves as a front end to the xinit command. The default location for both the startx shell script and the xinit program is /usr/X11R6/bin.

For a production system, especially a user's workstation, you will most likely want Linux to boot into the X-Window system. Fortunately, you don't have to rerun the Xconfigurator to change this. You can change the mode Red Hat Linux boots into by editing the /etc/inittab file and changing the default runlevel. In Red Hat Linux, the X-Window system is defined as runlevel 5. To make the X-Window system your default runlevel at boot time, use your favorite text editor and change the line in /etc/inittab that reads:

```
id:3:initdefault:
```

to:

```
id:5:initdefault:.
```

Note that this change will not take effect until you reboot. If you are running as the root user, you can also use the init command to switch between X-Window runlevel 5 and non-X-Window runlevel 3.

```
init 3
```

switches your display from X-Window back to text terminal mode.

```
init 5
```

TABLE 7-2

Key Combinations Controlling X-Window Session

Key Combination	Function
CTRL-ALT-F1 through F6	Switch from X-Window GUI to virtual console 1, 2, … .
CTRL-ALT-F7	Switch from text console to X-Window GUI.
CTRL-ALT-+	Toggle between X-Window video modes.
CTRL-ALT-BACKSPACE	Terminate X-Window GUI.

switches you from text terminal mode to X-Window. You can find more information on changing runlevels in Chapter 5.

You can still use the virtual console feature of Red Hat Linux when you're running the X-Window system. You can switch between six text consoles and one GUI console. Table 7-2 shows several key combinations you can use to control your X-Window session.

xdm, gdm, kdm

In order to gain access to a Linux system, you must first pass an authentication check. On most systems, this consists of identifying yourself to the system by typing in a username and password combination. When you log in to Linux from a text terminal, you make use of the services of the getty (get tty) program. The getty program monitors the terminal, waiting for someone to press a key indicating they wish to log in. When this happens, the getty program spawns the login program, which asks you for your username and password.

When you log in from the X-Window GUI, the login and authentication task is handed over to another special type of X-client, the display manager. The display manager is a fairly simple program. Its primary purpose is to display a dialogue box on the screen that asks you for your username and password combination. You have a choice of display managers to use with Red Hat Linux. The default display manager is the GNOME display manager. To change your display manager, change the name of the file pointed to by the prefdm symbolic link in the /etc/X11 directory:

ln -fs /usr/bin/gdm /etc/X11/prefdm	Use the GNOME display manager (default).
ln -fs /usr/bin/kdm /etc/X11/prefdm	Use the KDE display manager.
ln -fs /usr/X11R6/bin/xdm /etc/X11/prefdm	Use the X11 display manager.

How you start the X-Window system affects how it behaves. The most noticeable difference is that when you start the X-Window GUI using startx, exiting your X-Window session doesn't log you out but returns you to the command line from which you entered the startx command. Exiting an X-Window session that was started by logging in through a display manager is effectively the same as logging out of a command line login session. The startup process for an X-Window session launched by startx also differs slightly from one started through a display manager.

The default behavior for the gdm window manager is to launch a GNOME session for you. The kdm window manager launches a KDE session. As an alternate to using the switchdesk utility, both the gdm window manager and the kdm window manager have option buttons to allow you to log in under a different desktop environment other than the default.

There are a number of configuration files you can use to customize the behavior of your X-Window session. These files are hidden files that reside in your home directory. Typically these files are shell scripts that are read and executed by the X-Window startup routines. If the X-Window startup program doesn't find a particular configuration file in your home directory, it will use a systemwide default version of the same file.

When you start the X-Window system with the startx command, the xinit program looks for a file to run named .xinitrc in your home directory. Using the shell's file name generation shorthand character for your home directory, the full pathname for this file is ~/.xinitrc. If the startx command cannot find ~/.xinitrc it will run the file /etc/X11/xinit/xinitrc. This file in turn will run either the file ~/.Xclients or, if that file doesn't exist, /etc/X11/xinit/Xclients.

The ~/.xinitrc file usually contains a series of commands that start various X-clients. Figure 7-8 shows an example of a simple ~/.xinitrc file.

The first line tells Linux which shell program to use to run the ~/.xinitrc script. The next two lines are comment lines. The first line after that starts up an xterm terminal client. The next line starts up the xclock application to display a clock on your screen. The line after that brings up an X-Window calculator. Notice that the three command lines end with an ampersand. This is important; it tells the shell to run each command line and return control to the calling program (~/.xinitrc) without waiting for the program started on the command line to finish running. The final line in the ~/.xinitrc file uses the exec command to start the fvwm window manager. This tells Linux to run the fvwm program and that fvwm should take control of the process that is running the .xinitrc shell script so that when the fvwm process exits—that is, when you choose to exit the X-Window system—the other programs that were started by the ~/.xinitrc process will be terminated.

You can create a ~/.xinitrc file with any text editor. After you have saved the file and exited the editor, you should make sure the file is executable by issuing the command:

```
chmod a+x ~/.xinitrc
```

If you log in using a display manager, the initialization of your X-Window session takes place in a somewhat different manner than it does when you run startx. When you run startx, your X-Window session runs as a child process of your text based login shell. You can verify this with the runlevel command; even though the X-Window system is running, Linux is

FIGURE 7-8

The .xinitrc file can be used to customize the behavior of startx

```
#!/bin/bash
#A simple ~/.xinitrc shell script
#/usr/X11R6/bin should also be in your PATH
xterm &
xclock -geometry 200x200-20+20 &
xcalc -geometry 300x300-20-20 &
exec fvwm
```

still at runlevel 3. After you exit the X-Window system, you still have to log out of this shell to terminate your login session.

When you log in from a display manager, Linux does not start an interactive shell. Instead, the display manager launches a program, called the session manager, that is the controlling process for your X-Window login session. If you are running the GNOME desktop, this program is /usr/bin/gnome-session; if you are running KDE, it is /usr/bin/kwm. The standard X-Window session manager is /usr/bin/xsession. All X-clients that you run from your X-Window session are child processes of the session manager process. When you exit the session manager, all child processes of the session manager are terminated also. When you log in via a display manager, the session manager does not execute the contents of ~xinitrc.

Both the GNOME and the KDE display manager allow you to choose the desktop environment you wish to start through the use of option buttons. From the GNOME display manager, you click the Options button and then select the Sessions menu and select the session manager you want to use. Both GNOME and the KDE environment use their own startup files.

If you start a window session using the default xsession program, you can customize your session using the ~/.xsession file or the ~/.Xclients file; xsession looks for ~/.xsession first and then looks for ~/.Xclients. If neither file exists, then it will use system defaults. The system defaults for most window managers and desktop environments are stored in directories under /etc/X11 (Figure 7-3).

EXERCISE 7-3

startx

In this exercise, we will start the X-Window system using startx with a customized .xinitrc file.

1. If the X-Window system is running, stop it using the command:

   ```
   init 3
   ```

2. Log in to a text console.
3. Make sure you're in your home directory. Use your favorite text editor to create a .xinitrc file such as the example we saw earlier.
4. Make sure the .xinitrc file is executable:

   ```
   chmod  a+x  .xinitrc
   ```

5. Start the X-Window system by typing:

```
startx
```

Your X-Window session should automatically start the applications in your .xinitrc file.

CERTIFICATION OBJECTIVE 7.04

Remote Display of X-Apps

One of the most powerful features of the X-Window system is the strength of its networking support. The X-Window system was designed from the beginning to run in a networked environment. If you are a system manager with a number of Red Hat Linux systems under your care, there's no need to leave your office and make a journey to the server room every time you want to run a GUI administration tool. With the X-Window system, you can connect to any number of systems and redirect the output from X-clients running on those systems back to the X-server running on your desktop.

X-Security

Before you can run remote clients and have them redirect their output back to your X-server, we need to take a look at some basic X-Window security. When working with remote X-applications, you should also keep in mind that all other Linux security features are still in effect. You will still need a user account and password, or the equivalent such as an entry in a .rhost file on the remote system, in order to connect to the remote system to start an X-client. Authorization problems or network problems at layers below the X-Window system can prevent your X-Window client applications from running.

Part of the job of the X-server running on your system is to listen for requests from X-clients that want to send their output to your display. Those requests can come from local client applications, those that are running on your system, or they can come from remote client applications running on another system. Without some form of access control, any X-client application on any system on your network can send its output to the display controlled by your X-server. This includes client applications started up by other users on other systems. Although on a small network you might want to allow indiscriminate network access to your display, in a larger network environment or in a production network environment, you will want to limit who can send client output to your X-server.

The simplest way to control access to your display is with the xhost command. The xhost command controls access to your X-server display on a machine-by-machine basis. Table 7-3 shows how you use the xhost command to secure your X-server.

The xhost command provides you with a basic security mechanism. The X-Window system can also make use of more sophisticated methods to control access to X-servers. These methods use DES encrypted authorization strings and other mechanisms to validate remote users trying to access a local X-server display. Some of these methods have the advantage over xhost-based access control of allowing you to restrict or allow access to your display to specific users from specific machines or network domains. Access information for these other validation methods is stored in the hidden file ~/.Xauthority. You use the xauth program to manipulate the information in this file.

X-Remote

Running a remote X-client requires that you have access to the remote system on which the client will run. In turn, the remote system, and possibly the account you are using on the remote system, must have permission to connect to the X-server display that the X-client you start will use for its console. In the following example, we will take a step-by-step look at running an X-client on a remote system, server1.xyz.com, and sending the output back to our local workstation, work1.xyz.com.

TABLE 7-3

Securing X-Server with xhost Command

xhost	Show current security settings.
xhost +	Disable security; allow connections from any system.
xhost -	Enable security.
xhost +server1.xyz.com	Allow connection from server1.xyz.com.
xhost –server1.xyz.com	Disable connections from server1.xyz.com.

The first step in the process is to make sure you allow server1 access to the display on our local system:

```
xhost +server1.xyz.com
```

Of course, if you have already granted server1 access to our display then you can skip this step.

The next step in the process is to log in to server1. Here, you will use the telnet command, but this could be done using any remote login program, such as rsh or rlogin, that allows us to establish a remote login session on server1:

```
[root@work1]$ telnet server1.xyz.com
Trying 192.168.1.2...
Connected to server1.xyz.com.
Escape character is '^]'.
Red Hat Linux release 6.0 (Hedwig)
Kernel 2.2.5-15 on an i486
login: root
Password: Fizzbin7
[root@server1]$
```

Since you are going to be running X-Window client applications, you will probably want to make sure the X-Window binary directory is in your search path:

```
[root@server1]$ (echo $PATH | grep '/usr/X11R6/bin') >/dev/null  \
|| PATH=$PATH:/usr/X11R6/bin
```

The final step in the process is to start your remote X-client, or X-clients if you plan to start up more than one remote program. At this point, you can choose to start our X-client in one of two ways. For this example, you will start the same X-client application using each method. The X-client program you will run is xclock.

Since X-Window clients behave like Linux applications, all you need to do to run the xclock program is type the program name on the command line. Since this program is an X-Window client application, however, you need to provide it with one crucial piece of information: the name of the X-server it is going to use. You can provide this information on the command line when you start the application by specifying the -display option (see Table 7-1):

```
[root@server1]$ xclock -display work1.xyz.com:0.0
```

This starts the xclock application on server1, but the output from the program is displayed on work1. At this point, your telnet session on server1 appears to be locked up. This is because the xclock application is running as your foreground process. Unless you received an error message when you started the application, you don't see any indication that anything is happening on server1 because the output from xclock is being sent to the X-server on work1. To regain control of your telnet session, you can either terminate xclock by typing CTRL-C, or you can suspend it by typing CTRL-Z. If you are going to be starting multiple client applications, you should end each command line with an ampersand (&) to tell Linux to run the X-client as a background process.

The other method for starting an X-client from the command prompt uses a shell environment variable to pass the display information to the X-client. When you start an X-client without the -display option, the X-client looks for the DISPLAY environment variable in your current process. In fact, this is how X-clients you run on your local system determine where to send their output. When you log in to your workstation from the display manager, the DISPLAY variable is automatically set to point to the X-server running on your workstation. If you are connecting to a remote host and will be starting multiple X-clients, you should set this variable so that you don't have to specify the -display option for every X-client you run. Having typed a CTRL-C to regain control of your telnet session, you can set the a DISPLAY variable and rerun xclock:

```
[root@server1]$ export DISPLAY=work1.xyz.com:0.0    #sh,ksh,bash
[root@server1]$ xclock
```

The first part of the display specification is the X-server the X-client should connect to. The second part of the display specification requires further explanation. A single X-Server can control multiple GUI consoles attached to a single system. Each GUI console has its own set of input and output devices (monitor, keyboard, and mouse). In addition, each GUI console can have multiple monitors. When you are redirecting the output for an X-client, you must tell it not only which system to connect to but also which GUI console and which display on that console to display to.

On most systems this will be console 0, display 0 (0.0). The server portion of the display can be a host name, a fully qualified domain name, or an IP address. The following are all valid specifications for a remote display:

- work1:0.0
- work1.xyz.com:0.0
- 192.168.1.5:0.0

Troubleshooting

The X-Window system is very robust and stable, but occasionally problems can arise. There are several things you can try when you troubleshoot X-Window problems.

- Session managers create log files in your home directory such as ~/.xsession-errors. Check these log files as well as /var/log/messages and /var/log/Xerrors for error messages from your X-Server.
- Problems with the .xinitrc or .Xclients shell scripts may cause problems. Try deleting or renaming these files.
- Check the DISPLAY environment variable to make sure it is set correctly. If you are running X-clients locally, programs still use this variable. You can set it with the command:

  ```
  export DISPLAY=localhost:0.0
  ```

  or

  ```
  export DISPLAY=:0.0
  ```

- Make sure /usr/X11R6/bin is in your search path.
- Check for underlying system problems or network problems that could be causing problems with the X-Window system.
- Even if your X-server is not responding or you can't read the display, don't forget that you can switch to a text console to gain access to the system.

- If you are troubleshooting X-server problems on a remote system, try starting an X-client from your workstation using the remote X-server's display. Note that you will need appropriate X-security access to do this:

```
xclock -display remotesys:0.0
```

EXERCISE 7-4

Troubleshooting DISPLAY Problems

In this exercise, we will see what happens if you unset the DISPLAY variable.

1. Log in to an X-Window session.
2. Bring up a terminal window from the panel or a menu.
3. Start the xclock application using the command:

```
xclock  &
```

4. Unset your DISPLAY variable:

```
unset DISPLAY
```

5. Start another xclock:

```
xclock  &
```

6. You should get an error message saying that the X-client can't find your display. Reset the DISPLAY variable with the command:

```
export DISPLAY=localhost:0.0
```

7. Try starting the xclock application again.

The X-server and most X-clients have associated man pages. You should also consult these;* man X *is a good place to start. Note that you may have to install the RPMs for the man pages. There are also several helpful text documents in /usr/doc and /usr/doc/*HOWTO *that explain various aspects of configuring the X-Window system.

Now that you have seen how X-Window clients and the X-Window server work together, here are some common situations that you may encounter and their solutions.

QUESTIONS AND ANSWERS

I'm having problems getting XFree86 to run on my hardware.	Check the Red Hat hardware support site. Run SuperProbe.
I want to use a different desktop environment.	Use the switchdesk utility to change your desktop environment.
I want to stop the X-Window system without halting Linux.	Use the init command to change the system runlevel.
I'm having problems starting an X-client.	Check the that the DISPLAY variable is set and exported. Check for underlying network problems. Check X-security problems.
My X-Window display is acting strangely and I can't log in.	Switch to a virtual console.

CERTIFICATION SUMMARY

The X-Window system provides a state-of-the-art graphical user interface and offers features that are not found in other GUI environments. Although the X-Window system can be complicated, the Xconfigurator program simplifies the process of setting up the X-Window system. One of the most important steps you can take in setting up the X-Window system on Red Hat Linux is to select hardware that the XFree86 X-server supports.

The look and feel of the X-Window interface is determined by your choice of window manager. Red Hat Linux comes with several desktop environments including GNOME, KDE, AfterStep, WindowMaker, and fvwm. The GNOME desktop interface is the default for Red Hat Linux.

The X-Window system is designed to run on networked systems. You run client applications, both locally and remotely, that use the X-server on your workstation for their console.

TWO-MINUTE DRILL

- One of the most important aspects of getting a Red Hat Linux system up and running is configuring the user interface. On most systems, this means configuring the X-Window interface.
- The X-Window system is designed as a flexible, powerful client-server architecture. In order to configure and troubleshoot the X-Window interface it is important that you understand the client-server nature of the X-Window system.
- In the X-Window world, the meanings of the terms *client* and *server* have been somewhat reversed. The X-server is the component of the X-Window system that you run on your desktop. The X-Window applications that you run make use of these services that are provided by the X-server to display their output; hence they are referred to as clients or X-clients.
- One of the most important steps you can take to ensure that you wind up with a working X-Window configuration is selecting the proper hardware.
- Red Hat Linux has support for hundreds of video cards and monitors. The best place to check to see whether your video card and monitor are supported is the Red Hat support site at http://www.Red Hat.com/corp/support/hardware/index.html.
- If you don't find your video card or monitor among the list of Red Hat–supported hardware, you can also check http://www.XFree86.org/cardlist.html.
- The X-Window server program that is shipped with Red Hat Linux is an open-source program called XFree86.
- The Red Hat Linux distribution includes precompiled versions of the XFree86 server for the most common types of video cards. These images are stored in Red Hat package files (RPMS).
- The Xconfigurator program is a character-based GUI that leads you through a series of menus aiding you in configuring your video hardware.
- If you are planning to install Red Hat Linux on a laptop, in addition to consulting the Red Hat support site, you should also check the

Linux laptop page at http://www.cs.utexas.edu/users/kharker/linux-laptop.

- As an alternate to using Xconfigurator, you may wish to use the XFree86 XF86Setup program.
- The Red Hat Certified Engineer exam is primarily a performance-based exam. It is very important, therefore, that you try out the concepts presented in this chapter and experiment with them. Don't just read about them.
- You need to be familiar with both the /etc/X11 directory and the /usr/X11R6 directory. This is the directory where the X-Window software is stored. Of particular importance is the /usr/X11R6/bin directory, where the X-Window executable images are stored.
- X-Window clients, or X-clients, are the application programs you run that use the windowing services provided by your X-server to display their output.
- Starting an X-client is very easy. When you start the X-Window system for the first time on Red Hat Linux, several X-clients will already be started for you. You can start additional X-clients by using the mouse and selecting a program to start from a menu, or you can start an X-client from a command line.
- One of the most useful X-clients is a program called xterm. As its name implies, xterm is an X-client application that creates a terminal window on your X-display.
- One of the most popular window managers available for Linux is the fvwm window manager. The fvwm window manager was developed specifically for Linux and can be configured to emulate other window environments such as the commercial Motif window manager or even Windows 95. This can make *fvwm* a good choice if you are migrating users from a Microsoft Windows platform to Linux.
- WindowMaker is another very well done window manager that comes with Red Hat Linux. The WindowMaker interface is designed to resemble the commercial NEXTSTEP interface.
- Two other powerful virtual desktop environments that come with Red Hat Linux are the GNOME (GNU Network Object

Model Environment) desktop environment and the KDE desktop environment. Both GNOME and KDE are designed to emulate the look and feel of the Common Desktop Environment (CDE).

- You can configure the X-Window interface to start automatically when your system boots, or you can choose to start the X-Window system manually.
- In order to gain access to a Linux system, you must first pass an authentication check. On most systems, this consists of identifying yourself to the system by typing in a username and password combination.
- One of the most powerful features of the X-Window system is the strength of its networking support. The X-Window system was designed from the beginning to run in a networked environment.

SELF TEST

The following Self Test questions will help you measure your understanding of the material presented in this chapter. Read all the choices carefully, as there may be more than one correct answer. Choose all correct answers for each question.

1. Which of the following are true about the X-Window system? (Choose all that apply.)
   - A. The X-server runs on your workstation; X-clients run on your workstation or on other computers on the network.
   - B. If an X-server is running on your workstation then X-client applications running on your computer cannot send their output to an X-server running on another system on the network.
   - C. An X-client application gets its input from the keyboard and mouse that are attached to the same X-server where the client is sending its output.
   - D. Aside from the steps necessary to start the remote application, there is no difference between running an X-client locally and running one remotely.
2. Your supervisor comes to you and says he is thinking of purchasing some new workstations for the graphics department and that he has decided they will run Red Hat Linux. He has a requirement to have them purchased and installed as quickly as possible. He has found what appears to be a good deal on some brand-name systems and would like you to determine whether they will be suitable for the planned task. You follow up on his suggestion and discover that the video card for the systems is built around a completely new video chip design. What recommendation do you make regarding the purchase?
   - A. Go ahead and purchase the systems "as-is."
   - B. Since these systems will be used by the graphics department, make sure they have plenty of disk space to store graphic files.
   - C. Purchase the systems, but have the vendor replace the new video cards with a model that is listed on the Red Hat Linux support site.
   - D. Make sure the systems have 100MB/s Ethernet cards so that graphics files can be shipped across the network as quickly as possible.
3. You performed a new install of Red Hat Linux and ran into problems when you tried to install the X-Window system. Your system is now up and running, and you can get logged in to a command prompt. How do you go about reconfiguring the X-Window system?
   - A. Use the vi editor and modify the /etc/X11/XF86Config file.

B. Run the Xconfigurator utility from the command line.

C. Restart the X-Window GUI and run XF86Setup.

D. Reinstall Red Hat Linux.

4. When you run Xconfigurator, it is unable to determine the type of video card installed in your system. You are unable to find the documentation for your system anywhere. What can you do to determine the type of video hardware installed on your system?

A. Rerun the Xconfigurator program to see whether it will recognize your video card the second time around.

B. Try running XF86Setup.

C. Run linuxconf.

D. Run the SuperProbe program.

5. A user who is new to the X-Window system calls you with a question about his mouse. He has been reading some documentation, and it keeps referring to his middle mouse button, but he only has a two-button mouse. What do you tell him?

A. Hold down the CTRL key and click the left mouse button.

B. He will have to purchase a three-button mouse to use the X-Window interface.

C. Click the left and right mouse buttons simultaneously.

D. He will have to run Xconfigurator and configure the X-Window system to use a two button mouse.

6. Your X-Window configuration appears to be working, and you have an xterm terminal window open on your desktop. Whenever you try to start other X-clients from the command line, however, you keep getting the error message "command not found." What is probably causing the problem?

A. You have too many X-clients running, and Linux is unable to start any additional applications.

B. The /usr/X11R6/bin directory is missing from your PATH.

C. The /etc/X11/XF86Config directory is missing from your PATH.

D. You need to use the xhost command to allow X-clients to access your server.

7. You want to start an xterm X-client that is 80 columns wide by 30 lines high from the command line and position it in the upper right corner of your display when it starts. What command would you use?

A. xterm -geometry +0-0 -font 80x30

B. xterm -geometry 80x30-0+0

C. xterm -geometry 80+30+0+0

D. xterm -display 80x30-0+0

8. Which of the following are valid X-client command line options? (Choose all that apply.)

A. -display

B. -windowsize

C. -background

D. -forecolor
E. -bordercolor

9. When you migrate a Windows 95 user to a Linux workstation, what steps can you take to minimize the learning curve for this person?
   A. Install the full set of online documentation.
   B. Install the KDE desktop environment.
   C. Use the switchdesk utility and set the user's desktop environment to AnotherLevel.
   D. Set Linux to boot to runlevel 3.

10. You are using the GNOME desktop environment. You know that you just started up the GNOME spreadsheet application, but now it seems to have disappeared from your screen. How can you get it back?
   A. Use the pager applet and select the virtual display on your desktop that shows it has an open client window.
   B. Log out and log back in, and GNOME will restart the application.
   C. Use the main menu button to restart the application.

11. You are troubleshooting a system that appears not to have been set to boot into the X-Window system but you know that the system has been configured to run an X-server. What is the first step you should try?
   A. Type **X** to start the X-server.
   B. Run the startx command to start the X-Window system.
   C. Edit /etc/X11/XF86Config and set the X-Window system to start on system boot.
   D. Run the file .xinitrc in your home directory.

12. When you installed Red Hat Linux, you configured the X-Window system but chose not to have Linux boot up with the X-Window system running. You have been starting the X-Window system with the startx command and everything is working without any problems. You would now like to make the X-Window GUI the default runlevel for your system. How would you do this?
   A. Edit /etc/inittab and look for the line that reads 'id:3:initdefault' and replace it with a line that reads 'id:5:initdefault' and reboot.
   B. Run Xconfigurator.
   C. Change the /etc/X11/prefdm link.
   D. Execute the runlevel 5 command.

13. You are troubleshooting a Linux server that boots into runlevel 5 and need to temporarily shut down the X-Window system. How would you do this?
   A. Use the ps command to obtain the process of the XFree86 server and use the kill command to stop it.
   B. Edit /etc/inittab and look for the line that reads 'id:3:initdefault' and replace

it with a line that reads 'id:5:initdefault' and reboot.

C. Use the command init 3.

D. Use the stopx command.

14. Your system is using the xdm display manager. You want to use the GNOME display manager (gdm). How can you do this?

A. Change the /etc/X11/prefdm link.

B. Run Xconfigurator.

C. Edit /etc/X11/XF86Config.

D. Use the GNOME control panel to change the display manager.

15. You would like to automatically start up the xclock application whenever you start up an X-Window session with startx. How would you do this?

A. Create or edit the file .Xdefault and add the command:

```
xclock &
```

B. Create or edit the file xinitrc in the system root directory with the command:

```
xclock -geometry 200x200-0+0 &
```

C. Edit /etc/X11/XF86Config and add the command:

```
xclock -geometry 200x200-0+0 &
```

D. Create or edit the file .xinitrc in your home directory and add the command:

```
xclock &
```

16. How could you start a KDE session from a system running the gdm display manager?

A. Relink /etc/X11/prefdm.

B. Click the Options button on the gdm login message box and select Sessions -> KDE.

C. Log in normally and use switchdesk to change your default desktop.

D. You can't log in to the KDE environment from the gdm display manager.

17. What command would you issue to allow X-clients running on the system with an IP address of 172.16.200.99 to access your X-server?

A. xauth +172.16.200.99

B. xhost -172.16.200.99

C. xhost +

D. xhost +172.16.200.99

18. You log in to a remote system via telnet with the intention of starting up several remote X-clients that will send their output to your display (admin1.xyz.com). What can you do to make this easier?

A. Use the -display admin1.xyz.com option.

B. Create a DISPLAY variable with the command:

```
DISPLAY=admin1.xyz.com:0.0
```

C. Create a DISPLAY variable with the command:

```
export DISPLAY=admin1.xyz.com
```

D. Create a DISPLAY variable with the command:

```
export DISPLAY=admin1.xyz.com:0.0
```

19. A user calls up to report that she is having problems getting a remote molecular modeling application to display to her screen. Assuming she has disabled all security on her X-server, how could you use the display option to help troubleshoot the situation? Your workstation is admin1.xyz.com; her workstation is ws97.xyz.com.

A. Tell her to run the SuperProbe utility with the -display option so you know what kind of monitor she is using.

B. Have her try to start an X-client and direct its display to her X-server with the command:

```
xclock -display localhost:0.0
```

C. Have her try to start an X-client and direct its display to your X-server with the command:

```
xclock -display admin1.xyz.com:0.0
```

D. You start an X-client from the command line and direct its display to her X-server with the command:

```
xclock -display ws97.xyz.com:0.0
```

20. The X-server on your company's Web server appears to be locked up. How might you gain access to the console?

A. Press CTRL-ALT-+.

B. Press CTRL-ALT-F1 .

C. Press ALT-F1.

D. Press CTRL-ALT-DEL to reboot the system.

8

Network Client Services

CERTIFICATION OBJECTIVES

8.01 HTTP/Apache

8.02 FTP

8.03 Samba

8.04 Mail Services

8.05 Printing

Linux was designed with networking as its heart and soul. The extensive network services available with Red Hat Linux are not only the top dogs in their fields, they create one of the most powerful and useful Internet-ready platforms available today.

Red Hat Linux includes the Apache Web Server. The Apache Web Server is currently used by more Internet Web sites than all the other Web servers combined. It is based on the NCSA code with so many "patches" that it was referred to as a "patchy" server. The Apache Web Server continues to advance the art of the Web, and it provides one of the most robust and reliable Web services.

The anonymous FTP and the WU_FTP (Washington University FTP) packages provide both a general and a real fortress of an FTP server service. With WU-FTP, you can lock down users, directories, subdirectories, and files with various levels of access control.

Other standard services in the UNIX/Linux world are those using SMTP, and the POP and IMAP services. These are the de facto standards on the Internet for the world's largest distributed mail delivery systems.

Along with the traditional network services already mentioned, Red Hat Linux also provides interoperability packages for all of the most popular operating systems, including Windows (Samba), Novell (MARS-NWE), and Macintosh (MacUtils) networking.

The Windows-based operating systems use the SMB protocol within the TCP/IP realm to provide file and print services. Samba services provide an excellent SMB service that allows your machine to participate in a Microsoft Workgroup or an NT Domain network as a client of the Windows-based services, and as a server of local resources, both file and print, as Windows SMB-based services.

Additionally, you have a Novell set of client utilities, a Novell "look-alike" server service, a set of Mac client utilities, and a Mac "look-alike" server available. These are not discussed in this chapter.

Printing is a fundamental service with all operating systems. Linux provides the BSD utilities and daemon services for local and remote print services. Linux also provides connectivity to most other network print services via their native protocols.

The next section deals with the basic concepts surrounding the use of these services, and shows a basic level of configuration. In all cases, the assumption is that your network settings are correct and functioning properly. You can run either linuxconf or the netcfg command to reconfigure the network settings.

CERTIFICATION OBJECTIVE 8.01

HTTP/Apache

Web services are the easiest way to provide simple, secure access to documents of any type. The Apache Web Server provides both normal and secure Web services using the HTTP and HTTPS protocols, respectively. The Apache Web Server has extensive functionality and can be further extended using add-ins and macros to provide additional services.

Installation

If you selected a Server installation, you already have the Apache Web Server installed. If you selected a Workstation installation or a Custom installation and did not select the Web Server optional package set, you will need to install it. You can use the packages from the installation CD-ROM or from any network service that shares these RPM (Red Hat Package Manager) installation files. Figure 8-1 shows how to install the Apache Web Server package from a local CD-ROM.

FIGURE 8-1

Installing the Apache Web Server package from a local CD-ROM

```
===============================================================
(make sure the Red Hat Install CD is in the local CDROM drive)
[root@linux6 /root]#  mount   /dev/cdrom
[root@linux6 /root]#  rpm  -iv  /mnt/cdrom/RedHat/RPMS/apache*
(lots of info scrolls by, omit option v to run silent)
[root@linux6 /root]#  umount   /dev/cdrom
===============================================================
```

FIGURE 8-2

Installing the Apache Web Server from an NFS share

```
=================================================================
[root@linux6 /root]#     # you need a directory point to mount to
[root@linux6 /root]#  mkdir   /mnt/nfs  # if it does not already exist
[root@linux6 /root]#     # assuming nfsserver is the remote host
[root@linux6 /root]#     # sharing the file service /nfs/RedHat
[root@linux6 /root]#  mount  -t nfs  nfsserver:/nfs/RedHat  /mnt/nfs
[root@linux6 /root]#     # the package name begins with 'apache'
[root@linux6 /root]#  rpm  -i  /mnt/nfs/RPMS/apache*
(no info scrolls by, add option v for verbose mode)
[root@linux6 /root]#  umount   /mnt/nfs   # no further need for mount
=================================================================
```

Figure 8-2 shows how to install the Apache Web Server from an NFS share.

Setup Files

The files installed are maintained in:

/home/httpd	Most of the HTTPD files
/etc/httpd	Much of the network-side setup information

EXERCISE 8-1

Install Apache Server

1. Put the Red Hat Installation CD into the local CD-ROM reader.
2. Check to make sure /mnt/cdrom exists and is available.
3. Mount the CD on /mnt/cdrom.
4. Locate the Apache RPM package.
5. Load the Apache RPM package.
6. Unmount the CD-ROM device.

Basic Apache Configuration for a Simple Web Server

There are three main configuration files for your Web server. The installation creates a generic Web server service that you can further customize and optimize if desired. As installed, it will function just fine for a basic Web service. You can fine-tune your Web server by making changes to the configuration files, as shown in Figure 8-3.

FIGURE 8-3

Apache Web Server configuration file list and usage

```
==================================================================
/etc/httpd/conf/srm.conf        DocumentRoot for the main server
/etc/httpd/conf/access.conf     access control by host, hosts, nets.
/etc/httpd/conf/httpd.conf      main configuration file
==================================================================
```

The configuration of your Apache Web Server can be spread out between these three files, or it can be in just one. In order for the Apache Web Server to start, all three files must exist, even if they are empty. The installation contains a default configuration you can begin with.

The config files listed in Figure 8-3 are located under the directory `/etc/httpd/conf`. Each file can be used for a specific purpose in the management scheme of the Web server. The main configuration file usually contains most of the setup information (see Figure 8-4).

FIGURE 8-4

A few key settings from srm.conf

```
========================================================================
# See the tutorials at http://www.apache.org/ for
# more information as well as supplied html files with server software.
# DocumentRoot: The directory out of which you will serve your
# documents. This establishes the base to all other aliases.
# You can use any directory; for big sites, use a separate partition

DocumentRoot /home/httpd/html

# UserDir: The name of the directory appended onto a user's home
# directory if a ~user request is received.

UserDir public_html  # ie. /home/username/public_html/

# DirectoryIndex: Name of the file or files used as pre-written HTML
# directory index.  Separate multiple entries with spaces.

DirectoryIndex index.html index.shtml index.cgi

# FancyIndexing for fancy directory indexing (on) or standard (off)

FancyIndexing on          # use icons listed below

# AddIcon tells the server which icon to show for different filenames
# and extensions. (This is a sampling from a long list)
```

FIGURE 8-4

A few key settings from srm.conf *(continued)*

```
# There are 3 related parts: ByEncoding, ByType, by extension.

# displays the compressed.gif picture for compress or gzip files
AddIconByEncoding (CMP,/icons/compressed.gif) x-compress x-gzip

# displays the text.gif picture for all basic text files
AddIconByType (TXT,/icons/text.gif) text/*
..    # many entries removed for brevity

# displays the binary.gif picture for all files ending in .bin, .exe
AddIcon /icons/binary.gif .bin .exe
# displays the layout.gif picture for the specified extensions
AddIcon /icons/layout.gif .html .shtml .htm .pdf
..    # many entries removed for brevity

# adds icons to screen for specific actions, Go Back, a Directory, etc.
AddIcon /icons/back.gif ..
AddIcon /icons/hand.right.gif README
AddIcon /icons/folder.gif ^^DIRECTORY^^
AddIcon /icons/blank.gif ^^BLANKICON^^

# DefaultIcon is which icon to show for files which do not have an icon
# explicitly set.

DefaultIcon /icons/unknown.gif

# ScriptAlias: This controls which directories contain server scripts.
# Format: ScriptAlias fakename realname
# This is to protect your file system from intruders. A virtual root
# for the cgi-bin directory is created that translates to a local dir

ScriptAlias   /cgi-bin/   /home/httpd/cgi-bin/

..    # many entries removed for brevity
=====================================================================
```

on the job

You need all three Apache configuration files to exist, or the server will refuse to start.

Notes About access.conf

The access configuration file, access.conf, defines control modes and which types of services are allowed, on a directory-by-directory basis. These controls are for directories directly accessed by the server, not necessarily for the whole system.

These restrictions are recursive from the parent directory. The first directory to configure is the root, '/'. You should configure the "default" to be a very restrictive set of permissions. You can then adjust these permissions on other selected directory subtrees such as the DocumentRoot, as defined in srm.conf, and the cgi-bin directory if using cgi scripts.

```
=====================================================================
<Directory />           # complete restrictions start at root
Options None            # no options
AllowOverride None      # no bypass allowed
</Directory>            # end of options for this directory
                        # NOTE: looks like HTML tags
=====================================================================
```

The next directory to put restrictions on is the one containing your HTML files. The example in the next section uses the /home/httpd/html directory, the default directory for your HTML documents. This should be changed to match DocumentRoot in srm.conf if you use another directory, or if you have additional virtual Web sites that have their own DocumentRoot assignments.

PER DIRECTORY CONTROL— .HTACCESS There is a way to override these passed-down permission controls in any directory below a restricted directory DocumentRoot. You create a hidden file, called .htaccess, in the directory, and it can override the permission settings unless the AllowOverride option is set to None. You can put an .htaccess control file in every directory that can be accessed by your Web server and customize the access differently from the primary subtree root access.

```
===============================================================
<Directory /home/httpd/html>
Options Indexes Includes FollowSymLinks
AllowOverride None      #.htaccess in a directory is ignored
order allow,deny        # in which to test, first is allow tests, then deny
allow from all          # in this case no restrictions
</Directory>            # end of this directory's settings
===============================================================
```

The Options line can have many choices, in many combinations:

"None" or "All"	No options in force or All of the ones below

or any combination of

```
"Indexes"
```

Allow the use of the directive's controlling directory indexing (AddDescription, AddIcon, AddIconByEncoding, AddIconByType, DefaultIcon, DirectoryIndex, FancyIndexing, HeaderName, IndexIgnore, IndexOptions, ReadmeName, etc.).

"Includes"	Server side "includes" permitted
"FollowSymLinks"	Can access symbolic links in other directories
"ExecCGI"	Directories containing cgi scripts; these scripts are available "MultiViews" executables

A resource may be available in several different representations. For example, it might be available in different languages, different media types, or a combination of both. This allows the server to choose the best representation of a resource based on the browser-supplied preferences for media type, languages, character set, and encoding.

You should also control any ScriptAlias CGI directories if they are configured in srm.conf. The default cgi-bin directory is/home/httpd/cgi-bin. If you configured another directory, you should change the directory reference to whatever your ScriptAlias points to.

```
===========================================================================
<Directory /home/httpd/cgi-bin>
AllowOverride None   # .htaccess files ignored
Options ExecCGI        # allow execution of any CGI scripts
</Directory>
===========================================================================
```

The Server installation includes access to documentation, but through an alias name. The actual directory with the documentation has restricted access options.

```
========================================================================
# Allow access to local system documentation from localhost
Alias /doc /usr/doc  # /doc is the alias to /usr/doc
<Directory /usr/doc> # must restrict real directory, not the alias
order deny,allow
deny from all
allow from localhost # allows local interaction
Options Indexes FollowSymLinks
</Directory>
========================================================================
```

Finally, you can add access control for any other directories that are available via your Web interface.

```
========================================================================
<Directory /??your/choice/here??/>
Options Indexes FollowSymLinks
order deny,allow                # order of testing
deny from .badones.net          # full restrictions
allow from .yourdomain.net      # allows local domain interaction
</Directory>
========================================================================
```

For more information on any of these details, you can look at the HTML-based documentation included in the installation in /home/httpd/html/manual/core.html and the related links within this file.

Main Configuration File—httpd.conf

This is where most of the configuration changes are needed. The defaults are fine as a starting point, but for a large, heavily trafficked Web site, some may need to be changed. The /etc/srm.conf and /etc/access.conf files usually only need to be changed as your system grows and your security needs to expand to cover more possible "leaks."

Another important aspect of the httpd.conf file is the creation of virtual Web sites. The httpd.conf configuration file is shown in Figure 8-5. Virtual

Web sites allow this server to respond to more than one Web site name, such as www.corp1.net, www.company2.org, and so forth.

FIGURE 8-5

Synopsis of httpd.conf configuration file

```
=======================================================================
##
## httpd.conf -- Apache HTTP server configuration file
##
# A complete explanation of all directives and their options is in
#     /home/httpd/manual/mod/core.html

# These are selected hi-lites from the main server httpd.conf file.
# See URL http://www.apache.org/ for instructions.

# Dynamic Shared Object (DSO) Support
# this feature provides very specific customization modules
# Requires a 'LoadModule' and 'AddModule' line for each DSO
# Please read the file README.DSO in the Apache 1.3 distribution
#      'httpd -l' for the list of currently built-in modules
#
# Example:       modulename  relative location of source
# LoadModule  foo_module  libexec/mod_foo.so
#
# Documentation for modules is in "/home/httpd/manual/mod/*.html"

# Modules that are available but not yet used are commented out as in:
#LoadModule mmap_static_module modules/mod_mmap_static.so

# Note: most entries have been removed for brevity here

# modules that are loaded at startup are not commented out as in:
LoadModule env_module         modules/mod_env.so

# Extra Modules         # these are new features/modules you may want
# all of these are commented out and are NOT loaded in this instance
#LoadModule php_module         modules/mod_php.so
#LoadModule php3_module        modules/libphp3.so
#LoadModule perl_module        modules/libperl.so

#  [WHENEVER YOU CHANGE THE LOADMODULE SECTION, UPDATE HERE, TOO]

ClearModuleList
#AddModule mod_mmap_static.c
AddModule mod_env.c
..    # should have one line match here for each line in LoadModule
```

FIGURE 8-5

Synopsis of httpd.conf configuration file *(continued)*

```
# Extra Modules   # corresponding reference from LoadModule section
#AddModule mod_php.c
#AddModule mod_php3.c
#AddModule mod_perl.c

# ServerType is either inetd, or standalone. Using inetd is slower.

ServerType standalone

# Port: The port the standalone listens to. For ports < 1023, you will
# need httpd to be run as root initially.
# If you want to be more secure, you can use some alternate port.
# A common one is 8080 but anything over 1023 can be used.
# Why? Only requests directed specifically at the port 8080 are
# accepted. This also slows web crawlers from 'finding' the site.

Port 80     # default port number, best initial choice.

# HostnameLookups: Log the names of clients or just their IP numbers
#   e.g.   www.apache.org (on) or 204.62.129.132 (off)

HostnameLookups off     # with on, can check country of origin for ex.

# If you wish httpd to run as a different user or group, you must run
# httpd as root initially and it will switch.

# User/Group: The name (or #number) of the user/group to run httpd as.

User nobody          # no privileges, no directory access privileges
Group nobody      # should also be a no privilege account

# ServerAdmin: Address, where problems with the server should be
# e-mailed. Does not have to be local, can be anywhere on your net

ServerAdmin root@linux6.vaddac.com

# ServerRoot: The directory the server's config, error, and log files
# are kept in. NOTE! All but LockFile can reside on NFS, SMB, etc.

ServerRoot /etc/httpd   # can be a separate file system

# ErrorLog: The location of the error log file. If this does not start
# with /, ServerRoot is prepended to it.

ErrorLog logs/error_log          # could be a separate file system

# LogLevel: Control the number of messages logged to the error_log.
```

FIGURE 8-5

Synopsis of httpd.conf configuration file *(continued)*

```
# Possible values include: debug, info, notice, warn, error, crit,
# alert, emerg. (From least to most verbose)

LogLevel warn     # adequate level, higher for more, lower for less

# The following directives define some format nicknames for use with
# a CustomLog directive (see 'Log Configuration Options' below).
# The last argument of all 'Log' options indicates the log reference
# as in: referer, agent, common, combined

LogFormat                  (the next line goes here, like all the others)
"%h %l %u %t \"%r\" %>s %b \"%{Referer}i\" \"%{User-Agent}i\"" combined
LogFormat "%h %l %u %t \"%r\" %>s %b" common
LogFormat "%{Referer}i -> %U" referer
LogFormat "%{User-agent}i" agent

# The location of the access logfile (Common Logfile Format).
# If this does not start with /, ServerRoot is prepended to it.
# If you would like to have an agent and referer logfile uncomment the
# last 2 directives. (Creates separate logs instead of combined)

CustomLog logs/access_log combined          # include referer, agent OR
#CustomLog logs/referer_log referer
#CustomLog logs/agent_log agent

# PidFile: The file the server should log its pid to

PidFile /var/run/httpd.pid

# ScoreBoardFile: stores internal server process information.
# NO OTHER invocation of Apache can share the same scoreboard file.

ScoreBoardFile /var/run/httpd.scoreboard

# ServerName 'ThisName' allows sent back to clients
# Note: ServerName must be a valid DNS name for your host.

#ServerName new.host.name

# CacheNegotiatedDocs: By default, Apache sends Pragma: This asks proxy
# servers not to cache the document. Uncomment to allow caching

#CacheNegotiatedDocs

# Timeout: The number of seconds before receives and sends time out

Timeout 300
```

FIGURE 8-5

Synopsis of httpd.conf configuration file *(continued)*

```
# KeepAlive: Whether or not to allow persistent connections (more than
# one request per connection). Set to "Off" to deactivate.

KeepAlive On

# MaxKeepAliveRequests: The maximum number of requests to allow
# during a persistent connection. Set to 0 to allow an unlimited.
# We recommend you leave this number high, for maximum performance.

MaxKeepAliveRequests 100

# KeepAliveTimeout: Number of seconds to wait for the next request

KeepAliveTimeout 15

# Apache maintains enough server processes to handle the current load
# plus a few spare servers to handle transient, it
# periodically checks how many servers are waiting for a request.

MinSpareServers 8          # currently not handling requests
MaxSpareServers 20         # kill off extras as necessary

# Number of servers to start --- expand if heavy traffic level.

StartServers 10

# Intended mainly as a brake to keep a runaway server from taking
# your Linux with it as it spirals down...

MaxClients 150

# MaxRequestsPerChild: the number of requests each child process is
# allowed to process before the child process dies.

MaxRequestsPerChild 100

# VirtualHost: Allows responses to requests for more than one
# server address. This can be accomplished with the ifconfig
# alias flag, or through kernel patches like VIF.
# Any httpd.conf or srm.conf directive may go into a VirtualHost
# command. The following is commented out by default.

#<VirtualHost host.some_domain.com>
#ServerAdmin webmaster@host.some_domain.com
#DocumentRoot /www/docs/host.some_domain.com
#ServerName host.some_domain.com
```

FIGURE 8-5

Synopsis of httpd.conf configuration file *(continued)*

```
#ErrorLog logs/host.some_domain.com-error_log
#TransferLog logs/host.some_domain.com-access_log
#</VirtualHost>
======================================================================
```

Web Server Log Files

The log files are listed as being in /etc/httpd, but they are linked to /var/logs/httpd. You can change both their number and format. By default, there is only one log file for all events. If you want more detail about your Web site for tuning or statistical reasons, you can have the Web server generate more information, and break the data up more granularly by month, week, day, or any other period of time.

There are three lines in the default /etc/httpd.conf file. Notice only the "combined'"entry is not commented out. This forces all log entries into the one file, access_log.

```
CustomLog logs/access_log combined
#CustomLog logs/referer_log referer
#CustomLog logs/agent_log agent
```

LOG CONFIGURATION OPTIONS The log files have a very specific format for the information stored in them as per the HTTP RFP. You probably do not need to change these. Figure 8-6 is an excerpt from the /home/httpd/html/manual/mod/mod_log_config.html help file supplied with the Server installation that explains the various macro reverence meanings.

The "..." can be nothing at all (e.g., "%h %u %r %s %b"), or it can indicate conditions for inclusion of the item (which will cause it to be replaced with "-" if the condition is not met). Note that there is no escaping performed on the strings from %r, %...i, and %...o;.

The forms of condition are a list of HTTP status codes, which may or may not be preceded by "!". Thus, "%400,501{User-agent}"" logs User-agent: on 400 errors and 501 errors (Bad Request, Not Implemented) only; and"%!200,304,302{Referer}"" logs Referer: on all requests that did ***not*** return some sort of normal status.

FIGURE 8-6

Log format options

```
=====================================================================
%...b:          Bytes sent, excluding HTTP headers.
%...f:          Filename
%...{FOOBAR}e:  The contents of the environment variable FOOBAR
%...h:          Remote host
%...a:          Remote IP-address
%...{Foobar}i:  The contents of Foobar: header line(s) in the request
                sent to the server.
%...l:          Remote logname (from identd, if supplied)
%...{Foobar}n:  The contents of note "Foobar" from another module.
%...{Foobar}o:  The contents of Foobar: header line(s) in the reply.
%...p:          The canonical Port of the server serving the request
%...P:          The process ID of the child that serviced the request.
%...r:          First line of request
%...s:          Status.  For requests that got internally redirected, this
                is status of the *original* request --- %...>s for the last.
%...t:          Time, in common log format time format
%...{format}t:  The time, in the form given by format, which should
                be in strftime(3) format.
%...T:          The time taken to serve the request, in seconds.
%...u:          Remote user (from auth; may be bogus if return status (%s) is 401)
%...U:          The URL path requested.
%...v:          The canonical ServerName of the server serving the request.
%...V:          The server name according to the UseCanonicalName setting.
```

Note that the common log format is defined by the string "%h %l %u %t \"%r\" %s %b", which can be used as the basis for extending the format if desired (*e.g.,* to add extra fields at the end). NCSA's extended/ combined log format would be:

```
"%h %l %u %t \"%r\" %s %b \"%{Referer}i\" \"%{User-agent}i\"".
=====================================================================
```

This log format is consistent with the standard NCSA format and does not need to be changed in most cases.

Starting the Apache Web Server

The actual binary file is /usr/sbin/httpd. The binary file is normally started at system initialization. You can also stop and start the service using the control script provided with the installation. With no arguments, a syntax usage statement is printed, as shown in Figure 8-7.

FIGURE 8-7

Controlling the Apache Web Server daemon

```
===================================================================
[root@linux6 /root]# /etc/rc.d/init.d/httpd
Usage: /etc/rc.d/init.d/httpd {start|stop|restart|reload|status}
[root@linux6 /root]# /etc/rc.d/init.d/httpd  status
httpd (pid 535 534 533 532 531 530 529 528 527 526 525) is running...
[root@linux6 /root]#
```

Requesting the status of the Web server simply shows the 10 initial processes started by the server to handle requests. The output also indicates that your server is "running." The "stop" option shuts down all server processes; the "start" option can then be used to restart all functionality as indicated by the configuration files. The "restart" option is equivalent to a stop-and- start request. A "reload" forces the main server to re-read the configuration files and update them accordingly. This reload is normally only done if you do not want to kill a busy service.

ALTERNATE CONFIGURATION FILE LOCATION When you start /usr/local/apache/httpd, it looks for its configuration information in the file /usr/local/apache/conf/httpd.conf. You can change the location of this file if you want, but you will need to update all system startup references to reflect the new location by using the -f option, location of configuration file, as in:

```
/usr/local/apache/httpd  -f  /usr/local/apache/conf/httpd.conf
```

Assuming there were no problems, you should be able to connect to your local service with a browser request:

```
http://localhost/            # even if no network hosts defined
http://206.195.1.222/   # if no hosts resolution, use IP address
http://www.yourweb.org/      # use DNS or hosts resolution of address
```

If you were to check your system processes, you would notice that there are a number of child processes. These child processes are created by the parent httpd program and should not be terminated individually, because the httpd will just restart identical processes. Assuming that you started the httpd server as root, these child processes will be started under the user account specified in the configuration file. These extra processes handle the incoming requests to the server, and are regenerated as needed, based on the parameters specified in the httpd.conf file as outlined earlier.

```
MinSpareServers 8           # currently not handling requests
MaxSpareServers 20          # kill off extras as necessary
StartServers 10             # initial processes
MaxClients 150              # processes are renewed regularly
```

SOME POSSIBLE PROBLEMS The installation will normally create a running system. Always make backups of the configuration files before introducing any changes. If you make changes to any of the configuration files and the resultant setup fails, here are a few suggested starting points to look at, per the documentation supplied with the server. If all else fails, go back to the originals and start over if necessary.

If, when you run httpd, it complains about being unable to "bind" to an address, then either some other process is already using the port you have configured Apache to use, or you are running httpd as a normal user but are trying to use a port below 1024 (such as the default port 80).

- If the server is not running, read the error message displayed when you run httpd. You should also check the server error_log for additional information (with the default configuration, this will be located in the file error_log in the logs directory).
- If you want your server to continue running after a system reboot, you should add a call to httpd to your system startup files (typically, rc.local or a file in an rc.N directory). This will start Apache as root. Before doing this, make sure that your server is properly configured for security and access restrictions.
- To stop Apache, send the parent process a TERM signal. The PID of this process is written to the file httpd.pid in the logs directory (unless configured otherwise). Do not attempt to kill the child processes, because they will be renewed by the parent. A typical command for stopping the server is:

  ```
  kill -TERM `cat /usr/local/apache/logs/httpd.pid`
  ```

Web Site Content

The actual HTML pages and pictures, CGI scripts, and the supplied documentation is in /home/httpd/html. Note that Linux uses .html, not .htm files. The top directory files supplied with the installation are :

```
index.html        the default page returned by server
poweredby.gif     picture logo of RedHat (in index.html)
manual/           manual pages and gif's
```

Home Page Is index.html

Whenever a browser requests a site without a specific page, the Web server has a defined default page to send back. It can have any name; common choices are home.html and index.html. Even the extensions have changes. The file index.asp represents Active Server Pages from a Windows host and is in a different format than pure HTML.

Your Web server has a default Web page that is included when you install the Web server. This page can be changed using any text- or HTML-specific editor. If you use a text editor, you need to know something about the basic tags used by a browser.

BASICS OF HTML CODING A basic Web page can be a simple text file. Tags represent requests to the client browser to display something a special way. The HTML coding came from a long line of markup languages that evolved on many platforms. An example of a simple Web page is provided in the following section.

Note: if you are not familiar with HTML tags, don't worry, you can just edit the supplied files and customize them your way. The HTML format is relatively straightforward. Most tags have a start-of-format and an end- of-format tag reference. For example, the title bar of the Web browser comes from the text between the tag <HEAD> and an end tag </HEAD>. Notice that the same tag name is used in both; the start-of-format-tag is just the name, and the end-of-format-tag has the tag name preceded by a slash.

Browsing Your Homepage

You can use any browser from the network if your machine is reachable, or you can use a local browser to connect to the main Web page of your server. If you do not have X working, do not worry; there is a text-based browser installed that can be used quite effectively to 'browse' the main Web page of your server.

TEXT-BASED BROWSER LYNX You can connect to any Web site on your network, if accessible, using the lynx browser. This browser simply ignores the font and font size requests, and displays the HTML strings as single lines. URL tags are shown in a different color or shade if your terminal supports this feature, and can be located with the UP and DOWN arrow keys. To connect to the indicated URL, press the RIGHT ARROW key; to go back, press the LEFT ARROW key. To quit, press q or Q as shown here:

```
===============================================================
[root@linux6 /root]# lynx localhost
Test Page for Red Hat Linux's Apache Installation (p1 of 2)

                                 It Worked!

   If you can see this, it means that the installation of the Apache
   software on this Red Hat Linux system was successful. You may now add
   content to this directory and replace this page.

                     ___________________________________

     If you are seeing this instead of the content you expected, please
     contact the administrator of the site involved. If you send mail
     about this to the authors of the Apache software or Red Hat
     Software, who almost certainly have nothing to do with this site,
     your message will be ignored.

                     ___________________________________

   The Apache documentation has been included with this distribution.

   For documentation and information on Red Hat Linux, please visit the
   web site of Red Hat Software. The manual for Red Hat Linux is
   available here.
-- press space for next page --
  Arrow keys: Up and Down to move. Right to follow a link; Left to go back.
 H)elp O)ptions P)rint G)o M)ain screen Q)uit /=search [delete]=history list
q
[root@linux6 /root]#
===============================================================
```

USING NETSCAPE TO BROWSE A HOMEPAGE You can connect to your new Web service using any browser. If you have your X Windows services running, you can use the supplied Netscape browser to connect to localhost, the Web name, or use the IP address directly.

EXERCISE 8-2

Update and Test the Main Apache Web Page

1. Copy the file /home/httpd/html/index.html to /home/httpd/html/index2.html.
2. Edit the file /home/httpd/html/index.html.
3. Change the title of the page to reflect your personal or corporate name.
4. Use the lynx text-based browser to connect to localhost (or 127.0.0.1).

Hosting a Virtual Web Site

You can add virtual hosts to /etc/httpd/conf/httpd.conf by adding a set of entries for each virtual host, including the local host itself:

```
Here is what the original configuration file contains:
#<VirtualHost host.some_domain.com>
#ServerAdmin webmaster@host.some_domain.com
#DocumentRoot /www/docs/host.some_domain.com
#ServerName host.some_domain.com
#ErrorLog logs/host.some_domain.com-error_log
#TransferLog logs/host.some_domain.com-access_log
#</VirtualHost>

You can change this as follows
The pfr.net virtual web site might look like this:

<VirtualHost  pfr.net>
ServerAdmin   guru@pfr.net          # admin email
DocumentRoot  /pfr                  # your choice, must have index.html
ServerName    www.pfr.net           # net access
ErrorLog      /pfr/logs             # your choice
TransferLog   /pfr/logs-tr          # transaction logs
ScriptAlias   /cgi/     /pfr/cgi    # associates virtual with real dir.
  <Directory  /pfr/html>            # document root
```

```
    Options      ExecCGI   Indexes   Includes      # described above
</Directory>
</VirtualHost>
```

To test your new virtual host setup, you can restart the Apache Web Server with the following control script request:

```
[root@linux6 /root]#    /etc/rc.d/init.d/httpd   restart
```

You should now be able to check the Web content page of all of your virtual Web sites by using any browser. You should create an appropriately specific index.html page for each virtual host.

Once you create one virtual host, even the local host must be made virtual, or it will disappear. Create another entry for localhost or your local Web name BEFORE all other virtual host entries but AFTER the NameVirtualHostline, as shown in Figure 8-8.

Patches, Upgrades, Need More Info

You can get the latest information, documentation, upgrades, options, patches, bug fixes, and more from the Apache Web site at http://www.apache.org/.

FIGURE 8-8

Sample virtual LocalHost setup

```
================================================================
NameVirtualHost 127.0.0.1
<VirtualHost localhost>
 ServerNamelocalhost
 ServerAdmin root@localhost
 DocumentRoot/home/httpd/html/
 ErrorLoglogs/error_log
 TransferLoglogs/access_log
 <Directory /home/httpd/html>
 OptionsExecCGI Indexes Includes
 </Directory>
</VirtualHost>
================================================================
```

EXERCISE 8-3

Create and Test a Virtual Web Site

1. Add a virtual Web site for the fictional company SnoBard called www.snobard.net.
2. Create a DocumentRoot directory called /snobard.
3. Copy the file /home/httpd/html/index.html to /snobard/index.html.
4. Edit the file /snobard/index.html.
5. Change the title of the page to reflect the SnoBard corporate name.
6. Test accessing the virtual Web site and the local Web site.

CERTIFICATION OBJECTIVE 8.02

FTP

The FTP (File Transfer Protocol) service has been around a long time. There are two application-related sides to FTP, the client and the server. The client application is available and, usually, freely supplied on all other operating systems when they support the TCP/IP protocol suite. The server application is common on most Web hosting machines and predates the actual Web as the normal Internet method of transferring files between any types of systems.

The FTP service is a subservice of the inetd "superserver" service. The inetd service listens for a list of services and launches the services as needed for each subservice, such as telnet, FTP, talk, finger, and so forth. The configuration file, /etc/inetd.conf, indicates which services are listened for.

FTP Client

The original FTP client software was a basic command-line, text-oriented client application that offered a simple but efficient interface. Most Web browsers offer a more graphical interface and can be used as the interface if desired.

The client allows you to access the directory tree and all files within it. The graphical client is optimized for download from the remote host. By simply clicking on a file, you initiate a transfer download; by clicking on a directory, you initiate a "cd targetdirectory" command and the interface updates with the local files in the new director.

In the text-based interface, you must enter each command at the FTP prompt, one at a time. Almost all commands are run at the remote host, similar to a telnet session. To run commands locally, precede the command with an "!". Basic FTP client commands are shown in Figure 8-9.

Installation of FTP

There are two packages that you can install, anonftp and wu-ftp. The anonftp package provides anonymous access to anyone without the need for specific user accounts. You can install the anonftp rpm package if it is not already installed. The installation creates a /home/ftp tree and populates it with a minimal set of directories and files. You should add files to the /home/ftp/pub directory that are to be made available to anonymous logins for download to their machines only.

You can upgrade the anonymous FTP by also installing the wu-ftp service.

The wu-ftp provides sophisticated features related to user management. With it, you can establish many more features and controls on many more objects. Additional features include control of transfer and command logs,

FIGURE 8-9

Basic FTP client commands

```
=================================================================
Remote Commands (Process on remote host)
cd       to change the current working directory at the remote host
ls      commands to list files at the remote host
get      to retrieve one file from the remote host
mget      to retrieve many files using wildcards or full file names.
    (if logged in with a local login account, not anonymous)
put      to upload one file from your machine to the target host
mput      to upload many files to the target remote host
pwd      print working directory on remote host
quit      end the FTP session
Local Commands (Process on your host)
!ls      list files on your host machine, current directory
lcd      change local host directory for upload/download
!pwd      print working directory on local host
=================================================================
```

on-the-fly compression and archiving (using gzip), user type and location classification, limits on a per-class (local, remote) basis, directory upload permissions, restricted guest accounts, messages per directory and system, and virtual name support.

One of the other excellent advanced features of wu-ftp is its ability to provide full user and group specific authorization of FTP services. wu-ftp adds a third group of "guest" users. You can specify specific access for various users and groups in /etc/ftpaccess.

Installed During System Installation

If you used the Server Installation option, you should already have the FTP service installed and running. If you used the Workstation Installation option, you probably do not have the FTP service installed. If you used the Custom Installation option, you would have had to select the Anonymous FTP Server package, which is not selected by default.

You can check for the installed packages by using grep to look for the string "ftp" or "anon" from the output of the "rpm query all" command: "rpm –qa", as shown in Figure 8-10.

You can install the anon-ftp and wu-ftp RPM packages if they are not already installed. You need to mount the CD-ROM drive and access the /RedHat/RPMS directory for the installation files, as shown in Figure 8-11.

FIGURE 8-10

Checking to see if FTP is already installed

```
=================================================================
[root@linux6 /root]# rpm -qa| grep ftp
ftp-0.10-22
gftp-1.13-4
ncftp-3.0beta18 -3
tftp-0.10-23
anonftp-2.8-1
wu-ftpd-2.4.2vr17-3
[root@linux6 /root]#
=================================================================
```

FIGURE 8-11

Installing the FTP and WU_FTP RPM packages

```
=================================================================
[root@linux6 /root]# mount /dev/cdrom
[root@linux6 /root]# cd /mnt/cdrom/RedHat/RPMS/
[root@linux6 RPMS]# rpm-iv anonftp-2.8-1.i386.rpm
anonftp-2.8-1
[root@linux6 RPMS]# rpm-iv wu-ftpd-2.4.2vr17-3.i386.rpm
wu-ftpd-2.4.2vr17-3
[root@linux6 RPMS]# umount /dev/cdrom
=================================================================
```

exam Watch

Workstation and Custom installations do not include any FTP server; these packages can be installed at any time using the RPM package manager.

Configuring a Simple Anonymous FTP Server

The basic installation of the FTP packages creates an FTP service that allows for anonymous access. You can test your installation from any host on the network.

The anonymous FTP service uses the /home/ftp/ directory as the only accessible tree. You should customize the content of this tree as the final step in configuration of this anonymous service. For example, you could put some RPM packages in the pub directory for all users to download to their Linux hosts, as shown in Figure 8-12. The default installation does not add any files to the pub directory.

TESTING YOUR FTP SERVICE The last step is to test anonymous login of the FTP service. From any command line, you can use the client application to connect to any host, including your own host machine. It does not matter which host you ftp to, assuming it has an FTP service running. Windows 9*x* and NT workstations by default do not have an FTP service, only the FTP client application. NT Server has an FTP service that is not installed by default.

FIGURE 8-12

Example listing of /home/ftp with RPM packages

```
==================================================================
[root@linux6 ftp]# ls -R
binetclibpub
bin:
compresscpiogziplsshtarzcat
etc:
groupld.so.cachepasswd
lib:
ld-2.1.1.solibc-2.1.1.solibnsl-2.1.1.solibnss_files-2.1.1.so
ld-linux.so.2libc.so.6libnsl.so.1libnss_files.so.2
pub:
206.195.1.hosts vga_cardgames-1.3.1-7.i386.rpm
bsd-games-1.3-8.i386.rpmvga_gamespack-1.3-7.i386.rpm
xv-3.10a-9.i386.rpm
[root@linux6 ftp]#
==================================================================
```

Like any network connection, the FTP client needs a valid network address. If you use a host "name," the system must be able to resolve the name to an IP address. The typical method is by a simple lookup of the /etc/hosts file. Every machine has at least one entry in this file called localhost that points to the local machine. To test your connection, without knowing the name of your host or its IP address, you can use the name "localhost."

Note that in Figure 8-13, the login name is anonymous and the system complains when the password is root@localhost, even though this is the suggested e-mail-based password. In fact, root@anydomain.anygroup would have been acceptable instead of the suggested e-mail address.

Super Daemon Configuration /etc/inetd.conf

The FTP service daemon is actually started from the inetd super daemon. The inetd daemon usually listens for all configured protocols other than HTTP. Each service protocol to listen for is specified in /etc/inetd.conf. The inetd (INET Daemon) process launches the specific service whenever an incoming packet is received for that service.

Figure 8-14 shows a truncated view of the /etc/inetd.conf file with just the first few lines, and then the FTP and telnet control lines. Most of the configuration information has been deleted in this example. You usually do not need to change anything in this file.

FIGURE 8-13

Test anonymous login to FTP

```
==================================================================
[root@linux6 RPMS]#ftplocalhost
Connected to localhost.
220 linux6.4egans.com FTP server (Version wu-2.4.2-VR17(1) Mon Apr 19 09:21:53 EDT 1999) ready.
Name (localhost:user01): anonymous
331 Guest login ok, send your complete e-mail address as password.
Password:(do not use 'root@localhost')
230-The response 'root@localhost' is not valid
230-Next time please use your e-mail address as your password
230-for example: root@localhost
230 Guest login ok, access restrictions apply.
Remote system type is UNIX.
Using binary mode to transfer files.
ftp> ls
total 6
drwxr-xr-x   6 root     root        1024 Sep 24 07:08 .
drwxr-xr-x   6 root     root        1024 Sep 24 07:08 ..
d--x--x--x   2 root     root        1024 Sep 24 07:08 bin
d--x--x--x   2 root     root        1024 Sep 24 07:08 etc
drwxr-xr-x   2 root     root        1024 Sep 24 07:08 lib
drwxr-sr-x   2 root     ftp         1024 Mar 21  1999 pub
226 Transfer complete.
ftp> ls pub
200 PORT command successful.
150 Opening ASCII mode data connection for /bin/ls.
total 1609
drwxr-sr-x   2 root  ftp     1024 Sep 24 17:06 .
drwxr-xr-x   6 root  root     1024 Sep 24 07:08 ..
-rw-r--r--   1 root  root     280 Sep 24 17:04 206.195.1.hosts
-rw-r--r--   1 root  ftp   498168 Sep 24 16:56 bsd-games-1.3-8.i386.rpm
-rw-r--r--   1 root  ftp    27866 Sep 24 16:56 vga_cardgames-1.3.1-7.i386.rpm
-rw-r--r--   1 root  ftp    23064 Sep 24 16:56 vga_gamespack-1.3-7.i386.rpm
-rw-r--r--   1 root  ftp  1081477 Sep 24 16:50 xv-3.10a-9.i386.rpm
226 Transfer complete.
ftp> quit
221-You have transferred 0 bytes in 0 files.
221-Total traffic for this session was 2886 bytes in 6 transfers.
221-Thank you for using the FTP service on linux6.4egans.com.
221 Goodbye.
[root@linux6 RPMS]#
==================================================================
```

The leading remarks in Figure 8-14 indicate how to force the super daemon to refresh if any changes have been made to this file. To force the inetd service to refresh, send it the sigHUP, value is 1, signal as indicated.

FIGURE 8-14

Truncated /etc/inetd.conf—FTP entry shown

```
================================================================
[root@linux6 RPMS]#  less  /etc/inetd.conf
#
# inetd.conf    This file describes the services that will be available
#               through the INETD TCP/IP super server.  To re-configure
#               the running INETD process, edit this file, then send the
#               INETD process a SIGHUP signal.
# Version:      @(#)/etc/inetd.conf     3.10    05/27/93
..        # all other services have been deleted from this file.
#
ftp     stream  tcp     nowait  root    /usr/sbin/tcpd  in.ftpd -l -a
telnet  stream  tcp     nowait  root    /usr/sbin/tcpd  in.telnetd
..
(within the less program: press f=forward, b=back-a-page, h=help, q=quit)
[root@linux6 RPMS]# ps   -ax   |   grep   inetd     # locate inetd pid
  383 ?        S      0:00 inetd
[root@linux6 RPMS]# kill    -HUP    383      # force refresh of inetd
[root@linux6 RPMS]#
================================================================
```

You do not need to reboot, but this would also work as a means of forcing a refresh.

Home Office FTP Service

Working from a home-based office and traveling the world can sometimes leave you missing some important files. To remedy this, install a basic anonymous FTP service on your Red Hat Linux server. Put any files for customer downloads under the anonymous public access directory. Use wu-ftp to manage access by privileged users to specific directories. With this setup, you can support your and your customers' needs with quick downloads of files from anywhere in the world, assuming you are connected to the Internet full time.

If you are not connected to the Internet, you could set up a PPP-type dial-in access connection to your machine. This would allow you or your customers to dial in to your machine to download files using FTP.

Configuring wu-ftpd

The anonymous FTP service only allows downloads from the public site. If you have users who want remote access to their home directory files or any generally accessible files on your system, the wu-ftp service provides a very secure control over what login names or groups can get on or off your system.

There are a few files that control the many security aspects of the wu-ftp. They can be used to restrict or control basic service access, allow additional groups, and allow guest users to access the site—and all with different access privileges. These files are in the /etc directory. The most notable of these are /etc/ftpaccess and /etc/ftpusers, shown in Figure 8-15.

FIGURE 8-15

The basics of the FTP control files in /etc

```
=================================================================
[root@linux6 /root]# ls -l /etc/ftp*
-rw-------   1 root     root       484 Apr 19 06:22 /etc/ftpaccess
-rw-------   1 root     root       456 Apr 19 06:22 /etc/ftpconversions
-rw-------   1 root     root        39 Apr 19 06:22 /etc/ftpgroups
-rw-------   1 root     root       104 Apr 19 06:22 /etc/ftphosts
-rw-------   1 root     root        79 Apr 19 06:22 /etc/ftpusers
[root@linux6 /root]# cat  /etc/ftpaccess
class   all   real,guest,anonymous   *  # create a 'list' = class
email root@localhost        # change this to correct hostname
loginfails 5                # closes connection
readme  README*    login
readme  README*    cwd=*
message /welcome.msg              login    # at login, display message
message .message                  cwd=*
compress        yes               all      # class named all
tar             yes               all
chmod           no                guest,anonymous  # specific groups
delete          no                guest,anonymous
overwrite       no                guest,anonymous
rename          no                guest,anonymous
log transfers anonymous,real inbound,outbound
shutdown /etc/shutmsg
passwd-check rfc822 warn
[root@linux6 /root]#
[root@linux6 /root]# cat /etc/ftpusers  # NOT ALLOWED to use FTP
root            # list of default names installed with Linux
bin
daemon
adm
lp
sync
shutdown
halt
mail
```

FIGURE 8-15

The basics of the FTP control files in /etc *(continued)*

```
news
uucp
operator
games
nobody
[root@linux6 /root]# cat /etc/ftpgroups    # NOT ALLOWED to access FTP
# test:ENCRYPTED PASSWORD HERE:archive     # this is a sample line
[root@linux6 /root]#
[root@linux6 /root]# cat /etc/ftphosts     # NOT ALLOWED access to host
# Example host access file
#
# Everything after a '#' is treated as comment,
# empty lines are ignored

[root@linux6 /root]# cat /etc/ftpconversions    # rules thereof
 :.Z:  :  :/bin/compress -d -c %s:T_REG|T_ASCII:O_UNCOMPRESS:UNCOMPRESS
 :   : :.Z:/bin/compress -c %s:T_REG:O_COMPRESS:COMPRESS
 :.gz: :  :/bin/gzip -cd %s:T_REG|T_ASCII:O_UNCOMPRESS:GUNZIP
 :   : :.gz:/bin/gzip -9 -c %s:T_REG:O_COMPRESS:GZIP
 :   : :.tar:/bin/tar -c -f - %s:T_REG|T_DIR:O_TAR:TAR
 :   : :.tar.Z:/bin/tar -c -Z -f -
%s:T_REG|T_DIR:O_COMPRESS|O_TAR:TAR+COMPRESS
 :   : :.tar.gz:/bin/tar -c -z -f -
%s:T_REG|T_DIR:O_COMPRESS|O_TAR:TAR+GZIP
[root@linux6 /root]#
=================================================================
```

Most of the files in Figure 8-15 contain lists that are DENIED access to the FTP site.

The /etc/ftpconversions file is a special file that the FTP service uses to automatically compress and/or decompress files for transfer. The executables for these conversions are found in the /home/ftp/bin directory. Each line in /etc/ftpconversions represents a rule of action for specific filename extensions. More details are available from the user documentation files. (See Figure 8-16.)

FIGURE 8-16

Basic example for wu-ftp configuration files

```
================================================================
[root@linux6 /root]# cat  ftpaccess.heavy
loginfails 2   # drop connection quickly

class   remote  real,guest,anonymous *

# limit local accesses to 20 any day of week or display message
limit   local    20  Any               /etc/msgs/msg.toomany
# limit remote accesses to 100 users
#          All day Saturday and Sunday, any day from 6 pm to 6am
#               After 100 connections, display message msg.toomany
limit   remote  100 SaSu|Any1800-0600   /etc/msgs/msg.toomany
# limit remote accesses to 60 (rest of time) or display message
limit   remote  60  Any                /etc/msgs/msg.toomany

readme  README*    login
readme  README*    cwd=*

message /welcome.msg            login
message .message                cwd=*

compress        yes             local remote   # execution allowed
tar             yes             local remote

# allow use of private file for SITE GROUP and SITE GPASS?
private         yes

# passwd-check  <none|trivial|rfc822>  [<enforce|warn>]
passwd-check    rfc822  warn     # security 'level' from rfc822

log commands real
log transfers anonymous,real inbound,outbound
shutdown /etc/shutmsg

# all the following default to "yes" for everybody
# all the basic file manipulation commands are restricted use
# only logged on 'local' users can run these commands.
delete          no      guest,anonymous          # delete permission?
overwrite       no      guest,anonymous          # overwrite permission?
Rename          no      guest,anonymous          # rename permission?
chmod           no      anonymous                # chmod permission?
umask           no      anonymous                # umask permission?

# specify the upload directory information
# action  rootdir  dir(def=*)  allow  group    via     perm permit/not
upload  /var/ftp  *           no     nobody   nogroup 0000 nodirs
upload  /var/ftp  /bin        no
```

FIGURE 8-16

Basic example for wu-ftp configuration files *(continued)*

```
upload  /var/ftp  /etc         no
upload  /var/ftp  /incoming    yes     root    daemon  0600 dirs

# directory aliases...  [note, the ":" is not required]
alias   inc:    /incoming

# cdpath
cdpath  /incoming
cdpath  /pub
cdpath  /

# path-filter...
path-filter  anonymous  /etc/pathmsg  ^[-A-Za-z0-9_\.]*$  ^\.  ^-
path-filter  guest      /etc/pathmsg  ^[-A-Za-z0-9_\.]*$  ^\.  ^-

# specify which group of users will be treated as "guests".
guestgroup ftponly

email user@hostname      # should change to a real email address
[root@linux6 /root]#
================================================================
```

exam Watch

You need to install the anonftp package to provide an anonymous FTP service. You only need wu-ftp if you want to add security settings for various group and user login access.

CERTIFICATION OBJECTIVE 8.03

Samba

Starting with Windows 3.11, Windows clients could "'share" their file systems and printers for other Windows clients to "map to" as remote resources. This sharing was provided through a facility called SMB, Server Message Block, a.k.a. NetBIOS. Through the collective works of Andrew Tridgell and many others, Linux systems provide SMB support over TCP/IP via a package known as Samba.

There are four basic "things" that one can do with Samba:

- Share a Linux directory tree with Windows machines
- Share a Windows drive with Linux machines
- Share a Linux printer with Windows machines
- Share a Windows printer with Linux machines

Samba imitates many of the advanced network features and functions associated with the Win9*x* and NT operating systems via the use of the SMB protocol. Complete information can be found at ftp://nimbus.anu.edu.au/pub/tridge/samba/

Samba can be easily configured to:

- Share user home directory shares
- Be the WINSserver or a client of any WINS service
- Link to or manage a workgroup browse service
- Be the master browser service if multiple workgroups exist
- Authenticate access from the local login security or from an NT PDC authority for all share access requests
- Provide local directory connections as mounted SMB file systems
- Provide domain logon validation services
- Provide synchronization of passwords between Windows and Linux systems

There are more aspects, but you get the idea. This is all done from one long file. The first time you see the file, you may be overwhelmed by the detail. The next section will dissect this file into more palatable morsels.

Installing Samba Services

If you did a Server installation, the Samba package is already installed. If you did a Workstation installation, Samba is not installed by default. If you did a Custom installation, you may have selected Samba Services. You can query all packages installed by RPM and then grep for Samba to see if it is installed. A Samba installation is shown in Figure 8-17.

Basics of Samba Services

Samba services provide interoperability between the Microsoft Windows network clients and Linux (or any UNIX, for that matter) clients. You need to have a basic understanding of how Microsoft Windows networking works in the TCP/IP realm.

Windows networking started with NetBIOS hostnames containing 15 characters or less. These unique hostnames provided a simple, flat hostnaming system for their network identification. All identification requests were made through broadcast packets. Windows defaulted to using NetBEUI as the protocol to transport packets between hosts. NetBEUI is not "routeable," as it does not contain any network segmentation information.

Windows networks could also use IPX/SPX, which is routeable, but the widest support of services and WAN connectivity was with TCP/IP. Windows could not give up on their established design, so they added some features to TCP/IP via the usual RFP process. One of the nice features of Windows networks was the browser service. All machines registered their NetBIOS names with one "elected" browse master, the keeper of the database. A browse database is maintained by some "elected" host for every protocol running on the network. For instance, if NetBEUI, IPX/SPX, and TCP/IP protocols were

FIGURE 8-17

Installation of Samba services

```
=================================================================
[root@linux6 /root]#  rpm  -qa |  grep  -i  samba
(No output if not found by grep)
[root@linux6 /root]#  mount   /mnt/cdrom
[root@linux6 /root]# cd  /mnt/cdrom/RedHat/RPMS/
 [root@linux6 RPMS]# rpm -iv samba-2.0.3-8.i386.rpm
samba-2.0.3-8
[root@linux6 /root]#  rpm  -qa  |  grep  -I  samba
samba-2.0.3-8
[root@linux6 /root]#  umount   /mnt/cdrom
=================================================================
```

installed on a host, then three duplicate browse databases were required—one per protocol.

Originally, the Windows network only used NetBEUI for the Local Area Network (LAN). Current Windows networking uses TCP/IP as the primary protocol. Connecting two or more LAN networks together creates a Wide Area Network (WAN). The Internet is the world's largest WAN. Trying to keep a single database of all hostnames was not practical.

NAME RESOLUTION—DNS The Internet evolved a distributed service to provide hostname-to-IP resolution called the Domain Name Service (DNS). The DNS design distributes the databases across any number of servers. Each server runs a local DNS service with a static (text file) database of DNS records. A DNS record is simply a hostname and the related IP address.

DNS Name	Type	IP Address
www.foo.bar	A	10.1.1.1
ftp.foo.bar	A	10.1.1.2

*(2 DNS A=Address records)

You enter www.foo.bar, and DNS returns the IP address 10.1.1.1; whatever name this record represents from whichever DNS server that has the record.

Each DNS service maintains a list of the local LAN hosts only. DNS is manually administered in most cases; each record is added by an administrator into a text configuration file.

The Windows gurus decided to create their own centralized service that was dynamically updated by each host when the hosts booted up. This dynamic Windows-only based service was called the Windows Internet Naming Service (WINS). WINS is a database of IP addresses and the related NetBIOS names. The Internet does not use WINS; it only uses DNS.

For almost all network clients, there is an automatic IP configuration service, called the Dynamic Host Configuration Protocol (DHCP). When a DHCP client boots, it sends a request to a network service for IP configuration information. The DHCP server can supply all the network information for the client plus the additional Windows IP parameters information, notably the WINS IP address, if the client is a Windows-based system.

NAME RESOLUTION—WINS WINS was designed as a dynamic (records added by client at bootup), centralized (all records on one or more central servers), and robust service, an alternative to using DNS, that provided WAN "browsing" of Windows-based client LANs if properly configured.

Each WINS server maintained a central database with multiple records for all machines. On a large network, this was a big data file. For each host, at least three and as many as 10 records or more could be added to WINS to satisfy all the Windows networking needs. Naturally, this multirecord-per-machine format became very cumbersome as the network's size grew. Over the next few releases of Windows, WINS will be phased out.

UNIX systems also have their own authentication services for users and network access. Windows has the NT Domain or LAN Manager Domain authentication system designs. They are based on different strategic designs, and interoperability was not originally one of them.

WHAT ABOUT SAMBA? This is where Samba fits in. Samba on Linux provides all the Windows networking services that are available on any Windows TCP/IP client or server. You can configure Samba services so your Linux workstation looks like another Windows host, participating in browse lists and in WINS. You can also configure Samba to be a look-a-like NT Domain server, validate logon authentication requests, be the WINS server itself, be the file and print server of Windows services, be the Master Browser (another browser list of all the other network group browser lists), and much, much more.

To configure Samba, as shown in Figure 8-18, you simply need to know what an NT Domain or workgroup is, and configure the parameters accordingly for your Linux workstation or server to match the local network needs. The variations are too numerous to mention. A basic workstation participating in a workgroup and a server acting as part of a domain are discussed here.

FIGURE 8-18

Samba service "pieces"

```
==================================================================
/usr/bin/smbd           - main SMB service daemon
/usr/bin/nmbd           - NetBIOS name service daemon
/etc/smb.conf           - main configuration file
/usr/bin/smbclient      - connects to SMB shares, ftp-like syntax
/bin/testparm           - tests validity of /etc/smb.conf file
/etc/rc.d/init.d/smb    - daemon start and stop control script
/usr/bin/smbmount       - used to mount SMB share on local directory
smbfs                   - file system extension to mount SMB shares on directories
/usr/bin/smbprint       - A script to print to a printer on an SMB host
/usr/bin/smbstatus      - Lists current SMB connections for the local host
/usr/bin/smbrun         - Facilitates running applications on SMB hosts
==================================================================
```

Samba Has Two Daemons

The actual running daemons that make up Samba services are the smbd and nmbd, both located in /usr/bin. Their configuration comes from one file, /etc/smb.conf. There is a simple test program that checks the basic syntax of your /etc/smb.conf, /bin/testparm. The testparm utility only looks at the format; it does not test the actual connectivity of any shares.

Main Configuration File of Samba—/etc/smb.conf

The main configuration file is rather long-winded and contains many parts that require a good understanding of the Windows world. There are some very helpful documents, mentioned in the default supplied smb.conf filem in the Samba manual entriesm and supplied additional documentation files.

The Samba configuration file in Figure 8-19 covers most of the major Windows-oriented global settings. Many more details about Samba services can be found in the documentation. Use either the main pages on Samba or look in /usr/doc for samba How-Tos.

In Figure 8-19, a few options and a few example sections have been removed for brevity. Some of the comments have been shortened, and additional comments are shown in bold.

FIGURE 8-19

Main Samba configuration file—/etc/smb.conf

```
=================================================================
# This is the main Samba configuration file. You should read the
# smb.conf(5) manual page in order to understand the options listed
# here. Samba has a huge number of configurable options (perhaps too
# many!) most of which are not shown in this example
#   (even more have been removed for this example)
# Any line which starts with a ; (semi-colon) or a # (hash)
# is a comment and is ignored. In this example we will use a #
# for commentry and a ; for parts of the config file that you
# may wish to enable
#
# NOTE: If you modify this file you should run the command "testparm"
# to check that you have not many any basic syntactic errors.
#
#==================== Global Settings =======================
[global]

# workgroup = NT-Domain-Name or Workgroup-Name
   workgroup = MYGROUP      # this is the 'browser' group name
     # you can join an existing workgroup or domain,
# or samba will create a new group for you

# server string is the equivalent of the NT Description field
   server string = Samba Server  # the comment when browsing

# This option is important for security. It allows you to restrict
# connections to machines which are on your local network. The
# following example restricts access to two C class networks and
# the "loopback" interface. For more examples of the syntax see
# the smb.conf man page
;   hosts allow = 192.168.1. 192.168.2. 127.

# if you want to automatically load your printer list rather
# than setting them up individually then you'll need this
   printcap name = /etc/printcap    # default config file for printers
   load printers = yes                 # automatically shares printers

# It should not be necessary to spell out the print system type unless
# yours is non-standard. Currently supported print systems include:
# bsd, sysv, plp, lprng, aix, hpux, qnx
;   printing = bsd    # you do not have to change this for linux

# Uncomment this if you want a guest account, add this to /etc/passwd
# otherwise the user "nobody" is used
  guest account = pcguest  # uncomment this for 'easy' access
            # you still need to create the actual user account
```

FIGURE 8-19

Main Samba configuration file—/etc/smb.conf *(continued)*

```
# LOG FILES : create a separate log file for each machine that connects
   log file = /var/log/samba/log.%m          # excellent idea
# Put a capping on the size of the log files (in Kb).
   max log size = 50                   # excellent control

# Security mode. Start with (local /etc/passwd) 'user' level security.
# Could be 'share' for simple password access control
   security = user    # uses local /etc/passwd to authenticate

# Use password server option only with security = server
# if 'server' security requests passed to 'password server'
# use these 2 lines if you wanted an NT Domain security validation
;   security = server                  # to use NT-Server-Name
;   password server = <NT-Server-Name> # sends authentication here

# You may wish to use password encryption. Please read
# ENCRYPTION.txt, Win95.txt and WinNT.txt in the Samba documentation.
# Do not enable this option unless you have read those documents
;  encrypt passwords = yes             # allows syncronization
;  smb passwd file = /etc/smbpasswd          # except with NIS

# The following are needed to allow password changing from Windows to
# update the Linux login system passwords also.
# NOTE: Use these with 'encrypt passwords' and 'smb passwd file' above.
# NOTE2: You do NOT need these to allow workstations to change only
#        the encrypted SMB passwords. They allow the Unix password
#        to be kept in sync with the SMB password.
# this assumes you have related users on each system
;  unix password sync = Yes
;  passwd program = /usr/bin/passwd %u
#the next line is wrapped onto 2 lines, it should be one long line
;  passwd chat = *New*UNIX*password* %n\n *ReType*new*UNIX*password* %n\n
*passwd:*all*authentication*tokens*updated*successfully*

# Unix users can map to different SMB User names
;  username map = /etc/smbusers     # what login = what Win. logon

# Most people will find that this option gives better performance.
# See speed.txt and the manual pages for details
   socket options = TCP_NODELAY

# Configure Samba to use multiple interfaces, for multi-homed system
;   interfaces = 192.168.12.2/24 192.168.13.2/24

# Browser Control Options:
# set local master to no if you don't want Samba to become a master
# browser on your network. Otherwise the normal election rules apply
```

FIGURE 8-19

Main Samba configuration file—/etc/smb.conf *(continued)*

```
;   local master = no    # does a good job, browsing is a waste of time

# OS Level determines the precedence of this server in master browser
# elections. The default value should be reasonable
;   os level = 33           # this values exceeds NT, therefore always wins

# Domain Master specifies Samba to be the Domain Master Browser. This
# allows Samba to collate browse lists between subnets. Don't use this
# if you already have a Windows NT domain controller doing this job
;   domain master = yes     # use if you do logon authentication

# Preferred Master causes Samba to force a local browser election
# and gives it a slightly higher chance of winning the election
;   preferred master = yes

# if you enable domain logons then you may want a per-machine or
# per user logon script
# run a specific logon batch file per workstation (machine)
;   logon script = %m.bat
# run a specific logon batch file per username
;   logon script = %U.bat
# this is a neat feature if you want Linux to 'really look like' NT
# you can setup custom login scripts for machines and users

# All NetBIOS names must be resolved to IP Addresses
# the default order is "host lmhosts wins bcast". "host" uses the unix
# system /etc/hosts OR DNS or NIS depending on the settings

# Windows Internet Name Serving Support Section: to be WINS or not
# WINS Support - NMBD component enables it's WINS Server
;   wins support = yes    # must be off if a WINS client

# WINS Server - Tells the NMBD components of Samba to be a WINS Client
#      Note: can be either a WINS Server, or a WINS Client, but NOT both
   wins server = 206.195.1.1 # use the correct IP of WINS server here

# WINS Proxy - Help out non-WINS clients. The default is NO.
;   wins proxy = yes # only in special legacy windows networks

# DNS Proxy - try to resolve NetBIOS names via DNS nslookups.
   dns proxy = no     # unless this method preferred choice

# due to the 8.3 name convention of Windows, you may need this
# Case Preservation can be handy - system default is _no_
# NOTE: These can be set on a per share basis
;  preserve case = no
;  short preserve case = no
```

FIGURE 8-19

Main Samba configuration file—/etc/smb.conf *(continued)*

```
# Default case is normally upper case for all DOS files
;  default case = lower
# Be very careful with case sensitivity - it can break things!
;  case sensitive = no

#================= Share Definitions ======================
[homes]
   comment = Home Directories
   browseable = no    # only logged on user sees their home dir
   writable = yes           # They can write to it, no one else

# NOTE: If you have a BSD-style print system there is no need to
# specifically define each individual printer
[printers]
   comment = All Printers
   path = /var/spool/samba     # spooling directory used
   browseable = yes      # shows up in browse list
   public = yes              # to allow user 'guest account' to print
   guest ok = yes
   writable = no             # not a file system
   printable = yes    # this is a print service

# This one is useful for all users to share files
[tmp]
   comment = Temporary file space
   path = /tmp
   read only = no
   public = yes            # everyone gets access

# A publicly accessible directory, but read only
[public]
   comment = Public FTP Stuff
   path = /home/ftp/pub
   public = yes
   writable = no              # 'read only = yes' does this too
   printable = no

================================================================
```

SHARE DECLARATIONS The final parts in the smb.conf file are the share declarations. Each starts with a section name, such as [tmp]. This section name contains the name that will be seen if the service is set to browseable.

There are three reserved names for special sections that smb.conf uses. These special names are [global], for all global settings; [homes], which automatically shares all user home directories with any user who connects with a specific username; and [printers], which automatically shares out the printers on this system with NetBIOS names set to their primary queue name.

In Figure 8-19, there are four final sections; the additional comments from the original file have been removed. The top two sections are the reserved section names for homes and printers. The last two sections are the local directory shared services. The first section, [tmp], creates a read-write share of the /tmp directory. Everyone has read and write on the tmp share. Normally, the /tmp directory has the *sticky bit* set. The sticky bit restricts file deletion to the owner of the file only. The final section, [public], is a read-only share named public that will be available to all users.

These shares are set to browseable, meaning that they should appear in any Windows Network Neighborhood or equivalent "view" of shared resources.

What to Do with Samba?

The configuration of /etc/smb.conf, as shown in Figure 8-19, has many aspects that are important. In this case, many groups of lines were removed from the file supplied by the installation that are not even discussed. In a basic installation, you may not need to change much except for the actual file and print shares. You could, for instance, share the same file trees via Samba as you share with NFS. For print shares, just create the printers and let Samba share them all automatically to any and all Windows clients.

Note: Samba print shares are not like NT print queues; drivers are not downloaded to the host when print requests are received from certain Windows-based clients. All Windows hosts will need to install the correct driver for the Linux printer queues.

Here are a few additional options to consider, but these are completely dependent on your actual Windows network settings and services. Not all of these options are discussed here; check the full Samba documentation supplied with the system.

- Be a Client of WINS if it is used locally by Windows clients
- Allow your host to be visible in the local browse list

- Configure a log file for each machine that connects to any share
- Configure automatic printer shares for all configured printers
- Create browseable shared directories

Adding Linux to an NT network can be smoothed over by configuring the Samba service to "look like" another Windows host on the network. You can configure Samba services to be a client of the WINS server, share out print services and file systems just like all the other Windows hosts, and participate in the browser service.

Basic SMB Configuration

Configuration of the main service is in a text file named /etc/smb.conf. The system comes with a preconfigured file that has most of the Windows-like characteristic services commented out. Changes can be made using any editor, such as vi, pico, or joe.

Some of the names of options are not necessarily properly spelled according to some observers. You need to be careful about the spelling you use:

Correct	Incorrect	Means
writable	writeable	Can write to a file share (not a print share)
browseable	browsable	Appears in Windows browsing if set to "yes"

General Samba "Windows" Settings

The configuration file has a top [global] section that provides the system characteristics. This sets how Samba will mimic the Windows network characteristics. The minimum set of options to change or modify are usually:

```
   Related to Browsing
Workgroup             'LAN' name browse list to be a part of
server string  the comment string seen when browsed
```

"'Browsing" means the service will appear in Windows Network Neighborhood, or equivalent service request, just like any Windows shared service that is not "hidden." A hidden service in Windows networking has a dollar sign ($) as the last character of the filename. The browsing mechanism does not display shared services with a $ as the last character. In Samba, you can get the same hidden property by setting the "browseable" option to "no", effectively making the shared service "hidden" to browsing.

```
   Related to Printing
printcap name = /etc/printcap   # default for Linux
load printers = yes          # automatically shares printers
;    printing = bsd          # Linux uses bsd, no need to set

   Related to Connection Authentication
   You can either use the local Linux authentication
   (If you do not know NT, this is the best choice)
security = user        # uses local /etc/passwd to authenticate

         OR you can use a Domain Controller authentication
         (If you have NT experience, this may be a better choice)
security = server                  # to use NT-Server-Name
password server = <NT-Server-Name>     # sends authentication here

   Related to NT Based WINS Service or Support
   EITHER
wins support = yes          # is WINS SERVER
OR
wins server = 206.195.1.1 # is WINS client
(NOT both, if it is a server, it is automatically a client)
wins proxy = yes     # 'helps' in special legacy windows networks
dns proxy = no       # unless this method preferred choice
```

Client Configuration for File Services

The bottom part of the Samba configuration file, /etc/smb.conf, contains the actual shared services: home directories, printers, and specific SMB shares that may or may not be browseable by Windows clients.

There are a few reserved section words: homes, printers, and global. These three names represent sections of related options that are special to the Samba configuration. For each share that you create, you must give it a section name, as in [public]. The service will appear as the string "'public". For example, if your server was named linux66, the access to this share would be \\linux66\public from any Windows client.

MAKING CONNECTIONS FROM WINDOWS At a Windows command prompt, you could make a permanent connection to the file share named public on the linux66 host, and assign as local drive U:, with the following command:

```
$ net use U: \\linux66\public
```

At a Windows command prompt, you could make a permanent connection to the public printer share named lp on the linux66 host, assigned as local printer lpt2:, with the following command:

```
$ net use lpt2: \\linux66\lp
```

You could also make these same connections via the Windows Explorer interface.

There are a few more file-sharing options that are available. Check the documentation for more details on group or user specifications, mask value, and other information that may be useful in some instances. These shares are simple examples of a write-enabled share and a read-only share. (See Figure 8-20.)

You can test for client connectivity using the smbclient utility.

Client Configuration for Print Services

There is a simple option line in the /etc/smb.conf file that shares out all local printer systems as if this were another Windows host. The only difference is that it does not support the NT style of downloading the driver to the host. Any Windows host would have to have the correct driver locally installed in order to use the Linux-based printer.

There is a special control option for printers that starts with the section heading [printers]. Using the same standard share options, Samba will create a shared print service for each installed print queue available through the local print control service. In the case of Linux, the local print service is based on the BSDLPD (Line Print Daemon) service.

```
(in the [global] upper characteristics section)
# Currently supported print systems include:
# bsd, sysv, plp, lprng, aix, hpux, qnx
;   printing = bsd  # you do not have to change this for linux

(at the end of the configuration file, near top of all share definitions)
[printers]
```

```
comment = All Printers
path = /var/spool/samba  # spooling directory used
browseable = yes # shows up in browse list
public = yes           # to allow user 'guest account' to print
guest ok = yes
writable = no          # not a file system
printable = yes  # this is a print service
```

There is a slight difference in configuration between a file and a print service. File services are "writable" but not "printable"; print services are "printable" but not "writable."

FIGURE 8-20

Synopsis of setting up Samba shares

```
#================== General Services ======================
[homes]
   comment = Home Directories
   browseable = no    # only logged on user sees their home dir
   writable = yes          # They can write to it, no one else

[printers]
   comment = All Printers
   path = /var/spool/samba  # spooling directory used
   browseable = yes  # shows up in browse list
   public = yes            # to allow user 'guest account' to print
   guest ok = yes
   writable = no           # not a file system
   printable = yes  # this is a print service

#================= Share Definitions ======================
# This one is useful for all users to share files
[tmp]
   comment = Temporary file space
   path = /tmp
   read only = no
   public = yes            # everyone gets access

# A publicly accessible directory, but read only
[public]
   comment = Public Stuff
   path = /home/ftp/pub
   public = yes
   writable = no           # 'read only = yes' does this too
   printable = no
============================================================
```

Although this simple "share all" design is the easiest for printer options, you could selectively share out any printer instead by creating a section title for each printer to be shared. For more details, check the Samba documentation.

Testing Changes to /etc/smb.conf

After making any changes to /etc/smb.conf, it is always a good idea to test your system before putting it into production.

TESTING A NEW SMB.CONF CONFIGURATION—TESTPARM You can do a simple syntax check using the supplied test utility, testparm, as shown in Figure 8-21. This does not actually check to see if the service is running or functioning correctly; it only checks basic text syntax and groupings.

Stopping and Restarting the Samba Services

After making any changes to the configuration file, /etc/smb.conf, you could wait for the Samba service to re-read the configuration file at some later point, or you can force the issue using the /etc/rc.d/init.d/smb control script.

/etc/rc.d/init.d/smb UTILITY The script /etc/rc.d/init.d/smb is used to start, stop, and restart the Samba daemons, as shown in Figure 8-22.

FIGURE 8-21

Running testparm

```
=================================================================
[root@unix34 /root]# testparm
Load smb config files from /etc/smb.conf
Processing section "[homes]"
Processing section "[printers]"
Processing section "[tmp]"
Processing section "[public]"
Loaded services file OK.  # this is what to look for: 'OK'
Press enter to see a dump of your service definitions
CTRL+C   # you could press return to watch 10+ pages of output
[root@unix34 /root]#
=================================================================
```

This utility may be used whenever the configuration file changes to force an instant update of the Samba services.

Checking Samba File and Print Services

You can test actual connectivity using the smbclient utility. Before testing actual connectivity, you should force the Samba daemons to re-start as shown in Figure 8-22.

CLIENT TOOL—smbclient The last tool is the client access tool, smbclient. With this tool, you can test connectivity to any SMB host, Windows based or Samba based. It even provides an FTP-like interface that will be familiar to most Linux and UNIX users. You smbclient to an SMB share, you get an SMB prompt much like in FTP, and you use the same basic movement and file manipulation commands. The only difference is that the remote host is not running FTP services; this is all done through the SMB protocol service. This means you can connect to any Win9*x* / NT based system and get or put any files from their shares, assuming you have a valid logon name and password if required for the Windows share.

The listing in Figure 8-23 connects to a Win98 host named W98LAPTOP and to the share named DOCS on host W98LAPTOP. After listing all the .zip files, it "gets" the file named UNIX1IG.ZIP. The quit command disconnects the service connection. Notice the similarity of the interface to a typical FTP client session.

FIGURE 8-22

Restarting the Samba daemons—/etc/rc.d/init.d/smb

```
==================================================================
[root@unix34 /root]# /etc/rc.d/init.d/smb    # print syntax
statement
Usage: smb {start|stop|restart|status}
[root@unix34 /root]# /etc/rc.d/init.d/smb  restart
Shutting down SMB services:                              [  OK  ]
Shutting down NMB services:                              [  OK  ]
Starting SMB services:                                   [  OK  ]
Starting NMB services:                                   [  OK  ]
[root@unix34 /root]#
==================================================================
```

FIGURE 8-23

Viewing shares and connecting with smbclient

```
================================================================
[root@linux6 /root]# smbclient -L linux6 -U user01
Added interface ip=206.195.1.222 bcast=206.195.1.255 nmask=255.255.255.0
Password:                  #enter appropriate user01 password
Domain=[LINUX] OS=[Unix] Server=[Samba 2.0.3]

        Sharename      Type      Comment
        ---------      ----      -------
        tmp            Disk      Temporary file space
        public         Disk      Public Directory
        IPC$           IPC       IPC Service (Samba Server onRH6)
        lp             Printer
        bubblejet      Printer   bj200
        user01         Disk      Home Directories

        Server              Comment
        ---------           -------
        LINUX6              Samba Server on RH6

        Workgroup           Master
        ---------           -------
        LINUX
[root@linux6 /root]#
[root@linux6 /root]# smbclient -L w98laptop
Added interface ip=206.195.1.222 bcast=206.195.1.255 nmask=255.255.255.0
Got a positive name query response from 206.195.1.23 ( 206.195.1.23 )
Password:                  # no password needed on Win98 hosts

        Sharename      Type      Comment
        ---------      ----      -------
        DOCS           Disk      Read Only
        DRIVEC         Disk      Password Restricted
        IPC$           IPC       Remote Inter Process Communication

        Server              Comment
        ---------           -------

        Workgroup           Master
        ---------           -------
[root@linux6 /root]#
[root@linux6 /root]# smbclient \\\\w98laptop\\docs
Added interface ip=206.195.1.222 bcast=206.195.1.255 nmask=255.255.255.0
Got a positive name query response from 206.195.1.23 ( 206.195.1.23 )
Password:
smb: \> dir *.zip
  UNIX1IG.zip                         A    56022  Fri May  7 18:45:38 1999
  VirtualNTMachineOnLinux.zip         A   113261  Fri Jul  2 09:27:20 1999
```

FIGURE 8-23

Viewing shares and connecting with smbclient *(continued)*

```
  PERL4DAVE.zip                    A  115070  Wed May 19 18:37:30 1999
                 57942 blocks of size 16384. 31261 blocks available
smb: \> get unixlig.zip
getting file unixlig.zip of size 56022 as unixlig.zip (99.652 kb/s) (average 99.
6521 kb/s)
[root@linux6 /root]#
==================================================================
```

There are both client and server portions to Samba services. You should be familiar with the basic steps of how to configure the server characteristics and the shared services.

Creating Local SMB Mounts to Remote File Services

The system reads the text file /etc/fstab at every reboot to mount all the file systems local to the machine. This file may also contain mounts of remote file systems using the NFS and SMB file systems.

You can update the /etc/fstab file with a permanent connection to each SMB share on the network you want to make available to local users. This is similar to a permanent NFS network connection. The main difference between SMB and NFS connections in the /etc/fstab file is that the type of file system for the SMB shares is the SMB file system, denoted as smbfs, instead of the NFS File Share, nfsfs, as with an NFS connection. You can get more details by reading the man page on smbmount and fstab.

THE SMB FILE SYSTEM If you do not want a permanent connection, you can use the smbmount command to make a temporary smbfs connection to any network-accessible share. You can create a directory and then "'mount" an SMB remote share service on it using the smbmount command (see Figure 8-24).

In Figure 8-24, a directory is created to act as the mount point for the SMB share. The root user can then make a long-term connection (until reboot) of

FIGURE 8-24

Sample smbmount of Windows-based service

```
================================================================
[root@linux6 /root]# mkdir  /mnt/docs  # make sure a directory exists
[root@linux6 /root]# smbmount \\\\w98laptop\\docs -c 'mount /mnt/docs'
Added interface ip=206.195.1.222 bcast=206.195.1.255 nmask=255.255.255.0
Got a positive name query response from 206.195.1.23 ( 206.195.1.23 )
Server time is Sat Oct  2 16:34:56 1999
Timezone is UTC-7.0
security=share
[root@linux6 /root]# ls  -l  /mnt/docs/*.zip
-rwxr-xr-x   1 root     root       115070 May 19 18:37 /mnt/docs/PERL4DAVE.zip
-rwxr-xr-x   1 root     root        56022 May  7 18:45 /mnt/docs/UNIX1IG.zip
-rwxr-xr-x   1 root     root       113261 Jul  2 09:27 /mnt/docs/VirtualNTMachin
eOnLinux.zip
[root@linux6 /root]#
[root@linux6 /root]# mount    # list all mounted file systems
/dev/hda8 on / type ext2 (rw)
none on /proc type proc (rw)
/dev/hda7 on /boot type ext2 (rw)
/dev/hda1 on /dosC type vfat (rw)
/dev/hda6 on /dosE type vfat (rw)
none on /dev/pts type devpts (rw,mode=0622)
//W98LAPTOP/DOCS on /mnt/docs type smbfs (0)
[root@linux6 /root]# umount /mnt/docs     # disconnect from share
[root@linux6 /root]#
================================================================
```

the service named DOCS on the (Win98) host named W98LAPTOP on the directory point named /mnt/docs. This connection is then available to all users on the Linux host as a local directory. This connection would be permanent until the next reboot. To make this connection persist after a reboot, an entry such as the following should be added to the /etc/fstab file:

```
//W98LAPTOP/DOCS    /mnt/docs    smbfs    defaults    0
```

If your host connection is going to an NT Domain service, then a username and password may be necessary to make the connection in all cases. You can specify the username with the "-U username" optional string on all of the commands in Figure 8-24.

Other Samba Configuration Utilities—linuxconf, swat

All of the configuration in the preceding section was done from a command-line viewpoint. For a small installation, this is probably the easy ways to learn the basics. If the network becomes large and the service offerings extensive, you may want to try one of the more advanced GUI-based interfaces.

There is a Web-based interface, called SWAT (Samba Web Admin Tool) that can be used to configure any Samba server from any client on the network. You need to install, compile, and configure this optional product before you can use it (see Figure 8-25). See the documentation for SWAT on your system. The actual SWAT interface can be accessed through port 901 of the server.

The linuxconf X Windows interface offers a GUI-based interface to configure Samba services. The linuxconf utility is already configured on your server by default. You can start linuxconf in the background at any xterm command line with:

```
# linuxconf  &
```

The interface allows you to create and manage all of the Samba services from one central interface.

FIGURE 8-25

Configuration for linuxconf and SWAT in /etc/inetd.conf

```
=======================================================================
...   # at the end of /etc/inetd.conf, these are added, uncomment swat
linuxconf stream tcp wait root /bin/linuxconf linuxconf --http
swat      stream  tcp     nowait.400      root /usr/sbin/swat swat
# turned on swat by uncommenting (remove leading '#') line above
=======================================================================
```

EXERCISE 8-4

Create Samba File and Print Shares

1. Put the Red Hat Installation CD in the local CD-ROM reader.
2. Install the Samba RPM.
3. If you have a WINS server configured, authorize Samba to participate as a WINS client; use the IP of your WINS server.
4. Configure Samba to share as public, in read-only mode, the /home/ftp/pub directory tree.
5. Configure Samba to share all installed print queues to all users.
6. Allow guest access to all public shares, create a guest account with UID 500, GID 500, password is anonymous.
7. Share all user home directories.
8. Create separate log files for each host that connects.
9. Make all print and file shares browseable, but not home directories.

CERTIFICATION OBJECTIVE 8.04

Mail Services

If you have Linux, you have a powerful mail server. The Internet is predominantly using sendmail, and Linux has a very current version of this service and some of the other popular mail services.

There is a huge configuration file associated with the sendmail daemon, but there are only a few entries you need to change for your system to work with other systems. Linux can also be configured to respond to many popular remote mail user agent protocols such as POP3 and IMAP requests.

There are three major independent but interrelated "parts" to the mail service world. You need all of them to have the mail system "'work" as a mail system (see Table 8-1).

On the hub server, you will need to configure the sendmail service for various outbound services related to mail, including forwarding, relaying, method of transport between systems, lists of hosts to exchange mail with, optional aliases for lists of names, and the spooling directories.

Mail is very dependent on your network name resolution working correctly. This can be either through /etc/hosts for a small network or via DNS on a large network. Make sure that name resolution is functioning correctly before trying to configure mail.

You can use linuxconf to create a specific POP mail user account.

SMTP

SMTP, Simple Mail Transfer Protocol, has become one of the most important service protocols of the modern era. Much of the Internet-connected world lives and dies by their e-mail, and SMTP is the heart of it. SMTP is a *protocol*, a set of rules for transferring data packets, that is used by some Mail Transfer Agents.

In Linux, there is an smtpd (SMTP daemon) service running to handle these requests. smtpd is configured at boot time along with the Sendmail daemon. In earlier versions of Red Hat Linux, smtpd was configured in /etc/inetd.conf.

TABLE 8-1 Mail System Components

MTA	Mail Transfer Agent	sendmail, pop, imap, …
MUA	Mail User Agents	mail, Netscape, elm, …
MDA	Mail Delivery Agents	UUCP, TCP, SMTP, …

The Sendmail daemon is configured from a set of files in /etc:

/etc/sendmail.cf	Main configuration file
/etc/sendmail.cw	List of hosts to receive mail for
/etc/aliases	List of groups, group of names is an "alias"

You should be able to configure a basic POP mail account.

Basic Sendmail Configuration

If this server is to handle all mail as local, then the default installation of sendmail is already set up to do this. If mail is to be transferred between hosts, your network must be configured correctly on all hosts and you will need to add some configuration information to the /etc/sendmail.cf file, as shown in Figure 8-26.

Essentially, you configure each workstation to forward all nonlocal mail messages to a central relay host. The relay host acts as a central repository hub. Messages are then forwarded to the gateway system (if not for local network) or to the local system as per the configuration "'rules" defined in the sendmail configuration file.

BASIC DECLARATION TYPES There are many entries, each one starting with a capital letter representing the size or use of the next letter,

FIGURE 8-26

How big is sendmail.cf?

```
================================================================
[root@linux6 /root]# wc  -l  /etc/sendmail.cf
   1055     /etc/sendmail.cf  # current line count of this file
[root@linux6 /root]#
================================================================
```

the actual variable, string, or option. For example, Dw is a single variable/string (D) called "w." (See Table 8-2.)

There are a few notable variables that need to be set on each system. These variables are only needed if mail is to be forwarded to other hosts via specific transport methods. The basic configuration in sendmail.cf is shown in Figure 8-27.

INCORRECT MAIL SETUP When your name resolution is not working, your mail messages get stuck in a queue that will try to resend them at regular intervals. This is standard practice. If the host or network connectivity is down for some segment, then the mail forwarder or relay host will store the message and forward at the next interval. The user does not need to do anything. The administrator needs to make sure this queue does not regularly fill up. If so, he or she may want to reconfigure messages for that network to be sent at more irregular times. (See Figure 8-28.)

Command-Line Mail

To simply test your mail system, you can use the built-in command-line mail utility. This is a very simple text-based interface. The system keeps each user's mail in a system directory. Once users read a message, they can reply, forward, or delete it. If they do not delete the message, when they quit the mail utility, the system stores the message in their home directory in a file called mbox. Any messages that are not read during a session remain in the system area.

TABLE 8-2

Some common declaration types in sendmail.cf

D	Single variable
C	"Classes" have multiple variables, strings
O	sendmail options
F	Next argument is a file containing more information for this option

FIGURE 8-27

Basic configuration options in sendmail.cf

```
=================================================================
Cvotherhost1  otherhost2 ..   # forward mail to these
Dwyourname              # your host name
Cwyourothername            # your alternate host name: mailhost
# file containing names of hosts for which we receive email
Fw/etc/sendmail.cw
# my official domain name
Dj$w.yourname.org     # must be defined in /etc/hosts or dns
# "Smart" relay host (may be null, typically your ISP host)
DShostISPname
# Relay host
Drrelayhostname   # must be defined in /etc/hosts or dns
=================================================================
```

FIGURE 8-28

Unable to transport mail—root is notified

```
==================================================================
[root@linux6 /etc]# mail
Mail version 8.1 6/6/93.  Type ? for help.
"/var/spool/mail/root": 1 messages 1 unread
>U  1 MAILER-DAEMON@linux6  Sun Oct  3 03:55  67/2221  "Warning: could not se"
&     # simply press <ENTER> key to see each message
Message 1:
From MAILER-DAEMON@linux6.4egans.com  Sun Oct  3 03:55:39 1999
Date: Sun, 3 Oct 1999 03:55:39 -0700
From: Mail Delivery Subsystem <MAILER-DAEMON@linux6.4egans.com>
To: root@linux6.4egans.com
MIME-Version: 1.0
Content-Type: multipart/report; report-type=delivery-status;
        boundary="DAA03153.938948139/linux6.4egans.com"
Subject: Warning: could not send message for past 4 hours
Auto-Submitted: auto-generated (warning-timeout)
This is a MIME-encapsulated message
--DAA03153.938948139/linux6.4egans.com
    **********************************************
    **      THIS IS A WARNING MESSAGE ONLY      **
    **  YOU DO NOT NEED TO RESEND YOUR MESSAGE  **
    **********************************************
The original message was received at Sat, 2 Oct 1999 23:55:21 -0700
from root@localhost
----- The following addresses had transient non-fatal errors -----
```

FIGURE 8-28

Unable to transport mail—root is notified *(continued)*

```
root@rh6laptop.4egans.com

   ----- Transcript of session follows -----
root@rh6laptop.4egans.com... Deferred: Name server: rh6laptop.4egans.com.: host
name lookup failure
Warning: message still undelivered after 4 hours
Will keep trying until message is 5 days old

--DAA03153.938948139/linux6.4egans.com
...  # internal message format removed from here
--DAA03153.938948139/linux6.4egans.com--
& d   # delete current read buffer
& q   # quit mail
[root@linux6 /etc]# mail
=================================================================
```

To send mail to another user, you can use the mail command-line utility. You can either enter the body of the text as prompted by mail, or you can redirect a file to the mail utility as the body of the text:

```
======================================================================
[root@rh6laptop /root]# mail root   # assumes local host
Subject: First message
Sent to you by me
cheers.
Cc: user01@rh6laptop
[root@rh6laptop /root]# mail root@rh6linux -s 'hosts file' < /etc/hosts
[root@rh6laptop /root]#
======================================================================
```

READING MAIL MESSAGES You must have mail messages pending in the system in order to read mail. The mail utility is only interactive when there is mail to be read. You can read pending messages by running mail with no arguments.

To read any message, you can enter the number of the message at the mail prompt and press ENTER. If you press ENTER with no argument, the mail utility assumes you want to read the next unread message. (See Figure 8-29.)

FIGURE 8-29

Using command-line e-mail

```
=============================================================
[root@rh6laptop /root]# mail   # start mail in interactive mode
Mail version 8.1 6/6/93.  Type ? for help.
"/var/spool/mail/root": 1 message 1 new   # system stores mail here
>N  1 root@rh6laptop.4egan  Sat Oct  2 16:43  15/418   "First message"
&         # press <RETURN> key to read current 'N' (not-read) message
Message 1:
From root  Sat Oct  2 16:43:26 1999
Date: Sat, 2 Oct 1999 16:43:25 -0700
From: root <root@rh6laptop.4egans.com>
To: root@rh6laptop.4egans.com
Subject: First message
Cc: user01@rh6laptop.4egans.com
Sent to you by me
cheers.
& d         # delete current message
& q         # quit mail
[root@rh6laptop /root]#
===================================================================
```

Workstation

If you installed as a Workstation, you have basic mail services installed. If you selected Server or Custom install, you needed to select the Mail/News group packages option. If you did not install them yet, you can use RPM to install the mail and news RPM packages.

```
===================================================================
[root@rh6laptop /root]# mail root
Subject: First message
Sent to you by me
cheers.
Cc: user01@rh6laptop
[root@rh6laptop /root]# mail
Mail version 8.1 6/6/93.  Type ? for help.
"/var/spool/mail/root": 1 message 1 new
>N  1 root@rh6laptop.4egan  Sat Oct  2 16:43  15/418   "First message"
&         # press <RETURN> key to read current message
Message 1:
From root  Sat Oct  2 16:43:26 1999
Date: Sat, 2 Oct 1999 16:43:25 -0700
From: root <root@rh6laptop.4egans.com>
To: root@rh6laptop.4egans.com
Subject: First message
Cc: user01@rh6laptop.4egans.com
```

```
Sent to you by me
cheers.
& d          # delete current message
& q          # quit mail
[root@rh6laptop /root]#
==================================================================
```

Mail Hub

A central mail hub is configured as the relay host for all mail messages to be delivered to other hosts. All workstations relay their external mail messages to the central host if they are not configured to be sent directly to each host in the network. A centralized hub is most beneficial when there is another network to go to. In years past, it was common to have mail sent via a uucp dial-up connection at specified times each day. This was common for networks that were independent of the Internet but participated in news and discussion groups by connecting once a day in the evening to get all updates.

Location and Description of sendmail Files

The sendmail configuration files are located in /etc/, as shown in Table 8-3.

MAIL GROUP "ALIAS" LISTS—ALIASES The /etc/aliases is compiled by the newaliases command into a random access database for fast alias expansions during processing. The basic format is:

```
groupname:  user01, user02, othergroupname, …
```

Once a groupname has been created, it can be included in subsequent newgroupname entries rather than having to add all the same usernames again.

TABLE 8-3

Configuration Files for sendmail

sendmail.cf	Main configuration file
aliases	List of alias names (blank initially)
sendmail.mc	m4 configuration (used to recreate sendmail.cf)
sendmail.cw	Hosts to forward to (blank initially)

REBUILD FILE—SENDMAIL.MC If your sendmail.cf file ever corrupts, fails, or becomes unusable after an edit session, you can rebuild it back to a default set of settings using the m4 configuration file sendmail.mc. The first few commented-out lines in Figure 8-30 indicate how to rebuild the sendmail.cf file. The uncommented lines at the end of the file are expanded by the m4 pre-processor to the equivalent sendmail.cf sections.

POP

The POP (Point of Presence) is a mail delivery protocol. It has very basic commands, including retrieve and send messages. A mail service can be configured to be a central depository (POP) for incoming mail messages from any other MTA service. Client applications then download the mail messages off the POP server for processing at the local host. The ipop3d daemon service handles all requests.

You can configure the ipop3d daemon service to listen for requests within the /etc/inetd.conf configuration file of the inetd service (see the code listing in the IMAP section that follows).

FIGURE 8-30

How to use the sendmail.mc file

```
======================================================================
[root@linux6 /etc]# head -9 sendmail.mc
dnl This is the macro config file used to generate the /etc/sendmail.cf
dnl file. If you modify this file you will have to regenerate the
dnl /etc/sendmail.cf by running this macro config through the m4
dnl preprocessor:
dnl
dnl        m4 /etc/sendmail.mc > /etc/sendmail.cf
dnl
dnl You will need to have the sendmail-cf package installed for this to
dnl work.
[root@linux6 /etc]# m4 sendmail.mc > sendmail.cf # rebuilts it
[root@linux6 /etc]#
======================================================================
```

You can configure user accounts that are only designed to service POP user accounts (users that log in and receive mail only), for which no interactive service is provided. The easiest method for this is to use linuxconf to configure the POP account.

IMAP

The IMAP daemon service provides another client access method: an imapd service (daemon) listens for all imap requests for mail. With IMAP, the server maintains all mail messages for the user locally, acting as the central repository of all IMAP account mail messages. This is the common service used by Web-based mail services. You do not need to have a client utility such as Netscape or Outlook. The mail user agent service is a browser-based "Web" interface. All user messages remain on the server. This makes it easy for someone traveling the world to access their mail without having to carry a laptop or hand-held computer; they can log in from any Internet terminal to retrieve their mail messages using any browser.

Configured POP and IMAP in /etc/inetd.conf

To configure a basic workstation, you need to remove the comments from the pop and imap configuration lines in /etc/inetd.conf so they look as follows:

```
==============================================================
[root@linux6 /etc]# egrep  'pop|imap' /etc/inetd.conf
# pop-2    stream  tcp     nowait  root    /usr/sbin/tcpd ipop2d
pop-3    stream  tcp     nowait  root    /usr/sbin/tcpd ipop3d
imap     stream  tcp     nowait  root    /usr/sbin/tcpd imapd
[root@linux6 /etc]#
================================================================
```

Using linuxconf

There is a /sbin/linuxconf module that can be used by experts to reconfigure the /etc/sendmail.cf file. Once manipulated by this method, there is no going back to manual editing. You need to have a fairly good understanding of the basic syntax of the sendmail configuration file to use this utility.

There are many fine books available on the subject of configuring sendmail, few of which are for the beginner. There are a few key parts that you can set up either using linuxconf or via any text editor modifying /etc/sendmail.cf directly.

CERTIFICATION OBJECTIVE 8.05

Printing

The Linux printing utilities are modeled after the BSD printing service and use the LPD service. LPD uses the /etc/printcap text file to define the printer queues, their characteristics, and destinations.

In general, a defined "printer" is a queued delivery system of data to a port or device. Most original UNIX hosts used serial ports for data connections. Printers were attached to serial ports, and print queues "fed" the data at the prescribed baud rate to the print device.

Another key feature was the ability to create a local queue name that actually redirected the print request to a network printer on another host.

The Printing Subsystem

The printing subsystem uses the LPD service. The LPD service daemon listens for requests and spawns a child process for each event so it can continue to listen for more requests.

Access Control to Printing

By default, access to printing is open to all users. To restrict access, control is provided by two means:

- Only from machines listed in the file /etc/hosts.equiv or /etc/hosts.lpd.
- If the rs capability is specified in the printcap entry for the printer being accessed, lpr requests will only be honored for those users with accounts on the machine with the printer.

Print Device Location

You do not need a printer on every machine. You can have one on any machine and have any number of remote hosts print to it. For that matter, the print queue does not even have to be a paper printer; it can be any output device such as a terminal, X Windows terminal, fax device, plotter, CAD/CAM system, and so forth. For any device other than a simple line printer, you will need a filter program to convert the input stream to the specific output stream.

exam Watch

Installation of a printer on a PC is usually to the /dev/lp0, parallel port.

Printer Configuration—/etc/printcap

You can configure printers manually or by using the graphical printtool utility if you have X Windows running. Manual printer additions require that you know what you are doing and that you know what parameters to change. For simple line printers, this can be just as quick as using the GUI interface.

Figure 8-31 shows that a queue named lp has been defined. The printer device is a BJC-600 or BJC-4000 type printer attached directly to the parallel port /dev/lp0. The default name for the first printer is normally lp in the BSD print system. You can actually have any number of alternate names for this printer if desired. This can all be configured in /etc/printcap either manually or with printtool.

Using the Print Configuration Utility—printtool

The printtool X Windows tool can be used to display, change, and add printers to the local system. The syntax of the /etc/printcap file is very specific. Once you have used printtool to modify this file, you should avoid manually changing /etc/printcap.

You can start the printtool utility either from linuxconf or directly from the command line by its name. You would run it in the background if your

FIGURE 8-31

GUI setup of printers—printtool

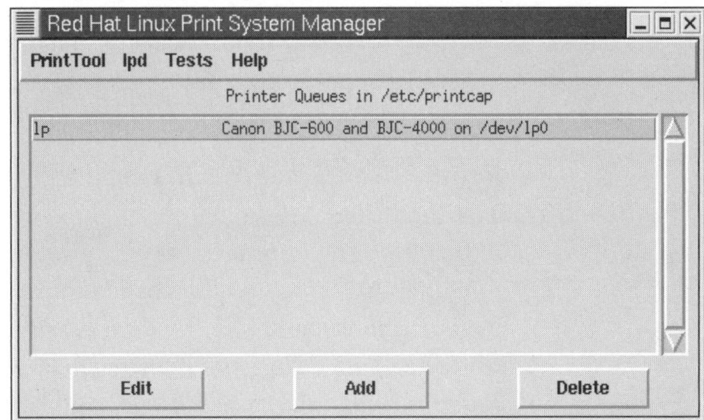

system is running X Windows, as it automatically detects the environment as terminal or X mode.

```
[root@rh6laptop /root]# printtool &
```

Adding Local and Remote Printers

Using the printtool utility is the safest practice. This utility has an easy-to-understand interface. When the printtool is invoked, you are shown any current configured printers and are given a choice of Add, Edit, Remove, Cancel, or Quit

If you click Add Printer, you are walked through the following steps:

1. What type of printer: Local, Remote LPD, SMB, or NetWare?
2. Name(s) for this queue:

   Separate each name with a "|" symbol (e.g., lp2|slow|ttyprinter).
   The first name is the primary name for all options.
   The default is to number printers as lp, lp1, lp2, etc.
3. Spooling directory (defaults to /var/spool/lpd/*firstname*).

4. File size limit (defaults to 0, allows any file size, up to you).
5. Lists known devices (defaults to lp0: parallel port 1).
6. Input filter (you must select from the many options).

Print Filter System for Local Printers

The print filter file is only required for newer printers. Basic line printers, such as dot matrix printers that only print text, do not need a filter. Anything that can do graphics of any sort will need a print filter. Most modern printers need a filter. Not every printer will appear on the list. You will have to use the closest alternate model, usually one or at most two revisions behind the current driver. Updated filters can be gotten from the Web when they are made available.

In Figure 8-32, you can see the wide assortment of printers that have print filters already created for them. Select the model closest to your product if it is not one of the choices presented.

FIGURE 8-32

Selecting a print filter with printtool

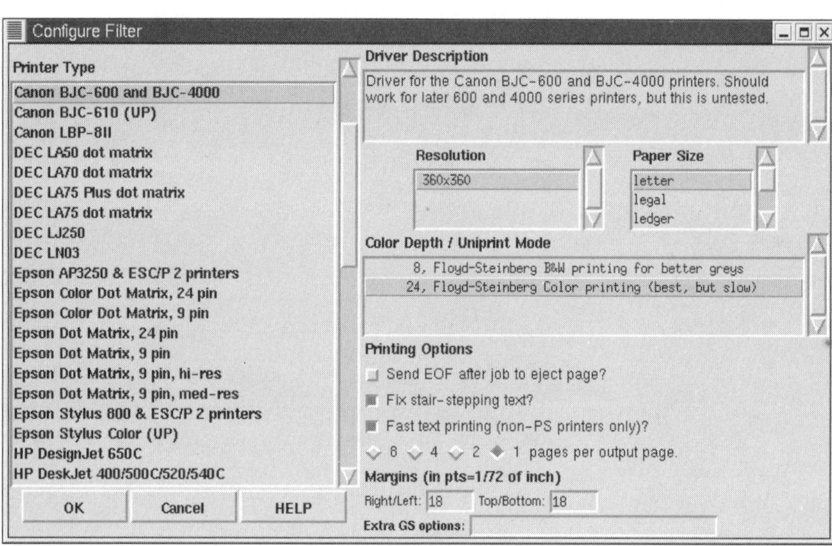

You also have printer characteristics to select from: tray size, resolution, color resolution if applicable, quick bug fix options, margin sizes, and so forth.

The final details of the installed printer are shown in Figure 8-33. A Canon BJC4100 printer on the parallel port was the device that the print queue named lp will print to.

To edit any printer entry, click on the entry, then click Edit.

/etc/printcap File

This is the basic configuration file that is read by the print system daemon at initialization. It is a simple text file with one long entry for each printer. Usually, these long entries are spread across many lines by using the backslash as the last character on a line, thus extending the command syntax to the next line. An example is given in Figure 8-32; the three lines that make up the remote printer access control are actually one line.

Each entry represents one print queue. If this is a local printer, it can have any number of names, but it requires a local spooling directory for the data files submitted, and at least a destination file representing the port. Additionally, it may require a value for "if", the input filter, that translates the character stream to specific device request format.

The entries for the local printer BJ4100 printer and a remote printer in the /etc/printcap file are shown in Figure 8-34.

FIGURE 8-33

Add or edit a printer with printtool

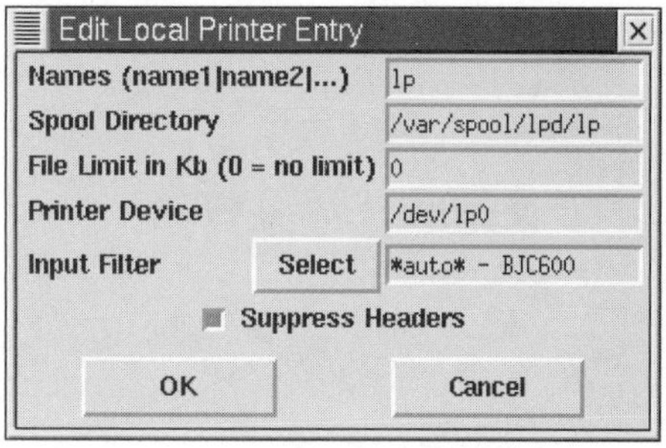

Edit Local Printer Entry
Names (name1|name2|...) lp
Spool Directory /var/spool/lpd/lp
File Limit in Kb (0 = no limit) 0
Printer Device /dev/lp0
Input Filter Select *auto* - BJC600
Suppress Headers
OK Cancel

FIGURE 8-34

Printer entries in /etc/printcap

```
============================================================
[root@rh6laptop /root]# cat /etc/printcap
#
# Please don't edit this file directly unless you know what you are doing!
# Be warned that the control-panel printtool requires a very strict format!
# Look at the printcap(5) man page for more info.
#
# This file can be edited with the printtool in the control-panel.


##PRINTTOOL3## LOCAL bjc600 360x360 letter {} BJC600 24 1
lp:\
    :sd=/var/spool/lpd/lp:\
    :mx#0:\
    :sh:\
    :lp=/dev/lp0:\
    :if=/var/spool/lpd/lp/filter:
#
# NEXT entry is for a remote LPD printer service
##PRINTTOOL3## REMOTE ljet4 300x300 letter {} LaserJet4 Default {}
lp0|hp6|laser:\
        :sd=/var/spool/lpd/lp0:\
        :mx#0:\
        :sh:\
        :rm=206.195.1.222:\
        :rp=lp:\
        :if=/var/spool/lpd/lp0/filter:
[root@rh6laptop /root]#
============================================================
```

Figure 8-34 has one local and one remote entry. The remote entry is using the IP address. You could also use the hostname if it was resolvable by either /etc/hosts or DNS.

/etc/hosts.lpd File

Access can be restricted by implementing the access control file list, /etc/hosts.lpd. For each host or network, put one line entry into this file.

Using lpc, lpq, and lprm

The lpd service includes three user utilities that are used to add print requests, list queued print requests, and remove print requests: lpr, lpq, and lprm, respectively. There is also a single administration control and management utility called lpc.

lpc—LINE PRINT CONTROL (OF QUEUES) UTILITY You can use lpc to control, start, and stop all local queues if you have the privilege. The lpc utility is not commonly available to users, just superusers.

To view all known queues, use the status option to lpc as illustrated in Figure 8-35.

lpr—LINE PRINT REQUEST UTILITY Any user can use the lpr utility to send print requests to any local queue name. You can lpr any files to a queue, or you can redirect any output via lpr. To print to any specific-named queue, precede the queue name with "-P", (with no space between this and the queue name). Figure 8-36 illustrates this feature.

lpq—LINE PRINT QUEUE (PRINT STATUS) UTILITY To view jobs that have not printed or are currently being printed, you can use

FIGURE 8-35

Using lpc

```
==========================================================
[root@rh6laptop /root]# lpc status
lp:
        queuing is enabled
        printing is enabled
        no entries
        no daemon present
lp0:
        queuing is enabled
        printing is enabled
        no entries
        no daemon present
[root@rh6laptop /root]# lpc stop lp
lp:
        printing disabled
[root@rh6laptop /root]# lpc stop lp0
lp0:
        printing disabled
[root@rh6laptop /root]#
============================================================
```

FIGURE 8-36

Using lpr

```
==========================================================================
[root@rh6laptop /root]# lpr /etc/hosts
[root@rh6laptop /root]# lpr -Plp0 /etc/printcap
[root@rh6laptop /root]#
==========================================================================
```

the lpq command. You can use the same printer queue name specification, but precede the queue name with "-P", as illustrated in Figure 8-37.

lprm—LINE PRINT REMOVE (QUEUED JOBS) UTILITY

The final user utility is used to remove currently nonprinting jobs. You need to know the print queue entry number, as obtained with the lpq utility shown in Figure 3-36. You can specify the specific queue by preceding the queue name with "-P" as illustrated in Figure 8-38.

There are more options to most of these utilities. See the man pages for more details.

FIGURE 8-37

Using lpq

```
==========================================================================
[root@rh6laptop /root]# lpq
Warning: lp is down: printing disabled
Warning: no daemon present
Rank   Owner      Job  Files                                 Total Size
1st    root       0    /etc/hosts                            125 bytes
[root@rh6laptop /root]# lpq -Plp0
rh6laptop: Warning: lp0 is down: printing disabled
rh6laptop: printing disabled
Rank   Owner      Job  Files                                 Total Size
1st    root       0    /etc/printcap                         620 bytes

connection to 206.195.1.222 is down
[root@rh6laptop /root]#
==========================================================================
```

FIGURE 8-38

Using lprm

```
===========================================================================
[root@rh6laptop /root]# lprm 0
dfA000AGAeb31 dequeued
cfA000AGAeb31 dequeued
[root@rh6laptop /root]# lprm -Plp0 0
dfA000AzPEIcp dequeued
cfA000AzPEIcp dequeued
connection to 206.195.1.222 is down
[root@rh6laptop /root]#
===========================================================================
```

Using Other Print Services

Linux can also connect to remote printer services such as any LPD service on any other host (UNIX, Linux, NT running LPD, etc.), any SMB type printers from Windows or Samba services, and any Novell-based print services. For Novell-based print services, you will not be able to print to a NetWare printer without ncpfs (Novell File System) installed. If you are not interested in Novell printers, you do not need to install ncpfs. If you are not interested in Windows-based printers, you do not need Samba services installed.

Selecting a Network Print Service

Other print services can also be attached to using the printtool utility, as illustrated in Figure 8-39.

When you add a network printer queue, you can use any name you want locally that is unique. You are not required to use the same name as the remote queue.

Remote LDP Service

To connect to any LPD type service, you will need the IP (or equivalent resolvable name for the host) and the name of the queue at the remote site.

FIGURE 8-39

Adding a network print service

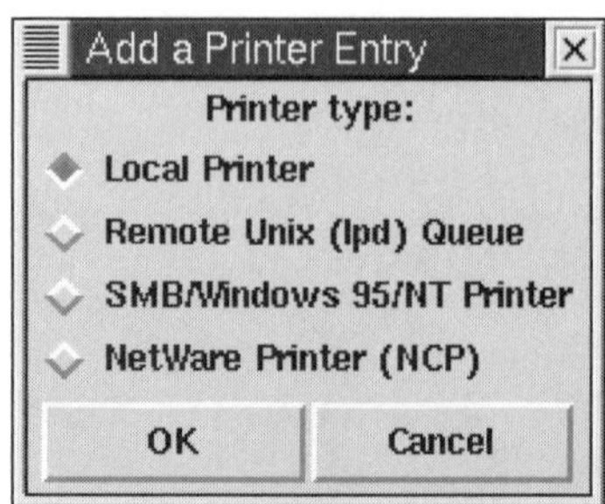

You may need to know the filter program if it is on a foreign operating system, such as NT.

Most network print devices can be accessed as though they were an LPD service, such as HP Jetdirect ports. These can also be reached via NetWare if configured that way.

Printing with Samba

To connect to an SMB service, you will need either the NetBIOS name or the IP address and the name of the shared print service. You will most likely need a print filter for the remote printer to be installed locally. This may vary, so test before using.

Connect to Novell Print Service

If your network already contains a NetWare server providing print services, you can create a printer connection using the printtool interface.

You will need to have installed the ncpfs. You will then need to know the name of the preferred server and the printer name, and a valid username and related password. Add the print filter if needed.

Remember to always test your printers thoroughly before putting them into production.

QUESTIONS AND ANSWERS	
Your boss has decided that everyone in the company should have easy access to the human resources information pertaining to all employees, such as their benefits and services.	Set up the Apache Web Server to share all the HR documents only to the local network. Let HR figure out how to create the HTML. Then fix it.
The benefits package for most new hires has two 50-page parts to it that the human resources people want the users to be able to download from anywhere.	Set up the wu-ftp service with restricted access to the HR site documents for only logged-on users. Do not allow anonymous login to access this site.
Human Resources would like all users to be able to post their ideas and complaints to a central service that they can easily deal with on a day-by-day basis	Set up interoffice mail services and create two specific accounts to handle ideas and complaints.
Naturally, everyone wants to be able to print to the latest and greatest color laser printer hanging off the newest PC on the network.	Depending on the host operating system of the new PC, you have several options: Samba, if it is NT/Win9x; LPD, if it is Linux/UNIX; or NetWare (or Macintosh) services. Set up as appropriate.

CERTIFICATION SUMMARY

Most of the services that you would want as a basic user are configured during a Workstation installation. As an administrator, you would probably have to configure a few additional aspects for access or use of any centralized services like e-mail, DNS or hosts table, Web, print, and Samba services.

After a Server installation, you will need to configure all of the centralized services that this, and every other, server will offer, such as e-mail, Web, Samba services, anonymous and/or controlled FTP services, and print services.

Most of these services have a main configuration file as well as some security control files, commonly all found in /etc, but this varies. These services use text-based configuration files that can be manipulated using any text editor individually or all together via linuxconf.

TWO-MINUTE DRILL

- ❑ Red Hat Linux includes the Apache Web Server. The Apache Web Server is currently used by more Internet Web sites than all the other Web servers combined.
- ❑ Web services are the easiest way to provide simple, secure access to documents of any type. The Apache Web Server provides both normal and secure Web services using the HTTP and HTTPS protocols, respectively. The Apache Web Server has extensive functionality and can be further extended using add-ins and macros to provide additional services.
- ❑ If you selected a Server installation, you already have the Apache Web Server installed. If you selected a Workstation installation or a Custom installation and did not select the Web Server optional package set, you will need to install it.
- ❑ You can get the latest information, documentation, upgrades, options, patches, bug fixes, and more from the Apache Web site at http://www.apache.org/.
- ❑ The FTP, or File Transfer Protocol, service has been around a long time. There are two application-related sides to FTP, the client and the server. The client application is available and, usually, freely supplied on all other operating systems when they support the TCP/IP protocol suite. The server application is common on most Web hosting machines and predates the actual Web as the normal Internet method of transferring files between any types of systems.
- ❑ There are two packages that you can install, anonftp and wu-ftp. The anonftp package provides anonymous access to anyone without the need for specific user accounts. You can install the anonftp rpm package if it is not already installed. The installation creates a /home/ftp tree and populates it with a minimal set of directories and files. You should add files to the /home/ftp/pub directory that are to be made available to anonymous logins for download to their machines only.
- ❑ The wu-ftp provides sophisticated features related to user management. With it, you can establish many more features and

controls on many more objects. Additional features include control of transfer and command logs, on-the-fly compression and archiving (using gzip), user type and location classification, limits on a per-class (local, remote) basis, directory upload permissions, restricted guest accounts, messages per directory and system, and virtual name support.

- ❑ The FTP service daemon is actually started from the inetd super daemon. The inetd daemon listens for all configured protocols other than HTTP usually. Each service protocol to listen for is specified in /etc/inetd.conf. The inetd, INET Daemon process, launches the specific service whenever an incoming packet is received for that service.
- ❑ Starting with Windows 3.11, Windows clients could '"share" their file systems and printers for other Windows clients to "map to" as remote resources. This sharing was provided through a facility called SMB, Server Message Block, a.k.a. NetBIOS. Through the collective works of Andrew Tridgell and many others, Linux systems provide SMB support over TCP/IP via a package known as Samba.
- ❑ There are both client and server portions to Samba services. You should be familiar with the basic steps of how to configure the server characteristics and the shared services.
- ❑ If you have Linux, you have a powerful mail server. The Internet is predominantly using sendmail, and Linux has a very current version of it as well as some of the other popular mail services.
- ❑ You can configure user accounts that are only designed to service POP user accounts, users that log in and receive mail only, no interactive service is provided. The easiest method is to use linuxconf to configure the POP account.
- ❑ The Linux printing utilities are modeled after the BSD printing service and use the LPD service. LPD uses the /etc/printcap text file to define the printer queues, their characteristics, and their destinations.

SELF TEST

The following Self Test questions will help you measure your understanding of the material presented in this chapter. Read all the choices carefully, as there may be more than one correct answer. Choose all correct answers for each question.

1. What service would you use to provide human resource documents to any or selected users on the network?

   A. Samba
   B. Apache
   C. X Windows
   D. FTP

2. The human resource department wants to restrict access to its Web site. What features of the Apache Web Server could you incorporate?

   A. Virtual Host
   B. Port 4001
   C. access.conf
   D. All of the above

3. The sales department wants to amalgamate its Web service with the HR department to save money. What is the easiest way to do this?

   A. Virtual Host
   B. .htaccess
   C. DocumentRoot
   D. memory

4. The sales department wants to keep detailed and separate log files about page hits and error messages. Which options should it use?

   A. Virtual Host
   B. CustomLog
   C. DocumentRoot
   D. ErrorLog

5. When you view all system processes, you notice there are over 35 HTTP daemons running. You thought you configured 10. What has happened?

   A. It is spiraling out of control.
   B. Each virtual service can call up to three times its base number of daemons.
   C. There may be some FTP service requests.
   D. Apache is dynamically configuring for current load needs.

6. You copy over the Windows-based Web site to your site, set up the virtual host, and try to hit the homepage, but it fails. Which of these could be the problem if this was a straightforward Web site copy of existing files that worked?

   A. DocumentRoot
   B. Port Number
   C. index.html
   D. Wrong browser settings

7. Finally, you accessed your site, late at night, from your home office. Too bad you have a slow modem connection. How can you test the Web site without a graphical interface?

   A. SWAT

   B. lynx

   C. linuxconf

   D. netscape -text

8. The sales department wants to make test results, FAQs, and new product data sheets available to resellers for their own sales literature. How would you make the material available to them for quick downloads?

   A. Samba

   B. Apache

   C. FTP

   D. Anonymous FTP

9. The sales department wants to know if it can selectively give access to certain users to certain directories. Which FTP options could be used?

   A. .htaccess

   B. ftpaccess

   C. rpm

   D. hosts.allow

10. When a user logs in anonymously, she cannot access any of the sales documents. There are no documents available at all. Why might that be?

    A. Virtual host points to wrong system.

    B. DocumentRoot set incorrectly.

    C. Ftpaccess file does not point to correct directory.

    D. Anonymous FTP is separate from wu-ftp.

11. You notice no ftpd service running when you randomly check your system, but no complaints have been made. Why is there no daemon?

    A. It is awakened by inetd as needed.

    B. It only runs at designated intervals of the day.

    C. Nobody uses it; system cleans house regularly.

    D. It runs out of memory.

12. The sales force complains occasionally that they are refused an FTP connection even though their customers never see this. What may be set too low?

    A. Access times

    B. Local login limit

    C. Limited number of daemons

    D. System memory

13. There is a rogue set of users on the curriculum development team who insist on using their own equipment on their own network. Corporate wants to share information with their Windows-only network without having to retrain them. Which service should you install on Linux to "'join" with theirs?

A. Apache Web Services
B. FTP GUI Clients
C. Samba Services
D. There is nothing you can do

14. The rogue curriculum people have set up an NT server to handle their printing and file services. It uses WINS for name resolution, and all user logins are at the domain server. You just want to make connections to some server-hidden shares and back up these files for them. What options would you configure in Samba?

A. BrowseMaster
B. WINS Server IP as Client
C. NT Server for Authentication
D. Special Backup share service from your machine to copy files to

15. Which is not a component of the Samba File Sharing Service?

A. /usr/bin/smbd
B. /usr/bin/nmbd
C. /usr/bin/smbclient
D. /etc/smb.conf

16. You made a couple of quick changes to your Samba configuration file and you need to test it quickly for syntax errors. Which utility should you run?

A. smbmount
B. smbclient
C. smbfs
D. testparm

17. You are asked to share the HR downloadable documents to Windows users who are not that familiar with FTP and want a shared drive connection. How do you force the Samba service to reread the configuration file immediately?

A. testparm
B. /etc/smb.conf
C. /etc/rc.d/init.d/smb
D. /etc/samba/restart

18. The Windows users are complaining that they cannot see the HR document share in their Network Neighborhood diagram. What option is missing from smb.conf?

A. Hidden = no
B. Browseable = yes
C. NetworkDisplay = on
D. Viewable = no

19. One of your Linux workstation clients needs to get at a file from one of the curriculum developers who has a basic Win98 machine and has created a shared service to the files that are to be retrieved. What utility would you introduce to the Linux user that she would probably know how to use if you showed her once?

A. smbmount
B. smbfs
C. smbclient
D. smb

20. Suddenly, many more users are requesting access to the curriculum development files because they need to make some technical changes on a regular basis. If they are all connecting to just one server host, how could you make the service "'local"?

    A. smbclient-all

    B. smbmount

    C. smbfs

    D. /etc/rc.d/init.d/smbstatus

21. A few other departments have been using their own DOS-based mailing systems. The company wants to use a standard service so both employees and customers can all use the same system. What would be the best choice?

    A. Internet Explorer 53

    B. DaVinci Mail

    C. DaMail Mail

    D. sendmail

22. Some of the salespeople are no longer local, and they need to be able to get their mail from any Web-based server in the world. What option would you configure for this?

    A. sendmail—Web interface

    B. POP3 daemon

    C. IMAP daemon

    D. Apache Mail interface

23. Your system has become very large. You want to look at your current printer configuration in X Windows. What utility might you use?

    A. smbclient

    B. /etc/printcap

    C. printtool

    D. lprsetup

24. The HR and sales departments want to restrict the users who can print to their printers. What file can be used to restrict access to print services?

    A. printtool

    B. /etc/printcap

    C. /etc/lpraccess

    D. /etc/hosts.lpd

9

Network Management

CERTIFICATION OBJECTIVES

9.01	DNS/Bind
9.02	Squid Proxy Server
9.03	NFS
9.04	Internet News
9.05	DHCP/Bootp
9.06	Other File-Sharing Methods
9.07	Time Synchronization
9.08	PPP Configuration (as a Client) Using netcfg and the Files Generated

More complex networking services in Red Hat Linux require more advanced administration methods. While graphical tools such as linuxconf are available to assist in configuring all aspects of Linux networking, a more concrete knowledge of the concepts is gained by appreciating the command-line environment of the network services.

The first section of this chapter discusses the Domain Name System (DNS). This service allows human-readable domain names (e.g., www.redhat.com) to be translated into machine-readable IP addresses (e.g., 206.132.41.202), and vice versa. The next section goes into the Squid proxy server, which serves as a mediator between an end user and a Web site. The caching server can make a user's performance in Net surfing increase considerably. A large section on the Network File System (NFS) discusses a powerful and versatile way of sharing file systems between servers and workstations. The section on Internet News outlines the old familiar Usenet, and how to run a server on your network for local users. DHCP allows a Linux server to serve out dynamic IP addresses. The PPP section demonstrates how a Linux server can use a dial-up connection for individual or network Internet access.

CERTIFICATION OBJECTIVE 9.01

DNS/Bind

DNS is the Domain Name System. DNS converts machine names and IP addresses. It maps from name to address and from address to name, and provides other useful information to machines and their users.

In this section, two server configurations will be discussed: a caching-only server and a primary DNS server for a domain. Files such as /etc/nsswitch.conf, /etc/resolv.conf and /etc/hosts should already be set up properly on the DNS server. This setup also assumes the server is not behind any kind of firewall that blocks name queries.

A program called named does name serving on Red Hat Linux. This is a part of the BIND (Berkeley Internet Name Daemon) package that is coordinated by Paul Vixie for the Internet Software Consortium. Named is included in most Red Hat Linux installations and is usually installed as /usr/sbin/named. If named is not on the server, download a binary from a Linux FTP site, or get the latest source from ftp://ftp.isc.org/isc/bind/src/cur/bind-8/. There are two versions of BIND currently available, BIND 4 and BIND 8. BIND 8 uses a configuration file known as /etc/named.conf, and BIND 4 uses /etc/named.boot. These two versions are radically different, so only BIND 8 will be discussed here. BIND 4 has serious security concerns associated with it, so BIND 8 is highly recommended. Red Hat 6.*x* ships with BIND 8.

A Caching-Only Name Server

A caching-only name server will find the answer to name queries and remember the answer the next time you need it. This will shorten the waiting time of the next inquiry significantly, especially for a slow or shared connection. The first file to look at is /etc/named.conf. This is read when named starts. For now, it should simply contain:

```
// Config file for caching only name server
  options {
          directory "/var/named";
          // Uncommenting this might help if you have to go through a
          // firewall and things are not working out:
          // query-source port 53;
  };
  zone "." {
          type hint;
          file "root.hints";
  };
  zone "0.0.127.in-addr.arpa" {
          type master;
          file "pz/127.0.0";
  };
```

The "directory" line tells named where to look for files. All files named subsequently will be relative to this. For example, pz is a directory under /var/named; in other words, /var/named/pz. /var/named is the right directory according to the Linux File Hierarchy Standard. The file named /var/named/root.hints is named in this. /var/named/root.hints should contain:

```
;
.                    6D IN NS        G.ROOT-SERVERS.NET.
.                    6D IN NS        J.ROOT-SERVERS.NET.
.                    6D IN NS        K.ROOT-SERVERS.NET.
.                    6D IN NS        L.ROOT-SERVERS.NET.
.                    6D IN NS        M.ROOT-SERVERS.NET.
.                    6D IN NS        A.ROOT-SERVERS.NET.
.                    6D IN NS        H.ROOT-SERVERS.NET.
.                    6D IN NS        B.ROOT-SERVERS.NET.
.                    6D IN NS        C.ROOT-SERVERS.NET.
.                    6D IN NS        D.ROOT-SERVERS.NET.
.                    6D IN NS        E.ROOT-SERVERS.NET.
.                    6D IN NS        I.ROOT-SERVERS.NET.
.                    6D IN NS        F.ROOT-SERVERS.NET.

G.ROOT-SERVERS.NET.     5w6d16h IN A    192.112.36.4
J.ROOT-SERVERS.NET.     5w6d16h IN A    198.41.0.10
K.ROOT-SERVERS.NET.     5w6d16h IN A    193.0.14.129
L.ROOT-SERVERS.NET.     5w6d16h IN A    198.32.64.12
M.ROOT-SERVERS.NET.     5w6d16h IN A    202.12.27.33
A.ROOT-SERVERS.NET.     5w6d16h IN A    198.41.0.4
H.ROOT-SERVERS.NET.     5w6d16h IN A    128.63.2.53
B.ROOT-SERVERS.NET.     5w6d16h IN A    128.9.0.107
C.ROOT-SERVERS.NET.     5w6d16h IN A    192.33.4.12
D.ROOT-SERVERS.NET.     5w6d16h IN A    128.8.10.90
E.ROOT-SERVERS.NET.     5w6d16h IN A    192.203.230.10
I.ROOT-SERVERS.NET.     5w6d16h IN A    192.36.148.17
F.ROOT-SERVERS.NET.     5w6d16h IN A    192.5.5.241
```

The file describes the root name servers in the world. This changes over time and must be maintained. A shell script for maintaining this file can be found at the end of this section.

The next section in named.conf is the last zone. A file named 127.0.0.0 in the subdirectory pz should contain:

```
@     IN   SOA   ns.your-domain.com. hostmaster.your-domain.com. (
                                 1        ; Serial
                                 8H       ; Refresh
                                 2H       ; Retry
                                 1W       ; Expire
                                 1D)      ; Minimum TTL
                           NS    ns.your-domain.com.
 1                         PTR   localhost.
```

Next, */etc/resolv.conf* should look something like this:

```
search subdomain.your-domain.com your-domain.com
nameserver 127.0.0.1
```

The "search" line specifies what domains should be searched for any hostnames that may be required. The "nameserver" line specifies the address of the local nameserver; in this case, the local server, since that is where named runs (127.0.0.1 is right, no matter if the machine has another address as well). If a list of several nameservers is required, put in one "nameserver" line for each. (Note: named never reads this file, the resolver that uses named does.)

Here's an example to illustrate what this file does: If a client tries to look up host, then host.subdomain.your-domain.com is tried first, then host.your- domain.com, then finally host. If a client tries to look up ftp.redhat.com, ftp.redhat.com.subdomain.your-domain.com is tried first, then ftp.redhat.com.your-domain.com, and finally ftp.redhat.com. Do not put too many domains in the search line; it takes time to search them all.

The example assumes that the server belongs in the domain subdomain.your-domain.com; the server is probably called your-machine.subdomain.your-domain.com. The search line should not contain a TLD (Top Level Domain, "com" in this case). If there is a frequent need to connect to hosts in another domain, that domain can be added to the search line like this:

```
search subdomain.your-domain.com your-domain.com other-domain.com
```

Obviously, real domain names should be used. Please note the lack of periods at the end of the domain names. This is important, and will be explained momentarily.

Next look at /etc/nsswitch.conf. This is a long file specifying where to get different kinds of data types, from what file or database. It usually contains helpful comments at the top, which should be read. After that, find the line starting with "hosts:". It should read:

```
hosts:      files dns
```

If there is no line starting with "hosts:", then put in the one above. It says that programs should first look in the /etc/hosts file, then check DNS according to resolv.conf.

Starting Named

After all this, it's time to start named. The server should be connected to the Internet before starting named. Type **ndc start**, and press RETURN, no options. If that does not work, try **/usr/sbin/ndc start** instead. If you view the syslog message file (usually called /var/log/messages) while starting named (do tail -f /var/log/messages), you should see something like:

```
        Oct 10 12:23:34 ns named[2795]: starting.  named 8.1.1
Sun Oct 10 12:23:34 EDT 1999 root@ns:/var/tmp/bind-8.1.1/named
        Oct 10 12:23:34 ns named[2795]: cache zone ""
(IN) loaded (serial 0)
        Oct 10 12:23:34 ns named[2795]: master zone
"0.0.127.in-addr.arpa" (IN) loaded (serial 1)
        Oct 10 12:23:34 ns named[2795]: listening [127.0.0.1].53 (lo)
        Oct 10 12:23:34 ns named[2795]: listening [10.0.0.1].53 (eth0)
        Oct 10 12:23:34 ns named[2795]: Forwarding source address is
 [0.0.0.0].1040
        Oct 10 12:23:34 ns named[2795]: Ready to answer queries.
```

If there are any messages about errors, then there is a mistake. named will name the file with the error (one of named.conf and root.hints). Stop named, and go back and check the files.

Now test the setup. Start nslookup to examine the work.

```
$ nslookup
Default Server:  localhost
Address:  127.0.0.1
>
```

If something other than the above appears, go back and check everything. Each time the named.conf file is changed, restart named using the ndc restart command. Now enter a query:

```
> mail.redhat.com
Server:  localhost
Address:  127.0.0.1

Name:    mail.redhat.com
Address:  199.183.24.239
```

nslookup now asks named to look for the machine mail.redhat.com. It then contacts one of the nameserver machines named in the root.hints file and asks its way from there. It might take a little while before the result comes back, as nslookup may need to search all the domains in /etc/resolv.conf.

If the same query is made again:

```
   > mail.redhat.com
 Server:  localhost
 Address:  127.0.0.1

Non-authoritative answer:
Name:    mail.redhat.com
Address:  199.183.24.239
```

Note the "Non-authoritative answer:" line that appears this time around. This means that named did not go out on the network to ask this time; the information is in the cache now. However, the cached information might be out of date (stale). So nslookup announces this (very slight) possibility by saying "Non-authoritative answer:". When nslookup says this the second time a host is queried, it's a sure sign that named cached the information and that it's working. Exit nslookup by giving the command "exit".

A Simple Domain

Now a simple domain can be defined. The domain will be your-domain.com, and it will define machines in it. Not all characters are allowed in hostnames. DNS is restricted to the characters of the English alphabet a–z, and numbers 0–9 and the character - (dash). Upper and lowercase characters are the same for DNS, so Mail.Your-Domain.Com is equivalent to mail.your-domain.com. You've already seen the named.conf file set up in an earlier code example. Note the lack of a period (.) at the end of the domain names in this file. This says that the zone 0.0.127.in-addr.arpa will be defined, that the localhost is the master server for it, and that it is stored in a file called pz/127.0.0. You've already seen that file set up in an earlier code example.

Please note the period (.) at the end of all the full domain names in pz/127.0.0, in contrast to the named.conf file. Some people like to start each zone file with a $ORIGIN directive, but this is superfluous. The origin (the place in the DNS hierarchy that it belongs) of a zone file is specified in the zone section of the named.conf file; in this case, it's 0.0.127.in-addr.arpa.

This *zone file* contains three *resource records* (RRs): an SOA RR, an NS RR, and a PTR RR. SOA is short for Start of Authority. The @ is a special notation meaning the origin, and since the "domain" column for this file says 0.0.127.in-addr.arpa, the first line really means:

```
0.0.127.in-addr.arpa.    IN      SOA ...
```

NS is the Name Server RR. There is no @ at the start of this line; it is implicit since the last line started with a @. So, the NS line could also be written:

```
0.0.127.in-addr.arpa.    IN      NS      ns.your-domain.com.
```

It tells DNS that ns.your-domain.com is the nameserver of the domain 0.0.127.in-addr.arpa. "ns" is a customary name for nameservers, but as with Web servers, which are customarily named www.something.com, the name may be anything. Finally, the PTR record says that the host at address 1 in the subnet 0.0.127.in-addr.arpa (i.e., 127.0.0.1) is named localhost.

The SOA record is the preamble to all zone files, and there should be exactly one in each zone file. It describes the zone, where it comes from (a machine called ns.your-domain.com), who is responsible for its contents (hostmaster@your-domain.com, insert the proper e-mail address here), which version of the zone file this is (serial: 1), and other things having to do with caching and secondary DNS servers. For the rest of the fields (refresh, retry, expire, and minimum), the numbers described here are safe, but the files should be individualized for each network. Now insert a new "'zone" section in named.conf:

```
      zone "your-domain.com" {
type master;
          file "pz/your-domain.com";
  };
```

Note again the lack of an ending period (.) on the domain name in the named.conf file. Now populate the your-domain.com zone file:

```
;
; Zone file for your-domain.com
;
; The full zone file
;
@    IN    SOA  ns.your-domain.com. hostmaster.your-domain.com. (
                199910101  ; serial, todays date + todays serial #
                         8H              ; refresh, seconds
```

```
                        2H              ; retry, seconds
                        1W              ; expire, seconds
                        1D )            ; minimum, seconds
;
     TXT      "your-domain.com, your domain"
     NS       ns.your-domain.com. ; Internet Address of name server
     NS       ns2.your-domain.com.
     MX       10 mail.your-domain.com. ; Primary Mail Exchanger
     MX       20 mail2.your-domain.com. ; Secondary Mail Exchanger

localhost         A        127.0.0.1

gw                A        192.168.196.1
                  HINFO    "Cisco" "IOS"
                  TXT      "The router"

ns                A        192.168.196.2
                  MX       10 mail.your-domain.com.
                  MX       20 mail2.your-domain.com.
                  HINFO    "Pentium" "Linux 2.2"
www               CNAME    ns

ns2               A        192.168.196.3
                  MX       10 mail.your-domain.com.
                  MX       20 mail2.your-domain.com.
                  HINFO    "i486"       "Linux 2.0"
                  TXT      "DEK"

mail              A        192.168.196.4
      MX          10 mail.your-domain.com.
                  MX       20 mail2.your-domain.com.
                  HINFO    "386sx" "Linux 1.2"

mail2               A        192.168.196.5
       MX         10 mail.your-domain.com.
                  MX       20 mail2.your-domain.com.
                  HINFO    "P6" "Linux 2.1.86"

ftp               CNAME    mail2
```

Two things must be noted about the SOA record. ns.your-domain.com must be an actual machine with an A record. It is not legal to have a CNAME (Canonical NAME) record for the machine mentioned in the SOA record. Its name need not be "ns"; it could be any legal hostname. Next, hostmaster.your-domain.com should be read as hostmaster@your-domain.com—this should be a mail alias, or a mailbox, where the person(s) maintaining DNS should read mail frequently. Any mail regarding the domain will be sent to the address listed here. The name need not be "hostmaster"; it can be a normal e-mail address, but the e-mail address "hostmaster" is often expected to work as well.

There are a number of new RRs here: HINFO (Host INFOrmation) has two parts; it's a good habit to quote each. The first part is the hardware or CPU on the machine, and the second part is the software or OS on the machine. The machine called "ns" has a Pentium CPU and runs Linux 2.2.

CNAME is a way to give each machine several names. For example, www is an alias for ns. CNAME record usage is a bit controversial; however, it's safe to follow the rule that an MX, CNAME, or SOA record should never refer to a CNAME record, they should only refer to something with an A record. It's also safe to assume that a CNAME is not a legal hostname for an e-mail address: webmaster@www.your-domain.com is an illegal e-mail address given the setup shown previously (that is what MX (Mail eXchanger) records are for). Expect many mail administrators to enforce this rule even if it works for some. The way to avoid this is to use A records (and perhaps some others too, like an MX record) instead. Many DNS administrators recommend not using CNAME at all.

The MX RR tells mail systems where to send mail that is addressed to someone@your-domain.com; namely, to mail.your-domain.com or mail2.your-domain.com. The number before each machine name is that MX RR's priority. The RR with the lowest number (10) is the one that mail should be sent to if possible. If that fails, the mail can be sent to one with a higher number, a secondary mail handler (i.e., mail2.your-domain.com, which has priority 20 here). Restart named by running ndc restart. Examine the results with nslookup:

```
$ nslookup
Default Server:  localhost
Address:  127.0.0.1

> ls -d your-domain.com
```

This means that all records should be listed. The results should look very similar to the zone file itself.

The Reverse Zone

Now programs can convert the names in your-domain.com to addresses that they can connect to. Also required is a *reverse* (or *inverse*) *zone*, one making DNS able to convert from an address to a name. This name is used by many servers of different kinds (FTP, IRC, WWW, and others) to decide if they want to talk to a given server or not, and if so, maybe even how much priority it should be given. For full access to all services on the Internet, a reverse zone is required. Add another zone to named.conf:

```
zone "196.168.192.in-addr.arpa" {
type master;
          file "pz/192.168.196";
  };
```

This is exactly as with the 0.0.127.in-addr.arpa, and the contents are similar:

```
@    IN    SOA   ns.your-domain.com. hostmaster.your-domain.com. (
           199910101 ; Serial, todays date + todays serial
                          8H       ; Refresh
                          2H       ; Retry
                          1W       ; Expire
                          1D)      ; Minimum TTL
                NS        ns.your-domain.com.

  1             PTR       gw.your-domain.com.
  2             PTR       ns.your-domain.com.
  3             PTR       ns2.your-domain.com.
  4             PTR       mail.your-domain.com.
  5             PTR       mail2.your-domain.com.
```

Once again, restart named and examine the output of nslookup. If the results do not look similar to the actual zone file, look for error messages in the syslog.

Common DNS Pitfalls

DNS is a net-wide database. Make sure the information that goes into the database is up to date and well formatted. Many network outages can be traced to poorly administered DNS servers. A few examples of common DNS errors are shown in the following sections.

The Serial Number Wasn't Incremented

The single most common DNS error occurs when an administrator makes updates to a zone file, restarts DNS, and notices that no one else on the Internet knows about the updates. If a DNS server doesn't detect a new serial number on a zone file, it assumes the file is the same, and sticks with its cache. The serial number is the first thing that should be edited when updating a zone file. Be sure to put the current date (with a four-digit year!) on it, and increment the last number if necessary.

The Reverse Zone Isn't Delegated

When a service provider assigns a network-address range and a domain name, the domain name is normally delegated as a matter of course. A *delegation* is the glue NS record that helps you get from one nameserver to another. The reverse zone also needs to be delegated. If the 192.168.196 net with the your-domain.com domain came from a provider, they'd need to put NS records in for the reverse zone and the forward zone. If the chain is followed from in-addr.arpa and up to the assigned net, a break in the chain will be discovered at the service provider. If you find the break in the chain, contact the service provider and ask them to correct the error.

exam Watch

From an end-user perspective, DNS might be considered the glue that holds the Internet together. Pay special attention to the nuances of the configuration files, so that network-wide problems are avoided.

Keep It Working

There is one maintenance task to do on DNS other than keeping it running: keeping the root.hints file updated. The easiest way to do this is by using *dig*. First, run dig with no arguments. You will get the root.hints according to the local server. Then ask one of the listed root servers with dig @rootserver. Note that the output looks like a root.hints file. Save it to a file (dig @e.root-servers.net . ns >root.hints.new) and replace the old root.hints with it. Remember to reload Named after replacing the cache file.

The following script can be run automatically to update root.hints. Install a crontab entry to run it once a month, and forget about it. The script assumes mail is working, and that the mail-alias "hostmaster" is defined.

```
#!/bin/sh
 #
 # Update the nameserver cache information file once per month.
 # This is run automatically by a cron entry.
 #
 # Original by Al Longyear
 # Updated for bind 8 by Nicolai Langfeldt
 # Miscellaneous error-conditions reported by David A. Ranch
 # Ping test suggested by Martin Foster
 #
 (
  echo "To: hostmaster <hostmaster>"
  echo "From: system <root>"
  echo "Subject: Automatic update of the root.hints file"
  echo

  PATH=/sbin:/usr/sbin:/bin:/usr/bin:
  export PATH
  cd /var/named

  # Are we online?  Ping a server at your ISP
  case `ping -qnc some.machine.net` in
    *'100% packet loss'*)
         echo "The network is DOWN. root.hints NOT updated"
         echo
         exit 0
         ;;
  esac

  dig @rs.internic.net . ns >root.hints.new 2>&1

  case `cat root.hints.new` in
    *NOERROR*)
         # It worked
         :;;
    *)
         echo "The root.hints file update has FAILED."
         echo "This is the dig output reported:"
         echo

         cat root.hints.new
```

```
        exit 0
        ;;
esac

echo "The root.hints file has been updated to contain the following
information:"
echo
cat root.hints.new

chown root.root root.hints.new
chmod 444 root.hints.new
rm -f root.hints.old
mv root.hints root.hints.old
mv root.hints.new root.hints
ndc restart
echo
echo "The nameserver has been restarted to ensure
that the update is complete."
echo "The previous root.hints file is now called
/var/named/root.hints.old."
) 2>&1 | /usr/lib/sendmail -t
exit 0
```

EXERCISE 9-1

DNS/Bind

Following the example files shown previously, set up your own DNS server. Serve the domain called rhce.test.

1. Edit the /etc/named.conf file to reflect the new information. Name the zone file pz/rhce.test, and set it to be a master domain.
2. Edit the file /var/named/pz/rhce.test and place the proper zone information in it. Start by adding in the header with the serial number and expiration information.
3. Add the SOA RR with a proper hostmaster contact to the zone file.
4. Add NS and MX RRs for the domain. Use the 192.168.*.* address range.
5. Add several hosts with A, HINFO, and TXT RRs. Use www, ftp, and mail for a few.
6. Save the zone file, and then restart Named with the ndc restart command.
7. Bring up nslookup to check the rhce.test domain.

CERTIFICATION OBJECTIVE 9.02

Squid Proxy Server

Squid is a high-performance HTTP and FTP caching proxy server. It conforms to the Harvest Cache architecture and uses the Inter-Cache Protocol (ICP) for transfers between participating peer and parent/child cache servers. It can be used as either a traditional caching proxy, or as a front-end accelerator for a traditional Web server. Squid accepts only HTTP requests, but speaks FTP on the server side when FTP objects are requested.

Squid is most useful for reducing bandwidth utilization (via cache hits) and load-leveling (via having better-connected parent request objects and then feeding them back to bandwidth-limited downstream clients). Extremely large studies have shown bandwidth reduction of 10–20% for all HTTP and FTP traffic, which is economically compelling for large installations. A worldwide hierarchy of Harvest Cache sites can be joined by those so inclined (see http://ircache.nlanr.net/Cache/joining.html for more details).

Required Packages

The following packages should already be installed on your Linux server. Squid will not operate without them all, so check the list now.

- /etc/rc.d/init.d/squid Start/stop script
- /etc/squid/ Configuration directory
- /usr/doc/squid-version Documentation, mostly in HTML format
- /usr/lib/squid/ Support files and internationalized error messages
- /usr/sbin/client Command-line diagnostic client program
- /usr/sbin/squid Main daemon program
- /var/log/squid/ Log directory
- /var/spool/squid/ Cache directory (100 MB or more in hundreds of hashed directories)

Initialization

When started for the first time from the Red Hat 6.*x* Squid package, /etc/rc.d/init.d/squid automatically runs squid -z to create the cache directories under /var/spool/squid/, and then proceeds to actually start Squid. Squid will then be running as a caching proxy server listening on port 3128. Web clients can then point to it at port 3128 as their explicit Web proxy.

Starting and Stopping Squid on a Linux Server

On Red Hat 6.*x* systems, Squid is started and stopped via /etc/rc.d/init.d/squid start and /etc/rc.d/init.d/squid stop. It may take a while to start as it first inspects its many hashed directories.

Configuration Options

Advanced configuration features are adjusted via the /etc/squid/squid.conf configuration file. This allows many tuning and security parameters to be adjusted. A key configuration section contains *cache_host* lines, which specify parent and sibling Squid cache servers, and which should be consulted before fetching a new object. The following example set specifies one parent and three sibling cache hosts:

```
#  squid.conf - On the host: childcache.example.com
#
#  Format is: hostname  type  http_port  udp_port
#
cache_host parentcache.example.com   parent  3128 3130
cache_host childcache2.example.com   sibling 3128 3130
cache_host childcache3.example.com   sibling 3128 3130
```

Squid first checks its own cache, then queries its siblings and parents for the object. If neither the cache host nor its siblings have the object, it asks one of its parents to fetch it from the source (or fetches it itself if it has no parents that responded to its request).

Squid can greatly improve the performance of a corporate intranet. If your company has many employees who surf the Net, a Squid server will decrease the bandwidth usage of your ISP connection.

CERTIFICATION OBJECTIVE 9.03

NFS

NFS is a file-sharing protocol originally developed by Sun Microsystems in the mid-1980s. It is based on Sun's XDR (external data representation, a byte-order-independent data formatting standard) and RPC (remote procedure call) technologies. Sun provided working reference source code, which enabled NFS to quickly become the preferred file-sharing protocol in nearly all versions of UNIX, and in other multiuser operating systems such as VMS. Linux has supported NFS (both as a client and a server) since quite early on, and NFS continues to be popular in organizations with UNIX- or Linux-based networks.

Variants of NFS

Like most other server protocols, NFS has several common variants that prove useful in different circumstances. A general familiarity with the most common variants will lead to more stable systems that can be configured on a case-by-case basis.

Universal NFS Daemon (UNFSD)

The UNFSD NFS server runs as a user-mode process, as opposed to the kernel. This provides some advantages in terms of flexibility, but tremendous disadvantages in performance and scalability. A UNFSD can only effectively handle one to two clients even on a strong server; and even with a single client, throughput is a fraction of what it would be on the same server using a kernel-mode NFS daemon. Bottlenecks in UNFSD include the filename lookups, extra copies between the kernel and user address space, and a single threaded NFS daemon.

One of the "flexibility" advantages of UNFSD (over kernel-mode NFS daemons) is that it can export any number of mount points that are in the same file system, which are subsets or supersets of each other. This is a minor point, however, and administrators who learned NFS on commercial

UNIX variants will generally find UNFSD a bit alien. Also, the daemon processes in UNFSD only read their configuration file when they start; the entire NFS service must be stopped and started again (potentially disrupting clients) to change the list of exported file systems.

All major Linux distributors shipped UNFSD through 1998. With the advent of the 2.2 kernel series, UNFSD is being quickly phased out, and is no longer being maintained as actively as KNFSD.

Kernel-Mode NFS Daemon (KNFSD)

The Linux kernel-mode NFS server, like the NFS server implementations in most commercial UNIX implementations, runs kernel processes to serve the NFS requests from clients. This means that the NFS daemon processes use kernel data structures (dentries, inodes, and devices) rather than their user-mode equivalents (filenames, file descriptors). This eliminates some serious bottlenecks present in UNFSD, enabling an inexpensive server to achieve full 100Mb/sec throughput and to efficiently serve dozens of simultaneous, active clients (limited more by disk and network I/O than by CPU usage or protocol bottlenecks).

The Linux KNFSD implementation started as a patch to the 2.0.*x* kernels, and was worked on heavily in the 2.1 development series. It became a standard kernel feature as of the 2.2 kernels, and has quickly become the default NFS implementation in most Linux distributions.

NFS Version 3 (NFS v3)

Version 2 of the NFS protocol has been in use since the late 1980s. By the early 1990s, higher-bandwidth networks and demands for better performance prompted Sun Microsystems to revise the protocol. NFS v3's key features include support for client-side caching of data, the use of larger block sizes for more efficient transfers, the ability to have multiple outstanding write requests, and the ability to run over TCP instead of UDP. Taken together, NFS v3 greatly improves write performance and scalability on large busy networks, and it makes modest improvements to read performance on low-traffic networks.

NFS v3 requires changes to both client and server implementations. Some NFS v3 features are implemented in the Linux 2.2 kernel, both on the client side and in KNFSD, with the important exception that KNFSD does not yet support TCP. Servers and clients automatically negotiate whether to use v3 or v2, and whether to use TCP or UDP, so compatibility between newer and older implementations is rarely an issue.

PC-NFS

In the late 1980s, Sun and several third parties developed an NFS client for single-user, single-tasking operating systems such as MS-DOS and Microsoft Windows. Unfortunately, the NFS authentication model is best suited for secure, multiuser client machines, and PC-NFS has always been a difficult protocol to support reliably. Typically, PC-NFS servers must run one or more extra "helper" processes (called something like rpc.pcnfsd) that handle logins from the single-user client machines, act like rpc.mountd to process mount requests, and handle printing. The helper processes are generally specific to a particular implementation of the PC-NFS clients they will be working with, and the vendor often provides source to the pcnfsd. A world-writeable spool directory is generally needed in /var to handle print requests (typically, /var/spool/pcnfs).

Due to the flaws in the PC-NFS concept, most organizations today prefer to use Samba to serve files to the single-user clients (like Windows 9*x*) using the clients' own native file- and print-sharing protocols. Samba is a very strong implementation, and should be used instead of PC-NFS given the choice.

WebNFS

WebNFS, another Sun-designed variant of NFS, is intended for Internet use. It differs from ordinary NFS in that clients do not have to "mount" the file systems, and they receive only read-only access. It may be suitable for publishing data to the public in a transparent manner, but is rarely used.

Secure NFS

Since about 1990, Sun and other vendors have supported versions of NFS using public-key based strong authentication. Secure NFS has proven itself extremely tedious and complex to administer, and is still not sufficient to keep data safe in hostile environments. As a result, Secure NFS is rarely used outside of specialized government installations.

NFS Server Configuration and Operation

NFS servers are relatively easy to configure. All that is required is to export a file system, either generally or to a specific host, and then mount that file system remotely.

Required Packages

Most of the NFS package should have been installed already, but double-check the required file list below just to be sure.

knfsd (server daemons and control programs)

- /etc/rc.d/init.d/nfs (start/stop script)
- /usr/doc/knfsd-<version> (documentation, mostly in HTML format)
- Server daemons in /usr/sbin: rpc.mountd, rpc.nfsd, rpc.rquotad
- Control programs in /usr/sbin: exportfs, nfsstat, nhfsstone (a benchmark)
- Status files in /var/lib/nfs: etab, rmtab, xtab

knfsd-clients (client daemons and control programs)

- /etc/rc.d/init.d/nfslock (start/stop script for lockd and statd)
- Server daemons in /sbin: rpc.lockd, rpc.statd
- Control program in /usr/sbin: showmount

portmap (Sun RPC portmapper, a prerequisite to both NFS client and server)

- /etc/rc.d/init.d/portmap (start/stop script)
- /usr/doc/portmap-<version> (documentation)
- Server daemon in /sbin: portmap
- Control programs in /usr/sbin: pmap_dump, pmap_set

Starting and Stopping NFS on a Linux Server

NFS is normally started at boot time, and in the case of knfsd it is not normally stopped or restarted during configuration (the exportfs command is normally used instead). However, if NFS or its main configuration file, /etc/exports, was not installed when the machine booted, it may be necessary to start it using /etc/rc.d/init.d/nfs start. When NFS must be shut down (perhaps for testing or upgrades), use /etc/rc.d/init.d/nfs stop. Generally, the portmapper (controlled via the /etc/rc.d/init.d/portmap start/stop script) should be started before NFS, and shut down after NFS, because NFS depends on it to function and may time-out if portmapper is not running.

This script starts the following processes:

- rpc.mountd Handles mount requests
- rpc.nfsd Spawns the specified number of nfsd kernel processes and exits.
- rpc.rquotad Reports disk quota statistics to clients

The /etc/exports File

/etc/exports is the only major configuration file for NFS on Linux. It explicitly lists which parts of which file systems are to be exported to clients via the exportfs command. The file format is similar to that used in SunOS 4.*x*, except that some additional options are permitted. Each line lists one directory that may be exported, the hosts it will be exported to, and the options that apply to this export. A given directory may only be exported once. With KNFSD, there are additional restrictions: Directories that are parents or children of each other cannot both be exported unless they are in different file systems, and only directories in the same file system are exported (KNFSD will not traverse mount points).

```
/pub                    (ro) someone.mylocaldomain.com(rw)
/home                  *.mylocaldomain.com(rw)
/opt/diskless-root      diskless.mylocaldomain.com(rw,no_root_squash)
```

In the preceding example, /pub is exported to everyone as read-only and to just one specific machine as read-write; /home is exported to any host whose inverse DNS pointer (IN PTR) is for a hostname ending in *.mylocaldomain.com*; and /opt/diskless-root is exported with full read-write privileges (even for the root account) to just one specific machine.

Changing the List of Exports

Simply changing /etc/exports does not automatically change anything right away. This file is simply the default set of exported directories for the exportfs -a command, which is typically run at boot time or by hand whenever /etc/exports has been changed. File systems can also be exported directly (and temporarily) via the exportfs command without modifying /etc/exports.

If exports are only being added to, running exportfs -a is sufficient to add them. However, if any exports are being modified, moved, or deleted, it is safest to first do exportfs -ua to temporarily unexport all file systems (potentially inconveniencing users) followed by exportfs -a. If many different directories are being exported and actively used, and only one is being changed, the exportfs command can explicitly unexport just the one being modified.

NFS Client Configuration and Operation

Now the client side mounts can be done. This is accomplished in a manner similar to mounting local file systems.

Configuration Files

NFS clients normally mount their remote file systems at boot time, based on entries in /etc/fstab. For example:

```
## Server Directory  Mount Point  Type  Mount Options  Dump Fsckorder
nfsserv:/homenfs      /nfs/home    nfs  soft,timeout=100  0    0
```

Alternatively, an automounter such as autofs or amd can be used to dynamically mount NFS file systems as they are referenced on the client, and to later unmount them when they have not been recently accessed.

Starting/Stopping

The startup script for remote NFS file systems specified in /etc/fstab, as of Red Hat 6.*x*, is /etc/rc.d/init.d/netfs. This script also manages remote SMB and NetWare file systems that are specified in /etc/fstab.

Client-Side Helper Processes

You may notice a few new system processes in the main process status ('ps aux'). These are required for proper client-side NFS mounts.

- rpc.statd Tracks the state of servers, for use by rpc.lockd in recovering locks after a server crash.
- rpc.lockd Manages the client side of file locking.

Diskless Clients

NFS supports diskless clients, which use either a boot floppy or a boot PROM to get started and then mount their root file system, swap space, a shared read-only /usr file system, and other shared read-write file systems such as /home. If "net-booting" from a boot PROM is used, the client will need bootp (or DHCP) and tftp services to obtain its network information and then download its kernel. See the Diskless-HOWTO for details on setting up diskless clients.

Quirks and Limitations of NFS

NFS does have its problems. An administrator who controls NFS mounts would be wise to take note of these limitations.

Statelessness

Unlike most other file-sharing protocols, NFS is designed to be (at least theoretically) completely "stateless." Thus, there is no separate login phase prior to gaining access to NFS resources. Instead, the NFS client normally contacts rpc.mountd on the server, which checks the request against currently exported file systems and provides an *NFS file handle* (a "magic cookie" that is generally hard to guess), which is then used for subsequent I/O. The advantage of this stateless protocol is that if the server must be rebooted, the client can simply wait for it to come back up without any of its software failing. The stateless concept, however, does not work well when insecure single-user clients are involved; makes file-locking very complex, and is counterintuitive to most people trained on other file-sharing technologies.

Superset/Subset Exports and Mount Points

As mentioned earlier, KNFSD processes NFS requests from a kernel internal data structure perspective, not from a user perspective. This has two important implications for exported directories. First, any mount points that are under an exported directory are not automatically exported, which has the interesting side effect that the real contents of the directory that is the mount point is seen instead. Second, it is impossible to export two directories in the same file system if one is inside the other. For example, /usr and /usr/local cannot both be exported unless /usr/local is on a separate file system from /usr.

Absolute and Relative Symbolic Links

Symbolic links over NFS are interpreted by the client, not the server. Thus, any absolute symbolic links are evaluated starting at the root directory of the client, usually leading to somewhere else on the client, which is often not what is expected or desired. This problem should generally be worked around via the thoughtful use of relative symbolic links inside exported file systems. There is also a server-side export option (link_relative) that automatically converts absolute symbolic links to relative; this can have nonintuitive results if the client mounts a subdirectory of the exported directory.

Root Squash

For security reasons, NFS servers normally translate access by the root account (UID 0) on clients to an unprivileged account (on Red Hat 6.*x*, user and group *nobody*). This behavior can be disabled (via the no_root_squash server export option) or modified in various ways; see the exports(5) man page.

NFS Hangs

Because NFS is stateless, clients normally wait for a server for up to several minutes; in some cases they'll wait indefinitely if the server stops responding. While this is occurring, any reference to the file system(s) on the unresponsive server will cause a process to hang, and it is generally difficult or impossible to unmount the offending file systems once the problem starts. Several steps can be taken to reduce the impact of this problem:

- Take great care to ensure the reliability of NFS servers and the network.
- Avoid mounting many different NFS servers at once, especially in a circular fashion.
- Clients should mount infrequently used NFS file systems only when needed, and unmount them after use.
- Mission-critical systems should avoid doing any NFS mounts at all if possible.
- Keep NFS mounted directories out of the search path for users, especially that of *root.*
- Keep NFS mounted directories out of the root (/) directory; instead, segregate them to somewhere else that is not accessed as often, (e.g., /nfs/home, /nfs/share).
- Consider using the soft option when mounting NFS file systems. This causes accesses to file systems mounted from unresponsive NFS servers to fail rather than hang; however, this risks making long-running processes fail due to temporary network outages. The time-out interval before requests are made to fail, in tenths of seconds, is set with the additional option timeo. The following example sets the timeout to 30 seconds:

```
mount -o soft,timeo=300 myserver:/home /nfs/home
```

Inverse DNS Pointers

When KNFSD checks a mount request against the current list of exports, it looks up the client's IP address in DNS to find the hostname associated with that client. This hostname is then finally checked against the list of exports. If the IP address to hostname lookup fails (because that IP address does not have an IN PTR record listed with whoever is the authority for its IP address range), rpc.mountd will deny access to that client. It leaves a message in /var/log/messages reporting a "request from unknown host." Another way to detect this problem is to directly look up the client's IP address, which must be turned backwards and must have .in-addr.arpa. appended. For example, this command would look up the inverse DNS pointer for 192.168.1.2:

```
nslookup -type=ptr 2.1.168.192.in-addr.arpa.
```

If there is no inverse DNS pointer, you'll get a message like this:

```
*** ns1.tux.org can't find 2.1.168.192.in-addr.arpa.: Non-existent host/domain
```

File Locking

Most NFS implementations have historically had serious problems making file locking work reliably and correctly, particularly between the implementations of different vendors. Any applications depending on file locking over NFS should be tested thoroughly before depending on their use.

Performance Tips

There are several suggestions to follow that will keep NFS running in a stable and reliable manner. Make sure you are aware of these pointers:

- Do not even consider using the user-mode NFS daemon if performance is an issue, or if you will have more than one or two simultaneously active clients.
- Eight kernel NFS daemons (the default) are sufficient for good performance even under fairly heavy loads. For extremely busy NFS servers, it may be worth increasing the number of NFS daemons beyond eight, keeping in mind that the extra kernel processes consume valuable kernel resources.
- In any network in which packet retransmissions are common, it is more efficient to use NFS over TCP than UDP, if available.

- NFS write performance can be extremely slow, particularly with NFS v2 clients, because the client waits for each block of data to be written to disk. Specialized hardware with nonvolatile RAM for holding writes pending their being physically written to disk is the best solution to this problem. In applications where data loss is not a big concern, the file system can be mounted by the client with the async option, which effectively removes this bottleneck as well.
- Hostname lookups are performed frequently by the NFS server; run the Name Switch Cache Daemon (nscd) to improve performance here.

Understand the implications of NFS. It is a powerful file-sharing system, but should not be used lightly.

NFS Security

The NFS introduces a number of serious security problems, and should never be used in hostile environments (such as on a server directly exposed to the Internet) without taking extreme precautions.

Shortcomings and Risks

NFS is an easy-to-use yet powerful file sharing system. However, it is not without its problems. A few security risks to keep in the forefront of your mind:

- **Authentication** NFS normally relies on the client host to accurately report the client's credentials (user ID and group IDs). This model breaks down if there is a possibility of users with root access to their own boxes, or even users with the capability of adding a computer to the network, or booting an existing computer off a boot floppy of their choice. The implications are that any data that is accessible via NFS to *any user* can potentially be accessed by *any other* user.
- **Privacy** Not even Secure NFS encrypts its network traffic.
- **SunRPC Infrastructure** Both the client and server parts of NFS depend on the RPC portmapper daemon. Portmapper has in the past had a number of serious security holes, and is not recommended for use on machines directly exposed to the Internet or other potentially hostile networks.

Security Tips

If NFS *must* be used in or near a hostile environment, these approaches can reduce the corresponding security risks:

- Educate yourself in detail about NFS security. If you do not clearly understand the risks, you should restrict your NFS use to friendly, internal networks that are behind a good firewall.
- If an Internet-exposed server needs to access internal files via NFS, use separate network interfaces on the server for the Internet (untrusted) network and the internal (trusted) network. Use ipchains to prevent the untrusted network from accessing the TCP and UDP ports that portmapper, mountd, and nfsd use.
- Export as little data as possible, and export file systems as read-only if possible.
- Use root squash to prevent clients from having root access to exported file systems.
- Use ipchains to deny access to the portmapper, mountd, and nfsd ports, except from explicitly trusted hosts or networks. The ports are:

```
111   TCP/UDP   portmapper   (server and client)
745   UDP       mountd       (server)
747   TCP       mountd       (server)
2049  TCP/UDP   nfsd         (server)
```

- Use a port scanner to verify that these ports are not accessible from untrusted network(s).

CERTIFICATION OBJECTIVE 9.04

Internet News

Network News Transport Protocol (NNTP) uses TCP port 119, as documented in RFC 977. It is a high-performance, low-latency message transfer protocol based on SMTP. A collection of NNTP servers accept posts and distribute them worldwide, moving billions of characters daily. Newsgroups are the organizational unit, with hierarchies existing for almost any subject area one can imagine. The major groups are alt, comp, gnu, misc, news, rec, sci, soc, and talk. Other newsgroups include commercial feeds and local distributions.

INND

INND was written in 1991 by Rich Salz to replace Cnews; the volume of NNTP traffic had risen to the point that Cnews was not able to keep up due to its architectural limitations.

INND is now maintained by ISC at www.isc.org. Red Hat supplies INND 2.2 in rpm format. Release 2.2 supports circular message buffers as well as file system based spooling. This is a performance advantage if a large number of newsgroups are being carried. Other major news servers include Cnews, and Cyclone.

The top 1000 NNTP servers by influence are tracked monthly at http://grasp.insa-lyon.fr/.

Configuring INND (Leafnode Services)

Red Hat keeps the INND configuration files in /etc/news. The minimal leafnode setup requires that you edit inn.conf, incoming.conf, and newsfeeds. Edit nnrp.access if you want to allow readers on other computers. It is good to edit motd and put a welcome banner for your readers along with any policies you may have.

You should set the organization directive in inn.conf. The defaults for the remainder are okay, but can be set as desired.

```
organization: Your Organization Here
```

Your ISP typically supplies NNTP services. Put their e-mail and telephone number in your incoming.conf file. This can be handy when troubleshooting.

You need a peer definition for your ISP in incoming.conf:

```
# A peer definition.
# Myisp.net (800) 555 1212 joenews@myisp.net
peer myisp {
       hostname: news.myisp.net
      }
```

If you want to post articles, you need an entry in newsfeeds. This example will use nntpsend to transmit your outbound traffic. nntpsend is run hourly from /etc/cron.hourly/inn-cron-nntpsend:

```
# Myisp.net (800) 555 1212 joenews@myisp.net
news.myisp.net:!junk/!foo:Tf,Wnm:news.myisp.net
```

Articles will be kept in /var/spool/news, so make sure there is enough space available. Your newsfeed will determine how quickly the files fill and what expire policies will be required. If possible, make /var a file system and allocate plenty of inodes with -i 1024.

If you find that performance is an issue and file systems are slowing you down, investigate cycbuffs. Enabled in *inn.conf* with the storageapi: true directive, you will have to set up *cycbuff.conf* and allocate some space for circular buffers.

- Run inncheck and correct any permissions problems or other conditions detected before starting INND.
- Start INND with /etc/rc.d/init.d/innd start.
- Stop INND with ctlinnd shutdown "Some Reason or Other".
- Check status with innstat.

Most of the INND files have man pages.

Troubleshooting

Here are a few common news errors and their solutions.

News Won't Start

If INND won't start at all, check the following:

- Try inncheck.
- If ININD starts manually but not at reboot, then confirm that INND is in /etc/rc.d/rc?.d/S95innd or similar, and that the runlevel is appropriate.
- See /var/log/news/news.err.

Readers Can't Read

If INND is running, but no one can read any news articles, check:

- Check nnrp.access and confirm that the desired reader is allowed.
- Confirm that INND is running by typing **ps ax | grep innd**.
- Telnet to port 119 and see if the banner comes up.
- See /var/log/news/news.err.

Posters Can't Post

If posters can't post:

- Check nnrp.access and confirm that the desired poster is allowed.
- Telnet to port 119 from the problem host and see if the banner comes up with (posting allowed).
- See /var/log/news/news.err.

News logs are in /var/log/news. Read them when there is a problem, especially /var/log/news/news.err. News databases are in /var/lib/news and can get very large. Keep an eye on /var disk space.

Telnet port 119 is always helpful, and it gives an indication of responsiveness. The banner should come up immediately. Typing **mode reader** in INNP will switch to NNRP. Type **help** for syntax, and **quit** to exit. Here's an example debugging session:

```
telnet localhost 119
Trying 127.0.0.1...
```

```
Connected to localhost.
Escape character is '^]'.
200 localhost InterNetNews server INN 2.2 21-Jan-1999 ready
mode reader
200 localhost InterNetNews NNRP server INN 2.2 21-Jan-1999 ready (posting ok).
503 Timeout after 10 seconds, closing connection.
Connection closed by foreign host.
```

CERTIFICATION OBJECTIVE 9.05

DHCP/Bootp

DHCP (Dynamic Host Configuration Protocol) and bootp are protocols that allow a client machine to obtain network information (such as an IP number) from a server. Many organizations are starting to use dynamic host control because it simplifies and centralizes network administration, especially in large networks or networks that have a significant number of mobile users. DHCP is backward compatible with bootp. Therefore, this section will only cover the configuration of DHCP.

DHCP Operational Overview

As with most network services, there is a server side and a client side to DHCP. The following examples use the DHCPd daemon on the server side, and the pump executable on the client side. There are other packages available, but these binaries are the ones that are installed with Red Hat.

Server Configuration

First, make sure that multicast is running on the server's network interface. Type **ifconfig–a**. The output should look something like:

```
eth0      Link encap:10Mbps Ethernet  HWaddr 00:B0:5F:D2:C4:34
            inet addr:192.168.248.45  Bcast:192.168.248.255/
Mask:255.255.255.0
            UP BROADCAST RUNNING MULTICAST  MTU:1500  Metric:1
            RX packets:43557 errors:0 dropped:0 overruns:0
```

```
          TX packets:52646 errors:0 dropped:0 overruns:0
          Interrupt:10 Base address:0x300
```

If MULTICAST doesn't appear, the kernel will need to be recompiled to add multicast support. On most systems, this will not be necessary.

In order for DHCPd to work correctly with picky DHCP clients (e.g., Windows 95), it must be able to send packets with an IP destination address of 255.255.255.255. Unfortunately, Linux insists on changing 255.255.255.255 into the local subnet broadcast address. This results in a DHCP protocol violation, and while many DHCP clients don't notice the problem, some (e.g., all Microsoft DHCP clients) do. Clients that have this problem will appear not to see DHCPOFFER messages from the server. Issue the command:

```
route add -host 255.255.255.255 dev eth0
```

eth0 is the name of the network interface card (NIC) that connects the server to the network. If the name on your server differs, make the appropriate change.

Now configure DHCPd by creating or editing /etc/dhcpd.conf. Most commonly, IP addresses are assigned randomly. The following sample file illustrates the configuration.

```
# Sample /etc/dhcpd.conf
default-lease-time 600;
max-lease-time 7200;
option subnet-mask 255.255.255.0;
option broadcast-address 192.168.1.255;
option routers 192.168.1.254;
option domain-name-servers 192.168.1.1, 192.168.1.2;
option domain-name "mydomain.org";

subnet 192.168.1.0 netmask 255.255.255.0 {
   range 192.168.1.10 192.168.1.100;
   range 192.168.1.150 192.168.1.200;
}
```

This will result in the DHCP server giving a client an IP address from the range 192.168.1.10–192.168.1.100 or 192.168.1.150–192.168.1.200. It will lease an IP address for 600 seconds if the client doesn't ask for a specific timeframe. Otherwise, the maximum (allowed) lease will be 7200 seconds. The server will also "advise" the client that it should use

255.255.255.0 as its subnet mask, 192.168.1.255 as its broadcast address, 192.168.1.254 as the router/gateway, and 192.168.1.1 and 192.168.1.2 as its DNS servers.

If you need to specify a WINS server for your Windows clients, include the netbios-name-servers option:

```
option netbios-name-servers 192.168.1.1;
```

You can also assign specific IP addresses based on a client's Ethernet address:

```
host dragonfire {
     hardware ethernet 08:00:12:23:4d:3f;
     fixed-address 192.168.1.201;
  }
```

This will assign the IP address 192.168.1.201 to a client with the Ethernet address 08:00:12:23:4d:3f.

DHCP can be customized to an individual machine's needs. Machines such as servers can get static IP addresses, and mobile users with laptops can be allotted dynamic IPs. There are a number of other options, such as NIS server addresses, timeserver addresses, and so on. The dhcpd.conf man page goes into detail on these options.

In most cases, DHCP installation doesn't create a dhcpd.leases file. This file is used by DHCPd to store information about current leases. The file is in plain text form, so you can view it during the operation of DHCPd. To create dhcpd.leases, type:

```
touch /var/state/dhcp/dhcpd.leases
```

on the command line. This will create an empty file for DHCPd to write its information into. Some of the older versions of DHCPd 2.0 placed the file in /etc/dhcpd.leases. If you get a message saying that the file exists, simply ignore it. Start up DHCPd by typing:

```
/usr/sbin/dhcpd
```

This will invoke DHCPd on the eth0 device. If you want to invoke it on another device, supply it on the command line:

```
/usr/sbin/dhcpd eth1
```

To verify that everything is working, turn on debugging mode and put the server in the foreground by typing:

```
/usr/sbin/dhcpd -d -f
```

Bring up one of the clients and watch the console of the server. A number of debugging messages will come up to indicate that a client has been leased an IP address.

Client Configuration

Configuring DHCPd under Red Hat is done from the Control Panel. Simply type **control-panel** as root from a terminal window. Note that the root user will need permission to display the Control Panel on the X-Windows screen. Display permissions are covered in the XWindow-User-HOWTO.

In the Control Panel

1. Select Network Configuration.
2. Click Interfaces.
3. Click ADD.
4. Select Ethernet.
5. In the Edit Ethernet/Bus Interface, select "Activate interface at boot time," and select DHCP as the Interface configuration protocol.

For the new configuration to take effect, reboot the machine, or type as root:

```
/sbin/ifup eth0
```

Client Issues

If the configuration according to the preceding steps does not work, there may be a problem with the setup. Here are a few possibilities for what's wrong:

- The NIC is not configured properly. Consult the Ethernet-HOWTO to double-check the functionality of the NIC.
- If the network works for a few minutes and then stops responding, check to see if gated (gateway daemon) is running. There have been

reports of gated breaking routes on Linux boxes, which results in this type of problem.

- If the machine is still not able to connect, you may have firewall rules (ipfwadm or ipchains rules) that disallow port 67/68 traffic used by DHCP to distribute configuration information. Check your firewall rules carefully.

CERTIFICATION OBJECTIVE 9.06

Other File-Sharing Methods

There are many other methods of file sharing on a Red Hat Linux system. The most popular ones in NFS and Samba have already been covered. Several minor ones, such as Coda and Andrew, fall outside the parameters of this book. Linux can also speak IPX, the language of Novell NetWare. Configuring a simple Linux-based NetWare server will be covered briefly.

IPX (mars_nwe)

There are two packages available that allow Linux to provide the functions of a Novell Fileserver, lwared and mars_nwe. This section will briefly explain how to configure mars_nwe. Using mars_nwe, files can be shared on a Linux machine with users using Novell NetWare client software. Users can attach and map file systems to appear as local drives on their machines, just as they would to a real Novell fileserver. Martin Stover <mstover@freeway.de> developed mars_nwe to enable Linux to provide both file and print services for NetWare clients. The name mars_nwe stands for Martin Stovers NetWare Emulator.

Configuring the Server

Edit the /etc/nwserv.conf file. The format of this file may at first look a little cryptic, but it is fairly straightforward. The file contains a number of single-line configuration items. Each line is whitespace delimited and begins with a number that indicates the contents of the line. All characters following a # character are considered a comment and ignored. A thorough example is listed:

```
     # Sample /etc/nwserv.conf file by Kevin Thorpe.
     # VOLUMES (max. 5)
     # Only the SYS volume is compulsory. The directory
containing the SYS
     # volume must contain the directories: LOGIN, PUBLIC,
SYSTEM, MAIL.
     # The 'i' option ignores case.
     # The 'k' option converts all filenames in NCP requests to
lowercase.
     # The 'm' option marks the volume as removable (useful for cdroms etc.)
     # The 'r' option set the volume to read-only.
     # The 'o' option indicates the volume is a single mounted
filesystem.
     # The 'P' option allows commands to be used as files.
     # The 'O' option allows use of the OS/2 namespace
     # The 'N' option allows use of the NFS namespace
     # The default is upper case.
     # Syntax:
     #    1 <Volumename> <Volumepath>   <Options>

     1   SYS         /home/netware/SYS/               # SYS
     1   DATA        /home/netware/DATA/      k       # DATA
     1   CDROM       /cdrom                   kmr     # CDROM

     # SERVER NAME
     # If not set then the linux hostname will be converted to
upper case
     # and used. This is optional, the hostname will be used if
this is not
     # configured.
     # Syntax:
     #    2 <Servername>

     2   LINUX_FS01

     # INTERNAL NETWORK ADDRESS
     # The Internal IPX Network Address is a feature that simplifies
IPX routing
     # for multihomed hosts (hosts that have ports on more than one
IPX network).
     # Syntax:
     #    3 <Internal Network Address> [<Node Number>]
     # or:
     #    3 auto
     #
     # If you use 'auto' then your host IP address will be used.
```

```
NOTE: this may
     # be dangerous, please be sure you pick a number unique to
your network.
     # Addresses are 4byte hexadecimal (the leading 0x is required).

     3   0x49a01010  1


     # NETWORK DEVICE(S)
     # This entry configures your IPX network. If you already
have your
     # IPX network configured then you do not need this. This is
the same as
     # using ipx_configure/ipx_interface before you start the server.
     # Syntax:
     #    4 <IPX Network Number> <device_name> <frametype> [<ticks>]
     #                 Frame types: ethernet_ii, 802.2, 802.3, SNAP

     4  0x39a01010  eth0  802.3  1

     # SAVE IPX ROUTES AFTER SERVER IS DOWNED
     # Syntax:
     #    5 <flag>
     #       0 = don't save routes, 1 = do save routes

     5 0

     # NETWARE VERSION
     # Syntax:
     #    6 <version>
     #      0 = 2.15, 1 = 3.11

     6 1
     # PASSWORD HANDLING
     # Real Novell DOS clients support a feature which encypts your
     # password when changing it. You can select whether you want your
     # mars server to support this feature or not.
     # Syntax
     #    7 <flag>
     #    <flag> is:
     #        0 to force password encryption. (Clients can't
change password)
     #        1 force password encryption, allow unencrypted
password change.
     #        7 allow non-encrypted password but no empty passwords.
     #        8 allow non-encrypted password including empty
passwords.
     #        9 completely unencrypted passwords (doesn't work
with OS/2)
```

```
7 1

# MINIMAL GID UID rights
# permissions used for attachments with no login. These
permissions
# will be used for the files in your primary server attachment.
# Syntax:
#    10 <gid>
#    11 <uid>
#    <gid> <uid> are from /etc/passwd, /etc/groups

10  200
11  201

# SUPERVISOR password
# May be removed after the server is started once. The server
# will encrypt this information into the bindery file after it
# is run. You should avoid using the 'root' user and instead use
# another account to administer the mars fileserver.
#
# This entry is read and encrypted into the server bindery files,
# so it only needs to exist the first time you start the server
# to ensure that the password isn't stolen.
#
# Syntax:
#    12 <Supervisor-Login> <Unix username> [<password>]

12  SUPERVISOR  chris  secretpassword

# USER ACCOUNTS
# This associates NetWare logins with unix accounts. Password are
# optional.
# Syntax:
     13 <User Login> <Unix Username> [<password>]

13  CHRIS chris
13  DAVE  dave

# LAZY SYSTEM ADMIN CONFIGURATION
# If you have a large numbers of users and could not be bothered
# using type 13 individual user mappings, you can automatically
# map mars_new logins to linux user names. BUT, there is
# currently no means of making use of the linux login password
# so all users configured this way are will use the single
# password supplied here. My recommendation is not to do this
# unless security is absolutely no concern to you.
# Syntax:
#    15 <flag> <common-password>
```

```
#    <flag> is: 0  - don't automatically map users.
#         1  - do automatically map users not configured above.
#               99 - automatically map every user in this way.

15  0  password

# SANITY CHECKING
# mars_nwe will automatically ensure that certain directories
# exist if you set this flag.
# Syntax:
#    16 <flag>
#    <flag> is 0 for no, don't, or 1 for yes, do.

16  0

# PRINT QUEUES
# This associates NetWare printers with unix printers. The queue
# directories must be created manually before printing is
# attempted. The queue directories are NOT lpd queues.
# Syntax:
#    21 <queue_name> <queue_directory> <unix_print_cmd>

21  EPSON  SYS:/PRINT/EPSON lpr -h
21  LASER  SYS:/PRINT/LASER lpr -Plaser

# DEBUG FLAGS
# These are not normally needed, but may be useful if are you
# debugging a problem.
# Syntax:
#    <debug_item> <debug_flag>
#
#    100 = IPX KERNEL
#    101 = NWSERV
#    102 = NCPSERV
#    103 = NWCONN
#    104 = start NWCLIENT
#    105 = NWBIND
#    106 = NWROUTED
#                 0 = disable debug, 1 = enable debug

100 0
101 0
102 0
103 0
104 0
105 0
106 0

# RUN NWSERV IN BACKGROUND AND USE LOGFILE
```

```
# Syntax:
#    200 <flag>
#        0 = run NWSERV in foreground and don't use logfile
#        1 = run NWSERV in background and use logfile

200  1

# LOGFILE NAME
# Syntax:
#    201 <logfile>

201  /tmp/nw.log

# APPEND LOG OR OVERWRITE
# Syntax:
#    202 <flag>
#        0 = append to existing logfile
#        1 = overwrite existing logfile

202  1

# SERVER DOWN TIME
# This item sets the time after a SERVER DOWN is issued that the
# server really goes down.
# Syntax:
#    210 <time>
#        in seconds. (defaults 10)

210  10

# ROUTING BROADCAST INTERVAL
# The time is seconds between server broadcasts
# Syntax:
#    211 <time>
#        in seconds. (defaults 60)

211  60

# ROUTING LOGGING INTERVAL
# Set how many broadcasts take place before logging of routing
# information occurs.
# Syntax:
#    300  <number>

300  5

# ROUTING LOGFILE
# Set the name of the routing logfile
# Syntax:
```

```
#    301 <filename>

301  /tmp/nw.routes

# ROUTING APPEND/OVERWRITE
# Set whether you want to append to an existing log file or
# overwrite it.
# Syntax:
#    302 <flag>
#        <flag> is 0 for append, 1 for create/overwrite

302  1

# WATCHDOG TIMING
# Set the timing for watchdog messages that ensure the network
# is still alive.
# Syntax:
#    310 <value>
#        <value> =   0 - always send watchdogs
#                  < 0 - (-ve) for disable watchdogs
#                  > 0 - send watchdogs when network traffic
#                        drops below 'n' ticks

310  7

# STATION FILE
# Set the filename for the stations file which determine which
# machines this fileserver will act as the primary fileserver
# for. The syntax of this file is described in the 'examples'
# directory of the source code.
# Syntax:
#    400 <filename>

400  /etc/nwserv.stations

# GET NEAREST FILESERVER HANDLING
# Set how SAP Get Nearest Fileserver Requests are handled.
# Syntax:
#    401 <flag>
#   <flag> is: 0 - disable 'Get Nearest Fileserver' requests.
#              1 - The 'stations' file lists stations to be excluded.
#              2 - The 'stations' file lists stations to be included.

401 2
```

If the server is configured to expect external programs to configure the network and/or provide the routing function, then start those before starting the server. If the server is configured so that it will configure the interfaces itself and provide the routing services, then type the command **nwserv**. To test the server, try to log in from a NetWare client on the network. Set a CAPTURE from the client and attempt a print. If both the login and print are successful, then the server is working.

CERTIFICATION OBJECTIVE 9.07

Time Synchronization

Several applications that can be run on a Linux server require accurate timestamps for logging, system accounting, and many other operations. Time synchronization with a centralized server is available through two protocols: XNTP and rdate.

XNTP

XNTP is a complete implementation of the NTP (Network Time Protocol) Version 3 specification, as defined in RFC 1305. The approach used by NTP to achieve reliable time synchronization from a set of possibly unreliable remote timeservers is somewhat different from other protocols. In particular, NTP does not attempt to synchronize clocks to each other. Rather, each server attempts to synchronize to Universal Coordinated Time (UTC) using the best available source and the available transmission paths to that source.

Time is distributed through a hierarchy of NTP servers, with each server adopting a stratum that indicates from how far away an external source of UTC it is operating. Stratum-1 servers, which are at the top of the hierarchy, have access to some external time source, usually a radio clock synchronized to time signal broadcasts from radio stations that explicitly provide a standard time service. A stratum-2 server is one that is currently obtaining time from a stratum-1 server, a stratum-3 server gets its time from a stratum-2 server, and so on. To avoid long-lived synchronization loops, the number of strata is limited to 15.

Each client in the synchronization subnet (which may also be a server for other, higher stratum clients) chooses exactly one of the available servers to synchronize to, usually from among the lowest stratum servers it has access to. NTP prefers to have access to at least three sources of lower stratum time. It then applies an agreement algorithm to detect discrepancies on the part of any one of the lower stratum servers. Normally, when all servers are in agreement, NTP will choose the best one in terms of lowest stratum, shortest network delay, claimed precision, and several other considerations. Synchronization takes place over TCP or UDP port 123.

NTP has the distinct advantage over other time protocols in its accuracy. However, one point worth noting is that NTP will never run a system clock backwards. If NTP detects that a client's clock is running faster than a lower stratum server, it will slow the clock down to allow it to catch up with UTC. This provides a more stable system clock for time-dependent applications.

NTP Configuration

The configuration file for NTP is /etc/ntp.conf. A good example configuration file would contain:

```
# peer configuration for host www
# (expected to operate at stratum 2)

server clock.llnl.gov
server norad.arc.nasa.gov
server tock.usno.navy.mil

driftfile /etc/ntp.drift
```

This particular host is expected to operate as a client at stratum 2 by virtue of the server keyword and the fact that all of the servers declared run at stratum 1. When configured using the server keyword, this host can receive synchronization from any of the listed servers, but can never provide synchronization to them. Unless restricted, this host can provide synchronization to dependent clients, which do not have to be listed in the configuration file.

A timeserver that is expected to receive synchronization from another server, as well as to provide synchronization to it, is declared using the peer keyword instead of the server keyword. It is usually considered unwise to use the peer keyword excessively.

One of the things the NTP daemon does when it is first started is to compute the error in the intrinsic frequency of the clock on the computer it is running on. It usually takes about a day or so after the daemon is started to compute a good estimate of this drift. Once the initial value is computed, it will only change by relatively small amounts during the course of continued operation. The driftfile keyword indicates to the daemon the name of the file where it may store the current value of the frequency error. If the daemon is stopped and restarted, it can reinitialize itself to the previous estimate and avoid the day's worth of time it would take to recompute the frequency estimate.

rdate

A much more simplistic way of setting the date from a network server is by using rdate. rdate uses TCP to retrieve the current time of another machine using port 13, as described in RFC 868. The time for each system is returned in ctime format (Sun Oct 17 20:36:19 1999). The default mode for rdate simply prints the time as taken from the requested server. The command rdate www will return the date from the server on the local subnet named www. Adding the –s option to the command line and running rdate as root will set the local system clock to the time retrieved from the server. rdate is not as accurate as NTP, but it has the disadvantage of setting the system clock backwards if the reported time is earlier than the current system time. Some applications, such as databases, may suffer serious consequences if they perceive "negative time." NTP is therefore recommended for general use.

CERTIFICATION OBJECTIVE 9.08

PPP Configuration (as a Client) Using netcfg and the Files Generated

A working hardware communication link is a prerequisite for a network connection. Such links include residential phone lines, ISDN and xDSL lines, leased communication links, exotic media like radio, laser, and fiber optic connections, as well as traditional networking systems like Ethernet.

Each such raw physical data link must have a protocol that defines atomic data units (packets), that specifies packet addressing and checksums, and so forth. Ethernet hardware provides this protocol transparently; other communication links require explicit protocol, which is handled by software.

For simplicity, this section will refer to all point-to-point communication devices as "modems." The official specification of the link protocol for modems is provided by RFC 1171, "The Point-to-Point Protocol for the Transmission of Multi-Protocol Datagrams Over Point-to-Point Links." The PPP protocol is designed to be reliable on a variety of communication links; it achieves this by including data checksums, and negotiating optimum link parameters. These features introduce slight overhead into PPP, but they also make it into a reliable protocol that is widely deployed on most existing computing platforms; it practically displaced SLIP, the simple point-to-point protocol that was a precursor to PPP.

The daemon pppd is the most common implementation of the PPP protocol. When started, pppd sequences through several stages to make a Sworking network connection. First, the link has to be brought up—in the case of a modem, by dialing out to the ISP's number. Next, the existing raw connection is authenticated, so that the ISP can identify its customer. Finally, the PPP protocol negotiates such link parameters as MTU, IP addresses/masks, and protocol compression mode.

It should be noted that the PPP protocol is symmetric; in other words, both nodes connected by PPP can originate all the protocol phases. In practice, however, the ISP usually runs a dial-in server that satisfies the requests from remote clients.

The Link Setup

The method used to open up the link is very device specific. The simplest point-to-point link is a direct hardware connection: a simple serial port cable linking two computers, or a leased communication circuit that is always connected.

If the link is not always up, we need to send appropriate commands to the communication device when we need to open it. There is enough variety in the details of this process that pppd uses a general-purpose program, called "chat." This program will attempt to send the appropriate commands and data, such as telephone numbers, to the communication device—as specified in the configuration file for "chat," called a "dialup script." It also captures and reacts in response to various return codes that may be received from the server.

In some cases, "chat" might actually also be involved in setting up the simple authentication of the login:/password: kind, since this dialog looks very similar to the question/response scenario that "chat" is handling while setting up the communication device.

The Authentication

Some communication links implicitly authenticate their participants. A dedicated line is a trivial example—there is no doubt which computers are on both ends. A non-obvious example might be a radio modem such as Ricochet for which the identity of the calling station is implicitly defined to be "the owner of the Metricom's proprietary radio modem." On the public telephone network, however, anyone can call the ISP's number; therefore, callers have to authenticate themselves before they are allowed to connect to the ISP's network.

Such authentication can be a simple userid/password query, issued after the telephone connection is made. Such simplistic methods are being replaced by authentication methods that are part of PPP specification, namely Password Authentication Protocol (PAP) and Challenge-Handshake

Authentication Protocol (CHAP and its illegitimate cousin, MS-CHAP). Strictly speaking, these methods are part of the next phase, the negotiation.

The Negotiation

The next step in setting up the PPP link is the negotiation of protocol parameters. This is done by exchanging messages of the Link Control Protocol (LCP). It is mostly transparent to the user, unless there are protocol version problems. This is rather unlikely at this point, since the PPP protocol is quite mature.

The Link

After completing the negotiation, the pppd program creates a network device in the kernel and starts accepting IP (and other network protocols) packets to be shipped via the PPP interface to the server.

It should be noted that, while Linux uses the routing information from PPP, it does not obtain the DNS server information this way, but instead uses the information from /etc/resolv.conf.

Setup the Easy Way

Modern Linux environments have fairly sophisticated tools for setting up the PPP; KDE ships the kppp program, and Red Hat Linux provides:

- modemtool For setting up modems
- netcfg For setting up network parameters and the dial-up scripts
- usernetctl For starting up and shutting down the PPP link

The first two tools are used once, to configure PPPD. The last one allows nonprivileged users to turn on and off the PPP device.

The modemtool program helps discover existing serial ports and sets up the /dev/modem link mentioned earlier. netcfg is a general-purpose network configuration tool for setting network names, host lists, interface properties, and routing. The network interface properties for the ppp0 device include the dial-up script setup, and in particular, the phone number and the name/password combination.

Setting up the ppp0 interface creates the shell script /etc/sysconfig/network-scripts/ifup-ppp, containing the instructions to start up the interface. This script requires root privileges to run successfully, which is inconvenient if we want to be able to control networking from a regular account. The SUID-root usernetctl program helps here—it will run the startup/shutdown scripts from any account on the system.

Detailed Setup and Debugging Instructions

Obviously, a prerequisite for a PPP connection is a working point-to-point hardware, normally a modem/serial COM port. The Linux naming scheme for such devices is /dev/ttyS0 (and ttyS1, ttyS2, etc.), which correspond to the DOS names of COM1, COM2, COM3, and so on, respectively. Such a COM port has to have its own address, and it shouldn't share interrupts with other devices. By convention, there should be a symbolic link /dev/modem pointing to a port that has the modem associated with it; if that is not the case, ln -s /dev/ttyS1 /dev/modem will create it, assuming that the modem is connected to the second serial port /dev/ttyS1. This is basically what the graphical shell 'modemtool' does.

Another prerequisite is information from the ISP about their setup:

- The phone numbers to their modem bank, with all the appropriate prefixes (area codes, PABX codes, etc.)
- Whether they use Dynamic IP or Static IP address assignment
- The DNS hosts used by the ISP
- The authentication method, and the username and password
- The commands used to start PPPD on the server, if needed

A useful program, minicom, can be used to test the serial port and the modem. After starting it up, type **ATH**, and a working modem should respond with the string "OK". Minicom can be even used to check serial ports without modems: all it takes is shorting pins 2 and 3 of the serial port connector, and all characters typed and sent out are coming back and should appear in the minicom window.

If the serial port works correctly, we may try to dial up the remote host, by typing the ATDT command followed by the phone number:

```
ATDT 1-800-MODEMS
```

This should be followed by the sound of modem dialing tones emanating from the modem's speaker, and by the screeching sound of an opening modem connection.

The remote system might simply start up with the PPP protocol right away, in which case we will see gibberish text in the minicom window. It could also ask us for name/password, and/or show a command-line prompt, requiring us to run PPPD on the remote end.

Having established the method to get to the stage where the remote system is sending PPPD traffic to our computer, we have to configure the dial-up script to automate this process. An extremely useful feature here is the verbose debugging option: chat –v and pppd –d. The debugging messages will appear in the syslog file /var/log/messages; a convenient method of watching this file is to open another window (or another text console) and run tail -f /var/log/messages in it.

Setting the PPP Server

Setting the PPP server for dial-in connections is only slightly more complicated. Most commonly, the server will forward traffic coming via the modem connections to the Internet via the Internet-connected second interface. Therefore, the kernel must have IP forwarding built into it.

Additional Information

A very good source of detailed information about PPP is the Linux PPP HOWTO by Robert Hart. This file is provided as /usr/doc/HOWTO/PPP-HOWTO.

CERTIFICATION SUMMARY

Networking services are an integral part of Red Hat Linux. DNS, Squid, NFS, News, NTP, and PPP are a few of the services that can be configured.

DNS serves as the name resolution standard of the Internet. The service runs as a network-wide database with many administrators. Each administrator is responsible for keeping the zone files that he or she supervises in working order. The diagnostic tool for DNS is nslookup.

Squid is a proxy server that allows a network to filter its HTTP and FTP traffic through a single caching server. This has the distinct advantage of reducing the load on the main Internet connection of the network.

NFS shares file systems across networks. This is a powerful method of controlling data and distributing I/O load, but there are many security concerns involved with its use. Care should be taken when setting up an NFS share on an unprotected network.

News services provide users with an open forum of information exchange with other users on the Internet. Internet news is easy to set up and maintain. A watchful eye should be kept out for full disk volumes or a lack of inodes.

DHCP allows a network administrator to easily manage the IP addresses and network information of many clients from a centralized server. DHCP requires some specialized setup on both the client and server sides, but is easy to maintain once it is configured.

NTP enables each machine on a network to be synchronized to a central time standard. This standard is not a single machine, but rather several machines that serve out UTC. The algorithms included with NTP allow for a highly accurate representation of time to an individual machine or a whole network.

PPP connects a machine to the Internet through a dial-up connection to an ISP. The daemon can be run as a single user on a single workstation, or it can be run on a network server with IP forwarding to allow the entire network to connect to the Internet.

TWO-MINUTE DRILL

- DNS is the Domain Name System, and it converts between machine names and IP addresses.
- The SOA record is the preamble to all zone files, and there should be exactly one in each zone file.
- CNAME is a way to give each machine several names.
- DNS is a net-wide database.
- The single most common DNS error occurs when an administrator makes updates to a zone file, restarts DNS, and notices that no one else on the Internet knows about the updates.
- A *delegation* is the glue NS record that helps you get from one nameserver to another.
- Squid is a high-performance HTTP and FTP caching proxy server. It conforms to the Harvest Cache architecture and uses the Inter-Cache Protocol (ICP) for transfers between participating peer and parent/child cache servers.
- On Red Hat 6.*x* systems, Squid is started and stopped via /etc/rc.d/init.d/squid start and /etc/rc.d/init.d/squid stop.
- NFS is a file-sharing protocol originally developed by Sun Microsystems in the mid-1980s. It is based on Sun's XDR (external data representation, a byte-order-independent data formatting standard) and RPC (remote procedure call) technologies.
- The startup script for remote NFS file systems specified in /etc/fstab, as of Red Hat 6.*x*, is /etc/rc.d/init.d/netfs.
- DHCP (Dynamic Host Configuration Protocol) and bootp are protocols that allow a client machine to obtain network information (such as an IP number) from a server.
- eth0 is the name of the network interface card (NIC) that connects the server to the network.
- Time synchronization with a centralized server is available through two protocols: XNTP and rdate.
- The configuration file for NTP is /etc/ntp.conf.
- A working hardware communication link is a prerequisite for a network connection.

SELF TEST

The following Self Test questions will help you measure your understanding of the material presented in this chapter. Read all the choices carefully, as there may be more than one correct answer. Choose all correct answers for each question.

1. Which program checks the DNS setup?
   A. dnscheck
   B. BIND
   C. nslookup
   D. resolve
2. You have added several new servers into your primary DNS server. The zone files are formatted properly, and you've restarted named. You advertise the new servers, and your help desk immediately starts getting calls that no one outside your domain can see the new servers. What is the most likely cause?
   A. Your servers are not connected to the network.
   B. The serial number was not incremented in the zone file.
   C. Someone has changed the zone files without your knowledge.
   D. The users at the other end are having ISP problems.
3. Which is an example of a properly formatted MX record?
   A. MX10.mail.domain.com.
   B. MX mail.domain.com.
   C. MX10 mail.domain.com
   D. MX10 mail.domain.com.
4. Squid serves as a caching server for which Internet protocols?
   A. FTP
   B. News
   C. HTTP
   D. DNS
5. Which is not a variant of NFS?
   A. KNFSd
   B. PCNFS
   C. MacNFS
   D. UNFSd
6. In the /etc/exports file, if we want to export /data as read-only, but grant write permission to the supervisor, the proper line is:
   A. /data (rw) superv.domain.com(ro)
   B. /data (ro) superv.domain.com(rw)
   C. /data (ro) *.domain.com(rw)
   D. /data superv.domain.com(rw)
7. On bootup, the system will check what file for NFS shares to mount?
   A. /etc/exports
   B. /etc/nfs.conf
   C. /etc/fstab
   D. /nfs/conf

8. /var fills up. What will restore operation of News?

   A. Remove /var/spool/news/articles/alt/binaries.
   B. Remove /var/lib/news/history.pag.
   C. Expire aging news articles.
   D. Make more inodes.

9. A message pops up that News is out of space, but *df -k* shows plenty remaining on /var. What's wrong?

   A. Out of inodes on file system.
   B. Hackers.
   C. Invisible files on file system.
   D. df is broken.

10. No new traffic has come in but innd is running. What's happened?

   A. Your ISP has dropped the connection.
   B. The TCP/IP link is down.
   C. The Internet has vanished and no one is posting.
   D. innd is overloaded

11. DHCP has been installed and configured properly. The network is responding. There are no firewalls or extraneous server processes. Clients are not getting their network information, though. What could be the cause?

   A. Not enough disk space.
   B. The dhcpd.leases file was not created.
   C. DHCP is in loopback mode.
   D. DHCP has phased the multicast server array.

12. You wish to configure a new IPX user to share a printer. What line should be inserted into the nwserv.conf file?

   A. User roger Pass changeme
   B. 100 roger changeme
   C. roger changeme
   D. 13 roger changeme

13. Which are proper keywords that can be used in a ntp.conf file?

   A. server
   B. client
   C. peer
   D. child

14. The driftfile in NTP serves as:

   A. A calculation of the average drift from true UTC of the local system clock.
   B. A random constant used to synchronize the clock with itself.
   C. A measure of the Earth's rotational drift.
   D. The "zero" from which system time is determined.

15. What naming scheme describes a serial port on a Linux system?

   A. /modem
   B. /dev/modem
   C. /dev/ttyS0
   D. COM1

16. You work at a large company. Every day at about noon, the network slows to a crawl. The CEO just noticed he has trouble

reading and sending email at that time and wants answers. What should you do?

A. Reconfigure your DNS servers to increase their local cache.
B. Upgrade your network.
C. Route all web surfing through a Squid server.
D. Route the CEO's mail over a different subnet.

17. Your company has just suffered an external security breach. As a result, the security department has tightened the screws on all the servers, routers, and firewalls. Up until this point, all user data had been mounted over NFS, but now, nothing works. What happened?

A. The hackers erased the NFS data, and they got the backups too.
B. The NFS ports are no longer allowed through the necessary firewalls.
C. The two are unrelated, check your disk space.
D. The file system is no longer shared from the server.

18. You add a new workstation to your dhcpd.conf file. You're in a hurry to finish, so you save and go to lunch. When you return, your phone mail is full of user complaints that they can't access the Internet, but the local network is fine. You surmise that you accidentally changed something in the dhcpd.conf file that you shouldn't have. What is the most likely cause?

A. The absence of a "routers" line.
B. The subnet mask was changed.
C. The IP range was thrown off.
D. The broadcast address was changed.

19. You've set up a PPP dialup for your small company's Internet connection. The dialup server is connected to the network so that all may share the connection. You can see the Internet from the dialup server, and you can see your internal network as well. However, the users are unable to access the Internet. What's wrong?

A. The users each need their own modems.
B. Be sure routed or gated is running on the dialup server.
C. Check to see that the network card knows about the modem.
D. Make sure IP forwarding is turned on.

20. You have the printer in your office set up as a NetWare printer for all to share. Your hard drive crashes and you have to restore from backup. Everything works from your console, and all the users use a default password, but no one can print but you. What is the fix?

A. Hook the printer directly to the network.
B. Have everyone reboot his or her machine to reestablish the connection.
C. Make sure the last backup caught the "21" directive in the nwserv.conf file.
D. Add in each individual user instead of using a default password.

RHCE

RED HAT CERTIFIED ENGINEER®

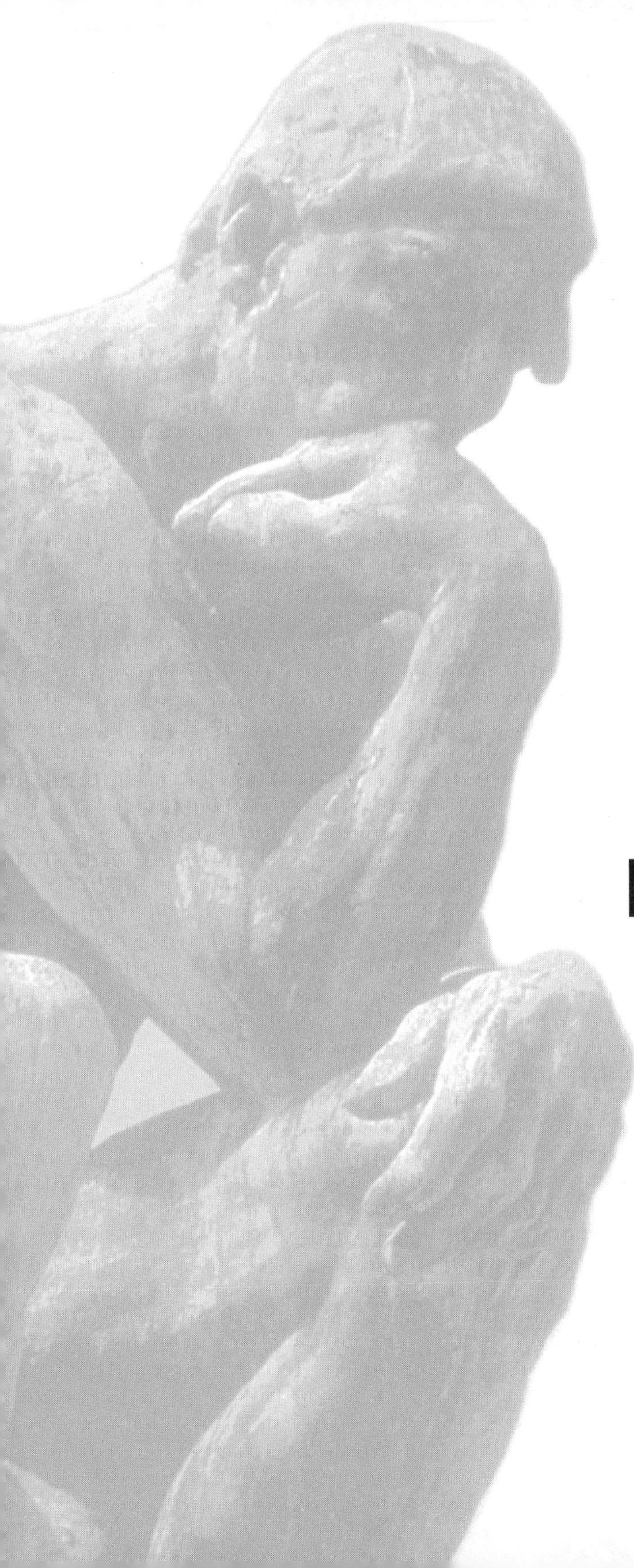

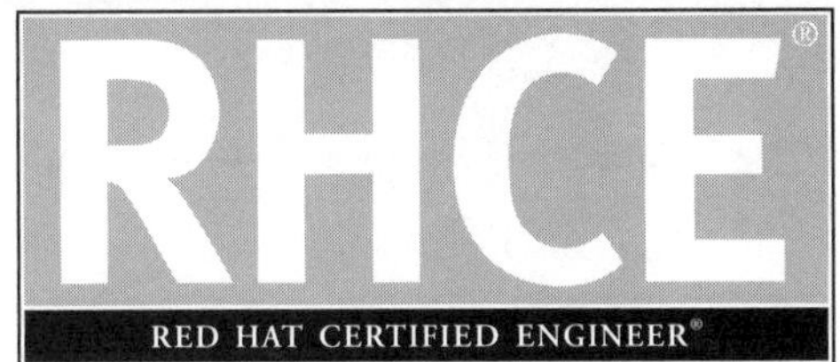

10

Systems Administration and Security

CERTIFICATION OBJECTIVES

10.01 Configuring NIS (yp)

10.02 Basic Host Security

10.03 System Logging

10.04 inetd

10.05 IP Aliasing and Virtual Hosts

10.06 Firewall Policy Elements—ipfwadm

10.07 NAT (Network Address Translation)

10.08 Routing, Static Routes

As a Red Hat Linux systems manager, you probably wear several hats, one of which is that of a security manager. This is especially so if you work for a small company. Even if you work for a large organization that has a dedicated network or systems security staff, as a systems administrator, you will probably be the person responsible for implementing the security policies on the Linux systems you manage.

You can spend very little time worrying about Linux security, or that may be your full-time job. For most Linux systems administrators, the amount of time spent on securing systems falls somewhere between these two extremes. The level of security you decide to impose on systems under your care depends on many factors, including what the system is used for and the security policies your company or organization has in place. If you are using your Red Hat Linux system for a home computer, you probably have much lower security requirements than for a system that is being used to process credit card orders for a Web site.

Red Hat Linux comes with a large and varied assortment of tools for managing security. This includes tools for managing the security on individual Linux hosts and tools for managing the security for an entire network of systems, both Linux and otherwise. In this chapter, you are introduced to some of the tools Red Hat Linux provides for managing security. First are tools for controlling access to individual Linux host systems, and then tools for securing networks.

CERTIFICATION OBJECTIVE 10.01

Configuring NIS (yp)

In order to access a system running Red Hat Linux, you usually must identify yourself by providing a valid username and password. One of the potential problems with managing a large network of Linux systems is that in order to allow a user access to any system on the network, you must provide that user with an account on every individual system.

The Network Information System, or NIS, provides you with a way to manage this. NIS allows you to share one centrally managed authorization database with other Linux systems in the network. With NIS, you maintain one password database on a NIS server, and you configure the other systems on the network to be NIS clients. When a user initiates a login session on the NIS client, that system consults its authorization file (usually /etc/passwd), and if the username that was entered doesn't exist there, the system will look up the authorization information on the NIS server.

NIS clients and NIS servers participate in NIS domains. You can have multiple NIS domains on a single network, but clients and servers can only participate in one domain. Note that a NIS domain is not the same as a BIND domain; in fact, for security reasons, your NIS domain name should be different from your BIND domain name. If you are coming from the Microsoft Windows NT world, NIS domains are analogous to LAN manager domains. If you are using NIS, you can find out the name of your NIS domain with the command:

```
domainname
```

NIS provides you with more than a shared authorization database. With NIS, you can provide shared access to any kind of information. By default, NIS under Red Hat Linux shares the following files:

- /etc/passwd
- /etc/group
- /etc/hosts
- /etc/networks
- /etc/services
- /etc/protocols
- /etc/netgroup
- /etc/rpc

You can configure NIS to share other files as well.

To provide NIS services, you must have at least one system that serves as the NIS master server. The NIS master server is where the centralized NIS database files, referred to as *maps*, are stored. To make a change to a NIS database, you must update the appropriate map on the master server. You can only have one NIS master server per NIS domain. The NIS maps are stored in /var/yp/DOMAIN, where DOMAIN is the name of your NIS domain.

In order to reduce the load on the NIS master server and provide some redundancy in case the master server goes down, you can also have Linux systems that serve as NIS slave servers. Slave servers receive copies of the NIS maps from the master server. NIS clients that need to validate a user can then validate against either the master server or a slave server. You can have multiple NIS slave servers on a network. If your network is subnetted, a recommendation is to have one slave server per subnet.

NIS clients are systems that use a NIS server to authenticate users. NIS clients don't store any information that is contained in the NIS databases; whenever that information is needed, it is retrieved from a server.

exam Watch

You will notice that most NIS commands start with yp. This is a holdover from the previous name of NIS when it was known as the Yellow Pages service.

NIS Components on Red Hat Linux

The directory /usr/lib/yp contains utilities used to configure and manage NIS services. You use the ypinit program in this directory to configure a NIS server. Table 10-1 lists the files needed to configure a NIS server.

Although NIS was designed to allow you to manage security by controlling who has access to your systems, NIS is not a very secure product. One thing you need to be aware of if you use NIS is that anyone who knows your NIS domain name and can connect to your network has access to all of the information stored in your NIS databases. There are a couple of mechanisms you can use to limit this vulnerability. You can use the file /var/yp/securenets to control who can connect to your NIS server. If your system is configured to use tcp_wrappers, the NIS software will detect this when it is installed, and you can use this method to limit access to your

TABLE 10-1

NIS Configuration Files and Commands

/usr/lib/yp/ypinit	Shell script to build initial database maps in /var/yp; ypinit -m builds the databases for a master server.
/var/yp/Makefile	Configuration file. Edit this file to control which maps are shared via NIS. You should edit this file and run *make* from the /var/yp directory.
/usr/lib/yp/makedbm	Convert text database files to NIS maps. Called by /var/yp/Makefile.
/sbin/ypserv	NIS server daemon, usually started at boot time in /etc/rc.d/rc?.d.
/sbin/yppasswdd	NIS password change daemon. You must run this in order for users to be able to change their NIS passwords with the yppass command. Usually started in /etc/rc.d/rc?.d.
/etc/ypserv.conf	ypserv daemon configuration file.
/var/yp/securenets	Controls which systems can access NIS databases.

NIS domain. Tcp_wrappers is covered later in this chapter. There is a variant of NIS, called NIS+ or NIS plus, that uses encryption and performs secure RPC authentication. Red Hat Linux has support for NIS+ clients but cannot be a NIS+ server.

To configure your workstation as a NIS client, use the authconfig utility or the linuxconf utility. Figure 10-1 shows the authconfig screen used to configure NIS. This will configure your system to use the ypbind daemon. The ypbind daemon queries the NIS server whenever a NIS lookup is needed. The authconfig window will require you to enter some information for the NIS domain that you want to join. You must at least know the name of the NIS domain. If you do not know the name of your NIS server, select the Request via broadcast option.

The other command you need to know about when running a NIS client is yppasswd. This is the command you will need to use in order to change your NIS password.

on the Job

One security risk to keep in mind if you use NIS is that anyone with access to the root account on any system that uses NIS can use the su command to switch user to any account in your NIS database.

FIGURE 10-1

The authconfig utility is used to configure a NIS client

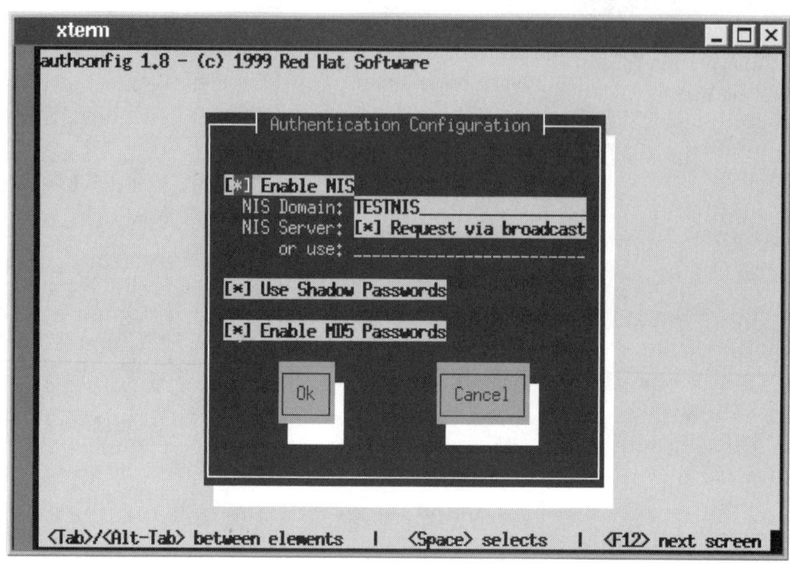

/etc/nsswitch.conf

The Name Service Switch file (/etc/nsswitch.conf) is used to control the order in which the various configuration databases available to the system are searched when information is requested. For example, consider the following entry from /etc/nsswitch.conf:

```
hosts: files nisplus nis dns
```

When an application requests a host name lookup (perhaps something as simple as ping host22), this entry tells the system that it should resolve the hostname as follows:

1. Check the local host table /etc/hosts.
2. If not found, try to locate the host name in a shared hosts map using NIS+.

3. If not found, try to locate the host name in a shared hosts map using NIS.
4. If not found, do a DNS lookup for the host name.

CERTIFICATION OBJECTIVE 10.02

Basic Host Security

A network is only as secure as the most open system in that network. Although no system can be 100-percent secure, you can follow certain basic host security measures to enhance the security on any given system and, consequently, your network. When devising security measures, you have to plan for accidental and intentional security violations.

Accidental security violations occur because users lack adequate training, or because someone tries to speed up completion of a task by not following procedures. In fact, an important consideration to make in any security measures you devise is how much of an extra burden they place on the end users of your system. Tighter security usually equates to more difficulty in getting productive work done. If security procedures are too stringent, they may backfire because users try to avoid them because they complicate their jobs. The amount of security you impose on a system should be directly proportional to the importance of what you are protecting.

Intentional security violations are deliberate attempts by someone to either gain access to information or deny the legitimate users of information access to that information. These types of attacks can range from someone who is simply "browsing around," to someone trying to destroy or bring down your system for revenge or notoriety, to a competitor trying to access trade secrets or confidential financial information.

There are several things you should be in the habit of doing to ensure your host is secure. The first is practicing good password security. Good password security consists of requiring your users to use passwords that aren't easily guessed, and requiring that they change their passwords on a regular basis. This also means closely guarding your root password.

Another step you can take to minimize security breaches is to keep your password database current. Unused accounts lying around can make good springboards for crackers trying to access your system.

You should also check system log files and accounting files and look for any unusual patterns or occurrences. You can also use utilities such as the swatch program to scan log files for certain types of messages and notify you when certain types of activity occur. Knowledge of your users' work patterns can also aid you in detecting security violations. If you notice that someone who normally works a nine-to-five workday has been logging in for long periods after midnight, you should consider investigating the reason. It could simply be that he is trying to meet a deadline on an important project, or it could be that a cracker has been logging on using his username and password after hours.

Another step you can take to keep your Red Hat Linux system secure is to install the latest errata releases from Red Hat. These contain patches or fixes for problems in applications or the operating system that could result in security violations.

Pluggable Authentication Modules (PAM) and the /etc/pam.d/... Files

Red Hat Linux comes with an authentication mechanism called "Pluggable Authentication Modules" or PAM. PAM consists of a set of dynamically loadable library modules that allow you, as the system administrator, to determine how applications perform user authentication. The idea behind PAM is to separate the process of authenticating users from the development of an application.

In traditionally written applications, the authentication mechanism is usually written into the code and compiled as part of the application. If you want to change authentication mechanisms, you have to modify the application source code and recompile. Programs that use PAM function calls to perform authentication tasks are said to be "PAM-aware." With PAM-aware applications, you can change the authentication mechanism an application uses without rewriting the application. All that is required to change the authentication mechanism an application uses is to simply modify a configuration file. Another advantage to using PAM is that you can use modules to extend the capabilities of your software. As an example, suppose you have an application that is only capable of using /etc/passwd for authentication. If you rewrite the application to use PAM modules for authentication, then the application can authenticate against any database that you have a PAM module for, such as a Novell password database or an NT password database.

PAM breaks the process of authenticating a user into four separate tasks. Modules are provided to handle these tasks. In addition to the provided modules, you can also develop your own modules. The PAM authentication tasks are:

1. **Authentication management** Establish the identity of a user (by prompting for a username/password combination, for example).
2. **Account management** Allow or deny access based on the account policies, such as no access at a certain time of day, no access when too many users are on the system, no root access from a network terminal.
3. **Session management** Apply settings for a user before he is given access to a service.
4. **Password management** These modules are required to update the user's associated authentication token. There is usually one of these for each challenge/response authentication module.

You can require PAM to use any combination of these four authentication steps when authorizing a user. When you use multiple modules to authenticate access to an application, the modules are said to be *stacked.*

You configure PAM using files in /etc/pam.d. Each file in this directory controls one service. Each line in the authorization file has the following format:

```
module_type      control_flag      module_path      [arguments]
```

Figure 10-2 shows an example PAM configuration file for configuring the login program. The # character is a comment; the backslash character \ continues the line on which it occurs to the next line in the file.

When a user logs in, the authentication process proceeds through each step in the /etc/pam.d/login file in the order they are listed. The control flag

FIGURE 10-2

The file /etc/pam.d/login configures how login authenticates users

```
#%PAM-1.0
auth       required   /lib/security/pam_securetty.so
auth       required   /lib/security/pam_pwdb.so shadow nullok
auth       required   /lib/security/pam_nologin.so
account    required   /lib/security/pam_pwdb.so
password   required   /lib/security/pam_cracklib.so
password   required   /lib/security/pam_pwdb.so nullok   \ use_authtok md5 shadow
session    required   /lib/security/pam_pwdb.so
session    optional   /lib/security/pam_console.so
```

in the second field controls whether the authentication process skips some steps or terminates immediately if one of the modules returns with a failure. When a step in the authentication process fails, the application doesn't know which module failed; it only knows that the authentication process failed. Table 10-2 explains each of the fields in a PAM configuration file.

You use the control flag field to determine how the authentication process reacts when a module returns a failure code. A value of *required* means that this module must return a success code for the authentication to succeed; however, if a particular module fails, other modules of the same type will still execute. A value of *requisite* indicates that the entire authentication process should terminate and fail immediately if the module returns a failure code. A value of *sufficient* indicates that if no other module of this type has failed, then the success of this module is sufficient enough to guarantee that the security requirements have been met. If the control flag for a module is marked as *optional*, the module is not considered crucial

TABLE 10-2

The PAM Configuration File Fields

module type	The type of authentication task being performed as outlined previously. Can be auth, account, password, or session.
control_flag	How PAM should handle module success or failure. Can be required, requisite, sufficient, or optional.
module_path	The path of the module. Most modules will be in /lib/security.
arguments	Optional arguments used by the module being invoked.

FIGURE 10-3

/etc/pam.d/shutdown—second and third *auth* modules skipped for root

```
#%PAM-1.0
auth        sufficient   /lib/security/pam_rootok.so
auth        required     /lib/security/pam_console.so
auth        required     /lib/security/pam_pwdb.so
account     required     /lib/security/pam_permit.so
```

to granting a user access to a service, and PAM ignores the success or failure code from that module.

As an example of how the control flags work, Figure 10-3 shows the /etc/pam.d/shutdown configuration file that controls access to the shutdown command. Notice that the first auth module that is checked is the rootok module. If you invoke this command from the root account, PAM will skip the other two auth modules and proceed to the account module on the last line of the file.

/etc/securetty and PAM

If you refer back to the first code example (PAM configuration file for configuring the login program), you will notice that the first module in the PAM configuration file for the login program is pam_securetty.so. This module is used to control which terminals the root account may log in from. Whenever the root account initiates a login, this module reads the file /etc/securetty. This file contains a list of the terminals that are permissible for root login and fails if the terminal that is being used to log in is not in this list. By default, the Red Hat Linux virtual consoles are the only terminals listed in this file. You should be careful which terminals you add to this file; restricting root access to terminals that are physically connected to your Linux system makes it that much more difficult for someone to attack your system via the Internet or a dial-up line.

EXERCISE 10-1

Configuring PAM

In this exercise, we experiment with some of the PAM security features of Red Hat Linux.

1. Make a backup copy of /etc/securetty: enter **cp /etc/securetty /etc/securetty.sav**.
2. Edit /etc/securetty and remove the lines for tty3 through tty8. Save the changes and exit.
3. Use ALT-F3 (CTRL-ALT-F3 if you're running an X-Window) to switch to virtual console number 3. Try to log in as *root*. What happens?
4. Use ALT-F2 to switch to virtual console number 2, and try to log in as root.
5. Restore your original /etc/securetty file: **mv /etc/securetty.sav /etc/securetty**.

exam Watch

Make sure you understand how Red Hat Linux handles user authorization.

Buffer Overruns and Security Problems

One method of attacking systems that has been successfully exploited is that of making use of *buffer overruns* in improperly written applications. Some server applications don't check the size of the input data stream they are receiving, and allow the input to overwrite other areas of the program's memory. When this happens, the server program behaves unpredictably and will often allow the user of the client application to obtain access to the system on which the server program is running.

CERTIFICATION OBJECTIVE 10.03

System Logging

An important part of maintaining a secure system is keeping track of the activities that take place on the system. Knowing the normal patterns of use on your system can help you spot unusual activity. Red Hat Linux comes with several utilities you can use to monitor the activity that takes place on a system and can help you identify the responsible party if security violations do occur.

Red Hat Linux comes with two daemons that perform logging. The klogd daemon logs kernel messages and events. The syslog daemon logs all other process activity. You can use the log files that syslogd generates to track activities on your system. If you are managing multiple Red Hat Linux systems, you can configure the syslogd daemon on each system to log messages to a central host system. Typically, you configure syslogd to start up at boot time using a file in /etc/rc.d.

/etc/syslog.conf

You choose the events that syslogd will log using the file /etc/syslog.conf. This file is a text file that consists of lines of rules. Each rule has two fields separated by one or more spaces: a selector field, and an *action* field. The selector field is a two-part field that tells syslogd which events (facilities) to log and the severity level (priority) at which events should be logged. The action field tells syslogd whether to write the message to a file or send it to someone immediately. The format of a rule in syslogd is:

```
facility.priority    action
```

Table 10-3 lists the valid entries for each field in /etc/syslog.conf.

You can use the asterisk as a wildcard in both the facility and priority subfields. For example, a specification of *.* indicates you want to log everything. A specification of auth.* means you want to log all messages

TABLE 10-3

Entries in /etc/syslog.conf are Used to Configure System Logging

facility	priority	action
auth, auth-priv, cron, daemon, kern, lpr, mail, news, syslog, user, uucp, local0 – local7, *	debug, info, notice, warning, err, crit, alert, emerg, * modifiers: !, = =debug !debug !=debug	absolute path—log event to specified file /dev/console /dev/ttyN—log event to specified terminal @host—log event to remote host user1, user2,…—send message to specified users *—do a write-all (wall) to all users

from the auth facility. You can modify the priority subfield with the ! and = characters. The default behavior for syslog is to log any message from a facility that has a priority equal to or higher than the one you specify. If you only want to see error messages from a facility, use the = modifier to specify only messages of that severity; auth.=err means only log error messages from the auth facility. The ! character negates a priority, so auth.!err means ignore any message coming from the auth facility with a priority of err or higher; auth.!=err means log all messages from the auth facility except messages with a priority of err.

Most messages from syslogd are written to files in the /var/log directory. You should scan these logs on a regular basis and look for changes in activity patterns that could indicate a break-in or attempts at breaking in to your system. If you are logging the activity on many systems, or if your system is very busy, wading through the log files and maintaining them can become a time-consuming process. Red Hat Linux comes with utilities that you can use to leverage the effectiveness of your log files.

Managing Logs (logrotate)

The logrotate utility allows you to set up automatic management tasks for log files. These include rotating log files, compressing log files, mailing log files, and removing log files. The logrotate utility is run via cron, and you can specify the frequency at which any given log file is modified. You configure the logrotate utility using the /etc/logrotate.conf file. The package file for the logrotate utility is logrotate-3.2-1.i386.rpm.

Monitoring Logs (swatch)

The swatch utility is another very useful utility that you can use to help you keep an eye on what is being sent to your log files. The swatch utility monitors log files and takes action when certain events occur. You configure the events to monitor and the type of action to take. The action can be as simple as sending a message to your terminal, or something more involved such as calling a pager number. By default, swatch looks for its configuration information in the hidden file .swatchrc in your home directory. The package file for the swatch utility is swatch-2.2-7.noarch.rpm.

CERTIFICATION OBJECTIVE 10.04

inetd

On a TCP/IP network, communication occurs between clients and servers. For example, when you use the telnet application to establish a login session on a remote system, the telnet application you are using communicates with the telnet server daemon on the remote system. A client application needs two pieces of information to establish a connection to a remote system: the address of the remote system, and the port number (or socket number) of the server process that is running on the remote system. Every commonly used TCP/IP application has a standard defined port number. For example, the standard port number for the telnet server daemon is always 23. The reason you don't normally have to specify the port number when telnetting to another system is that the telnet client application assumes you are connecting to port number 23 on the remote system. The file /etc/services lists port numbers and the services they address.

For a client to connect to a service on a remote system, the corresponding server program for that service must be running on the remote system. The port number for that application is the address of the *running* server application. If you are using a telnet client, you will connect to the telnet daemon at port 23; if you are using a Web browser, you will connect to the httpd daemon at port 80. If you look at the list of defined port numbers, you will see that there are potentially dozens of services that client applications could request connections to. If you are managing a server, it appears that in order to allow connections to these services, you will have to start the dozens of different server applications at system boot.

The inetd (for Internet daemon) program provides a way around this problem. Inetd is a special server program that is usually started at boot time. The startup script is /etc/rc.d/init.d/inet; there should be links to this program in the appropriate /etc/rc.d/rc?.d directories. The inetd program listens for connection requests from client applications to these socket addresses. When it receives a connection request, inetd starts up the server program for that port, hands the port over to the server application, and then goes back to waiting for another connection request. Once the client finishes with the service, the server application terminates until another client requires that service. The advantage this mechanism provides is that you don't have to have a server daemon running for every possible type of client request you might wish to satisfy; the inetd server will start up servers as they are needed.

You configure which services inetd will start using the /etc/inetd.conf file. Each line in the file specifies a particular service that you want to allow inetd to start. Inetd will listen for connection requests coming to the ports for those services. As a security measure, you should remove or comment out lines for services that you do not use. Figure 10-4 shows a sample inetd.conf file.

Each line in /etc/inetd.conf has the format:

```
service  socket_type  protocol  wait/nowait  user  server_program
[arguments]
```

FIGURE 10-4

The */etc/inetd.conf* file is used to configure inetd

```
# Example /etc/inetd.conf file
#Lines beginning with a '#' are comments
discard   stream  tcp   nowait  root  internal
discard   dgram   udp   wait    root  internal
daytime   stream  tcp   nowait  root  internal
daytime   dgram   udp   nowait  root  internal
telnet    stream  tcp   nowait  root  /usr/sbin/in.telnetd
ftp       stream  tcp   nowait  root  /usr/sbin/in.ftpd
talk      dgram   udp   wait    root  /usr/sbin/in.talkd
smtp      stream  tcp   nowait  root  /usr/sbin/in.smtpd
nntp      stream  tcp   nowait  news  /usr/sbin/in.nntpd
pop-3     stream  tcp   nowait  root  /usr/sbin/in.pop3.d
```

TABLE 10-4

Each Line in /etc/inetd.conf Controls a Single Service

service	A service that inetd should start by monitoring its assigned port number for connection requests. The port numbers for each service are listed in /etc/services.
socket type	One of stream, dgram, raw, rdm, or seqpacket.
protocol	One of udp, tcp, rpc/tcp, or rpc/udp.
wait/nowait	Should be wait only for datagram (UDP) sockets; all others should be nowait.
user	Account under which server should run.
server program	Path of server program or internal if the service is supplied by inetd.
arguments	Optional arguments for server program.

The fields are explained in Table 10-4.

You should only use inetd to start infrequently used services. Daemons for services such as a Web server, which receive constant connection requests, should be started as background processes at boot time to avoid the overhead involved in starting them through inetd.

When you modify /etc/inetd.conf, you must use the kill command to tell inetd to reread its configuration file. The PID for the inetd daemon is stored in /var/run/inetd.pid, so the easiest way to do this is:

```
kill -HUP `cat /var/run/inetd.pid`
```

EXERCISE 10-2

Configuring inetd

In this exercise, you will remove a service from inetd and then add it back. Make sure you have access to the system console before trying this exercise.

Establish a telnet session using the command **telnet localhost** and log in using a nonprivileged user account. Once you have verified that you can telnet to the system, log out.

Edit /etc/inetd.conf and comment out the line for the in.telnetd daemon.

1. Tell inetd to reread its configuration file using the command:

   ```
   kill -HUP `cat /var/run/inetd.pid`
   ```

2. Try to establish a telnet session now. Are you able to?
3. Edit /etc/inetd.conf and uncomment the in.telnetd line. Tell inetd to reread its configuration file.

tcp_wrappers and /etc/hosts.allow and /etc/hosts.deny

Although you can achieve some measure of security by commenting or removing unused services in /etc/inetd.conf, there is still the possibility of someone mounting an attack against the services you left enabled. Red Hat Linux comes with a package called tcp_wrappers that is enabled by default and allows you to limit access to the services you offer via inetd. Tcp_wrappers fits between inetd and the applications it starts up. With tcp_wrappers enabled, when inetd receives a network request for a service, it passes the request to tcp_wrappers. Tcp_wrappers logs the request and then checks its access rules. If the request is from a client that is allowed to access your server, then tcp_wrappers starts the requested server program and exits.

In addition to the security it provides, tcp_wrappers has some other advantages. It is invisible to the client, it is application independent, and the only time it is active is when inetd is establishing a session—it doesn't impose any overhead on the running server program. Applications can also be built using the tcp_wrappers library routines. Network access to these applications can then be controlled through the tcp_wrappers configuration files.

exam Watch

Under Red Hat Linux, the NFS* portmap *program has been built with tcp_wrappers, but any access rules you write for portmap can only use IP addresses.

The tcp_wrappers image is /usr/sbin/tcpd. You use tcp_wrappers by replacing the server program in /etc/inetd.conf with the tcp_wrappers daemon tcpd. The server program and its arguments then become arguments to tcpd. For example, in a standard inetd.conf file without tcp_wrappers, the entry to start the ftp daemon is:

```
ftp  stream  tcp  nowait  root  /usr/sbin/in.ftpd -l -a
```

With tcp_wrappers, the entry to start the same service becomes:

```
ftp  stream  tcp  nowait  root  /usr/sbin/tcpd  in.ftpd -l -a
```

You configure the access rules for tcp_wrappers using two files: /etc/hosts.allow and /etc/hosts.deny. Clients listed in hosts.allow are allowed access; clients listed in hosts.deny are denied access. An important point to remember is that if a client is not listed in either file, then it is automatically granted access. When tcp_wrappers searches its access files, the search stops on the first match that is found for a client. If either file is missing, then it is treated as an empty file; you can turn off access control by deleting hosts.allow and hosts.deny. The search order is:

1. hosts.allow
2. hosts.deny
3. no match = access granted

You use the same access control language in both /etc/hosts.allow and /etc/hosts.deny to tell tcp_wrappers which clients to allow or deny. The basic format of the lines in both files is:

```
daemon_list : client_list
```

For example, the line:

```
in.telnetd : 192.168.1.5
```

in the file /etc/hosts.allow tells tcp_wrappers that a client with the IP address 192.168.1.5 is allowed to telnet in to your system. The same line in /etc/hosts.deny tells tcp_wrappers that the client is *not* allowed to telnet into your system. You can specify clients a number of different ways, as shown in Table 10-5.

The ALL wildcard listed in the table can be used to represent any client or any service. Multiple lists can be separated by commas. Restrictions or exceptions can be applied to both daemon lists and client lists using the

TABLE 10-5 Ways to Specify Clients in /etc/hosts.allow and /etc/hosts.deny

.xyz.com	NOTE: begins with a dot. Matches any client where the last part of the host name contains '"xyz.com". Matches both ws1.xyz.com and server1.engr.xyz.com.
172.16.	NOTE: ends with a dot. Matches any client with an IP of 172.16.x.y.
172.16.72.0/255.255.254.0	IP network with subnet mask. Matches any client with an IP of 172.16.72.0 through 172.16.73.255.
ALL	Match any client, match any daemon.
LOCAL	Match any client host name that doesn't contain a dot.

EXCEPT operator. We will use a sample hosts.allow file (Figure 10-5) and hosts.deny file (Figure 10-6) to see how lists can be built to control access.

The first line in the hosts.allow file is simply a comment. The next line specifies that any client that is in the same domain as this system or any client from the .asafe.dom.com can connect to any service. The third line specifies that any client on the 192.168.25 subnet except for the client with an IP of 192.168.25.73 can ftp to this system. The last line specifies that the client with an IP of 192.168.1.10 can finger this host or use ftp.

The first line in the hosts.deny file is a comment. Comment lines begin with a number sign (#) and can appear anywhere in either file. The second line specifies that any client in the .xyz.com domain can't do anything other than run finger on our host. The third line specifies that no one other than the client with an IP of 192.168.1.10 is allowed to telnet to our host. The last line specifies that any other client that doesn't match any other rule will be denied all access to all inetd services.

FIGURE 10-5 A sample hosts.allow file

```
#hosts.allow
ALL : LOCAL, .asafe.dom.com
in.ftpd : 192.168.25.0/255.255.255.0 EXCEPT 192.168.25.73
in.fingerd, in.ftpd : 192.168.1.10
```

FIGURE 10-6

A sample hosts.deny file

```
#hosts.deny
ALL EXCEPT in.fingerd : .xyz.com
in.telnetd : ALL EXCEPT 192.168.1.10
 ALL:ALL
```

The tcp_wrappers access control language also allows you to specify a shell command to execute for a given client list. The format for a rule like this is:

```
daemon_list : client_list : shell_command
```

There are a number of expansion patterns you can use with these rules. When you include these as part of a shell command to be run, they will be expanded before the command is run. Some of the patterns you can use are listed in Table 10-6.

Tcp_wrappers also comes with some optional extensions that you enable when you build tcp_wrappers. The most interesting of these is the twist operator. An example of using this operator in hosts.deny is shown here:

```
in.telnetd : .hack.org : twist /bin/echo Sorry %c, access denied
```

The twist operator replaces the current process with the shell command and connects stdin, stdout, and stderr to the client process. In the preceding example, if someone from the hack.org domain tries to telnet to your system, he will receive a customized error message.

Tcp_wrappers also comes with two programs that you can use to check your configuration. The first of these is tcpdcheck. Tcpdcheck scans your /etc/hosts.allow and /etc/hosts.deny files and reports potential problems. The other program that you can use to check your configuration is

TABLE 10-6

Possible tcp_wrappers Expansion Patterns

%a	Client address	%h	Client host name
%A	Host address	%H	Server host name
%c	Client information	%p	Daemon process id
%d	Daemon process name	%s	Server information

tcpdmatch. Tcpdmatch allows you to test your rules to see if they behave as you expect. As an example, suppose you have added the rule for the in.telnetd daemon shown earlier, but you would really like to see what happens when someone from the hack.org domain tries to telnet to your system. You can test your system's response with the command:

```
tcpdmatch in.telnetd ws1.hack.org
```

and tcpdmatch returns:

```
client:   host name ws1.hack.org
client:   address  192.168.200.200
server:   process  in.telnetd
matched:  /etc/hosts.deny line 9
option:   twist /bin/echo Sorry ws1.hack.org, access denied
access:   delegated
```

EXERCISE 10-3

Configuring tcp_wrappers

In this exercise, you will use tcp_wrappers to control access to network resources. Since Red Hat Linux ships with tcp_wrappers enabled, you shouldn't have to make any modifications to /etc/inetd.conf.

1. Verify that you can telnet to the system using the address localhost.
2. Edit /etc/hosts.deny and add the following line:

   ```
   ALL : ALL
   ```

3. What happens when you try to telnet to the address localhost?
4. Edit /etc/hosts.allow and add the line:

   ```
   in.telnetd : localhost
   ```

5. Now what happens when you try to telnet to the address localhost?
6. If you have other systems available to you, try restricting access to the telnet service using some of the other tcp_wrappers rules.
7. Undo your changes when you are finished.

CERTIFICATION OBJECTIVE 10.05

IP Aliasing and Virtual Hosts

If you have more than one network interface card (NIC) in your Red Hat Linux system, you can attach your system to multiple networks and use it as a router between two physical subnets. At times, you may find it necessary or useful to use a Linux system as a router between logical subnets; that is, you wish to route packets between two different IP subnets that exist on the same physical network.

This is actually a quite useful capability, and one that is used very often. As an example, suppose that you have two official Class-C IP network addresses for your company. All of the systems in your company are on the same LAN, but half of the systems have IP addresses in one subnet, and the other half have IP addresses in the other subnet. In order for a system on one subnet to communicate with a system on the other subnet using IP, a router is required, even though both systems are on the same physical network.

In order to accomplish this, you need to be able to assign multiple IP addresses to a single NIC. To assign more than one IP address to a NIC, you need to enable the IP aliasing kernel module.

The first step in using IP aliases is to load the IP alias module:

```
insmod  /lib/modules/`uname -r`/ipv4/ip_alias.o
```

If the module has been compiled into the kernel, you can skip this step.

The next step in the process is to assign IP addresses to your network interfaces using the ifconfig command. When you specify an Ethernet interface, the interface name for the first Ethernet card in your system is eth0. The first IP address you assign to this interface will be the primary address for that interface. Subsequently assigned IP addresses will be aliases.

To specify the interface for the alias addresses, you specify the interface name followed by a colon and the alias number. As an example, here is how to assign three IP addresses to an Ethernet card:

```
ifconfig eth0 192.168.10.5
ifconfig eth0:0 192.168.200.5
ifconfig eth0:1 10.20.15.80
```

The final step in the process is to set up the appropriate routing information for the networks you have defined. We will look at setting up static routes later in this chapter.

Another use for IP aliases is using them to set up virtual host services. When you assign multiple IP addresses to an interface, that system can participate in multiple DNS domains.

With virtual host services, you can use one system as a server for multiple virtual domains.

To set up virtual domains, you must create an entire copy of the root directory structure of your system for each domain you create. This includes all library, binary, dev, and configuration directories. You can use the virtfs shell script to create virtual domain directories.

You use a program called virtuald in /etc/inetd.conf to start virtual host services. The virtuald program looks at the IP address that it is being called as and does a chroot to the virtual directory that has been assigned to that IP address in the configuration file for that service. The command chroot newdir sets the root directory for the process that executed the command to the path referenced by newdir; everything above the new root directory is hidden from the process.

To set up virtual host services, you modify /etc/inetd.conf. For example, the line in inetd.conf to start the ftp server would normally look like this:

```
ftp stream tcp nowait root /usr/sbin/tcpd in.ftpd -l -a
```

If you are configuring virtual host services, the same line would look like this:

```
ftp stream tcp nowait root /usr/local/bin/virtuald \
        /virtual/conf.ftp in.ftpd -l -a
```

Each virtual service is controlled by a configuration file that tells the virtuald program which virtual domain to chroot to for a given IP address. An example configuration file for the ftp service might read:

```
192.168.10.5 /virtual/xyz.com
192.168.200.5 /virtual/netzine.org
10.20.50.80 /virtual/widgetsrus.com
```

If you are providing virtual host services for Web services, you should use the virtual domain mechanism built into the Apache Web server. This will provide faster response for your users and allow Apache to use its built-in mechanisms for controlling traffic.

CERTIFICATION OBJECTIVE 10.06

Firewall Policy Elements—ipfwadm

If your organization's network is connected to the Internet or another external network, you probably have a firewall in place between your network and the external network (or have at least considered putting one in). A system running Red Hat Linux can make a very good firewall system even if the other systems on your network are running some other operating system such as Windows NT or the Macintosh OS. Firewalls are used to secure an internal network by controlling who can connect to systems on the internal network, and by controlling what kind of information is allowed out of the internal network.

A firewall sits between your company's internal LAN and an outside network. It is the job of the firewall to examine every network packet that passes into or out of your LAN and to filter out those packets that you, as the security administrator, have deemed a security risk. To understand this *packet filtering* process, you have to understand a little bit about how information is sent across networks.

When you send a message over a network, the message isn't sent as a single unit. Instead, the message is broken down into smaller-sized units called *packets*, and these packets are sent. When the packets reach their final destination, they are reassembled into the complete message. In addition to containing a portion of your message, each packet also contains some "'administrative" information, including the source address of the packet (where it came from), the destination address of the packet (where it's going), and the type of information contained in the packet. A firewall examines these administrative fields in each packet to determine whether to allow the packet to pass.

Red Hat Linux comes with everything you need to configure a system to be a firewall. On earlier versions of Red Hat Linux, ipfw was used to configure a Linux firewall configuration, and ipfwadm was the utility that was used to manage the firewall configuration. Under version 6.0, ipfw has been replaced by ipchains, which has several improvements over ipfw.

Packet filtering has to be compiled into the kernel to use Linux as a firewall system. To check that packet filtering is present, look for the file /proc/net/ip_fwchains. If this file isn't present, you will probably need to rebuild the kernel (using make xconfig is the easiest way) and make sure that the *CONFIG_FIREWALL* option is set to "y".

Configuring ipchains

The "chains" in ipchains are sets of rules that are applied to each network packet that passes through your Linux firewall system. Each rule does two things: it specifies the conditions that a packet must meet to match the rule, and it specifies the action or target to take if the packet matches. Ipchains has three default chains:

- **input** All incoming packets are checked against the rules in this chain.
- **output** All outgoing packets are checked against the rules in this chain.
- **forward** All packets being sent to another machine are checked against the rules in this chain.

These default chains cannot be deleted. You configure your firewall by modifying these default chains and by adding your own rules. You can also add and delete your own chains.

You use the ipchains command with the appropriate command options to manage rules and chains. Table 10-7 lists some of the commands you can use.

You can be very specific when telling ipchains which packets to match for a given rule. Some of the criteria that you can use to filter packets include the packet's source address, the packet's destination address, and the protocol type of the packet. Table 10-8 summarizes some of the parameters you can use to specify packets to filter.

The target that you specify with the -j parameter is the action the firewall should take if the packet matches the criteria for that rule. In addition to your own user-defined targets, you can use one of the predefined targets:

- **ACCEPT** Allow packet to pass
- **DENY** Drop packet; client doesn't receive any indication of packet's fate
- **REJECT** Drop packet; send client an ICMP "destination unreachable" message
- **MASQ** Used for network address translation

TABLE 10-7

Ipchains Commands

-N	Create a new chain
-X	Delete an empty chain
-L -v -n	List rules in a chain print counters no address lookups, use IP only
-F	Flush rules for a chain
-P	Change policy for a chain
-Z	Zero counters for all rules in a chain
-A	Append new rule to a chain
-I	Insert new rule in a chain
-R	Replace a rule in a chain
-D	Delete a rule in a chain

- **REDIRECT** Send a TCP or UDP packet to a local port on the firewall system
- **RETURN** Return to previous calling chain or jump to chain's policy target

We will look at some examples of defining some IP chains to see how you can use them to configure firewall services. To list all of the rules in all of the chains defined on the system, use the command:

```
ipchains -L
```

To define a rule that would prohibit any access from the 192.168.75.0 subnet and send a "destination unreachable" message back to any client that tried to connect, use the command:

```
ipchains -A input -s 192.168.75.0/24 -j REJECT
```

TABLE 10-8 Specifying Packets to Filter with ipchains

parameter	argument	explanation
-s	source address	Can be specified four ways full name: host1.xyz.com IP address: 192.168.1.1 group of IP addresses: 192.168.1.0/24 or 192.168.1.0/255.255.255.0 match any address: 0/0
-d	destination address	Same as for source address
-p	protocol	TPC, UDP, or ICMP
-I	interface	
-j	<target>	Action to perform on packet if it matches, can be one of ACCEPT, DENY, REJECT, MASQ, REDIRECT, RETURN, or user defined
-y		Block TCP SYN packet
!	can precede any parameter argument	Inversion operator -p TCP—match any TCP packet -p ! TCP—match any non-TCP packet

To define a rule that would prohibit users on the host 192.168.25.200 from "pinging" our system (remember that ping uses the ICMP protocol), use the command:

```
ipchains -A input -s 192.168.25.200 -p icmp -j DENY
```

To guard against TCP SYN attacks, from outside our network (assuming our network address is 192.168.190.0), use the command:

```
ipchains -A input -s !192.168.190.0/24 -p tcp -y
```

To delete the first rule we added, use the command:

```
ipchains -D input -s 192.168.25.200 -p icmp -j DENY
```

The policy for a chain is the default action or target to apply if no rule matches. By default, the policies for all three built-in chains are ACCEPT. To change the policy for the forward chain to be more secure, use the command:

```
ipchains -P forward DENY
```

You can save your firewall configuration to a file using the command:

```
ipchains-save >firewall.conf
```

To restore the configuration, use the command:

```
ipchains-restore <firewall.conf
```

Knowing how to secure a Red Hat Linux system against unauthorized access is vital knowledge. Be sure you understand the concepts and commands discussed in this chapter.

EXERCISE 10-4

Configuring IP Chains

In this exercise, you will restrict access to network services using IP chains.

1. Verify that you can send ICMP packets to your system using the command:

```
ping localhost
```

2. Add a firewall rule to deny all ICMP packets from localhost (127.0.0.1):

```
ipchains -A input -s 127.0.0.1 -p ICMP -j DENY
```

3. What happens when you try to ping localhost now?
4. Modify the rule you added above using the command:

```
ipchains -R input -s 127.0.0.1 -p ICMP -j REJECT
```

5. Now what happens when you try to ping localhost?
6. Delete the rule you added using the command:

```
ipchains -D input -s 127.0.0.1 -p ICMP -j REJECT
```

CERTIFICATION OBJECTIVE 10.07

NAT (Network Address Translation)

Network address translation (NAT) is a firewall feature that allows you to connect systems to the Internet and disguise their true IP addresses. NAT works by modifying the header information in IP packets as they pass through the firewall. As each packet passes through the firewall, the internal source address in the header is replaced with a public address. When the firewall receives incoming packets destined for a host on the internal network, the process happens in reverse. As the packets pass through the firewall, the header of each packet is modified so that the public address in the packet's destination field is replaced with the internal address of the system it is destined for.

There are several reasons why this is useful. Most obvious is the fact that disguising your internal IP addresses makes it harder for someone to attempt a break-in on your network. One of the major uses for NAT is that it allows you to connect systems to the Internet without having to have an officially assigned IP address for each system you want to have access to the Internet. Many organizations use the RFC1597 free IP network addresses to set up their internal IP networks. RFC1597 sets aside the networks 10.0.0.0, 172.16.0.0, and 192.168.0.0 for private use. Systems using addresses cannot directly connect to the Internet. With the aid of NAT, however, these systems can access the Internet as if they had an officially assigned IP address.

IP Masquerading

Red Hat Linux supports a variation of NAT called *IP masquerading*. IP masquerading allows you to provide Internet access to multiple computers with a single officially assigned IP address. Like NAT, the masquerade process is invisible to both your internal systems and systems on the Internet. Unlike NAT, which is basically a one-to-one mapping of an internal IP address to a valid external IP address, IP masquerading lets you map multiple internal IP addresses to a single valid external IP address.

Connecting multiple systems to the Internet using IP masquerading is a fairly straightforward process. Your firewall will need a NIC to connect to your LAN, and you will have to configure a SLIP or PPP interface to connect to the Internet. The basic outline of the process is:

- Assign your official IP address to the interface connected to the Internet.
- Assign your LAN systems addresses from one of the RFC1597 networks. Reserve one address for the NIC on your firewall.
- Assign this reserved address to the NIC on your firewall.
- Use ipchains to set up IP masquerading.
- Configure the systems on your LAN to use your firewall for their Internet gateway.

When an internal client system on your LAN sends a packet addressed to a host on the Internet, the packet will be handed off to the firewall. The firewall will modify the packet's header by replacing the source address with the firewall's official IP address and assigning a new port number to the packet. The firewall will remember the original packet header information. When a packet comes in from the Internet to the firewall that is addressed to the port number that was assigned to the outgoing packets from the internal client, the process is reversed. The firewall will replace the destination field and port with the internal client's private IP address and original port number, and then forward the packet back onto the LAN.

In order to use IP masquerading, IP forwarding must be enabled as outlined in the next section on IP forwarding. The next step in the process is using the ipchains command to enable masquerading. In this example, we will assume that your internal LAN is using the RFC1597 address of 192.168.80.0. The commands necessary to enable masquerading are:

```
ipchains -P forward DENY       # Turn OFF forwarding for everybody
ipchains -A forward -s 192.168.80.0/24 -j MASQ
```

IP Forwarding

IP forwarding is more commonly referred to as *routing*. Routing is critical to the operation of the Internet or any IP network. To be a router, a system must have multiple network connections. A router is not usually the final destination for a network packet; instead, it is simply a waypoint for that packet on its way to its final destination. A router works by examining the destination address of each packet it receives from a network interface. The router then decides which network interface to send the packet back out on in order to get it to its final destination. To use a Red Hat Linux system as a router, you must enable the built-in routing support. You must also enable routing to support IP masquerading.

To enable IP forwarding, edit */etc/sysconfig/network* and change the line that reads:

```
FORWARD_IPV4=false
```

to

```
FORWARD_IPV4=true
```

and reboot.

Work is underway to build a complete Linux router that will fit on a single floppy. Visit http://www.psychosis.com/linux-router/ to find out more.

CERTIFICATION OBJECTIVE 10.08

Routing, Static Routes

Even systems that don't serve as routers must know how to route packets in order to reach systems outside of their subnet. Any system that uses IP keeps a list of rules, called a *routing table*, that it uses to determine where to send packets. Each entry in the routing table contains at least three fields. The first field is a destination address. If a packet's destination address matches this field, then this rule will be used to forward the packet. The second field is the interface to which the packet will be sent. The third field is optional and contains the address of a router that will route the packet further along its journey across the network. Keeping routing tables current and accurate on all the systems on a network is crucial to keeping the network running. There are many methods for doing this automatically, but that discussion is beyond the scope of this study guide.

The simplest method for managing routing tables is through the use of *static routes*. Static routes are entries that you enter to the routing tables manually. If your network is small, if your network configuration doesn't change very frequently, or if your system is an end system, static routes can be adequate for managing your routing configuration. You manage static routes using the *route* command. Table 10-9 shows the route commands you can use to manage your routing table.

TABLE 10-9 Commands for Managing Your System's Routing Table

Command	Description
route -n	Display the current routing table.
route add -net 192.168.1.0\ netmask 255.255.255.0 eth0	Add a route to the 192.168.1.0 subnet via interface eth0.
route add -host\ 192.168.50.10 gw 192.168.1.1	Add a route to the host 192.168.50.10 via the gateway (gw) or router 192.168.1.1. The gateway must be reachable (you should be able to ping it) in order to specify it in the route.
route add default gw\ 192.168.1.1 eth0	Set default gateway. Every system should have a default gateway. If the destination address for a packet doesn't match any of the other entries in the routing table, then it will be sent to this system. The default gateway will show up with a destination address of 0.0.0.0 when you display the routing table with route -n.
route add -net 172.16.64.0\ netmask 255.255.224.0\ gw 192.168.1.1	Add a route to the 172.16.64.0 subnet via the router 192.168.1.1

Figure 10-7 shows the routing table that results when the commands in Table 10-9 are issued.

Now that you have seen some of the security capabilities of Red Hat Linux, here are some possible scenario questions and their answers.

FIGURE 10-7 A typical routing table. Host IP is 192.168.1.80; default route is 0.0.0.0

```
[root@localhost HOWTO]# route -n
Kernel IP routing table
Destination    Gateway        Genmask         Flags Metric Ref Use Iface
192.168.1.80   0.0.0.0        255.255.255.255 UH    0      0     0 eth0
192.168.50.10  192.168.1.1    255.255.255.255 UGH   0      0     0 eth0
192.168.1.0    0.0.0.0        255.255.255.0   U     0      0     0 eth0
172.16.64.0    192.168.1.1    255.255.224.0   UG    0      0     0 eth0
127.0.0.0      0.0.0.0        255.0.0.0       U     0      0     0 lo
0.0.0.0        192.168.1.1    0.0.0.0         UG    0      0     0 eth0
```

QUESTIONS AND ANSWERS	
You have installed an ftp server on your company network, but you would like to restrict access to certain departments. Each department has its own subnet.	Use tcp_wrappers to block access to the ftp service for unwanted subnets.
You only have one official IP address, but you need to provide Web access to the Internet for five systems.	Use ipchains to implement IP masquerading.
You are having trouble connecting to network services from your workstation.	Use the route -n command to make sure your default gateway is set.

CERTIFICATION SUMMARY

Being able to ensure that a Red Hat Linux system and the information it contains is adequately protected from attack from both inside and outside sources is a normal responsibility for most Red Hat Linux system administrators. Red Hat Linux comes with a variety of utilities that can be used to establish a secure computing environment. You must select the tools and determine the level of security that is appropriate for your environment.

Red Hat Linux can be a powerful tool for securing networks from outside attack. With tcp_wrappers and ipchains, you can turn your Red Hat Linux system into a nearly impenetrable firewall. You can also use Red Hat Linux as a secure portal to the Internet for your LAN using the IP masquerading features that are built into the kernel.

TWO-MINUTE DRILL

- The Network Information System, NIS, allows you to share one centrally managed authorization database with other Linux systems in the network.
- The directory /usr/lib/yp contains utilities used to configure and manage NIS services. You use the ypinit program in this directory to configure a NIS server.

- NIS is not a very secure product. Anyone who knows your NIS domain name and can connect to your network has access to all of the information stored in your NIS databases.
- Red Hat Linux comes with an authentication mechanism called "Pluggable Authentication Modules" or PAM. PAM consists of a set of dynamically loadable library modules that allow you, as the system administrator, to determine how applications perform user authentication.
- The first module in the PAM configuration file for the login program is pam_securetty.so. This module is used to control which terminals the root account may log in from. Whenever the root account initiates a login, this module reads the file /etc/securetty. This file contains a list of the terminals that are permissible for root login, and fails if the terminal that is being used to log in is not in this list.
- Red Hat Linux comes with two daemons that perform logging. The klogd daemon logs kernel messages and events. The syslog daemon logs all other process activity.
- The logrotate utility allows you to set up automatic management tasks for log files. These include rotating log files, compressing log files, mailing log files, and removing log files.
- The swatch utility is another very useful utility that you can use to help you keep an eye on what is being sent to your log files. The swatch utility monitors log files and takes action when certain events occur.
- A client application needs two pieces of information to establish a connection to a remote system: the address of the remote system, and the *port number* (or *socket number*) of the server process that is running on the remote system.
- For a client to connect to a service on a remote system, the corresponding server program for that service must be running on the remote system.
- Red Hat Linux comes with a package called tcp_wrappers that is enabled by default and allows you to limit access to the services you offer via inetd.

- ❑ Under Red Hat Linux, the NFS portmap program has been built with tcp_wrapper, but any access rules you write for portmap can only use IP addresses.
- ❑ If you have more than one network interface card (NIC) in your Red Hat Linux system, you can attach your system to multiple networks and use it as a router between two physical subnets.
- ❑ If your organization's network is connected to the Internet or another external network, you probably have a firewall in place between your network and the external network (or have at least considered putting one in). A system running Red Hat Linux can make a very good firewall system even if the other systems on your network are running some other operating system such as Windows NT or the Macintosh OS.
- ❑ The "chains" in ipchains are sets of rules that are applied to each network packet that passes through your Linux firewall system. Each rule does two things: it specifies the conditions that a packet must meet to match the rule, and it specifies the action or *target* to take if the packet matches.
- ❑ Network address translation (NAT) is a firewall feature that allows you to connect systems to the Internet and disguise their true IP addresses. NAT works by modifying the header information in IP packets as they pass through the firewall.
- ❑ Red Hat Linux supports a variation of NAT called *IP masquerading*. IP masquerading allows you to provide Internet access to multiple computers with a single officially assigned IP address.
- ❑ IP forwarding is more commonly referred to as *routing*. Routing is critical to the operation of the Internet or any IP network. To be a router, a system must have multiple network connections. A router is not usually the final destination for a network packet; instead, it is simply a waypoint for that packet on its way to its final destination. A router works by examining the destination address of each packet it receives from a network interface.
- ❑ The simplest method for managing routing tables is through the use of *static routes*. Static routes are entries that you enter to the routing tables manually.

SELF TEST

The following Self Test questions will help you measure your understanding of the material presented in this chapter. Read all the choices carefully, as there may be more than one correct answer. Choose all correct answers for each question.

1. You have a network consisting of 50 Linux workstations and 5 Linux servers. Most of the workstations are in public areas, and your users need to be able to log in from any workstation on the network. How might you satisfy this requirement?
   A. Keep a master copy of /etc/passwd on one of the servers, and do a backup and restore of that copy to all of the workstations every evening,
   B. Set one of the servers up to be a NIS server. Set another server up to be a NIS slave server. Make the workstations NIS clients.
   C. Set the workstations up to be NIS clients.
   D. Create a common account on every workstation and give everyone the password to this account.
2. How would you set up the workstations to be NIS clients?
   A. Edit /etc/passwd and add the line USE_NIS at the end of the file.
   B. Start the ypbind daemon.
   C. Add a line to start ypbind to /etc/inetd.conf.
   D. Run authconfig and enable NIS.
3. A user on of the NIS workstations calls you and tells you that she is having trouble changing her password using the passwd command. What should you tell her?
   A. You'll change her password for her.
   B. Try picking a more secure password.
   C. Make sure the CAPS LOCK key isn't on.
   D. She must use the yppasswd to change her NIS password.
4. Which of the following are *not* good basic host security measures?
   A. Jotting down the root password on your desk blotter.
   B. Checking system log files regularly for unusual activity.
   C. Hanging on to unused accounts in case their original users want to reactivate them.
   D. Providing users with adequate training so they know how to properly use the tools at their disposal.
5. What are the four steps that PAM breaks the authentication process into?
   A. Authentication management, account management, session management, and password management.
   B. Authentication management, account management, network management, and password management.

C. Authentication management, account logging, session management, and password management.

D. Authentication management, account management, session management, and firewall management.

6. You are editing the PAM configuration file by adding a module. How would you indicate that the authentication process should immediately terminate and fail if the module fails?

   A. Make sure the module is either an auth module or a password module, since these must always succeed.

   B. Use the required control flag.

   C. Use the requisite control flag.

   D. It doesn't matter; the authentication process always stops as soon as a module fails.

7. You experience a moment of forgetfulness and try to log in to the root account of your server via telnet from your Internet connection at home. Why doesn't this work?

   A. You are using IP chains to filter out telnet access to the root account.

   B. You miskeyed your password.

   C. Login to the root account is never allowed from any terminal other than the console.

   D. The network terminal device that you are trying to log in from is not listed in /etc/securetty; therefore, the root account will not be allowed to log in from that terminal.

8. Assume you normally work from a user account called sysadm. How might you configure your Red Hat Linux System to notify you whenever there is a serious problem with the kernel?

   A. Edit /etc/syslog.conf and add an entry such as:

   ```
   kern.err          root,sysadm
   ```

   B. Recompile the kernel to include error notification and specify sysadm as the user to be notified.

   C. Write a C program to monitor the /proc/err directory and send any messages that appear there to sysadm.

   D. Edit /etc/syslog.conf and add an entry such as:

   ```
   *.*          root,sysadm
   ```

9. You would like to have your system page you when certain events occur. How could you do this?

   A. Configure the paging feature of the logrotate utility.

   B. Install the swatch utility and set it up to do this.

   C. Not possible.

   D. Install the GNUpage utility.

10. You have a server application that is only used about once a day. How would you configure this service to start so that it didn't have to run continuously?

   A. Add an entry in the system cron table to start the service at about the time you think that service will be needed.

Add another entry to stop the service a few minutes later.

B. Write a shell script to start the service at boot time with a file in /ect/rc.d, but use a sleep command to put the process to sleep until it's needed.

C. Start the service by adding an entry for it in /etc/services.

D. Add an entry for the application in /etc/inetd.conf.

11. Below is a configuration line from inetd.conf :

```
smtp   tcp   nowait   root\
    /usr/sbin/in.smtpd
```

What is missing from the line?

A. The arguments for the smtp service.

B. The type of socket the service will use.

C. Nothing.

D. The type of protocol the service will use.

12. You would like to restrict access to your ftp site to clients in a particular subnet. How can you do this?

A. Use ipchains to filter out ftp requests for all but the given subnet.

B. Comment out the configuration line for the ftp service in /etc/inetd.conf.

C. Edit /etc/ftp.conf and add a reject line for all networks other than the given subnet.

D. Use tcp_wrappers and add the appropriate lines to /etc/hosts.allow and /etc/hosts.deny.

13. You are using the tcpd program to start services in inetd.conf. How could you restrict telnet access to be available only to clients on the 192.168.170.0 network? Assume that no other configuration has been done for tcpd.

A. Edit inetd.conf and add *-DENY EXCEPT 192.168.170.0* to the entry for the telnet daemon.

B. Edit /etc/hosts.allow and add the line:

```
in.telnetd :\
192.168.170.0/255.255.255.0
```

C. Edit /etc/hosts.deny and add the line:

```
in.telnetd :\
192.168.170.0/255.255.255.0
```

D. Edit /etc/hosts.deny and add the line:

```
in.telnetd : ALL EXCEPT\
192.168.170.0/255.255.255.0
```

14. You work at the headquarters of a company that has several divisions. Each division is part of the headquarters LAN, but each division has its own logical subnet and its own domain. You would like to set up an internal ftp server for each division, but you don't want to have to configure and manage multiple systems. What solution can you devise?

A. Set up a user's workstation in each division to be the ftp server and delegate the management of that server to the user of that workstation.

B. Use NIS and set up shared virtual ftp directories.

C. Use IP aliasing and set up virtual host services for each division.

D. Edit /etc/inetd.conf and change all occurrences of tcpd with virtuald.

15. You have just recently connected your organization's network to the Internet, and you are a little worried because there is nothing other than your router standing in the way between your network and the Internet. You have a spare 200MHz PC lying around doing nothing that just happens to have two Ethernet cards. You also have a mixture of systems on your network that includes Macintosh, Windows 95, and Linux. What might you do to ease your mind?

    A. Nothing; you're not advertising the systems on your LAN via DNS, so no one will ever find them.

    B. Install Red Hat Linux on the 200MHz PC and use ipchains to set it up as a firewall.

    C. Install Red Hat Linux on the 200MHz PC and use tcp_wrappers to set it up as a firewall.

    D. Install Linux on all systems on your network.

16. Which of the following are correct ways to specify a source address or a destination address when configuring IP chains?

    A. 192.168.188.0/255.255.255.0

    B. 192.168.188.0/24

    C. 192.168.188.5

    D. server1.xyz.org

    E. 0/0

17. Consider the following command:

```
ipchains -A input -s\
192.168.77.77 -j REJECT
```

What effect will this have when the client with an IP of 192.168.77.77 tries to connect to your system?

    A. No effect at all.

    B. Access will be denied, and the client application will not receive any indication of what happened.

    C. Access will be denied, and the client application will receive a message about the target destination being unreachable.

    D. You will receive a notification message on the system console.

18. You are setting up a small office and you would like to provide Internet access to a small number of users, but you don't want to pay for a dedicated IP address for each system on the network. How could Linux help with the problem?

    A. Assign the official IP address to a Linux system, and create accounts on that system for all of the office personnel.

    B. Install Linux and configure it for IP forwarding.

    C. Install a Linux router.

   D. Use the Linux system to connect to the Internet, and then use IP chains to set up IP masquerading.

19. Which of the following are correct?

   A. Only routers need to maintain route tables.

   B. You enter static routes manually.

   C. The system bases its decision on where to route a packet by looking at the packet's destination address.

   D. You don't need to worry about changing your routing tables when your network changes.

20. You are trying to connect to a remote system, but you can't make a connection. You are using the ping command to troubleshoot, and you notice that you can ping your own system and you can ping other systems that are on the same subnet as you. When you try to ping a system outside your subnet, however, you get no response. What steps can you take to resolve the problem?

   A. Contact the system administrator for the remote system and tell him to remove the ipchains DENY rule he has for your system.

   B. Disable tcp_wrappers for on your system.

   C. Use the route -n command and check to see that you have a default gateway set.

   D. Reconfigure your network setup.

RHCE®

RED HAT CERTIFIED ENGINEER®

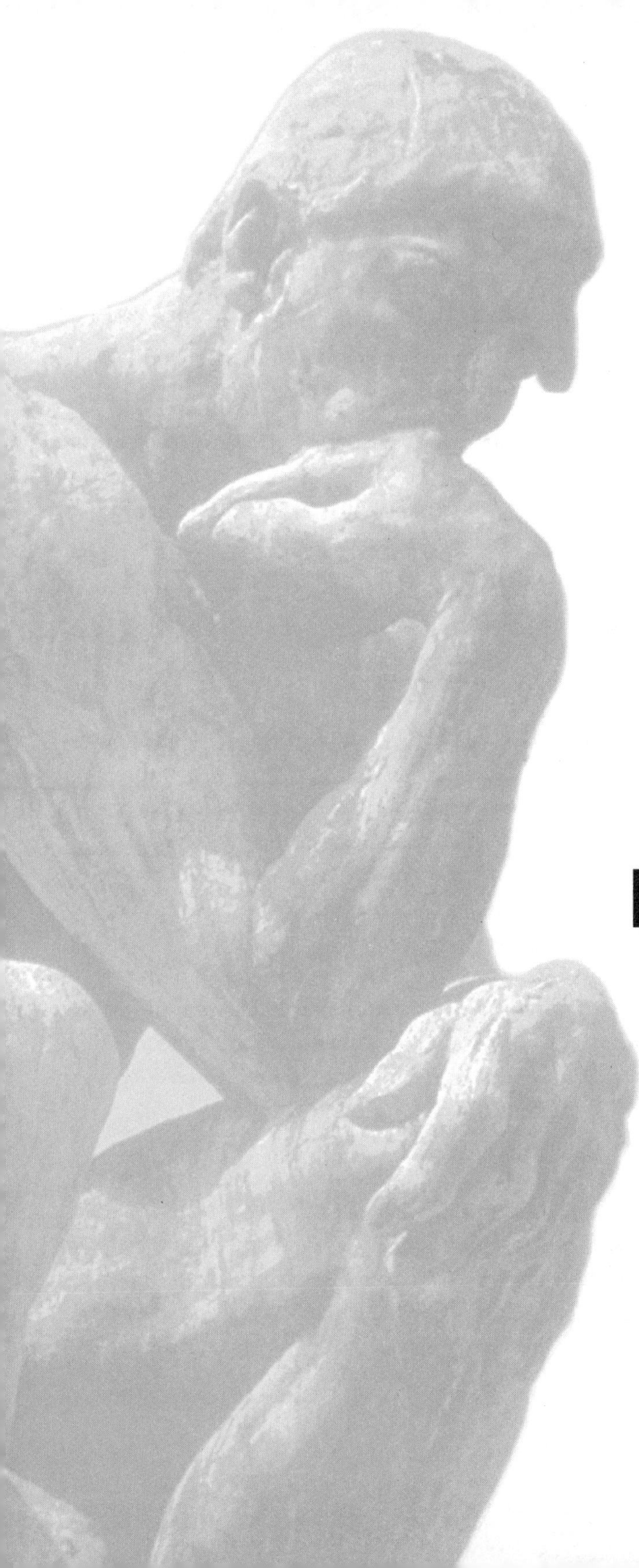

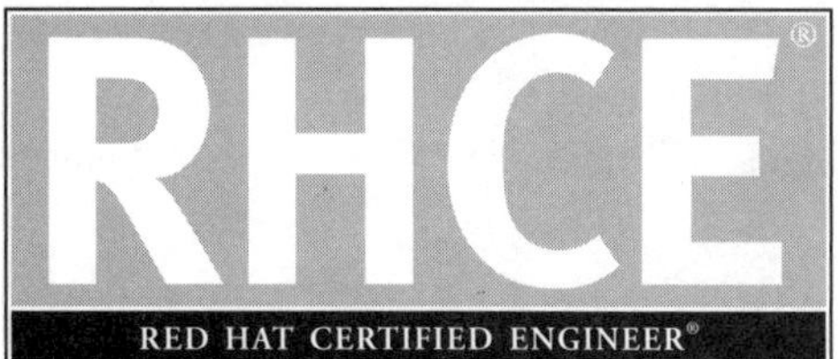

11

Operational Administration Recovery and Security

CERTIFICATION OBJECTIVES

11.01 Services Should Run as Users or Nobody, Not Root

11.02 Sgid Red Hat Scheme

11.03 COPS

11.04 Interaction of CMOS Clock Time and Linux System Time

11.05 User Process Accounting

11.06 tmpwatch

11.07 Emergency Boot Procedures

11.08 Obtaining Encryption Packages in RPM Format

11.09 Linuxconf

In this final chapter of the Red Hat Linux certified study guide, we will continue the discussion of system security we started in the last chapter. This will include taking a look at secure ways to run certain network services, a Red Hat Linux specific way of specifying file security, installing security packages.

We will also discuss one of the most fundamental and important topics of concern to any systems administrator: what to do when a system will not boot. When the inevitable happens, knowing the right things to look for and having some tricks up your sleeve may help you avoid a nightmare for you as a system administrator and a major loss of service for your users.

CERTIFICATION OBJECTIVE 11.01

Services Should Run as Users or Nobody, Not Root

When a Red Hat Linux system boots, a special process, *init*, is the first process started. The init process is responsible for starting all the other processes that comprise a working Linux system, including your own interactive shell process or X-Windows session. Since the init process is responsible for keeping things going, it runs with the user ID of the root account.

If you are a new systems administrator, or are new to the UNIX or Linux world, and are configuring your first Linux system, you might make the logical assumption that any network services you install should also be run under the user ID of the root account since they are system-wide services. However, this is not the case if you are at all concerned about network security.

Suppose you have configured a system to start several network services running under the root user ID. Although you did your homework and made sure to load the latest security patches, a daemon for one of the services you configured has a security hole that slipped your attention. A cracker stumbles upon your system on the Internet and starts plying his craft. He soon discovers the hole in the service and, using information published on the Internet, soon has root access to your system through the service daemon. Using this access, he is able to run a remote program on your system that gives him login access to a little-used user account.

To circumvent this sort of thing, any services you run, whether local or network, should run under their own user accounts. That way, if a cracker does succeed in exploiting a security hole in a particular application, the damage he can do is limited because the service he has broken into is running as a normal, unprivileged user. If you do not want to create an account for every single network service you start, there is an account called *nobody* that is often used to run services. The following code listing shows a typical /etc/passwd file. Notice that most common network services have their own user accounts under which to run.

```
root:x:0:0:root:/root:/bin/bash
bin:x:1:1:bin:/bin:
daemon:x:2:2:daemon:/sbin:
adm:x:3:4:adm:/var/adm:
lp:x:4:7:lp:/var/spool/lpd:
sync:x:5:0:sync:/sbin:/bin/sync
shutdown:x:6:0:shutdown:/sbin:/sbin/shutdown
halt:x:7:0:halt:/sbin:/sbin/halt
mail:x:8:12:mail:/var/spool/mail:
news:x:9:13:news:/var/spool/news:
uucp:x:10:14:uucp:/var/spool/uucp:
operator:x:11:0:operator:/root:
games:x:12:100:games:/usr/games:
gopher:x:13:30:gopher:/usr/lib/gopher-data:
ftp:x:14:50:FTP User:/home/ftp:
nobody:x:99:99:Nobody:/:
gdm:x:42:42::/home/gdm:/bin/bash
xfs:x:100:233:X Font
server:/etc/X11/fs:/bin/false
```

EXERCISE 11-1

Verifying That Services Have Their Own Accounts

In this exercise, you will verify that certain system and network services run with their own accounts. You should try this exercise on a system that is configured to offer various network services.

At a shell prompt, issue the command:

```
ps -aux --headers | less
```

What account is the Web server (httpd) running under? What account is the X-Windows display manager (gdm) running under?

exam Watch

You should get as much hands-on experience as you can before taking the exam.

CERTIFICATION OBJECTIVE 11.02

Sgid Red Hat Scheme

One major difference between Red Hat Linux and other versions of UNIX or UNIX-like operating systems that you should be aware of is how new users are assigned to groups. Using the traditional way of creating user accounts, you create one or more groups in /etc/group and then assign one of these groups to be the *primary group* for each new user account that is added. For example, you may create one group for the accounting department, and a group for the information systems department in your organization. When you create accounts for new hires in the accounting department, each user account receives a unique identifier, but receives the same group identifier as the other accounts that are in the accounting group. Note that user accounts can belong to more than one group; the primary group for an account is simply the default group for that account.

The user and primary group identifiers for a user are stored in the third and fourth fields, respectively, in /etc/passwd. When you look through this file on a traditional UNIX system, you will usually notice several user accounts that share a common group identifier. If you examine the /etc/passwd file on a Red Hat Linux system, however, you will notice that each user account appears to be assigned to its own group. This *user private group* scheme is the default behavior for creating accounts under Red Hat Linux. The idea behind user private groups is to make it easier to use groups.

The purpose of having groups in the first place is to allow users who are members of a particular group to share files. Typically, this is done by creating a directory and changing the group ownership of the directory to that of the group that is going to share files in the directory. For example, suppose you have a group set up for the users in the accounting department called accgrp, and you would like to create a shared called accshared under /home:

```
mkdir  /home/accshared
chown  nobody.accgrp  /home/accshared
chmod  775  /home/accshared
```

Any user who is a member of the accgrp group can now create files in the /home/accshared directory.

Several problems can arise when sharing files. For example, suppose that a user, who happens to be a member of accgrp but whose primary group is something other than accgrp, creates a file in the /home/accshared directory. The user who created the file will be the owner of the file, and the group ownership of the file will be the user's_primary group. Unless the user who created the file remembers to issue a chgrp command on the file to set the ownership of the file to the accgrp group, other users in that group may not have the necessary permissions to access the file.

The solution to this particular problem is to use something called the set group id bit, or setgid bit. The setgid bit is applied to a directory with the chmod command. When the setgid bit is set for a directory, any files that are created in that directory automatically have their group ownership set to be that of the group owner of the directory. The command to set the setgid bit for the /home/accshared directory is:

```
chmod  g+s  /home/accshared
```

or, alternately:

```
chmod  2775 /home/accshared
```

Setting the setgid bit solves the problem of making sure all files that are created in a shared directory belong to the correct group. The other problem that can arise has to do with permission settings. Typically, most users run with a umask setting of 022, which specifies that any files that they create are not modifiable by any account that is a member of the user's group or by anyone else on the system. If the user is creating a file in a shared directory and he wishes to allow others update access to the file, he will have to remember to issue a chmod command to make the file group writeable. The way around this problem is to set the default umask (usually in /etc/profile) to be 002. With this umask, any files a user creates will be modifiable by the user and any member of the group assigned the file.

At this point, especially if you are coming from a traditional UNIX environment, you may be saying to yourself, "Wait a minute, with a umask of 002, anyone who is a member of that user's primary group will automatically have write access to any file that user creates in his home directory!" This is the advantage behind the user private group scheme. Since every user account is the only member in its own private group, having the umask set to 002 has no effect on file security.

EXERCISE 11-2

Controlling Group Ownership with the setgid Bit

In this exercise, you will verify the effect the setgid bit has on file creation.

1. Add a user called *test*. Check the /etc/passwd and /etc/group files to verify that the user's private group was created.
2. Edit the /etc/group file and add a group called tg1. Make the *test* account a member of this group. The line you add should look like this:

   ```
   tg1::999:test
   ```

   Make sure the gid you assign to the group is not already in use.
3. Create a shared director for the tg1 group:

   ```
   mkdir  /home/testshared
   ```

4. Change the ownership of the shared directory:

   ```
   chown  nobody.tg1  /home/testshared
   ```

5. Log in as test. Change directory to the testshared directory and create a file. Check the ownership on the file:

   ```
   date  >test.txt
   ls  -l  test.txt
   ```

6. From the *root* account, set the setgid bit on the directory:

   ```
   chmod  g+s  /home/testshared
   ```

7. Switch back to the *test* account and create another file. Check the ownership on this file:

   ```
   :date  >test2.txt
   ls  -l
   ```

CERTIFICATION OBJECTIVE 11.03

COPS

Properly securing any computer system, whether Red Hat Linux or otherwise, requires attention to many details. Even the most experienced system administrator can occasionally overlook something when it comes to system security. One of the tools you may wish to employ if you are securing your system from network attacks is the *Computer Oracle and Password System*, or COPS.

COPS is actually a suite of programs that perform a variety of security checks. If COPS finds a potential problem, it will warn you. COPS does not fix any problems it finds, although it does have an option that will generate a shell command file that can be run manually. Among the types of things COPS will check for are:

- Permission settings on files, directories, and devices
- Bad passwords (i.e., those that are easily guessed)
- Files that are owned by root and have the SUID bit set
- Important binary files that have changed
- Holes in network service configurations

COPS is available from ftp.cert.org as a GNU-zipped tar file. You must perform some minor manual configuration to run the program. You can configure COPS to mail its output to you, or you can have it leave its reports in a directory. A very effective way to use COPS is to put an entry for it in your system crontab, so that you get periodic updates on the security status of your system. The following code listing shows a sample report generated by COPS.

```
    ATTENTION:
    Security Report for Thu Oct 14 05:28:30 EDT 1999
    from host localhost.localdomain


Warning!  /etc/security is _World_readable!
```

CERTIFICATION OBJECTIVE 11.04

Interaction of CMOS Clock Time and Linux System Time

Most personal computers have provisions in hardware for keeping track of the date and time. Among other purposes, the date and time values are used to record the time a file was created or modified. This date and time value is also used by the various logging utilities to timestamp events.

Knowing when something happened or when a given file was changed or accessed can be a vital tool if you are tracking down a security breach or debugging system problems. If your system time is more than a few minutes out of synch with real time, then the information in your log files and any other information that is marked with a timestamp may be nearly worthless if you are trying to determine the chronological order in which something happened.

One of the places you can change your system time is from the BIOS setup routine that is usually invoked by pressing a function key or the DEL key as the system is loading in the BIOS prior to booting into Linux. The time that you see here is the time that is actually stored in hardware. On many systems, this time will be the same as the local time. Other systems may have a requirement to keep this time in Greenwich Mean Time (GMT). If your system's hardware clock is set for GMT, then you will need to tell Linux to compensate by adding or subtracting the appropriate number of hours depending on how far east or west of the prime meridian you are.

Fortunately, this is easy to do; in fact, if you'll recall, you were asked to supply this information when you installed Red Hat Linux. If you need to change this information later, though, simply use the timeconfig command from a shell prompt. This will bring up the Configure Timezones screen shown in Figure 11-1. Use the SPACE BAR to check the Hardware clock set to GMT box, and then TAB down to the time zone list and select your

FIGURE 11-1

Use the Timezone Configuration screen to adjust your timezone offset

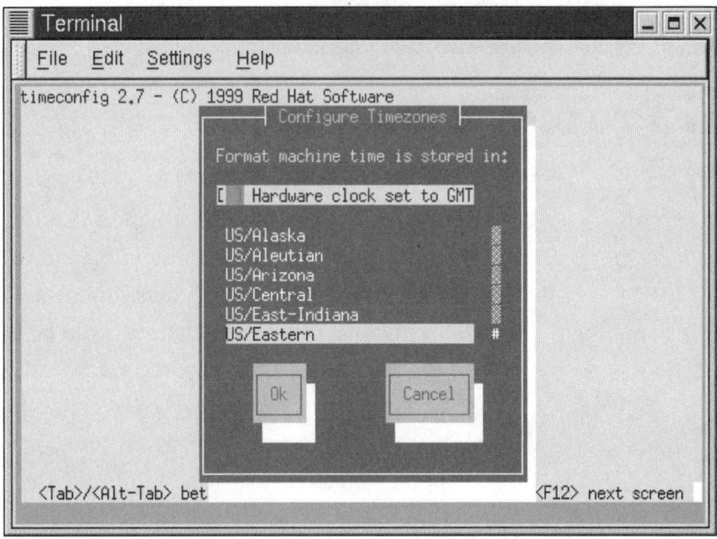

time zone using your arrow keys. Tab to OK, press ENTER, and you're done. The next time you reboot, your system time will be offset from the GMT time stored in your hardware clock.

EXERCISE 11-3

Adjusting Your Time Zone

In this exercise, you will use the timeconfig command to reconfigure your system's time offset.

1. On a test system, run the timeconfig command. Set or unset the Hardware clock set to GMT check box accordingly, TAB down to OK, and press ENTER.
2. Use the date command to check the current system time.
3. Reboot your system.
4. Use the date command to check the current system time. It should have changed by however many time zones away from Greenwich, England you are.

CERTIFICATION OBJECTIVE 11.05

User Process Accounting

One resource that you may not immediately think about when planning security for your site is the information that can be obtained by keeping track of user processes. The original intent behind user process accounting tools was to provide a mechanism for IS departments to keep track of the resources each account on a system used so charges could be billed back to the account owner. With the accounting utilities you can track such useful information as when your system was last rebooted, the last time a particular user account logged in and the specific commands a user executed.

Support for accounting is built into the Red Hat Linux kernel, but you will need to install the psacct RPM to use some of the tools mentioned here. Under Red Hat Linux 6.0, the specific RPM to install is psacct-6.3-10.i386.rpm.

After you have installed the process accounting rpm, you will need to turn on process accounting using the accton command along with the specification for the process accounting log file. The default file used for storing accounting information is /var/log/pacct, so the command to enable accounting is:

```
/sbin/accton  /var/log/pacct
```

If you plan on running process accounting as part of your normal system configuration, you will want to add the accounting command to your /etc/rc.d/rc.local system initialization script.

There is some small overhead associated with running process accounting, but the wealth of information it provides can easily offset any small loss in performance. You can disable process accounting at any time by using the accton command without any arguments.

The information in /var/log/pacct file is written in binary, so you must use the process accounting utilities to view this information. The two commands you have for viewing the information in this file are ac and sa.

The ac command is used to print out a report of connect time. This type of information could be useful in pinpointing suspicious activity. For example, if you know that one of your users left last week for a two-week vacation in Hawaii, but notice that his account has accumulated 30-plus hours of connect time since the last time you checked, it might be a tip-off that some sort of illicit activity is occurring on your system. Of course it could also be an indication that the user in question was so excited about his upcoming vacation that he forgot to log out, which in itself is a potential security breach.

The default action for the ac command is to print a summary of the total connect time for the system. You use options to control what information is displayed. Two of the most useful are the -d option, which provides a day-by-day summary of connect time, and the -p option, which breaks down the connect time by user. The following code listing shows an example of using the *ac* command to obtain a report of connect times for users on a system.

```
        root                               2.61
Oct 12  total    2.61
        root                              14.32
        zippy                              1.01
Oct 13  total   15.33
        zippy                              2.83
        hank                               5.47
        root                              27.03
Oct 14  total   35.34
        zippy                              1.02
        hank                               2.50
        root                               5.70
Today   total    9.22
```

The sa command is also a part of the psacct rpm. You can use it to summarize information contained in the /var/log/pacct file. In terms of security, however, a more useful command is the lastcomm command. You can use the lastcomm command to display which commands have been executed on your system. You can restrict the information that lastcomm returns by specifying arguments for the username, command name, or a specific terminal. For example, to view a list of users who have used the *su* command, you would type:

```
lastcomm  su
```

In addition to the process accounting utilities, you can also glean useful information from a couple of files that exist on Red Hat Linux, regardless of whether accounting is enabled. The files are /var/run/utmp and /var/log/wtmp. Both files store information in binary format, so you must use special utilities to access the information they contain.

The /var/run/utmp file must always exist on Red Hat Linux systems. This file is used to store information about currently running processes. It is used by utilities, such as the who command. In fact, if you feel that the who command represents a security risk, you can disable it by removing world read access from this file. Note that this file should never be writeable by any account other than root.

The /var/log/wtmp file is used by the init process and the login command to record logins and logouts. If you want to disable this feature, simply remove /var/log/wtmp. To view the information in this file, use the last command. Simply issuing the command without any arguments displays the entire contents of the login database to your screen. You can limit the information that is returned by specifying a list of usernames or terminals as arguments to the last command. The following code listing shows an example of using the last command.

```
[root@localhost /root]$ last hank
hank     pts/0     192.168.1.1     Fri Oct 15 10:35   still logged in
hank     tty4                      Thu Oct 14 21:09   still logged in
hank     tty5                      Thu Oct 14 12:51 - down    (00:21)
hank     tty3                      Thu Oct 14 12:51 - down    (00:21)
hank     pts/0     localhost       Thu Oct 14 01:59 - 03:55   (01:55)

wtmp begins Tue Oct 12 21:22:49 1999
```

Reading from left to right, the information that is displayed in the output from the last command is the username of the account, the terminal at which this user logged in (tty terminal means either a console terminal or possibly a serial terminal; pts is a network terminal), the location the user logged in from if the terminal is a network terminal, the login time for the session, and how long the user stayed logged in. The word *down* in some of the entries indicates the session was terminated by a system shutdown. You can use the command last reboot to list when your system has been booted.

Another useful command for detecting suspicious activity is the lastb command. If you create the file /var/log/btmp (using the touch command), Linux will record failed login attempts in this file. You use the lastb command to display the records in this file. If you notice an unusually large number of failed login attempts for a user, it may be an indication that someone is trying to break into your system via that account.

EXERCISE 11-4

User Process Accounting

In this exercise, you will try some of the user accounting tools.

1. Use the last command to view the record of logins on your system.
2. Create the file /var/log/btmp if it does not exist:

```
touch /var/log/btmp
```

3. Try to log in to an account on the system, but supply a bad password:

```
telnet -l someuser localhost
```

4. Use the lastb command to view your bad login history file.

CERTIFICATION OBJECTIVE 11.06

tmpwatch

The tmpwatch command (/usr/sbin/tmpwatch) is used to remove files that have not been accessed in a specified number of hours. As its name implies, you normally run it on directories such as /tmp and /var/tmp. The tmpwatch command works recursively, so if you specify the top-level directory in a tree, tmpwatch will search through the entire directory tree looking for files to remove. To use tmpwatch to delete all files in the /tmp directory that haven't been accessed within a week, you would use the command:

```
/usr/sbin/tmpwatch 168 /tmp
```

Although you can run the tmpwatch command interactively, you can automate this kind of housekeeping task with cron. If you do a standard install of Red Hat Linux, the /etc/cron.daily file will contain an entry to run tmpwatch on the /tmp, /var/tmp, and /var/catman directories.

CERTIFICATION OBJECTIVE 11.07

Emergency Boot Procedures

At some point in your career as a Red Hat Linux systems administrator, you're going to be faced with a system that will not boot. It will be up to you to determine the cause of the problem and implement a fix. Sometimes the problem may be due to hardware failure: the system in question has a bad power supply or has experienced a hard disk crash. Quite often, however, the failure of a system to boot can be traced back to the actions of a user: you, the system administrator! When you are editing certain system configuration files, leaving off a character or adding a character in the wrong place can render your system unbootable. Improperly configured system files probably cause more boot failures than actual hardware problems. A corollary to this bit of knowledge is that anytime you make any substantial modifications to your system or change certain configuration files (we'll discuss which ones later), you should actually reboot your system rather than assume that it will boot up the next time you need a reboot. It's much better to encounter problems while you can still remember exactly which changes you made.

Alternate Methods for Booting a System

To prepare for boot failures, you should make sure you have a valid boot floppy for your system, and a valid rescue floppy. When you installed Red Hat Linux, one of the last things you were asked was whether to make a boot disk. If you answered *no* to this prompt, you can use the mkbootdisk command to create a valid boot floppy. The mkbootdisk command reads your /etc/lilo.conf file to create a boot image that can be used to boot your system from a floppy. To use the mkbootdisk command, you must specify which version of the kernel (in /boot) to store on the floppy disk. For example, to make a boot disk for the standard Red Hat Linux 6.0 kernel, use the command:

```
mkbootdisk  2.2.5-15
```

You may be able to fix some problems that arise, such as accidentally deleting your master boot record, by simply booting from your boot disk. Other problems may require the use of a rescue disk. If the kernel can't locate the root file system, or if the root file system is damaged, the Linux kernel will issue a kernel panic and halt as shown in the following code listing.

```
.
.
.
.Partition check:c
 had: hda1 hda2 < hda5 hda6 hda7 >
autodetecting RAID arrays
autorun …
… autorun DONE.
VFS: Cannot open root device 00:30
Kernel panic: VFS: Unable to mount root fs on 00:30
```

Although this may look very bad the first time you encounter it, often the problem can easily be fixed with a rescue disk and a bit of work.

To create a rescue disk, you need to mount your Red Hat Linux distribution CD and dump the rescue disk image to a floppy disk. Assuming you mounted your distribution CD to /mnt/cdrom, the easiest way to do this is with the command:

```
cat /mnt/cdrom/images/rescue.img >/dev/fd0
```

The rescue disk contains a compact version of a root file system that has a minimal set of utilities that will allow you to mount a disk and either repair the problem with the disk or pull files off of the disk. If you do not have a functioning Linux system from which to make a rescue disk, you can also create a rescue disk from DOS using the rawrite.exe program located in the dosutils directory on your Linux distribution CD. You can also use this program to make a copy of the generic boot disk, boot.img, if you did not make a specific boot floppy for your system.

To boot into rescue mode, first boot your system using your boot floppy. At the boot: prompt, type, **rescue** and press ENTER. After the kernel is loaded from your boot floppy, you will be prompted to enter your rescue disk. The minimal root image on the rescue disk will be loaded into the RAM disk created by the kernel, and you will be at a root shell prompt (#). At this point, you have access to a basic set of commands. You can mount file systems, create directories, move files, edit files using the pico editor, and perform other functions. The file doc/rescue.txt on your distribution CD has a complete list of the commands that are available to you.

The great difficulty in working from the rescue environment is that you are working with a minimal version of the Linux operating system. Many of the commands that you are used to having at your disposal are not available to you at this level. If your root partition has not been completely destroyed, you may be able to mount this partition to your temporary root directory in memory and access commands from there. One important thing to make note of is that if you mount partitions from your hard drive from rescue mode and then make changes to files on those partitions, you will need to use the sync command to manually flush changes you make to files from memory to the disk drive. The other step you will want to remember to perform is to unmount any partitions that you mounted so that you could work on them. This will save you the wait of having to sit through a file system check when you reboot the system. When you have finished working in rescue mode, you must use the exit command to halt the system, and then restart the system to reboot.

One other option that is available to you if you are experiencing system problems is to boot into single-user mode. Your system may not have problems finding its root partition and starting the boot process, but may encounter problems when changing into one of the higher runlevels. If this is the case, you can still use the boot partition and root partition on your hard drive, but you want to tell Linux to perform a minimal boot process. To boot into single-user mode, issue the command:

```
linux  s
```

at the LILO prompt. Linux will boot into a minimal runtime environment and you will receive a bash shell prompt (bash#). Note that when you boot into single-user mode, no password is required to access the system. Running your system in single-user mode is very similar to running a system booted from a rescue disk. Many of the commands and utilities you normally use are unavailable. You may have to mount additional drives or partitions and specify the full pathname when running some commands. When you have corrected the problem, you can reboot the system or use the init or telinit commands to bring the system up to its normal runlevel.

What to Look For When Things Go Wrong

Although there are potentially many things that can go wrong that will cause a system not to boot, they can roughly be categorized as either hardware problems or software and configuration problems. The most common hardware-related problem you will probably encounter is a bad hard disk drive; like all mechanical devices with moving parts, these have a finite lifetime and will eventually fail. Hardware problems can sometimes be fairly easy to diagnose; you turn the power switch on and nothing happens. Software and configuration problems can be a little more difficult to diagnose. They can sometimes appear to be hardware problems at first glance. Often, the hardest part of fixing a system that won't boot is figuring out what the cause of the problem is.

One place you can look for information when diagnosing problems with a system is the LILO boot loader. When you see the LILO prompt on your screen before your system boots, LILO is actually conveying the information to you that it was able to successfully load its components into memory. If you do not see the LILO prompt, or only see part of the LILO prompt, that indicates that LILO had problems finding everything it needs to do its job. Table 11-1 summarizes how to interpret the LILO boot prompt for error information.

In addition to knowing how to mount disk partitions, edit files, and manipulate files, there are several other commands that you will need to know how to use in order to be able to fix problems from rescue mode or single-user mode. Three of the most useful are the fdisk command, the e2fsck command, and the lilo command. Unfortunately, the commands you don't have access to at this level include the man pages and the info utility, so in the event that you do not have a hardcopy manual nearby or

TABLE 11-1

The LILO Boot Prompt Can Provide Useful Debugging Information

Nothing	LILO not loaded
L	First stage loaded but not second stage; usually indicates disk problems or invalid parameters in /etc/lilo.conf
LI	Second stage loaded but invalid parameters in /etc/lilo.conf, or /boot/boot.b was moved without running /sbin/lilo
LIL	Second stage started but can't load descriptor table because of a bad disk or invalid parameters in /etc/lilo.conf
LIL?	Second stage loaded at wrong address, caused by invalid parameters in /etc/lilo.conf, or /boot/boot.b was moved without running /sbin/lilo
LIL-	Invalid parameters in /etc/lilo.conf, or /boot/boot.b moved without running /sbin/lilo
LILO	LILO successfully loaded

another working Linux system at your disposal, it helps to know how to use these commands at a rudimentary level at least.

fdisk

You may have already encountered the fdisk utility when you installed Red Hat Linux. The fdisk utility is one of the choices you are given when you are setting up disk partitions during the install process. You can invoke fdisk at any time from a command prompt. When you issue the command without any arguments, fdisk starts up in an interactive mode that lets you edit the partition table on a disk. One of the first things you will want to know if you are trying to rescue a system is what partitions you have available for mounting. You can use the fdisk -l command to obtain this information. The following code listing shows an example of using the fdisk command to display the partition information for a system.

```
[root@localhost /root]# fdisk -l

Disk /dev/hda: 240 heads, 63 sectors, 559 cylinders
Units = cylinders of 15120 * 512 bytes

   Device Boot    Start       End    Blocks   Id  System
/dev/hda1   *         1        41    309928+   6  FAT16
/dev/hda2            42       559   3916080    5  Extended
```

```
/dev/hda5              42        44     22648+  83  Linux
/dev/hda6              45        53     68000+  82  Linux swap
/dev/hda7              54       192   1050808+  83  Linux
```

Looking at the output from the fdisk command in this example, you can immediately see that if you were searching for the appropriate partitions to mount in rescue mode, that /dev/hda5 and /dev/hda7 would be the most logical choices. Furthermore, you could probably intuit that, based on the size of the partitions, /dev/hda5 is the partition that is normally mounted to /boot, and /dev/hda7 is the root partition.

e2fsck

You should also know how to use the e2fsck command. The e2fsck command performs the same function on the Linux second extended file system as the fsck command does on a standard UNIX file system; it is used to check the file system on a partition for consistency. In order to effectively use the e2fsck command, you need to understand something about how file systems are laid out on disk partitions.

When you format a disk partition under Linux using the mke2fs command, the mke2fs command sets aside a certain portion of the disk to use for storing inodes, which are pointers that are used to locate the actual disk blocks that make up the files that are created on that device. The mke2fs command also stores information about the size of the files system, the file system label, and the number of inodes in a special location at the start of the partition called the superblock. If the superblock is corrupted or destroyed, the remaining information on the disk is unreadable. Because the superblock is so vital to the integrity of the data on a partition, the mke2fs command makes duplicate copies of the superblock at fixed intervals on the partition. The copies are usually made at intervals of 8192 blocks, so the first copy of the superblock is at block 8193, the second copy is at block 16385, and so on.

The e2fsck command checks for, and corrects problems with, file system consistency by checking for things such as disk blocks that are marked as free but are actually in use and vice versa, inodes that don't have a corresponding directory entry, inodes with incorrect link counts, and a number of other problems. The e2fsck command will also fix a corrupted superblock. Normally, this will happen automatically, but if it doesn't and you can't mount a disk because of a corrupt superblock, you can use the e2fsck command with the -b option to specify an alternate superblock. For example, the command

```
e2fsck -b -y 8193 /dev/hda5
```

tells e2fsck to perform a consistency check and repair on the file system on disk partition /dev/hda5. The -y option is used to tell e2fsck to automatically assume you answered yes to all questions and prompts. If you are running e2fsck on a large partition, this can keep you from having to type y every time e2fsck asks a question.

lilo

You should run lilo whenever you rebuild your Linux kernel, change disk partitions, or do anything else that might affect the physical location of the files in /boot. If you make changes and forget to do this, you will have to boot into rescue mode and fix the problem. Although you may be familiar with using the lilo command when your system is running normally, you will have to make some adjustments when running lilo from rescue mode.

As an example, suppose you have a Linux system and have configured a separate /boot and a separate root partition. The /boot partition is on /dev/hda1, and the root partition is on /dev/hda5. You forgot to run lilo after rebuilding your kernel, so you have had to boot into rescue mode to fix the problem. Since you are running in the rescue environment, the rescue RAM disk is mounted as your root file system. The first thing you will probably want to do is to make some directories to use for mount points for the partitions you will need to access to fix the problem. Since the lilo command will need to update information on your /boot partition, you will need to mount /dev/hda1. The lilo command and /etc/lilo.conf are stored on the root file system, so you will need to mount /dev/hda5 as well:

```
mkdir  tmpmnt
mkdir  tmpmnt/boot
mount  /dev/hda5  tmpmnt
mount  /dev/hda1  tmpmnt/boot
```

At this point, if necessary, you could edit the lilo.conf file and make changes:

```
cd  tmpmnt/etc
pico  lilo.conf
#make changes to lilo.conf if necessary
```

Now you're ready to run lilo. Since you're in rescue mode, you will have to specify the path for the lilo command. The other thing you will need to do is use the *-r* option to tell lilo to use an alternate root (remember, your current root is the RAM disk file system). This will enable lilo to locate its configuration file and the /boot directory:

```
..      /sbin/lilo  -r  /tmpmnt
```

You should receive confirmation from lilo that the boot block was written. The only thing left to do is to flush your changes from memory to the disk drive, unmount the partitions, and reboot:

```
sync    #repeat several times to be sure

sync
sync
cd  /
umount  /dev/hda1
umount  /dev/hda5
exit
```

Places to Look First

Two places where you are likely to make errors that result in a nonbootable system are in the files /etc/lilo.conf and /etc/fstab. In both of these files, identifying the wrong partition as the root partition (specifying /dev/hda when you meant /dev/hda1, for example) can result in a kernel panic like the one shown in the code example you saw in the "Alternate Methods for Booting a System" section. Other configuration errors in /etc/lilo.conf will also cause a kernel panic at boot time. Any time you make changes to these files, you should reboot your system if at all possible, and test that things work as you intended.

As a Red Hat Linux administrator, you will be expected to know how to fix systems when things break. For this reason, a substantial portion of the exam is devoted to testing your troubleshooting and analysis skills.

Summary of the Rescue Process

To summarize, here are the basic steps to follow when you are trying to restore a system from a rescue disk:

- Boot using your system's boot floppy.
- Insert your rescue disk when prompted.
- At the rescue shell prompt, use fdisk -l to identify your partitions.
- If file system problems are suspected or indicated, run e2fsck on the afflicted partitions.
- If the problem is with a configuration file:
  - Create (a) temporary mountpoint(s).
  - Mount the appropriate partition(s).
  - Use the pico editor to fix the problem.
  - Run lilo if you are making changes to lilo.conf or the /boot partition.
- Sync your changes to the drive.
- Unmount any mounted partitions.
- Exit and restart the system.

Whenever you're working in rescue mode or single-user mode, always remember to sync your drives before halting.

EXERCISE 11-5

Performing an Emergency Boot Procedure

To do this exercise, you should have a test system at your disposal. Do not try this exercise on any system from which you are not prepared to lose all of the data.

In this exercise, you will "break" your system by purposely misconfiguring a file and then reboot into rescue mode to fix the problem. You will have to replace the partitions used in the commands for the /boot and root partitions with the actual partitions that are used for the /boot and root partitions on your system.

1. Make sure you have the Red Hat Linux distribution cd mounted:

   ```
   mount  /dev/cdrom  /mnt/cdrom
   ```

2. If the mkbootdisk RPM is not installed, install it:

   ```
   rpm  -i  /mnt/cdrom/RedHat/RPMS/
   mkbootdisk-1.2-2.i386.rpm
   ```

3. If you do not have a boot disk and a rescue disk, make those. Insert a floppy into the disk drive and type:

   ```
   mkbootdisk  2.2.5-15
   ```

4. Insert another floppy and type:

   ```
   cat  /mnt/cdrom/images/rescue.img  >/dev/fd0
   ```

   You will want to label the disks accordingly.

5. Edit the file /etc/lilo.conf and make a copy of your boot stanza. Label this stanza badboot. Change the location of the root device to point to an invalid partiton. For example, if your original lilo.conf looks like this:

   ```
   boot=/dev/hda
   map=/boot/map
   install=/boot/boot.b
   prompt
   timeout=50
   image=/boot/vmlinuz-2.2.5-15
           label=linux
           root=/dev/hda7
           read-only
   other=/dev/hda1
           label=dos
           table=/dev/hda
   ```

   Your new version should look like this:

   ```
   boot=/dev/hda
   map=/boot/map
   install=/boot/boot.b
   prompt
   timeout=50
   image=/boot/vmlinuz-2.2.5-15
   ```

```
        label=linux
        root=/dev/hda7
        read-only
image=/boot/vmlinuz-2.2.5-15
        label=badboot
        root=/dev/hda
        read-only
other=/dev/hda1
        label=dos
        table=/dev/hda
```

6. Run lilo to update your boot mappings:

```
lilo
```

   You should see a message similar to this:

```
Added linux *
Added badboot
Added dos
```

7. Reboot your system. At the LILO prompt, select badboot. You should see the boot process start, and then receive a kernel panic message.
8. Since you left a valid boot stanza, your system isn't really broken. To fix the problem, however, we're going to boot into rescue mode. Insert your boot disk, and reboot the system. At the boot: prompt type **rescue**. Insert your rescue disk when prompted.
9. Although you know the source of the problem, once you boot into rescue mode you should familiarize yourself with some of the repair utilities:

```
        fdisk  -l
   Device  Boot     Start         End     Blocks   Id  System
/dev/hda1   *           1          41     309928+   6  FAT16
/dev/hda2              42         559    3916080    5  Extended
/dev/hda5              42          44      22648+  83  Linux
/dev/hda6              45          53      68000+  82  Linux swap
/dev/hda7              54         192    1050808+  83  Linux
```

10. e2fsck -y /dev/hda5 # your output will vary
    e2fsck 1.14, 9-Jan-1999 for EXT2 FS 0.5b, 95/08/09
    /dev/hda5: clean, 23/5664 files, 3008/22648 blocks

11. Create (a) temporary mount point(s) for your /boot and root partitions, and mount those partitions:

```
mkdir  tmpmnt
mkdir  tmpmnt/boot
mount  /dev/hda7  tmpmnt
mount  /dev/hda5  tmpmnt/boot
```

12. Edit the bad stanza in lilo.conf and fix the problems:

```
pico  tmpmnt/etc/lilo.conf
```

The badboot stanza should now read

```
image=/boot/vmlinuz-2.2.5-15
        label=badboot
        root=/dev/hda7
        read-only
```

Save your changes to the lilo.conf file. Now you must run lilo to update your boot block:

```
/tmpmnt/sbin/lilo  -r  tmpmnt
```

13. Sync your changes and unmount any mounted partitions:

```
sync
sync
cd
unmount  /dev/hda5
unmount  /dev/hda7
```

14. Remove any boot media from your disk drives. Type **exit** to halt the system. Restart the system. You should now be able to boot from the badboot stanza.

CERTIFICATION OBJECTIVE 11.08

Obtaining Encryption Packages in RPM Format

Because of the U.S. government's restriction on shipping any encryption software that uses encryption keys larger than 56 bits outside of the United

States or Canada, Red Hat Linux does not ship with packages such as the Secure Shell. These packages are available from the Internet, however. Among the encryption packages you might wish to obtain are the Secure Shell (ssh) and secure copy program (scp). These programs are secure replacements for the rsh, telnet, and rcp programs. You will need the corresponding secure daemon, sshd, to use them.

Import and Export Restrictions on Encryption Software

Software that incorporates "strong" encryption technology (anything that uses more than 56 bits for encryption) must carry this warning or one similar to it: "This software is subject to United States export controls. You may not export it, in whole or in part, or cause or allow such export, through act or omission, without prior authorization from the United States government. In particular, you may not make any part of this software available for general or unrestricted distribution to others, nor may you disclose this software to persons other than citizens and permanent residents of the United States and Canada."

Rather than having to impose this somewhat heavy-handed label on every copy of Linux they sell and having to maintain separate distributions for domestic and international release, Red Hat has chosen not to include encryption technology in their distribution of Linux.

The ftp.replay.com Site

RPMs containing the Secure Shell programs as well as other encryption software can be found at http://ftp.replay.com. The site is located in the Netherlands, so it is not subject to U.S. export laws.

Validating RPMs with pgp

If you download an RPM from some location on the Internet and would like to verify that it is an official Red Hat RPM and has not been tampered with, you can verify the package's PGP-encrypted checksum using the rpm -K command. To obtain Red Hat's public key, point your browser to http://www.redhat.com/about/contact.html.

CERTIFICATION OBJECTIVE 11.09

Linuxconf

The linuxconf utility is a graphical utility that ties together most system administration tasks under a common interface. You can use linuxconf to do everything from adding user accounts to rebuilding the kernel. You start linuxconf from the Start menu, or you can start it from the command line by typing **linuxconf**.

System administration tasks in linuxconf are grouped by hierarchy. Items listed with a plus sign next to them have subtasks. You view these subtasks by clicking on the plus sign to expand the higher-level item. Expanded items have a minus sign next to them. Clicking on the minus sign collapses the subtasks so that only the higher level item is visible. Clicking on a subtask that doesn't have a plus sign next to it will bring up a configuration window for that particular task. Figure 11-2 shows the linuxconf utility being used to add user accounts.

FIGURE 11-2

linuxconf provides an integrated interface for system administration

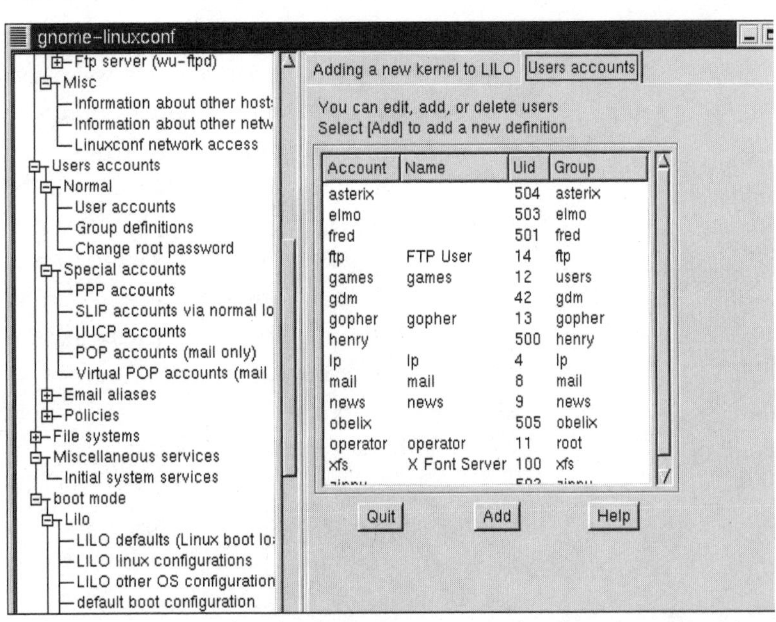

Now that you have a better idea of steps you can take to make your system more secure and reliable, and the process to go through when problems arise, here are some possible scenario questions and their answers.

QUESTIONS AND ANSWERS	
You come into work one morning and find that an extended power failure caused your Web server to shut down even though it was on a UPS. When you try to reboot the system, you get a "kernel panic" message on the console. What is the first thing you should try?	In this situation, the first thing you should try is to see if you can boot the system from a boot floppy. If the boot floppy fails, then you will have to boot into rescue mode to repair whatever problem is causing the kernel panic.
You suspect that someone from outside your organization has gained access to one of your accounts and is using the account for cracking purposes late at night. What could you do to help verify your suspicions?	Use the command last <username> to obtain a record of the login times and session duration for the username in question.

CERTIFICATION SUMMARY

As you've seen in this chapter and the last chapter, there are many facets to system security. Making sure that network services run under nonprivileged accounts is one of the most important things you can do to ensure your system remains secure from outside attack. The standard process accounting tools that come with Red Hat Linux can also be used to monitor your system for security problems.

One of the most valuable skills you can have as a Red Hat Linux systems administrator is knowing how to fix configuration problems that may prevent a system from booting. When systems break, you are often placed in a highly visible position in your organization as the person expected to fix the problem. Compounding the stress and difficulty of being under the gun to solve a problem is the fact that you are lacking a complete system when you are working in repair mode. Taking a test system and experimenting with the various ways to break and repair things is good practice for the time when things go wrong for real.

TWO-MINUTE DRILL

- When a Red Hat Linux system boots, a special process, init, is the first process started.
- The user and primary group identifiers for a user are stored in the third and fourth fields, respectively, in /etc/passwd.
- Setting the setgid bit solves the problem of making sure all files that are created in a shared directory belong to the correct group.
- COPS is a suite of programs that perform a variety of security checks.
- Support for accounting is built into the Red Hat Linux kernel, but you will need to install the psacct RPM to use some of the tools mentioned here. Under Red Hat Linux, the specific RPM to install is psacct-6.3-10.i386.rpm.
- The *ac* command is used to print out a report of connect time.
- The /var/run/utmp file must always exist on Red Hat Linux systems. This file is used to store information about currently running processes.
- The /var/log/wtmp file is used by the *init* process and the login command to record logins and logouts.
- The tmpwatch command (/usr/sbin/tmpwatch) is used to remove files that have not been accessed in a specified number of hours.
- The e2fsck command performs the same function on the Linux second extended file system as the fsck command does on a standard UNIX file system; it is used to check the file system on a partition for consistency.
- The linuxconf utility is a graphical utility that ties together most system administration tasks under a common interface.

SELF TEST

The following Self Test questions will help you measure your understanding of the material presented in this chapter. Read all the choices carefully, as there may be more than one correct answer. Choose all correct answers for each question.

1. You are setting up a Red Hat Linux system and are configuring several network services. What can you do to make sure your system is more secure from outside attack?

   A. Set up individual user accounts to run the services under.

   B. Pick a really secure password for the root account.

   C. Run the services under the user nobody account.

   D. Make sure the system is locked away in a machine room somewhere.

2. What should you do to a shared directory to ensure that all user accounts who are members of the group that owns the directory will have access to files created in that directory?

   A. Make sure the root account owns the directory.

   B. Make sure the nobody account owns the directory.

   C. Make sure directory is in every user's PATH.

   D. Make sure the setgid bit is set on the directory.

3. How would you set the setgid bit on the /home/developer directory? Assume that you have already issued the command chown nobody.developgrp /home/developer.

   A. chmod 2775 /home/developer

   B. chgrp 2775 /home/developer

   C. chmod 775 /home/developer

   D. chmod g+s /home/developer

4. How would you ensure that all files that are created by your users are automatically created with full access for the owner and group owner of the file?

   A. Have your users type the command umask 002 <filename> whenever they create a file.

   B. Place the command umask 002 in /etc/profile.

   C. Have your users type the command **chmod 002 <filename>** whenever they create a file.

   D. Place the command umask in /etc/profile.

5. You are concerned about the security of your system and would like some way to ensure you haven't overlooked some minor configuration setting that could result in a potential toehold for a cracker. What could you do to check the security of your system?

   A. Publish an invitation on the Internet for crackers to attempt to break into your system as a test of your security measures.

B. Hire a security consultant.

C. Download and install the Computer Oracle and Password System.

D. Assume your system was secure enough, and hope for the best.

6. Which of the following are not true?

   A. System time is stored in a hardware clock.

   B. Some systems store the time value in 24 hour GMT format.

   C. You cannot change your system's time zone offset once you have installed Linux.

   D. The timeconfig utility can be used to change your system's time offset.

7. You installed the psacct process accounting RPM and issued the command /sbin/accton, but nothing shows up when you issue the ac command or the sa command. You've checked and you have a /var/log/pacct file, but its size is 0 bytes. What is wrong?

   A. You will have to reboot to start the accounting process.

   B. Nothing is happening on your system, so nothing is being logged.

   C. You turned accounting off.

   D. The /var/log/pacct file is corrupt.

8. Your manager has asked you for a report of all the system reboots in the past week. How will you obtain this information?

   A. Check the /var/log/messages file.

   B. Issue the command last reboot >reboot.rpt.

   C. Check the /var/log/reboot file.

   D. Issue the command lastb >reboot.rpt.

9. You suspect someone has been trying to break into several accounts on your system. How could you check on this?

   A. Configure system logging to notify you whenever a failed login attempt occurs.

   B. Use the sa command to get a summary of failed login attempts.

   C. Use the command cat /var/log/btmp.

   D. Use the lastb command to display failed login attempts.

10. What would you use the *tmpwatch* command for?

    A. To monitor the system for break-in attempts.

    B. To clean up unused user account directories.

    C. To scan system-wide temporary directories and clean up old temporary files.

    D. To monitor the /tmp directory for the appearance of certain files.

11. The junior system administrator at your site has just come to you to report a suspected bad hard drive on the system he was working on. Whenever he tries to boot the system, he gets a kernel panic with a message saying the root partition

cannot be found. What do you suspect the problem is?

A. The hard drive has crashed.

B. The I/O bus is going bad.

C. Intermittent RAM problems are masquerading as disk problems.

D. The junior system administrator was modifying a system configuration file and has managed to configure the system so it will not boot.

12. What emergency repair items should you always have on hand?

A. A custom boot floppy for your system

B. A repair boot disk

C. Documentation on the partition layouts for the disk drives on your system

D. Documentation on using the repair utilities

13. How would you obtain a rescue disk if you don't have one?

A. Order one from Red Hat.

B. Run the mkrescuedisk utility.

C. Place a floppy in the floppy drive, mount the Red Hat distribution CD-ROM, and issue the command cp /mnt/cdrom/images/rescue.img /dev/fd0.

D. Place a floppy in the floppy drive, mount the Red Hat distribution CD-ROM, and issue the command cat /mnt/cdrom/images/rescue.image >/dev/fd0.

14. How can you boot a damaged Linux system to perform repairs?

A. Boot from your system's custom boot floppy.

B. Boot into rescue mode.

C. Boot into single-user mode using the command linux s.

D. Boot into runlevel 4.

15. When you boot your Linux system, the boot process gets as far as displaying the word *LIL* on the screen. What should you do?

A. Boot into rescue mode and run e2fsck.

B. Boot into rescue mode, and check /etc/fstab for errors.

C. Boot into rescue mode and check /etc/lilo.conf for errors.

D. Reinstall Linux.

16. You are a consultant and are helping a client who has managed to render his system unbootable. You have booted into rescue mode, but the client doesn't have any documentation on the partition layout on his disk drive. What can you do?

A. Use the fdisk -l command to display the partition table for the drive.

B. Reinstall Linux.

C. Use the e2fsck command and look for the superblock.

D. Use the fdisk command in interactive mode.

17. You are trying to boot a system and keep receiving a message about a corrupted

partition. You have booted into rescue mode. Now what might you do to fix the problem?

A. Use fdisk and delete the partition, then add it back.

B. Use the fdisk -l command.

C. Run lilo to rebuild the boot block.

D. Run the command e2fsck -b 8193.

18. What should you remember to do when running lilo from rescue mode?

A. Use the -r option to tell lilo to use an alternate root location.

B. Use the correct path to locate the lilo utility.

C. Use the sync command to flush changes you make to disk.

D. All of the above.

19. Where are some likely places for configuration errors that can prevent your system from booting?

A. /etc/lilo.conf

B. /etc/fstab

C. /etc/passwd

D. /boot

20. You have trouble remembering all of the dozens of different commands and options required to administer a system. What can you do?

A. Become adept at using the man pages and info utility.

B. Make copious notes to remind you how things work.

C. Use linuxconf to manage your system.

D. Write a shell script menu program for the tasks you most commonly perform.

RHCE®

RED HAT CERTIFIED ENGINEER®

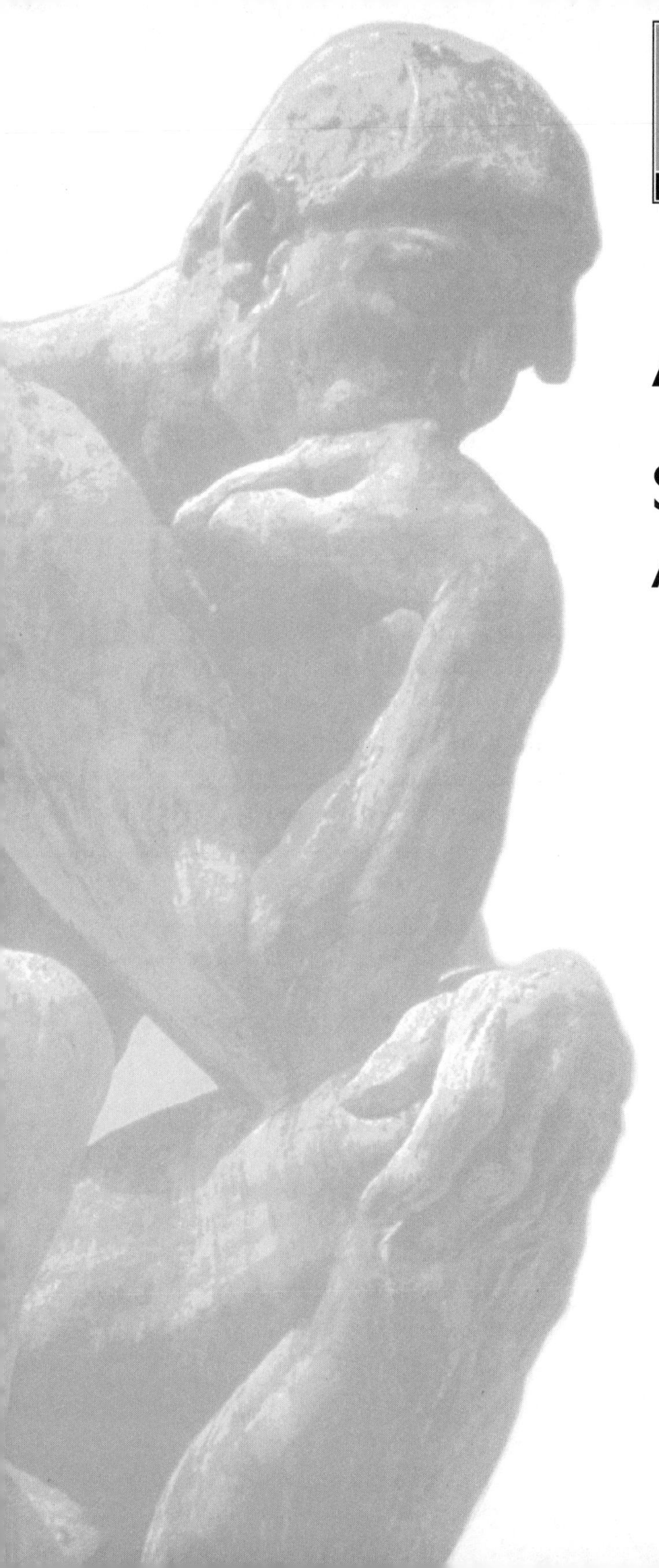

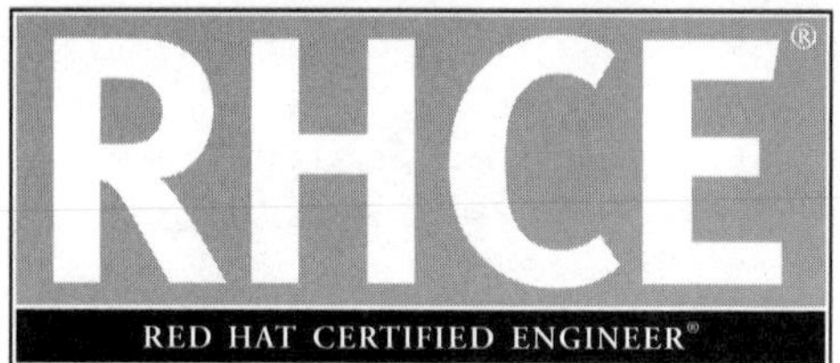

A

Self Test Answers

Chapter 1 Answers

1. Although originally intended to run on the Intel platform, Linux has been ported to which other platform?

   A. Sparc

   B. Alpha

   C. Power PC

   D. All of the above

   D. All of the above. Linux has been ported to the Sparc, Alpha, and Power PC platforms, as well as many others.

2. Currently, Linux scales up to how many processors?

   A. 2

   B. 8

   C. 16

   D. 32

   C. 16. Linux currently scales up to 16 processors.

3. The memory management system Linux uses is:

   A. Swapping

   B. Paging

   C. Preemptive multitasking

   D. Byte-swapping

   B. Paging. Linux uses paging, a method that intelligently allocates memory when system memory is running low by prioritizing memory tasks.

4. Although Linux is a direct descendent of UNIX, it was originally modeled around what operating system?

   A. MS-DOS

   B. Minix

   C. POSIX

   D. OSF/1

   B. Minix. Linux was originally modeled after the Minix operating system.

5. Linux uses what type of kernel architecture?

   A. Static

   B. Microkernel

   C. Distributed

   D. Monolithic

   D. Monolithic. The Linux kernel uses a monolithic kernel architecture.

6. Linux was the first real free operating system and spawned further free efforts such as the HURD kernel and BSD ports.

   A. True

   B. False

   B. False. At the time Linux was being developed, the HURD kernel was being developed, and BSD was actively being ported to the Intel architecture.

7. The term "Free Software" implies that:

   A. The software is free of cost.

   B. The distributor cannot charge you for the software.

   C. The software is freely modifiable and distributable.

   D. Only the software's author can charge a fee for using it.

   C. The software is freely modifiable

and distributable. Free software isn't about cost, but about freedom.

8. Most of the software and utilities in distributions such as Red Hat Linux are:

   A. GNU utilities

   B. Red Hat RPMs

   C. Proprietary

   D. Linux kernel utilities

   A. GNU utilities. GNU utilities make up the majority of software included in most Linux distributions today.

9. Most e-mail on the Internet passes through what free/open source mail transport software?

   A. Microsoft Exchange

   B. Netscape

   C. Open Mail

   D. Sendmail

   D. Sendmail. Most e-mail on the Internet passes through Sendmail, a free mail transport agent written by Eric Allman.

10. Although there are many Linux distributions, the term "Linux" refers to:

    A. Red Hat Linux

    B. The Linux kernel

    C. Linus Torvalds

    D. Free operating systems

    B. The Linux kernel. All Linux distributions are built around the Linux kernel.

11. The protocol used by the Internet is:

    A. TCP/IP

    B. Ethernet

    C. IPX

    D. AppleTalk

    A. TCP/IP. Linux was built from the ground up to support TCP/IP, and many other networking protocols.

12. Advantages of Free/Open Source software are:

    A. Stability

    B. Support

    C. Freedom

    D. All of the above

    D. All of the above. Free/Open Source software gives end users stability, support, freedom, and also the ability to make modifications to the source code.

13. A Workstation installation of Red Hat Linux gives you:

    A. An easy and fast install with maximum flexibility in configuration

    B. A somewhat more complicated install with maximum flexibility in configuration

    C. An easy and fast install with minimum flexibility in configuration

    D. A somewhat more complicated install with minimum flexibility in configuration

    C. An easy and fast install with minimum flexibility in configuration.

Selecting a Workstation install gives you the fastest and easiest install, but sacrifices flexibility in configuration.

14. DOS partitions are removed on what types of Red Hat Linux installations?

A. Workstation

B. Server

C. Workstation and Server

D. None of the above

B. Server. DOS partitions are removed on Server installs only. You may remove them on Custom installs.

15. What type of install gives you the most flexibility in configuration?

A. Workstation

B. Server

C. Custom

D. Server and Custom

C. Custom. The Custom install option gives the most flexibility in configuration.

16. Approximately how much disk space is needed for a Red Hat Linux Workstation install?

A. 250MB

B. 500MB

C. 600MB

D. 700MB

C. Approximately 600MB of free disk space is needed for a Red Hat Linux Workstation install.

17. The kernel and associated files reside on which partition?

A. /boot

B. /etc

C. /usr

D. /var

A. /boot. The kernel and associated files reside on the /boot partition.

18. In his paper, "The Cathedral and the Bazaar," Eric S. Raymond likened traditional software companies to:

A. Linux kernel developers

B. A bazaar

C. Cathedral builders

D. UNIX developers

C. Cathedral builders. Eric S. Raymond likened traditional software companies to cathedral builders.

19. Hardware to avoid using with Linux would be:

A. SCSI drives

B. Intel 486 systems

C. IDE CD-ROMs

D. Winmodems

D. Winmodems. You should avoid attempting to use Winmodems with Linux.

20. When selecting disk drives for a Linux install, the following information should be documented:

A. Capacity

B. Drive type (SCSI or IDE)

C. Manufacturer

D. All of the above

D. All of the above. Capacity, drive type, and manufacturer should be documented when selecting a hard drive for a Linux install.

Chapter 2 Answers

1. You install Linux onto a laptop and discover that there are two PCMCIA cards that you will need to install drivers for: an Ethernet card and a modem. What do you need to do in order to get these cards working?

   A. Recompile the Linux kernel to support Ethernet. Setting up the modem should be as easy as configuring the serial port it uses.

   B. Install the Card Services package to get the needed kernel modules and utilities to manage PCMCIA.

   C. Run the ifconfig and route utilities to configure the cards.

   D. Edit the file /proc/devices to reflect the new hardware, then configure the files in /etc/sysconfig to get them up and running.

   B. The Card Services package is needed in order for any PCMCIA device to work. The standard Linux kernel source code does not come with the required modules and drivers needed by PCMCIA devices. Also, the Card Services package includes a daemon to manage the cards for such things as loading, unloading, and inserting and removing cards.

2. A co-worker bought a brand new mouse to use on his Linux workstation. He tells you that the person he bought it from said it would work, but he is very frustrated because it doesn't. The old mouse had a rectangular 9-pin connector, and the new mouse has a round 6-pin mini DIN connector. What is most likely the reason why your coworker's new mouse doesn't work?

   A. The person who sold him the mouse sold him the wrong type. Your coworker should take it back and get a refund.

   B. The new mouse needs an adapter to change the round 6-pin mini DIN connector to the rectangular 9-pin connector.

   C. Your coworker's Linux workstation isn't set up to use a PS/2 mouse.

   D. Your coworker's Linux workstation isn't configured to use a busmouse.

   B and C. The new mouse is a PS/2 mouse. Therefore, the Linux workstation will have to be configured to use a PS/2 mouse with the PS/2 port. You may have to add support for PS/2 mice in the Linux kernel. Once there is support in the kernel, the mouse can be configured to use the PS/2 port using the XF86Setup or mouseconfig tool. You can get an adapter to change DIN to 9 pin.

3. What do you need to do in order to be able to use a third or fourth serial port in Linux? (Choose all that apply.)

   A. Obtain and install a hardware card that has more ports.

   B. Linux kernel 2.2 already handles this for you.

   C. Add a new entry to the file /etc/serial.conf.

   D. Use the setserial utility to assign resources to the new serial port.
   B and **D**. Use the setserial utility for Linux kernels earlier than 2.2.*x*. To configure the serial ports at boot time, edit the /etc/rc.d/rc.serial file to run the setserial command for each serial port you use. With kernel version 2.2.*x*, you don't need to assign unique IRQs for each serial port.

4. After installing an ISA plug-and-play device into a computer running Linux, what needs to be done in order to get the card working?

   A. Install and configure the isapnptools package for Linux.

   B. Nothing. Since it's a plug-and-play card, Linux will be able to install the device drivers and kernel modules automatically.

   C. The card will not work. Plug-and-play ISA cards are not supported in Linux.

   D. Run the pnpprobe utility, then set the resources that the card should use.
   A. While support for ISA plug-and-play devices is still somewhat lacking in Linux, the isapnptools package contains utilities that can be used to get the cards working. Try running man isapnp in Linux for more information.

5. You installed a printer onto a Linux workstation. After experiencing a lot of trouble trying to make it print, you're finally successful. However, now the sound card has stopped working. What most likely went wrong?

   A. The sound card was probably a plug-and-play device, and since Linux doesn't handle plug and play well, it couldn't detect the card after the new printer was installed.

   B. There is an IRQ conflict between the printer and the sound card.

   C. The sound card and printer are using the same device file in the /dev directory. You need to create a new device in the /dev directory to use both devices.

   D. None of the above.
   B. The default IRQ for a parallel port (what the printer is using) is 5 or 7. Many sound cards will try to use one of these IRQs as well. Try running cat /proc/interrupts to see what IRQs are being used, then choose a free one to assign to the sound card.

6. Which of the following RAID levels provides both redundancy and performance increases?

   A. RAID-5

   B. RAID-4

C. RAID-1

D. RAID-0
A. RAID-5 will provide both. There is no redundancy in RAID-0. Performance can actually be decreased in levels 1 and 4.

7. What problems could you come across when using systems that mix (E)IDE and SCSI technologies?

A. You can't mix them together.

B. There are potential IRQ conflicts between the controllers for each device.

C. The computer's BIOS may not be able to access SCSI devices.

D. SCSI disks cannot use LBA translation as (E)IDE devices can.
C. Depending on the computer's BIOS, SCSI disks may not be accessible to the computer's BIOS, which can cause troubles when trying to boot Linux. This means that you might not be able to boot off of a SCSI disk, or that your BIOS will assign a different order to your hard disks than Linux will, confusing Linux as to which disk is which.

8. How would an EIDE drive's geometry be changed, using LBA translation, if the drive had 1136 cylinders, 16 heads, and 63 sectors?

A. 1024 cylinders, 128 heads, 63 sectors

B. 1024 cylinders, 16 heads, 175 sectors

C. 284 cylinders, 64 heads, 63 sectors

D. 568 cylinders, 32 heads, 63 sectors
D. By doubling the amount of heads, the value of cylinders is halved, bringing the geometry within acceptable limits for the BIOS to understand.

9. You are setting up a Linux Server to be a file server for an office of 30 people. The server has 64MB of memory. How much of that memory should you reserve to be used as buffer cache?

A. Find out the maximum memory requirements of the system, then subtract the amount of RAM (64MB). The remaining value should be used to buffer cache.

B. You don't need to. Linux handles the buffer cache automatically.

C. About 1MB per user should be sufficient; therefore, use 30MB.

D. Always use double the amount of available RAM.
B. The Linux kernel will dynamically use all of the available memory in RAM to be used as buffer cache. The update daemon manages disk buffering by calling the sync command and running bdflush periodically.

10. What does LDP stand for?

A. Linux Development Project

B. Linux Development and Planning

C. Linux Documentation Project

D. None of the above
C. Linux Documentation Project. It can be your best friend. You'll use it often.

11. Of the following hardware, which would be the easiest to install Red Hat Linux on?

    A. A Toshiba laptop with an Intel Pentium II 266MHz CPU
    B. An IBM PC XT
    C. A 486DX/100 IBM Clone
    D. A PowerMac G3

    C. The 486 computer is supported by Red Hat. Toshiba has only recently released specifications for its hardware, so support is limited. Linux was originally developed for the 386 architecture. There are separate download areas and CD-ROMs for these other architectures and Linux does run on PPC, PowerMac G3 CPUs and sparc architectures.

12. What downside is there to extensive partitioning?

    A. Slower disk access.
    B. Unused disk space is wasted.
    C. Data fragmentation.
    D. The root partition might not be able to be accessed at boot time.

    B. If you allocate too much space on a partition than will ever be used, then that space is wasted.

13. You attempt to install Linux on an old 80386 computer. You manage to scavenge an 800MB hard drive to use. However, when you boot the computer, it reports the hard drive to be only 504MB. Why?

    A. The BIOS can access only the first partition, which must be 504MB.
    B. The hard drive must have bad sectors.
    C. The BIOS only supports IDE, not EIDE.
    D. An 80386 CPU can only address 504MB of data.

    C. The IDE (or ATA) standard does not support hard disks larger than 504MB. The 80386 computer was most likely manufactured before support for large drives was added with EIDE (ATA-s, or Fast-ATA).

14. What do you need to do in order to get past the 504MB barrier with an EIDE hard disk controller?

    A. Add a SCSI controller.
    B. Upgrade to an ATA-2 controller.
    C. Set jumpers on the hard disks to support EIDE.
    D. Set the hard drive translation mode to LBA in the BIOS.

    D. EIDE controllers support hard disks larger than 504MB, but your computer's BIOS may not be able to access the entire drive unless LBA translation is used.

15. You get a phone call from a frustrated user who just bought a new modem. The modem is a Lucent 56k Winmodem, and the user is having trouble making it work in Linux. Which of the following is most likely the source of his trouble?

    A. An IRQ conflict is preventing Linux from using the modem.

B. Winmodems are specific to Windows operating systems. Linux cannot use them.

C. The modem is a plug-and-play device, and the user does not have the isapnptools package installed/configured.

D. Linux does not support 56k modems.
B. Winmodems are not supported under Linux. They are hardware devices that are incomplete in design. This is made up for through software programming. In the case of Winmodems, the software only works for Windows operating systems.

16. When planning your Red Hat Linux installation, which of the following information is the least important to take note of?

A. The speed of your CD-ROM.

B. What type of mouse you will be using.

C. The frequency specifications of your monitor.

D. The model of your network card.
A. The only thing the speed of your CD-ROM will affect is the amount of time the install will take if you are installing from a CD-ROM.

17. RAID is an acronym for:

A. Redundant Array of Independent Disks

B. Redundant Array of Inexpensive Disks

C. Reliable Array of Independent Disks

D. Redundant Assortment of Inexpensive Disks
A or **B.** Independent or Inexpensive have both been acceptable for the "I" in RAID.

18. What is the maximum number of partitions that you can create for (E)IDE and SCSI disks?

A. There is no maximum.

B. 16 for (E)IDE and 15 for SCSI.

C. 24 for (E)IDE and 16 for SCSI.

D. Linux only supports a total of 64 partitions of all disks together.
B. Of course, you need to use extended and logical partitions to reach these limits. Otherwise, you are limited to using only four partitions.

Chapter 3 Answers

1. When you try to boot your newly created installation, with a root, /boot and swap partition, the system complains that there is no active boot drive. What should you do?

A. Reboot with the installation diskette and redo the installation.

B. Reboot with a DOS boot diskette and run FDISK /MBR.

C. Reboot with the installation diskette and run fdisk to activate the proper boot partition.

D. Reboot with the bootup diskette created during installation.
C. You can use the Linux supplied fdisk utility (*not* the DOS-based

utility fdisk) supplied on the BOOT.IMG diskette to mark the active (where boot block is located) partition. Use option p to print the current partition table, then a, and select the appropriate partition, usually hda1.

2. If you already have a PC with a previous version of Linux on it that you do not want to keep, which installation option will automatically delete only the Linux partitions and install a basic network and X-Windows-ready Linux system?

   A. Workstation

   B. Server

   C. Custom

   D. Dual Boot
   A. This is the main benefit of the Workstation option, little user interaction, the system creates the partitions from unused or previous Linux type partitions and everything installs for a basic network-ready system. There is no such option as Dual Boot.

3. After you have completed your installation, during bootup, the following appears on the console, and then the system seems to hang. What appears to be the problem?

   A. Cannot find second part of boot loader. /boot may be beyond 1024 cylinder.

   B. Other operating system boot loader interfering with lilo.

   C. Did not configure an active (boot) partition.

   D. System is waiting for special options to the command line.
   A. /boot is beyond the 1024 cylinder count as seen by the DOS level loader at this point in the bootup. You will need to use the emergency boot diskette created during the installation (assuming you created it), or reinstall the system again.

4. You have installed different versions of Linux before. During the installation, you are given a second option to create disk partitions, but you are only familiar with the text-based disk partition management program called:

   A. fixdisk

   B. rdisk

   C. fdisk

   D. druidisk
   C. During an installation, there is Disk Druid from Red Hat and the universal fdisk utility (NOT the DOS BASED UTILITY).

5. You are asked to install on a machine that has several versions of UNIX on it. There are many different partitions. You only want to use the same type of partitions that Linux already uses. What is the native file system format used by Linux?

   A. ufs

   B. ext2fs

   C. dos

D. fat

B. Although the system usually denotes it as Linux Native, the conventional name is the Extended 2 File System, ext2fs or ext2, denoted with an ID of 0x83 (swap is ID 0x82).

6. You have configured a new Workstation installation so that it dual boots with Win95. However, you have forgotten the name you used. When you enter Win95, lilo complains it cannot find that installation. You need to display all possible boot choices.

A. Press SPACE BAR-h ENTER

B. Help ENTER

C. TAB

D. ESC1B ENTER

C. You use the TAB key (or the ? (question mark) to display the listed label names).

7. Your main Linux Web server has been diagnosed as having to use swap on a regular basis. You notice that there is only one big swap file on the same physical disk as the root file system. There are three other disks with space available. How many swap partitions can be utilized, what is the maximum size for any one, and what is the maximum overall swap space allowed per system?

A. Eight partitions, max 2GB any one, 4GB total

B. Six partitions, max 3GB any one, 4GB total

C. Four partitions, max 4GB any one, 8GB total

D. Two partitions, max 5GB any one, 8GB total

A. Up to eight partitions, max 2GB for any one, 4GB for all swap space total.

8. Your MIS manager is concerned about the installation of Linux on the hundreds of workstations in the company. She thinks it requires someone to install from a CD-ROM on every machine, and only a few machines have CD-ROM drives. You want to reassure her that there will not be any problem using currently running network services. (Select all that apply.)

A. NFS

B. Samba

C. FTP

D. HTTP

E. DNS

F. DHCP

A, C, D. NFS, FTP, HTTP (Samba does not currently work well with RHLinux 6).

9. Your current user of this workstation could not get Windows to run so she ran the DOS FDISK.EXE with /MBR to put the boot sector back in place. Now you cannot run Linux. You boot up with the emergency startup disk you created. You need to update the MBR with the Linux Loader program with:

A. /etc/lilo.conf
B. /bin/configlilo
C. /sbin/lilo
D. /bin/sys/liloconf
C. /sbin/lilo resets the MBR to linux and, depending on /etc/lilo.conf, can provide access to the other operating system.

10. After you update the MBR, it only indicates one entry. You need to fix the setup file to include both options. What system file is used to set and create boot entries?

A. /bin/sys/liloconf
B. /sbin/liloconf
C. /etc/lilo.conf
D. /usr/sys/liloconf
C. /etc/lilo.conf contains all boot entries, the time-out, and which labeled entry is chosen by default.

11. Your MIS manager has heard that there is another boot loader capable of loading many different operating systems. What is an alternate boot loader available for Linux?

A. syslinuz
B. bootfs
C. loadlin
D. pmagic
C. loadlin can boot many different operating systems; syslinux is used only at installation.

12. You are told to check the Web server drive table after installation. There are eight partitions. Your MIS manager asks how that can be; DOS can only create one primary and one extended. How many primary partitions can any one disk drive contain?

A. 4 primary, 1 extended, 16 total partitions
B. 3 primary, 2 extended, 12 total partitions
C. 12 primary, 1 extended partition
D. 16 extended partitions
A. 4 total, 3 that are called primary and one extended that can contain 12 logical at most for a total of 16 named partitions.

13. A new product you are to add to the server asks you to go into single-user mode to run a system check on the file system. How do you start your system in single-user mode?

A. lilo : boot 1
B. lilo : init 1
C. lilo : single user
D. lilo : linux single
D. lilo: linux single (this assumes you used the default name tag for the boot image, linux. It could actually be anything, but this is the default. lilo : linux 1 would also work).

14. The MIS manager wants a further explanation of the drive table on the

server, specifically, the type of partition that can contain logical partitions.

A. ext2fs

B. nfs

C. primary

D. extended
D. The first three partitions are referred to as primary; the fourth is called an extended partition and can contain up to 12 logical partitions.

15. During the installation, you are asked to configure your network card to access the installation source files from an NFS server. Assuming you have already input the IP address and netmask for this host, you need to have:

A. DNS Server IP, BOOTP Server IP, NFS export name

B. DNS export name, BOOTP Server IP, NFS Server IP

C. DHCP Server IP, DHCP name, NFS export name

D. NFS export name, NFS Server IP
D. The IP address or full domain name of the NFS server and the export directory name. You must already have an IP address, netmask (and optional gateway IP if the services are on another network), or be using DHCP or BOOTP to obtain it, for the install host.

16. Your MIS manager has asked you to put Linux on a laptop for a CEO. The laptop has about 1GB of free disk space, but there is one partition with all available space allocated to it. What free utility is supplied with the installation that allows you to resize a partition?

A. fdisk

B. fips

C. bootp

D. syslinux
B. fips is on the installation disk, but you need to read the documentation carefully.

17. What program allows you to manage a dual boot between Linux and Win98?

A. lilo

B. syslinux

C. bootp

D. fdisk
A. lilo

18. During installation, you create the first six partitions and then you allocate the file system directory to them sequentially. But there is one partition that you cannot assign as a file system:

A. hda4

B. hda1

C. hda5

D. had
A. hda4 is the extended partition name and cannot contain a file system, just logical drives.

19. You are in a rush to install a workstation with the minimum number of partitions. What partitions are absolutely required?

    A. /boot, swap, /system
    B. root (/), swap
    C. swap , /boot, /usr
    D. /boot, /root

    B. The minimum partition set is a swap and a root (/) partition.

20. A Windows administrator is puzzled by the amount of swap space configured and wants to know what is recommended for Linux.

    A. Same as RAM memory.
    B. 40–90MB.
    C. Same as the server uses.
    D. Two to three times the RAM.
    E. There is no recommended amount of swap space; you need to know exactly how much space will be required.

    D. Although it is recommended to have two to three times the amount of RAM, this varies depending on the machine's peak load. For machines with small amounts of RAM, big swap files help it cope with large jobs, and is optimal if the machine is under-powered for some peak performance hits. In actual fact, you do not want the system to use the swap space if at all possible. If you do use swap space regularly, then you need more RAM for the system.

21. What partitions are created by a Workstation installation?

    A. /boot, swap, / root
    B. /, swap, /root
    C. swap, /boot, /usr
    D. /boot, /root, /usr

    A. There are three partitions made: /boot, swap, and a root, /, partition

22. What partitions are created by a Server installation?

    A. /boot, swap, /, /usr
    B. /, swap, /var, /boot
    C. swap, /boot, /usr, /home
    D. /boot, /, /usr, /home, swap, /var

    D. There are six partitions created out of all available disk space: the root, /, a swap, /var, /boot, /usr, and /home.

23. During your installation, you are not presented with any option to get to the NFS share where you provided access to the installation files. You do not have a CD-ROM available on this workstation. How do you remedy this?

    A. Create the RESCUE.IMG diskette, then reboot with this diskette in the floppy drive.
    B. Create the PCMCIA.IMG diskette, then reboot with this diskette in the floppy drive.
    C. Create the BOOTNET.IMG diskette, then reboot with this diskette in the floppy drive.

D. Create the SCSI.IMG diskette; enter when prompted.
C. There is no choice but to start all over. You must use the BOOTNET.IMG file to create your installation diskette; only it provides network based access.

24. You have a PC that already contains a different version of Linux. During the installation, you are asked where to put the boot loader, lilo. You know there is already another loader called loadlin installed. Where should you put the installation boot record?

A. In any partition except /boot

B. In any partition except /

C. In partition /boot

D. You do not need to install the lilo boot loader
C. Since loadlin is probably already in hda1, the first partition, you should put your boot reference in /boot, and then update loadlin to point to it.

25. During the installation, the authentication screen provides three options. You remember what the shadow password is and MD5, but forget exactly what the third option NIS is.

A. Network Inode Slave—Provides shared disk resources

B. Network Information Service—Provides centralized authentication

C. New Internet Standard—Centralized authentication of shared access

D. Newton Interrupt Sequence—File sharing protocol
B. NIS is a standard centralized master copy of the authentication files that is distributed to all other hosts in a trusted network.

Chapter 4 Answers

1. When adding a user using Linuxconf, what field is required to be filled in?

A. Full name

B. Login name

C. Command interpreter

D. Home directory
B. Login name. The only required field for a new user is the login name. Linuxconf will use defaults for the rest of the fields, if required.

2. When deleting a user account using Linuxconf, if "Archive the account's data" is selected, where is the deleted user's data archived?

A. /home/oldaccounts

B. /root/oldaccounts

C. /home/oldusers

D. /root/oldusers
A. /home/oldaccounts. All files stored in a deleted user's account are archived to /home/oldaccounts when the "Archive the account's data" option is selected.

3. Window manager configuration files for the fvwm2 window manager are stored in which directory?

   A. /usr/lib/X11/fvwm2

   B. /etc/X11/wmconfig/fvwm2

   C. /etc/fvwm2/config

   D. /etc/X11/fvwm2

   D. /etc/X11/fvwm2. Window manager configuration files are stored in /etc/X11/<windowmanager>, where <windowmanager> is the name of the window manager.

4. To change the mount options for a local filesystem, which file would you edit?

   A. /etc/filesystems

   B. /etc/fstab

   C. /etc/group

   D. /etc/mnttab

   B. /etc/fstab. Information regarding local filesystems, including mount options, is stored in /etc/fstab.

5. Which option would you mount a filesystem with, such that binaries cannot be executed on it?

   A. nouser

   B. nosuid

   C. noauto

   D. noexec

   D. noexec. The noexec option does not allow binaries to be executed on the filesystem.

6. Which of the following commands correctly installs the package "penguin-3.26.i386.rpm"?

   A. rpm -I penguin-3.26.i386.rpm

   B. rpm -i penguin

   C. rpm -i penguin-3.26.i386.rpm

   D. rpm --install penguin.rpm

   C. rpm –i penguin-3.26.i386.rpm. When installing a package, the -i option is used, followed by the name of the RPM file.

7. Checking the Red Hat Corporation's Errata Web page, you find a package listed that is currently on your system. A good strategy to update your system would be:

   A. Check to see the ramifications of upgrading the affected package.

   B. Watch for warnings when updating the package for config file replacements.

   C. Test the new package to ensure it's been configured correctly.

   D. All of the above.

   D. All of the above. Answers A, B, and C are good strategies when updating an RPM on your system.

8. Source RPMs are by default installed in which directory?

   A. /usr/lib/rpm

   B. /usr/src/rpm

   C. /usr/src/redhat

   D. /usr/src/redhat/rpm

   C. /usr/src/redhat. When installing SRPMs, they are by default extracted into the /usr/src/redhat directory structure.

9. What subdirectories are in the /usr/src/redhat directory?

   A. SOURCES, SPECS, BUILD, RPMS, SRPMS

   B. SOURCES, SPECS, LIBS, RPMS, DESC

   C. SOURCES, SPECS, BINS, RPMS, DESC

   D. SOURCES, SPECS, ETC, RPMS, SRPMS

   A. SOURCES, SPECS, BUILD, RPMS, SRPMS are the subdirectories within the /usr/src/redhat directory structure.

10. Which section of an RPM spec file is used to compile the source code?

   A. clean

   B. prep

   C. build

   D. install

   C. Build. The build section of the spec file is used to compile the source code.

11. The prep section of an RPM spec file serves what purpose?

   A. Describes what information users see when they request information about this package.

   B. Contains commands to compile and build the binaries from source code.

   C. Takes care of extra tasks to be performed when a verify command is issued.

   D. Unpacks the source code and configures it for building.

   D. Unpacks the source code and configures it for building. The prep section is performed just before the build section, and usually is used to unpack the source code and run any configuration commands.

12. When building an RPM from a tar archive, the tar file should be placed in what directory?

   A. /usr/src/redhat

   B. /usr/src/redhat/SOURCES

   C. /usr/src/redhat/TAR

   D. /usr/src/redhat/SRPMS

   B. /usr/src/redhat/SOURCES. Tar files should be placed in /usr/src/redhat/SOURCES when building a SRPM from a tar archive.

13. Issuing the command rpm -bc foo-2.2.spec causes what to happen?

   A. A binary and source RPM is created based on the spec file.

   B. Only the SRPM is built.

   C. Only the install section of the spec file is executed.

   D. Only the build section of the spec file is executed.

   D. Only the build section of the spec file is executed. The "c" modifier to the build option (-b) causes only the build section to be executed.

14. The /etc/sysconfig/network file contains information about:

    A. Your system's host name and NIS domain.
    B. The devices used for your network connections.
    C. Chat scripts for PPP and SLIP connections.
    D. The status of the network.

    A. Your system's host name and NIS domain. It also contains information regarding IPV4 forwarding, and whether or not your system uses networking.

15. What command is used to configure and display network devices?

    A. netstat
    B. arp
    C. ifconfig
    D. ifup

    C. ifconfig. The ifconfig command is used to configure and display network devices.

16. The netstat -r command is used to:

    A. Display kernel routing tables.
    B. Display gateway metrics.
    C. Configure kernel routing tables.
    D. Configure gateway metrics.

    A. Display kernel routing tables using netstat -r.

17. The command arp -d rhino causes the following to happen:

    A. All ARP tables are removed on the host rhino.
    B. All ARP information for the host rhino is removed.
    C. All ARP tables on the host rhino are displayed.
    D. All ARP information pertaining to the host rhino is displayed.

    B. All ARP information for the host rhino is removed. The -d option to arp tells the kernel to remove all arp info regarding a specified host.

18. Upon boot, the kernel invokes init, which in turn runs

    A. /etc/rc.d/init.d
    B. /etc/inittab
    C. /etc/rc.d/initdefault
    D. /etc/rc.d/rc.sysinit

    D. /etc/rc.d/rc.sysinit. init runs /etc/rc.d/rc.sysinit, which performs a number of tasks, including configuring the network, setting up keymapping, swapping, and the host name.

19. If you want to see what runlevels crond is configured to start in, you issue which command?

    A. chkconfig -list -crond
    B. chkconfig -l crond
    C. chkconfig --list crond
    D. chkconfig crond

    C. chkconfig --list crond. The output of

this command is the following: crond 0:off 1:off 2:on 3:on 4:on 5:on 6:off

20. To switch from the current virtual console to virtual console 4, you press:

 A. ALT-4
 B. ALT-F4
 C. CTL-4
 D. CTL-F4

 B. Press ALT-F4. Each virtual console has an ALT function key associated with it to move to that virtual console.

Chapter 5 Answers

1. You are creating a dual boot NT/Linux system. You already have NT installed and plan to use the NTLDR to load Linux on the second drive. Linux is installed and you have made a bootdisk that properly boots Linux. What command would you issue from Linux to copy the bootsector from the floppy?

 A. dd if=bootsect.lnx of=/dev/fd0 bs=512 count=1
 B. dd if=/dev/fd0 of=bootsect.lnx bs=512 count=1
 C. dd if=bootsect.lnx of=/dev/fd0 bs=512
 D. dd if=/dev/fd0 of=bootsect.lnx count=512

 B. dd if=/dev/fd0 of=bootsect.lnx bs=512 count=1. The options for the disk dump command need to be as follows: input file (if) needs to point to the floppy drive, output file (of) needs to point to the file you want to create, block size (bs) should be 512, and count should be 1 because we only need the bootsector from the disk.

2. You are dual booting an NT/Linux system. You have successfully copied a working bootsector over the NT boot partition and named it bootsect.lnx. What do you need to do so that the NTLDR loads Linux as an operating system?

 A. Edit the NTLDR file with C:\bootsect.lnx="Linux".
 B. Edit the BOOT.INI file with "Linux"=C:\bootsect.lnx.
 C. Edit the BOOT.INI file with C:\bootsect.lnx="Linux"
 D. Do nothing; NTLDR will detect any bootsector file that has the bootsect.xxx syntax.

 A. Edit the NTLDR file with C:\bootsect.lnx="Linux". The BOOT.INI file is loaded by NTLDR and parsed using the following syntax: <drive>:<filename>=<label>.

3. You have a mirrored RAID system with three drives. The first two are mirrored and the third is supposed to be a spare. When you look at the /etc/raidtab file you see that it says spare-disks 0. What does this entry tell you?

 A. The raidtab entry is set up correctly.
 B. Spare-disks support is turned off. To turn it on change spare-disks to 1.
 C. Currently no spare disks are loaded.

D. The mirror failed and had to use the spare disk.
A. Spare-disks start counting at 0 and we only have one spare disk so the raidtab entry is set up correctly.

4. You need to set up multiple Red Hat Linux systems over the network. You decided to have a bootdisk connect to your DHCP/BOOTP server and load a kickstart file. The kickstart file resides on the DHCP/BOOTP server with the following syntax: <client_ip-kickstart>. You plan to have the kickstart install Linux from an FTP server that does not reside on the DHCP/BOOTP server. What is the problem with this plan?

   A. You cannot have the FTP server on a different server from your DHCP/BOOTP servers.
   B. The kickstart file name is wrong.
   C. A BOOTP server can only be used to load kernels and will not load a kickstart file.
   D. You cannot install from an FTP server.
   D. You cannot install from an FTP server. Kickstart installs can only be done via CD-ROM or NFS servers. You can not use kickstart to load from FTP, HTTP or SMB.

5. You have several remote branches that you need to have Linux installed on. You decide the best way to do this is to have all the answers preconfigured on a kickstart file on a DHCP/BOOTP server and have it set up to install off an NFS server at the main branch. You plan to ship a bootdisk that has the kickstart file but are concerned that somebody on the network will see the root password in the file. What can you do?

   A. Encrypt the kickstart file that resides on the DHCP/BOOTP server.
   B. Boot the disk with **linux ks=encrypted**
   C. Use rootpw --iscrypted in the kickstart file.
   D. There is nothing you can do.
   C. Use rootpw --iscrypted in the kickstart file. If you paste an encrypted password after this line then the encrypted version will be sent and network ease droppers will not be able to read a clear text version of the root password.

6. When trying to load a sound module you get a device busy error message. You feel that it is your ISA Plug and Play sound card. You would like to view its Plug and Play configuration options so you can edit them to nonconflicting values. What command would you use to create a file of all your ISA Plug and Play device options?

   A. dumppnp > isapnp.conf
   B. pnpdump > isapnp.conf
   C. displaypnp > isapnp.conf
   D. showpnp > isapnp.conf
   B. pnpdump > isapnp.conf. This command will dump all of your Plug and Play devices with all of their possible settings to a file called

isapnp.conf. From here you can edit the file and reset your Plug and Play cards.

7. You run Linux on a laptop. The cardmgr daemon for your PCMCIA cards is stomping on an IRQ that you want reserved. What file do you use to tell the cardmgr to exclude this IRQ from its list?

   A. /etc/pcmcia/config.opts

   B. /etc/sysconfig/pcmcia

   C. /etc/pcmcia/config.exclude

   D. /etc/rc.d/rc.sysinit

   A. /etc/pcmcia/config.opts. This file is used to exclude any memory, IO addresses, and IRQs you want excluded.

8. You frequently use your laptop as a server during work hours. Many users come in and work on special project files throughout the day. You are concerned that there could be a loss of power and would like to warn the other users when the battery is about to run out. What would be the best way to handle this?

   A. Tell each user to run **apm** as often as possible to check battery life.

   B. Set up a user policy that instructs all users to save every five minutes.

   C. Use the wall option in the /etc/sysconfig/apmd file.

   D. Edit the shutdown script that runs at runlevel 0.

   C. Use the wall option in the /etc/sysconfig/apmd file. You can tell the apmd to notify the users before the battery runs out of power with the -W option.

9. What runlevel should you switch to in order to run X11 automatically at startup?

   A. 1

   B. 2

   C. 3

   D. 5

   A. 5. By default runlevel 5 will load X11 at startup.

10. Which runlevel would you need to load start single user mode?

    A. 1

    B. 2

    C. 3

    D. 5

    A. 1. By default runlevel 1 will switch Linux into single user mode.

11. What would happen if you modified the initdefault entry in the /etc/inittab file to look like this: id:5:initdefault:/usr/games/fortune?

    A. It would display a fortune every time you logged on.

    B. It would boot into X11 and display a fortune.

    C. It would display a fortune only when it booted.

    D. The fortune line would be ignored.

    D. The fortune line would be ignored. The initdefault keyword ignores any process entries that are listed. All initdefault does is set the default runlevel.

12. What startup file loads the modules?

A. /etc/rc.d/rc.modules

B. /etc/init.d/S10modules

C. /etc/rc.d/rc.sysinit

D. none of the above

C. /etc/rc.d/rc.sysinit. The /etc/rc.d/rc.sysinit file checks for pre-defined aliases in the /etc/conf.modules and loads them.

13. Which of the following does NOT describe kernel modules?

A. They make the kernel size smaller.

B. They increase your kernel speed.

C. You can dynamically unload modules from memory.

D. Modules have .dll extensions.

D. Modules have .dll extensions. Modules actually have .o extensions.

14. You have a network card that needs to have options specified at the command line when loading the module. You only need this network card on occasion so you want to leave it as a module. What can you do to simplify the loading of the module?

A. Add a bind command to the conf.modules file.

B. Add an options command to the conf.modules file.

C. Add the options to the end of the alias command in the conf.modules.file.

D. None of the above.

B. Add an options command to the conf.modules file. Once you have added an options command with your options to it you can simply type **modprobe <module>** and it will add the options for you.

15. When you type in **lsmod** and see a list of running modules, you notice that some of them say (autoclean). What does this mean?

A. The module will automatically remove its own files in the /tmp directory.

B. The module is not in use and should be removed.

C. The kerneld will automatically take care of removing it from memory.

D. The modprobe command has set the module to autoclean.

C. The kerneld will automatically take care of removing it from memory. You do not need to worry about modules that have (autoclean) listed because kerneld will remove and add them from memory when needed.

16. You are on a foreign computer and are not sure what network card is inside of it. You have checked dmesg and no network cards are listed. You have a bunch of compiled network modules but none are currently loaded. What could you do to quickly load the unknown network device?

A. Try loading each module manually.

B. modprobe *

C. Kerneld will load the module when the network card is accessed.

D. modprobe -t net
D. Modprobe -t net. This command will run through your /lib/modules/ .../net directory and try each module. It will stop when a module successfully loads.

17. You want to conserve as much memory as possible. When doing some checking you notice that there are some modules that are loaded but unused. What command could you use to remove these modules? (Choose all that apply)

A. rmmod

B. rmmod -r

C. modprobe -r

D. modprobe -d
A, B, C. rmmod, rmmod -r, and modprobe -r will remove modules. Only rmmod -r and modprobe -r will remove the module and all of its dependencies; rmmod will only remove the module specified.

18. You notice that a module you want to load will not load because its dependencies fail. When you examine the /lib/modules/.../ directory closer you notice that the modules.dep file does not exist. What would be the easiest way to recreate this file?

A. Add the dependencies by hand.

B. In the /usr/src/linux directory type **make modules_install**.

C. Depmod -a

D. None of the above.
C. Depmod -a. This command will go through all of your modules and find all dependencies for all of your modules. It then creates the modules.dep file for you.

19. With a default Red Hat install what is the name of the first script that runs on a system?

A. /etc/rc.d/rc.sysinit

B. /etc/init.d/rc.sysinit

C. /etc/rc.d/rc.0

D. /etc/rc.d/rc.1
A. /etc/rc.d/rc.sysinit. This is the first script that is called. This script is specified in the /etc/inittab file.

20. If you wanted to change the initial boot script, what entry in the /etc/inittab file would you modify?

A. boot

B. bootwait

C. sysinit

D. initdefault
C. Sysinit. This option runs during system boot but before any boot or bootwait entries. Initdefault merely sets the runlevel which are ignored at this level of booting.

Chapter 6 Answers

1. You have several users on your system. You want to restrict their disk space in their home directory, but because of the complexity of some of their programs, they need large temporary space. How could you restrict their disk usage in their home directories, but allow them unlimited access to the /tmp directory?

   A. Use edquota /home to edit the users' quota for their home directory.

   B. Use edquota and specify only the home directories in the text file.

   C. Mount the /tmp directory to a separate partition and use edquota on the partition that contains the home directory.

   D. None of these options will work.

   D. Mount the /tmp directory to a separate partition and use edquota on the partition that contains the home directory. You can only specify one quota per partition. If you move /tmp to its own partition, you can control it separately.

2. You are running an ISP service and provide space for users Web pages. You only want them to use 40 MB, but will allow up to 50MB until they can clean up their stuff. How could you use quotas to enforce this policy?

   A. Enable grace periods, set the hard limit to 40MB, and the Soft Limit to 50MB.

   B. Enable grace periods, set the Soft Limit to 50MB, and the Hard Limit to 40MB.

   C. Enable grace periods, set the Soft Limit to 40MB, and the Hard Limit to 50MB.

   D. None of the above.

   C. Enable grace periods, set the soft limit to 40MB, and the hard limit to 50MB. This will warn the users that they are over their limit after the grace period, but will make sure they do not exceed the 50MB true maximum barrier.

3. The CIO of your company wants to see a full report on how much disk space each user on the system is using up. What command would you use to display this information?

   A. repquota -a

   B. quotareport -a

   C. quotareport -all

   D. quotashow -a

   A. repquota will display a report of all users on your system. It shows the used space and their soft and hard limits.

4. You recently received a notice from your legal department. They want all servers to have a message to thwart off unauthorized access at the login prompt. How would you go about doing this? (Choose all that apply.)

   A. Modify /etc/banner.net

   B. Modify /etc/issue

   C. Modify /etc/issue.net

D. Modify /etc/login.msg
B and C. The /etc/issue file is used to log in on locally to the machine. The /etc/issue.net file is used when connecting remotely to a PC.

5. Your system currently boots into runlevel 3. After looking into the /etc/rc.d/rc3.d/ directory, you want to know what script will run first. Of the following links, what script will be the first to run when entering runlevel 3?

A. K20rwhod

B. S30syslog

C. K96pcmcia

D. S99linuxconf
B. S30syslog. Links that begin with an S will start a service when entering a runlevel, while links that begin with a K will kill a service. The earlier number will load first.

6. How would you set the runlevel so that your server boots into X Windows when you boot?

A. Modify the /etc/inetd.conf file and uncomment startx.

B. Modify the /etc/inittab file and set the initdefault to 5.

C. Modify the /etc/inittab file and set the initdefault to 6.

D. Modify the /etc/inittab.conf file and set the initdefault to 5.
B. Modify the /etc/inittab file and set the initdefault to 5. Runlevel 5 is used by Red Hat to load X Windows automatically.

7. Which commands would you NOT execute when building a monolithic kernel? (Choose all that apply.)

A. make bzImage

B. make lilo

C. make modules

D. make modules_install
C and **D.** make modules and make modules_install. These two commands are only necessary when building a modular kernel. A monolithic kernel contains all the drivers directly in the main kernel itself.

8. You are compiling a new kernel for a machine with an older BIOS that does not support large hard drives. The hard drive you plan to use is 4GB. Below is a simple description of your partitions:

/boot	(15 Meg)
/usr	(1 Gig)
/home	(1.9 Gig)
/	(1 Gig)

Where could you place the kernel to avoid problems with the older BIOS?

A. /usr/src/linux/arch/i386/boot

B. /usr/src/linux

C. /

D. /boot
D. /boot. Boot is a small partition that the BIOS can recognize and boot from. Once the kernel has loaded, it can then use the rest of the large disk.

9. You are almost finished building a new router for your company. You have both network cards properly set up to two different networks. Each side can successfully ping its network card, but neither side can ping the other network. After checking your firewall and forwarding rules, you feel they are set up correctly. All the kernel configuration settings such as IP Firewalling are enabled. What is most likely the problem?

   A. You didn't load the router module.

   B. You need to enable the environmental variable, ENABLE_ROUTING=1.

   C. You need to add a "1" to the kernel variables file /proc/sys/net/ipv4/ip_forward.

   D. None of the above.
   C. You need to add a "1" to the kernel variables file /proc/sys/net/ipv4/ip_forward. By default, routing is not enabled by the kernel. To enable it, you can simply add a "1" to this file with the following command: echo 1 > /proc/sys/net/ipv4/ip_forward.

10. Which one of these kernels is a developer's kernel?

   A. 2.0.0

   B. 1.2.25

   C. 2.3.4

   D. 3.0.13
   C. The second number determines if it is a stable release or a developer's kernel. If the second number is an odd number, then it is a developer's kernel. If it is an even number, then it is a stable kernel release.

11. When compiling a kernel, what are the valid configuration options used by make? (Choose all that apply.)

   A. config

   B. menuconfig

   C. windowconfig

   D. xconfig
   A, B, and **D.** config, menuconfig and xconfig. config is a basic text-based utility. Menuconfig is a text-based menu utility, and xconfig is a graphical X Windows utility.

12. After specifying all of your options for your kernel, you type in your final command, make zImage. The kernel goes through all of its final stages of compiling, but at the end it complains that the kernel is too large. What steps could you use to fix this problem? (Choose all that apply.)

   A. Edit your kernel configurations and make as many options as you can modules.

   B. Compile the kernel on a bigger system, then copy to your new system.

   C. Use make bzImage instead.

D. Use make zImage -compress.
A and **C.** Creating modules will greatly decrease the size of your kernel. Making a bzImage will allow you to create larger kernels than you normally could with make zImage.

13. What does the command **mkinitrd /boot/initrd 2.0.35** do?

A. Creates a list of kernel modules for kernel 2.0.35.

B. Appends the system's /boot/initrd to kernel 2.0.35.

C. Nothing, because the /boot directory is only referenced by the kernel during boot time.

D. Creates an initial ramdisk to load necessary modules during boot time.
D. Creates an initial ramdisk to load necessary modules during boot time.

14. You have just compiled a new kernel and now you want to upgrade your old kernel using LILO. You compiled the kernel with the command make zImage. You need to copy the kernel to the /boot directory. Where is the kernel currently located?

A. /usr/src/linux/

B. /boot/

C. /usr/src/linux/kernel/zImage/

D. /usr/src/linux/arch/i386/boot/
D. /usr/src/linux/arch/i386/boot/. The kernels are always compiled to this directory and will have a name of zImage or bzImage depending on which make command you specified.

15. You have just compiled a new kernel and you want to set up LILO to boot your new kernel by default but still have the option to boot the old kernel if necessary. You have already copied your kernel to the /boot directory. What section do you need to add to the /etc/lilo.conf file?

A. boot=

B. image=

C. install=

D. map=
B. image=. You will need to add another image=<your_new_kernel> before the image=<your_old_kernel> section. The rest of the options can stay the same.

16. What command could you use to easily create a rescue disk for your system?

A. fdrescue

B. mkrescuedisk

C. mkbootdisk

D. none of the above
C. mkbootdisk. This command will allow you to make a boot disk for your system that has the option of typing **rescue** at the LILO prompt.

17. Where could you look to find out how Pluggable Authentication Modules (PAM) are installed on your system? (Choose all that apply.)

A. /etc/pamd.conf

B. /etc/pam.conf
C. /etc/pam.d/
D. /etc/pamd.conf/
B and **C**. /etc/pam.conf file and /etc/pam.d/ directory. The older version of Red Hat uses the /etc/pam.conf, while the newer version uses the directory system, /etc/pam.d/.

18. The directory system for PAM and the older PAM configuration file are almost the same format. The older configuration file contains an additional column of information that is not in the directory-style PAM setup. What is the additional column?

A. module-type
B. module-path
C. service-name
D. service-path
C. service-name. You need to specify the service name with the /etc/pam.conf file because there is only one file for all of the different services. This is not necessary with the directory structure because each file's name is also the service's name.

19. What is the difference between a required PAM module and a module that is a requisite?

A. If a user fails to authenticate a required section, then he will be immediately rejected.
B. If a user fails to authenticate at a requisite section, then he will be immediately rejected.
C. Requisite sections are accumulated, and after all the requisites are checked, if one fails then access is denied.
D. None of the above.
C. Requisite sections are accumulated, and after all the requisites are checked, if one fails then access is denied.

20. You want to schedule a maintenance job to run on the first of every month at 4:00 A.M. Which of the following cron entries are correct?

A. 00 4 1 * * ~/maintenance.pl
B. 4 1 * * ~/maintenance.pl
C. 0 4 31/1 * * ~/maintenance.pl
D. 1 4 00 ~/maintenance.pl
A. 00 4 1 * * ~/maintenance.pl. The syntax for cron is minute, hour, day of month, month, day, and then the command.

Chapter 7 Answers

1. Which of the following are true about the X-Window system? (Choose all that apply.)

A. The X-server runs on your workstation; X-clients run on your workstation or on other computers on the network.
B. If an X-server is running on your workstation then X-client applications running on your computer cannot send their output to an X-server running on another system on the network.
C. An X-client application gets its input from the keyboard and mouse that are

attached to the same X-server where the client is sending its output.

D. Aside from the steps necessary to start the remote application, there is no difference between running an X-client locally and running one remotely.

A, C, and **D** are all true.

2. Your supervisor comes to you and says he is thinking of purchasing some new workstations for the graphics department and that he has decided they will run Red Hat Linux. He has a requirement to have them purchased and installed as quickly as possible. He has found what appears to be a good deal on some brand-name systems and would like you to determine whether they will be suitable for the planned task. You follow up on his suggestion and discover that the video card for the systems is built around a completely new video chip design. What recommendation do you make regarding the purchase?

A. Go ahead and purchase the systems "as-is."

B. Since these systems will be used by the graphics department, make sure they have plenty of disk space to store graphic files.

C. Purchase the systems, but have the vendor replace the new video cards with a model that is listed on the Red Hat Linux support site.

D. Make sure the systems have 100MB/s Ethernet cards so that graphics files can be shipped across the network as quickly as possible.

C. Since the workstations are going to be used by the graphics department, they are going to be running the X-Window system. Although you might be able to get the new video cards working given ample time for experimentation, the requirement to have the new workstations up as quickly as possible precludes this. To be sure you don't have any problems configuring the X-Window system, you choose to replace the newer video card with a supported video card.

3. You performed a new install of Red Hat Linux and ran into problems when you tried to install the X-Window system. Your system is now up and running, and you can get logged in to a command prompt. How do you go about reconfiguring the X-Window system?

A. Use the *vi* editor and modify the /etc/X11/XF86Config file.

B. Run the Xconfigurator utility from the command line.

C. Restart the X-Window GUI and run XF86Setup.

D. Reinstall Red Hat Linux.

B. You should use the Xconfigurator program any time you need to make changes to your X-Window configuration. Although you could use XF86Setup also, it wouldn't be necessary, nor would it be possible in this case, to try to start the X-Window system first. XF86Setup will start up a VGA X-server if the X-Window system isn't available.

4. When you run Xconfigurator, it is unable to determine the type of video card installed in your system. You are unable to find the documentation for your system anywhere. What can you do to determine the type of video hardware installed on your system?

   A. Rerun the Xconfigurator program to see whether it will recognize your video card the second time around.

   B. Try running XF86Setup.

   C. Run linuxconf.

   D. Run the SuperProbe program.
   D. The SuperProbe program will probe your video card and report on the type of video chip it uses and the modes it uses.

5. A user who is new to the X-Window system calls you with a question about his mouse. He has been reading some documentation, and it keeps referring to his middle mouse button, but he only has a two-button mouse. What do you tell him?

   A. Hold down the CTRL key and click the left mouse button.

   B. He will have to purchase a three-button mouse to use the X-Window interface.

   C. Click the left and right mouse buttons simultaneously.

   D. He will have to run Xconfigurator and configure the X-Window system to use a two button mouse.
   C. To emulate the missing middle button on a two-button mouse, click the left and right mouse buttons at the same time.

6. Your X-Window configuration appears to be working, and you have an xterm terminal window open on your desktop. Whenever you try to start other X-clients from the command line, however, you keep getting the error message "command not found." What is probably causing the problem?

   A. You have too many X-clients running, and Linux is unable to start any additional applications.

   B. The /usr/X11R6/bin directory is missing from your path.

   C. The /etc/X11/XF86Config directory is missing from your path.

   D. You need to use the xhost command to allow X-clients to access your server.
   B. Any time you receive the message "command not found," that is an indication that your search path is set incorrectly. In order to run X-client applications without having to specify an absolute pathname, make sure the /usr/X11R6/bin directory is in your search path.

7. You want to start an xterm X-client that is 80 columns wide by 30 lines high from

the command line and position it in the upper right corner of your display when it starts. What command would you use?

A. xterm -geometry +0-0 –font 80x30

B. xterm -geometry 80x30-0+0

C. xterm -geometry 80+30+0+0

D. xterm -display 80x30-0+0

B. The correct option is -geometry 80x30-0+0. Since you are creating a terminal window, the size specification 80x30 refers to the number of columns and lines. The offset specification -0+0 specifies that the right border of the xterm window should be offset 0 pixels from the right edge of the display and that the top border of the xterm window should be offset 0 pixels from the top of the display.

8. Which of the following are valid X-client command line options? (Choose all that apply.)

A. --display

B. --windowsize

C. --background

D. --forecolor

E. --bordercolor

A, C, and **E** are valid command line options for X-clients.

9. When you migrate a Windows 95 user to a Linux workstation, what steps can you take to minimize the learning curve for this person?

A. Install the full set of online documentation.

B. Install the KDE desktop environment.

C. Use the switchdesk utility and set the user's desktop environment to AnotherLevel.

D. Set Linux to boot to runlevel 3.

C. The AnotherLevel desktop (available as an option box) from switchdesk closely resembles the look and feel of Windows 95. This interface would be a good choice for someone migrating from that operating system.

10. You are using the GNOME desktop environment. You know that you just started up the GNOME spreadsheet application, but now it seems to have disappeared from your screen. How can you get it back?

A. Use the pager applet and select the virtual display on your desktop that shows it has an open client window.

B. Log out and log back in, and GNOME will restart the application.

C. Use the main menu button to restart the application.

A. Most of the desktop environments that set up a virtual desktop also start up a pager applet that indicates which portions of the desktop contain open windows. Use the pager to move the focus of your display to the area of your desktop that shows up as having open windows in the pager.

11. You are troubleshooting a system that appears not to have been set to boot into the X-Window system but you know that the system has been configured to run

an X-server. What is the first step you should try?

A. Type **X** to start the X-server.

B. Run the startx command to start the X-Window system.

C. Edit /etc/X11/XF86Config and set the X-Window system to start on system boot.

D. Run the file .xinitrc in your home directory.

B. The startx command is used to start the X-Window system if it is not already started.

12. When you installed Red Hat Linux, you configured the X-Window system but chose not to have Linux boot up with the X-Window system running. You have been starting the X-Window system with the startx command and everything is working without any problems. You would now like to make the X-Window GUI the default runlevel for your system. How would you do this?

A. Edit /etc/inittab and look for the line that reads 'id:3:initdefault' and replace it with a line that reads 'id:5:initdefault' and reboot.

B. Run Xconfigurator.

C. Change the /etc/X11/prefdm link.

D. Execute the runlevel 5 command.

A. The easiest way to change the default runlevel for your Linux system is to edit the /etc/inittab file and change the initdefault setting to runlevel 5.

13. You are troubleshooting a Linux server that boots into runlevel 5 and need to temporarily shut down the X-Window system. How would you do this?

A. Use the ps command to obtain the process of the XFree86 server and use the kill command to stop it.

B. Edit /etc/inittab and look for the line that reads 'id:3:initdefault' and replace it with a line that reads 'id:5:initdefault' and reboot.

C. Use the command init 3.

D. Use the stopx command.

C. You use the init command to change from the X-Window runlevel to runlevel 3. This will shut down the X-server. You can restart the X-Window system by issuing an init 5.

14. Your system is using the xdm display manager. You want to use the GNOME display manager (gdm). How can you do this?

A. Change the /etc/X11/prefdm link.

B. Run Xconfigurator.

C. Edit /etc/X11/XF86Config.

D. Use the GNOME control panel to change the display manager.

A. The file /etc/X11/prefdm is a link that points to the display manager your X-Window system will use. To use the GNOME display manager, run the command:

```
ln -fs /usr/bin/gdm /etc/X11/prefdm
```

15. You would like to automatically start up the xclock application whenever you start up an X-Window session with startx. How would you do this?

    A. Create or edit the file .Xdefault and add the command:
    xclock &

    B. Create or edit the file xinitrc in the system root directory with the command:

    ```
    xclock -geometry 200x200-0+0 &
    ```

    C. Edit /etc/X11/XF86Config and add the command:

    ```
    xclock -geometry 200x200-0+0 &
    ```

    D. Create or edit the file .xinitrc in your home directory and add the command:

    ```
    xclock &
    ```

    D. The startx command can be run by any user, not just the root account. You should put any customization commands in .xinitrc hidden file in your home directory.

16. How could you start a KDE session from a system running the gdm display manager?

    A. Relink /etc/X11/prefdm.

    B. Click the Options button on the gdm login message box and select Sessions -> KDE.

    C. Log in normally and use switchdesk to change your default desktop.

    D. You can't log in to the KDE environment from the gdm display manager.

    B and C. The advantage to option B is that you do not have to log out and log back in.

17. What command would you issue to allow X-clients running on the system with an IP address of 172.16.200.99 to access your X-server?

    A. xauth +172.16.200.99

    B. xhost -172.16.200.99

    C. xhost +

    D. xhost +172.16.200.99

    D. The xhost command is used to grant other systems access to your X-server. The command xhost + turns on security but doesn't grant any access.

18. You log in to a remote system via telnet with the intention of starting up several remote X-clients that will send their output to your display (admin1.xyz.com). What can you do to make this easier?

    A. Use the -display admin1.xyz.com option.

    B. Create a DISPLAY variable with the command:

    ```
    DISPLAY=admin1.xyz.com:0.0
    ```

    C. Create a DISPLAY variable with the command:
    export DISPLAY=admin1.xyz.com

    D. Create a DISPLAY variable with the command:

```
export DISPLAY=admin1.xyz.com:0.0
```

D. X-client applications use the *DISPLAY* environment variable to determine where to send their output. It must be an environment variable so you must use the export command to create it.

19. A user calls up to report that she is having problems getting a remote molecular modeling application to display to her screen. Assuming she has disabled all security on her X-server, how could you use the display option to help troubleshoot the situation? Your workstation is admin1.xyz.com; her workstation is ws97.xyz.com.

    A. Tell her to run the SuperProbe utility with the -display option so you know what kind of monitor she is using.

    B. Have her try to start an X-client and direct its display to her X-server with the command:

    ```
    xclock -display localhost:0.0
    ```

    C. Have her try to start an X-client and direct its display to your X-server with the command:

    ```
    xclock -display admin1.xyz.com:0.0
    ```

    D. You start an X-client from the command line and direct its display to her X-server with the command:

    ```
    xclock -display ws97.xyz.com:0.0
    ```

    D. One of the first things you can try in this situation is to see whether you can start an X-client and have it display on her workstation. If the user can see the display from xclock then the problem is probably not with her workstation.

20. The X-server on your company's Web server appears to be locked up. How might you gain access to the console?

    A. Press CTRL-ALT-+.

    B. Press CTRL-ALT-F1 .

    C. Press ALT-F1.

    D. Press CTRL-ALT-DEL to reboot the system.

    B. Since your company Web server is running on the system, you want to try to avoid rebooting. If your X-Window display doesn't appear to be working, you can switch to a standard text console with CTRL-ALT-F1.

Chapter 8 Answers

1. What service would you use to provide human resource documents to any or selected users on the network?

    A. Samba

    B. Apache

    C. X Windows

    D. FTP

    B. Apache. The Apache web server is the best choice here. You could use FTP or Samba to share the resources, but the easiest retrieval would be through a web browser interface.

2. The human resource department wants to restrict access to their web site. What features of the Apache Web server could you incorporate?
   A. Virtual Host
   B. Port 4001
   C. access.conf
   D. All of the above
   D. All of the above. Using all these techniques would provide the most secure control.
3. The sales department wants to amalgamate their web service with the HR department to save money. What is the easiest way to do this?
   A. Virtual Host
   B. htaccess
   C. DocumentRoot
   D. memory
   A. Virtual Host. By creating a virtual host for the other machine, even with a completely different IP address, you can host their site with very little disruption of service.
4. The sales department wants to keep detailed and separate log files about pages hit and and error messages. Which options should they use?
   A. Virtual Host
   B. CustomLog
   C. DocumentRoot
   D. ErrorLog
   B and D. CustomLog and ErrorLog. Within the Virtual Host, you can identify the ErrorLog. You can also use CustomLog to separate Referrer and Sender info if required.
5. When you view all system processes, you notice there are over 35 http daemons running. You thought you configured 10. What has happened?
   A. It is spiralling out of control.
   B. Each virtual service can call up to 3 times its base number of daemons.
   C. There may be some FTP service requests.
   D. Apache is dynamically configuring for current load needs.
   D. Apache is dynamically configuring for current load needs. The base is 10 but the limit is much higher and the server adds more as needed to keep a minimum available to listen at all times.
6. You copy over the Windows based web site to your site, set up the virtual host, and try to hit the home page, but it fails. Which of these could be the problem if this was a straightforward Web site copy of existing files that worked?
   A. DocumentRoot
   B. Port Number
   C. index.html
   D. Wrong browser settings
   C. index.html. Windows uses 3-character extensions. Check the file name expected for the default page; it is usually .html in Linux/UNIX.

7. Finally, you got it up, late at night, from your home office. Too bad you have a slow modem connection. How can you test the Web site without a graphical interface?

   A. SWAT

   B. lynx

   C. linuxconf

   D. netscape -text

   B. lynx. The lynx web browser works on any terminal interface.

8. The sales department wants to make available test results, FAQ's, and new product data sheets available to resellers for their own sales literature. How would you make the material available to them for quick downloads?

   A. Samba

   B. Apache

   C. FTP

   D. Anonymous FTP

   D, maybe C. Anonymous FTP. FTP is the fastest way to just get documents. These same documents can be viewed via an html document, but for download of a long document, a zipped up file is the fastest way to get it. You might use anonymous if you were not worried about who got the documents.

9. The sales department wants to know if they can selectively give access to certain users to certain directories. Which FTP options could they use?

   A. htaccess

   B. ftpaccess

   C. rpm

   D. hosts.allow

   B. ftpaccess. The file /etc/ftpaccess can be used to restrict user and group access to specific directories.

10. When a user logs in anonymously, they cannot access any of the sales documents. There are no documents available at all, why might that be?

    A. Virtual Host points to wrong system.

    B. DocumentRoot set incorrectly.

    C. Ftpaccess file does not point to correct directory.

    D. Anonymous FTP is separate from WU-FTP.

    D. Anonymous FTP is separate from WU-FTP. Anonymous login has an empty /home/ftp/pub directory. You need to add files or provide proper logins for service users.

11. You notice no ftpd service running when you randomly check your system, but no complaints have been made. Why is there no daemon?

    A. It is awakened by inetd as needed.

    B. It only runs at designated intervals of the day.

    C. Nobody uses it; system cleans house regularly.

    D. It runs out of memory.

    A. It is awakened by inetd as needed.

The supernet daemon inetd listens for the incoming requests and launches the service as needed.

12. The sales force complains occasionally that they are refused an FTP connection even though their customers never see this. What may be set too low?

    A. Access times

    B. Local login limit

    C. Limited number of daemons

    D. System memory
    B. Local login limit. It is common to limit local logins as well as remote logins to keep the load balanced during the heavy day times and let many more access evenings. You may want to allow more but you do not have to; if the system is running fine, leave it alone.

13. There is a rogue set of users in the curriculum development team who insist on using their own equipment on their own network. Corporate wants to share information with their Windows only network without having to retrain them. Which service should you install on Linux to 'join' with theirs?

    A. Apache Web Services

    B. FTP GUI Clients

    C. Samba Services

    D. There is nothing you can do
    C. Samba services provides transparent access to the Windows networking services for any Linux host.

14. The rogue curriculum people have set up an NT server to handle their printing and file services. It uses WINS for name resolution and all user logins are at the domain server. You just want to make connections to some server hidden shares and back up these files for them. What options would you configure in Samba?

    A. BrowseMaster

    B. WINS Server IP as Client

    C. NT Server for Authentication

    D. Special Backup share service from your machine to copy files to
    B. WINS Server IP as Client. You could become a WINS client so that your host name is resolved in the usual method by their hosts. You probably do not need to use NT authentication.

15. Which is not a component of the Samba File Sharing Service?

    A. /usr/bin/smbd

    B. /usr/bin/nmbd

    C. /usr/bin/smbclient

    D. /etc/smb.conf
    C. /usr/bin/smbclient. The service consists of the two daemons and the configuration file. smbclient is a client application, with an FTP like interface, used to connect to an SMB share anywhere on the network.

16. You made a couple of quick changes to your Samba configuration file and you need to test it quickly for syntax errors. Which utility should you run?

A. smbmount

B. smbclient

C. smbfs

D. testparm

D. testparm. The testparm utility is a quick syntax check.

17. You are asked to share the HR downloadable documents to the Windows users who are not that familiar with FTP and want a shared drive connection. How do you force the Samba service to re-read the configuration file immediately?

A. testparm

B. /etc/smb.conf

C. /etc/rc.d/init.d/smb

D. /etc/samba/restart

C. /etc/rc.d/init.d/smb. The control script is /etc/rc.d/init.d/smb. You can start, stop, restart, or display status of the services with this script.

18. The Windows users are complaining that they cannot see the HR document share in their Network Neighborhood diagram. What option is missing from smb.conf?

A. Hidden = no

B. Browseable = yes

C. NetworkDisplay = on

D. Viewable = no

B. Browseable = yes. This option must be set in each share declaration that is to be made visible to windows clients.

19. One of your Linux workstation clients needs to get at a file from one of the curriculum developers who has a basic Win98 machine and has created a shared service to the files that are to be retrieved. What utility would you introduce to the Linux user that they would probably know how to use if you showed them once?

A. smbmount

B. smbfs

C. smbclient

D. smb

C. smbclient. The smbclient utility has an interface that mimics FTP. The average Linux user would be familiar with the interface and would only need to be shown the slightly different syntax needed to make the actual connection.

20. Suddenly many more users are requesting access to the curriculum development files because they need to make some technical changes on a regular basis. If they are all connecting to just one server host, how could you make the service 'local'?

A. smbclient -all

B. smbmount

C. smbfs

D. /etc/rc.d/init.d/smb status

B. smbmount. You could smbmount it (using smbfs, this is not a command) on a local directory for all users to access easily.

21. A few other departments have been using their own DOS based mailing systems. The company wants to use a standard service so both employees and customers

can all use the same system. What would be the best choice?

A. Internet Explorer 53

B. DaVinci Mail

C. DaMail Mail

D. sendmail
D. sendmail. The Internet primarily connects the whole world with sendmail mail services.

22. Some of the sales people are no longer local, and they need to be able to get their mail from any web based server in the world. What option would you configure for this?

A. endmail - web interface

B. POP3 daemon

C. IMAP daemon

D. Apache Mail interface
C. IMAP daemon. Only the IMAP interface allows a web based system, not the server itself but the web programs, to provide mail services to users anywhere.

23. Your system has become very large. You want to look at your current printer configuration in X Windows. What utility might you use?

A. smbclient

B. /etc/printcap

C. printtool

D. lprsetup
C. printtool. The printtool X window interface is a quick overview of your printer setup but not your current queue status. Use lpq or 'lpc status' to see current print job and spooling status.

24. The HR people and sales want to restrict the users who can print to their printers. What file can be used to restrict access to print services?

A. printtool

B. /etc/printcap

C. /etc/lpraccess

D. /etc/hosts.lpd
D. /etc/hosts.lpd. This file can be used to restrict hosts or networks from accessing print services locally.

Chapter 9 Answers

1. Which program checks the DNS setup?

A. dnscheck

B. BIND

C. nslookup

D. resolve
C. nslookup. Nslookup checks the configuration of the nameserver based on the resolv.conf file.

2. You have added several new servers into your primary DNS server. The zone files are formatted properly, and you've restarted named. You advertise the new servers, and your help desk immediately starts getting calls that no one outside your domain can see the new servers. What is the most likely cause?

A. Your servers are not connected to the network.
B. The serial number was not incremented in the zone file.
C. Someone has changed the zone files without your knowledge.
D. The users at the other end are having ISP problems.
B. Make absolutely sure that the serial number at the top of the zone file is incremented each time you change a zone file. If it is not changed, external DNS servers will think that nothing changed in your domain, and they will not bother to pull new RRs.

3. Which is an example of a properly formatted MX record?

A. MX10.mail.domain.com.
B. MX mail.domain.com.
C. MX10 mail.domain.com
D. MX10 mail.domain.com.
D. Make sure the preference is defined, and the trailing '.' is included at the end of the record.

4. Squid serves as a caching server for which Internet protocols?

A. FTP
B. News
C. HTTP
D. DNS
A and C. HTTP and FTP sessions are cached by squid.

5. Which is not a variant of NFS?

A. KNFSd
B. PCNFS
C. MacNFS
D. UNFSd
C. There is no such thing as NFS for the Mac.

6. In the /etc/exports file, if we want to export /data as read-only, but grant write permission to the supervisor, the proper line is:

A. /data (rw) superv.domain.com(ro)
B. /data (ro) superv.domain.com(rw)
C. /data (ro) *.domain.com(rw)
D. /data superv.domain.com(rw)
B. export the file system as a general read-only, and then specify the machines that have read-write permission.

7. On bootup, the system will check what file for NFS shares to mount?

A. /etc/exports
B. /etc/nfs.conf
C. /etc/fstab
D. /nfs/conf
C. /etc/fstab contains all the necessary information for NFS to mount its file shares.

8. /var fills up. What will restore operation of News?

A. Remove /var/spool/news/articles/alt/binaries.
B. Remove /var/lib/news/history.pag.
C. Expire aging news articles.

D. Make more inodes.
   C. Run /usr/bin/news.daily delayrm as the news user. This should be run daily by /etc/cron.daily/inn-cron-expire.

9. A message pops up that News is out of space, but df -k shows plenty remaining on /var. What's wrong?

   A. Out of inodes on file system.

   B. Hackers.

   C. Invisible files on file system.

   D. df is broken.
   A. No more inodes. Run mkfs with a smaller -i (bytes-per-nodes) option or use cycbuffs. Confirm this diagnosis with df -i.

10. No new traffic has come in but innd is running. What's happened?

   A. Your ISP has dropped the connection.

   B. The TCP/IP link is down.

   C. The Internet has vanished and no one is posting.

   D. innd is overloaded
   D. Use ctlinnd mode to confirm this. The reason can then be traced through the error logs.

11. DHCP has been installed and configured properly. The network is responding. There are no firewalls or extraneous server processes. Clients are not getting their network information, though. What could be the cause?

   A. Not enough disk space.

   B. The dhcpd.leases file was not created.

   C. DHCP is in loopback mode.

   D. DHCP has phased the multicast server array.
   B. Make sure the dhcp.leases file is created before DHCP is started.

12. You wish to configure a new IPX user to share a printer. What line should be inserted into the nwserv.conf file?

   A. User roger Pass changeme

   B. 100 roger changeme

   C. roger changeme

   D. 13 roger changeme
   D. The '13' directive should be followed by the username and password.

13. Which are proper keywords that can be used in a ntp.conf file?

   A. server

   B. client

   C. peer

   D. child
   A and C. server denotes a lower stratum server and peer denotes an equal stratum machine.

14. The driftfile in NTP serves as:

   A. A calculation of the average drift from true UTC of the local system clock.

   B. A random constant used to synchronize the clock with itself.

   C. A measure of the Earth's rotational drift.

D. The "zero" from which system time is determined.
A. NTP takes about a day to calculate the contents of the driftfile. This assures accurate restart if the daemon is shut down for some reason.

15. What naming scheme describes a serial port on a Linux system?
    A. /modem
    B. /dev/modem
    C. /dev/ttyS0
    D. COM1
    B and C. /dev/modem can be a symbolic link to /dev/ttys0 (or ttyS1 and so forth) which is the main hardware designator for a serial port.

16. You work at a large company. Every day at about noon, the network slows to a crawl. The CEO just noticed he has trouble reading and sending email at that time and wants answers. What should you do?
    A. Reconfigure your DNS servers to increase their local cache.
    B. Upgrade your network.
    C. Route all web surfing through a Squid server.
    D. Route the CEO's mail over a different subnet.
    C. The users are most likely surfing the web on their lunch hour. All 500 of them just hit their favorite stock quote site. A great deal of bandwidth can be recovered by routing web traffic through a Squid server.

17. Your company has just suffered an external security breach. As a result, the security department has tightened the screws on all the servers, routers, and firewalls. Up until this point, all user data had been mounted over NFS, but now, nothing works. What happened?
    A. The hackers erased the NFS data, and they got the backups too.
    B. The NFS ports are no longer allowed through the necessary firewalls.
    C. The two are unrelated, check your disk space.
    D. The file system is no longer shared from the server.
    B. Ports 111, 745, 747, and 2049 must be allowed through the network security to function. Consider the possibility that NFS may have been to blame for the break-in, and restrict its use to isolated or protected subnets.

18. You add a new workstation to your dhcpd.conf file. You're in a hurry to finish, so you save and go to lunch. When you return, your phone mail is full of user complaints that they can't access the Internet, but the local network is fine. You surmise that you accidentally changed something in the dhcpd.conf file that you shouldn't have. What is the most likely cause?
    A. The absence of a "routers" line.
    B. The subnet mask was changed.
    C. The IP range was thrown off.

D. The broadcast address was changed.
A. The lack of a router declaration would cause an Internet outage. Any of the other choices would probably cause a general network outage.

19. You've set up a PPP dialup for your small company's Internet connection. The dialup server is connected to the network so that all may share the connection. You can see the Internet from the dialup server, and you can see your internal network as well. However, the users are unable to access the Internet. What's wrong?

    A. The users each need their own modems.

    B. Be sure routed or gated is running on the dialup server.

    C. Check to see that the network card knows about the modem.

    D. Make sure IP forwarding is turned on.
    D. IP forwarding passes packets from one network to another. You don't need to have the server setup up as a router, but it needs to know that it can forward packets from the network to the modem, and vice versa.

20. You have the printer in your office set up as a NetWare printer for all to share. Your hard drive crashes and you have to restore from backup. Everything works from your console, and all the users use a default password, but no one can print but you. What is the fix?

    A. Hook the printer directly to the network.

    B. Have everyone reboot his or her machine to reestablish the connection.

    C. Make sure the last backup caught the "21" directive in the nwserv.conf file.

    D. Add in each individual user instead of using a default password.
    C. Double-check the print queue (21) in the nwserv.conf file. You may have added the printer after your last backup.

Chapter 10 Answers

1. You have a network consisting of 50 Linux workstations and 5 Linux servers. Most of the workstations are in public areas, and your users need to be able to log in from any workstation on the network. How might you satisfy this requirement?

    A. Keep a master copy of /etc/passwd on one of the servers, and do a backup and restore of that copy to all of the workstations every evening,

    B. Set one of the servers up to be a NIS server. Set another server up to be a NIS slave server. Make the workstations NIS clients.

    C. Set the workstations up to be NIS clients.

    D. Create a common account on every workstation and give everyone the password to this account.
    B. This would be an ideal situation for NIS. A is incorrect because it is labor

intensive and would lead to many password database inconsistencies. **C** is incorrect because you need at least one NIS server. **D** is incorrect because this is obviously an insecure way to run a network.

2. How would you set up the workstations to be NIS clients?

   A. Edit /etc/passwd and add the line USE_NIS at the end of the file.

   B. Start the ypbind daemon.

   C. Add a line to start ypbind to /etc/inetd.conf.

   D. Run authconfig and enable NIS.
   D. Although you can configure NIS clients manually, the easier way is to use either the authconfig utility or the linuxconf utility.
   A is incorrect because this is invalid syntax. **B** is incorrect because you need to do more than start ypbind. **C** is incorrect because ypbind should be started from /etc/rc.d/init.d.

3. A user on one of the NIS workstations calls you and tells you that she is having trouble changing her password using the passwd command. What should you tell her?

   A. You'll change her password for her.

   B. Try picking a more secure password.

   C. Make sure the CAPS LOCK key isn't on.

   D. She must use the yppasswd to change her NIS password.
   D. You must use the NIS yppasswd command to change your NIS password.
   A, B, and **C** are all incorrect because the user's account is a NIS account; therefore, the only valid choice is **D.**

4. Which of the following are *not* good basic host security measures?

   A. Jotting down the root password on your desk blotter.

   B. Checking system log files regularly for unusual activity.

   C. Hanging on to unused accounts in case their original users want to reactivate them.

   D. Providing users with adequate training so they know how to properly use the tools at their disposal.
   A and **C** are both not recommended. **B** and **D** are both good security practices.

5. What are the four steps that PAM breaks the authentication process into?

   A. Authentication management, account management, session management, and password management.

   B. Authentication management, account management, network management, and password management.

   C. Authentication management, account logging, session management, and password management.

   D. Authentication management, account management, session management, and firewall management.
   A. PAM breaks the authentication process into these four steps.

6. You are editing the PAM configuration file by adding a module. How would you indicate that the authentication process should immediately terminate and fail if the module fails?

   A. Make sure the module is either an *auth* module or a *password* module, since these must always succeed.

   B. Use the *required* control flag.

   C. Use the *requisite* control flag.

   D. It doesn't matter; the authentication process always stops as soon as a module fails.

   C. The *requisite* flag is used to indicate that the authentication process should end immediately if the module fails. **A** is incorrect because any PAM module can fail and the authorization process will continue. **B** is incorrect because *required* is not a valid flag. **D** is incorrect because the control flag determines when the authorization process terminates.

7. You experience a moment of forgetfulness and try to log in to the root account of your server via telnet from your Internet connection at home. Why doesn't this work?

   A. You are using IP chains to filter out telnet access to the root account.

   B. You miskeyed your password.

   C. Login to the root account is never allowed from any terminal other than the console.

   D. The network terminal device that you are trying to log in from is not listed in /etc/securettys; therefore, the root account will not be allowed to log in from that terminal.

   D. The root account is only allowed to log in from terminals listed in /etc/securettys. **A** is incorrect because this is not a typical firewall function. **B** is obviously incorrect. C is incorrect because of answer **D.**

8. Assume you normally work from a user account called sysadm. How might you configure your Red Hat Linux System to notify you whenever there is a serious problem with the kernel?

   A. Edit /etc/syslog.conf and add an entry such as:

   ```
   kern.err          root,sysadm
   ```

   B. Recompile the kernel to include error notification and specify sysadm as the user to be notified.

   C. Write a C program to monitor the /proc/err directory and send any messages that appear there to sysadm.

   D. Edit /etc/syslog.conf and add an entry such as:

   ```
   *.*          root,sysadm
   ```

   A. Although **D** might seem like a good choice, this would also show you all messages from every facility. It would be very difficult to pick out just the kernel messages from everything else that would be coming to your screen. **B** and

C are obviously incorrect because there is too much effort involved.

9. You would like to have your system page you when certain events occur. How could you do this?

   A. Configure the paging feature of the logrotate utility.

   B. Install the swatch utility and set it up to do this.

   C. Not possible.

   D. Install the GNUpage utility.
   B. The swatch utility monitors system log files. Among its capabilities is the ability to page you when certain events that you have specified occur.
   A is incorrect because the logrotate utility doesn't handle paging. **D** is incorrect because there is no such utility.

10. You have a server application that is only used about once a day. How would you configure this service to start so that it didn't have to run continuously?

   A. Add an entry in the system cron table to start the service at about the time you think that service will be needed. Add another entry to stop the service a few minutes later.

   B. Write a shell script to start the service at boot time with a file in /ect/rc.d, but use a sleep command to put the process to sleep until it's needed.

   C. Start the service by adding an entry for it in /etc/services.

   D. Add an entry for the application in /etc/inetd.conf.
   D. Inetd is used to start services on an as-needed basis. You tell inetd which services to start by placing them in inetd.conf.
   A and **B** obviously won't work very well. **C** is incorrect because the /etc/services file is used to associate a service name with a port number.

11. Below is a configuration line from inetd.conf :

```
smtp   tcp   nowait   root
/usr/sbin/in.smtpd
```

   What is missing from the line?

   A. The arguments for the smtp service.

   B. The type of socket the service will use.

   C. Nothing.

   D. The type of protocol the service will use.
   B. The second field in the configuration line should contain the type of socket the server application will use. Since the service is using TCP, the socket type should be stream.

12. You would like to restrict access to your ftp site to clients in a particular subnet. How can you do this?

   A. Use ipchains to filter out ftp requests for all but the given subnet.

   B. Comment out the configuration line for the ftp service in /etc/inetd.conf.

   C. Edit /etc/ftp.conf and add a reject line for all networks other than the given subnet.

D. Use tcp_wrappers and add the appropriate lines to /etc/hosts.allow and /etc/hosts.deny.
D. This is a good situation for tcp_wrappers.
A is incorrect because ipchains is better used to filter entire protocols. B is incorrect because this would disable ftp completely. C is incorrect because there is no ftp.conf file.

13. You are using the tcpd program to start services in inetd.conf. How could you restrict telnet access to be available only to clients on the 192.168.170.0 network? Assume that no other configuration has been done for tcpd.

A. Edit inetd.conf and add -DENY EXCEPT 192.168.170.0 to the entry for the telnet daemon.

B. Edit /etc/hosts.allow and add the line:

```
in.telnetd : \
192.168.170.0/255.255.255.0
```

C. Edit /etc/hosts.deny and add the line:

```
in.telnetd : \
192.168.170.0/255.255.255.0
```

D. Edit /etc/hosts.deny and add the line:

```
in.telnetd : ALL EXCEPT \
192.168.170.0/255.255.255.0
```

D. Although B would allow the requested access, since no other configuration has been done for tcp_wrappers, /etc/hosts.deny will be empty, so other clients will be allowed access by default. The best choice is to restrict all access to the telnet daemon and then make an exception for clients in the requested subnet. A is incorrect because the syntax is wrong. C is incorrect because it would result in telnet access being *denied* to the 192.168.170.0 network.

14. You work at the headquarters of a company that has several divisions. Each division is part of the headquarters LAN, but each division has its own logical subnet and its own domain. You would like to set up an internal ftp server for each division, but you don't want to have to configure and manage multiple systems. What solution can you devise?

A. Set up a user's workstation in each division to be the ftp server and delegate the management of that server to the user of that workstation.

B. Use NIS and set up shared virtual ftp directories.

C. Use IP aliasing and set up virtual host services for each division.

D. Edit /etc/inetd.conf and change all occurrences of tcpd with virtuald.
C. Since each network has its own domain and its own subnet, this is the perfect situation for IP aliasing. With IP aliasing, you can use one system as the server for multiple domains.
A is incorrect because this is an insecure way to accomplish this and would require knowledgeable users. B is incorrect because this isn't what NIS is used for. D is incorrect because you

should only need to virtualize the ftp daemon.

15. You have just recently connected your organization's network to the Internet, and you are a little worried because there is nothing other than your router standing in the way between your network and the Internet. You have a spare 200MHz PC lying around doing nothing that just happens to have two Ethernet cards. You also have a mixture of systems on your network that includes Macintosh, Windows 95, and Linux. What might you do to ease your mind?

    A. Nothing; you're not advertising the systems on your LAN via DNS, so no one will ever find them.

    B. Install Red Hat Linux on the 200MHz PC and use ipchains to set it up as a firewall.

    C. Install Red Hat Linux on the 200MHz PC and use tcp_wrappers to set it up as a firewall.

    D. Install Linux on all systems on your network.

    B. Your best choice would be to take the unused PC and turn it into a firewall using Linux and IP chains. If you use a router to connect to the Internet, then your firewall system sits between your LAN and the router. This results in a two-node network consisting of the router and one of the network interfaces in your firewall that serves as a buffer zone between the Internet and your LAN. You assume that any traffic on this side of the firewall is potentially unsafe. This buffer network is sometimes referred to as the "demilitarized zone," or DMZ.

    A is incorrect because this is a poor way to secure a network. **C** is incorrect because although you might also want to use tcp_wrappers as part of your security strategy, it is designed to secure individual machines, not an entire network. Although **D** might be a good option in general, it won't necessarily make your network more secure.

16. Which of the following are correct ways to specify a source address or a destination address when configuring IP chains?

    A. 192.168.188.0/255.255.255.0

    B. 192.168.188.0/24

    C. 192.168.188.5

    D. server1.xyz.org

    E. 0/0

    All are correct.

17. Consider the following command:

    ```
    ipchains -A input -s \
    192.168.77.77 -j REJECT
    ```

    What effect will this have when the client with an IP of 192.168.77.77 tries to connect to your system?

    A. No effect at all.

    B. Access will be denied, and the client application will not receive any indication of what happened.

C. Access will be denied, and the client application will receive a message about the target destination being unreachable.

D. You will receive a notification message on the system console.

C. Because of the REJECT target, the client will receive an ICMP error message. If the target was DENY, the client would receive no indication of what happened to the packet.

18. You are setting up a small office and you would like to provide Internet access to a small number of users, but you don't want to pay for a dedicated IP address for each system on the network. How could Linux help with the problem?

A. Assign the official IP address to a Linux system, and create accounts on that system for all of the office personnel.

B. Install Linux and configure it for IP forwarding.

C. Install a Linux router.

D. Use the Linux system to connect to the Internet, and then use IP chains to set up IP masquerading.

D. If you need to connect several systems to the Internet, but only have one official IP address to use, IP masquerading is the perfect solution. A is incorrect unless your users want to telnet to a single system and use a command-line interface. B and C are essentially the same answer and are both incorrect because a router will not help in this situation.

19. Which of the following are correct?

A. Only routers need to maintain route tables.

B. You enter static routes manually.

C. The system bases its decision on where to route a packet by looking at the packet's destination address.

D. You don't need to worry about changing your routing tables when your network changes.

B and C are correct. A is incorrect because every system must maintain some routing information. D is incorrect because when your network changes is when you really need to make sure your routing tables are correct.

20. You are trying to connect to a remote system, but you can't make a connection. You are using the ping command to troubleshoot, and you notice that you can ping your own system and you can ping other systems that are on the same subnet as you. When you try to ping a system outside your subnet, however, you get no response. What steps can you take to resolve the problem?

A. Contact the system administrator for the remote system and tell him to remove the ipchains DENY rule he has for your system.

B. Disable tcp_wrappers for on your system.

C. Use the route -n command and check to see that you have a default gateway set.

D. Reconfigure your network setup.
C. In this situation, the first thing you should check is that you have a default route (or default gateway) set and that the system is up. Any packet you send that is addressed to a network other than your system's subnet must go through the router to get to its destination. If the router is down, or your system doesn't have an entry for it in its routing table, then your packets aren't going anywhere.
A, B, and **D** are all incorrect because anytime you experience this type of situation, the most likely cause is a routing problem.

Chapter 11 Answers

1. You are setting up a Red Hat Linux system and are configuring several network services. What can you do to make sure your system is more secure from outside attack?

   A. Set up individual user accounts to run the services under.

   B. Pick a really secure password for the root account.

   C. Run the services under the user nobody account.

   D. Make sure the system is locked away in a machine room somewhere.
   A and **C.** You should run network services under their own accounts or the nobody account. If someone does succeed in exploiting a security hole in the server application, his actions will be limited to those of a normal user.

2. What should you do to a shared directory to ensure that all user accounts who are members of the group that owns the directory will have access to files created in that directory?

   A. Make sure the root account owns the directory.

   B. Make sure the nobody account owns the directory.

   C. Make sure directory is in every user's PATH.

   D. Make sure the setgid bit is set on the directory.
   D. When the setgid bit is enabled for a directory, all files that are created in that directory are created with the same group owner as that of the directory.

3. How would you set the setgid bit on the /home/developer directory? Assume that you have already issued the command chown nobody.developgrp /home/developer.

   A. chmod 2775 /home/developer

   B. chgrp 2775 /home/developer

   C. chmod 775 /home/developer

   D. chmod g+s /home/developer
   A and **D.** Both commands will set the setgid bit. The advantage to **D** is that you don't have to worry about affecting the other permission settings.

4. How would you ensure that all files that are created by your users are automatically created with full access for the owner and group owner of the file?
   A. Have your users type the command **umask 002 <filename>** whenever they create a file.
   B. Place the command umask 002 in /etc/profile.
   C. Have your users type the command **chmod 002 <filename>** whenever they create a file.
   D. Place the command umask in /etc/profile.
   B. Placing the command umask 002 will set the default umask for all users. Typing the umask command without any arguments displays the current umask setting for your process.
5. You are concerned about the security of your system and would like some way to ensure you haven't overlooked some minor configuration setting that could result in a potential toehold for a cracker. What could you do to check the security of your system?
   A. Publish an invitation on the Internet for crackers to attempt to break into your system as a test of your security measures.
   B. Hire a security consultant.
   C. Download and install the Computer Oracle and Password System.
   D. Assume your system was secure enough, and hope for the best.
   C. The COPS package will perform a scan of your system and look for configuration settings that could potentially compromise your system's security.
6. Which of the following are not true?
   A. System time is stored in a hardware clock.
   B. Some systems store the time value in 24 hour GMT format.
   C. You cannot change your system's timezone offset once you have installed Linux.
   D. The timeconfig utility can be used to change your system's time offset.
   C. Is false.
7. You installed the psacct process accounting RPM and issued the command /sbin/accton, but nothing shows up when you issue the ac command or the sa command. You've checked and you have a /var/log/pacct file, but its size is 0 bytes. What is wrong?
   A. You will have to reboot to start the accounting process.
   B. Nothing is happening on your system, so nothing is being logged.
   C. You turned accounting off.
   D. The /var/log/pacct file is corrupt.
   C. By default, when you issue the accton command without any arguments, accounting is disabled. To enable accounting, you need to

specify the accounting log file to use: /sbin/accton /var/log/pacct.

8. Your manager has asked you for a report of all the system reboots in the past week. How will you obtain this information?

   A. Check the /var/log/messages file.
   B. Issue the command last reboot >reboot.rpt.
   C. Check the /var/log/reboot file.
   D. Issue the command lastb >reboot.rpt.
   B. The last reboot command will list the times your system has been rebooted. Edit the file reboot.rpt and remove all but the last week's entries.

9. You suspect someone has been trying to break into several accounts on your system. How could you check on this?

   A. Configure system logging to notify you whenever a failed login attempt occurs.
   B. Use the sa command to get a summary of failed login attempts.
   C. Use the command cat /var/log/btmp.
   D. Use the lastb command to display failed login attempts.
   D. The lastb command is used to display failed login attempts. You must have a /var/log/btmp file in order to record failed login attempts.

10. What would you use the tmpwatch command for?

    A. To monitor the system for break-in attempts.
    B. To clean up unused user account directories.
    C. To scan system-wide temporary directories and clean up old temporary files.
    D. To monitor the /tmp directory for the appearance of certain files.
    C. The tmpwatch command is usually run as a cron job. It is used to recursively search through temporary directories and remove files that have not been accessed within a specified time frame.

11. The junior system administrator at your site has just come to you to report a suspected bad hard drive on the system he was working on. Whenever he tries to boot the system, he gets a kernel panic with a message saying the root partition cannot be found. What do you suspect the problem is?

    A. The hard drive has crashed.
    B. The I/O bus is going bad.
    C. Intermittent RAM problems are masquerading as disk problems.
    D. The junior system administrator was modifying a system configuration file and has managed to configure the system so it will not boot.
    D. In a situation like this, the cause is most likely human error.

12. What emergency repair items should you always have on hand?

    A. A custom boot floppy for your system

B. A repair boot disk

C. Documentation on the partition layouts for the disk drives on your system

D. Documentation on using the repair utilities

All of the above are good to have on hand if you have to perform a system rescue.

13. How would you obtain a rescue disk if you don't have one?

A. Order one from Red Hat.

B. Run the mkrescuedisk utility.

C. Place a floppy in the floppy drive, mount the Red Hat distribution CD-ROM, and issue the command cp /mnt/cdrom/images/rescue.img /dev/fd0.

D. Place a floppy in the floppy drive, mount the Red Hat distribution CD-ROM, and issue the command cat /mnt/cdrom/images/rescue.image >/dev/fd0.

D. is the correct way to make a rescue disk.

14. How can you boot a damaged Linux system to perform repairs?

A. Boot from your system's custom boot floppy.

B. Boot into rescue mode.

C. Boot into single-user mode using the command linux s.

D. Boot into runlevel 4.

A, B, and **C** are all correct.

15. When you boot your Linux system, the boot process gets as far as displaying the word LIL on the screen. What should you do?

A. Boot into rescue mode and run e2fsck.

B. Boot into rescue mode and check /etc/fstab for errors.

C. Boot into rescue mode, and check /etc/lilo.conf for errors.

D. Reinstall Linux.

C and possibly **A.** LILO is telling you that it got part of the way through the boot process but couldn't continue because of errors in lilo.conf or possible disk errors. If you suspect disk problems, you might run e2fsck on the /boot partition. If your disk isn't having problems, then you should investigate lilo.conf for errors. The boot process has not gotten far enough at this point for /etc/fstab to have anything to do with the problem.

16. You are a consultant and are helping a client who has managed to render his system unbootable. You have booted into rescue mode, but the client doesn't have any documentation on the partition layout on his disk drive. What can you do?

A. Use the fdisk -l command to display the partition table for the drive.

B. Reinstall Linux.

C. Use the e2fsck command and look for the superblock.

D. Use the fdisk command in interactive mode.
A and **D** will both work.

17. You are trying to boot a system and keep receiving a message about a corrupted partition. You have booted into rescue mode. Now what might you do to fix the problem?

A. Use fdisk and delete the partition, then add it back.

B. Use the fdisk -l command.

C. Run lilo to rebuild the boot block.

D. Run the command e2fsck -b 8193.
D. Try running a file system check using an alternate superblock. **A** might fix the problem, but would have the unfortunate side effect of deleting all of the data on the partition.

18. What should you remember to do when running lilo from rescue mode?

A. Use the -r option to tell lilo to use an alternate root location.

B. Use the correct path to locate the lilo utility.

C. Use the sync command to flush changes you make to disk.

D. All of the above.
D. You should keep all of these in mind when using lilo in rescue mode. You should always remember to use the sync command when you are running in rescue mode or single-user mode to make sure your changes are written to disk.

19. Where are some likely places for configuration errors that can prevent your system from booting?

A. /etc/lilo.conf

B. /etc/fstab

C. /etc/passwd

D. /boot
A, B, and **D.** The omission of a single character in /etc/lilo.conf or /etc/fstab can mean the difference between a bootable system and one that will not boot. Any time you make changes that affect the files in /boot, you should rerun lilo to ensure that the boot loader can locate the files in that directory it needs.

20. You have trouble remembering all of the dozens of different commands and options required to administer a system. What can you do?

A. Become adept at using the man pages and info utility.

B. Make copious notes to remind you how things work.

C. Use linuxconf to manage your system.

D. Write a shell script menu program for the tasks you most commonly perform.
C. The linuxconf utility provides you with an easy-to-use interface for system management.

RHCE®
RED HAT CERTIFIED ENGINEER®

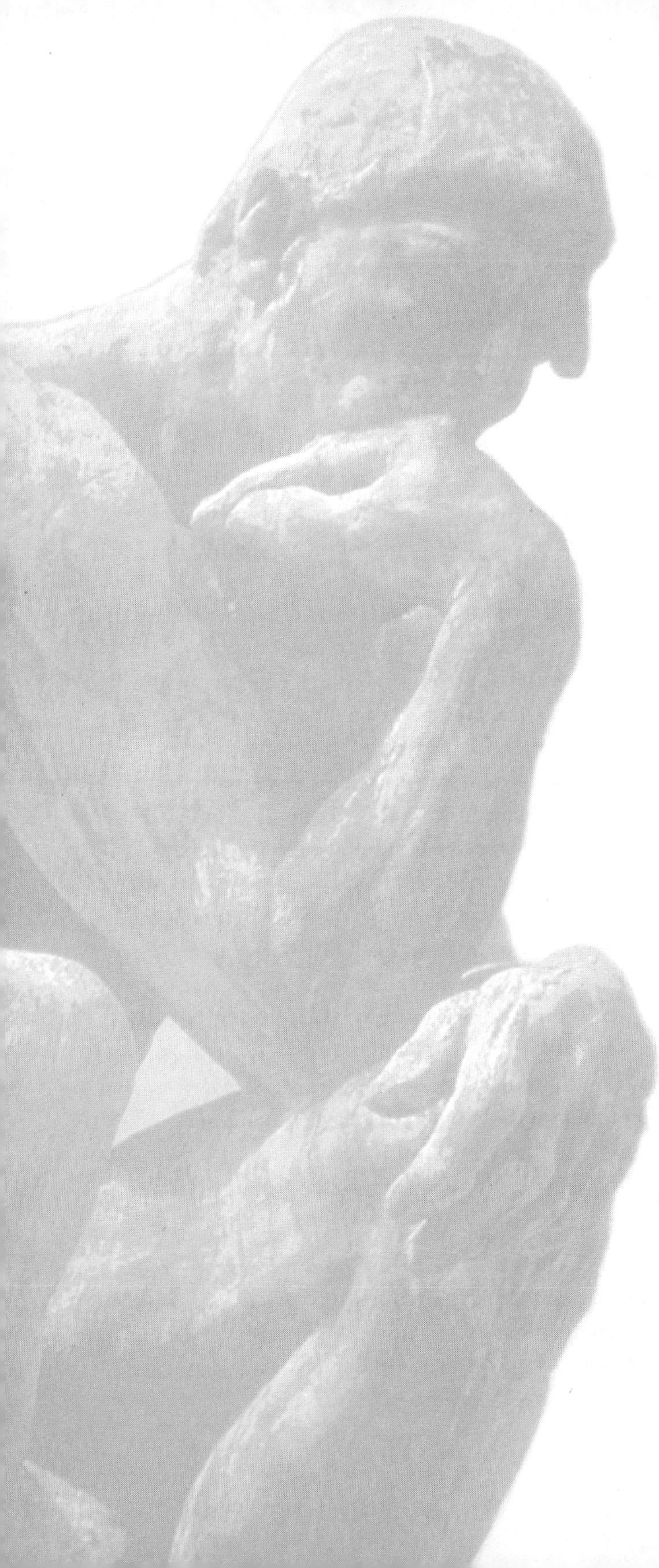

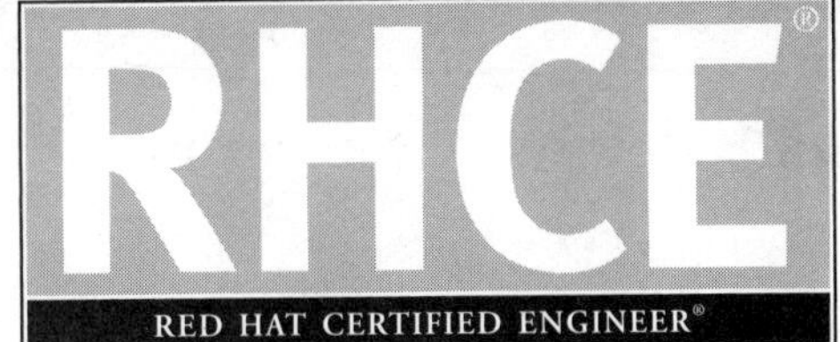

B

About the CD

This CD-ROM contains a browser-based testing product, the Personal Testing Center. The Personal Testing Center is easy to install on any Windows 95/98/NT computer.

Installing the Personal Testing Center

Double-clicking on the Setup.html file on the CD will cycle you through an introductory page on the Test Yourself software. On the second page, you will have to read and accept the license agreement. Once you have read the agreement, click on the Agree icon and you will be brought to the Personal Testing Center's main page.

On the main page, you will find links to the Personal Testing Center, to the electronic version of the book, and to other resources you may find helpful. Click on the first link to the Personal Testing Center and you will be brought to the Quick Start page. Here you can choose to run the Personal Testing Center from the CD or install it to your hard drive.

Installing the Personal Testing Center to your hard drive is an easy process. Click on the Install to Hard Drive icon and the procedure will start for you. An instructional box will appear, and walk you through the remainder of the installation. If installed to the hard drive, the "Personal Testing Center" program group will be created in the Start Programs folder.

Should you wish to run the software from the CD-ROM, the steps are the same as above until you reach the point where you would select the Install to Hard Drive icon. Here, select Run from CD icon and the exam will automatically begin.

To uninstall the program from your hard disk, use the add/remove programs feature in your Windows Control Panel. InstallShield will run uninstall.

Test Type Choices

With the Personal Testing Center, you have three options in which to run the program: Live, Practice, and Review. Each test type will draw from a pool of over 200 potential questions. Your choice of test type will depend on whether you would like to simulate an actual RHCE exam, receive instant feedback on your answer choices, or review concepts using the testing simulator. Note that selecting the Full Screen icon on Internet Explorer's standard toolbar gives you the best display of the Personal Testing Center.

Live

The Live timed test type is meant to reflect the actual exam as closely as possible. You will have 120 minutes in which to complete the exam. You will have the option to skip questions and return to them later, move to the previous question, or end the exam. Once the timer has expired, you will automatically go to the scoring page to review your test results.

Managing Windows

The testing application runs inside an Internet Explorer 4.0 or 5.0 browser window. We recommend that you use the full-screen view to minimize the amount of text scrolling you need to do. However, the application will initiate a second iteration of the browser when you link to an Answer in Depth or a Review Graphic. If you are running in full-screen view, the second iteration of the browser will be covered by the first. You can toggle between the two windows with ALT-TAB, you can click your task bar to maximize the second window, or you can get out of full-screen mode and arrange the two windows so they are both visible on the screen at the same time. The application will not initiate more than two browser windows, so you aren't left with hundreds of open windows for each Answer in Depth or Review Graphic that you view.

Saving Scores as Cookies

Your exam score is stored as a browser cookie. If you've configured your browser to accept cookies, your score will be stored in a cookie named History. If you don't accept cookies, you cannot permanently save your scores. If you delete the History cookie, the scores will be deleted permanently.

Using the Browser Buttons

The test application runs inside the Internet Explorer 4.0 browser. You should navigate from screen to screen by using the application's buttons, not the browser's buttons.

JavaScript Errors

If you encounter a JavaScript error, you should be able to proceed within the application. If you cannot, shut down your Internet Explorer 4.0 browser session and re-launch the testing application.

Practice

When choosing the Practice exam type, you have the option of receiving instant feedback as to whether your selected answer is correct. The questions will be presented to you in numerical order, and you will see every question in the available question pool for each section you chose to be tested on.

As with the Live exam type, you have the option of continuing through the entire exam without seeing the correct answer for each question. The number of questions you answered correctly, along with the percentage of correct answers, will be displayed during the post-exam summary report. Once you have answered a question, click the Answer icon to display the correct answer.

You have the option of ending the Practice exam at any time, but your post-exam summary screen may reflect an incorrect percentage based on the number of questions you failed to answer. Questions that are skipped are counted as incorrect answers on the post-exam summary screen.

Review

During the Review exam type, you will be presented with questions similar to both the Live and Practice exam types. However, the Answer icon is not present, as every question will have the correct answer posted near the bottom of the screen. You have the option of answering the question without looking at the correct answer. In the Review exam type, you can also return to previous questions and skip to the next question, as well as end the exam by clicking the Stop icon.

The Review exam type is recommended when you have already completed the Live exam type once or twice, and would now like to determine which questions you answered correctly.

Questions with Answers

For the Practice and Review exam types, you will have the option of clicking a hyperlink titled Answers in Depth, which will present relevant study material aimed at exposing the logic behind the answer in a separate browser window. By having two browsers open (one for the test engine and one for the review information), you can quickly alternate between the two windows while keeping your place in the exam. You will find that additional windows are not generated as you follow hyperlinks throughout the test engine.

Scoring

The Personal Testing Center post-exam summary screen, called Benchmark Yourself, displays the results for each section you chose to be tested on, including a bar graph similar to the real exam, which displays the percentage of correct answers. You can compare your percentage to the actual passing percentage for each section. The percentage displayed on the post-exam summary screen is not the actual percentage required to pass the exam. You'll see the number of questions you answered correctly compared to the total number of questions you were tested on. If you choose to skip a question, it will be marked as incorrect. Ending the exam by clicking the End button with questions still unanswered lowers your percentage, as these questions will be marked as incorrect.

Clicking the End button and then the Home button allows you to choose another exam type, or test yourself on another section.

C

About the Web Site

Access Global Knowledge

As you know by now, Global Knowledge is the largest independent IT training company in the world. Just by purchasing this book, you have also secured a free subscription to the Global Knowledge Web site and its many resources. You can find it at http://access.globalknowledge.com.

You can log on directly at the Global Knowledge site, and you will be e-mailed a new, secure password immediately upon registering.

What You'll Find There. . .

The wealth of useful information at the Global Knowledge site falls into three categories:

Skills Gap Analysis

Global Knowledge offers several ways for you to analyze your networking skills and discover where they may be lacking. Using Global Knowledge's trademarked Competence Key Tool, you can do a skills gap analysis and get recommendations for where you may need to do some more studying. (Sorry, it just might not end with this book!)

Networking

You'll also gain valuable access to another asset: people. At the Access Global site, you'll find threaded discussions, as well as live discussions. Talk to other MCSD candidates, get advice from folks who have already taken the exams, and get access to instructors and MCTs.

Product Offerings

Of course, Global Knowledge also offers its products here, and you may find some valuable items for purchase—CBTs, books, or courses. Browse freely and see if there's something that could help you take that next step in career enhancement.

RHCE®
RED HAT CERTIFIED ENGINEER®

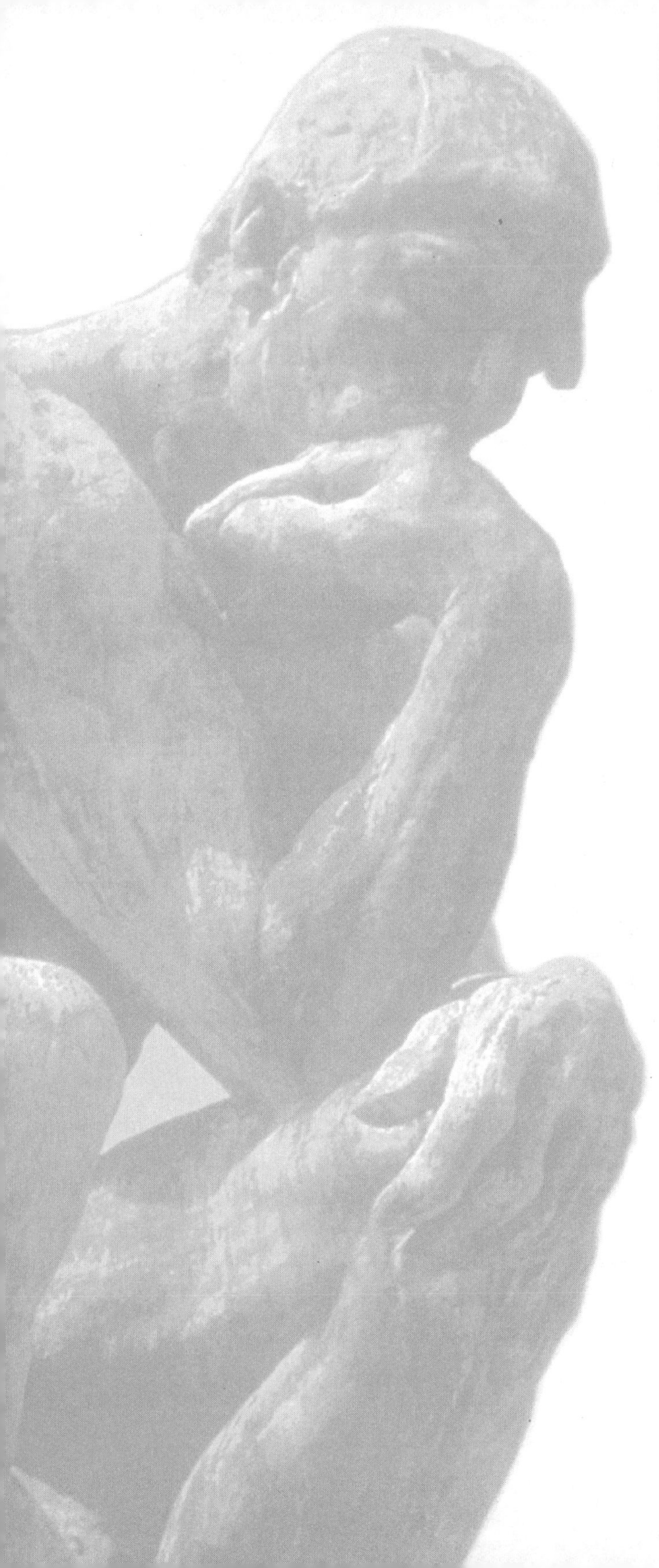

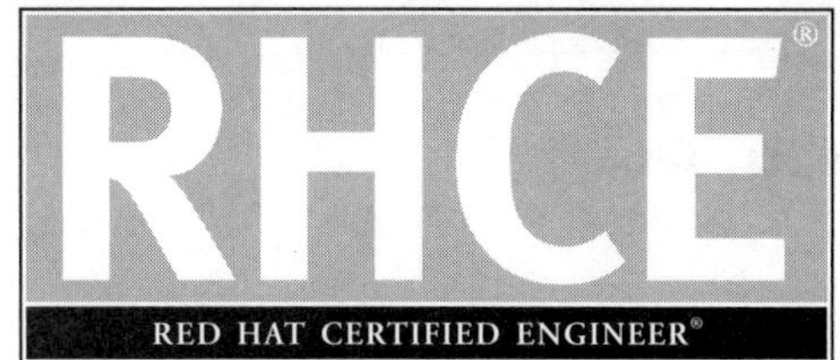

Glossary

Access configuration file The access configuration file, access.conf, defines control modes and allowed types of services on a directory-by-directory basis. These controls are for directories directly accessed by the server, not for the whole system necessarily.

Accidental security violation Accidental security violations occur because users lack adequate training, or because someone tries to speed up completion of a task by not following procedures. In fact, an important consideration to make in any security measures you devise is how much of an extra burden they place on the end users of your system.

Acorn Disc Filing System (ADFS) The standard filesystem of the Acorn's RISC-PC systems and the Archimedes line of machines. Currently, Linux supports ADFS as read-only.

Acorn Econet/AUN Acorn Econet is an older protocol, used by Acorn computers to access file and print servers.

Address Resolution Protocol (ARP) An Internet Protocol (IP) that maps Internet addresses dynamically to the actual addresses on a Local Area Network (LAN).

Advanced Power Management (APM) An Application Program Interface (API) which regulates the speed of programs in battery-powered computers.

Aliasing support Aliasing support allows you to have multiple Ips on one network card.

Apache Web server The Apache Web server provides both normal and secure Web services using the http and https protocols respectively. The Apache Web server has extensive functionality and can be further extended using add-ins and macros to provide additional services.

AppleTalk A Local Area Network (LAN) standard developed by Apple Computer capable of linking as many as 32 Macintosh computers, IBM PC-compatible computers, and peripherals.

arp The arp command is used to view or modify the kernel's Address Resolution Protocol (ARP) table. Using arp, you can detect problems such as duplicate addresses on the network, or manually add arp entries when arp queries fail.

AT Attachment Packet Interface (ATAPI) The specification and standards for IDE and CD-ROM drives.

Authentication The process by which a user or an incoming message is identified.

Basic Input/Output System (BIOS) The BIOS is a set of programs (encoded in Read Only Memory (ROM) on IBM PC-compatible computer programs) that handle startup operations such as the Power-On Self Test (POST) and low-level controls. Some system components have a separate BIOS.

Berkeley Internet Name Domain (BIND) A Domain Name Service (DNS) available to the public and for most Unix-based computers.

Berkeley Software Distribution (BSD) A version of the Unix operating system that was developed and formerly maintained by the University of California at Berkeley. BSD helped to establish the Internet in colleges and universities because the distributed software included Transmission Control Protocol/Internet Protocol (TCP/IP).

BOOTstrap Protocol (BOOTP) A Transmission Control Protocol/Internet Protocol (TCP/IP) for network and diskless computers used to obtain Internet Protocol (IP) addresses and miscellaneous network information.

Buffer A temporary storage space for data. A buffer is ordinarily used as a timing coordination device to compensate for the difference in the speeds of two or more processes.

Build section Like the prep section, the build section is also a shell script. This script will handle building binary programs out of the source code.

Busmouse You can usually identify a busmouse from its round 9-pin connector. The mice usually plug into a card, which might have jumper settings or some software (for DOS) to set IRQs and base I/O addresses. While most busmice use the BusMouse protocol, there are some older mice that use other protocols such as MouseSystems or Logitech. The device files for Inport, Logitech, and ATI-XL busmice are /dev/inportbm, /dev/logibm, and /dev/atibm respectively.

Caching-only name server A caching-only name server will find the answer to name queries and remember the answer the next time you need it. This will shorten the waiting time the next time significantly, especially for a slow or shared connection.

Chains Chains in ipchains are sets of rules that are applied to each network packet that passes through your Linux firewall system. Each rule does two things: it specifies the conditions that a packet must meet to match the rule, and it specifies the action or target to take if the packet matches.

Challenge Handshake Authentication Protocol (CHAP) A protocol (e.g., Point-to-Point Protocol or PPP) in which a password is required to begin a connection as well as during the connection. If the password fails any of these requirements, the system breaks the connection.

Character devices Character devices are where to specify support for a wide variety of things. These things include virtual terminals, serial ports, parallel ports, mice, joysticks, and non-SCSI tape drives.

Checksum A checksum is a field created by adding bits or characters for a result that claims for error checking. Checksums are used to determine if a file has been modified, which comes in handy if you need to verify the integrity of one or more packages.

chkconfig utility The chkconfig command gives you a simple way to maintain the /etc/rc.d directory structure. With chkconfig, you can add, remove, and change services, list startup information, and check the state of a particular service.

Client A client is a computer, such as the workstation on your desk, that you use to access and process the information that is stored on the server.

Coda Coda is a networked filesystem similar to NFS. Currently Linux supports Coda clients only.

Common Desktop Environment (CDE) A Graphical User Interface (GUI) for open systems.

Common Gateway Interface (CGI) How HTTP daemon-compatible (HTTPD-compatible) World Wide Web (WWW) servers access external programs. If this process is followed, data will be returned to the user as a generated Web page. CGI programs or scripts are commonly employed as a user fills out an on-screen form. The form generation or search process then brings other programs into play.

Common Object Request Broker Architecture (CORBA) A distributed object communication standard suited for multiple-tier client/server applications.

Computer Oracle and Password System (COPS) COPS is a suite of programs that you run that perform a variety of security checks. If COPS finds a potential problem, it will warn you. COPS does not fix any problems it finds although it does have an option that will generate a shell command file that can be run manually. Among the types of things COPS will check for are:

1. Permission settings on files, directories, and devices
2. Bad passwords (i.e., those that are easily guessed)
3. Files that are owned by root and have the SUID bit set
4. Important binary files that have changed holes in network service configurations

Consultative Committee for International Telephony and Telegraphy (CCITT) The CCITT is a defunct international organization that designed analog and digital communication standards involving modems, computer networks, and fax machines, such as V.21, V.22, V.32bis, and V.34.

Copyleft Known as GNU Public License.

Daemon A Unix process designed to handle a specialized function (such as handling Internet server requests) and requiring a limited user interface.

Desktop The desktop is a workspace where the X-server places all of your windows and icons.

/dev/pts The /dev/pts filesystem is the Linux implementation of the Open Group's Unix98 PTY support.

Direct Memory Access (DMA) channel A channel used to transfer data from the RAM memory to peripheral devices such as hard disk controllers, network adapters, and tape backup equipment. Requests for data are handled by a special chip called a DMA controller, which operates at half the microprocessor's speed.

Disk buffering Disk buffering is what happens when information from a disk is stored in memory until it is no longer needed. The memory that is used for disk buffering is called the buffer cache.

Disk Druid One of the excellent additional programs supplied on the Red Hat Linux installation disk is the more graphical Disk Druid program that provides a more intuitive interface. The actions are similar but the interface hides the need to know about the partition ID (just uses a text ID) and has an optional called Growable. This option allows the system to determine how much disk space a partition will take based on available free space.

Display Manager The display manager displays a dialogue box on the screen that asks you for your username and password combination. You have a choice of display managers to use with Red Hat Linux. The default display manager is the GNOME display manager.

Domain Name System (DNS) Because the unique Internet Protocol (IP) address of a web server is in the form of a number difficult for humans to work with, text labels, separated by dots (domain names), are used instead with the DNS responsible for mapping these names to the actual IP numbers in a process called resolution.

Dynamic Host Configuration Protocol (DHCP) A software utility that is designed to assign Internet Protocol (IP) addresses to clients and their stations logging onto a Transmission Control Protocol/Internet Protocol (TCP/IP) and eliminates manual IP address assignments.

e2fsck command The e2fsck command performs the same function on the Linux second extended file system as the fsck command does on a standard Unix file system; it is used to check the file system on a partition for consistency.

edquota To specify disk quotas you need to run edquota. Edquota will edit the quota.user or quota.group file with the vi editor.

Enhanced Industry Standard Architecture (EISA) A bus architecture supportive of 32-bit peripherals compatible with 16-bit peripherals, transferring data at 33MB/s.

Enhanced Integrated Drive Electronics (EIDE) To work around the access limitations of IDE, the Enhanced IDE (EIDE) was created. As well as being able to support hard disks larger than 504MB, EIDE also improved access speeds to hard drives.

Environment The environment defines where a user looks for programs to be executed, what the login prompt looks like, what terminal type is being used, and more.

/etc/exports /etc/exports is the only major configuration file for NFS on Linux. It explicitly lists which parts of which file systems are to be exported to clients via the exportfs command. The file format is similar to that used in SunOS 4.*x*, except that some additional options are permitted.

/etc/ftpconversions The /etc/ftpconversions file is a special file that the ftp service uses to automatically compress files and/or decompress files for transfer. The executables for these conversions are found in the /home/ftp/bin directory. Each line in /etc/ftpconversions represents a rule of action for specific file name extensions.

Ethernet The networking protocol linking up to 1,204 nodes in a bus topology.

eXternal Data Representation (XDR) A networking standard used for interchange formats in networking by employing certain data formats.

Fast switching Fast switching is an option that allows you to connect two computers directly together with a network cable. This is an extremely fast way for two computers to communicate.

fdisk A DOS and Windows utility designed to partition a hard drive before formatting can begin.

Fiber Distributed Data Interface (FDDI) Fiber-optic networks running at 100 megabits per second, utilizing wiring hubs as prime servers for network monitoring and control devices.

File Allocation Table (FAT) An area on a disk indicating the arrangement of files in the sectors.

File server A computer within a Local Area Network (LAN) allowing access to a main system of files for all computers on the network.

File Transfer Protocol (FTP) An Internet protocol allowing the exchange of files. A program enables the user to contact another computer on the Internet and exchange files.

File Transfer Protocol (FTP) client The client basically allows you to access the directory tree and all files within it. The graphical client is optimized for download from the remote host. By simply clicking on a file, you initiate a transfer download; by clicking on a directory, you initiate a "cd targetdirectory" command and the interface updates with the local files in the new directory.

Files section This is a list of files that will become part of a package. Any files that you want to distribute in the package must be listed here.

Firewall A utility preventing unauthorized users from entering a restricted database or server via a Local Area Network (LAN) and/or the Internet for security reasons.

Free software Free software is the term typically used to refer to software that has been released under the GNU Public License (GPL). Richard Stallman's definition allows the following parameters

1. You can run the program for any purpose.
2. You can modify the program to suit your needs.
3. You can redistribute copies, either gratis or for a fee. You can distribute modified versions of the program.

fvwm window manager The fvwm window manager was developed specifically for Linux and can be configured to emulate other window environments such as the commercial Motif window manager or even Windows 95. This can make fvwm a good choice if you are migrating users from a Microsoft Windows platform to Linux.

getty program The getty program monitors the terminal waiting for someone to press a key indicating they wish to log in. When this happens, the getty program spawns the login program, which asks you for your username and password.

GNU The acronym stands for GNU's Not Unix.

GNU Network Object Model Environment (GNOME)
GNOME is the default desktop for Red Hat Linux 6.0 and is the desktop you first see after you install the X-Window system.

GNU Public License (GPL) GPL is also called Copyleft. As stated in the preamble, "The GNU General Public License is intended to guarantee your freedom to share and change free software—to make sure the software is free for all its users." It can be found at http://www.gnu.org.

Graphical User Interface (GUI) An overall and consistent for the interactive and visual program that interacts (or interfaces) with the user. GUI can involve pull-down menus, dialog boxes, on-screen graphics, and a variety of icons.

Hard Limit The maximum space allowed by quota management software.

High Performance File System (HPFS) A large-disk file and filename handling system able to coexist with File Allocation Table (FAT) systems.

Home directory The home directory is the initial directory in which users are placed when they first log on to a Red Hat Linux 6.0 system. For most normal users this will be /home/*username*, where *username* is the user's login name. Users typically have write permission in their own home directory, so they're free to read and write their own files there.

HyperText Markup Language (HTML) The language used for Web documents in the World Wide Web (WWW); it defines the tags, codes, etc., for that particular Web page.

HyperText Transfer Protocol (HTTP) An Internet standard supporting World Wide Web (WWW) exchanges. By creating the definitions for Universal Resource Locators (URLs) and their retrieval usage throughout the Internet, HTTP allows Web authors the ability to embed hyperlinks and also allows for transparent access to an Internet site.

HyperText Transfer Protocol Daemon (HTTPD) A Web server developed at the Swiss Center for Particle Research (CERN) and called CERN HTTPD. HTTPD was also developed at the National Center for Supercomputing Applications (NCSA). Unlike the CERN version, the NCSA version allowed for authentication, clickable imagemaps, forms, and word searches.

IMAP With IMAP, the server maintains all mail messages for the user locally, acting as the central repository of all IMAP account mail messages. This is the common service used by Web based mail services.

Inetd program The Inetd server program is usually started at boot time. The startup script is /etc/rc.d/init.d/inet; there should be links to this program in the appropriate /etc/rc.d/rc?.d directories. The inetd program listens for connection requests from client applications to these socket addresses. When it receives a connection request, inetd starts up the server program for that port, hands the port over to the server application, and then goes back to waiting for another connection request.

/etc/inittab inittab describes what process should be started when booting as well as what should be running at normal operations levels.

Install section Another shell script like the build and prep sections, the install section allows you to build install targets within the source distribution.

Integrated Drive Electronics (IDE) drive An IDE drive is a hard disk drive for 80286, 80386, and 80486 processors containing most controller circuitry within the drive. IDE drives combine Enhanced System Device Interface (ESDI) speed with Small Computer System Interface (SCSI) hard drive interface intelligence. It is on the IBM PC ISA 16-bit bus standard, and it was adopted as a standard by ANSI in 1990 as Advanced Technology Attachment (ATA). A setback to IDE was that it could only access 504MB of disk space.

Integrated Services Digital Network (ISDN) ISDN is a set of standards still evolving for a digital public telephone network. Integrated Services Digital Networks (ISDN) lines are a fairly popular and inexpensive high-speed digital line. Adding ISDN support will allow you to use an ISDN card for inbound or outbound dialing connections. The ISDN device has a built in AT compatible modem emulator, autodial, channel-bundling, callback, and caller-authentication without the need for an external daemon to be running.

Intentional security violation Intentional security violations are deliberate attempts by someone to either gain access to information or deny the legitimate users of information access to that information. These types of attack can range from someone who is simply browsing around, to someone trying to destroy or bring down your system for revenge or notoriety, to a competitor trying to access trade secrets or confidential financial information.

Internet Cache Protocol (ICP) When a proxy server queries another about an incoming Web page, this is the protocol used enabling the server to avoid going to the Internet to get the page.

Internet Control Message Protocol (ICMP) A protocol for sending error/control messages. ICMP employs Transmission Control Protocol/Internet Protocol (TCP/IP).

Internet Packet eXchange (IPX) IPX is Novell NetWare's built-in networking protocol for Local Area Network (LAN) communication and was derived from the Xerox Network System protocol. IPX moves data between server and/or workstation programs from different network nodes.

Internet Protocol (IP) The IP was originally developed by the U.S. Department of Defense for internetworking of dissimilar computers across a single network. This connectionless protocol aids in providing a best-effort delivery of datagrams across a network.

Internet Protocol (IP) Masquerading IP Masquerading allows you to provide Internet access to multiple computers with a single officially assigned IP address. Like Network Address Translation (NAT), the masquerade process is invisible to both your internal systems and systems on the Internet. Unlike NAT, which is basically a one-to-one mapping of an internal IP address to an valid external IP address, IP Masquerading lets you map multiple internal IP addresses to a single valid external IP address.

Internet Relay Chat (IRC) A process enabling computers to communicate (chat) with one another similar to a telephone conference call.

Interrupt ReQuest (IRQ) An IRQ is a computer instruction designed to interrupt a program for an Input/Output (I/O). In other words, an interrupt request (IRQ) is a signal that is sent to the computer to request some processing time.

Inverse zone A zone in which DNS is able to convert from an address to a name.

K Desktop Environment (KDE) A Graphical User Interface (GUI) for Unix computers.

kdbconfig The kbdconfig utility allows you to set the type of keyboard you have.

Kernel The kernel is the heart of the whole operating system. This is what boots and loads up your different system level device drivers. With the ability to recompile your kernel you can greatly improve the speed and lower the memory consumption of your kernel. In essence you can build a specific kernel for your architecture. Increasing the size of your kernel decreases your systemwide available memory; moreover some systems need to have the kernel smaller than a certain size in order to boot.

Kernel module A kernel module is not compiled directly into the kernel but as a plugable driver that can be loaded and unloaded into the kernel as needed.

Kernel Network File System Daemon (KNFSD) The KNFSD server, like the NFS server implementations in most commercial Unix implementations, runs kernel processes to serve the NFS requests from clients. This means that the NFS daemon processes use kernel data structures (dentries, inodes, and devices) rather than their user-mode equivalents (filenames, file descriptors). This eliminates some serious bottlenecks present in Universal Network File System Daemon (UNFSD), enabling an inexpensive server to achieve full 100MB/s throughput and to efficiently serve dozens of simultaneous, active clients (limited more by disk and network I/O than by CPU usage or protocol bottlenecks).

Kickstart Red Hat's solution to automated installation of Red Hat's Linux. Kickstart installation files can reside on the boot floppy or on a DHCP/BOOTP server. If the file resides on the floppy you can initialize it with linux ks = floppy. Kickstart installations can only be performed from a CD-ROM or NFS server.

Line Print Control (LPC) You can use LPC to control, start and stop all local queues if you have the privilege. The LPC utility is not commonly available to users, just to superusers.

Line Print Queue (LPQ) To view jobs that have not already been printed or are currently being printed, you can use the LPQ command.

Line Print Remove (LPRM) This utility is used to remove currently nonprinting jobs.

Line Print Request (LPR) Any user can use the LPR utility to send print requests to any local queue name.

Linear mode Linear mode is the combination of one or more disks to work as one larger device. There is no redundancy in linear mode—the disks are simply filled up in the order they appear (e.g., disk 1, disk 2, etc.). The only performance gain linear mode will experience is when several users access data that reside on different disks.

Linux Linux is a preemptive multitasking operating system allowing symmetrical multiprocessing, networking, multiple users, advanced memory management, POSIX support, and multiple filesystems.

Linux Documentation Project (LDP) The LDP is a global effort to produce reliable documentation for all aspects of the Linux operating system, including hardware compatibility. Within the LDP, you can find the Linux Hardware HOWTO.

Linux Hardware HOWTO The Linux Hardware HOWTO is a document that lists most of the hardware components supported by Linux. The list is updated regularly with added hardware support, so it is an up-to-date source of information. The latest version of the Linux Hardware HOWTO can be found at http://users.bart.nl/~patrickr/hardware-howto/Hardware-HOWTO.html, or within the LDP, which can be found at Sun Microsystems' Sunsite at http://metalab.unc.edu/LDP/HOWTO/Hardware-HOWTO.html or any mirror sites of Sunsite.

linuxconf The linuxconf utility is a graphical utility that ties together most system administration tasks under a common interface. You can use linuxconf to do everything from adding user accounts to rebuilding the kernel. You start linuxconf from the start menu or you can start it from the command line by typing linuxconf.

Logical Block Addressing (LBA) LBA involves a special way of addressing sectors. Instead of referring to a cylinder, head, and sector for a location on the hard disk, each sector is assigned a unique number from 0 to N-1, where N is the number of sectors on the disk. LBA mode allows geometry translation, which means that the BIOS can be fooled into believing that the hard disk's geometry is acceptable.

logrotate The logrotate utility allows you to set up automatic management tasks for log files. These include rotating log files, compressing log files, mailing log files, and removing log files. The logrotate utility is run via cron, and you can specify the frequency at which any given log file is modified. You configure the logrotate utility using the /etc/logrotate.conf file. The package file for the logrotate utility is logrotate-3.2-1.i386.rpm.

Master Boot Record (MBR) The original Intel motherboard design provided for the loading of a bootup program.

Message Digest 5 (MD5) A one-way hash function designed to create message digests. MD5 is fast but less secure than Secure Hash Algorithm 1 (SHA-1).

Microsoft Windows Windows is an Application User Interface (AUI) for the Disk Operating System (DOS) that brings to IBM (and IBM compatible) computing such Macintosh-type Graphical User Interface (GUI) features as pull-down menus, multiple typefaces, desk accessories, and other capabilities. Windows does not allow for stability, modifications, support, and freedom to the degree allowed by free and open software.

Minix Minix is a microkernel-based teaching operating system. Also, the standard filesystem for the Minix operating system. This is the original default Linux filesystem, although the ext2 filesystem has since superceded it.

Mkbootdisk Mkbootdisk is a utility that can create a bootdisk. This is basically a rescue disk. After you create this disk it can be used to simply boot your system, or you can specify the word *rescue* at the LILO prompt.

Modular kernel A modular kernel has greater flexibility than a monolithic kernel. You can compile almost all of your drivers as modules. A module can be inserted into the kernel whenever you need it. Modules keep the initial kernel size low, which decreases the boot time and increases overall performance.

Monolithic kernel A monolithic kernel is a kernel where all of the device modules are built directly into the kernel. The modular kernels have all of their devices as separate loadable modules. A monolithic kernel can talk directly to its devices faster than a module. But it will increase the size of your kernel.

mouseconfig The mouseconfig utility allows you to set your mouse to the correct type.

Netstat command The netstat command is used to display a plethora of network connectivity information. The more commonly used option to netstat, -r, is used to display the kernel routing tables.

Netware Control Protocol (NCP) NCP is the network filesystem used by Novell, over the IPX protocol. NCP allows Linux to use NCP as a client.

Network Address Translation (NAT) NAT is a firewall feature that allows you to connect systems to the Internet and disguise their true IP addresses. NAT works by modifying the header information in IP packets as they pass through the firewall. As each packet passes through the firewall, the internal source address in the header is replaced with a public address. When the firewall receives incoming packets destined for a host on the internal network, the process happens in reverse. As the packets pass through the firewall, the header of each packet is modified so that the public address in the packet's destination field is replaced by the internal address of the system it is destined for.

NETwork Basic Input/Output System (NETBIOS) A program included in the MS-DOS versions 3.1 and later for linking personal computers to a Local Area Network (LAN). NETBIOS was originally developed by IBM and Sytek; a version of NETBIOS is now offered by many hardware vendors so that their products can be networked.

NETwork Basic Input/Output System Extended User Interface (NetBEUI) The transport layer for NETBIOS.

Network block support Network block support lets you use a physical disk on the network as if it were a local disk.

Network File System (NFS) A file access utility developed by Sun Microsystems, which released it to the public as an open standard, allowing users on Unix and Microsoft Windows NT networks to access files and directories on other computers as if they were on their own workstations. NFS translates the remote users to local users.

Network File System (version 3) Version 2 of the NFS protocol has been in use since the late 1980s. By the early 1990s, higher-bandwidth networks and demands for better performance prompted Sun Microsystems to revise the protocol. NFS v3's key features include support for client-side caching of data, use of larger block sizes for more efficient transfers, the ability to have multiple outstanding write requests, and the ability to run over Transmission Control Protocol (TCP) instead of User Datagram Protocol (UDP). Taken together, NFS v3 greatly improves write performance and scalability on large busy networks and makes modest improvements to read performance on low-traffic networks.

Network Information System (NIS) NIS allows you to share one centrally managed authorization database with other Linux systems in the network. With NIS, you maintain one password database on a NIS server, and you configure the other systems on the network to be NIS clients. When a user initiates a login session on the NIS client, that system consults its authorization file (usually /etc/passwd), and if the username that was entered doesn't exist there, the system will look up the authorization information on the NIS server.

Network Interface Card (NIC) A NIC is a board with encoding and decoding circuitry and a receptacle for a network cable connection that, bypassing the serial ports and operating through the internal bus, allows computers to be connected at higher speeds to media for communications between stations.

Network News Transport Protocol (NNTP) The standard governing the distribution of UseNet newsgroups through the Internet.

NT File System (NTFS) A Windows file system using the Unicode character set. NTFS allows file names up to 255 characters in length. NTFS has the advantage of supposedly being able to recover from disk crashes, especially hard disk crashes.

ntsysv utility The ntsysv command takes the functionality of chkconfig and wraps it into an easy-to-use screen interface. By default, ntsysv configures the current runlevel. You can specify a different runlevel with the -level flag.

Object Linking and Embedding (OLE) A set of standards, developed by Microsoft and incorporated into Microsoft Windows and Apple Macintosh System software, for creating dynamic automatically updated links between documents and for embedding documents created by another. With OLE, changes made in a source document can be automatically reflected in a destination document.

Open Source software Open Source software, like Free software, requires that software source code be provided and readable, redistribution be free, modifications can be done, etc. What Open Source does not promote, however, are the philosophical reasons behind Free software. Where the GPL makes freedom a central point, Open Source sidesteps the philosophy and sets only the guidelines for software to fit the Open Source definition. The official definition is much closer to the definition of Free software. The GNU GPL, BSD, X Consortium, and Artistic licenses conform to the Open Source definition. The definition can be found at http://www.opensource.org.

Operating System/2 (OS/2) A multitasking operating system for IBM PC and compatible computers that uses flat memory to emulate separate DOS machines; it can run DOS, Windows, and OS/2 programs concurrently, protecting the others if one program crashes and allowing dynamic exchange of data between applications.

Package A package is a container. It includes the files needed to accomplish a certain task, such as the binaries, configuration, and documentation files in a software application. It also includes instructions on how and where these files should be installed and how the installation should be accomplished. A package also includes instructions on how to uninstall itself. RPM packages are often identified by filenames that usually consist of the package name, the version, the release, and the architecture for which they were built.

Partition A section of storage on a hard disk, usually set aside before the disk is formatted.

Password Authentication Protocol (PAP) The protocol used when logging onto a network.

Personal Computer Memory Card Interface Adapter (PCMCIA) An interface standard for plug-in cards for portable computers; devices meeting the standard (for example, fax cards, modems) are theoretically interchangeable.

Personal Computer Network File System (PCNFS) In the late 1980s, Sun and several third parties developed an NFS client for single-user, single-tasking operating systems such as MS-DOS and Microsoft Windows. Unfortunately, the NFS authentication model is best suited for secure, multiuser client machines, and PCNFS has always been a difficult protocol to support reliably. Typically, PCNFS servers must run one or more extra "helper" processes (called something like *rpc.pcnfsd)* that handle logins from the single-user client machines, act like *rpc.mountd* to process mount requests, and handle printing.

Plug and Play (PnP) An emerging standard that requires add-in hardware to carry the software to configure itself in a given way supported by the operating system. Plug and play has been available for Macintosh computers for quite some time and has been incorporated into Microsoft's Windows operating systems.

Pluggable Authentic Module (PAM) PAM is not very useful on a single-user environment or where the users are trusted, but it is perfect for a multiuser system where users are not trusted. PAM allows for more granularity in defining security. You can use PAM to control access to certain resources with means that are not actually coded into the program. PAM consists of a set of dynamically loadable library modules that allow you, as the system administrator, to determine how applications perform user authentication. The idea behind PAM is to separate the process of authenticating users from the development of an application.

Point Of Presence (POP) The point in a Wide Area Network (WAN) where the local phone call provides access to the network. It has very basic commands including retrieve and send messages. A mail service can be configured to be a central depository (POP) for incoming mail messages from any other MTA service. Client applications then download the mail messages off the POP server for processing at the local host. The ipop3d daemon service handles all requests.

Point-to-Point Protocol (PPP) One of two standards for dial-up telephone connection of computers to the Internet, with better data negotiation, compression, and error corrections than the other Serial Line Internet Protocol but costing more to transmit data and unnecessary when both sending and receiving modems can handle some of the procedures.

POSIX POSIX defines a minimum interface for Unix-type operating systems.

prefdm Prefdm is a link that points to the proffered display manager. This is typically xdm, kdm, or gdm. Xdm is X-Windows' default window manager, Kdm is KDE's window manager, and gdm is Gnome's window manager.

Prep section The prep section prepares the source files for packaging. Usually the prep section starts out by removing the leftovers from any previous builds and unarchives the source files.

Pretty Good Privacy (PGP) A cryptographic software package designed by Phil Zimmerman that uses RSA cryptographic methods.

/proc The /proc filesystem is the Linux virtual filesystem. Virtual means that it doesn't occupy real disk space. Instead, files are created on the fly when you access them. /proc is used to provide information on kernel configuration and device status.

Process Identifier (PID) A nonpermanent number created by a computer's operating system for a variety of internal purposes.

PS/2 mouse A PS/2 mouse (used on newer PCs and on most laptops) has its own port and uses IRQ 12. A PS/2 mouse uses a 6-pin mini DIN connector and communicates using the PS/2 protocol. The device file for PS/2 mice is /dev/psaux.

QNX An operating system from QNX Software Systems that uses less memory with quicker response times.

Query mode Using RPM's (Red Hat Package Manager) query mode, you can determine which packages are installed on your system, or what file belongs to a particular package. This can be a big help if you want to locate a file that belongs to a certain package. Query mode can also be used to identify what files are in an RPM file before you install it. This lets you see what files are going to be installed on your system before they're actually written.

rc.sysinit The rc.sysinit script runs almost all crucial system dependent bootup operations.

rdate rdate uses TCP to retrieve the current time (ctime) of another machine using port 13, as described in RFC 868. The time for each system is returned in ctime format (Sun Oct 17 20:36:19 1999). The default mode for rdate simply prints the time as taken from the requested server. The command rdate www will return the date from the server on the local subnet named www.

Red Hat Hardware List The Red Hat Hardware List is specific to all hardware that has been tested on systems running Red Hat Linux. Red Hat will provide installation support for any hardware that is listed as "supported." There is also an "unsupported" list. This list does not necessarily mean that the specified hardware will not run on Linux; it just means that Red Hat will not provide installation support for that hardware.

Red Hat Package Manager (RPM) With RPM, software is managed in discrete "packages," a collection of the files that make up the software, and instructions for adding, removing, and upgrading those files. RPM also makes sure that you never lose configuration files by backing up existing files before overwriting. RPM also tracks which version of an application is currently installed on your system. A key feature of RPM is that filenames can be specified in Uniform Resource Locator (URL) format. You may use these formats anywhere a filename is called for in RPM.

Redundant Array of Inexpensive Disks (RAID) A system backup method, common on network servers, using software working with several hard drives to assure data redundancy and security.

Redundant Array of Inexpensive Disks Level Zero (RAID-0) RAID-0 reads and writes to the hard disks are done in parallel, increasing performance, but filling up all hard drives equally with the same data. There is no redundancy in this level, since a failure of any one of the drives will result in data loss. This level is used for speed increases. If one disk is busy, the data can be accessed from another. The limit to the speed of a RAID-0 system is the bus speed that connects to the disks. RAID-0 is also called "stripe mode."

Redundant Array of Inexpensive Disks Level Four (RAID-4)
This level requires three or more disks. Like RAID-0, data reads and writes are done in parallel, except that there must be one extra disk that keeps parity information of all the data. If one drive fails, then the parity information can be used to reconstruct the data. Reliability is improved, but since parity information is updated with every write operation, the parity disk can be a bottleneck on the system.

Redundant Array of Inexpensive Disks Level Five (RAID-5)
RAID-5 works on three or more disks, with optional spare disks. With this level, several disks can be combined with both performance and reliability increases. Like RAID-4, parity information of the data is recorded. However, instead of dedicating one disk to store the parity information, it is distributed evenly across all disks. If one disk fails, the data can be reconstructed onto a spare disk.

Refresh rate This is the rate at which the image you see on your screen is redrawn. The refresh rate is expressed in terms of Hertz (Hz). A refresh rate of 60 Hz means that an image is redrawn 60 times in one second. Computer monitors have both a vertical and a horizontal refresh rate. Some monitors, known as multisync monitors, support multiple vertical and horizontal refresh rates.

Remote Procedure Call (RPC) Software tool developed by a consortium of manufacturers for developers who created distributed applications that automatically generate code for both client and server.

Reverse zone A zone in which DNS is able to convert from an address to a name.

Router The node that determines how best to transfer a message from one station to another, based on the address provided by the sending station. Unlike a bridge, the router services packets or frames containing certain protocols and can handle multiple protocol stacks simultaneously. Routers can connect networks that use different topologies and protocols.

Routing table A list of rules used by any system using Internet protocols. The routing table uses to determine where to send packets. Each entry in the routing table contains at least three fields. The first field is a destination address. If a packet's destination address matches this field, then this rule will be used to forward the packet. The second field is the interface to which the packet will be sent. The third field is optional and contains the address of a router that will route the packet further along its journey across the network. Keeping routing tables current and accurate on all the systems on a network is crucial to keeping the network running.

Samba Starting with Windows Version 3.11, Windows clients could 'share' their file systems and printers for other Windows clients to 'map to' as remote resources. This sharing was provided through a facility called Server Message Block (SMB). Linux systems provide SMB support over TCP/IP via a package known as Samba. Samba services provide interoperability between the Microsoft Windows network clients and Linux (or any Unix, for that matter) clients. You need to have a basic understanding of how Microsoft Windows Networking works in the TCP/IP realm.

Secure Network File System (SecureNFS) Since about 1990, Sun and other vendors have supported versions of NFS using public-key based strong authentication. Secure NFS has proven itself extremely tedious and complex to administer and is still not sufficient to keep data safe in hostile environments. As a result, Secure NFS is rarely used outside of specialized government installations.

Sendmail Sendmail is a free program written by Eric Allman in 1979.

Sequenced Packet eXchange (SPX) The NetWare communications protocol controlling network message transport.

Serial Line Internet Protocol (SLIP) The standard for how a workstation or personal computer can dial up a link to the Internet that defines the transport of data packets through an asynchronous telephone line, allowing computers not part of a Local Area Network (LAN) to be fully connected to the Internet.

Server A computer that makes printer and communication services available to other network stations.

Server Message Block (SMB) A network protocol developed by Microsoft and adopted by many other vendors that allows one computer to use the files and peripherals of another as if it were local.

Session aware The ability for the application to remember the location in the document where you were last working and reposition your cursor at that point when you restart the application.

Simple Internet Protocol Plus (SIPP) Switched Multi-megabit Data Services (SMDS) interface protocol, one of three Internet Protocol ng (Ipng) candidates.

Simple Mail Transfer Protocol (SMTP) A U.S. Department of Defense standard for electronic mail systems that have both host and user selections. User software is often included in Transmission Control Protocol/Internet Protocol (TCP/IP) packages; host software is available for exchanging SMTP mail with mail from proprietary systems.

Small Computer System Interface (SCSI) SCSI is a complete expansion bus interface that accepts such devices as a hard disk, CD-ROM, disk drivers, printers, or scanners. SCSI is faster and more flexible than (E)IDE, with support for up to 7 or 15 devices, depending on the bus width. Data transfer speeds for SCSI range from 5 to 80MB per second.

Soft limit This is the maximum amount of space a user can have on that partition. If you have set a grace period this will act as the borderline threshold. The user will then be notified that they are in quota violation.

Spec file The spec file controls the way a package is built and what actions are performed when it is installed or removed from a system. There are eight different sections in a spec file. The spec file is stored in /usr/src/redhat/SPECS/<packagename>.spec.

Squid Squid is a high-performance HTTP and FTP caching proxy server.

startx The startx command to start the X-Window interface manually from a command line prompt.

Static routes Static routes are entries that you enter to the routing tables manually. If your network is small, if your network configuration doesn't change very frequently, or if your system is an end system, static routes can be adequate for managing your routing configuration. You manage static routes using the route command.

Stripe mode Also called Redundant Array of Inexpensive Disks Level Zero (RAID-0).

Super Video Graphics Array VGA (SVGA) An enhancement of the Video Graphics Array (VGA) display standard for IBM personal computers that can display at least 800 pixels horizontally and 600 lines vertically, and up to 1,024 pixels by 768 lines with 16 or 256 colors; it can use as much as 1MB of video memory.

Swap file A file used to store instructions and data that do not fit in Random Access Memory (RAM).

swatch The swatch utility monitors log files for certain types of messages and takes action when certain events occur. You configure the events to monitor and the type of action to take. The action can be as simple as sending a message to your terminal, or something more involved such as calling a pager number. By default, swatch looks for its configuration information in the hidden file .swatchrc in your home directory. The package file for the swatch utility is swatch-2.2-7.noarch.rpm.

switchdesk A utility that easily switches your default desktop from one environment to another.

Tape ARchive (TAR) A Unix utility for archiving files most often in conjunction with the compress utility.

TELNET A virtual terminal protocol from the U.S. Department of Defense that interfaces terminal devices and terminal oriented processes (MIL-STD-1782).

timeconfig The timeconfig utility allows you to set your time zone.

Tmpwatch command The tmpwatch command (/usr/sbin/tmpwatch) is used to remove files that have not been accessed in a specified number of hours. As its name implies, you normally run it on directories such as /tmp and /var/tmp. The tmpwatch command works recursively so if you specify the top level directory in a tree, tmpwatch will search through the entire directory tree looking for files to remove.

Token Ring A Local Area Network (LAN) technology that circulates a special message (the token) among network nodes, giving them permission to transmit.

Transmission Control Protocol/Internet Protocol (TCP/IP) TCP/IP is a set of communcations standards created by the U.S. Department of Defense in the 1970s that has now become an accepted way to connect different types of computers in networks.

Transparent proxy support Transparent proxy support allows for the router to secretly forward packets to a proxy server.

UFS The standard filesystem for BSD and BSD derivatives, SunOS, and NeXTstep.

UMSDOS UMSDOS allows you to run Linux from a DOS partition (not currently supported by Red Hat).

Uniform Resource Locator (URL) A string of characters precisely identifying the type and location of an Internet resource, one of two basic kinds of Universal Resource Identifiers (URIs) and the standard way to find a resource.

Uninterruptible Power Supply (UPS) The UPS is a battery that can supply continuous power to a computer system if the power fails; it charges while the computer is on and if the power fails, it provides power allowing the user to shut down the computer properly to preserve crucial data.

Universal Network File System Daemon (UNFSD) The UNFSD server runs as a user-mode process, as opposed to the kernel. This provides some advantages in terms of flexibility, but tremendous disadvantages in performance and scalability. A UNFSD can only effectively handle one to two clients even on a strong server; and even with a single client, throughput is a fraction of what it would be on the same server using a kernel-mode NFS daemon. Bottlenecks in UNFSD include the filename lookups, extra copies between kernel and user address space, and a single threaded NFS daemon.

Universal Time Coordinated (UTC) Formerly Greenwich Mean Time (GMT), which is the international time standard.

Unix-to-Unix Copy Program (UUCP) A standard utility for exchanging information between two Unix nodes, allowing Unix users to exchange files, electronic mail, and UseNet articles via long-distance telephone uploads and downloads.

UseNet UseNet is the news distribution and bulletin board channel of the Unix-to-Unix Control Program (UUCP), the international Wide Area Network (WAN) that links Unix computers.

User Datagram Protocol (UDP) A Transmission Control Protocol/Internet Protocol (TCP/IP) normally bundled with an Internet Protocol layer software that describes how messages received reach application programs within the destination computer.

VFAT VFAT allows you to read Windows 95 partitions.

Virtual Desktop The virtual desktop allows the area where you can place windows to be larger than the area of your display hardware.

Virtual Memory System (VMS) An operating system for VAX computers with multiusers and multitasking requirements.

Web Network File System (WebNFS) WebNFS, another Sun-designed variant of NFS, is intended for Internet use. It differs from ordinary NFS in that clients do not have to "mount" the file systems, and they receive only read-only access. It may be suitable for publishing data to the public in a transparent manner, but it is rarely used.

Window Manager The window manager is a special type of X-client. A window manager cannot run on its own; it needs the services of an X-server to do its job. It is the job of the window manager to control how other X-clients appear on your display. This includes everything from placing title bars and drawing borders around the window for each X-client application you start to determining the size of your desktop.

Write-back buffer cache There are two types of buffer caches. With a write-back buffer cache, writes are done at a later time, usually in the background, so as not to slow down other programs. While a write-through cache is less efficient, a write-back cache is more susceptible to errors.

Write-through buffer cache There are two types of buffer caches. With a write-through buffer cache, any changes to blocks of data in the cache are written to disk at once. While a write-through cache is less efficient, a write-back cache is more susceptible to errors.

X.25 A Consultative Committee on International Telephony and Telegraphy (CCITT) standard for computer access to and data handling in a packet switched network.

Xconfigurator program The Xconfigurator program is a character-based GUI that leads you through a series of menus aiding you in configuring your video hardware. The Xconfigurator program will automatically probe your video card and try to pick the appropriate X-server image for it. If Xconfigurator cannot determine what make of card you have, then you must select your video card from the list of video cards supported under Red Hat Linux 6.0.

X-server The X-server is the component of the X-Window system that you run on your desktop. The X-server is responsible for drawing images on your screen, getting input from your keyboard and mouse, and controlling access to your display.

xterm application xterm is an X-client application that creates a terminal window on your X-display. So, after all the hard work you've gone through to get a nice windowing display, you're right back where you started, with a command line interface.

X-Window clients X-Window clients, or X-clients, are the application programs you run that use the windowing services provided by your X-server to display their output. You run one X-server process to control your display. In contrast, you can run as many X-clients as your hardware resources, primarily RAM, will support.

X-Window system X-Window system is the graphical user interface (GUI) for Linux. Unlike other operating systems in which the GUI interface is an integral part of the operating system itself, the X-Window system is not a part of Red Hat Linux but is a layered application. Thus you can have a fully functioning Linux system without running the X-Window interface.

INDEX

A

B

C

D

I

J

K

L

M

N

Q

R

S

T

U

V

W

X

Z

Custom Corporate Network Training

Train on Cutting Edge Technology We can bring the best in skill-based training to your facility to create a real-world hands-on training experience. Global Knowledge has invested millions of dollars in network hardware and software to train our students on the same equipment they will work with on the job. Our relationships with vendors allow us to incorporate the latest equipment and platforms into your on-site labs.

Maximize Your Training Budget Global Knowledge provides experienced instructors, comprehensive course materials, and all the networking equipment needed to deliver high quality training. You provide the students; we provide the knowledge.

Avoid Travel Expenses On-site courses allow you to schedule technical training at your convenience, saving time, expense, and the opportunity cost of travel away from the workplace.

Discuss Confidential Topics Private on-site training permits the open discussion of sensitive issues such as security, access, and network design. We can work with your existing network's proprietary files while demonstrating the latest technologies.

Customize Course Content Global Knowledge can tailor your courses to include the technologies and the topics which have the greatest impact on your business. We can complement your internal training efforts or provide a total solution to your training needs.

Corporate Pass The Corporate Pass Discount Program rewards our best network training customers with preferred pricing on public courses, discounts on multimedia training packages, and an array of career planning services.

Global Knowledge Training Lifecycle Supporting the Dynamic and Specialized Training Requirements of Information Technology Professionals

- Define Profile
- Assess Skills
- Design Training
- Deliver Training
- Test Knowledge
- Update Profile
- Use New Skills

College Credit Recommendation Program The American Council on Education's CREDIT program recommends 53 Global Knowledge courses for college credit. Now our network training can help you earn your college degree while you learn the technical skills needed for your job. When you attend an ACE-certified Global Knowledge course and pass the associated exam, you earn college credit recommendations for that course. Global Knowledge can establish a transcript record for you with ACE, which you can use to gain credit at a college or as a written record of your professional training that you can attach to your resume.

Registration Information

COURSE FEE: The fee covers course tuition, refreshments, and all course materials. Any parking expenses that may be incurred are not included. Payment or government training form must be received six business days prior to the course date. We will also accept Visa/MasterCard and American Express. For non-U.S. credit card users, charges will be in U.S. funds and will be converted by your credit card company. Checks drawn on Canadian banks in Canadian funds are acceptable.

COURSE SCHEDULE: Registration is at 8:00 a.m. on the first day. The program begins at 8:30 a.m. and concludes at 4:30 p.m. each day.

CANCELLATION POLICY: Cancellation and full refund will be allowed if written cancellation is received in our office at least six business days prior to the course start date. Registrants who do not attend the course or do not cancel more than six business days in advance are responsible for the full registration fee; you may transfer to a later date provided the course fee has been paid in full. Substitutions may be made at any time. If Global Knowledge must cancel a course for any reason, liability is limited to the registration fee only.

GLOBAL KNOWLEDGE: Global Knowledge programs are developed and presented by industry professionals with "real-world" experience. Designed to help professionals meet today's interconnectivity and interoperability challenges, most of our programs feature hands-on labs that incorporate state-of-the-art communication components and equipment.

ON-SITE TEAM TRAINING: Bring Global Knowledge's powerful training programs to your company. At Global Knowledge, we will custom design courses to meet your specific network requirements. Call 1 (919) 461-8686 for more information.

YOUR GUARANTEE: Global Knowledge believes its courses offer the best possible training in this field. If during the first day you are not satisfied and wish to withdraw from the course, simply notify the instructor, return all course materials, and receive a 100% refund.

In the US:

CALL: 1 (888) 762-4442
FAX: 1 (919) 469-7070
VISIT OUR WEBSITE:
www.globalknowledge.com
MAIL CHECK AND THIS FORM TO:
Global Knowledge
Suite 200
114 Edinburgh South
P.O. Box 1187
Cary, NC 27512

In Canada:

CALL: 1 (800) 465-2226
FAX: 1 (613) 567-3899
VISIT OUR WEBSITE:
www.globalknowledge.com.ca
MAIL CHECK AND THIS FORM TO:
Global Knowledge
Suite 1601
393 University Ave.
Toronto, ON M5G 1E6

REGISTRATION INFORMATION:

Course title______________________________________

Course location_________________________ Course date________

Name/title____________________________ Company________

Name/title____________________________ Company________

Name/title____________________________ Company________

Address__________________ Telephone ________ Fax________

City__________________ State/Province______ Zip/Postal Code________

Credit card__________ Card #________________ Expiration date________

Signature________________________________

LICENSE AGREEMENT

THIS PRODUCT (THE "PRODUCT") CONTAINS PROPRIETARY SOFTWARE, DATA AND INFORMATION (INCLUDING DOCUMENTATION) OWNED BY THE McGRAW-HILL COMPANIES, INC. ("McGRAW-HILL") AND ITS LICENSORS. YOUR RIGHT TO USE THE PRODUCT IS GOVERNED BY THE TERMS AND CONDITIONS OF THIS AGREEMENT.

LICENSE: Throughout this License Agreement, "you" shall mean either the individual or the entity whose agent opens this package. You are granted a non-exclusive and non-transferable license to use the Product subject to the following terms:

(i) If you have licensed a single user version of the Product, the Product may only be used on a single computer (i.e., a single CPU). If you licensed and paid the fee applicable to a local area network or wide area network version of the Product, you are subject to the terms of the following subparagraph (ii).

(ii) If you have licensed a local area network version, you may use the Product on unlimited workstations located in one single building selected by you that is served by such local area network. If you have licensed a wide area network version, you may use the Product on unlimited workstations located in multiple buildings on the same site selected by you that is served by such wide area network; provided, however, that any building will not be considered located in the same site if it is more than five (5) miles away from any building included in such site. In addition, you may only use a local area or wide area network version of the Product on one single server. If you wish to use the Product on more than one server, you must obtain written authorization from McGraw-Hill and pay additional fees.

(iii) You may make one copy of the Product for back-up purposes only and you must maintain an accurate record as to the location of the back-up at all times.

COPYRIGHT; RESTRICTIONS ON USE AND TRANSFER: All rights (including copyright) in and to the Product are owned by McGraw-Hill and its licensors. You are the owner of the enclosed disc on which the Product is recorded. You may not use, copy, decompile, disassemble, reverse engineer, modify, reproduce, create derivative works, transmit, distribute, sublicense, store in a database or retrieval system of any kind, rent or transfer the Product, or any portion thereof, in any form or by any means (including electronically or otherwise) except as expressly provided for in this License Agreement. You must reproduce the copyright notices, trademark notices, legends and logos of McGraw-Hill and its licensors that appear on the Product on the back-up copy of the Product which you are permitted to make hereunder. All rights in the Product not expressly granted herein are reserved by McGraw-Hill and its licensors.

TERM: This License Agreement is effective until terminated. It will terminate if you fail to comply with any term or condition of this License Agreement. Upon termination, you are obligated to return to McGraw-Hill the Product together with all copies thereof and to purge all copies of the Product included in any and all servers and computer facilities.

DISCLAIMER OF WARRANTY: THE PRODUCT AND THE BACK-UP COPY OF THE PRODUCT ARE LICENSED "AS IS." McGRAW-HILL, ITS LICENSORS AND THE AUTHORS MAKE NO WARRANTIES, EXPRESS OR IMPLIED, AS TO RESULTS TO BE OBTAINED BY ANY PERSON OR ENTITY FROM USE OF THE PRODUCT AND/OR ANY INFORMATION OR DATA INCLUDED THEREIN. McGRAW-HILL, ITS LICENSORS, AND THE AUTHORS MAKE NO GUARANTEE THAT YOU WILL PASS ANY CERTIFICATION EXAM BY USING THIS PRODUCT. McGRAW-HILL, ITS LICENSORS AND THE AUTHORS MAKE NO EXPRESS OR IMPLIED WARRANTIES OF MERCHANTABILITY OR FITNESS FOR A PARTICULAR PURPOSE OR USE WITH RESPECT TO THE PRODUCT. NEITHER McGRAW-HILL, ANY OF ITS LICENSORS, NOR THE AUTHORS WARRANT THAT THE FUNCTIONS CONTAINED IN THE PRODUCT WILL MEET YOUR REQUIREMENTS OR THAT THE OPERATION OF THE PRODUCT WILL BE UNINTERRUPTED OR ERROR FREE. YOU ASSUME THE ENTIRE RISK WITH RESPECT TO THE QUALITY AND PERFORMANCE OF THE PRODUCT.

LIMITED WARRANTY FOR DISC: To the original licensee only, McGraw-Hill warrants that the enclosed disc on which the Product is recorded is free from defects in materials and workmanship under normal use and service for a period of ninety (90) days from the date of purchase. In the event of a defect in the disc covered by the foregoing warranty, McGraw-Hill will replace the disc.

LIMITATION OF LIABILITY: NEITHER McGRAW-HILL, ITS LICENSORS NOR THE AUTHORS SHALL BE LIABLE FOR ANY INDIRECT, SPECIAL OR CONSEQUENTIAL DAMAGES, SUCH AS BUT NOT LIMITED TO, LOSS OF ANTICIPATED PROFITS OR BENEFITS, RESULTING FROM THE USE OR INABILITY TO USE THE PRODUCT EVEN IF ANY OF THEM HAS BEEN ADVISED OF THE POSSIBILITY OF SUCH DAMAGES. THIS LIMITATION OF LIABILITY SHALL APPLY TO ANY CLAIM OR CAUSE WHATSOEVER WHETHER SUCH CLAIM OR CAUSE ARISES IN CONTRACT, TORT, OR OTHERWISE. Some states do not allow the exclusion or limitation of indirect, special or consequential damages, so the above limitation may not apply to you.

U.S. GOVERNMENT RESTRICTED RIGHTS: Any software included in the Product is provided with restricted rights subject to subparagraphs (c), (1) and (2) of the Commercial Computer Software-Restricted Rights clause at 48 C.F.R. 52.227-19. The terms of this Agreement applicable to the use of the data in the Product are those under which the data are generally made available to the general public by McGraw-Hill. Except as provided herein, no reproduction, use, or disclosure rights are granted with respect to the data included in the Product and no right to modify or create derivative works from any such data is hereby granted.

GENERAL: This License Agreement constitutes the entire agreement between the parties relating to the Product. The terms of any Purchase Order shall have no effect on the terms of this License Agreement. Failure of McGraw-Hill to insist at any time on strict compliance with this License Agreement shall not constitute a waiver of any rights under this License Agreement. This License Agreement shall be construed and governed in accordance with the laws of the State of New York. If any provision of this License Agreement is held to be contrary to law, that provision will be enforced to the maximum extent permissible and the remaining provisions will remain in full force and effect.